MW00759196

**Nikita Khrushchev
and the
Creation of a Superpower**

Nikita Khrushchev

AND THE
CREATION OF A
SUPERPOWER

Sergei N. Khrushchev

Translated by
Shirley Benson

Foreword by
William Taubman

Annotations by
William C. Wohlforth

The Pennsylvania State University
University Park, Pennsylvania

Library of Congress Cataloging-in-Publication Data

Khrushchev, Sergeĭ.
  [Nikita Khrushchev. English]
  Nikita Khrushchev and the creation of a superpower /
Sergei N. Khrushchev.
      p.   cm.
  Abridged and translated from: Nikita Khrushchev : krizisy i
rakety.
  Includes bibliographical references and index.
  ISBN 0-271-01927-1 (alk. paper)
  1. Khrushchev, Nikita Sergeyevich, 1894–1971.   2. Heads
of state—Soviet Union—Biography.   3. Soviet Union—
Politics and government—1953–1985.   4. Khrushchev,
Sergeĭ.   5. World politics—1945–   I. Title.
DK275.K5K4874213
947.08—dc21   98-54931
                                                                      CIP

It is the policy of The Pennsylvania State University Press to use
acid-free paper for the first printing of all clothbound books. Pub-
lications on uncoated stock satisfy the minimum requirements of
American National Standard for Information Sciences—
Permanence of Paper for Printed Library Materials, ANSI
Z39.48–1992.

CONTENTS

FOREWORD

BY WILLIAM TAUBMAN

Even before *glasnost* lifted the curtain on Soviet secrecy, and the fall of the USSR opened the information floodgates, much was known about Nikita Khrushchev, more perhaps than about any other Soviet leader. Khrushchev himself revealed a great deal. He gave endless speeches (those on agriculture alone fill eight volumes) and countless interviews; he diverged from prepared texts more than he followed them; he was often indiscreet. And after his ouster from power in 1964 he disclosed even more. Not only did he dictate several thousand pages of memoirs over the course of several years, but he managed to get many of them published in the West before and just after his death in 1971. Another portion appeared in the West two decades later as a third volume of *Khrushchev Remembers*, and a nearly full Russian text of Khrushchev's memoirs, edited by his son, Sergei Khrushchev, and his grandson, Nikita Khrushchev, was published in the Moscow scholarly journal *Voprosy istorii* (Questions of history) between 1990 and 1995, and then in 1999 in four volumes by the publishing house "Moscow News."

In the last few years, even more information about Khrushchev has seen the light of day. Beginning in the late Soviet period, former officials and others have published memoirs. Since 1991, party and state archives (but not police and military archives or the Presidential Archive, where the most sensitive material of all on Soviet leaders is located) have opened to researchers. The secrets thus revealed make it possible to study Soviet history with a breadth and depth that was impossible for decades. But the flood of new information also poses difficulties (How to find real nuggets in all the archival dross? How to recognize revelations distorted to settle old scores?) while leaving key questions about Khrushchev's life and career unanswered: How did he manage not only to survive Stalin but to succeed him? What led him to denounce his former master? How could a man of minimal formal education direct the affairs of a vast transcontinental empire in the nuclear age? Why did Khrushchev's attempt to ease East-West tensions result in two of the worst crises of the Cold War in Berlin and Cuba? To resolve these and other contradictions, we need more than policy documents from archives and memoirs from associates. We need firsthand testimony by family members who knew Khrushchev best, especially by his only surviving son, Sergei, in whom he often confided.

Sergei Khrushchev was born in 1935 when his father was Moscow party chief. His recollections go back to the Second World War and beyond. As he grew up, he became fascinated with Soviet politics, and especially military matters. In the Khrushchev family, as in other Kremlin households, such subjects were off limits. But Nikita Khrushchev conveyed a lot nonetheless. Sergei wasn't present at Kremlin meetings, but when he and his father took long walks in the evening, Khrushchev sometimes talked about events of the day. Sergei also accompanied his father on major foreign trips—to Great Britain in 1956, East Germany in 1958, the United States in 1959, France, India, Indonesia, Burma, and Afghanistan in 1960, and Egypt in 1964, among others. And after he himself became a control systems engineer and went to work for a leading Soviet missile designer, Vladimir Chelomei, Sergei attended many meetings at which his father transacted business with key leaders of the Soviet defense establishment.

Sergei Khrushchev has previously written a book (called *Pensioner soiuznogo znacheniia* in Russian, and *Khrushchev on Khrushchev* in English) that narrates his father's last years: his long decline and sudden fall from power, his bleak time in forced retirement, his herculean effort to prepare his memoirs, his death, and his family's struggle to obtain a suitable memorial. In this new two-volume work, Khrushchev's son provides much more. It is not a full-scale biography, but without this book such a biography would be far more difficult to write. Sergei's book includes memories of Ukraine (where his father was Stalin's viceroy) before and after the war and of Khrushchev's return to Moscow in late 1949. Beginning in 1953, it covers key domestic developments (Stalin's death, Beria's fall, Khrushchev's 1956 speech unmasking Stalin, the abortive 1957 coup against him, his 1957 firing of Marshal Georgy Zhukov, the new 1961 Communist Party program, the 1962 Novocherkassk riots) and foreign turning points (the 1955 Geneva summit; the 1956 Polish, Hungarian, and Suez crises; the Berlin Crisis of 1958–61; the 1959 American trip; the 1960 U-2 crisis; the 1962 Cuban Missile Crisis; and the 1963 partial nuclear test-ban treaty).

But the heart of this book is the story of Khrushchev's efforts to build up the Soviet Union as a viable superpower. When Stalin died, he left the USSR isolated in a hostile world, with a war machine it couldn't afford. Khrushchev wasn't the only post-Stalin leader who wanted to ease Cold War tensions and reduce the defense burden, but his approach was unique. As Sergei Khrushchev shows, his father was a true believer in communism and in his country's mission to overtake and surpass the West. But he was not a believer in war, having seen too much of it firsthand himself. Nor did he think the Soviet Union could afford to match the United States in defense spending without breaking its promise of better times to the Soviet people. So Khrushchev embarked on deep cuts in Soviet conventional forces, including bombers, surface ships, artillery, and troop strength itself, while eschewing tactical nuclear weapons for fear they would lower the atomic threshold and thus risk nuclear war.

Given all these constraints, what kind of military superpower could the USSR be? Khrushchev's answer was to rely mainly on strategic nuclear weapons and the missiles that delivered them, or rather, since reliable Soviet intercontinental missiles weren't ready for deployment in substantial numbers, on the appearance of having more rockets than in fact he possessed. Khrushchev was convinced he could play on the nerves of his adversaries by threatening nuclear strikes he had no intention of undertaking. He tried out that tactic during the Suez Crisis, and was convinced that it worked; he used it again during the Berlin Crisis and tried to repeat it in Cuba. But instead of cowing his adversaries, his bluster and bluff alarmed them and mobilized them to undertake resistance that forced him to back down. Not only that, it alienated his own military—to the point where, far from helping to save him from an attempted coup as they had done in 1957, they stood aside and gladly accepted his ouster in 1964.

Sergei Khrushchev doesn't just present his general picture. He chronicles Khrushchev's conduct of Soviet foreign and military policy year by year, week by week, even (in the case of the Cuban Crisis) hour by hour. What advanced weaponry did the Soviets have and when did they have it? No information was more classified during the Cold War. Now it's all here. How much did Khrushchev really know about military affairs, how did he use what he knew to manage the military-scientific-industrial complex, and how did it maneuver to try to manage him? With Sergei's help, we look over his father's shoulder as he tours missile design facilities and observes trials of new weapons at test ranges. We listen in as rocket designers and military planners lobby Khrushchev relentlessly, and then recoil from his repeated criticism of out-of-date conventional weapons, his constant touting of the miraculous potential of nuclear weapons, his dream, expressed during his last two years in power, of replacing the mammoth draft-based Red Army with smaller professional forces based on regional militias.

Despite Sergei Khrushchev's deep admiration for his father, he does not depict him as a paragon. He is an accomplice of Stalin's; he is divided in his own mind about how to handle Stalin's legacy, and how to respond to the American U-2 spy flight; he fails fully to think through both his Berlin and his Cuba policies; and he is too reckless and emotional for his own good. But unlike Stalin's other lieutenants, he somehow retains his humanity, his concern for his people's welfare (as he understands it), and the courage to take risks for what he thinks is right.

The period from 1953 to 1964 was a critical one in the history of our country, a period that witnessed the turn from preparations for a third world war to peaceful coexistence, a period of sharp (almost 50 percent) reduction in the armed forces of the USSR. It was also the time when the United States officially, in the words of its president, John F. Kennedy, acknowledged that the United States and the Soviet Union were equal in military might and were equally capable of destroying each other. It was during those years that the Soviet Union became a superpower while simultaneously making a drastic reduction in its military expenditures. Was such a thing possible? Apparently so. It was only necessary to relinquish the standard approach of military professionals to the concept of security, an approach based on maintaining a balance in everything: in tanks, ships, and planes. This balance required that every tank and every plane of a probable, and even improbable, adversary be countered by our own tank or plane, along with some extras. The Soviet Union simply did not possess the strength or the resources for that. "You'll ruin us, leave us naked," said Father, trying to persuade his opponents in the General Staff and the Ministry of Defense.

During those years Father brought about a sharp change in military doctrine, a change toward asymmetrical assurance of security based on the priority development of only those weapons which would make it senseless for the opposing side to attack us—because the price to be paid for some hypothetical victory would be unacceptable to a civilized state.

The new strategy made it possible to forgo the development of entire types of weapons, such as a surface fleet and long-range aviation, while preparing to reduce the number of tanks and make still greater cuts in the number of men under arms, to one-tenth of that during Stalin's time.

The resources made available were directed toward food production, housing construction, and improvement of the standard of living. At that time, a time of harsh confrontation, we had to produce everything ourselves. Trade with the rest of the world was only beginning, and no one would sell us grain, meat, or equipment.

This book does not aspire to shed light on all the events of those years. I write only about those events I was fated to witness. I have tried to avoid drawing conclusions or judging my own Father—that's not appropriate for a son. However, I very much hope that what I have written will make it possible to restore a connection between those times and today. Now as then we must concentrate our energies and our resources where they will do the most good. If we try to do everything, we will only add new misfortunes to the old.

In conclusion I wish to thank those who helped me in the writing and publication of this book: first of all my wife, Valentina Nikolayevna and my son Nikita Sergeyevich. Then my colleagues at the Machine-Building research bureau, especially the late Mark Bendetovich Gurevich, who took on the work of reviewing the manuscript. To Colonel Sergei Yevgenyevich Sokolovsky, who checked many of the facts, I owe a special debt.

Many thanks to my friend Professor William Taubman, who not only read the manuscript in its many incarnations but was also kind enough to provide a foreword. I would also like to thank Shirley Benson, who took on the huge task of translating the manuscript into English, and Raymond Benson, who helped edit the translation. Many thanks are due to my friend Doctor Karl Zaininger; to Asif Siddiqi and Pyotr Gorin, historians of Soviet space research; and to Dr. Rodney Hall, all of whom read the manuscript and made many valuable comments.

I am especially grateful to Penn State Press, its director Sandy Thatcher and its editors, Cherene Holland and Andrew Lewis, who turned the manuscript into a book.

I would also like to thank Mark Garrison, the first director of the Center for Foreign Policy Development, Brown University, and Thomas J. Watson Jr., founder of the Center, who invited me to work at his marvelous institution, which has afforded me a wonderful opportunity to think and write.

My thanks to Professor James Blight, who set me on the right track in my search for a publisher of my book.

And, of course, I would like to express sincere appreciation to the former chancellor of Brown University Artemis A. W. Joukowsky, the former president of Brown University Vartan Gregorian, director of the Thomas J. Watson Jr. Institute for International Studies Professor Thomas Biersteker, Professor P. Terrence Hopman, and Professor Stephen Shenfield, as well as my other colleagues at the Institute, who provided me with the opportunity to work without hindrance while preparing the book for publication.

Sergei Khrushchev

PROLOGUE

Typical Moscow autumn weather prevailed on that late Sunday afternoon of October 28, 1962. Summer's warmth was irrevocably past, but winter had not yet arrived.

Moscow's sidewalks overflowed with people hurrying about their business. The few cars on the streets drove by almost silently, since a new law prohibited blowing your horn inside city limits. So naturally everyone's attention was caught by a black government Chaika limousine that was impatiently blowing its horn at a red traffic light. It had already passed through many intersections and raced recklessly along Moscow streets and narrow lanes for a good half hour. The basso blare of the car's horn was starting to resemble a cry of despair. The driver was simply unable to find his destination and was growing increasingly nervous.

He had good reason to be nervous. His passenger was a very important comrade, a short, thick-set man with a big head on which a few strands of sparse red hair barely covered an expansive bald spot. His short, thick fingers were nervously fingering a red package embossed with five wax seals. Large black letters on the package read "Central Committee of the Communist Party of the Soviet Union."[1] There was no address.

The man sitting in the Chaika, Leonid Ilichev, was the secretary of the Central Committee who exercised total control over all Soviet newspapers and magazines, as well as all radio and television. In the package were typewritten pages containing the answer of the chairman of the Council of Ministers,[2] Nikita Sergeyevich Khrushchev, to a letter from the president of the United States, John Fitzgerald Kennedy.

---

1. "Central Committee." The Soviet Union was governed by the Communist Party, which was organized on the basis of congresses held roughly every five years. Those congresses elected a Central Committee comprising the three hundred or so most influential party officials in the country. The Central Committee elected from its membership an executive body of about a dozen top party leaders—the true cabinet of the Soviet Union—called the *Presidium* in Khrushchev's day. Before and after Khrushchev's tenure, this body was called by its better-known name, the *Politburo*. In addition, the Central Committee elected *secretaries* to manage the administrative apparatus ("the apparat") of the party. First among those secretaries was Khrushchev, the *first secretary* (called "general secretary" before and after Khrushchev's time), who chaired the Presidium and had the power to appoint lower-level officials (and thus influence the lower-level bodies to which he was formally beholden). Leonid Ilichev, mentioned in the text below, was the Central Committee secretary in charge of ideology.

2. "Chairman of the Council of Ministers." Though the Communist Party was the supreme political authority in the Soviet Union, the country was administered by complex governmental

The world was on the brink of catastrophe. Something terrible and irreparable could happen at any moment. It had therefore been decided not to send the answer through the usual channels for exchanging messages between heads of state, but to broadcast it at once on Moscow radio. This was an unusual, perhaps unprecedented, step in international practice, but an effective one. The answer would be on the president's desk in just a few minutes. It was widely known that American radio intercept services were very efficient and very fast.

The subject of the message was the installation on the island of Cuba of Soviet medium-range ballistic missiles tipped with nuclear warheads. In the opinion of the Soviet leadership, this desperate step was needed to keep the United States from repeating its adventure of the previous April, when a military force landed on the beaches of the Bay of Pigs.

However, neither Premier Khrushchev nor his colleagues in the Presidium of the Central Committee had anticipated the U.S. reaction to this step. After all, the missiles had been installed by mutual agreement between two allied states, Cuba and the Soviet Union, and did not seem to them to threaten anyone. It was hard to imagine that little Cuba presented a danger to its mighty neighbor, even with several dozen missiles sited in groves of palm trees.

But American thinking was based on different principles. The agreement between the USSR and the Republic of Cuba was viewed as an intolerable intrusion into the Western hemisphere. The United States could not allow that, and there was a tremendous reaction. The U.S. naval blockade, threats of air attack, repeated flights by reconnaissance aircraft over the island, and finally the announcement of a heightened degree of military readiness of the U.S. armed forces had brought the world to the brink of war.

The deadly nature of nuclear conflict was well understood on both sides

---

hierarchy. The mainly ceremonial parliament—called the *Supreme Soviet*—elected a Council of Ministers, which comprised the heads of all major government ministries and agencies. The Council of Ministers was managed by a *presidium*, distinct from the party's presidium but about the same size, which ran the governmental bureaucracy. The head of this presidium was called the chairman of the council of ministers—the person formally in charge of the government (and, hence, the Soviet economy) and often called "prime minister" by Westerners. Khrushchev, who had become first secretary of the party in 1953 after Stalin's death, assumed the chairmanship of the Council of Ministers in 1958.

A final, technical note: The Supreme Soviet also elected a presidium with a chairman, who was formally the head of state and had to perform the ceremonial functions associated with that office, such as signing treaties. Thus, in Khrushchev's Soviet Union there was a party presidium headed by the First Secretary (Khrushchev) who was the supreme political authority; a presidium of the Council of Ministers headed by a chairman (also Khrushchev) who was the supreme governmental authority; and a presidium of the Supreme Soviet, headed by a chairman (from 1953 to 1960, Kliment E. Voroshilov, and from 1960 to 1964, Leonid I. Brezhnev) who was technically head of state.

of the ocean. Both the chairman of the Council of Ministers of the Soviet Union and the president of the United States considered nuclear war to be unthinkable. But the desire to avoid such a war was not enough. They had to find and to implement steps to prevent it from breaking out. Both leaders realized that conflict was inevitable if they lost control over the situation.

Messages flew back and forth. Proposal after proposal was made and rejected. Soviet solutions to the crisis were unacceptable to the United States, American solutions unacceptable to the Soviet Union.

Tension grew. In the United States there was mounting pressure to punish the obstinate Cubans by ordering a surgical air strike to destroy the missile bases. The president disagreed with the hotheads. He realized that such an action would inevitably lead to a war too terrible to contemplate.

With emotions at the breaking point Robert Kennedy, the president's brother and the U.S. attorney general, met with Soviet ambassador Anatoly Dobrynin. The conversation was unofficial. Kennedy looked exhausted, his bloodshot eyes testifying to sleepless nights.

Kennedy called the situation extremely dangerous. He said that the military were intent on landing an invasion force in Cuba and that the president was resisting their pressure with some difficulty. He felt that the situation could spiral out of control at any moment. He therefore asked, in the president's name, for an immediate positive answer from the Kremlin to a message from the president—or else, he said, we will not be able to restrain the military. That was approximately the tone of his final words.

The Foreign Ministry was not the Kremlin's sole source of information. KGB and military intelligence reported that preparations were under way to intervene in Cuba, that troops had been moved to forward positions, and that the signal to attack would follow in short order. Their report soon lay on Khrushchev's desk. A coded message from Havana arrived almost simultaneously. Fidel Castro warned that Cuban intelligence thought an invasion would begin within hours.

After receiving these disturbing reports, as well as the letter from President Kennedy linking the withdrawal of Soviet missiles from Cuba to U.S. guarantees of nonintervention, the members of the Presidium of the Central Committee, Central Committee secretaries, and Khrushchev's closest aides gathered at a dacha near Moscow. The fate of millions of people, of all humanity, depended on their decisions, on their wisdom and restraint. Which would prevail, ambition or the voice of reason? Withdrawal of the missiles would undoubtedly be seen as yielding to U.S. pressure—even as a defeat. Reason won out.

Father formulated his proposal succinctly: If the president gave his word not to invade Cuba, then the missiles had fulfilled their purpose and they could be brought home. One must not trifle with the destinies of nations and peoples. His colleagues supported him, and he immediately began to dictate a letter to the president. Finally, after the last corrections were made, there was a final reading, and the text was ready. Everyone had approved it. It was ready to send.

Naturally, such important decisions should have been discussed with Fidel, but time was running out. By the time papers traveled to Cuba and back, there might not be anyone left. Speed was of the utmost importance.

Khrushchev proposed sending the letter to the president by radio. No one objected. The Chaika's passenger, who was at the meeting, offered to take it personally to Moscow's Radio Center. That would be the surest way. However, neither he nor his driver from the Kremlin garage knew exactly where the Moscow Radio Center was located. That was why they were wandering around the streets of Moscow, horn wailing. And time was passing.

They finally tracked down the building. Radio officials, who had been notified by telephone that their "Boss" was bringing an important message, were nervously milling about at the entrance. Announcer Yury Levitan was waiting upstairs.

The messenger jumped out before the car even came to a full stop. He moved swiftly, despite a noticeable paunch. "Which floor?" he asked hurriedly, almost running toward the elevator.

The building was old, and the elevator, in its wire cage, was visible to everyone. The door closed with a crash and the elevator began to creak as it moved slowly upward. For some reason it got stuck between floors—perhaps its impatient passenger had rattled the door.

Nothing seemed to work. The elevator wouldn't move up or down, and the door wouldn't open. The agitated hosts didn't know what to do and stood fretting on the stairs while their guest paced back and forth in the elevator. The repairman was sent for, but it was Sunday and he was not on the premises. Meanwhile more time was passing.

The messenger thought of a possible solution. He tried to slip the envelope through a crack in the elevator door, but the wax seals got in the way. Hurriedly tearing the envelope open, he began passing pages from the valuable document through the crack. A few minutes later the elevator finally started to rise.

As the high-ranking guest walked into the broadcasting studio, Yury Levitan cleared his throat and began testing his voice. Its dry and inflexible tones always alerted listeners to the fact that they were about to hear an important TASS communiqué or a protest note from the Soviet government.[3]

In this case, the tone grated on the ear of his guest, who said, "Yury

---

3. TASS—the Telegraphic Agency of the Soviet Union. That is, official radio.

Borisovich, a little softer, please. It's a matter of war or peace." Levitan nodded in agreement.

And so, after the usual portentous introduction, "*This* is Radio Moscow," Levitan read the words that would resolve what the West calls the Cuban Missile Crisis and Soviets usually referred to as the Caribbean Crisis. Reason prevailed. On this occasion there had been enough time.

Thus ended the most serious in a series of crises, one after another, in the course of those years. Fortunately, it ended peacefully.

The Caribbean Crisis has provoked many discussions, interpretations, and conjectures. For this account I have relied on the evidence of eyewitnesses, on testimony that has grown into legend. Today it is difficult to tell who may have invented improbable details attesting to their participation in high-level political events and who, after so many years, may have simply forgotten things. Whether there have been a few embellishments of the facts is not important. What we *can* say is that, thanks to the wisdom of both governments, we managed to survive.

After all, someone could have made a mistake. We could have run out of time.

I was told the elevator story by the eminent Soviet journalist Melor Sturua during a meeting in Moscow between scholars from the United States, the Republic of Cuba, and the Soviet Union in January of 1989 to discuss the events that had so worried us in 1962. Some even less likely events were recalled during that meeting.

Scholars from Harvard's John F. Kennedy School of Government and Brown's Thomas J. Watson Jr. Institute for International Studies and from the Soviet Academy of Sciences have spent years studying the causes, development, and resolution of the Caribbean Crisis. It is not a simple matter. Separating truth from imagination or discovering how the crisis arose is not as important as finding a medicine for the illness that threatened mankind with extinction.

There were crises long before Father entered the world of high-level politics, and there have been crises since his retirement. They are characteristic of our era and independent of the will of any single individual. However, the process reached its peak during the "Khrushchev era." The events of those years are, therefore, of special interest. If we understand what happened then, we can understand better what is happening now. After all, those who master the past, master the future.

The so-called missile race also began during those years. Since then the territory of what was once the Soviet Union has gradually been transformed from a possible target encircled by the air bases of a "potential foreign adversary" into a partner that must be taken into account.

I had the opportunity to observe Father in a variety of situations related to solving these crises. Of course, I don't know everything. I will leave it to the professional historians to do what they do best. I only wish to share what I personally saw and heard.

While I was only a witness to some, albeit extremely interesting, episodes in international affairs, I participated directly in developing our missile strike force. I worked for ten years in one of our missile design bureaus. There, in contrast to the case of political decisions, I could see what was happening from two perspectives: from above as though through Father's eyes and from below with my own. I hope that my account will be useful to the historians who study those turbulent years, as well as simply to those inquisitive readers who are interested in finding out why we are still alive on this earth.

PART ONE

CHAPTER ONE

START

Until 1953 Father had no direct connection either with political crises or with missiles. In 1944, he exchanged his general's greatcoat for an ordinary civilian suit and returned to Kiev to supervise the reopening of the coal mines and the factories. He was far more concerned that the sugar beets be planted on time than with problems in building new tanks and planes. The persistent confusion that prevailed during the harvest concerned him far more than the crises over Berlin. Of course, I should not be taken literally. As a member of the Politburo, he was involved in world affairs. But they were not among his personal responsibilities. Other people were in charge—Beria of the nuclear industry, planes, and missiles, and Malenkov of radar. Father was given the task of supplying the country with bread, coal, and steel.[1]

Distance from the center of activity played a role as well. Members of the top leadership in the capital, close to Stalin, were not their own men. In Kiev Father was relatively free. He was directly involved in economic matters. Naturally the "services" (the MGB, later the KGB)[2] followed his every move, but Father had established good—I would even say trusting—relations with their Ukrainian chief, Ivan Aleksandrovich Serov. There was no reason to expect dirty tricks from his direction.

MY EARLIEST MEMORIES

Of course my memories of the Kiev period of our lives, especially the prewar years, are rather sketchy—just a child's sensation of sun, warmth, and light.

---

1. Larentiy Pavlovich Beria. As head of the political police (People's Commissar for Internal Affairs) from 1938 to 1945, Beria was one of Stalin's most notorious henchmen. In the postwar period here, Beria was in charge of the Soviet nuclear program. Georgy Maksimilyanovich Malenkov—another one of Stalin's chief lieutenants who held top economic posts during the war and in the postwar period. Both men's relations to Khrushchev and eventual fate in the post-Stalin era are related below.

2. The MGB (*Ministerstvo gosudarstvennoi bezopasnosti*—Ministry of State Security) and MVD (*Minsterstvo vnutrennykh del*—Ministry of Internal Affairs) were successors of the NKVD (*Narodnyi komitet vnutrennykh del*—People's Commissariat of Internal Affairs) and precursors of the KGB (*Komitet gosudarstvennoi bezopasnosti*—Committee of State Security). The acronyms all refer to bu-

Father had unexpectedly been "bounced" from the Moscow Party Committee to the Ukrainian Central Committee to replace Stanislav Kosior. In those days such abrupt changes were considered routine. We traveled from Moscow to Kiev by train. Before the war that took about twenty-four hours. Father's aide, Pavel Gapochka, spent the entire day telling me a scary and interminable fairy tale, so that I always associate the journey with sweet emotions of apprehension and anticipation.

That was at the very beginning of 1938, winter or early spring. It was a year when frightening fairy tales could not compare to real life.

In Kiev we were installed in a tidy town house on Karl Liebknecht Street, across from the new building of the Ukrainian Supreme Soviet. A description of our daily lives is not the purpose of my book, but there is one thing I should mention. The windows of the one-story house where we lived faced the street. The previous owner had covered the bottom half of the windows with white paint to block the stares of inquisitive pedestrians. At the time I didn't know who had lived there, and at three or four years of age I could hardly have been interested. Nevertheless, I remember how the servants whispered in the corners: "What an ugly man he was! Hiding from people! Had the windows painted so nobody could see what he was doing."

What could have been going on here? At once I thought of Gapochka's frightening fairy tale, of scary faces, dungeons, and tightly sealed doors. Stanislav Vikentyevich Kosior, who was already being called an "enemy of the people,"[3] had lived in the house before us.

I don't know whether the furnishings were changed after he left. Probably not, since that was not the practice then; moreover, the inhabitants thought of themselves as guests who would not be staying in "official" housing for long. We had not brought our own furniture.

I remember a large grand piano in the dining room. Once, behaving childishly during dinner, I threw a crust of bread on the floor. What a disaster! As children we were not physically punished. I believe that such punishment would have been unnatural for my parents, not that it was a matter of principle. But at that moment they forgot themselves. Mother slapped my face hard. It was more humiliating than painful. Then Father dragged me off the chair and pushed me under the table: "Pick it up."

I refused. I sat under the table sobbing, then threw myself across the room and under the piano. No further physical punishment was forthcoming, and no one "hunted me down" in my sanctuary. Mama leaned over and,

reaucracies that were part political police, part internal and external spy organizations, and part traditional ministry of the interior.

3. Stanislav V. Kosior was head of the Ukrainian Communist Party from 1928 to 1938. An "enemy of the people" was the standard phrase applied to victims in Stalin's Great Terror. Kosior was shot on Stalin's orders in 1939.

looking toward the far corner where I was hiding, spoke in a sad and reproachful tone about how hard the peasants worked to grow and collect grain
and make bread. She concluded by asking: "How could you throw it on the
floor?"

I was ashamed and cried bitterly. From that day on I never left anything
on my plate. Throughout their lives, both Father and Mother had a special,
peasant attitude toward bread. Both had grown up in poor families and knew
how much work went into producing it.

In 1939 Father put on his military uniform for the first time since the civil
war.[4] The Red Army was preparing to advance into the Western Ukraine in
order to occupy the eastern part of Poland, which had been awarded to the
Soviet Union by the Ribbentrop–Molotov Pact.[5] Ukrainians did not view
this campaign as aggression, but as the restoration of justice: Ukraine was
reunited with its western lands, which for centuries had been under foreign
occupation. My memory of saying good-bye is associated more with Marshal
Semyon Timoshenko, commander of the Kiev Military District, than with
Father. I remember the strong odor of cologne and tobacco and feel of getting scratched by the medals on his tunic when he lifted me up, tossed me in
the air, and carefully lowered me to the ground. Father, on the other hand,
didn't like sentimental farewells or kisses. He just stroked my head and asked,
"What should I bring you?" I didn't know what to say, mumbled "a pencil,"
and buried my head in his side. He filled my request, bringing back an enormous bright yellow pencil almost as big as I was, with the name of some
Polish store printed on its side. He must have given the task to his guards,
who "requisitioned" the pencil from some nearby window. It was almost
impossible to write with, but I have kept it as a souvenir all my life. And I
have it to this day, though it is now far shorter than it was.

Aside from the pencil Father brought back a whole bunch of new relatives: grandmother and grandfather, an uncle, and cousins—a brother and
sister. After the First World War, Mother's whole family had remained behind in territory that became part of Poland.

But more about that later. After Father's death I tried for a long time to
get Mother to write about her life. I wanted to preserve all I could about the
past, not just for the sake of our family but for that of history in general. I
continued to live for Father's memoirs, on which work had been interrupted
when the manuscript was confiscated by the KGB and the Central Committee, but I had no doubt that Mama's recollections would add to what Father

---

4. Nikita S. Khrushchev joined the Red Army in early 1919 and served as a soldier and a party
worker until the end of the Russian Civil War in 1921.

5. "Ribbentrop-Molotov Pact." Better known as the Hitler-Stalin pact—a public treaty of non-
aggression with a secret protocol establishing spheres of influence between the Soviet Union and
Germany in Central Europe.

had dictated and would describe those times somewhat differently. However, Mama didn't respond. She wasn't attracted to the tape recorder I had brought to her at the dacha, where she whiled away the time alone between weekend visits from her children and grandchildren. But it turned out later that she had taken my advice and begun to make notes, not on tape but by hand in a school notebook. These were discovered only after her death in 1984, when my sister Rada and I sorted, divided up, and packed her things. We had to be quick about emptying her half of the small dacha given her by the Council of Ministers after Father's death, since the new occupant wanted to move in.

Rada took the notebook, because she had also tried to persuade Mama to write down her reminiscences, also without response. A year later she gave it to me, along with a whole basket of letters. Mama had corresponded with many people. She considered it a duty to reply to everyone who wrote her, whether they were acquaintances or strangers.

MAMA REMEMBERS

I make so bold as to give Mama's notes in full. She wrote laconically, sternly, dryly. That was precisely the way she viewed what had been important in her life. She never faltered, and continued to be guided by the ideals and principles of a revolutionary, one who had devoted herself entirely to the fight for people's happiness. That, incidentally, did not prevent her from taking care of her family, receiving guests with a radiant smile, and occupying herself with her grandchildren as they grew up.

This is what Mama wrote:

To my children and grandchildren
Nina Petrovna Kukharchuk (Khrushcheva):
    I was born on April 14, 1900, in the village of Vasilyev, Poturzhinsk *gmina* [the *gmina* was equivalent to the *volost*, the smallest administrative district in tsarist Russia—S.K.], Tomashovsky District, Kholmskaya Province, in the former Kingdom of Poland.[6] My brother Ivan was born three years later. The population of Kholmskaya Province was Ukrainian, and people spoke Ukrainian in the villages, but the administration in the village, the *gmina*, and above was Russian. In school children were taught in Russian, although they did not speak Russian at home. From history it is known that the government of the Kingdom pursued a policy of russification of the population. I remember that in the first grade of my village primary school, the teacher hit pupils across the palms of their hands with a ruler when they made a mistake, even

---

6. The Kingdom of Poland was the official name of Poland when it was part of the Russian empire.

when it was because they didn't understand the teacher's explanations in Russian (the children didn't know Russian). This was called "getting a paw."

Mama—Yekaterina Grigoryevna Kukharchuk (maiden name, Bondarchuk)—was married at sixteen and as a dowry was given one *morg* of land (0.25 hectares), several oak trees in the forest, and a chest for clothes and bedding. In the village such a dowry was considered very generous. Soon after the wedding my father was called up for military service. Mama had two married brothers: Pavel, with a wife and their three children, and Anton, with a wife and four children. The only one of Anton's children still alive is Vasily Antonovich Bondarchuk, who lives in the city of Lutsk. Uncle Anton and his daughter were tortured to death by Banderites [followers of Ukrainian nationalist Stjepan Bandera—S.K.] in 1946; one of his sons, Petro, was killed by bandits in Poland, and his son Ivan died from tuberculosis after the war. Pavel's sons went to work in Canada and were not heard from again. His daughter Nina now lives on a collective farm in Volynskaya Province.

Father—Pyotr Vasilyevich Kukharchuk—came from a poorer family than my mother. The family consisted of his parents, four brothers, and three sisters. It owned an indivisible allotment of 2.5 *morg*s (0.75 hectares), an old house, and a small orchard. They had no horses.

My father was the oldest in the family. When his mother, Grandmother Domna, died, Father inherited the land and should have paid his sisters and brothers one hundred rubles each (a large sum in those days). I think that the war that began in 1914 interfered with paying that sum.

I don't remember my grandfathers, Grigory and Vasily. They died before I was born.

Our village, Vasilyev, was poor, and most people worked for the landowner for wages. At that time he paid women ten kopecks for a whole day (from sunup to sundown) harvesting beets, while the men got twenty to thirty kopecks for mowing. I don't remember much from that time: I was supposed to prepare nettles and cut them up with a large knife for the pigs, which were being fattened for Easter or Christmas. The knife often hit my fingers instead of the nettles, and it left scars on my left index finger that didn't fade for a long time.

I still remember the garden, which was small and overgrown with grass and nettles. It had large plum trees, one cherry tree, and small young pear trees. I broke a small pear tree. Uncle Anton asked why I did that, and I replied: "Don't feel bad. Look how many you have left."

Mama—Yekaterina Grigoryevna—and I lived with her family at the time. Father was then away on military service in Bessarabia and later, in 1904, fought against Japan. Grandmother Kseniya's house was larger. Everyone sat on a wide bench, not at a table, and ate from the same dish. Mother's younger children were held, but there wasn't enough room for the older children and me, so we had to reach between the grownups' shoulders for the food. If you spilled anything, you got a spoon across the forehead. For some reason Uncle Anton always kidded me, saying that I would marry into a family with lots of children; the children would be snotty-nosed and I would have to eat with them out of one dish, reach for food over their heads, etc., etc.

In 1912 Father put me, a sack of potatoes, and a chunk of a hog on a cart and drove us to the city of Lublin, where his brother, Kondraty Vasilyevich, was a conductor on freight trains. Uncle Kondraty arranged for me to study at the Lublin gymnasium (a four-year school). I had already studied for three years before that at the village school. The village teacher had convinced my father that I was good at science and should study in the city, and my father had listened.

I studied for one year in Lublin. The next year Uncle began working as a senior watchman in the Kholm Fiscal Office and transferred me to the same type of school in the city of Kholm.

When the First World War broke out, I was in the village of Vasilyev on vacation from the Kholm Pro-Gymnasium, where I was a student in the second class.

Autumn 1914. Austrian troops slipped into our village and began to make trouble, stealing things and abducting girls. Mama put me behind the stove, ordered me to stay there and told the soldiers that I had typhus. Of course, they lost no time in leaving. Soon the Austrians were ousted by Russian troops, and we were ordered to evacuate the village—how and to where, we were not told. We had no horses, so we took what we could carry and left home carrying bags. We walked in the same direction as everyone else. I remember Mother carried a primus stove for a long time—it was her pride and joy—but there was no kerosene, so we had to abandon the primus. We walked for a long and difficult time ahead of the advancing Austrian troops. At a station we came across Father, who was serving in a militia unit. They were auxiliary troops. Because of his age, Father was no longer considered fit for combat service.

Father told his commander about meeting his family, and the commander allowed us to remain with the unit. Mama began working as a cook at the unit's command post and my brother and I went around on Father's wagon and helped him out as much as we could. I was fourteen and Vanya was eleven.

During a lull at the front the commander summoned Father, gave him a letter to Bishop Yevlogy of Kholm, and ordered him to take me to Kiev. Bishop Yevlogy headed some sort of refugee relief organization there. He arranged for me to study at government expense at the Kholm Maryinsky Girls' School, which had been evacuated from Kholm to Odessa. This was a seven-grade boarding school for girls. I studied there for four years and finished it in 1919. My parents spent those four years in evacuation in Saratovskaya *guberniya*.[7]

A few words about Bishop Yevlogy and the school. In Poland, Kholm Bishop Yevlogy was an important supporter of the autocracy and a fervent advocate of the policy of russification. He trained russified cadres from among children of the local population, from West Ukrainian villages. If he had not intervened, I would never have been able to study at government expense at that school, which did not accept the children of peasants. Specially selected daughters of priests and officials were the school's students. I chanced to be there because of the special circumstances of wartime, as I have described.

After the war, in 1918, my parents and my brother Ivan returned home from Saratovskaya *guberniya* through Odessa. Father came to visit me at the apartment where we students were living and looked over the place. The large hall caught his fancy and he said: "We could live here." But the administration only allowed him to spend the night, and that only reluctantly. Then my parents and brother left for home, in Poland, and I remained in Odessa to finish my schooling.

After graduating from the school I worked for a time in its office, writing out certificates and copying various papers—the school had no typewriter.

At the beginning of 1920 I joined the underground of the Bolshevik Party and began to work at the party's orders in Odessa and in the villages of Odessa Province. Communists were mobilized in June of 1920, and I was sent to the Polish front.[8] Since I knew the Ukrainian language and local conditions, I was initially chosen to be an agitator attached to a military unit, and I traveled around the villages and talked about Soviet rule. A Red Army soldier, also an agitator, went with me. When the Central Committee of the West Ukrainian Communist Party was formed, I was appointed to head the section for work among women. We were then in the city of Ternopol. As is well known, we had to leave Poland in the autumn of 1920. My army service ended at the same time. Together with the Party Central Committee Secretary Comrade Krasnokutsky and others, I arrived in Moscow and was assigned to attend the Yakov M. Sverdlov Communist University and to take the six-month courses recently organized by the Bolshevik Party Central Committee.

In the summer of 1921 I was sent to the Donetsk Basin, to the city of Bakhmut (now Artyemovsk), to teach the history of the revolutionary move-

---

7. A *guberniya* was a province in tsarist Russia.

8. "The Polish front." The events described in the paragraph occurred during the war with Poland, which attempted to wrest Ukraine from the Bolsheviks in April and May of 1920. The Red Army counterattacked, reconquered Ukraine, and approached Warsaw in August, only to be beaten back by the Poles, leading to the evacuation mentioned here by Nina Petrovna Khrushcheva.

ment and political economy at the provincial party school. Until my future
students arrived, I was assigned by the provincial party committee to work as
secretary of the provincial committee to purge party ranks. There I went
through my second purge, the first having occurred at the front, in Ternopol.

Party purges, which Mama refers to here, were conducted periodically
after the Revolution. Careerists, thieves, and other scoundrels tried to associate themselves with the ruling party as a way to improve their position and
material well-being. The party tried intermittently to purge itself, but as
happens after every revolution, the positions held by those purged were soon
filled by even worse scoundrels. They eventually took control of all the commanding heights, and in 1939 the Eighteenth Party Congress recognized
that carrying out purges was pointless.

To have survived a purge was like a confirmation of your honesty, so
Mama was proud that she had met the test.

One additional note: Immediately after the Revolution, those "purged"
from the party were generally not subject to repressions, in contrast to the
Stalin purges of the 1930s.

As is well known, the requisitioning of farm products stopped after the Tenth
Party Congress and markets began to appear.[9] They had various commodities
for sale—if you had the money to buy them. Once I went with two other
teachers to a market to buy some bread and we were all infected with typhus.
One of us (Abugova) died, while the other teacher and I were sick for a long
time and then suffered a relapse. However, our youth helped us to overcome
the disease and we recovered. We were not hospitalized, but were taken care
of at the school. We were fed by Serafima Ilyinichna Gopner, who was then
head of the Donetsk Provincial Party Committee's agitation and propaganda
section. She obtained miners' rations for us through the TsPKP (Central
Administration of the Coal Industry), which was under Pyatakov, the future
Trotskyite.[10] In the summer of 1922 Serafima Ilyinichna arranged for me to

---

9. "The requisitioning of farm products." This is a reference to "war communism"—the
abolition of markets and state seizures of grain. The party abandoned this policy at its Tenth
Congress, initiating the "New Economic Policy" of permitting market exchange and private agriculture.

10. Georgiy Leonidovich Pyatakov was indeed a "Trotskyite"—that is, a supporter of Leon
Trotsky—during the factional struggles in 1920–27. He was expelled from the party when Stalin
triumphed over the "united opposition" of Trotsky, Zinoviev, and Kamenev in 1927. But his membership was restored when he supported Stalin's rapid industrialization drive in 1928, and he went
on to hold leading economic posts during the first five-year plan. Pyatakov was the principal defen-
dant in the first show trial of 1937, which ushered in Stalin's Great Terror, and was subsequently
executed. By that time, the party leadership under Stalin had succeeded in distorting Trotsky's role
in the revolution and his actual views, and the designation "Trotskyite" had become an official
term of abuse that bore no relationship to a person's real beliefs or activities.

work in the provincial program of courses for teachers in Taganrog, on the shore of the Sea of Azov. I recuperated there from typhus.

In the autumn of 1922 I was sent to Yuzovka (now Donetsk) to teach political economy at the district party school. There I met Nikita Sergeyevich Khrushchev, who was studying at the workers' faculty in Yuzovka.

In 1924 we were married and began working together at the Petrovka Mine, in Yuzovsky District. Our district was called Petrovo-Maryinsky. It combined the Petrovsky Mine with the agricultural fields of Maryinka and its neighboring villages. The district executive committee of the Soviet of Workers' and Peasant Deputies was located in the village of Maryinka, while the district party committee was in Petrovka. The district committee secretary lived in Petrovka and the chairman of the district executive committee lived in Maryinka.

Earlier, I had spent a year taking courses for retraining teachers for Soviet and party schools (administered by the Krupskaya Academy of Communist Education). Then, at the end of 1923 I was sent as propagandist of the district party committee to the Rutchenkov mine. That was where Nikita Sergeyevich's parents and children (by his deceased first wife) and his sister and her family lived. He had worked there as deputy director of the mine administration and left from there to study at the workers' faculty in Yuzovka.

Father was married for the first time in 1914, to Yefrosinya Ivanovna Pisareva, who was from a workers' family. They had met three years earlier. Her father had taught young Nikita the difficult craft of metalworking.

Yefrosinya Ivanovna had two children: a daughter Yuliya in 1916 and a son Leonid one year later. In 1918, to save them from the Germans, Father left the Donbas mine and moved his family from Uspenka to his native village of Kalinovka, in Kursk Province on Russian territory.

The terms of the separate Brest Peace Treaty provided for the German army to occupy the Ukraine.[11] Father left Kalinovka for the civil war front. Soon, at the beginning of 1919, a misfortune occurred. Yefrosinya Ivanovna fell gravely ill, from typhus, as Father described it. During the civil war millions died of typhus. Father received permission to visit his sick wife; he was fighting on the Southern Front, not very far away. However, he did not arrive in time. Yefrosinya had died.

The young communist—Father had joined the Communist Party in 1918—ran into an unexpected problem. The Russian Revolution, after the example of the Great French Revolution, completely rejected religion and called it the opiate of the people. But now he was expected to carry the coffin

---

11. "The separate Brest Peace Treaty" refers to the treaty signed at Brest-Litovsk between the Bolshevik government and Imperial Germany, which ceded vast territories of the Russian empire to Berlin only to be nullified the subsequent year by the German defeat.

with his wife's body through the gate at the entrance to the cemetery, which happened to be across from a church. Father decided to bypass the church by not carrying the coffin through the gate, but passing it from hand to hand over the cemetery fence. He thought that he would thereby avoid offending those relatives who were believers and still not violate his atheistic communist principles. This was typical of his future behavior—unexpected, sometimes shocking, and always out of the ordinary. At the time the villagers all roundly condemned him. To this day they still shake their heads disapprovingly when they recall what happened.

Father returned to the front right after the funeral. The children—Yuliya, two and a half, and Leonid, eight months—were left with his parents. When the civil war ended, Father returned to the Donbas and was soon joined by his parents and the children.

"I conducted classes with the miners on political literacy, delivered lectures on political subjects in the club and carried out various orders from the district committee," Mother wrote.

> I moved into a house for new arrivals (something like a hotel of the mine administration), which was across the road from the club. After a heavy rain it was very hard to cross the road, since my boots would stick in the mud and my feet would "walk out" of them. You had to tie on the boots a special way. People frightened me, talking about the mud before I went to Rutchenkovka, and since I had no boots I had to find a private cobbler to make them. Many women came when I delivered lectures at the club. It turned out that they were interested in seeing the wife that their friend Nikita Khrushchev had found somewhere else, not at the mine.
>
> When N.S.[12] finished his studies, the workers' faculty of the high school sent him to be the secretary of the Petrovo-Maryinsky District Party Committee and I was transferred from Rutchenkovka to Petrovka, again as propagandist of the district party committee. An interesting detail: At the time propagandists were paid out of funds from the center, while district committee secretaries were paid from local funds. At one time I was paid more than N.S.
>
> There was still unemployment then, even among communist miners. After classes at the mine's political school my listeners accompanied me home and sometimes reproached me for the fact that I was working and my husband was working, while they had no work and had big families at home. But life gradually calmed down and the unemployed disappeared from the area of the mine.
>
> Lenin died in January of 1924. N.S. went to Moscow for the funeral as

---

12. Here and below, "N.S." refers to Nikita Sergeyevich Khrushchev's first name and patronymic.

a member of the Donetsk delegation. Following an appeal by the Central Committee, many workers joined the party. That was called the Lenin Appeal. Propagandists had more work; we had to teach semiliterate workers the fundamentals of political theory, and that was difficult. Moscow sent new propagandists, who were mobilized by the Central Committee from among graduates of various universities.

At the end of 1926 N.S. was transferred to work at the regional party committee, where he began to head the organizational department, while I went to Moscow to raise my qualifications at the Krupskaya Communist Academy. I studied in the department of political economy there until the end of 1927. After completing my courses I was sent to the Kiev Inter-regional Party School to teach political economy. I had to conduct courses in the Ukrainian language, since the students were members of the underground from the Western Ukraine.

During the year I was studying in Moscow, N.S. succeeded in working for a time in Kharkov in the Central Committee of the Ukrainian Communist Party (Bolshevik) and by the autumn of 1927 was already chairman of the organizational department of the Kiev Regional Committee. I was also sent to Kiev, even though a comrade from the department of the Central Committee that assigned personnel strongly insisted that I be sent to Tyumen. I was helped in this matter by the Kiev regional [okrug] committee secretary, Comrade N. Demchenko, who was later unjustifiably repressed.

In Kiev I taught political economy in the inter-district party school, where members of the underground from the Western Ukraine and Poland studied. That was from 1927 to 1929.

Rada was born in Kiev in 1929. That year N.S. left for the Industrial Academy in Moscow, and in the summer of 1930 we joined him and moved into the Academy's dormitory on the Petrovka, No. 40. We had two rooms on different ends of the corridor. We slept in one, with little Rada. Yuliya, Lenya, and the nanny, Matryosha (whom N.S. found before we arrived), slept in the other.

I was sent to work in the party committee at the Electric Lamp Factory. At first I organized and led the Soviet party school. A year later I was elected to the party committee and began to head the agitation and propaganda department of the plant's party committee.

About three thousand communists belonged to the factory's party organization. The plant worked in three shifts, and I had a great deal of work. I left home at 8 A.M. and returned after 10 P.M. As ill luck would have it, Radochka came down with scarlet fever and was put in the hospital next to the plant. In the evening I would run over to look through the window and see what the child was doing. I saw the nurse give her a bowl of kasha and a large spoon and then run off to gossip with her friends. Rada was small, not much more than a year old. I saw her standing with her feet in the bowl and crying, but the nurse ignored her and I couldn't do anything. We signed for her and took the child away early; she barely recovered.

I worked at the Electric Lamp Factory until the middle of 1935, when Seryozha was born. I completed the five-year plan in two and one-half years and received a certificate of honor from the factory organization. I went through my third regular party purge while at the factory. I became acquainted with a large circle of famous Muscovites, with writers, old Bolsheviks, former political convicts sent by their organizations to visit the factory, and collective farmers sponsored by our factory. I consider those to have been the most active years of my political and public life.

In 1935, after maternity leave, the district party committee sent me as the senior party official to the social organization VSNITO (All-Union Council of Scientific and Engineering-Technical Associations), where I worked until Lena was born in 1937.

N.S. was not allowed to complete the Industrial Academy but was transferred to party work, first as secretary of the Baumansky District Party Committee and then of the Krasnaya Presnya District Party Committee. At that time the party was engaged in a brutal struggle with the right-wingers. In 1927 N.S. was a delegate to the Fifteenth Party Congress from the Donetsk organization, and in 1930 he was a delegate to the Sixteenth Party Congress from the Moscow party organization. By 1932 he was already working as a secretary of the Moscow City Committee and after that as a secretary of the provincial party committee. In 1934 he was a delegate to the Seventeenth Congress of the All-Union Communist Party (Bolshevik) and was elected to the party Central Committee. In 1935 L. M. Kaganovich, who had been first secretary of the Moscow City Committee, left to become People's Commissar for Transportation, and they elected N. S. Khrushchev first secretary of the Moscow City party organization. He worked there until the beginning of 1938, when he was sent to the Ukraine as a secretary of the Central Committee of the Communist Party of Bolsheviks of the Ukraine.

Here Mama provides a chronology of Father's life. I will cite only part of it, the beginning of his life's course:

1894, April 17 [actually April 15—S.K.]—born in the village of Kalinovka, Kurskaya *guberniya*.

1909—moved to Yuzovka (the Donbas), where his father worked in the mines in Pastukhovka and Rutchenkovo.

1909–12—at the Bosse factory, student of a metalworker.

1912–18—metalworker at the mines in Pastukhovka and Rutchenkovo.

1915—began to read the newspaper *Pravda*.

February 1917—met L. M. Kaganovich at a meeting.

1918—joined the Russian Communist Party (Bolshevik).

1919–21—served in the Red Army.

1922—deputy director of the Rutchenkovo mine.

1923—studied at the Workers' Faculty in Yuzovka. Secretary of the party bureau.

1925—secretary of the district party committee in Petrovo-Maryinsky District; delegate to the Ninth Congress of the Communist Party (b) of the Ukraine in Kharkov; nonvoting delegate to the Fourteenth Congress of the All-Union Communist Party (b) in Moscow.

1928—worked in the organizational department of the Central Committee of the All-Union Communist Party (b), director of the organizational department of the Kiev District Committee of the Ukrainian Communist Party.

1929–30—student and secretary of the party organization of the Industrial Academy in Moscow, delegate to the Sixteenth Congress of the All-Union Communist Party (b).

1931—first secretary of the Bauman District Party Committee in Moscow (six months) and then first secretary of the Krasnaya Presnya District Party Committee in Moscow for the following six months.

1932—second secretary of the Moscow City Party Committee.

1933—second secretary of the Moscow City and Regional Communist Party Committees.

1934—elected to the Central Committee of the All-Union Communist Party (b) at the Seventeenth Party Congress.

1935—Kaganovich moves to the People's Commissariat for Transportation and N. S. Khrushchev is appointed first secretary of the Moscow City and Regional Party Committees.

1938—Elected first secretary of the Central Committee of the Communist Party (b) Ukraine.

And so on. The remaining stages in Father's career are well known.

In Moscow N.S. directed much of his work to the construction of the first metro line and the Moscow River embankments, as well as the creation of a breadmaking industry (by adapting old circular buildings, as the technology demanded). It was necessary to organize the city economy, baths, public toilets, and electric power for the enterprises of Moscow, and especially for those of the province. New floors were added to low-rise buildings to increase living space, and a great deal else was accomplished.

During this period we already had an apartment in the so-called Govern-

ment House on Kamenny Most (four rooms), and N.S.'s parents moved in
with us. At that time food was distributed by ration card. My distribution
center was located near the plant, while N.S.'s was located in what is today
Komsomolsky Lane. Sergei Nikanorovich, N.S.'s father, traveled to those
distribution centers for potatoes and other food products and carried them
on his back—there was no other possibility. One time he had a heavy load
and jumped off a streetcar while it was in motion and in the opposite direction—it was lucky he wasn't killed. He also used to carry Rada to the day
nursery on the second floor of our building when the elevator wasn't working.
Rada loved her grandfather very much.

Grandmother Kseniya Ivanovna spent most of her time in her room or
sitting on a stool on the street near our entrance. There were always people
standing around her, and she would talk with them. N.S. didn't approve of
her sitting there, but his mother wouldn't listen to him.

Grandmother Kseniya Ivanovna was totally unable to adapt to city life
and didn't want to change her habits. In the village she was used to sitting
outside on a *zavalinka* [mound of earth around peasant homes—Trans.] and
spending hours chatting with neighbors, and she continued this in Moscow.
But Moscow was not Kalinovka, and in the 1930s a heart-to-heart talk could
cost you your life. That was why Father worried.

We left for Kiev in the early spring of 1938, and I had to leave my job; everything I had done up until then was on a voluntary basis on instructions from
the district party committee. During our Kiev period I taught party history
in the district party school (under the Molotovsky District Committee in the
city of Kiev), gave lectures, and took evening courses in the English language.
I took care of the three children, who were small and often sick.

In 1938, in Kiev, I registered with the party organization of the Institute
of Traumatology and Orthopedics in Leninsky District. There I made the
acquaintance of Professor Anna Yevfremovna Frumina, who, beginning in the
spring of 1941, treated Seryozha for tuberculosis of the hip and supervised
his treatment until he was fully recovered. Seryozha was placed in a small bed
made of plaster (one leg, his arms and upper part of his chest were left free),
in which he spent more than two years. It was only in 1943 that he began
to walk with crutches, and then in a "tutor"—a corset specially adapted for
walking.

A curious digression: I don't remember the date, unfortunately. A dacha
was built for V. M. Molotov[13] according to a special design, with large rooms

13. Actually, the dacha was not built for Vyacheslav Molotov but for his predecessor in the
Council of People's Commissars, Aleksei Ivanovich Rykov. Father lived at this dacha, which was
listed in the KGB registry as No. 9, beginning in 1958, when he became chairman of the Council
of Ministers. Later it was the residence of Nikolai Ivanovich Ryzhkov, the next-to-last head of

for the reception of foreign guests. One day it was announced that there would be a government reception for People's Commissars (Ministers) and Moscow party leaders [my Father among them—S.K.] at that dacha. Officials were invited along with their wives, so I was also at the reception. The women were invited to the living room. I sat down near the door and listened to conversations among the Moscow guests. All the women had their own professions, and they chatted about their work and children.

Then we were invited to the dining room, where tables were arranged in a U shape. We were seated according to a prearranged order. I sat next to Valeriya Alekseyevna Golubtsova-Malenkova. The wife of Stanislav Kosior, who had just been transferred to work at the USSR Council of People's Commissars, was seated across from me.[14] It was already known that N. S. Khrushchev would replace him as secretary of the Ukrainian Communist Party. During dinner I started to ask Kosior's wife what kitchenware I should take with me. She was quite astonished by my questions and said that the house we would live in had everything and we didn't need to take anything with us. Indeed, it turned out that the cook and her staff had more fine kitchenware at their disposal than I had ever seen. The same was true in the dining room. We began to live with things supplied by the government: furniture, dishes, and beds. Food was delivered from a government warehouse and we were billed once a month.

To return to the reception: I found everything very curious. After the guests were seated, I. V. Stalin entered from the buffet room, followed by members of the Politburo, and they all sat down at the head table. Of course, they were greeted with applause for a long time. I don't remember exactly, but I think it was Stalin himself who said that many new people's commissariats had been formed recently, that new leaders had been appointed, and that the Politburo had decided it would be useful to bring everyone together in such a friendly setting, to talk and get to know one another better.

After that many people spoke, giving their affiliation and describing what they thought of their work. Women were asked to speak. Valeriya Alekseyevna Golubtsova-Malenkova talked about her scientific research, which provoked the women to criticize her. In contrast, the young wife of Kaftanov, the People's Commissar for Higher Education, said that she would do everything to help her husband work better in his new and responsible position. This met with general approval.

During the dinner I learned that Comrade Kosior had two sons. Kosior's

---

government of the Soviet Union. The dacha, renamed "Gorky-9," is now the country residence of the Russian president.

14. "Council of People's Commissars." "People's Commissar" was at that time the term for "minister." Hence, this body was the ancestor of the Council of Ministers.

wife made a very pleasant impression on me. I often thought of her when I found out years later that she had been unjustly sent into exile and shot, and that the instructions to shoot her had been personally signed by V. M. Molotov. N.S. told me this under the following circumstances: One day Polina Semyonovna Molotova met me in the courtyard of the house on Granovsky Street and asked me to pass on to N.S. her request to be received at the Central Committee on the subject of accepting V. M. Molotov back into the party—he had been expelled several years before. N.S. received Polina Semyonovna and showed her the document with Molotov's instructions to shoot the wives of Kosior, Postyshev, and other ranking officials of the Ukraine. He then asked whether, in her opinion, it was possible to talk about restoring Molotov's party membership or if he should be put on trial. N.S. told me this when I asked if Polina Semyonovna had visited him and how the conversation ended.

In 1935–36 enterprises worked on the basis of an uninterrupted week: people worked five days, with the sixth day off, on a sliding scale. It was a very inconvenient schedule for me. N.S. had a regular day off, so we were never free on the same day. The purpose of the uninterrupted work week was a good one: equipment was fully utilized, so labor productivity rose and people were less tired. But the system was not popular, and we later shifted to a six-day work week, with Sundays off.

I remember that in those years Yevgeniya Kogan, Kuibyshev's former wife, was the secretary for propaganda of the Moscow City Committee, and I remember her daughter, Galya Kuibysheva.[15] I remember how disappointed I was when Comrade Kogan arranged for her comrades to visit theaters, which happened often. But I couldn't go with them because I worked at the factory Sundays. And all cultural events in which N.S. participated were unavailable to me because of the "uninterrupted" week.

The secretary of the party committee at the Electric Lamp Factory was Comrade Yurov, a very energetic comrade. People in those days called each other by their last names and didn't take any particular interest in family matters. Yurov didn't know or care who my husband was. Late one evening he called our apartment. I answered and he said brusquely: "Who is speaking?" I automatically answered, "Kukharchuk." "But what are you doing there? I'm calling Comrade Khrushchev's apartment." He was very surprised to find out that I was, it turned out, Khrushchev's wife. He was calling on an urgent matter: the meadows of a collective farm supported by our factory were about to be trampled by an Army cavalry unit, and it was imperative that the Moscow City Committee of the Communist Party intervene before

---

15. Valerian Vladimirovich Kuibyshev—a top economic official in Stalin's Kremlin—died (of natural causes) in 1935.

morning. The next day he questioned me about how I managed to conceal my family connection with the secretary of the Moscow City Committee. I replied that I had not concealed it, but hadn't thought it necessary to inform my comrades at the factory in the absence of questions from them. Incidentally, with the assistance of the Moscow City Committee, the meadows were protected from the cavalry. Later on Comrade Yurov was unjustly subjected to repression and perished.

Members of the factory's party committee worked very hard. As I've already mentioned, I left home at eight in the morning and returned no earlier than ten in the evening. I traveled by streetcar from our apartment building to Elektrozavodskaya Street, which took at least an hour.

On the way to and from work I read new books. I remember reading *How the Steel Was Tempered* for the first time on the streetcar.[16] The factory worked in three shifts and the party, trade union, and Komsomol[17] organizations (committees) had to work during all three shifts: we held meetings, political classes, etc.

During the 1950s I kept in touch with the factory's workers through Varya Syrkova, who invited me to her home, where I saw former comrades. But after she died, and later Comrade Tsvetkov (former director of the lamp factory) died, personal contacts ended, though Tamara Tamarina, who had worked at the Electric Lamp Factory since 1916, would call on the telephone and pass on greetings.

This is how my parents got to know Nikita Sergeyevich:

In 1939 the Germans occupied Poland and were approaching my native village, Vasilyev. As is well known, our forces were moving west at that time and occupied regions of the western Ukraine, the city of Lvov and western Belorussia. N.S. called me in Kiev and said that my village, Vasilyev, and the surrounding region would pass to the Germans and that if I wanted to, I could take the opportunity to go to Lvov, and from there I would be taken to Vasilyev and could pick up my parents. N.S. added that Comrade Burmistenko, secretary of the Central Committee of the Communist Party (b) (Ukraine) was organizing my trip. Comrade Burmistenko told me that two women were traveling to Lvov on orders of the Central Committee, and that I could go with them. One young Komsomol member was going to work with youth and the other, a party official, was supposed to work with women in Lvov. We were ordered to put on uniforms and carry revolvers. They said

---

16. *How the Steel Was Tempered* (1934), the best-known work of the novelist Nikolai Alekseevich Ostrovsky, was a classic of the "socialist-realist" school. It is a semi-autobiographical yarn of a young tough who is eventually transformed into a selfless communist who triumphs over impossible odds only to die of a terminal illness.

17. Komsomol—the Young Communist League, the youth wing of the Communist Party.

that the change in dress was for convenience, so that military patrols would not stop us so often along the road.

Vanya Podosinov, an excellent driver from the Central Committee garage, took the wheel of our ZIS-101.

Our trip was more or less uneventful until we were near Lvov, where we were almost run over by an oncoming truck. The truck driver hadn't slept for three nights and had fallen asleep at the wheel. To avoid a collision, Vanya Podosinov turned the wheel sharply to the right and the car struck a telegraph pole. The only one hurt was the Komsomol member, who hit her nose on the window. An officer who happened to pass by (he checked our documents), picked us up in his car, sent the girl off to the hospital for treatment and the two of us were lodged in Lvov, in an apartment of the command post. Semyon Konstantinovich Timoshenko, commander of the Kiev Military District, was commanding the troops. N. S. Khrushchev was there also, in his capacity as a member of the Military Council. When N.S. and Timoshenko returned home and saw us in military uniform with revolvers they first started to laugh, but then N.S. got very angry and ordered us to change into dresses immediately. He continued indignantly: "What on earth were you thinking of? You want to persuade the local population to be in favor of the Soviet government and you come here with revolvers? Who's going to trust you? They've been taught for years that we're aggressors, and you'll confirm that slander with your revolvers."

I changed clothes and went to Vasilyev for my parents. I was accompanied by Vasily Mitrofanovich Bozhko, one of the officers from N.S.'s bodyguard. Our trip was uneventful and we arrived at my parents' house. Father and Mother were at home. A lot of people came running to see me and to ask for news. No one wanted to believe that the village would go to the Germans; not even the junior commanders of units had been told that yet. But Comrade Timoshenko had given me permission to say why I was coming for my parents. That night they moved a tank into Father's courtyard. All night long soldiers crowded into the house to get warm; Mama fed them and V. M. Bozhko sat down with them also. Toward morning representatives from the local government (still Soviet) came to arrest me as a spy and provocateur. Bozhko and the tank crew had a hard time persuading them that they were making a mistake. In the morning my parents and brother with his family loaded their belongings onto the truck and got in, and we headed for Lvov. A representative of the local government came with us as far as the first military command post. He wanted to get more precise information, but at the post they had not been told what territory would go to the Germans according to the treaty.

I brought my relatives to Lvov, to the *voevode*'s [governor's] palace, where N.S. was staying. They started to walk around the rooms, marveling at everything. For example, Father turned on the bathroom faucet and called to Mother: "Come see, water's flowing out of a pipe!" Everyone ran in, looked, exclaimed. Only my brother, Ivan Petrovich, said that he'd seen indoor plumbing during his army service.

When Comrade Timoshenko and N.S. walked into the room, Father pointed to Timoshenko and said: "Is this our son-in-law?" But he didn't seem disappointed when he found out that N.S. was his son-in-law. . . .

The beginning of the war, in June 1941, found us in Kiev.

THE WAR YEARS

Mama's chronological notes break off here. It's not clear whether she didn't want to describe later events or whether there simply hadn't been enough time to write everything down. Now there is no way to answer that question. However, individual notes have been preserved, and I have inserted them on various pages of this chapter.

As Mama already described in her notes, in the spring of 1941 misfortune struck. I contracted tuberculosis of the hip, which was called coxitis. It settled in my legs. I was forbidden, not just to walk, but to sit or move in general. I lay on my back on boards, tightly bandaged to a plaster form in the shape of my whole lower body.

In those days tuberculosis was not a rarity. Members of my Father's family suffered from it. Mother's parents and her brother had died of it. My older sister, Yuliya, became gravely ill from it. As Mama writes in one of her notes devoted to the children, "After the end of school, where Yuliya was studying in the second year of the Department of Geography (Kiev University), she had to interrupt her study because she came down with a severe form of tuberculosis. After an operation on her lungs, they performed a pneumothorax, in which condition she was evacuated in 1941."

There was no good treatment, since the medicines simply didn't exist. My parents went to all the doctors. Their prognosis was not reassuring, but they advised quiet, fresh air, and nourishing food. That temporary immobility left its mark on the rest of my life. During the most intensive period of development of a conscious self, I was deprived of the society of other children. Who needs a friend who is firmly tied to a bed? Only grownups, especially my Mother, spent time with me. I have always gratefully remembered the few friends who spent a few crumbs of their childish attention on me.

The war began while I was in this state of immobility. Then came the evacuation, from Kiev to Moscow, and from there to Kuibyshev, where families of high-ranking government officials were housed at the former sanatorium of the Volga Military District. We lived in the same building as Malenkov's family. When the Germans approached Stalingrad, the Malenkovs moved further on, to Sverdlovsk. Mama refused to move again. She simply lacked the strength to retreat further. Besides, in his letters from the front, from Stalingrad, Father expressed his conviction that the Germans were worn out and would not advance beyond the Volga.

The family gathered under Mama's wing was a large one. Besides me, hanging like an immobile weight around her neck, there were my two sisters—Rada, already an adolescent schoolgirl, and little four-year-old Lena— and Mama's parents and relatives—in all, fifteen persons.

My brother Leonid was in the Air Force, flying bombers. At the beginning of the war flying in bombers was considered a form of suicide. Fighter cover was virtually nonexistent, and the Germans shot point-blank at the slow and clumsy planes. According to his fellow fliers, Leonid fought well, didn't hide behind others' backs or behind his father's name. This is what his commander wrote in recommending him for an award:

> Aircraft Commander Leonid Nikitovich Khrushchev has performed twelve military missions. He has carried out all military tasks outstandingly. He is a courageous and fearless pilot. During an aerial battle on July 6, 1941, he fought bravely against the opponent's fighters until the attack was repelled.
>
> Khrushchev emerged from the battle with a bullet-riddled aircraft. He takes the initiative. . . . He has often gone into battle substituting for unprepared crews. I recommend that Comrade Khrushchev be awarded the Order of the Red Banner.
>
> (signed)
> July 16, 1941
> Colonel Pisarsky, commander of the Forty-Sixth Aviation Division

Leonid had ten days left as a bomber pilot.

The military report on the incident states: "On July 26 the remainder of the three squadrons of the 134th Bomber Group took off to bomb an airfield in the region of the Izoch station and artillery in the region of Khikalo. On returning, the undefended bombers were attacked by eight German Messerschmitt-109 fighters. Losses comprised four of the six planes."

Leonid's plane barely reached the front line and landed in a neutral zone with the fuselage shot away. One crew member was killed in the air, and Leonid broke his leg in the landing. Red Army soldiers rescued the crew of the downed plane. In the field hospital they wanted to amputate Leonid's leg, but he refused and threatened them with his gun. The leg healed very badly, and Leonid recuperated for more than a year in a hospital in the rear, in Kuibyshev. There I saw him for the last time, pale, smiling, wearing his new decoration.

When his leg knit, Leonid began agitating to return to the front, this time in fighters. By using all the contacts available to him, my brother got his wish. But then something very unfortunate occurred. Since I was only six at the time, naturally no one told me anything. But at home I heard people whispering that Leonid had killed someone. Much later I read the memoirs of General Stepan Mikoyan and found out what happened. Mikoyan was also in the Air Force and as a lieutenant had flown to Kuibyshev, where he met Leonid. Stepan Mikoyan writes as follows: "One evening a Navy officer turned up from the front. After everyone was really plastered, somebody mentioned that Leonid was a very accurate marksman. The officer dared Leonid to hit a bottle balanced on his head. Leonid refused for a while, but finally agreed and shot off the neck of the bottle. The sailor claimed that wasn't enough and said he had to hit the bottle itself. When Leonid fired again, he hit the officer in the forehead."

A court found Leonid guilty. At that time people were not put in prison, but were sent to the front to serve in penal battalions. They allowed Leonid to stay in the Air Force. He returned to the front in an air squadron, flying fighters, as he had always wanted. However, he was not fated to fight for long. Leonid completed only six more missions. During the seventh, on March 11, 1943, he was shot down in the vicinity of the village of Zhizdra, not far from Smolensk.

It was a common fate for young pilots untrained in the intricate techniques of aerial combat. It occurred over swampy, German-occupied terrain. In the heat of battle his disappearance was not noticed by his fellow pilots— one minute Leonid was there, the next he was gone. The front commander sent condolences to Father and offered to send a search party to the area where the plane was presumed to have crashed. Father thanked him, but asked him not to risk the lives of others. It would not help and would not bring back his son. So Leonid Khrushchev joined the ranks of the missing.

In 1995 a report appeared in Russian newspapers that a teacher in one of the local schools had found the remnants of a Soviet fighter in the Smolensk swamps. In its cabin they found the skeleton of the pilot in a decayed lieutenant's uniform and a fur helmet. According to his fellow pilots, Leonid had worn such a helmet with earphones, the only one in the whole regiment, and was very proud of it. Since the wooden fuselage had rotted away, the number of the plane is legible on the engine, and it only remains to compare it with records in the military archives. If the record has been preserved, there will be one less person missing in action.

Soon after Leonid's death, his widow, Lyubov Illariovna, was arrested in Kuibyshev and charged with working for foreign intelligence—a standard accusation. The diplomatic corps had also been evacuated to the Volga. I no longer remember whose spy, British or Swedish, she was supposed to be. She was not freed until the 1950s, after suffering a full measure of misfortune in the Karaganda camps. Their year-old daughter Yuliya was left to Mother's care. She grew up with us and was very unhappy to be put in a different category—that of grandchild. Mama was the first to notice this, so Yuliya became a daughter.

Mama's niece and nephew, Nina and Vasya, also lived with us. In Kuibyshev they attended school along with Rada, but toward the end of the war Vasya turned seventeen and joined the artillery. After only brief training he was sent to the front. Vasily Ivanovich Kukharchuk died during the advance on Vienna in 1945, just before victory was won.

My oldest sister was the only one to spend the evacuation far away from us. She was evacuated to Central Asia together with her husband, Viktor Petrovich Gontar, director of the Ukrainian "Dumka" ("Thought") State Choir. Viktor Petrovich was not sent to the front, , but was firmly barricaded in the rear, the life of someone in the "valuable" profession of theater administrator was not to be risked. He did not see Father again until after the liberation of Kiev.

Aleksei Ivanovich Adzhubei, my future brother-in-law, was also not in the fighting. In October 1941 he was seventeen and living in Moscow. Many of his schoolmates lost their lives as volunteers at the front during the German attack on Moscow in October 1941. During those terrible days young Aleksei was summoned to serve in the Song and Dance Ensemble of the all-powerful NKVD. His mother, Nina Matveyevna, sewed clothes for Beria's wife.

Besides the Malenkovs, the others living on the sanatorium's grounds in Kuibyshev included the Serovs, the Poskrebyshevs, the Litvinovs, and a few other no less privileged families.[18] I remember only those who showed any interest in me, since I was still attached to the stretcher.

I remember Pavlik Litvinov. He was always looking for something to eat. In the autumn he would dig up potatoes and treat himself to them, sometimes baked in the ashes left from a fire and sometimes eaten raw. Never before or since have I seen anyone eat a raw potato.

In 1941 a large construction project was going on in a narrow gully that dropped down to the Volga near our home. Floodlights were on all through the night. We didn't know what they were doing, but it was rumored that prisoners were working there. The secret was revealed after a fire left our family without a roof over our heads in January of 1943. Our wooden house was consumed in an hour's time, and we barely managed to escape in our nightclothes. I was carried out on the stretcher. A fire brigade came, but in temperatures of −30 degrees Centigrade (−22 degrees Fahrenheit) the

---

18. "Serovs, the Poskrebyshevs, the Litvinovs." The families of General Ivan Aleksandrovich Serov, who was People's Commissar of the NKVD in the Ukraine before the war; Stalin's assistant, A. N. Poskrebyshev; and Soviet Foreign Minister (People's Commissar for Foreign Affairs) Maksim Litvinov. His grandson Pavel became a well-known dissident in the 1960s.

water froze in their hoses, so they simply watched while the roof collapsed and the walls fell in. Less than an hour later nothing was left but embers. Officials from the NKVD, who were in charge of the former sanatorium, didn't know where to put us.

For several hours we hung around the entrance to the command post while urgent negotiations proceeded with Moscow. A decision was finally made. We were led down a meticulously cleared paved road leading to the forbidden zone where lights had so recently twinkled. A few minutes later we entered a handsome two-story stone house, fronted by columns.

It turned out that Stalin was to have moved here if Moscow had fallen. The house was surrounded by paved walks, with views of the Volga from benches set on the steep bank. An elevator inside the house led to a bunker with numerous rooms, passages, and service areas that had been built many meters below ground. In the summer of 1943, when it became certain that the "object" would not be needed by its proprietor, we were even taken on a tour of the underground site. The elevator was no longer working, puddles of water had formed in some places, and the furniture had been removed, leaving the rooms empty.

There, in Kuibyshev, I relearned how to walk and then to run, on crutches. I rejoiced in my newfound mobility. It even seemed to me that I ran faster on crutches than healthy children did without them. I was inexpressibly happy to reenter the world of movement.

In 1943 we left Kuibyshev, first for Moscow and then finally home to Kiev.

All those years I had not seen Father. Mama had visited him at the front several times, and I had carefully preserved his presents from Stalingrad: a trophy box of German medals, a shell casing, and SS daggers.[19]

This is how Mama recalled that time of troubles:

In Kuibyshev we lived at first in the city; then they gave us a dacha (which we shared with the Malenkov family) at a sanatorium of the Volga Regional Military District. Some factories—ball-bearing, aviation, and others—had been relocated not far from us, in the village of Bezymyanka. Rada, my relatives Vasya, Nina, and Rona attended school. Irma did not, because of her deafness.[20] Seryozha lay in the plaster cast, and we carried him from the fourth floor down to the street. Later, at the dacha, things were easier. I worked as a propagandist for the district party committee and took day courses in the

---

19. During the war, N. S. Khrushchev held the rank of lieutenant general in the Red Army and served in the defense of Stalingrad as the senior political officer.

20. Nina and Vasya were the children of Mama's brother, Ivan Petrovich. Rona and Irma were the daughters of Father's sister, Irina Sergeyevna.—S.K.

English language. I took part in various types of work to mobilize the district Soviet and went to a collective farm for a month to harvest grain.

I remember some difficult times listening to the radio, waiting for news from the front, especially the Stalingrad front. Those evenings I sewed a variety of table-napkins and pillow-covers, which helped to distract me somewhat from gloomy thoughts.

I flew to Moscow several times, when N.S. flew there on matters related to the Stalingrad front.

My last contact with the war occurred on April 17, 1944, in Kiev. We celebrated Father's fiftieth birthday, and on that day the Germans bombed Darnitsa heavily. We children collected splinters from the antiaircraft shells.

THE EARLY POSTWAR YEARS

Kiev

Life at peace began. Father had no time for foreign policy. The poor harvest of 1946 hit hard. In response to Father's request for a reduction in grain deliveries, Stalin sent Kaganovich to Kiev.[21] He became first secretary of the Central Committee, the granaries were swept clean, and hunger and cannibalism came to the Ukraine. I can't read Father's memoirs of that time without a shudder.

After accomplishing his mission, Kaganovich returned to Moscow.

Troubles travel in groups. Mama recalls: "In the spring of 1947 N.S. caught a cold in the Irpenskaya water meadows near Kiev, where he went to organize the cultivation of vegetables on peat bogs to feed residents of the capital. He fell gravely ill with pneumonia. We feared for his life. He lay at home, looked after by a doctor and nurse, with consultations by two professors (Zelenin and someone else) from Moscow."

They thought he might not survive. Neither the newly popular penicillin nor oxygen brought any relief. As they emerged from Father's bedroom, Professors Vovsi and Gubergrits (for some reason I remember those particular names), medical luminaries of the time, only shook their heads in distress.

I can still remember Father's motionless gray face on the pillows, the hoarse whistle of his breathing, and his uncomprehending look. But he had a strong constitution and at last recovered. They sent him to the sea to recuperate. Not to the Black Sea, to which Father was accustomed, but to the

---

21. Lazar Moisevich Kaganovich was the archetypical brutally efficient Stalinist manager who got things done regardless of the cost in blood. As head of the Ukrainian Communist Party (1925–26), and of the Moscow Party Committee (1930–35), he helped advance Khrushchev's career. This episode, however, in which Stalin sent Kaganovich to Ukraine to relieve Khrushchev of his duties as first secretary of the Ukrainian Communist Party, soured their relations permanently.

Baltic. For some reason I still cannot fathom, his doctors considered the southern sun to be contraindicated. So Father spent his first postwar vacation in the settlement of Mairi, near Riga, along with a whole flock of children. The sea seemed unusually shallow, uninviting, and frigid. But we, the children, paid no attention to the temperature and dashed into the water at the first opportunity, even when our parents and older sister Yuliya sat on the shore in coats, observing our "feats." Father quickly regained his strength. When the duck hunting season began he disappeared in the direction of the nearby lakes. In the middle of August he decided to fly to Königsberg, which had recently been renamed Kaliningrad. He took us, along with Rada. The city lay in ruins. Its center was completely burned out. We stayed in a general's residence on the outskirts.

Father asked the general whether the Germans were causing any trouble. "No, of course not, Nikita Sergeyevich, everything's quiet," responded the general quickly. But then he added: "I have a machine gun on the terrace outside my room on the second floor. When I wake up at night I shoot off a round, and then go back to bed." I didn't understand why he needed a machine gun if everything was peaceful.

We spent a couple of days in Kaliningrad. Father was very interested in how they were making fabrics out of brown coal. He was enthusiastic about what German chemists had achieved and took away a whole collection of samples to show Ukrainian scientists and try to introduce these technologies at home. We also visited a gigantic quarry where amber was being extracted. It made an indelible impression on me, especially the pieces with mosquitoes or flies trapped inside. Father was not interested. Upon arriving back in Riga, Father began preparing to go home. We returned to Kiev in early autumn, toward the start of the school year.

Life gradually returned to normal. That meant Father was busy working, but he found time to be with us children, to walk in the woods or go boating on the Dnieper River. Father loved company. On weekends secretaries of the Central Committee and deputy chairmen of the Council of Ministers usually gathered at our dacha, even if there was no special occasion. Generals were included. The Kiev district commander at the time was Colonel General Andrei Antonovich Grechko, an old friend of Father's from the front. Grechko was convivial and loved to tell jokes.

During these get-togethers serious conversation alternated with humor. They included swimming in the Dnieper during the summer and visits to nearby collective farms in the autumn, "to admire the harvest," as Father would say. It would all end with a noisy dinner, shared by the whole company.

But hunting was Father's favorite recreation. Today we've heard our fill of how government leaders amused themselves. In those years no one

thought twice about it. Everything was arranged very simply. Father's colleagues—I remember best Ivan Semyonovich Senin, Demyan Sergeyevich
Korotchenko, Nikifor Timofeyevich Kalchenko, Aleksandr Yevdokimovich
Korneichuk, and General Grechko—spread out in a line, ambling forward
through the autumn stubble and calling to one another in hopes of scaring
up a hare. When the older members of the group got tired, we children,
alternating with the guards, would whoop and chase the hares and foxes
toward our fathers, who were standing on the firing line. The bag was usually
not very big, but the satisfaction was great.

Such meetings brought people closer, transforming them from colleagues
to simply comrades, and sometimes into friends. In those complicated times
that meant a great deal. In all the postwar years no one in Father's circle
disappeared without a trace. Nobody searched among them for "enemies of
the people."

Moscow

We returned to Moscow at the very beginning of 1950, right after celebrating the New Year in Kiev. Mama arranged it so that we didn't miss a single
day in school. She was a strict disciplinarian. Father had left several weeks
earlier. Stalin summoned him in December for his seventieth birthday celebrations. Father barely managed to break away and return to Kiev for a few
days in order to turn over his affairs to his successor, Leonid Georgiyevich
Melnikov.

It was obvious that Stalin was seriously worried. The so-called Leningrad
Affair had just come to a conclusion.[22] Voznesensky and Kuznetsov, young
and increasingly influential members of the Politburo, were dead. It seems
very likely that this time Stalin genuinely believed in the existence of a plot.
He became concerned when, right after the Leningrad Affair concluded, he
was given materials indicating the existence of a similar "plot" in the capital,
headed by Georgy Mikhailovich Popov, chief of the Moscow party organization. I think this was the reason for the peremptory summons to Father.
During his first few days in Moscow, Stalin handed Father a pile of documents with charges of anti-Soviet activities not only against Popov and his
inner circle, but against all district committee secretaries and district execu-

---

22. The "Leningrad Affair" was the execution on fabricated charges of several high-level party
leaders who had been close to Leningrad party chief Andrei Zhdanov, who died in 1948. Among
its victims were Zhdanov's replacement in Leningrad—A. A. Kuznetsov—and one of his most
successful younger protégés, the economist and central planner N. A. Voznesensky. According to
the senior Khrushchev, the plot was carried out at the initiative of Zhdanov's enemies Malenkov
and Beria. It is emblematic of the postwar period: a morbidly suspicious Stalin surrounded by
backstabbing and cutthroat courtiers jockeying for position.

tive committee chairmen, as well as some enterprise directors. Father was aghast. He had never, thank heaven, run into such problems in the Ukraine after the war. The local vigilantes knew that they had better not poke their noses into the Ukrainian Party Central Committee with such denunciations.

Father decided not to change his ways just because he was no longer in Kiev. He realized that the affair might die down if he did not display any zeal—provided, naturally, that Stalin's interests were not involved. Had they been, nothing and no one could have helped the victims. In this case Father's experience, gained in the "meat grinder" of 1937, as he called it, suggested that Stalin was not the author of the intrigue, and so the hand of the executioner might be stayed.

Several weeks later, when Stalin, without waiting for Father's report, asked for the results of his investigation, Father tried to persuade him that the denunciation was false and all the evidence fabricated. Stalin did not pursue the matter, and it died down. Father arranged for his predecessor, Popov, to be sent far away. He was named a factory director, a position in which Stalin wouldn't view him as a threat and Popov's life would not be in jeopardy. Popov viewed his "exile" in a different light and remained in the camp of those hostile to Father to the end of his days.

With the move to Moscow our life style changed considerably. Guests stopped coming by. Father never said a word about hunting. In Moscow danger lurked in friends and friendship. No one knew how meetings would be reported to the "Boss" by the KGB guards or what he might think. An innocent meeting between old friends could end tragically.

We found this turn of events in our family lives unusual and unexpected. Father too had grown unused to Moscow customs during his period of freedom in the Ukraine.

I remember one particular occasion. In the summer of 1950 Father decided to visit his old friend Nikolai Aleksandrovich Bulganin. They had been friends since the 1930s, when Father was secretary of the Moscow Party Committee and Bulganin was chairman of the Moscow Soviet. Stalin dubbed them "The City Fathers."

After 1930, when Father left the capital, their paths diverged. Now they lived on the same stairwell, on the fifth floor of No. 3 Granovsky Street (Malenkov lived one floor below us), but rarely met outside the office. Sometimes they would return together after a late "dinner" with Stalin and sometimes the families would drop in on each other.

One time Father wangled an invitation to Bulganin's dacha. The whole family went. This meeting of old comrades was not a success. Our hosts put on a facade of cordiality and there was a groaning table, but the conversation went in fits and starts, with agonizing pauses.

It was one thing to meet in Kiev, far from the Kremlin. Here in Moscow the world was ordered on different principles. Why was Khrushchev suddenly visiting Bulganin at the dacha, where they went for a long walk in the woods, far from curious eyes and attentive ears? Without waiting for evening, we left for home.

Perhaps the fiasco of our visit had nothing to do with politics. The fact is that during the war, while he was a member of the Military Council on the Western front, Bulganin had acquired a new family. Divorces were not encouraged in the top party ranks; in fact they were frowned on more severely than in the Catholic church. Bulganin therefore could not bring himself to talk about, much less legalize, his new relationship. He received us at the dacha with his old family. What kind of cordiality could there be in that situation? At the time Father was not aware of the transformation in his friend's family life.

One way or another, Father did not visit Bulganin again and did not invite him to our dacha. Still, Father could not entirely break himself of old habits. He couldn't imagine living without social contacts. While Stalin was alive, Father saw Malenkov more than anyone else. We visited his dacha several times, went mushroom gathering and dined together. But we met more frequently in the city. Father got in the habit of dragging Georgy Maksimiliyanovich off for a stroll around Moscow in the evening, after work. He wouldn't object, and a bunch of us would set off, first the principals, behind them Mama with Malenkov's wife, Valeriya Alekseyevna, then Rada and her husband Alyosha, Malenkov's children, and I.

The guards arrayed themselves around us—Father's guards, who were used to such walks from our stay in Kiev, and the local guards, who saw a potential terrorist in every passerby. However, they didn't approach us or bother the passersby, since they knew that Father wouldn't put up with such behavior. Hardly anyone recognized Father or Malenkov. Our walks usually took place on autumn evenings (in summer we spent nights at the dacha), so it was hard to distinguish faces in the dark. In any case, the walks proceeded without incident.

We usually walked along Kalinin Street, then the Mokhovaya, turned onto Gorky (now Tverskaya) Street and then toward home. If we went into the Aleksandrovsky Gardens, farther on into Red Square and along the river bank below the Kremlin, the excursion lasted longer. Conversations on the street rarely touched on serious subjects, and Stalin was never mentioned. They usually gossiped about the children and chatted about their households. During those walks Valeriya Alekseyevna persuaded me to apply for study at the Electric Power Institute. She had been its director for a long time and had left a favorable impression there. At the time the Institute was assembling an up-to-date department for electro-vacuum technology and special instrument building.

Something else new appeared in Father's life in Moscow—an armored ZIS-110 limousine, the latest achievement of the Moscow Auto Plant. Even before the war armor-plated Packard automobiles had been purchased in the United States for Politburo members. One of these was offered to Father. However, he didn't believe there would be an attempt on his life, besides which he loved space and fresh air. He adamantly refused to shut himself up in a stifling, cramped box. He preferred an open car, with a canvas top in case of rain. In it Father traveled along Ukrainian fields, leaving behind a cloud of fine dust. He protected himself with a special canvas dust-coat buttoned tightly to the neck.

In Moscow other rules were observed. At first everything continued as before. Father waved off his guards' insistent suggestions to use the armored car. But one day a ZIS drove into our dacha courtyard. It was somehow different from the usual one—the same, but not quite the same. As always, I went out to meet Father and took hold of the handle to open the car door. It turned, but nothing happened. I pulled hard and a small crack appeared. Gradually the door opened. It turned out to be incredibly heavy and thick. The windows alone were four inches thick.

A disgruntled Father climbed out. Glancing scornfully at the car, he announced: "I'll be riding in this now. They made me."

"They" were not identified. Perhaps General Vlasik, the chief of Stalin's bodyguard, had complained to Stalin, who had issued a simple order. Or perhaps Father himself had decided it was not sensible to stand out as the only one not using an armored vehicle. I can't say. He rode in that car until March of 1953 and then discarded it for good.

Interestingly enough, only Mikoyan followed his example. The remaining members of the collective leadership, especially Voroshilov and Molotov, kept a tight grip on their armored monsters. Did they think there was a victim hiding behind every bush, thirsting for revenge? Or did they simply feel uncomfortable without an impenetrable wall between themselves and the surrounding world?

Another new factor in our lives were telephone calls from the "Boss." Actually, Stalin himself never called. Someone called from the Secretariat. But just the possibility of such a call caused nervous tension whenever the "Kremlin line" emitted its imperious ring.

Father felt especially uncomfortable on weekends. He was faced with a dilemma—should he eat with the family? He wouldn't feel comfortable if summoned to dinner on a full stomach. A great deal has been written about Stalin's dinners, and I don't want to repeat it. Sometimes the phone would ring and Father would leave hastily. Sometimes he was spared.

The last time Father waited for a call like that was at the beginning of March 1953. It was March 1, a Sunday. The evening before, or rather that morning, he had returned home to the dacha around five o'clock. He often came home at that hour after "dining" with Stalin. Father was sure that Stalin couldn't stand being alone on a day off and would call. Without having dinner, Father went for a walk, telling us to call him at once if he were summoned. That was said pro forma, since everyone knew perfectly well what to do in that case. The call did not come, and it began to get dark. He had a solitary snack and sat down to read some papers. It was already evening when Malenkov called to say that something had happened to Stalin. Father left hurriedly.

Naturally, we didn't know who had called or what had been said. Everyone was busy with his own concerns.

We were somewhat surprised when Father returned after only an hour or two. However, nobody asked any questions. He went quietly upstairs to his bedroom and resumed working on his papers.

I didn't hear him leave the second time. I had probably gone to sleep. This time Father was away for many hours—until the next morning. We still didn't know anything. The next day he said that Stalin was ill, that his condition was very serious, and that he and Bulganin would stay the night at the patient's bedside at a nearby dacha. An announcement about Stalin's illness did not appear in the newspapers until March 4. Apparently until then there was some faint hope for his recovery. Father didn't answer any of my questions clearly, responding with phrases like: "They're treating him; they're doing everything possible."

Such an announcement in the newspapers could mean only one thing— there was no hope. Ordinarily, everything relating to Stalin was kept in the utmost secrecy. Father confirmed the worst, saying: "Anything can happen. We must prepare the nation." I remember that he added: "Otherwise it would look like he's alive—he's alive and then suddenly he's dead. Who knows what people might imagine? You know, when Lenin fell ill, medical bulletins were issued and published regularly."

I tried to quiz Father for details, but he didn't want to provide any. Besides, what could he tell me? I was still just a kid.

What did Stalin mean to me? Like many people, I have often thought about that over the years. With the passage of time my attitude has changed dramatically. It is important not to substitute today's attitude for yesterday's. Our family hardly ever talked about Stalin. It was thought that there was nothing to explain. There was not a word of criticism. But Father's tension was always apparent. He tried not to show it, but sometimes it broke through in little things.

I remember the following episode. Toward the end of his life Stalin began to identify jazz music with counterrevolutionary activity. Perhaps nobody had been arrested yet for playing it, but things were drifting in that direction.

One summer Sunday at the dacha I put on a record of Leonid Utesov's, *The Steamship*. At the time it was considered an extreme "left-wing" work. Father was sitting at a table reading the newspapers. At first he didn't react, then he looked up and said, or rather ordered, "Turn that off."

I stopped the record player. Father paused, then added, "Best to break it."

I didn't answer. I was really sorry at the thought of losing the record. He didn't insist, but asked me not to play it again.

What did he know or suspect? What was he afraid of?

In those years Comrade Stalin remained for me the supreme leader for all times and all peoples. I attributed whatever seemed illogical in his *On Economic Problems* and *Questions of Linguistics*—books which I simply couldn't absorb—to my inability to comprehend the thinking of a genius. To doubt them would never have entered my mind.

STALIN DIES

On the evening of March 5 Father returned home about midnight, much earlier than on previous days, when it was usually almost morning.

"Why isn't he keeping watch?" I thought involuntarily.

Father took off his jacket and went to wash up, while we sat silently at the table in the dining room. He came in, sat down tiredly on the couch, and stretched out his legs. After a pause, he said: "Stalin died. Today. They'll announce it tomorrow."

He closed his eyes.

I went into the next room, a lump in my throat. I kept thinking: "What will happen now?"

I was truly upset, but it was as if a "second self" sat in judgment and was horrified by the shallowness of my emotions, by their inadequacy in comparison with the tragedy of the moment. However, nothing more came, and I returned to the dining room.

Father still sat on the couch, his eyes half-closed. The others sat motionless around the table. I saw only Father.

Hesitating, I asked: "Where will he lie in state?"

"In the Hall of Columns. It will be announced tomorrow." I thought Father sounded somehow indifferent and removed from it all. Then he added, after a pause: "I'm very tired after the last few days. I'm going to take a nap."

He rose heavily and headed slowly toward the bedroom.

I was upset and indignant: "How can he sleep at such a moment? And without saying a word about Stalin? As if nothing had happened!" I was amazed by his behavior.

Several days went by. In the course of those frosty days Stalin's body was placed in the Mausoleum and its inscription was changed. Now there were two names: "Lenin. Stalin." One after the other.

Restructuring

On March 7 a decree of the Plenum of the Central Committee of the CPSU, the Council of Ministers, and the Presidium of the Supreme Soviet informed the country of its new leaders and their duties.

G. M. Malenkov was to head the Council of Ministers; L. P. Beria, a new Ministry of Internal Affairs, combining the MVD and the MGB; and N. A. Bulganin was to concentrate on defense. Other appointments were also listed. The number of ministries was sharply reduced.

There was a vaguely worded reference to Father: "N. S. Khrushchev will concentrate on work in the Central Committee of the CPSU. In this connection he is relieved of his duties as secretary of the Moscow committee."

Father had become secretary of the Central Committee immediately upon returning to Moscow; at the same time he was elected to the Moscow committee. It had long been customary, indeed obligatory, for the head of the Moscow organization—the party's most prestigious and important body—to be a member of the Central Committee Secretariat. Now, though externally it seemed that nothing had changed, the short phrase about Father's new responsibility was in fact very significant. At the time the post of first secretary did not exist. Stalin had abolished it, allegedly in order to achieve greater internal party democracy—let all Central Committee secretaries, including Comrade Stalin, be equal.

Another persistent memory: a memorial issue of the magazine *Soviet Union*. It was filled with photographs of Stalin, with captions in various languages. An advance copy arrived at our apartment in a blank envelope, along with Father's ordinary—not secret—mail from the Central Committee, which is why I saw it first. The magazine's contents suited my mood in those days, so I took it in to show Father. He looked through the photographs, then returned to the colored picture of Stalin on the cover, as if weighing the contents. And put it aside without comment. I waited for a reaction. Father said nothing. I couldn't resist and said a few words in praise of the magazine. Father seemed to ignore what I said, so I fell silent.

He finally remarked, almost to himself, that it was not a good idea to publish the magazine in this format.

I was absolutely amazed and naturally asked why. He thought for a bit longer, then without saying anything very illuminating, replied that there was a great deal to think over at this time, and such a magazine, which would be distributed around the world, would not play a positive role. Frankly, I didn't understand a thing. I was astonished, but didn't ask any more questions.

Events unfolded very rapidly that spring. In April something happened that would have been unthinkable as recently as the previous winter—all the newspapers published a Soviet government statement with a proposal to end the protracted Korean war. Negotiations soon began on a truce and the exchange of prisoners. Then the country was stunned by an announcement that the case of the "Doctors' Plot" was closed.[23] As recently as January 13 we had read in *Pravda* about how the patriotic Dr. Lidiya Timashuk had warned Stalin that the doctors of the Kremlin hospital were planning to kill the leadership through improper medical treatment.

On April 25 newspapers published the full text (instead of the usual carefully digested commentaries) of a speech by U.S. president Dwight Eisenhower to a group of American editors. It was an unprecedented step in those days. In May there was an even more unusual occurrence—the No. 11 issue of *Pravda* published the complete text of a speech to the House of Commons by that "warmonger," Sir Winston Churchill. Stalin must have turned over in his grave.

Yes, the world had changed. A new leadership had taken the helm and was working out its own policies.

Father gradually began to play an ever more important role. After the elimination of Beria from the political arena there was a substantial increase in his level of activity. I don't wish to repeat that whole story, which Father describes in detail in his memoirs. I would only mention that it was he who initiated this complex operation and brought it to a conclusion. I remember that on June 26, the day of the decisive session of the Presidium of the Central Committee, he spent the whole morning sitting on a bench in the garden of his dacha alone with Anastas Ivanovich Mikoyan. He forbade anyone to approach, and I hung around with the heads of their security guards. We all strolled along nearby paths.

Everything seemed unusual that day. Father usually left for work about nine in the morning. If there were guests, they came in the evening, and the whole family, both adults and some not quite so grown up, participated (as listeners) in conversations with them. That morning's talk lasted for a long time. Father and Mikoyan finally stood up and walked toward the house. Both looked very intent. I still remember their expressions because they were

---

23. "Doctors' Plot." A fabricated case against the "Kremlin doctors" (most with Jewish surnames) accused of plotting to murder Stalin and other top leaders. When first announced in the press, the plot was taken by many as the harbinger of a new Great Terror.

so out of the ordinary—I was used to Father's farewell smile and Anastas Ivanovich's friendly glance. Skirting the house, they went toward the waiting car. Father opened the heavy door of the armored ZIS limousine with some difficulty and let his guest climb in before him. I was also surprised that, for the first time since Stalin's death, he was using the armored car. Father finally noticed me, smiled, and waved good-bye. A guard quickly closed the door with a quiet click and took the front seat. The car moved off.

We didn't suspect a thing. But that evening, when a tired Father returned to the dacha, he announced: "Today Beria has been arrested. It seems that he is an enemy of the people and a foreign spy."

We were stunned and speechless. Untypically, I didn't ask a single question. We only learned the details much later. At the time everything was kept secret. It was not until July 3 that a long lead editorial appeared in *Pravda*, entitled "The Teachings of Marx-Engels-Lenin-Stalin—Mighty Ideological Weapon of Our Party." To the trained eye it was a signal that something unusual had happened in the leadership. Then, on July 10, it was announced that a recent Central Committee plenary session (the exact date was a secret) had issued a decree "to remove L. P. Beria from the Central Committee and expel him from the party for criminal anti-party and antistate activities and as an enemy of the Communist Party and the Soviet people."

THE BERLIN CRISIS OF 1953

Ten days before Beria's arrest, the new leadership was confronted with its first serious crisis. Disturbances broke out on June 16 in Berlin, in the German Democratic Republic. They spread quickly to other parts of the country. Moscow reacted immediately. A session of the Presidium of the Central Committee decided to send Soviet forces, primarily tanks, into German cities. They were authorized to use weapons if necessary.

Beria was appointed the Soviet government's representative to Berlin and given emergency powers. There was a certain dark humor in this. After Stalin's death Beria had spoken out against supporting the GDR, which had been formed in 1949, and he proposed ceding it to the West. In this he was opposed by Molotov, who was energetically supported by Father. They thought that Beria's position was radically incorrect and that a socialist East Germany would serve as an attractive window to display the advantages of the "socialist way of life" and attract the proletariat of Western Europe—and not only Europe—by its example.

Now Beria was responsible for imposing order in the occupied zone with an iron fist. He succeeded. The situation quickly stabilized. Tanks were posted at all intersections of any importance in the rebellious cities, their exposed guns clear evidence of the soldiers' intentions.

There was shooting in a number of places; people were killed and wounded. The occupying army was not joking. It demanded the unconditional surrender of its prostrate enemy.

The uprising in the GDR and preparations for Beria's arrest coincided. Beria's assignment in Berlin was a true gift from fate for the plotters. In his memoirs, Father refers more than once to their fears that their efforts might come to light. In truth, all the members of the Presidium of the Central Committee were Beria's hostages—none of them could take a step without their MVD guards, who were loyal only to him.

In Beria's absence matters proceeded more quickly. By the time he returned everything had been agreed.[24] Only Mikoyan had doubts. It was on that morning of June 26 that Father made a last, unsuccessful attempt to win him over. Anastas Ivanovich did not support Beria's arrest.

The situation in Germany quickly stabilized, but the uprising was a grave warning. Father took what happened very seriously. Why were the workers opposing their own, workers' government? He saw as the basic reason for the clash the vagueness and inconsistency of our policy toward Germany, particularly in the economic sphere. By this time our allies had renounced their share of the payments stipulated by the documents that defined the status of the defeated German state. The economy in the Western zones had begun to improve dramatically.

In answer to my questions, Father willingly told me what he thought had happened in the GDR. As I remember, he pointed to the following aspects: First of all, it was wrong to continue exacting reparations after the formation of the German Democratic Republic, a workers' state. We were now friends, not enemies; nevertheless we were forcing them to pay large sums at a time when West Germany did not have a similar economic burden. As a result, East Germans were not living as well as West Germans, which naturally provoked irritation and dissatisfaction. Moreover, politically we were putting ourselves at a disadvantage by hauling away everything we could find.

He thought that dismantling the factories was a mistake. We were sending home obsolete equipment that would not help us to restore our ravaged national economy. Moreover, the policy was severely damaging relations with Germany. In his words, we were removing everything down to the bare ground, just as the Fascists had done in our country.

Father was particularly disturbed by the vagueness of our policy with respect to the future of Germany. At the time no one questioned the urgent need to sign a peace treaty and unify Germany, but on what terms? Two

---

24. In archive materials that are now accessible there is no mention of Beria's trip to the GDR (according to them, his deputy, Sergo Goglidze, went instead), but I decided to leave everything as I remembered it.—S.K.

German states, with differing systems—capitalist and socialist—already existed. Father thought that we were simply obligated to support the GDR and to declare that it could not be assimilated by the FRG. However, not everyone in the Soviet leadership agreed, and the Germans themselves were not unanimous. In both East and West they longed for the unification of their country. All of this provoked uncertainty and dissatisfaction; and now, on top of that, there were interruptions in the supply of provisions.

Western intelligence services played an important role too, according to Father.

I was satisfied by his explanations, since it all seemed to make sense. Today we see things very differently. But I wish to convey Father's views as faithfully as possible, not to comment on them from the vantage point of the present.

Perhaps I should remind readers that these events occurred in 1953. The war had not yet passed into history. The decisive intervention of our occupation forces and the rapid restoration of order had caused a great deal of satisfaction in Moscow. How did the Germans react to the punitive action? I remember Father's saying that according to reports from Berlin, once the situation stabilized, local people even showed some sympathy with the soldiers.

SUMMER AT THE DACHA

The stormy events of the summer of 1953 did not change Father's habits. As always, we spent that summer at the dacha. He needed life at the dacha to restore his strength, to be far from the noise and fumes of city streets. Father was drawn there by his love of nature, not simply by the desire to rest. In springtime he was enthralled by the flowering apple and cherry trees. He could sit for hours admiring them. Lilac and rose bushes, chestnut and white acacia trees—it's hard to list all his favorite bushes and trees. Spring was his favorite time of year. The rebirth of nature suited his creative peasant soul. And the opposite was true—the dying-off in autumn put him in a mood that not even the varied and beautiful colors of the falling leaves could lift.

Father also loved animals. Two dogs—German short-hairs—lived with us in Kiev. They were "war booty" given Father by some friends who were generals, after they returned from Germany. Mama didn't think much of animals. They created confusion and disturbed the order she had established in her household. However, she tolerated them and tried to hide her dislike. She vacillated between two points of view: On the one hand, the children's character would benefit from contact with animals. On the other, they might catch all kinds of infections.

In addition to dogs, we had rabbits, ducks, geese, and guinea hens, which were looked after by my grandmother, Yekaterina Grigoryevna, Mama's mother, who couldn't imagine not caring for the animals along with the rest of the family.

Knowing Father's fondness for animals, people were constantly bringing him young creatures that were lost in the woods. Squirrels roamed around in the house. Naturally, they did not contribute to an orderly household—they tended to gnaw holes in the tablecloths and break things. They loved to dig nuts out of my sisters' braids. The minute Father opened the door after returning home from work they appeared and began rummaging through his pockets for presents, which always put a blissful smile on his face.

A fox cub joined Father's foster children. The guards found him at the dacha. He gradually grew into a large, reddish fox. He was not sociable by nature and spent all day in the garden, where he found safe hiding places. He permitted us to feed him, but acknowledged only Father. When Father came home from work and took his usual evening stroll, the fox would follow in his footsteps. The instant Father turned up the steps to the house, however, he would disappear. Naturally, the fox was not without sin. He hunted Grandmother's menagerie. At night we were often awakened by heart-rending cries of bird in distress. In the morning we would find traces of the crime, a pile of feathers under a bush. Grandmother threatened terrible retribution, but the thief always got away with it by hiding behind Father's broad back.

The largest inhabitant of Father's "zoo" was a wild male deer. He was shy by nature and grazed on the grass. He would sometimes walk around with his master, but did not permit any liberties and kept his distance from people. However, in the spring his longing for a female overcame other emotions and he became extremely irritable. Then people, especially women, had to keep their wits about them. He would not allow a single skirt to pass him by. His style of wooing was original: First he would stare surreptitiously at the chosen victim. Then, picking the right moment, he would give chase and butt her in the lower back. Some people were amused and some outraged, especially the stout matrons who visited Father with their husbands. This way of expressing his emotions kept everybody on the alert in the spring. Quiet was not restored until the arrival of summer, when two-legged creatures lost their attraction for him.

Father found life oppressive in our Moscow apartment, which was on the fifth floor and had windows overlooking a stone well in the courtyard. Whenever possible he went off to the dacha. In winter he didn't always manage to get there—or rather, the tunnels of icy paths between high snowdrifts were less appealing. When spring began he spent nights outside the city more and more often, and moved there entirely when the weather warmed up.

The state dacha assigned to Father after the transfer from Kiev was in the former palace of Grand Duke Sergei Aleksandrovich, the governor-general of Moscow and uncle to the last tsar. Before the war the palace had served as an overnight rest home of the Moscow Party Committee. Moscow Committee secretaries, district committee secretaries, and Moscow Soviet officials were allowed to use it. Up until 1938 Father also occupied two rooms in the wing that had housed the grand duke's staff.

After the war, or perhaps even earlier, circumstances changed, and Aleksandr Sergeyevich Shcherbakov, Moscow Committee and Central Committee secretary, moved into the palace. His guards lived in the staff wing. After Shcherbakov's death the dacha passed to Popov, and then to us. It was a huge, two-story building in the pseudo-Gothic style popular in the late nineteenth century, with window-sashes in the form of crosses. An attached glassed-in greenhouse rose the entire height of the building.

The entrance to a bomb shelter (required at that time for all dachas belonging to members of the Presidium of the Central Committee) was across from the front door, hidden in the thick grass of the courtyard. A path ran across a small meadow and fell steeply down to the Moscow River.

Father tried to train squirrels in the new place too, but they didn't take to it and ran away into the woods as soon as possible. However, they did deign to eat nuts and bread crusts from your hands, but they paid a price for that—boys from the neighboring village of Usovo soon killed them.

A polar bear cub was our guest for a short time at the dacha. A navigator from Polar Aviation, Pyotr Georgiyevich Petukhov, brought him back from one of his flights in the North. The bear was quite small at the time, about the size of a dog. Petukhov couldn't manage to live with the cub in his apartment, so presented the bear, as a generous gift from an old acquaintance, to the head of Father's guard, Leonid Trofimovich Litovchenko. Knowing of Father's great fondness for animals, Litovchenko brought him to the dacha. Our enthusiasm knew no bounds. True, not everyone was so enthusiastic. My sister Rada's husband, Aleksei, regarded our new guest with suspicion and kept him at a respectful distance. He was, after all, a wild animal. Everyone else rubbed, patted, and stroked the little bear, who screwed up his eyes with pleasure. However, it wasn't long before trouble began. The bear cub had a difficult character and long, if not terribly sharp, claws. He demanded attention. His greatest enjoyment was to suck on a finger or button. At first that seemed amusing, but it quickly became tiresome. The bear cub couldn't understand why his favorite toy—perhaps his mother?—was being withdrawn. He would whimper and run after you, trying to stand on his hind legs, grasping his newfound friend with his front paws. Only your own agility could save you. One of Father's duty secretaries from the Central Committee heard about the bear and came to admire him. The bear's fervent interest in our astounded guest resulted in his jacket being torn to shreds.

Still another problem arose. The bear cub loved to lie in the sun. He would stretch out blissfully on the warm asphalt, and we were well advised not to bother him at such times. He picked out a favorite spot in front of the gate, where he loved to sunbathe in the morning, just when Father was ready to leave for work. We would tempt him with something and pull him by the paws; resisting at first, he would soon join in the game and run around with us children. The chauffeur would seize that opportunity to escape. Actually, Father never showed any irritation over these delays.

But a wild animal remains a wild animal. The bear grew up, and we had to give him to a zoo.

THE EARLY COLD WAR YEARS

The international situation Stalin's successors had inherited was an extremely grave one. A typical example of relations between the two powers during those years: On July 27, 1953, an American pilot, Ralph S. Barr, flying an F-86, shot down a Soviet IL-12 passenger plane on its way from Port Arthur to Vladivostok. Fifteen passengers and six crew members were killed. Of course, the pilot saw that it was a civilian aircraft, but war was raging next door, in Korea.

The Soviet Air Force repaid the debt. On July 30 an American B-50 was shot down near Vladivostok, in the area of Cape Gamov. An eye for an eye, a tooth for a tooth.

The Cold War was on, and in some places it was already fairly hot. The new leadership had to take over the wheel without stepping on the gas. Whereas some Presidium members had earlier been concerned with international relations and others with defense and new types of weapons, Father's work had long been totally unrelated to these issues. Now, while keeping informed about housing construction, about the effort to produce prefabricated reinforced concrete, and about his favorite square-cluster method of potato planting, he mastered these new areas. But it was not just a question of mastering new subjects. Immediate steps had be taken. Furthermore, any mistake could be very costly, since the international situation at the time was not simply tense, but was actually in crisis. A military clash seemed possible at any moment.

On one of our first trips to the dacha after moving to Moscow I noticed antiaircraft batteries located along the Rublyovskoye Highway, where the Molodyozhnaya subway station is located today. Like any young boy, I was more interested in the guns than in the sowing machinery Father pointed out operating on adjacent fields.

I mentioned the guns to Father, but he made no comment. Later I found that the batteries had live shells next to their guns. An air raid could be expected at any moment—it seemed likely. After all, the Soviet Union was surrounded by U.S. military bases and their nuclear-armed bombers were able to reach almost any point in our country. The United States itself was invulnerable. The Soviet Union had practically no nuclear warheads and did not possess a single airplane that could, even in theory, accomplish such a mission. The entire responsibility for the country's security now lay on the shoulders of the new leadership. Father had not yet become the leader, but he was one of those whose decisions would determine the future. There must be no repetition of 1941. His memories of that tragic rout remained fresh. He had lived through the war from its first day up until 1944, and for many years any decisions he made concerning national defense were influenced by the events of 1941.

Father considered national security to be of the utmost importance—fully as important as providing the people with food, clothing, and shelter. The Soviet Union had to acquire arms so modern that no adversary would even dream of invading. In those years policy was carried out only from a position of strength. However, the recent war had taught Father something else: hatred for every war. He genuinely sought to avoid conflict. Throughout his life he retained vivid memories of dead bodies, the fetid smell of decomposition arising from battlefields, and ruins, ruins, ruins. His peasant, pragmatic turn of mind couldn't admit any repetition of the nightmare. And yet our military doctrine at the time stated that a final struggle between socialism and a rotting, dying capitalism tenaciously fighting for its life was inevitable. Father had not yet rejected that theory, but he did base his foreign policy on actions to prevent the outbreak of war.

It is generally known that after the war Stalin had taken advantage of every opportunity to increase our military might. Creation of a nuclear bomb was the most important objective. But equally important was solving the problem of how to deliver it. The Soviet Union had no strategic bombers. The aircraft industry had always focused on the production of front-line aviation. The country didn't lack designs. Before the war Tupolev, Bartini, and Petlyakov had developed first-rate designs. But nothing had come of them. Stalin disliked large planes, and his word was law. He thought that they cost too much to build. Most generals agreed with him. All of them, including Georgy Konstantinovich Zhukov, had matured, achieved their ranks, and won their medals in front-line operations. Strategic aviation required thinking on a larger scale. During the war our forces had driven out the Fascists step by reconquered step. Everyone saw the results of military missions by fighters and tactical bombers. The infrequent raids carried out by the few Soviet long-distance bombers had more of a propaganda quality. The Soviet Air Force didn't so much bomb Berlin as demonstrate above it.

Of course, the mass shuttle-bombing raids by American Flying Fortresses made an impression on Soviet military commanders. They visited Poltava airfield as if it were a zoo, to take a look at the exotic marvels from across the ocean. They praised the planes and admired the technology, but said maliciously among themselves that they didn't need such luxuries.

Though Father was not immune to the interest in Western technology, he himself didn't go to Poltava. He was too busy. However, in the spring of 1944 a general sent him one of the inflatable rubber boats that were supplied to American bomber crews in case they had to ditch. The package was accompanied by a note: "Look what they've thought up! These things float on air bladders." We had not even dreamed of such things.

Father loved all technical innovations and immediately decided to try out his present. We inflated the boat and launched it on a small pond near the house where Father moved after the liberation of Kiev. It looked much too fragile to carry up to half a dozen passengers, as the description accompanying it claimed. Father tried it out with some colleagues from the Ukrainian Council of Ministers. I must say they crawled into it with some trepidation, but were soon reassured. The American instructions were correct. The clumsy vessel didn't founder, even after the most elephantine of the "experimenters"—Father's deputy in charge of agriculture, Vasily Fyodorovich Starchenko, a marvelous scientist and wonderful person—climbed in. I still have a photograph: Father at the oars, with Mikhail Sergeyevich Grechukha, Starchenko, and their wives, who were of equal heft and held bouquets of lilacs, sitting along the sides of the boat.

Father was so pleased that he wanted to arrange for inflatable boats to be produced in the Ukraine. However, that turned out to be beyond the capacity of our industry at the time. Besides which, admiration for American achievements quickly went out of style.

Claims of our superiority were made with increasing stridency in newspapers and over the radio. The war was receding further and further to the west. Everywhere you heard: "The Russian soldier is defeating the Germans without such tricks." There was no change in people's mentality. For a very long time the strategic effect of the massive bombing of German and Japanese economic centers was underestimated.

The "struggle against cosmopolitanism" played an important role here. People of my generation remember how attempts to show that everything had been invented in Russia, including the steamship, the airplane, and the radio—without exception, everything!—reached the height of absurdity. The military field was no exception. For years it was drummed into our heads that our allies had played an insignificant role in achieving victory. Tortured logic required evidence that strategic bombing was ineffective, and such evidence was found. The paradox is that the people who make up such stories are the first to believe them.

However, be that as it may, a powerful long-range bomber was required to carry an atomic bomb. The task of developing one was given to the design bureau of Andrei Nikolayevich Tupolev, who had created the largest Soviet planes, the TB-1 and TB-3, before the war. The legendary flight to America over the North Pole was made on his ANT-25. This tradition continued in succeeding years: Petlyakov, designer of the Pe-8, spent most of his career in Tupolev's design bureau.

The bureau began work on the project, but it turned out that Stalin was thinking along different lines. Some time earlier he had taken a fancy to the American Flying Super Fortress. There the question of cosmopolitanism, or of our priority, didn't concern him. He really wanted to get hold of that plane, but how?

As early as 1943 Soviet intelligence had obtained complete onboard documentation of the B-29 strategic bomber. It was translated into Russian and studied carefully. However, it told you how to fly the plane, not how to build one.

And then Stalin got lucky. Soon after or maybe just at the end of the war a B-29 strayed off course and landed at a Soviet airport in the Far East. Yankees love to name their planes, and inscribed on the fuselage of our guest was "The Tramp." This time it had certainly wandered far. The fact that we had been allies was not yet forgotten, so people did not impute any sinister meaning to the incident. Those involved thought the normal procedure was to feed the crew, refuel the plane, and send it on its way. Of course, Moscow was called, and Stalin was immediately informed. Instructions quickly came to detain the crew and seal the plane. Negotiations about returning the crew and the plane began. The end result was that we returned the crew, but Soviet representatives didn't even want to hear about the plane. The Americans gave up—why fight over an old bomber? However, the incident contributed to the deterioration in relations between our two countries.

A secret order to deliver the plane to Moscow soon followed. At that point the documents obtained earlier came in handy. They were used to brief Lieutenant Colonel Reydel and his crew, who studied them quickly and then flew "The Tramp" to Moscow, landing at Izmaylovo airport. Today that space is crisscrossed by the many streets of Izmaylovo Park.

A personal order from Stalin arrived at the Ministry of the Aviation Industry: "Make an exact copy." They were given very little time to do it. "Tourists" came frequently to inspect the exotic toy from across the seas. Celebrities like Tupolev and Ilyushin visited more than once. Separately, for Andrei Nikolayevich didn't like Sergei Vladimirovich. At one time they had been on opposite sides of barbed wire.[25] Tupolev thought Ilyushin was one

---

25. The great designer Andrei Tupolev was arrested in 1937 on false charges of selling aircraft

of those who had sent innocent people to prison. That's not for me to say, but relations between the two illustrious designers were far from good.

Specialists looked into every corner of the giant plane. They disassembled and reassembled the numerous instruments. Their conclusions were not reassuring, especially with respect to automation. The plane was packed with remote firing-control systems and a large number of sensors. Soviet experts could only guess how some of them operated. They had not dreamed of such luxuries in our aircraft. The Soviet Union had only recently mastered the production of electric automatic pilots, and there was great pride in that achievement. But all this? It was discouraging. And what was Stalin to be told?

It was decided to assign Tupolev to bring the matter to Stalin. His work on a strategic bomber was the furthest advanced; into his new plane he had built all the newest achievements in aerodynamics, engine construction, and everything else that we possessed. His native ingenuity had compensated for our technological shortcomings. Tupolev laid his proposals before Stalin. He marshaled impressive arguments against duplicating the American plane—by the time they studied it, made blueprints, and prepared a production line, it was bound to be obsolete. After all, the B-29 had been used since the middle of the war. Years would go by, and in the end we would have a museum piece. How much more sensible to concentrate on the plan for a new bomber able to satisfy the demands of a modern air war. One would think that Stalin was bound to agree with Tupolev, but that was not the case. He issued an exasperated command: "Copy it without changing a single detail."

Stalin tried to avoid even the slightest risk. Both the atomic bomb and its carrier must be exactly the same as the American ones. That would guarantee success. Nuclear scientists proposed their own variant for a bomb, more powerful and effective, but they also received strict orders not to deviate one iota from the American blueprints obtained by the intelligence service. The time to improve it would come only after the new weapon was in hand.

The B-29 was moved to Moscow's Tsentralny Airport and carefully dismantled. All the parts were neatly packed and shipped under guard to various corners of the country. Enormously painstaking work began. A complex technical system cannot be duplicated thoughtlessly and mechanically. The principles underlying the plane and its parts had to be understood down to their finest detail, and that was extremely difficult. It's sometimes easier to make a new instrument than to understand some ingenious foreign device. To decipher a puzzle often demands more skill than even its original author possessed. A lengthy government decree was prepared. The Politburo made

---

designs to Germany and spent several years "behind the barbed wire" in an NKVD-run prison design bureau. While imprisoned he developed the Tu-2 bomber, the success of which earned his release in 1943.

Beria personally responsible for the success of what was designated the TU-4. The American plane could be duplicated only by using American technology. You couldn't get around a problem by substituting water pipes for wing frames, as Aleksandr Yakovlev had done on his fighters during the war.

The TU-4 opened a new page in Soviet aircraft construction. It is no exaggeration to say that an entire modern aircraft industry had to be built in the effort to carry out Stalin's order to make an exact copy.

New research institutes and design bureaus were established to work on the plane's automated elements and new technologies and materials. As specialists tackled the American technological riddles, new factories were built and equipped with the most advanced technology of the time. Thus, Soviet avionics was born along with the TU-4. Most of today's Soviet planes use instruments, sensors, and electrical machinery descended from that B-29. So Stalin's decision could be considered beneficial. If you don't think about the cost, naturally.

But when the TU-4 appeared, everyone was convinced that Tupolev was right, the bomber wasn't suited to modern warfare. The Soviet Air Force received bombers to carry nuclear weapons that were identical to those which destroyed Hiroshima and Nagasaki.

However, the main task had yet to be solved. The territory of the United States remained invulnerable, while American military maps showed our country covered with the circles that represented possible targets for their bases scattered throughout Europe and Asia.

WEAPONS OF MASS DESTRUCTION

For those times Father's attitude toward the secrecy that permeated our lives could be called extremely liberal. Of course, we weren't allowed to look at the intelligence reports, messages from ambassadors, and other such documents he brought home in his fat brown leather folder crammed with papers. But the folder itself had no lock, only a leather catch that fastened to a knob. He would put the folder on a small table in the dining room and only at night take it with him to the bedroom. And that was not for reasons of security, but because he meant to glance over some papers before he went to sleep. No member of the household would have dreamed of touching the folder unless Father asked someone to bring it to the garden when he settled down there to read.

Father thought that the veil of secrecy drawn over planes, missiles, and tanks was to a large extent artificial. Of course, some secrecy was essential, but why classify as secret the external appearance of planes or ships, which many people could see in motion? In those years even the index designating the type of a missile was considered top secret. However, there were some curious exceptions. Articles sometimes appeared in scientific journals describing the behavior of a thin-walled cylindrical casing partly filled with a liquid. This scientific circumlocution for a missile was sufficient camouflage for the censors. The formulas used in publications meant far more to specialists than completely secret descriptions. Science cannot develop without cross-pollination.

After I began studying at the Institute, Father started to take me with him on visits to design bureaus and experimental factories. He thought it would be good schooling for a future engineer, but warned me to be inconspicuous and not to push myself forward: "And, of course, don't talk too much."

Father was beaming when he returned to the dacha one day in the first half of August 1953. It wasn't late yet; the sun was still rather high in the sky. While the household got ready for dinner, Father and I walked out to the meadow in front of the house, his favorite place to relax on summer evenings.

Father was bursting to share his secret: that day, August 12, Soviet nuclear scientists had exploded a hydrogen bomb. The experiments had been successful. Father simply couldn't contain himself. The Soviet Union had finally managed to get the better of the United States! True, the Americans had already tested such a bomb in 1952, but according to Father the American device was so heavy and cumbersome that no plane could lift it. It had to be tested on a gigantic tower. Soviet physicists had found a fundamentally new solution, and the country now possessed a weapon of unparalleled destructive force.

Neither then nor later did Father dream of using nuclear weapons. When he saw a film showing the explosion of an atomic bomb for the first time, apparently after Stalin's death, he returned home restless and depressed. He was proud of our scientists' achievements and of the growing power of our army, but employing them did not enter into his plans. Naturally, if we were attacked, if we were in a hopeless situation—well, that was another matter.

After telling me this sensational news, Father fell momentarily silent, and then began talking about what wonderful scientists and designers (he always said these two words in conjunction, so as not, God forbid, to insult someone), what talented people we had! He told me that a very young man, barely thirty years old, named Sakharov, had played an outstanding role in developing the hydrogen bomb. Father couldn't remember his first name and patronymic. It was Sakharov who had made the calculations that put us ahead of the Americans.

"What a mind!" exulted Father.

Father didn't describe Sakharov's breakthrough, perhaps because of secrecy, though possibly he himself didn't understand it.

I don't know whether Father ever met Andrei Dmitriyevich or corresponded with him at that time, but he was attracted to the young scientist. By nature, Father had strong and instinctive emotional feelings about scientifi-cally creative people. If he came to believe in them, Father stood wholeheart-edly behind them to the end. His enthusiasm knew no bounds, though this did not preclude arguments and sometimes even clashes. His choices were not always fortunate ones. His favorites included such a sinister person as Lysenko, along with people of unquestioned reputation, such as Academi-cians Lavrentyev, Kurchatov, Korolyov, Tupolev, and many others.[26]

Father concluded his exuberant words about Sakharov by saying that such a person deserved the highest awards: "Of course, we will confer on him the title Hero of Socialist Labor, but he deserves more. He has surpassed many others in the importance of the results he has achieved."

To the day of his death Father retained his enthusiastic attitude toward Andrei Dmitriyevich Sakharov. Neither their disagreements, nor the serious differences in their views of how our society should develop, affected his feelings.

Specialists proposed three methods for delivering the freight (as the nuclear warhead was modestly called) to the North American continent—by plane, by cruise missile, and by ballistic missile.

As the decade of the 1950s began, our country's principal strategic de-fense task was to make sure that its "potential foreign adversary" was de-feated. For a good many years that phrase referred to the United States.

No one knew which method would turn out to be the most effective. It was decided to hold a competition. Generous prizes and awards were prom-ised to the winning team. The largest rewards, in the form of dachas and cars built at government expense, the title Hero of Socialist Labor, noncompeti-tive "election" to the Academy of Sciences, Stalin Prizes, and simply enor-mous monetary prizes were promised to chief and general designers. To Stalin's way of thinking, no one would be able to resist such an approach, and scientists would do the impossible. I have never come across anything even remotely similar in any subsequent decree.

Work did not have to begin from scratch. The teams under Andrei Niko-layevich Tupolev and Vladimir Mikhailovich Myasishchev were working on the development of a bomber. After the successful testing of a hydrogen bomb, Vyacheslav Malyshev, deputy chairman of the Council of Ministers

---

26. Trofim Lysenko—the agronomist who built a career out of the claim that plants could inherit traits acquired at specific phases of their development. He (though not the agricultural policies he promoted) enjoyed spectacular success under both Stalin and Khrushchev by telling them what they wanted to hear—that there were simple and cheap ways to dramatically enhance agricultural productivity. Mikhail A. Lavrentyev was a distinguished mathematician and organizer of the "science city" at Novosibirsk. The careers of physicist and weapons designer Igor Kurchatov and missile designer Sergei Korolyov are discussed in detail below.

and the official responsible for nuclear development, proposed placing a three-megaton charge on an intercontinental missile. According to preliminary estimates by Andrei Dmitriyevich Sakharov, its weight should not exceed five and a half tons. Its enormous destructive power would compensate for any possible errors in delivering the missile to the target. Semyon Alekseyevich Lavochkin and the indefatigable Myasishchev were preparing proposals for intercontinental cruise missiles.

At the end of 1953 Malyshev visited Sergei Korolyov's design bureau. Estimates made by Mikhail Tikhonravov for a new long-range ballistic missile were especially interesting and seemed promising to Malyshev. On May 20, 1954, the government issued a decree on developing an intercontinental ballistic missile and placed Korolyov in charge of the work. He had been arrested and imprisoned right after the trial of Marshal Tukhachevsky. Research on rocket technology, which the marshal had supported and promoted in every possible way as the basis for developing a new and terrible weapon, was immediately curtailed. Prison doors slammed shut on those enthusiastically pursuing rocket research, and they remained shut for a long time.

Korolyov, having miraculously survived the Magadan camps, had spent the war in a *sharashka*[27] working on rocket boosters, which were to be mounted on the Pe-2 bomber and Lavochkin's fighters. According to designers, planes could dramatically increase their speed at the moment of attack by using boosters. The work did not go smoothly; they were unable to achieve consistent results. Korolyov himself was followed around the airfield by two armed guards.

In 1944 he was finally set free. Advancing troops seized what was left of the ballistic missiles with which Hitler had tried to frighten the British. There was an urgent need for specialists capable of understanding how they were made. In those years charges were dropped as easily as they had been made, if the "Boss" wanted it.

Sergei Pavlovich, in the uniform of a lieutenant colonel, left for postwar Germany together with a group of specialists on engines, guidance systems, and launch equipment, in order to study the captured parts of the V-2. The newly created bureau soon began designing its own duplicate. (To be precise, I should note that the first group, which flew to Germany in September of 1944, was composed of N. A. Pilyugin, A. Ya. Bereznyak, B. Ye. Chertok, L. A. Voskresensky, V. P. Mishin, M. K. Tikhonravov, and Yu. A. Pobedonostsev.)

Korolyov had always demonstrated extraordinary energy, and now in ad-

---

27. *Sharashka* was Soviet prison slang for the NKVD's special sites for political prisoners drafted to work in their areas of professional expertise rather than at hard labor. Magadan was among the most notorious and deadly camps in Stalin's gulag prison empire in Siberia.

dition he showed remarkable organizational talent and the ability to rally people and entire working teams and subordinate them to his will.

MOSCOW COMES TO LIFE

The first New Year without Stalin was celebrated at a Youth Ball in the Kremlin. This was not simply a great occasion, but a sign of changing times. Hundreds of Muscovites walked freely into what had been the most restricted area of Moscow, where previously no one had been admitted without a special permit, references, and painstaking checks.

A few months before Stalin's death, I tried to arrange a tour of the Kremlin for my classmates. What a fuss that caused! To begin with, I had to ask Father's permission. Without his approval no one would have even bothered to talk to me. The Kremlin guard unit simply wouldn't have dreamed of such a thing.[28]

The Kremlin was home to a few members of the Presidium of the Central Committee, who had moved there in the 1920s: Anastas Mikoyan, Kliment Voroshilov, and I think, Vyacheslav Molotov.[29] In the 1930s younger leaders were given apartments on Granovsky Street. The "Seniors" continued to live in the Kremlin.

After moving to Moscow I became friendly with Mikoyan's son, Sergo. The Khrushchev and Mikoyan dachas were located near each other and at one time Sergo was in the same class in school as my older sister Rada. Sergo has described the complications of inviting guests to their apartment. First, a request for a pass had to be submitted, giving detailed information about the guest: who he was, who his parents were, where he lived, what he did for a living. I don't remember what else. Next the guest had to pick up a form on watermarked paper from the Kremlin commandant's headquarters in the Kutafya Tower. He was then able to visit his friend for a cup of tea.

I myself was never in the Mikoyan apartment. We met only at the dacha. Everything was simpler there—no need for passes. The guards knew me by sight and let me in without any problem.

Probably those attending the Youth Ball were also checked. Invitations were not given out to just anybody, but distributed among active Komsomol

---

28. The conversation with Father turned out to be a simple matter. He said that he didn't see any problem. He immediately summoned the chief of his personal guard, Ivan Mikhailovich Stolyarov, and ordered him to help.

After a brief reply—"Yes, sir!"—the matter proceeded. We drew up lists and filled out forms. Then I gave Stolyarov typewritten information about the proposed participants, which was passed along to higher levels of authority. A long time went by, and I began to get nervous. Finally, permission was granted. To our general delight, no one's name was crossed out.—S.K.

29. Anastas Ivanovich Mikoyan and Kliment Yefremovich Voroshilov—top party leaders under Stalin who would later play crucial roles in support of and opposition to Khrushchev.

members. The ball was only Father's first step. The Kremlin was soon opened to visitors in general. That would seem like a natural step, but not everyone approved. Voroshilov was especially disturbed.

Father gave a humorous account of a conversation that had occurred after the meeting of the Presidium of the Central Committee during which he suggested returning to the custom before Stalin, when the Kremlin was open to visitors. During the session Kliment Yefremovich did not speak, but held his silence and voted "in favor." When the meeting ended he approached Father and began to complain that now he wouldn't be able to go for a walk. Father couldn't hide his surprise and asked Voroshilov with a smile, "Are you afraid of the people?"

"Walk as much as you like, do you think they'll bite you?" he joked.

Voroshilov walked off in a huff. After years of seclusion he really had begun to fear people. And the fact that Father took walks along city streets and visited collective farms and factories provoked his colleagues to constant whispers of disapproval behind his back. He stood out from the rank and file by this behavior, and such individuals are not easily forgiven.

After the Kremlin was opened up its remaining residents gradually departed: Voroshilov and Molotov moved to Granovsky Street and Mikoyan to Lenin Hills.

Little by little other places were also restored to their original use.

GUM's return to its building filled with shops on Red Square provoked much talk in Moscow.[30] Its windows, for many years covered by dusty gray curtains, were spruced up and attracted a crowd. The store had been closed many years before, in accordance with the NKVD's particular approach to security: GUM is located directly across from the Mausoleum rostrum, where Soviet leaders stood during holiday parades. What if a terrorist hid in GUM's long connecting passageways or shops? The NKVD's harsh nature was coupled with a military directness, so that the old shops were soon housing Kremlin offices, with guards posted at the doors to check the repeatedly verified passes of the absolutely trusted officials who filled its numerous offices.

Today it's hard to imagine GUM as an office building. That's true as well of the brilliantly lighted Praga Restaurant, which returned to life at the same time. Why was the restaurant closed? Stalin's route from the Kremlin along Dorogomilovskoye to Volynskoye, to the dacha close to town ran through the Borovitsky Gates, along Frunze Street, past the statue of a sitting Gogol on the boulevard, then along the Arbat right under the Praga's windows. The NKVD did not want to take any chances. What if some terrorist-cus-

---

30. GUM (*Gosudarstvennyi universal'nyi magazin*)—the giant "state department store" on Red Square.

tomer were to throw something from the restaurant's open balcony at the Leader's car passing below?

The adjacent Gogol monument had no better luck. For decades Stalin had ignored it. Gogol just sat there smiling sadly. Then one day, not long before his death, something about the statue irritated Stalin—and the sitting Gogol was hastily replaced by a standing Gogol.

The fate of the skyscraper Palace of Soviets was one of the concerns of the new authorities. Stalin had intended it to be the greatest building in the world, surpassing New York's skyscrapers and far outstripping Hitler's architectural ambitions to transform Berlin into the future center of the universe. Plans called for the building to be so tall that the statue of Lenin crowning it would be hidden in the clouds for most of the year.

Construction began in the mid-1930s on the Kropotkinskaya Embankment near the Kremlin, on the place where the Cathedral of Christ the Savior—a monument to the victory over Napoleon—had been blown up not long before. A massive foundation was laid down and they began to weld the metalwork, but then the war intervened. The steel in the frame was needed for the production of tanks.

After the war the work began again, but progress was slow. By the time of Stalin's death only the framework of the first five or six floors had been restored.

Father strongly objected to the construction of skyscrapers. They were far more expensive than five- or six-story buildings, and there was no problem with finding land in Moscow for construction. His colleagues in the Presidium of the Central Committee agreed with him. Work stopped again.

Workers began dismantling the unlucky Palace for the second time. It was decided to build an outdoor swimming pool in its place—the largest in the world. Why a swimming pool? Father explained to me that it would be a shame to put up an ordinary building on such a mighty foundation. But a swimming pool would provide people with enjoyment and protect the place for our descendants, who would decide what to do with their "heritage." So they decided to build a pool. At the time the decision went unremarked. Only people in nearby museums grumbled that the steam from water heated during the winter destroyed the balance of humidity in their storerooms.

In time the pool became a small part of Moscow life, and almost every one of the capital's residents had dipped into it at least once.

Years passed. The descendants made their decision. A copy of the old Cathedral of Christ the Savior is being resurrected on the old foundation.

"But how long will it be there?" Muscovites ask. An ancient legend says that at one time a small wooden chapel stood on this spot in the swampy vicinity of the Kremlin. In it lived a monk. His peace was disturbed by Tsar Ivan IV, nicknamed the Terrible because of all the blood he spilled. The tsar decided to tear down the chapel and build a monastery in its place. It is said that the hermit cursed both the tsar's messengers and the place itself, predicting that whatever was built there would not stand for long. The prediction seems to have come true. The monastery built by Ivan IV was torn down by order of Tsar Nicholas I, who had the Cathedral of Christ the Savior built in its place. Then the cathedral was razed to make room for the Palace of Soviets, which was abandoned in favor of a swimming pool, which has since been replaced by a copy of the old cathedral. And all on the same accursed spot.

GENEVA AND THE GERMAN QUESTION

A conference of the foreign ministers of the United States, Britain, France, and the Soviet Union opened in Berlin on January 25, 1954.

Many disputes had surfaced. Indeed, there wasn't a single question on which the viewpoints of the West and of our country coincided. But the issue of Germany dominated every other.

Father was noticeably nervous. He began to return home late and spent a lot of time on the telephone during the evening. That was unusual, since he rarely made calls from home and received calls even less often. He usually left the door to his study open. He seemed to talk most frequently with Molotov. Daily discussions about our position on Germany and Austria were continued on the phone.

One time, when Father came out of the study after such a call, I started to ask him some questions. He realized that I had overheard, but rather than getting angry he began to explain patiently that the state of war couldn't continue indefinitely and that a peace treaty must be concluded, that we had to establish good relations with our neighbors and that only friendship, equal rights, and mutual respect could preserve peace in the long run. In Austria there was a government; we had to sign a treaty with it and bring our troops home. An occupation army has never been a symbol of friendship.

I was upset. We had won the war, taken Vienna, but now we had to leave? Father explained the rudiments of international relations, but I had trouble understanding him. After all, our newspapers and radio had been saying something different for many years. They had called for victory, not for retreat. And now, without having achieved anything, we had agreed to a cease-fire in Korea and were preparing to leave Austria.

"But what will happen with Germany?" I continued.

Father seemed deep in thought. I thought he hadn't heard me, and repeated "What about Germany?"

"The situation in Germany is different," he said after a long pause. "There are two states in existence. The East Germans have chosen socialism, and we are simply obligated to support them in building a new society. That is our duty as Communists. The Americans want to destroy the GDR and unite it with West Germany. We will not agree to that."

Father went on to talk at length about serious inconsistencies: we had always been in favor of German unification, but now, under present conditions, the matter should only be solved by the Germans themselves, by the governments of the GDR and FRG. Apparently he had decided to use this conversation with me as an opportunity to rehearse his own arguments one more time.

Of course, the conference failed to reach an agreement. In those years we were not only disinclined to engage in dialogue, we had difficulty understanding the other parties. Each side presented its position mechanically. Many of our proposals were not meant for discussion but were directed, as Father put it, at exposing the aggressive essence of the policy of imperialism. The Americans behaved similarly. The German question was the most complex. Soviet proposals in those years reflected the status quo, but were absolutely unacceptable to the West. Not only did Konrad Adenauer refuse to consider holding a dialogue with Walter Ulbricht—the mere mention of the GDR threw him into a rage.

Father decided to act independently. He wished to convince the world of his determination that the GDR should have a status in no way inferior to that of the German state in the west. On March 20, 1954, the Soviet government took the decisive step: Moscow announced the end of the occupied status of East Germany and the establishment of diplomatic relations with the GDR. Actually, there was a self-conscious phrase about these agreements remaining in force until a decision was made on German unification. Father briefly explained his intentions to me: the Western powers should soberly evaluate the seriousness of our plans for the GDR, while our friends in Germany should appreciate our firmness and understand that we would not abandon them. He particularly stressed that Soviet support for the GDR was not a ruse in a diplomatic game, but derived naturally from our principled international position.

"All those who are fighting against imperialism and for their independence can rely entirely on our understanding and support," concluded Father in words that I was to hear from him often in the future.

THE DESIGNERS

It was in that year, 1954, that I first got to know the people who created our modern military technology.

One evening Father said that he was planning to visit Vladimir Mikhailovich Myasishchev's aviation design bureau the following day, and added casually, "If you want, I can take you with me."

The visit to Myasishchev was scheduled for the afternoon. Right after lectures at the Institute were over, I drove up to the Central Committee building. Father's ZIS limousine was parked at the entrance, which was used only by members of the Presidium of the Central Committee.

"Nikita Sergeyevich was asking about you," said the head guard. "I'll tell him you're here and we'll start off."

The trip took no more than half an hour. The design bureau was located in Moscow, but far from the center, in Fili. At the time its location was top secret, and it was called Plant No. 23. Now widely known, the M. V. Khruni-chev Plant is one of our space program's principal suppliers.

We walked as a group through the guard post and into a hangar. In the center was a huge airplane, strikingly unusual in appearance. Its wheels were not in the normal place along the sides, but jutted out of the fuselage, while four jet engines were tightly nestled against the fuselage and arrow-shaped wings hung down to the ground and were supported by small wheels. The plane combined power and speed. Father was being shown the newest strate-gic bomber, the 3M.

It made an indelible impression on me. Father was outwardly impassive, but he was also impressed by this marvel of modern technology. Myasishchev talked about the plane's ceiling, range, bomb-load capacity, and armament. Our group circled the plane slowly.

Father listened carefully to the chief designer's explanations, without ask-ing any questions. He simply nodded approvingly.

When Vladimir Mikhailovich had finished, Father thanked him and con-gratulated everyone on the magnificent aircraft.

We walked over to the design bureau's building and, going up to the third floor, seated ourselves in the chief designer's office (or in a conference hall, I don't remember which). Posters on the wall depicted various modifications of the bomber we had just seen, the new supersonic heavy bomber and the Buran super long-range cruise missile. There were many others too, evidence of the chief designer's inexhaustible imagination.

A general discussion followed. Myasishchev, as our host, spoke first and was followed by generals dressed in their summer uniforms and by subcon-tractors. On this occasion there were none of the mutual complaints, recrimi-nations, and appeals to higher authority to resolve the disputes that sometimes occurred. Everything went smoothly.

However, once in the office Father's behavior changed. He turned out to have quite a number of complicated questions. He became particularly atten-tive when Vladimir Mikhailovich referred to the use of his plane as an inter-continental bomber for carrying nuclear weapons.

As a point of information: At that time we had no idea that it was possible to refuel a plane in the air. I don't know about American pilots, but even years later our pilots thought in-flight refueling was some kind of acrobatic trick that only a chosen few could perform.

The 3M would have to perform its assigned mission with the fuel it took on at home. Despite every trick and contrivance they could think up, there would not be enough fuel, even in theory, for the plane to return. The design bureau had devised an original plan: A map hanging in the corner of the hall showed the flight path of Myasishchev's bomber from Soviet territory to the vitally important centers of the potential foreign adversary. Small circles over New York and Washington enclosed precisely drawn nuclear "mushroom" clouds. After accomplishing its mission, the small red plane symbol on the map was depicted turning in the direction of neighboring Mexico, not toward home. Small white caps represented parachutes dropping from the plane over Mexico.

This proposed diagram was supposed to represent a "solution" to the problem. After carrying out its mission, the crew was to be interned in neutral Mexico. Of course, there was no explanation of how Mexico could be considered neutral. It's hard to say what the plan's authors had been counting on—perhaps a lack of common sense in their audience.

Father listened attentively to Myasishchev's report and to the Air Force general's co-report. Then, smiling maliciously, he asked: "Did the Mexican government agree to this plan?" "Or maybe your mother-in-law lives there?" he joked mirthlessly.

Myasishchev and the generals, looking depressed, were silent. Then they began to talk incoherently about the special circumstances of wartime and Mexico's traditional neutrality. Father couldn't restrain himself: "How can you speak of neutrality when a country is sitting next to a giant hit by atomic bombs? And then the crew runs off to hide there?!" The tone of the conversation changed abruptly.

His next question was no easier to answer: "How likely is it that we will be able to penetrate U.S. air defenses?" Father began to talk about our air-defense missiles developed by the design bureau of Semyon Alekseyevich Lavochkin, and about how they would have prevented any such plane from reaching Moscow.

"Don't you think the Americans have something similar?" he asked, turning to Myasishchev.

There was a long silence. Father didn't even demand an answer. He recalled what happened when Stalin had asked Tupolev to build a similar plane. Tupolev possessed the courage and honesty to reply that modern aviation technology was not capable of building a bomber able to fly to the United

States, penetrate antiaircraft defenses, fulfill its mission, and return. Tupolev promised only to develop a bomber suited to military operations in Europe.

"And he did. The TU-16 is an outstanding plane," concluded Father.

No one else asked to speak. Both military officers and civilians looked morose. Father decided to clear the air. He said that the designers had not wasted their efforts; it was a good plane and it was needed, but we should not saddle it with missions it could not perform.

"There will have to be some other answer to the problem of reaching the U.S.," he said in conclusion, turning to ask Myasishchev: "But what future surprises are you preparing for us?"

Vladimir Mikhailovich told us about a completely new plane. Everything about it was unusual and out of the ordinary; it had super-thin wings and was made of stainless steel rather than aluminum. At supersonic speeds—three times the speed of sound—the usual aluminum alloys would melt like wax. His listeners sat mesmerized, staring at an attractive poster depicting a plane with a fantastic delta wing and four jet engines mounted on pylons beneath it.

Father nodded approvingly when Myasishchev concluded. He took great pleasure in hearing about projects for machines that weren't even dreamed of earlier. He was genuinely proud of being close to their creators. However, that did not keep him from being a demanding customer, quite capable of counting his money.

He asked the same question about the plane's range. Myasishchev replied simply that the plane was not capable of intercontinental flight, but that it could reach any place on the European continent.

Father nodded in agreement. The conference approved a proposal to develop the new bomber, which was designated the M-50.

Discussion then turned to a new project, the Buran cruise missile. It could undoubtedly reach any point on the territory of the potential foreign adversary, but could it succeed in carrying out its mission?

Father did not receive a satisfactory answer to his question: "How do you propose to penetrate the territorial antiaircraft system, with its missiles and interceptors?"

The Buran project was nevertheless approved, since in those years it was a "bird in the hand." It never went into construction, however. The need for it disappeared with the first test flights of intercontinental ballistic missiles.

The conference came to an end. Father said good-bye to those present and wished success to Vladimir Mikhailovich. He had obtained the information he needed. Unfortunately, it was not reassuring. Apparently we could not expect a quick and effective answer to the problem. Visits to Korolyov and Lavochkin still lay ahead.

CONTACTS WITH THE WEST

The strengthening of our military might was neither the only nor the chief factor in establishing new relations with the West. Father placed his main hope of improving international relations on expanded contacts; while a dialogue had not yet begun, at least we had made each others' acquaintance. The tour of the Paris theater "Comédie Française" caused a sensation in Moscow that April. When the entire Presidium attended the final performance of *Le Bourgeois Gentilhomme*, the tour was regarded as a major diplomatic step forward in those years of universal politicization.

Two days later, on April 17, 1954, Father celebrated his sixtieth birthday. The newspapers published appropriate congratulations and a decree that conferred the title "Hero of Socialist Labor" on him. A few greetings came from abroad.

That evening a reception was held in Father's honor at one of the state dachas. There were many toasts wishing him success and long life. The festivities went on and on, with the guests gathered on a large enclosed terrace (there was a frost that evening) singing soulful Ukrainian songs.

On April 26 the foreign ministers of the United Kingdom, France, the United States, and the Soviet Union convened in Geneva to discuss the situation on the Korean peninsula and in Indochina. The recently signed truce had just halted the bloodletting in Korea. The question of the country's unification remained unresolved.

The situation in Indochina was developing tragically. The Vietnamese were pouring out their life's blood in the struggle against the French, and the colonial expeditionary force was also barely holding on. Both sides longed for peace and, paradoxically enough, both sides were ready for defeat and surrender. The French were the first to yield. They surrendered after the defeat at Dien Bien Phu. Through joint efforts by all countries participating in the negotiations, a compromise was arrived at: Cambodia and Laos were declared to be sovereign states, and Vietnam was divided in half at the seventeenth parallel. At the time these decisions were greeted joyfully throughout the world, even though real peace in those regions was still a long way off.

The foreign ministers' conference lasted until July. Earlier, on May 1, my familiar giant—the 3M—flew over Red Square, accompanied by MIG fighters and leading a long column of TU-16s. The country was showing off its growing military power.

On May 8, the eve of the ninth anniversary of the victory over Fascism, all the newspapers published a sensational TASS report. I can't resist quoting an excerpt: "Press reports have appeared concerning a speech delivered by Mr. W. Churchill, the British prime minister, at the annual meeting of 'The Primrose League,' a Conservative Party organization, in which the prime minister calls for improving relations between Britain and the Soviet Union and for establishing goodwill contacts.

"TASS has learned that the British prime minister's speech is being read in leading circles of the Soviet Union." I will stop here, but simply note that all subsequent references to the recent "warmonger" were suffused with goodwill.

A vital shift in mood was taking place in the Soviet Union. Today the steps taken then seem timid and sometimes quite insignificant, but that is only from today's perspective.

In those days even the transition to coeducation of boys and girls in schools, as reported in the papers, was considered an incredibly daring step. It would contradict one of Stalin's decrees! On the other hand, only several months later, on Stalin's birthday, *Pravda* published an article with the title, "J. V. Stalin—Leading Theoretician of Marxism-Leninism," by Academician M. Mitin.

Nevertheless, when M. D. Ryumin, who had headed a Ministry of Internal Affairs department investigating especially important cases, was tried and executed, a report was issued stating that he had tortured people under investigation to force them to incriminate themselves. He had falsified evidence in cases under investigation. It took a lot of courage at the time to publish a report about people being tortured in our country.

In July *Pravda* published these words: "The peaceful coexistence of capitalism and socialism is entirely possible." That was the title of a special article by V. Kortunov that appeared on the twenty-seventh. The author supported his views with extensive quotations from Stalin. Kortunov and the newspaper's editors would never have made such a statement on their own initiative, since it contradicted the fundamental dogma of the inevitability of a clash between the two systems, the destruction of the obsolete structure, and its replacement by a new and progressive one.

At that time Father, as well as others, was beginning to wonder whether war between the two camps *was* inevitable. Didn't everything that was happening in the world contradict that thesis? Was it mistaken? Or more simply, outdated? Father's very nature rebelled against the inevitability of war. He was a man who preached the idea of creation, not destruction. The decision to revise a classic tenet of Marxism-Leninism was not made lightly. Still another seditious concept, that an armed uprising was not at all inevitable in the transition from capitalism to socialism, began to take shape, at first quietly and then more and more explicitly. A transfer of power might take place by parliamentary vote in civilized countries. I don't remember specifically how Father's colleagues reacted to these ideas and who agreed or disagreed with him, but he had to fight more than one battle over them.

Today a lot seems clear and obvious, even to a child. The population of the former Soviet Union is concerned with entirely different problems and lives in a different world. But the Soviet people had to follow a long and difficult path simply to continue to survive in this world. These seditious ideas had not yet taken shape in 1954; they were not to be fully expressed for another year and a half.

Newspapers published the Soviet government's "Note to the Governments of France, Britain and the United States on Collective Security in Europe" almost simultaneously with the article on peaceful coexistence.

MALENKOV

During those years my family socialized more with the Malenkov and Mikoyan families than with others. On Sunday Father went for walks in the neighborhood of the dacha, usually accompanied by the children. Mama didn't always come. She tired easily, and thought that these excursions sometimes lasted too long. We would walk down a hillside toward the red brick wall around the Mikoyan dacha, within the famous Zubalov estate. It had previously belonged to a wealthy native of Baku, who enclosed the entire estate with a very high stone wall and named it after himself. After the revolution Stalin's family had lived in some of the buildings, while Mikoyan got the others. Stalin's half had been empty for a long time.

Father used to knock loudly on the green iron gates. The guard would look out of his small square window, throw open the heavy gates, and disappear into the phone booth, saying "I'll announce you at once." The owner soon appeared, and we would go off on our walk.

Still, Father maintained closer ties with Malenkov. You couldn't call their relationship a friendship; it was more an alliance, a relationship tracing its roots to the many years these two very different people had known each other. Of course, Father had not forgotten Malenkov's negative reaction to Father's search for allies in the struggle against Beria on the day Stalin died. During those hours Malenkov had supported Beria. However, four months later he willingly agreed with the proposal to organize a plot against his former ally. As chairman of the Council of Ministers, he was assigned an important role in the affair.

The families also kept in touch. I have already described our walks together in Moscow. Mama had known Valeriya Alekseyevna, Malenkov's wife, since before the war and thought highly of her intellect and strong character. Malicious gossips said that Malenkov might run the Council of Ministers, but his wife ran him. That appeared to be true. Rada and Aleksei Ivanovich were friendly with Malenkov's daughter Volya and her husband, who were architects. I was friendly with Andrei and Yegor, their younger sons. After

1957 our paths diverged sharply and I never saw them again. I only know that they both became doctors of biology and are, by reputation, good scientists.

During those walks with the Malenkovs, Father often reminisced about Kiev, the garden on Osiyevskaya Street where he had lived after the war, and the fresh air, redolent with the fragrance of lilacs, such a contrast to the gasoline smell of Moscow's streets.

During one of these walks Malenkov suggested that Father take a look at plans for some new two-story residences. He had the idea of building them on Lenin Hills, far from the city center, as homes for members of the Presidium of the Central Committee. They would have more space and the air was cleaner; furthermore, the time had come for the Kremlin's last residents to move out. Malenkov's older children participated in planning this community, which Moscow wits later dubbed "The Path to Communism Collective Farm."

Father had no objection, and work got under way. Since construction was expected to take a few years, Georgy Maksimiliyanovich looked for a couple of houses for himself and Father to live in until the project was finished. Father was offered a two-story house behind a high stone wall on Yeropkinskaya Street, No. 3, next to the Institute of Foreign Languages. The Royal Thai Embassy is located there today. Malenkov found himself a similar house on Pomerantsev Street, No. 6, which is now the Embassy of the Republic of Guinea. The houses had connecting courtyards, so that they could pass through an inner gate and meet without interference. Memories of the time preparations were under way to arrest Beria were still fresh in both men's minds. At that time they were all panic-stricken that their meetings would attract attention and be reported to Lavrenty Pavlovich. It was easy to imagine what would have happened in that case, since even the guards assigned to the chairman of the Council of Ministers and the secretary of the Central Committee were wholly subordinate to the all-powerful Ministry of Internal Affairs.

There was good reason for the special decree issued after Beria's arrest, which removed the personal guard units of the members of the Presidium of the Central Committee from subordination to the reorganized Committee of State Security. From then on the guards were supposed to be under the sole orders of those whom they were guarding. In reality the decree remained mostly on paper, and the KGB apparatus retained complete power and influence over the guards.

Malenkov then took the next step. He decided to build a dacha right next to Father's dacha. Just in case—so he could always drop in and ask for advice.

Father had no objection to that, either. The estate was surrounded by a large park, the far corner of which was completely overgrown by a thick hazelnut grove. Mushroom pickers pushed their way in with difficulty and returned covered from head to foot by spiderwebs.

There was no reason to delay, so a picket fence was put up to divide the property and construction began. However, Malenkov never lived in the dacha. He had just moved in, during the stormy month of June 1957, when there was a change in his fate, as well as that of his country. Since that time the dacha has not been used as a residence. It was chosen as a place to hold negotiations with foreign delegations and for government receptions and was called Novo-Ogaryovo, after Father's dacha, which was for some reason renamed Ogaryovo after the Revolution. Earlier it had been the residence of the Moscow governor-general. Central Committee and government experts frequently gathered at Novo-Ogaryovo while working on important documents. The place was very suitable; it was some distance from the city, and Father could walk over at any time to see how things were progressing.

Meanwhile Father, full of energy and initiative, gradually squeezed out Malenkov, who was not very comfortable in such a high-ranking position. The center of gravity in making not just party decisions, but economic decisions as well, increasingly shifted to the Central Committee. I recall that decrees on economic matters were issued solely by the Council of Ministers while Stalin was alive and for the first few months after his death. The Central Committee didn't seem to be involved. Stalin was unconcerned about the "masthead" over any decree, since, whatever it concerned, everything in which he took an interest passed through his hands anyway. Now the situation had changed. Immediately after Beria's arrest and the September (1953) Central Committee Plenum, documents began to be issued under two signatures, Khrushchev's and Malenkov's. The most important decisions adopted in the country were entitled "Decrees of the Central Committee of the CPSU and the Council of Ministers of the USSR." At the September plenum it was Malenkov himself who proposed putting the word "First" before Father's title, "Secretary of the Central Committee." That profoundly altered the distribution of power.

Changes were also observable in their personal relations. Earlier, conversations and discussions were held as between equals. Now Father talked more, and I would even use the word "instructed," while Malenkov nodded his head, agreed, assented. I wasn't happy with these differences, which made me uncomfortable. Mama also frowned when Father adopted a didactic tone of voice.

At first Malenkov seemed satisfied with this new arrangement, or at least he revealed no dissatisfaction with it. It's possible that he was happy to shift some of his burden to others. That could not be said of his wife, Valeriya Alekseyevna. The changes taking place were obviously unpleasant to her strong and assertive character. But soon Georgy Maksimiliyanovich began to react differently. He still smiled at Father's jokes, but a scarcely concealed hostility began to flicker in his eyes. He did not, however, dare to protest.

Father also changed. He increasingly complained about the lack of initiative shown by the chairman of the Council of Ministers, about his attachment to paperwork. Yet if Malenkov had shown any initiative, Father would have been even more displeased. He wanted the position to be held by an executive assistant, not an independent partner. In the type of society existing at that time, the pitiless logic inherent in a struggle for power (for some reason we are embarrassed to use that phrase about our relatives) inevitably resulted in replacing all partners with assistants They were more reliable, at least in the short term.

Malenkov's days as head of state were already numbered by the autumn of 1954. He was not even included in the delegation sent to the Chinese People's Republic to celebrate its five-year jubilee, even though the meeting with Mao was thought to be of supreme importance. Father felt that Malenkov was too agreeable and submissive, traits that made him dangerous to his own side when negotiating with foreign leaders, even friendly ones. Bulganin took Malenkov's place on the delegation. The official explanation that someone had to stay behind to "mind the store" deceived no one. Malenkov looked grim. Though the crisis had not yet come to a head, the first signs were obvious.

FATHER ENGAGES THE SOVIET FLEET

October brought bad news. The smell of gunpowder was in the air. On October 6, the eve of the GDR's national holiday, Konrad Adenauer gave a speech outlining his plans for arming West Germany. The speech was interpreted as an overt threat, not only to the GDR but to all of Germany's former enemies to the east. Adenauer's remarks were not generalizations made by a careless politician. The plan existed, and it was soon to be approved by our former allies.

Father was away. He had left on September 29 for Beijing, accompanied by Bulganin, Mikoyan, and others in a large and representative government delegation.

Father often talked about relations with both a unified and divided Germany. I remember him saying: "The West Germans are the only ones who might bring about a new war in Europe." Those fears were shared by his colleagues in the Presidium. Adenauer's speech caused concern in Moscow and required an immediate response. But while notes and démarches were still being prepared in Moscow, an agreement on the remilitarization of West Germany, albeit on a limited scale, was signed on October 29 in Paris. The Soviet government considered it essential to take adequate defensive steps, and not just in relation to the GDR. I would, with some reservations, characterize Father's reaction to the Paris agreements as "alarm."

While participating in the Chinese ceremonial festivities, Father didn't neglect business. Since the war many negative elements had crept into our relations with the people's democracies, as our allies were called. Father thought that one of the most serious mistakes of the period was the unapologetic Soviet interference in their internal affairs. Examples of such interference included the establishment of joint companies and the extensive and continued Soviet military presence on their territory. He felt that friendship and cooperation were possible only on the basis of noninterference and equality. His words were soon put to some serious tests.

While in Beijing Father put an end to the joint Soviet-Chinese companies. The Soviet side relinquished its share in favor of its hosts. The naval base at Port Arthur was also transferred to its legitimate owner, the Chinese People's Republic.

That appeared to eliminate any reason or pretext for friction. Such was Father's naively straightforward thinking at the time. It seemed to him that socialist solidarity would ensure us against any trouble.

Father Inspects the Pacific Fleet

As the visit to China drew to a close, Father decided to use this convenient opportunity to become familiar with the Far East and to visit our Pacific Fleet. In those days, flying all the way from Moscow to Vladivostok on a small, two-engine IL-14 seemed like more than just a trip. It seemed like an expedition.

His inspection of the Navy began in Port Arthur, which was still a Soviet naval base. Father was accompanied by the commander in chief of the Soviet Navy, Admiral Nikolai Gerasimovich Kuznetsov, who had flown in from Moscow.

Everything went smoothly and according to plan: the visits to staff headquarters and to the ships were followed by firing demonstrations by shore defense artillery batteries.

Father congratulated the seamen on their skill. However, when looking down at the bay from commanding heights, he noted that the closed bay would become a trap for ships in case of nuclear attack, still more so in case of thermonuclear attack. The narrow passages, no matter how carefully guarded, would be no barrier to aviation. He reminded listeners of the tragic history of the attack on the U.S. fleet at Pearl Harbor by the Japanese. "And the Japanese didn't have the atomic bomb. They needed dozens and hundreds of planes. Now one would be enough," said Father, concluding his lecture.

His hosts began to object and to insist that they were taking every possible step to defend against a nuclear weapon. Father didn't insist on arguing. The base was, in any case, going to be handed over to the Chinese.

Until that moment Father hadn't taken much interest in the Navy. Now, with responsibility resting on his shoulders, he took a proprietary interest in calculating how the fleet could counter nuclear warheads and missiles.

His next meeting with Navy sailors was in Vladivostok, headquarters of the Pacific Fleet. On October 17 Father left on the cruiser *Kalinin* to view naval maneuvers. It was a hectic day. The ships' guns fired, destroyers captured an "enemy" submarine, torpedo boats emerged from a smoke screen and carried out a spirited attack on the cruiser (the torpedoes missed). A great deal was interesting and instructive. The maneuvers finally ended and the time came to sum up the results.

After thanking the crew, Father headed for the admiral's lounge with a crowd of officers at his back. When everyone was seated, he began to rake them over the coals. I'll mention only his main points. He thought that the military techniques they had demonstrated did not meet the new conditions created by the appearance of nuclear missiles. The admirals observing the exercises had been delighted by a well-rehearsed performance, said Father, but they hadn't realized that a conflict with a real enemy would be a catastrophe—not a trace of men or ships would be left.

Father also criticized the fact that the Fleet was crowded into its main base, Golden Horn Bay. His arguments duplicated what he'd said in Port Arthur, but his conclusions were even more pointed. He advised—really, ordered—that the Fleet be dispersed to various ports on the Sea of Okhotsk, the island of Sakhalin, and the Kamchatka peninsula. This decision had actually been made in Stalin's time, and Father was only strongly affirming it. Referring to his own experience, he said that before the war started the Kiev Military District had dispersed its planes among local airfields, so almost all survived unscathed. By contrast, planes in neighboring Belorussia, left on its main air bases, were blown to bits.

No one objected to this last point, and the ships were soon scattered to different ports. That caused serious supply problems, since almost all the warehouses were still at the main base. The seamen grumbled. From noisy Vladivostok, capital of the Maritime Territory, they had to move to the boondocks, where there were no apartments.

Father's statement that the Navy was unprepared for modern warfare infuriated Admiral Kuznetsov. He regarded it as a slap in the face and began to object sharply. He was very bold and accustomed to defending his own views to the bitter end. Kuznetsov didn't yield to anyone. After one talk with Stalin he was even demoted, but that didn't make him any more cautious. Father had a lot of experience dealing with the military. He had no doubt that he was right, and a reference to his lack of competence in naval matters only spurred him on. After agreeing that he was not trained in the art of naval warfare, Father immediately rejoined: Why is it that even a nonspecialist sees the absurdity of what is taking place, while admirals, graduates of the Naval Academy, don't see what is obvious?

Both parties insisted they were right. Kuznetsov was disconcerted. The demonstration of the Navy's power and training before the top leadership had been conceived of as a strategic operation. The naval shipbuilding program was soon to be discussed by the Presidium of the Central Committee. The admiral had put his whole heart into that program. If it were implemented, our country would venture onto the high seas with its own cruisers, battleships, and aircraft carriers. Kuznetsov knew that Father was trying to save every kopeck and that it would take very solid arguments to get the billions that would be needed.

Father clashed with Admiral Kuznetsov in Moscow soon afterward, during the debate on the long-term program for rearming the Navy.

Stalin's Daydream

I'd like to recall a little previous history. Generalissimo Stalin very much wanted the Soviet Union to become a great naval power, a mistress of the seas. Possibly he aspired to inherit the mantle of Peter the Great. Large ships began to be built even before the war, but that program was interrupted in 1941 when the Germans captured the Nikolayev docks and blockaded Leningrad. The war convincingly demonstrated that in a defensive war the Navy plays an auxiliary role for a continental power like ours. Our sailors did not participate in a single major naval battle during the entire four years of the war.

Nevertheless, work to finish the surviving cruisers resumed immediately after Germany surrendered. Stalin authorized lavish expenditures. Construction of new heavy cruisers and battleships began, and there was talk of building an aircraft carrier. This at a time when the Soviet Union's former allies were acting very differently. Having gained a great deal of experience in naval warfare, especially in the Pacific, both the Americans and the British were somewhat disillusioned about the importance of large ordnance ships. They decided not to build any more and to mothball many of those already built.

But in the Soviet Union intensive work went on day and night at the Black Sea, Baltic, Northern, and Far Eastern shipyards. Battleships and cruisers, unfortunately already outdated, were launched one after another or rested on the ways. They were equipped with 12- and 16-inch heavy-caliber guns, antiaircraft guns, torpedo launching chambers, and range finders. They would soon be called upon to perform military service.

By the mid-1950s the first stage of Stalin's program was nearing completion. The pride of the shipbuilders and the future flagship of the Navy, the battleship *Sovetskiy Soyuz*, was ready for launch.

Naval officers presented the new leadership with proposals that, if implemented, would have ensured that we had an oceangoing navy. The matter seemed to have been decided. In a film made at Stalin's personal order, the legendary Admiral Ushakov was shown on screens throughout the country predicting a glorious destiny for the Soviet fleet. The military never dreamed that Stalin's plans would be subject to revision.

The usual procedure for consideration by the Presidium of a new program got under way. All documents were distributed to the participants in the session in advance. Detailed information was provided on what ships were to be built, when and where, how much they would add to Fleet strength, and how much it would all cost. The proposal had already been thrashed out with all interested government departments and all the necessary signatures had been appended to the document. It needed only to be approved.

Strange Waters for Kuznetsov

In those years there were seventy to eighty items on the agenda of every session of the Presidium, which by tradition met after lunch on Thursdays. These varied from major issues, as on that occasion, to minor ones concerning various appointments and reassignments of officials. Naturally, sometimes there wasn't even time to bring up a question, much less discuss it. Far from everyone had read the materials that had been distributed, and members often relied on the authority and knowledge of experts.

Although Presidium sessions devoted only a few minutes to any particular question, the documentation for it was always prepared with what I would call the most meticulous care. First, the project's author slaved over it, polishing formulations, repeatedly recalculating balance sheets and scheduling deadlines for the numerous participants to complete various stages of work—then fitting it all into voluminous addenda. Everything had to be described there, down to the most minute detail. If any producer was left out, the author had only himself to blame. He would have to persuade it to undertake the work, but everyone already had more than enough to do and would resist undertaking additional responsibilities.

The next stage was to reach agreement with the various participants, each of whom tried to reduce the amount of work for which he was responsible and to postpone deadlines, but also to get more money for bonuses, housing, and other benefits. "Padding," as it was called.

This was a battle to the death. First, enterprise directors would argue to the point of exhaustion. Then unresolved questions were passed on to the relevant ministries, where the process of reaching agreement moved along bit by bit, until a draft decree eventually arrived at the appropriate minister's office.

Everything still unresolved went to the Council of Ministers, to the Military-Industrial Commission—the inner sanctum, behind the Kremlin walls. Its chairman, Dmitry Fyodorovich Ustinov, was more feared than the chairman of the Council of Ministers. Not only feared, but respected for his persistence and the pressure with which he pursued his objectives. It was there, in the quiet of the Kremlin offices, that the main battles unfolded, where ministers had to be prevailed upon to give their approval. Hardened and experienced men, they presented the greatest challenge.

I recall Ustinov's favorite method, to which he resorted in critical situations. He would closet directors of various ranks in his office and announce: "You're not leaving here until you sign off."

That usually succeeded. After all, every official was in command of his branch and was well aware of what could be done easily, what would require intensive work, and what was unrealizable. The last was very rarely the case. Those who composed draft documents were extremely well informed about the capabilities of their suppliers. Usually a minister bargained in the hope of reducing his contribution, but once convinced that his opponent's position was unassailable, he would pick up a gold-tipped pen and sign.

The next step was to obtain signatures of approval from the appropriate Central Committee department. Though furious discussions were unavoidable there as well, any complaints about the draft would be directed at the Council of Ministers. Such criticism almost never resulted in any changes. After the last official signature, that of the responsible Central Committee secretary, was obtained, the document was typed on a special machine and on special paper and sent to the inner sanctum: the office in charge of records for the Presidium. After the date for its consideration was set, the draft decree and "supplementary documentation" were distributed to participants in the session: the members and candidate members of the Presidium.

The provisions in the decree itself meant little to the uninformed reader; members of the Presidium could not, even theoretically, be equally conversant with all aspects of the country's life. Therefore an extremely important stage in the process was the compilation of authoritative and lucid supplementary documentation to accompany the draft decree. It alone enabled people to understand the subject, the purpose of the document, what would be achieved, and where the necessary resources would come from.

If the documentation did not answer all these questions fully, then during the session there could very well be some questions and arguments, which would result at a minimum in delaying the adoption of a final decision. Those initiating the decree composed the documentation. Those who had the greatest command of their material had the upper hand.

Competently prepared proposals went through like a flash, as the saying goes. Nevertheless, people with experience tried to have their business considered close to the end of a session, when its participants were tired and had quite lost the desire to ask questions.

Today, when historians rummage through the archives, they usually look for decrees. When they find them, they are disappointed; they can't understand what the decrees are all about. My point is that they're looking for the wrong thing—they need the supplementary documentation, not the decree. My advice is to study the proposal the same way members of the Presidium did. Start with the documentation.

Kuznetsov's Defeat

Father, who had somewhat earlier replaced Malenkov as chairman of Presidium meetings, unexpectedly broke with the customary routine. He asked the Navy's commander in chief to provide more details about which ships would be built, how much each project would cost, and most important, how the country's defense capability would be affected. What would we get in result?

Kuznetsov clearly had perfect command of the material, and it was apparent that he had suffered through every point himself and was not just reading a text prepared by subordinates.

Briefly, the whole thing boiled down to this: If the proposed program were successfully carried out in the next decade, we would have a modern navy capable of acting anywhere on the world's oceans. Aircraft carriers, battleships, cruisers, destroyers, transports, and supply tankers—they had not overlooked anything. Naturally, the cost of this achievement would be substantial: between one hundred and ten and one hundred and thirty billion rubles.

Father voiced doubt that we could afford such a project. Recalling his recent visit to our Pacific fleet, he brought up a sore subject: "Aren't all these battleships and cruisers out of date in the nuclear age? Won't all this money be thrown to the wind?" He asked his colleagues for their opinions.

Kuznetsov defended himself fiercely. He launched a general counterattack. An oceangoing fleet was the core of his dream of being a naval commander whose flag would fly at least as high as those of his rivals, if not higher.

Father continued to drive his point home. The oceans left him indifferent. What concerned him was the security of his own shores and, even more, how to find the money to restore our ruined agriculture and to build housing. How much housing could be built with the money for one cruiser!

The argument raged for more than an hour.

There had never been anything like this at a session of the Presidium of the Central Committee, where a special regime reigned: the "seniors" asked questions and voiced truths, while the "juniors" undertook to implement them. That day saw more than Father's first conflict with the military, with whom until then he had been in complete agreement. For the first time Father tried to move away from the doctrine of offensive war, which prevailed during Stalin's time. Kuznetsov simply couldn't understand him; he couldn't imagine that such a thing was possible. They were speaking different languages.

Finally both sides exhausted their arguments, but without reaching agreement. At that point neither Father nor Kuznetsov suspected that it was impossible to agree. They were counting on logic. In vain.

Father suggested postponing consideration of the question until the next session, so that the participants could weigh all the pros and cons once more. Presidium members agreed with feelings of relief, but Kuznetsov was simply beside himself.

Father recalled that Kuznetsov collared him in the hall after the meeting. The admiral took the postponement of discussion as a personal insult, and he had decided to lock horns with the main culprit.

Father headed for the door, the Navy's commander in chief walking beside him.

"How long do I have to put up with such an attitude toward *my* Navy," he practically shouted.

Father looked at him in surprise. Resisting the temptation to respond in kind, he tried to smooth over the situation, saying that Presidium members had to get a better idea of what it was on which they were being asked to spend such a vast sum of money. But Kuznetsov couldn't control himself. Father interrupted, and still trying to reason with the admiral, said: "But Comrade Kuznetsov, we have not rejected your program, we've only postponed discussing it. The Central Committee Presidium cannot mindlessly approve resolutions put before it. Calm down. We'll talk in more detail next week, then we'll understand each other and come to a decision."

Kuznetsov was too angry to respond. He seemed to have regained his composure when he and Father reached the main entrance of the building where the Presidium usually met. Father put his hand out to bid him good-bye. They shook hands. The guard standing at the curb opened the door of the ZIS limousine. Father sat down in the front seat. The car took off, leaving the admiral standing alone in front of the Kremlin.

This conversation in the corridor left a painful impression on Father, but in no way influenced his decision. During the week Father's resolution hardened; he simply could not permit such funds to be spent on what he thought was a doubtful project.

The following Thursday the argument flared up with renewed force. Because of its importance, this time it was the only item on the agenda.

Kuznetsov defended himself stubbornly: A powerful surface fleet was essential to the country, and victory in a future war could not be guaranteed without it. He conceded that the costs would be great, but the nation would just have to tighten its belt to achieve victory in a just cause.

At that point Father thought he'd found a way out. He asked Kuznetsov: "If today you get everything you're asking for in this decade—all these cruisers, battleships, and aircraft carriers—could our Navy then compete with the American Navy and oppose it on the seas?"

Kuznetsov thought briefly, seeming to vacillate. Finally, looking Father in the eye, he replied firmly: "No."

At that moment the fight was essentially over. The ensuing discussion dealt with trifles. People asked Kuznetsov some questions and he replied. But the whole basis of his argument had disappeared, and when the time came, the Presidium voted against the proposal.

Kuznetsov had been too inflamed by the argument to anticipate the possibility of defeat. Who knows what he was counting on? Probably the word "no" simply didn't exist in his vocabulary. Presidium members and guests drifted slowly out of the room. The admiral stood silently. He seemed not to comprehend that it was all over. By the time he had calmed down a little, he was alone in the room with Father, who sat signing some papers. Kuznetsov pulled himself together, his eyes glittered, and he angrily flung at Father: "You'll answer for this! History will never forgive you!!!" He then turned and stomped out the door. Father looked after him in astonishment.

Father Inspects the Black Sea Fleet

These events reinforced Father's conviction that things were not right with the Navy. He asked for information about the warships being built at shipyards. He took an interest in how much it cost to operate the fleet. He was especially astonished by fuel consumption: Every time the Black Sea Fleet went to sea, it used up as much fuel as the Ukraine was allotted for an entire year. Father clutched his head: If the cruisers, battleships, and destroyers included in a program adopted under Stalin and now either finished or still being built were put into service, costs would not only increase, they would multiply.

What to do? Father couldn't forget the Kometa, recently designed by Artyom Mikoyan's design bureau. It was an antiship cruise missile launched from planes—precisely the type of weapon that would change the face of the modern, or rather future, Navy. If missiles were installed on submarines and torpedo boats, the difference between large and small ships would be eliminated. Its automatic radar homing system would enable it to destroy a target over vast distances. Father was amazed that Kuznetsov and the admirals didn't understand such obvious things. Naturally, you couldn't do without a surface fleet if you wanted to send landing forces across the ocean. But not even Stalin had dreamed of such insane ventures.

Cruise missile installations on the coast, along with cruise missile-bearing torpedo boats, would make us invulnerable from the sea. At a deeper level, cruise missile-bearing submarines would dictate their will over sea and ocean communications. Choosing advantageous positions, they would hit even the most powerful and threatening battleships and disappear, vanishing into the depths. Furthermore, submarines were several times less expensive.

Father became increasingly convinced that he was right and that the surface fleet was obsolete. When the dream of Anatoly Petrovich Aleksandrov was realized, and diesel-powered submarines were replaced by nuclear powered ones, nothing would be able to compete with them. Then the victor in an ocean battle would be uncertain: the Americans with their aircraft carriers, or Soviet submarines with their missiles.

Preparing for a meeting of the Presidium, Father met with Aleksandrov and Kurchatov. Their conversation convinced Father that the nuclear engine would bring about a revolution in naval warfare. And once convinced of something, Father was a man of action and began to explore ways to realize it. He found supporters in the Navy, who began working on the theory. Kuznetsov considered them traitors. Father set about carrying out his ideas. Thus the concept of a new Russian fleet, a subsurface one, was born. It still had to be built. He was later to meet with both successes and bitter disappointments.

However, Father didn't hurry to make a decision, but thought to test his judgment one more time. A favorable opportunity soon arose, since early autumn—it was now September 1955—was approaching and it was time for vacation. Father prepared to go to the Crimea. Malenkov headed there at the same time.

This time he planned to visit Sevastopol. He wanted to talk with the Black Sea Fleet command. He was interested in finding out how they viewed modern war at sea. He also wanted to take a look at the ships and compare them with those he had seen in the Pacific. Initially, they planned to meet with a small group, the fleet commander and his deputies; but then Father thought it over and decided to invite unit commanders and department heads, and not just those attached to the Black Sea Fleet.

Officially, the subject of the meeting was "Operations of the Black Sea Fleet in the Event of War." I don't remember who was given the honor of delivering a report.

Quite a crowd gathered on the appointed day. The walls of the hall were festooned with diagrams, graphs, and maps of the Black and Mediterranean Seas, stippled by red arrows and dotted with black silhouettes representing Soviet and foreign naval warships.

The report began with a "storming" of the Dardanelles, a successful one this time. The Fleet bombarded the forts with heavy-caliber weapons and landed an invasion force. Cruisers and destroyers briskly repelled attacks by the opponent's ships, which steadily fell in number as the defenders' resistance weakened. Finally, having crushed its opponent, Black Sea forces broke through into the Mediterranean and set a course for North Africa.

At first Father listened without interrupting, but his expression darkened. He began to breathe heavily, like a rhinoceros preparing to attack. What was being described strongly reminded him of the cruiser *Kalinin*'s maneuvers in the Pacific the previous autumn. The same artillery fire, the same torpedo boats, and the same smoke screens, only there everything had happened at sea, while here the battle was unfolding on paper. Not a word was said about missiles or other innovations.

Everyone has his limits. When the speaker began describing a successful landing on the African coast, Father couldn't restrain himself. He inquired maliciously how the fleet planned to defend itself against homing missiles, such as our Kometa. There was dead silence. The speaker pulled at the pointer in his hands, like a pupil who hadn't studied his homework. Finally he brought himself to speak and announced loudly: "I don't know about them." Father was genuinely surprised: "What, you don't know about the Kometa?"

"No, not at all," he replied.

The fleet commander, who was sitting next to Father, whispered in his ear that, in accordance with existing regulations on secrecy, information on special types of armaments was not relayed to combat units and ships.

"To avoid leaks," he added.

"What?" Father erupted. "But then how are they going to fight?"

He looked at Zhukov, Malinovsky, and the admirals sitting on the dais. No one answered. Zhukov only laughed. He didn't like these Navy dandies.

"He's deluding us with talk about landing in Africa," Father continued to seethe. "They would have drowned him long before. There wouldn't be a trace of him left. How can you prepare for war if commanders don't have the slightest idea what weapons they will face?"

The question hung in the air.

I don't want to go over all the events of that day. The conference was ruined; even the colorful maps on the walls seemed to have faded.

They interrupted the report and announced a recess.

Father proposed meeting again several days later. In the interim those present should familiarize themselves with modern armaments; luckily they were located here, right under their noses. Then it would be possible to argue about methods for conducting modern warfare.

Father himself was only strengthened in his view that money was wasted on a surface fleet and that it could not be relied upon in case of misfortune.

The Old Navy Is Vanquished

When they met again, on October 13, 1955, not a word was said about North Africa. Father set a harsh tone. He talked about his idea of moving the Navy under water, to a safe depth. Minister of Defense Marshal Zhukov spoke in the same vein. They found quite a few supporters in the hall, mainly among those whose shoulder boards were not covered with gold braid.

Advocates of a surface fleet fought back, but their arguments sounded unconvincing. They had clearly suffered total defeat.

Father left the conference more than ever persuaded that he was right. He made up his mind to act decisively.

Father decided not to return to Yalta from Sevastopol by car, but asked the Navy to take him there by submarine. He wanted to see what it was like, to get a hands-on feel for it, so to speak. Father was pleased by the ride, but that was his first and last trip by submarine—with his stout build he had trouble negotiating the tight cylindrical hatchways connecting the submarine's compartments.

Now Father focused his attention on shipyards, where the program was being pushed hard. First of all, Father demanded a reduction in the number of surface ships being built. The list was cut in several stages. Kuznetsov fought for every destroyer, not to speak of every cruiser. Father stood firm. As a result, the list was reduced to almost nothing and a very large sum of money, an amount trailing ten zeros, was liberated.

The appetite grows as it feeds. The fates of the cruisers already under construction were decided after a great deal of wrangling. They were sentenced, as yet unborn, to be scrapped—even most of the ships that only needed "one last nail." The new fleet didn't need them.

The Navy went through a painful ordeal. Even the supporters of the concept of an underwater fleet shuddered at the prospect of destroying those magnificent cruisers.

The rumor that new warships at naval shipyards were being cut up for scrap spread quickly. When it reached me, I rushed to ask Father about it. I have already described his reasoning. While I couldn't think of any objections, I could not agree with him either. Even now, years later, it grieves me deeply when I think of those cruisers.

Perhaps Father was more upset than all the rest of us. His whole nature, that of an industrious manager, resisted destroying the fruits of human labor.

He tried to think of ways to use the cruisers and destroyers. At that time we were catastrophically short of all kinds of ships, including passenger ships, freighters, and fishing boats. And now we were putting such beautiful ships under the cutting torch.

From the start, specialists rejected Father's first idea of converting the cruisers into passenger liners. The tightly interlaced compartments of a ship designed to destroy people could not be reconfigured for even the most uncomplaining passengers. And operating costs would be unimaginably high.

Father did not retreat. At the time, the Slava whaling ship was enjoying nationwide fame. Stories were told about the profits it was reaping. Father became enthusiastic about the idea of converting a battleship into a mother ship and reclassifying destroyers as whalers. What could be simpler than replacing the hundred-millimeter bow guns with harpoon cannons? Why stop there? The idea of reclassifying the remaining ships as fishing boats really appealed to Father.

The Ministry of the Fishing Industry was told to draw up a proposal. A week later the minister requested a meeting with Father. He entreated Father: if you force us to take those ships, we'll go bankrupt! He was not referring to the cost of converting them, which he assumed the government would cover. He meant that his ministry would be ruined by the costs of operating them.

Father had to give up his plan. He realized that these ships could not be sent to sea, that we would only embarrass ourselves. However, he really wanted to avoid sentencing them to the scrap heap. He suggested, not very hopefully, that the obsolete warships be permanently at anchor and used as rest camps or, at worst, as dormitories. No one was enthusiastic about that idea either.

The ships were condemned to be scrapped. The guns, machinery, and anything else that might prove useful were removed from the finished cruisers, and what remained was sent for salvage. The bare hulls were left for years to rust in the back yards of naval shipyards, waiting in line for the next world.

The *Sovetskiy Soyuz* and a few other cruisers were spared. They were selected to be targets, and for years after were pounded by the large-caliber guns of their sister ships—those lucky enough to stay afloat. Bombs rained down on them like hail. Cruise missiles pierced their sides. This went on until one of the giants sank after being hit by a particularly lucky shot. Only then was it decided that using such a mass of valuable metal as a target was wasteful.

So the fate of these last monsters was decided. They were also sent to the smelter.

Time has shown that Father was right about the future. The old Navy had outlived its day, and a new one had to be born. The money saved was turned into houses, roads, and farms. Whether they were well managed is another matter.

The fate of the Navy's commander in chief was not an easy one. Having lost his previous influence, he discovered that his supporters of yesterday moved quickly over to the enemy camp. Denunciations of Kuznetsov rained down on Father from all directions, citing his strong words about the new leadership. Father maintained a sullen silence, but he became increasingly irritated.

Zhukov played an important role in deciding Kuznetsov's fate. He and Father were on the same side of the barricade. Zhukov didn't like the fleet and didn't hide his negative attitude toward it. Once when something angered him during a ship visit he announced ominously: "I'll soon put you in Army boots."

The seamen didn't forget his words. It would be hard to think of a worse insult to Navy pride. And the collision between two personalities also played a part. The Navy's commander in chief and the minister of defense were both hard men.

There is no doubt that Father took the initiative in dismissing Admiral Kuznetsov, and he never tried to conceal that. But at the time there was no talk of demoting him. According to witnesses, that was Zhukov's doing. That same year, 1955, at about 1:00 A.M. on October 29, an accident in the Bay of Sevastopol, the main base of the Black Sea Fleet, gave Zhukov the pretext he needed. The battleship *Novorossiysk* exploded and sank at its mooring, killing 608 sailors. It had recently borne the name *Julio Caesar* and was given to the Soviet Union after the war when the Italian fleet was divided up. Investigators were not sure what caused the catastrophe. Some talked of revenge by the legendary Italian underwater saboteurs of Count Borghese. But whatever caused it, the commander in chief had to answer for everything. Kuznetsov was relieved of his command, and Zhukov proposed demoting him to the rank of rear admiral, to which Father agreed. The action undoubtedly did neither of them any credit. Thank heaven, today justice has been done, and the monument over Kuznetsov's grave in Novodevichy Cemetery bears the title, "Admiral of the Fleet of the Soviet Union." Unfortunately, too late for Kuznetsov to have known about it.

Kuznetsov's dismissal was inevitable, and the fate of the *Novorossiysk* had no bearing on it. Proponents of two diametrically opposite viewpoints cannot conduct a common policy, and one must give way. Unfortunately, at the time people did not submit their resignations. A leader could go from being all powerful to being a nonentity in the course of a day.

The concept of a strike force submarine fleet prevailed. Admiral Kuznetsov was replaced as commander in chief by Admiral Sergei Georgiyevich Gorshkov, at the time a passionate advocate of a submarine fleet.

The last time Father thought about the desirability of having a surface strike force was during the conflict in the Congo. The Soviet Union was trying in every way possible to help the young republic and Prime Minister Lumumba, but the Congo was too far from the Soviet Union.

The Americans, who supported the opposition group, unambiguously showed the flag. An impressive squadron approached the shores of Africa. Father thought they might put troops ashore. We had no way to interfere or to help our friends.

Admiral Gorshkov proposed sending a cruiser and a pair of destroyers, but it became clear that they would run out of fuel and that it was doubtful that we could supply them at such a distance from Soviet bases. The idea smacked of adventurism and was quickly rejected.

Father fretted. The situation then was entirely different from today. Competition between the two countries was running high. The victory of one party in the Congo and the defeat of the other was viewed as a victory or defeat for the Soviet Union or the United States, as a victory or defeat for socialism or imperialism. Father followed events attentively and was distressed by every failure.

He could not, therefore, be indifferent to the situation in the Congo. His restless nature demanded action. He summoned Admiral Gorshkov—I was present at the meeting—and Boris Yevstafyevich Butoma, chairman of the Committee on Shipbuilding, and asked: "How much would it cost and how long would it take to build a rapid response squadron? One that would show the power and flag of the Soviet Union in support of our friends anywhere in the world?"

It took about a week to get a preliminary estimate. The report the specialists prepared for Father calculated that it would take about five years to build the fighting ships and auxiliary vessels, and that the squadron would cost about five billion rubles.

In reply, Father simply mumbled: "Rather a lot. We'll find better uses for all that money."

He never raised this question again.

FOREIGN AFFAIRS

The impending creation of a West German army and its inclusion in NATO was the main foreign policy problem in the autumn of 1954. The decisions being made would radically change the balance of forces in Europe. Father undertook feverish, but fruitless, attempts at least to delay, if not stop, the process.

On November 13 neighboring countries were sent a note with a proposal to hold an all-European conference on mutual security before ratification of the Paris Accords. The appeal went unanswered. In those years no one even thought such a thing was possible. Security was defined solely by the number and quality of opposing divisions. Even Father himself did not believe in the real possibility of reaching mutually acceptable agreements. The time was not ripe. His appeal was more of a propagandistic nature.

Nevertheless, on November 29 an All-European Conference on Security in Europe opened with great pomp in Moscow, but it was attended only by our allies, the people's democracies. The participants passionately assured each other of the danger of remilitarizing West Germany. An enviable correspondence of views prevailed at the sessions. After four days a unanimous resolution against the arming of Germany was adopted. But two months later Bonn ratified the Paris Accords, and they went into effect.

It was then the turn of the Soviet Union, which could no longer remain unconcerned. So, step by step, the course of events that later became known as the Berlin Crisis unfolded. It differed in nature from the Berlin blockade at the end of the 1940s, when Stalin was testing the strength of the Allies. Here the question was how to defend the interests of the countries that had chosen the path of building socialism, and primarily how to ensure the national security of the GDR, to get the West Germans to recognize the European realities established after the Second World War. Not the easiest of tasks.

I am deliberately employing the terminology used at that time. Whatever we think about our history and however we judge the actions of our fathers, it is impossible to change the past and senseless to refashion it in terms of the present. Let the past remain as it was, with all its mistakes and absurdities. We should not fear the fact that today we think differently, that much was not accomplished and could not be accomplished. Let the mistakes of the past serve as lessons for us and let us never repeat them. Therefore I ask the reader's indulgence for leaving the reasoning of those years without commentary throughout the text of my book, even if today both author and readers see that it was mistaken.

When crises are discussed—whether in Berlin, the Caribbean, Suez, Poland, or Hungary—attention is focused on their tragic stage, when shells begin to explode and bombs to fall, or at least when there is a real threat of that happening. Then matters which had seemed urgent only yesterday are put aside and a feverish search for solutions begins. Thank the Lord if we have time to think, and there is still time to put out the fire.

In fact, crises, like diseases, arise long before fever manifests itself. They develop slowly. Often years pass before the consequences of a decision become faintly visible.

The symptoms of more than one approaching crisis can be traced to the years when the first post-Stalin changes were being made. Unfortunately, even now they are not always easy to diagnose. Let's try to see them, at least in hindsight.

A report dated July 5, 1953, concerned a speech given by Hungarian prime minister Imre Nagy on the occasion of the election of a new government. Only two years later came the decision by a plenary session of the Hungarian Workers' Party Central Committee to remove Imre Nagy from all his posts, including that of chairman of the Council of Ministers, and to expel him from the Politburo and Central Committee for views deviating from the line set out by the Central Committee.

This was many months before the tragedy of the Hungarian crisis. How many lost opportunities and mistakes lay ahead!

Often it is precisely the period preceding an explosion that is of the greatest interest. Today we have the opportunity to determine how adequate the assessment of events at the time was to the actual circumstances; to investigate what lay at the basis of the decisions that were made; and finally, to try to understand the motives behind the acts of those making the decisions in those distant years.

The USSR was making every effort to show undeviating support for the GDR—there was no room for retreat or compromise. The government was acting with reserve toward its western partners. A decree of the Presidium of the Supreme Soviet titled "On Cessation of the State of War Between the Soviet Union and Germany" was published on January 26, 1955. The West was just as adamant about its intentions. Because of the decision to remilitarize West Germany, on April 10 the Soviet government annulled the Treaties on Alliance and Mutual Assistance with Britain and France. They were outdated anyway, since they dealt entirely with the past war, they were just paper. A few days earlier, the Soviet Union had announced the return to the GDR of the Dresden Gallery treasures, which had been seized as war booty. It was decided to return them ceremoniously as a gesture meant to show that we were now friends, not enemies. The confrontation reached its culmination in the signing on May 14 of the Warsaw Pact, making official the confrontation of two armed coalitions in Europe.

On April 15 Federal Chancellor Julius Raab was greeted cordially in Moscow and signed documents on the status of neutral Austria. Both sides were pleased with the result. Many years later, in recalling those days' events Father always spoke warmly about them.

Though the Twentieth Party Congress was not far off, it seemed as if Stalin's position was unshakable. Familiar quotations appeared in the editorial pages of *Pravda*. A grandiose monument to Stalin was unveiled in Prague on May 2 and now loomed oppressively over the city.

However, at the same time a very high level Soviet delegation prepared to leave for Yugoslavia. Besides Father and Bulganin, who had replaced Malenkov as chairman of the Council of Ministers on February 9, 1955, it included Anastas Ivanovich Mikoyan, Dmitry Trofimovich Shepilov, Andrei Andreyevich Gromyko, and an enormous retinue of advisers. Molotov was not among them, though he should have been because of his rank. After the events of 1947,[31] his presence in a delegation sent to make peace with Tito was unthinkable.

Father decided not just to improve relations between the two countries, but to apologize. This initiative did not meet with universal approval in Moscow. Indeed many considered a meeting with Tito to be near treason. Others thought that it was time to take the initiative in reestablishing relations and to "forgive" the apostate by inviting him to Moscow. However, Father thought that we, the Soviet Union, had to take the first step and go to Belgrade, thereby demonstrating our sincerity. In his opinion, Tito could not fail to appreciate the friendly gesture. After that, it wouldn't hurt to invite our neighbor to Moscow.

An awkward situation, very characteristic for those years, arose during the welcoming reception at the Belgrade airport. As Father put it, his brain was not yet "restructured," and so to shield Stalin it substituted a "scapegoat." He struck a false note in his speech.

"We sincerely regret what happened," said Father. "We resolutely reject all the extraneous features of that period. On our part, we attribute them to the provocative role played in relations between Yugoslavia and the USSR by Beria, Abakumov, and others, who have now been exposed as enemies of the people. We have thoroughly studied the documents that formed the basis of accusations and insults directed at the Yugoslav leadership at that time. Facts show that these materials were fabricated by enemies of the people, by the contemptible agents of imperialism who wormed their way into the ranks of our party by deceitful methods." And so on, in that vein.

The warm welcome almost broke off at the very start, but Tito saved the day. Leaning toward Father, he said quietly—in Russian—that since practically everyone in Yugoslavia speaks Russian, it was not necessary to interpret his remarks. Father began to object, but then quickly caught on.

In later years he loved to recall this episode. He cited it as an example of the pernicious influence of the lie. From then on he avoided any false notes.

I think that what happened at the Belgrade airport also influenced Father's thinking in the dramatic hours preceding his "secret" report to the Twentieth Party Congress.

---

31. "The events of 1947." This is a reference to the Stalin-Tito split over claims to Trieste, the Balkan Federation, and the Greek Civil War (1946–49), which culminated in a cold war in miniature between the Soviet Union and Yugoslavia (and Stalin's efforts to assassinate the Yugoslav leader).

THE GENEVA SUMMIT AND THE GERMAN QUESTION

In the midst of daily concerns, Father was preparing for his first international examination. A meeting of heads of state and government of the four powers was scheduled for July. The first since Potsdam.

There were certain difficulties in choosing the Soviet delegation. Father didn't hide his desire to go to Geneva. In those days his thoughts were always occupied by the forthcoming conference, and he constantly led conversations around to that subject.

There were several possible reasons for this. The main one was the question of the division of power, or the power struggle, if you like. Since Malenkov's resignation Father had become the pivotal figure in the Presidium. Both Bulganin and the new minister of war, the legendary Zhukov, and even the obstinate Molotov, acknowledged his leadership, at least outwardly. Father simply couldn't bear to miss the first meeting by heads of the great powers to be held since he became the nation's chief leader.

As a prudent administrator, he had other reasons for concern: although Malenkov, who easily deferred to others, had been replaced by the more steadfast (in Father's opinion) Bulganin, even the latter needed oversight. Father thought Bulganin could miss something, might not be vigilant and might quickly agree to some proposal without examining its political and class essence. True, Foreign Minister Molotov's participation in the negotiations was not in doubt, and he was famous for more than firmness—his resistance to compromise was common knowledge throughout the West. But Molotov was Molotov, and Father wanted to see things through his own eyes.

Simple human curiosity also played an important role. Father had never visited Western Europe. His trips abroad had been limited to a few visits to the people's democracies and one to friendly China. Although immediately after the war he had traveled incognito, under the pseudonym General Petrenko, through parts of occupied Germany and Austria selecting equipment to be sent to the Ukraine as reparations, that could hardly be called a visit.

Father played a key role in choosing the delegation, so including himself was not an issue, and his participation caused not the slightest concern among other members of the Presidium. So why was there a problem? The stumbling block was that he did not hold a government title corresponding to the occasion. It was only later that everything became less complicated and Western leaders meeting with the general secretary of the Central Committee of the Communist Party of the Soviet Union no longer worried about his other titles—it was enough that he possessed the real power.

At that time things were different. It can't be said that people simply didn't associate with communists. The war had destroyed the stereotypes of the

1930s. But a definite protocol was observed: the chairman of the Council of Ministers, though also a member of the Presidium of the Central Committee, was one thing. Someone who was only the first secretary of the Central Committee was quite another. They might, Father thought, not pay him the proper amount of attention. He was morbidly suspicious that he would not be shown the respect accorded a head of state by formal protocol. It always seemed to him that Western leaders were only looking for a pretext to humiliate the representatives of a socialist state. And that was not just his imagination.

So the question of whether or not to include him in the delegation grew into a serious problem. Molotov came to the rescue, suggesting the following solution: along with his other titles, Father was a member of the Presidium of the Supreme Soviet. He could therefore participate in the negotiations as a representative of our country's supreme legislative body. Father wasn't thrilled by the idea, but he accepted it as the only possibility.

At home he told us that the comrades had decided his presence on the delegation was essential. He went on to describe what they had thought up to get around the formal difficulties. Father was noticeably amused, although his title didn't seem terribly respectable compared with those of chairman of the Council of Ministers, minister of foreign affairs, and minister of defense. He kept referring indirectly to this painful subject, looking at it from various angles.

Bulganin had also hardly been out of the country. A whole host of problems relating to protocol arose: What to wear, how to greet people, which forks to use at official dinners, etc., etc. Father wasn't ashamed to ask questions, and Molotov became the chief expert on etiquette.

Officials from the Ministry of Foreign Affairs even suggested tailcoats. I imagined Father in tails and couldn't repress a smile; it was so incongruous. Apparently Father thought so too. He began talking about Mikoyan's trip to the United States in the 1930s and recalled how they had made fun of his tailcoat.

"And will you put on a tailcoat?" Mama interrupted in a funereal tone of voice.

After a moment's reflection, Father replied roughly: "No, they'll have to take us the way we are. We won't play up to them. If they want to talk with workers, they had better get used to us."

The question of tailcoats was dropped. Despite every effort, our fathers looked awkward. It would take years for them to feel comfortable in tailcoats.

An unusual period of "fraternizing" with the West began in Moscow before the four-power meeting. By the standards of those days, naturally. Nothing like it had been seen since the war. For the first time in a decade all more or less important Soviet leaders attended the U.S. ambassador's

Independence Day reception on July 4. The same thing happened at the French Embassy ten days later, on Bastille Day.

Three days after that the Soviet delegation left for Geneva. Minor annoyances, or more precisely jabs at Father's pride, began at the airport. Until the day he died, he never forgot how humiliated he felt when the delegation's modest, two-engine IL-14 landed. It looked like an insect next to the planes that delivered Dwight Eisenhower, Anthony Eden, and Edgar Faure.

And then another false step. The guests, or rather the heads of government, were welcomed by a Swiss honor guard, as required by protocol. When Bulganin was asked to step forward, "the chief of Swiss protocol, a hulking fellow, moved directly in front of me," writes Father in his memoirs. He was thus prevented from making any possible move forward.

Father often recalled this episode and made fun of the chief of protocol for suspecting him of planning to violate the rules. Both in his memoirs and in conversation, he was always true to this version. I can't say that it wasn't the case, and making conjectures is a thankless pastime. However, in view of arrangements at the time, my feeling is that at the least hint from his hosts Father would have moved forward at Bulganin's side. Not because he didn't understand the rules of behavior, but because he understood them perfectly and thought it would be useful to show where the real power lay. So perhaps the chief of protocol had made the right move.

I won't comment on the course of the negotiations, since everything possible has already been said. I would only note that Father did not regard them as an invitation for dialogue, but as an attempt by the West to feel out the new Soviet leadership, to test its solidity. In turn, Father was terribly afraid of showing any weakness, but at the same time thought it essential to demonstrate friendliness.

He was not called upon to speak at any official sessions, but he did not regret that; speaking from a written text according to protocol was not his style. He made up for it at the friendly evening gatherings with one or another delegation. At these Father, and not the head of the delegation, quickly became the center of attention. Bulganin seemed to accept that. Father increasingly pushed him into a secondary role, and Nikolai Aleksandrovich sometimes even played up to him. But inwardly Bulganin was offended and increasingly displeased. Father didn't seem to notice, or else didn't want to notice.

Father took away favorable impressions from the Geneva meetings. The reserved Anthony Eden, who invited him and Bulganin to make an official visit to Britain, upheld his good reputation in Father's eyes. Father did not forget (or perhaps someone told him) that in 1938 Anthony Eden, then a young diplomat, had resigned in protest when the Munich Agreement was signed. Father viewed both these steps, separated by almost twenty years, as a good sign. He hoped to find a basis for mutual understanding, keeping class distinctions in mind, naturally.

Father felt genuine sympathy for French premier Edgar Faure, or Edgar Ivanovich, as he asked the Russians to call him. Father retained that sympathy throughout his life and always received the ex-premier on his visits to our country. They always met as friends. If he came across Faure's name in the newspaper, Father would exclaim, "Oh, Edgar Ivanovich!"

In his own way, Dwight Eisenhower also pleased Father, who proudly remembered their brief meeting at the Victory Parade in Moscow, in June of 1945. It was hardly likely that the American general would remember the Ukrainian premier. Now they were meeting as equals.

For some reason Father attributed special significance to the meeting of the two wartime heroes, Eisenhower and Zhukov. He thought that memories of victory and wartime comradeship would create a special atmosphere of confidence, if not trust. Naturally, he didn't count on any concrete results. But perhaps, as meeting followed meeting, some ice might melt. Father was influenced by this thinking when he included Zhukov in the delegation.

Father later observed regretfully that nothing came of his plan. Eisenhower received Zhukov, and in his words, they chatted about this and that. The president presented him with a fishing rod, but the meeting ended without having had any effect on the relations between our two countries.

On the other hand, John Foster Dulles became a real hero in Father's eyes. Father hadn't liked him and had always thought of him as a sworn enemy and anticommunist. However, after their conversations he felt such respect for his opponent's intellect that he often said he felt calmer when Dulles was secretary of state than when the post was held by his more liberal successors. Dulles conducted a policy that bordered on war, but he understood precisely where the border was and never dreamed of crossing it.

What was Father most afraid of in Geneva? That the world might, God forbid, imagine that he could bow before the imperialists.

What did Father want most of all? To find common ground, a mutual understanding that would make it possible to avoid war.

It was that contradiction—not to yield, but to reach an agreement—which repeatedly brought negotiations to a halt and forced recesses in the search for a compromise. This process continued throughout the next decade. Fortunately, Father was always guided by the sensible conviction that a bad peace was better than a good quarrel. But a good peace would be even better.

The effort to try to understand each other, to make a step toward each other, won out in Geneva. The "Spirit of Geneva" was born. Unfortunately, it didn't last long. Father found the negotiations difficult, not only because of the need to find a solution to what seemed an insoluble situation and to reconcile irreconcilable positions, but because he was doing it all for the first time and was feeling his way.

The German problem was the overriding issue. Here there was no time for temporizing, since every mistake threatened unpredictable complications.

German unification was not to be contemplated, since it would contradict the Central Committee's decision to build socialism in the GDR. Nevertheless, both sides talked, insisted, fought for a unified Germany. But only in words.

Each side pursued its own goals: they wanted to strengthen the FRG and we wanted to strengthen the GDR. Both Germanys intently followed the slightest change in tone during the negotiations. Konrad Adenauer's greatest fear was that his allies would say the forbidden initials "GDR." Walter Ulbricht could not allow East Germany to be used as a pawn in trading between the two camps.

Naturally, they did not succeed in reaching an agreement. The final document was revised repeatedly in an effort to harmonize conflicting views. Sometimes a breakdown in negotiations seemed inevitable, but common sense prevailed and some formulaic language was finally agreed upon. But what phrasing! Both terse and equivocal—"free elections . . . unification of the two parts of Germany"—each side interpreted the seemingly unambiguous words to its own satisfaction.

After the Geneva Memorandum was signed, Father decided it had to be clarified before he returned home. In Berlin Ulbricht was worried, most of all by the possibility of holding all-German elections. There was no doubt that he would lose. The population of West Germany was almost double that of the GDR.

The Soviet delegation went from Geneva directly to Berlin. The visit impressed Father, despite his skeptical attitude toward organized events. He knew what they were worth. The crowds of people on the streets didn't particularly impress him; he knew that was not difficult to arrange. But after experiencing the war firsthand, he had expected a sullen reception and was touched by the smiles and welcoming faces.

After signing documents with the GDR that reiterated our determination to support its progress along the path to socialism, the delegation returned home.

Father was pleased with himself. He talked enthusiastically about the meetings and infected his listeners with his optimism. It seemed as if the world had turned toward peace. And he didn't forget presents. He had ordered that delegation members be given a little pocket money—not enough for them to splurge, but so they wouldn't be embarrassed if they dropped into a cafe.

Of course Father didn't go shopping in Geneva, but soon after arriving he sent the chief of his bodyguards to find out how much Swiss watches cost. From the time he lived in the Donbas he thought of watches, especially Swiss watches, as the height of luxury. He had acquired a "Pavel Bure" watch before the Revolution and remembered it with what can only be called veneration.

The scout returned with a report that simply astounded Father: watches cost practically nothing. He immediately ordered that they be purchased for everyone at home—but to look for an even lower price. We all received stylish gold-plated self-winding wristwatches. The last word in watches. You had to keep waving your arm around to make sure the watch wouldn't stop at some inopportune moment. But what people won't do in the name of progress!

Father wasn't the only purchaser. The entire Soviet delegation rushed out to buy watches. There was one to suit every taste. The bodyguards strutted around wearing watches that bore a smiling Stalin on the face and hands sticking out of his mustaches.

For himself Father picked out a small knife, suitable for slicing mushrooms or peeling apples. He kept it in his pocket until the day he died. In our recent moves the little knife somehow disappeared. Alas.

The world began to breathe more freely. What had seemed unimaginable only yesterday suddenly became a reality.

Contacts with West Germany began. Even before Geneva, in June, there was an exchange of notes between Moscow and Bonn on the question of establishing diplomatic and trade relations between the two countries.

And then Chancellor Konrad Adenauer arrived in Moscow on September 8. Many people compared his visit to Ribbentrop's arrival in August of 1939. At first negotiations were difficult. No mutual sympathy or trust was apparent; the past war was a heavy burden. But slowly the meeting made progress. Father was delighted. They agreed to establish diplomatic relations.

And then everything came to a halt again. Adenauer began talking about the unification of Germany or, more accurately, about the annexation of the GDR. Moscow didn't want to hear about it. The chancellor argued sensibly that the Soviet economy needed credits, and he proposed an interest-free loan of a billion marks. An enormous sum! But that did not have the desired effect—Father saw the West German gesture as an insult. For a billion they want to buy up the freedom of a people that had embarked on the road to socialism! He simply refused to discuss the idea.

On the other hand, the Soviet side satisfied their guests on another, no less painful, matter. We agreed to send home all Germans captured during the war, including those prisoners of war who had been convicted of crimes.

A total of 8,877 war criminals were freed, while 749 were transferred to the custody of the government of the FRG. The crimes they had committed were too grave to be forgiven.

The U.S. ambassador, Charles (Chip) Bohlen, introduced additional complications into the already difficult negotiations. He jealously followed every step taken by the chancellor. This is how Father remembered it:

> We continued our talks and began to work on a document that would be possible to sign. Our negotiating partners displayed especially stubborn resistance on one particular subject. We were surprised. Then they let slip that Charles Bohlen, the U.S. ambassador to the USSR, was exerting pressure on Adenauer. . . .
>
> As the negotiations were coming to a close, Adenauer boasted that, despite pressure put on him by Bohlen, he had still brought the negotiations to a successful conclusion, so that in the end we were agreeing on a text. The Germans told us of their desire to expedite the signing before Bohlen saw the final version. We agreed with their approach. If it was acceptable to us but not Bohlen, then of course we were on Adenauer's side. So the document was signed. Thereupon they informed me that Bohlen was extremely indignant about Adenauer's position, but the document had already been signed.[32]

Adenauer's departure was accompanied by a certain feeling of relief. Father was reassured by the talks with his high-ranking guest, and by his assurances that articles in the press about revenge and getting back the Eastern lands was one thing, but real government policy was quite another. The West German government had a sober appreciation of the situation in Europe; any change in borders was considered unrealistic, and its policy was based on the expectation of peace, not war.

An amused Father chuckled over the chancellor's age—he was already almost eighty—but was captivated by the clarity of his intellect. Adenauer assured Father of his sincerity, so that while Adenauer remained in the category of political opponents and fervent anticommunists, Father included him among politicians, such as John Foster Dulles, with whom you could do business.

---

32. In this book I give numerous quotations from Father's memoirs, which he dictated between 1967 and 1971. As fate would have it, I became the editor and custodian of the dictated materials. When I wrote this book the full text of Father's memoirs had not yet seen the light of day in Russia. It was published in four volumes by "Moscow News" only in 1999. I did not use the American edition of the 1970s either, since in preparing it the editors considerably rearranged the original text.

I quote Father from the manuscript and cannot therefore provide the reader with footnotes to any publication.—S.K.

CHAPTER TWO

ACCELERATION

As 1956 began Father was sure of his power and ready to take decisive political action. However, in order to carry out his plans to provide the country with an abundance of food, clothes, footwear, and housing, in other words everything a human being needs and the Soviet people had gone many years without—he needed not just peace and confidence in the future, but money, a great deal of money.

Father thought that one of the principal ways to obtain this money was to reduce the number of men in the armed forces, of which there were more than five million. To be exact, at the time of Stalin's death there were 5,394,038 persons under arms.[1] The previous year's reduction in the Army by 640,000 men[2] and the structural change in the Navy had shown that his plan was a practical one. In fact, reductions actually began before 1955, but they were the result of totally secret decisions and were not announced in the press. According to a report submitted to Father by the Ministry of Defense, a total of 1,116,216 men had been demobilized by January 1, 1956.[3]

Nevertheless, the country's defense capability had not been affected, while more than a million young workers, plus additional funds, had been returned to the national economy. Father thought the added manpower was more important than the money. He decided to take the next step. He ordered preliminary calculations to see if an additional reduction in the Army, of more than one million men, was feasible.

Father placed great hopes on negotiations with the West. The Geneva Summit seemed not to have had any practical results, but that was only superficially. It had given rise to the "Spirit of Geneva." The Army, naturally, continued to exert considerable influence on events in our country, but Father had rejected planning for victory in favor of planning for coexistence. Despite the optimism of the military, he was beginning to understand that

---

1. *Military Archives of Russia*, no. 1 (1993): 272–74. This was the first and only issue of the journal published.

2. "Statement of the Soviet Government," *Pravda*, May 15, 1956, Decree of the CPSU CC and Council of Ministers of the USSR issued on August 12, 1955.

3. *Military Archives of Russia*, no. 1 (1993): 194, 283–88, 305–7.

after a nuclear war the winner would not look very different from the loser. The Geneva Summit had proved that dialogue was not only possible, but productive as well. Father was determined to continue it.

I have already mentioned that Anthony Eden had invited the Soviet leaders to visit Britain, while the French premier planned to visit Moscow. For the first time in years representatives of many of the world's air forces—from the United States to China—were expected in Moscow. Only a year before, such a "frivolous" idea simply couldn't have been imagined. Now Father only laughed in response to the concerns of the military: "The more they see, the more they'll wonder if it's worth starting a war. Let them see that we're not going around in birchbark sandals any longer."

All of Father's behavior was indicative of the turn toward peace. War had disappeared from the agenda, and the question of who would win was now to be decided in factory workshops and on the fields of agriculture, not the fields of battle. This type of thinking smacked of dissidence at the time, since official Marxism continued to claim that victory of a new social system was impossible without revolution, without a bloody clash between the representatives of two incompatible ideologies. If that were true, the Army should be larger, not smaller, and it should receive still more money as it prepared for the decisive moment. The people could continue to do without. It was their duty to do so in the name of a shining future. Or so the "Orthodox Marxists" believed.

With his pragmatic nature, Father resisted such arguments. He asked himself specific questions: When will this clash happen? Who will begin it? We? Will the proletariat in the West rise against their oppressors? And if the class struggle comes to nuclear war, who and what will be left? Practice had not as yet confirmed the theory. People's lives there were improving. Palmiro Togliatti[4] insisted that change in the political structure of developed countries would occur peacefully, by votes in parliaments and not on the barricades. Father doubted that Togliatti's ideas were correct—the bourgeoisie would not give up its power without a struggle—but the very idea that a bloodless transition from capitalism to socialism was possible appealed to him.

Father's discussions with theoreticians did not make anything clearer. Both Mikhail Andreyevich Suslov and Pyotr Nikolayevich Pospelov answered his questions with obscure and wordy citations from the classics of Marxism-Leninism that did not satisfy him for long. The thought that war was inevitable seemed blasphemous to him. He resisted the idea that a different solution was impossible. He had never before doubted the theory, but

---

4. Reference here is to Italian Communist Party leader Palmiro Togliatti, who argued for greater "polycentrism" (e.g., freedom from Moscow) in the international communist movement.

now he was forced to. He was gradually coming to the conclusion that the theoreticians were wrong, that their dogmas were outdated and had to be revised and related to real life. His cautious remarks on the avoidance of war caused a storm of protest. The very idea of reconciliation with imperialism seemed treasonable, not only to professional Marxists but even to me, who was just being initiated into "the best traditions" of the social sciences.

In the end, Father won out. To support his new position his aides found the necessary citations in the works of the founding fathers of Marxism. He began to prepare his report to the Twentieth Congress of the CPSU planned for February. In it were arguments that up to the very day of the Congress many would have found unacceptable.

REVELATIONS ABOUT THE PAST

The best possible description of how Father decided on his famous report is given in his own memoirs, and I will not repeat it. But I cannot refrain from noting that the problems it dealt with had not arisen suddenly. Father had begun to have his doubts about orthodox Marxist theory right after Stalin died. When Roman Rudenko, the new Soviet prosecutor general, assumed his post, Father immediately posed to him what was a difficult question in those days: Could one believe the results of the open trials held during the 1930s?[5] The main unsettled question in his mind was: Could Nikolai Bukharin, for whom Father had cherished especially warm feelings, really have been guilty? Rudenko answered in the negative. Then Father broadened the scope of the inquiry. He ordered a special commission, headed by Central Committee secretary P. N. Pospelov, to search the archives and ascertain how such a large number of "enemies of the people" suddenly appeared in the 1930s.

Toward the beginning of 1956 Father received a memorandum with a description of Stalin's crimes. Today, and for those who have read *The Gulag Archipelago*, these initial revelations now seem like trifles. At the time, it was as if the walls had crumbled and the foundations were shaken. Father distributed the document to members of the Presidium of the Central Committee. Some reacted by fearing exposure, others were horrified by the scale of the crimes. All felt strongly that the information should be kept under lock and key. Father wavered. Tell everything? Attack Stalin? That would take exceptional courage. Remain silent? Try to emerge from the quagmire of lawless-

---

5. "The open trials." A reference to the show trials of the late 1930s, the climax of which was the trial of Nikolai Bukharin, Aleksei Rykov, and sixteen others in March 1938. (Khrushchev never rehabilitated Bukharin; Gorbachev took that step in 1988.) The show trials were part of the public propaganda surrounding Stalin's Terror. Most of the real action—including thousands of quick "trials"—took place in secret.

ness and lies by relying on a new lie? Father understood that such a step was doomed to fail, that concealing the truth about the monstrosity of Stalin's regime would lead, in the long run, to even greater monstrosities in order to stay in power or to a cowardly passivity while others investigated everything. Father could not even imagine the first alternative. The second did not suit his active nature. He was used to anticipating the blows of fate, not waiting for them to fall. Still, he could not make up his mind to act. Days passed. Pospelov's memorandum lay in his briefcase like a smoldering ember, but there was still nothing in the Central Committee report being prepared for the Congress about the repressions.

Naturally, Father did not doubt everything inherited from the past. He believed, and could not but believe, in the imminent victory of socialism in all countries. People could not fail to see that it was superior. He revered class solidarity and felt duty-bound to give international assistance to people freeing themselves from colonialism. In that cause, Father felt that our country did not have the right to remain on the sidelines. That was his opinion in 1953, and his views didn't change in 1956 or 1962. In 1964 he left power, still unshaken in those views, still convinced that he was right. And so he remained until his death in 1971.

THE TWENTIETH PARTY CONGRESS

The Twentieth Congress of the Communist Party of the Soviet Union opened on February 14, 1956. The report, following tradition, dealt mainly with economic matters. I reread it recently and it seemed pallid, though at the time people claimed that it raised many critical questions. By the standards of those days, it probably did.

An exception was the section touching on so-called theoretical questions. I have written of Father's desire to cut the Gordian knot of our relations with the West, with the capitalist countries. Where were we headed? Toward war, a military clash—or did we mean to search for a path to peace? Father declared that we had to choose peace, and the Congress confirmed that war was not the inevitable solution to the contradictions between socialism and capitalism, and what is more, that conspiracy, revolution, and armed insurrection were no longer to be viewed as the only legitimate ways to replace a rotting capitalist structure with a flourishing socialist one. Elections to bourgeois parliaments—voting, which had been unequivocally rejected in the recent past and equated with treachery—were no longer considered anathema. Now people had the right to choose their own fate. By its authority, the party's highest forum sanctioned a new approach to relations between two worlds and transformed a blasphemy into "a new word in developing the theory of Marxism." Thereafter, peaceful coexistence, a reduction in the armed forces, and negotiations in West and East were given the right to exist, and from being tactical tricks in the struggle against imperialism they were transformed into the basic strategic line of our policy.

Today all this sounds somewhat naive. But in 1956 Father's words caused some to sigh with relief, others to mutter covertly that revisionism was raising its head. But the main point lies elsewhere: the turn from war toward peace was becoming not only desirable but palpable. Father's human emotions no longer existed in contradiction to communist ideology. True, to bring this about, it had been necessary to correct the ideology.

In my opinion, the Twentieth Party Congress's approval as law of Father's "new word" on the peaceful coexistence of two systems, on the possibility of preventing war in our time, and on the forms for the transition from capitalism to socialism in different countries was fully as important as the exposure of Stalin's crimes.

Father would continue to act in this way. In a conflict of interests between a person and dogma, he chose the person whenever possible. Some taboos were simply too much for him.

The General Report took up an entire day. Father returned home dead tired, but extremely pleased. He was simply beaming. To deliver the General Report to a Congress was the highest honor imaginable.

The next morning sessions resumed and discussion began. Debates at the Congress followed a time-honored pattern, with speakers repeating and illustrating with examples the basic theses of the report. Only Mikoyan devoted part of his speech to doubts about the validity of some of the Stalinist repressions. It rumbled like distant thunder and fell silent. The delegates did not support him.

No one foresaw the approaching explosion. Only a few days separated us from Father's second, so-called secret speech. Like the other inhabitants of our country and of the entire world, even members of our family did not suspect that one of the most terrible and bloody myths of our time was about to collapse.

I don't remember those days very well. Father didn't share his thoughts with me. The other members of our household had no idea of his intentions either. Outwardly he gave nothing away. Mornings, as usual, he glanced through the newspapers, where the numerous speeches were given equal space, and then left for that day's session in the Kremlin.

That was Father's way. Open, direct, even loquacious in matters relating to construction and agriculture, he became taciturn and unapproachable when vital political concerns were at stake. We only learned afterward what happened, not before, just as when Beria was arrested.

During the decades since, Father's second report has been clouded in rumor, even myth. For example, for some reason many believe that the report was delivered at night. This lends the entire event a compelling aura of mystery; nevertheless, it isn't true. The delegates gathered in the morning as usual; however, on that day the numerous guests of the Congress were given a separate program, and they dispersed to various Moscow enterprises to speak at specially organized meetings.

Father himself is probably the most authoritative witness to the dramatic events of those days. This is how he describes what happened:

> The Congress convened. I read the General Report. . . . But I wasn't satisfied. I was tormented by the following thought: The Congress will soon end. A resolution will be adopted. All that is a formality. But then what? The hundreds of thousands of people who were shot, including two-thirds of the Central Committee elected at the Seventeenth Party Congress, will remain on our conscience. Very, very few held out, entire party groups were shot or repressed. There were very few lucky enough to survive. What should we do?
>
> I was haunted by the findings of Pospelov's commission. Finally I steeled myself, and during a recess, when only Presidium members were present in the room, I brought the matter up:
>
> "Comrades, what are we going to do about Comrade Pospelov's memorandum? What are we going to do about the executions and the arrests? The Congress is coming to a close and we'll all go away without having said anything. But we already know that the people who suffered under the repressions were innocent, that they were not enemies of the people. They were honest people, devoted to the party, devoted to the Revolution, devoted to the Leninist cause of building socialism and communism in the Soviet Union. People will be returning from exile, we won't keep them there any longer. We must figure out how to bring them back."
>
> At that point we had not yet made any decisions to reexamine the question and bring prisoners home. . . .
>
> As soon as I finished speaking, everyone started attacking me, especially Voroshilov:
>
> "What's the matter with you? How is that possible? You think you can tell all this to the Congress? How do you think that will reflect on the prestige of our party and our country? You won't be able to keep it secret! Then they'll point at us. What will we be able to say about our role?"
>
> Kaganovich also began to object very vehemently, along the same lines. His position wasn't one based on a profound party and philosophical analysis, it was selfish fear for himself. He was eager to avoid responsibility. If crimes had been committed, then hush it up, cover it up.
>
> I said:
>
> "Even looking at it from your position, that's impossible. Nothing can be covered up. People will be coming out of prison and returning to their rela-

tives in the cities. They'll tell their relatives, friends, acquaintances, and comrades everything that happened. The whole country and the whole party will find out that people have spent ten to fifteen years in prison, some even longer, for absolutely nothing. All the charges against them were lies. This is impossible.

"Then, Comrades, I ask you to think about the fact that we are holding the first Congress since Stalin's death. I think that at this Congress we must honestly tell the delegates the whole truth about the life and work of our party and of the Central Committee during the period covered by the report. We're now giving an account of the period after Stalin's death, but as members of the Central Committee, we must tell about the Stalin period as well. We were in the leadership together with Stalin, so how can we say nothing to the Congress delegates?

"The Congress is coming to an end. The delegates will soon disperse. Newly released prisoners will be coming back and starting to tell people in their own way about what happened. Then the Congress delegates, the entire party, will say: But excuse me, what's going on here? The Twentieth Congress was just held. Nobody said anything. How could you not have known these things that people back from exile and prison are talking about? You must have known!

"We will not be able to answer! To say that we didn't know anything would be a lie. We have Comrade Pospelov's memorandum, and now we know everything. We know that the repressions were not based on anything, that it was all Stalin's despotism."

Once again there was a very stormy reaction. Voroshilov and Kaganovich repeated in unison: "They'll hold us accountable! The party has the right to call us responsible. We were in the leadership and if we didn't know, that's our problem, but we're still responsible for everything."

I said: "If you consider our party to be founded on democratic centralism, then we, as leaders, didn't have the right *not* to know. Some of us were unaware of many things, since a system was established where you were supposed to know only what you were told. You weren't supposed to stick your nose into anything else. And we didn't. But not everyone was in that position. Some knew, and some even took part in these matters. So there are various degrees of responsibility.

"I'm prepared, as a member of the Central Committee since the Seventeenth Congress and of the Politburo since the Eighteenth Congress, to bear my share of responsibility before the party, if the party should see fit to hold responsible those who were in the leadership under Stalin, when this tyranny held sway."

Again they disagreed with me and objected: "Don't you see what will happen?"

Voroshilov and Molotov were especially vehement. Voroshilov kept saying that it needn't be done, it must not be done, and repeating: "Who's asking us to do this?"

I said: "The crimes were committed. We have to admit that much to ourselves. When people start asking about it, they'll already be sitting in judgment. I don't want that to happen. I don't want to take the responsibility."

But there was still absolutely no agreement. I saw that it would be impossible to get the Presidium members to reach a decision. We couldn't raise this question in the Congress Presidium until we arrived at an agreement within the Presidium of the Central Committee.

At that point I suggested the following:

"The party congress is proceeding, but the internal discipline required for unified leadership among members of the Central Committee and the Central Committee Presidium during the Congress has broken down. Now that the General Report has been given, every member of the Presidium and of the Central Committee has the right to speak at the Congress and to present his point of view, even if it doesn't coincide with that of the Report."

I didn't say that I would speak, but those who had objected understood that I could give a speech and present my views on the arrests and executions.

I don't remember precisely, but I think that Bulganin, Pervukhin,[6] and Saburov gave me their personal support. I'm not sure, but I think it's possible that Malenkov did also. Now I can't say exactly, because he was the Central Committee secretary for personnel and his role in these questions was quite an active one. He, in fact, helped Stalin promote cadres and then destroy them. I'm not saying that he showed any initiative in the repressions. That is not likely. But in the provinces and territories where Stalin sent Malenkov to establish order, dozens and hundreds of people were repressed and many of them executed. See what a state we sank to!

Years passed before Father talked about the agonizing thoughts that went through his mind that night. After his ultimatum he came home and went at once to his room. He could not share this explosive information with anyone, even his wife. And why would he? To warn them? What was the sense of that? He understood: the way back was cut off, and the only thing left was to move forward. Father thought that yesterday's criminals, driven into a corner, were capable of anything, even of arresting him. The telephone was still. He decided not to call anyone either. He didn't want to display any weakness. The night passed uneventfully. As always, Father came to breakfast a little after eight. As always. . . . Only Mama worried that he was sick (he looked

6. Mikhail Georgyevich Pervukhin—member of the Presidium who headed the Ministry of Medium Machine Construction, with responsibility for the nuclear program, who later joined the leadership cabal against Khrushchev in 1957.

tired, with circles under his eyes). Father reassured her: everything was all right. When the Congress was over, he would catch up on his sleep.

As always, toward nine he went off to work. Without any delays.

He was almost convinced that he had won. Almost . . .

Again the top leaders met before the session in the room set aside for the Presidium.

His opponents looked no better; apparently they too had spent a sleepless night. Where had their thoughts led?

We can't know. But one thing was clear: they were not able to unite against him; they didn't dare. Their fear of one another was too great.

As soon as he entered the room, Father threw himself into the battle.

He writes:

> I said: "Even among people who have committed a crime, there comes a moment when a confession will assure him leniency, if not acquittal. If we are going to make a report to a Congress on the abuses committed by Stalin, then we must do it now, at the Twentieth Congress. The Twenty-first Congress will already be too late, even if we get that far without being brought to task."
>
> The opposition gave in, or I should say, retreated for the time being:
>
> . . . Someone took the initiative and said: if that's the way things stand, apparently a report will have to be made. . . . Then the question came up, who should make the report. I proposed Comrade Pospelov. I argued that he had studied these questions, he was the Commission chairman, he drew up the memorandum which we would be using. . . . Others, I no longer remember exactly who, began to object and proposed that I deliver the report. . . .
>
> They said: "If Pospelov or another Central Committee secretary delivers the speech, it will make people wonder, why didn't Khrushchev say anything about this business in his General Report? Why is Pospelov bringing up such an important matter in the debates? How could Khrushchev not know, or if he knew, not have thought it was important? It follows that there may be disagreement in the leadership on this matter, and that Pospelov is just giving his own opinion."
>
> This argument was worth considering, and I agreed. . . .
>
> The Congress heard my report in silence. It was so quiet you could hear a fly buzzing. Everything was so unexpected, and you had to understand how shocked people were by the atrocities to which party members—honored old Bolsheviks and young people alike—had been subjected. . . . It was a tragedy for the party. . . .
>
> In my report to the Twentieth Congress nothing was said about the public trials attended by representatives of fraternal communist parties. That was when Rykov, Bukharin, and other national leaders were sentenced. . . .

The duplicity of our behavior was also apparent in the matter of the open trials. Again we were afraid to tell the whole story. There is absolutely no doubt that those people were innocent, that they were the victims of tyranny.

But leaders of the fraternal parties were present at the open trials, and they subsequently testified in their own countries that the sentences were just. We didn't want to discredit them, so we indefinitely postponed the rehabilitation of Bukharin, Zinoviev, Rykov, and others.

But it would have been better to have told everything. Murder will always out.

It is well known from historical accounts that the chronology of events was somewhat different. The decision to make a "secret" report on the basis of Pospelov's memorandum was adopted by a Central Committee plenum on the eve of the Congress. The memorandum contained devastating numbers, even by today's standards. During 1937–38 alone, 1,548,366 people were arrested, 681,692 of whom were shot. Top-level leaders in republics, territories, and provinces were arrested; then their replacements were arrested; and so on. Of the 1,966 delegates to the Seventeenth Congress of the All-Union Communist Party (Bolsheviks), 1,108 were arrested, 848 were shot, and so on.

On February 9, Pospelov delivered a report on his memorandum to the Central Committee Presidium. It was then, apparently, that the argument Father recalls broke out.

Father managed to get his way, and February 13, the day before the Congress convened, the Presidium decreed "to submit a proposal to the CPSU Central Committee plenum that the Central Committee Presidium considers it necessary to deliver a report on the cult of personality to a closed session of the Congress and appoints N. S. Khrushchev speaker." The plenum rubber-stamped this decision when it met the same day.

By February 18, Central Committee secretaries Pyotr Nikolayevich Pospelov and Averky Borisovich Aristov had prepared the first version of the report. It was limited to the prewar years and mainly concerned the extermination of leaders of the party.

Father was dissatisfied with this narrow focus and by the next day, February 19, had already dictated his own text to a stenographer. CPSU Central Committee secretary Dmitry Shepilov, at the time one of Father's trusted supporters, helped him edit the text—or, at any rate, that's what Shepilov writes in his memoirs. They didn't even have time to retype it before Father left for the Congress session in the Kremlin with the text, all covered with pencil marks in various colors.

From the speaker's rostrum, Father said a great deal more than was in the text. In his memoirs quoted above, two different topics are conflated: his concern about introducing at the plenum the very question whether to deliver a report on Pospelov's memorandum and the clash with his opponents in the Central Committee Presidium on the eve of the report, a clash evidently related to the "unsanctioned" expansion in the limits of the report. Apart from Father's memoirs, there is no direct testimony about the latter. But this seems to me the most probable supposition.

I have managed to resurrect the chronology of events from notes made at sessions of the Central Committee Presidium by Vladimir Malin, head of the Central Committee General Department.[7]

There is no doubt that it was the "secret" speech that united an anti-Khrushchev nucleus. A new crisis became inevitable; it would just take some time for the opposition to form and for a suitable moment to arrive.

The secret speech didn't remain secret for long. You can't hide something like that. I very much doubt that Father wanted it kept secret. On the contrary! His own words confirm the opposite—that he wanted to bring his report to the people. Otherwise all his efforts would have been meaningless. The secrecy of the sessions was only a formal concession on his part to the fears of his opponents.

Within days the report had taken on a life of its own. At first Father insisted that it be read to party members at closed meetings. The *Pravda* publishing house reproduced the text in thousands of copies stamped "Secret" and distributed them to party organizations. That year there were about seven million members of the Communist Party. Moscow was quickly flooded with rumors. Naturally I approached Father with questions, and he satisfied my curiosity beyond expectations by simply handing me a slim, dark red booklet and saying: "Well, read this. But give it back to me."

I was horrified by what I read. Of course, I already knew something about these matters. My "education" had begun with the bill of indictment against Beria, which had fallen into my hands at the end of 1953. I remember every detail of that dank autumn evening. Father returned home with a bulging folder. In the dining room he took out of it a thick, paperbound volume in the standard "government" gray-blue—the color of the KGB's dress overcoats—and, leaving the other papers in their usual place on the dining room table, headed to his study with the mysterious book.

I went after him. Eager to learn what was going on, I tried not to miss a minute in the evening and followed Father as if on a leash. This time I was especially curious, since Father as a rule didn't bring home such voluminous documents. In the evening he usually read the day's mail.

Leaving the book on his desk, he went into the bedroom to change.

7. R. Pikhoya, *The Soviet Union: A History of Power, 1945–1991* (Moscow: RAGS Publishing House, 1998), 138–53.

There was no question of even glancing into the book. I only tried to read the title on its cover, which was printed in small letters. Even to approach the table would have violated the same internal prohibition. All I could make out were some words in slightly larger print: "Bill of Indictment," but the other lines faded into the gray background.

Father found me standing with neck outstretched and eyes straining to make out the barely visible letters. There was no need to explain what had attracted my attention. Father went to the table, stood there for a moment as if thinking something over, and then handed me the volume. It was the bill of indictment prepared by the prosecutor's office for the forthcoming trial of Beria and his closest aides.

The trial was only a few days off (at the time I didn't know that), and according to a practice which I now know was established in the 1930s, the prosecutor general sent the results of the inquiry for approval at the highest level. Naturally, the gray-blue "brick" was sent to all members of the Central Committee Presidium—the collective leadership of the country and the party—and not Father alone.

"Do you want to read it?" asked Father, sounding rather dubious. He seemed unsure whether it was a good idea to put such an important document into my hands.

"Of course," I said hastily, fearing that it would be taken away.

I was overwhelmed with curiosity and the urge to find out what awful things had been done by a man whose portrait had been hanging on Moscow buildings as recently as May of that year.

"All right," said Father, finally making up his mind. "But remember that I'm trusting you with a state secret, so keep your mouth shut."

I nodded. I kept my word. I didn't dare share my impressions of what I read with anyone—except Father, of course.

I read all night, gripped by horror. The document detailed everything: ties with British intelligence, and cooperation with counterrevolution, violence toward women, and moral degeneration, which took the form of building houses for himself in someone else's name.

This last deed was especially disturbing, since Father considered that to display private property instincts was the most terrible sedition.

Nothing I read caused me any doubt. Beria was portrayed as a bloodthirsty thug, capable of anything.

When I returned the book to Father the next morning, I naively asked him how Beria had passed secret information to the British, and what it was. Father was still for a moment, and then mumbled something unintelligible. I didn't pursue the matter, thinking that I was prying into a secret not meant for my ears. In those years I was simply unable to doubt what I read.

Another question disturbed me even more: What punishment awaited the participants in all these crimes? They must suffer some punishment. After I said all this to Father, there was a long pause. I began to think that he had decided to avoid answering. But no . . .

He finally said in a strained voice: "You know, we have punished Beria's principal associates. Some have been shot, others are in prison. But millions were mixed up in that meat grinder. Millions of victims and millions of executioners—investigators, informers, guards. If we started to punish everybody who'd had a hand in it, there would be just as much bloodletting. And maybe even more."

Father stopped short. I was staggered by his answer—to exact no retribution from the butchers! I started to object, but Father had no intention of arguing with me.

"There's no need to talk about it," he said gloomily. "I'm tired, I don't feel like talking."

I never brought up the subject again. As the years went by, I became increasingly convinced that Father was right.

The "secret" speech was not restricted to party members for long; clearly, Father tried to ensure that it would reach as many ears as possible. It was soon read at Komsomol meetings; that meant another eighteen million listeners. If you include their relatives, friends, and acquaintances, you could say that the entire country became familiar with the speech. Representatives of fraternal parties, who had been guests at the Congress, took copies home with them.

Spring had barely begun when the speech began circulating around the world, initially in a form somewhat modified by journalists to their liking. That was reported to Father, but he ordered that no corrective measures be taken. Can anyone recapture words which have flown to freedom?

The complete text of the speech soon turned up in American hands. An investigation was undertaken, whose traces led to Poland. It was learned that the secret red booklet had fallen into the hands of Israeli intelligence, and from there journeyed across the ocean to the United States.

The CIA, Allen Dulles's agency, made an effort to make the text of the speech known to everyone, whether they were interested or not. In this case Allen Dulles served as an "unwitting" promoter of Father's interests. Now everyone learned of Stalin's crimes.

DELIVERING THE FREIGHT

Right after the Congress, on February 27, 1956, Father visited Korolyov's "firm," as part of his continuing investigation into the muddled military economy. He no longer thought of himself as a novice in missile technology.

He had received detailed reports on all its problems from Dmitry Ustinov, "Uncle Dima," as missile specialists called him. But reports are one thing, and seeing things with your own eyes is another.

Father liked very much to see things in person, to evaluate new things for himself, and to talk with the people involved in the making of them. Sometimes he gleaned more information from a person's remark, intonation, or expression than from a long, carefully edited document.

The trip was postponed several times when some urgent matter came up at the last minute. A final date was set. Father took along a representative group with him to visit Korolyov. Well, not a group, a commission . . . well, not a commission. . . . Specifically, Vyacheslav Molotov, Nikolai Bulganin, Lazar Kaganovich, Aleksei Kirichenko (recently, in July 1955, he became a full member of the CC Presidium), and as I remember, Pervukhin, got together to visit this new thing, a missile.

When Father suggested I accompany them, I agreed at once. To see real ballistic missiles! He also took along Aleksei Ivanovich Adzhubei. Since his graduation from the university four years earlier, Aleksei had achieved considerable success in the field of journalism and began to enjoy a certain degree of respect from Father.

Our destination, the small town of Kaliningrad (not to be confused with the Baltic port city of Kaliningrad), now renamed Korolev, was located not far from Moscow. At that time even its name was mentioned only in a whisper. The very location of the country's chief missile establishment was top secret, even after articles with its exact address had appeared in the American press.

It was a short trip. A solid fence with brick factory buildings behind it indicated that we had reached our goal. Our cars turned right through massive metal gates which swung open for us. After weaving between some buildings, we stopped at a workshop. At the door, which was many meters high, Father was met by the short and muscular chief designer, Sergei Korolyov. Father already knew him. The entourage invariably present during such visits—ministers, military officers and local persons, leaders of the design bureau and the plant—milled around some distance away.

Korolyov shook hands with his guests and invited them into the shop with a proprietary gesture. The still brief history of Soviet missiles began here, and it is from here that we were to look into the future.

The dimensions of the workshop were staggering. It seemed even larger than Myasishchev's hangar, but appeared to be rather empty. We looked around instinctively for an airplane. We saw nothing of the kind, only some long objects that looked like tanks or pipes. That was how one of the most carefully guarded military secrets looked to us. Following its host, our group walked to the center of the hall, where missiles, painted camouflage green, lay on holding rigs, their engines gleaming from the copper of their exhaust pipes. Those now familiar forms provoked surprise and even protest at that time: Could these things really fly?

Korolyov stopped at his first creation, the R-1. The missile was identical to the German V-2, Von Braun's handiwork. Its range was modest, only 270 kilometers, and its accuracy also left something to be desired. Sergei Pavlovich didn't try to claim priority, as often happens in such cases. He explained that our industry had no experience in creating such flying machines, so they needed something to start off with.

After the R-1 we came to their first original product, the R-2 missile. It duplicated the shape of its predecessor, but was larger and more massive. That was understandable, since it had a range of six hundred kilometers. "This is our history, we began with them," said Korolyov, concluding the first part of his account.

"And this is our present, the R-5," he said, pointing to the next exhibit.

On a holding rig lay something like an enormous pencil, but with a finely chiseled nose. It had something that looked like a soup bowl at the other end (the rocket engine), with small stabilizers arranged like the fletching on an arrow (the fins). The construction really looked utterly incapable of flight. The others at least had streamlined shapes and a certain refinement in the form of stabilizers.

Apparently I wasn't the only one to have this reaction, since Father looked surprised. However, he made no comment and simply examined the strange object closely. Korolyov explained that the missile had an estimated range of up to twelve hundred kilometers and that, unlike previous missiles, most of its flight path would be above the atmosphere.

"A streamlined shape is not very important in this case, since its engine capacity is more than sufficient to overcome air resistance in gaining velocity. The advantage of a cylindrical form is very obvious; it is a very technological shape," he concluded.

Father liked this rational approach and permitted himself a question: "Couldn't the body of the missile be welded, the way large-diameter pipes are welded?"

Our host smiled and replied that in principle that was possible, but it was something for the future.

Father lingered by the missile for a long time. First he was interested in learning which of our potential adversaries would be within range of them. Korolyov walked over to a map of Europe, which was hanging on a special stand. It looked just like the ones we had in school, except that this one had arcs of intersecting circles against the blue background of the Atlantic Ocean. Thin radii drawn with India ink stretched to the western borders, to the frontier of East Germany.

In the upper right-hand corner of the map there was a calligraphic inscription: "Highly classified. Of special importance." Slightly below that was, "Copy Number—." Of course, I don't remember that number, but it was no higher than three. This information was meant for a very narrow circle of people.

Korolyov explained the map: if the launch sites were moved forward to our borders it would be possible to strike Britain, and only Spain would still be out of range. Father chuckled with satisfaction. He looked at the map one more time, and drawled: "Excellent. Until recently we couldn't even dream of such a thing. But the appetite grows by what it feeds on. Comrade Korolyov, isn't it possible to extend the missile's range a little more?"

Korolyov shook his head. "That would require a different missile."

"It's not a question of Spain," continued Father. "I wouldn't want to put such a weapon on foreign territory, even that of friendly countries. Especially nuclear warheads. Furthermore, you've shown them very close to the border."

Father looked around at those present. No one objected. Everyone remembered how much we had lost in the recent past by carelessly moving warehouses and supply bases near our borders. They were all overrun by the Germans in the first days and even hours of the war.

"We have to think about this matter," he said, turning to Ustinov.

Ustinov said that developmental work going on at the new design bureau of Mikhail Kuzmich Yangel might solve the problem. His missile had a range of two thousand kilometers and could be based on Soviet territory. But for now we could not do without the R-5.

Father knew what Yangel was working on, of course. He glanced at Korolyov, hoping to hear his opinion. But Korolyov didn't want to encroach on someone else's bailiwick and made no comment. Father didn't insist. He respected the chief designer's delicacy.

Father turned to Korolyov and asked him the power of the nuclear warhead on his missile. Sergei Pavlovich hesitated. He glanced around rather distractedly at everyone, then looked questioningly at Ustinov.

In those years no one talked out loud about nuclear warheads. No subject was more secret and forbidden. And there were a lot of people in the hangar.

Noticing his hesitation, Father encouraged him: "Don't worry. I'll take the responsibility."

Ustinov nodded slightly. Korolyov finally came up very close to Father and said something in a low voice. We were standing a short distance away and couldn't hear what he said.

Father nodded with satisfaction, paused for a moment as if mentally debating, and then in a surprisingly loud voice repeated the figure for the nuclear warhead's explosive force. It was seventy kilotons. By today's measure, it was of moderate magnitude, but at the time even twenty kilotons was impressive.

Everyone fell silent. Father smiled, enjoying the effect produced by his words. After a pause, he commented: "Quite an impressive warhead. It will have a very sobering effect on those hotheads who dream about war. It wouldn't be a bad idea to inform NATO of its size." Korolyov continued: "By government decision, about three weeks ago, February 2, we carried out a test of the missile along with a special warhead [by specific instruction, the word nuclear was barred from the official lexicon]. We launched an R-5M [as the nuclear modification of the R-5 was called] from a special test site in the region of the Aral Kara Kumy, where everything was equipped to measure the parameters of the special explosion."

The test was not very successful. The heating element in the warhead section had been accidentally unplugged several hours before takeoff, and no one had detected it, so the nuclear warhead froze and, although the control relays of the explosive mechanism worked properly, the result was what is called a smoldering blast. The explosion did not achieve even half the expected power. But Father was not discouraged.

Anything can happen at the start of a program. In his report on the test, Igor Kurchatov stated that it had been verified that the nuclear warhead delivered to the target by the missile had worked properly. Father congratulated Korolyov on his enormous achievement and said that, thanks to the missile engineers, the country was feeling far more confident.

Tests of the R-5M equipped with a nuclear warhead had a noticeable influence on Father's behavior in the subsequent negotiations with our former allies, especially with Britain and France. The Soviet Union now possessed a weapon of unsurpassed power. While the United States remained out of range, the R-5 faced no barriers in Europe. The fact that there were only a few of them was unimportant. Father was not planning to wage war, and as a threat the mere existence of the new weapon was sufficient.

Father turned to the map and stared piercingly at it: "How many warheads would be needed to destroy England? Have you calculated that?" He turned to Korolyov. At the time Britain was considered the United States' main and most powerful ally, and consequently our enemy number two.

Before Sergei Pavlovich could answer, Ustinov said "five," adding after a moment: "A few more for France—seven or nine, depending on the choice of targets."

"Only five?" Father repeated, somewhat dubiously.

"Five would be enough to crush defenses and disrupt communications and transportation, not to mention the destruction of major cities." Ustinov's tone did not allow for even a shadow of doubt.

"It's terrible to think of," said Father, sounding neither horrified nor delighted. "During the war we couldn't even have imagined something like this."

He broke off abruptly. There was silence in the hangar. Korolyov shifted from one foot to the other, uncertain whether or not he should continue.

"Yes, a terrible force." Father seemed to collect himself. "The last war was bloody, but with such warheads it has become simply unthinkable. Five warheads and a whole country gone. Terrible."

Father fell silent again, but only for a few seconds.

"Well, what else have you prepared for us?" he said, turning to Korolyov.

Sergei Pavlovich led the group to the next platform.

He continued: "When we built the first two missiles, we were only learning, creating a new branch of industry. Now we have embarked on a new and important stage, organizing series production and introducing the new weapon into the Army on a mass scale."

Not everything was going smoothly, however, since making the transition from guns to missiles was not an easy one. Now and then Father interrupted the report to ask questions or, picking out one of the ministers from the group, started to discuss the solution of some urgent question. Ustinov invariably joined in. He was obviously well informed about everything and gave short, precise answers with no hesitation. He wrote Father's instructions down on a small pad.

Father was satisfied. Both the designer and the minister not only knew what they wanted but had a clear idea of how to achieve it.

Father had a special sympathy for such people; he became their partner, as it were. That was what happened this time. From then on Korolyov could phone Father directly, bypassing numerous bureaucratic obstacles. Just the possibility, even if not used, enabled him to overcome difficulties that had previously seemed insuperable. And in extreme cases, he could pick up the telephone and dial Father's four-digit number.

Another guard post was located at the door to the next section. We were entering the *sanctum sanctorum*. This new hall-hangar was even more impressive. Not as big as the previous one, it stretched upward like a many-metered glass tower-aquarium. Unlike the glass in an aquarium, however, the windows were covered by a thick layer of white paint—protection from curious eyes.

The size of the object inside amazed us. A single missile occupied the brightly lit well of the hangar. In size and outline it reminded me involuntarily of the Kremlin's Spasskaya Tower, with its combination of surging movement toward the sky and a heavy, earthbound foundation. There it stood, at its full height, the 270-ton "Seven," or R-7. Its weight would increase as the design process continued, and by the time testing began it weighed 283 tons.

Crowding together at the entrance, we all stared silently at this miracle of technology. Korolyov enjoyed the effect and didn't hurry to begin his presentation. Finally recovering from its daze, the main group moved around the missile, craning their heads. Then Korolyov began to talk, sometimes aiming his pointer up high, toward the ceiling, and sometimes crouching to point at something down low.

Sergei Pavlovich spoke at length about the strap-on boosters, which surrounded the slender shape of the central block like a wide flared skirt.

"It was only this one and one-half stepped configuration which enabled us to solve the engineering problems, because the thermonuclear warhead installed in the missile is extraordinarily cumbersome," concluded Korolyov.

He then fell silent and seemed to expect questions. His listeners were also silent. Father later admitted that he was simply numb, intimidated by the grandeur of such an object created by human hands.

Molotov was the only one to ask a question: "Why does the central block become thinner after the belt, where the strap-on boosters are attached, than it is higher up?"

Becoming animated, Korolyov explained that design factors called for that shape; otherwise the boosters would not attach properly and the missile would be overextended.

Molotov nodded with satisfaction. I remember this rather trivial question because of Father's reaction to it. For some reason it made him angry and irritated. He didn't say anything at the hangar, but at home he expressed himself freely.

His complaint amounted to: Why did Molotov have to make a fool of himself by asking such a simple-minded (as Father put it) question?

"It's obvious that he doesn't know a thing about missiles. What difference does it make to him where the missile is thicker or thinner? Specialists know what diameter they need," he fumed.

I was puzzled. Vyacheslav Mikhailovich's question had not sounded so misplaced to me. He could certainly have kept silent. But why not ask a question?

Father continued indignantly: "Leaders on our level shouldn't interfere in specialized fields. Everyone should stick to his own work. Does he really expect to correct engineers?"

Such arguments sounded strange coming from him, since Father tended to bombard engineers and scientists with questions about the particular features of any machine that attracted his interest.

The real reason for Father's irritation was undoubtedly different. The brief friendship with Molotov—arising from their joint fight against Beria in 1953—had, with their mutual enemy eliminated, entirely unraveled by 1956. They didn't agree about developing the virgin lands. Father's visit bearing

apologies to Tito offended Molotov. Mutual hostility grew. While the reserved Molotov kept it bottled up, such behavior was much harder for emotional Father. So he was letting off steam.

A discussion got under way right there in the hangar, near the missile.

At the time it was estimated that missiles needed a range of eight thousand kilometers in order to destroy targets on U.S. territory. Korolyov had
no doubt that he could meet this challenge.

Father simply beamed upon hearing Sergei Pavlovich's report. I had
rarely seen him in such a mood. He was particularly impressed by the missile's velocity, about twenty-five thousand kilometers an hour. Until then
everyone was used to talking about airplanes, so that when they encountered
a fundamentally new type of flying apparatus they still used the old parameters. The figure impressed and somehow hypnotized. Father inquired how
long it would take the missile to fly from Moscow to Kiev. He had covered
that route repeatedly during the previous fifteen or so years in an old Doug-
las aircraft, which took three hours. Korolyov answered that the missile
would take only minutes. Father grunted with satisfaction and nudged Kirichenko, who was standing beside him. With the appearance of such rockets,
the problem of overcoming an air defense system simply disappeared. That
whole system, with its missiles, radars, and interceptors, would be far below,
and the R-7 would, as it were, jump over it.

In conclusion, Father asked when test flights would begin, adding somewhat apologetically: "We're not hurrying you. Everything should be thoroughly worked out and verified, but you know yourself how urgently we need
the missile."

Korolyov nodded. He was proceeding as fast as possible. Tests were
planned for spring of the next year. They could not be held any sooner. The
missile itself still required a great deal of work, and a test site had to be
prepared.

Moving on to the next visual display, Sergei Pavlovich explained that the
existing well-used test site in the Volga's lower reaches, at Kapustin Yar,
could not be used for launching such long-range missiles. Three remote
radio stations for flight control of the missile (*radio upravlenie punkt*, or
RUP), which ensured accuracy in hitting the target, would have to be placed
in a special sequence: two symmetrically on either side of the launch site at a
distance of 150 to 200 kilometers, and a third 300 to 500 kilometers to the
rear. However you configured it, from Kapustin Yar one or the other RUP
would lie either on the surface of the Caspian Sea or, even worse, in Iran. It
had been necessary to prepare a new test site in the Aral Sea region, at Tyura-
Tam station. Work was in full swing, but there was still much to do. Father
was fully informed about the construction, but didn't go into the details. He
lapsed into an account of how the location of the first missile test site was

chosen, right after the war. Many of those present probably remembered that history. After all, they had selected the site. Still, everyone listened attentively. Such are the privileges of leadership.

As I mentioned earlier, rocket development was supervised by Beria in his day. And he didn't like being contradicted. The guns of the war against Fascism had hardly fallen silent when a commission entrusted with extraordinary powers visited the Ukraine. They were to choose a place for the country's first missile test site.

They decided to settle down in comfort. At the beginning they were poised to strike at a huge piece of the Black Earth region near Mariupol. They began doing research and drawing maps. Father knew nothing about it. In those years it was not a good idea to stick your nose into your neighbor's affairs, particularly if your neighbor wielded such power. The provincial party committee secretary brought alarming news: "The military are crisscrossing our most fertile fields, measuring something. It's rumored that most of the population will be moved out of the area and something extremely secret will be built there, either a plant or a test site."

Father summoned the commission's chairman to inform him that, as of now, he was still the chairman of the Council of Ministers and the first secretary of the Communist Party of the Ukraine. The interview was not a success. The chairman was guided by instructions from Moscow, and references to fertile lands and wealthy villages had no effect. In those years whole ethnic groups could be exiled far from their native places at a whim, and in this instance only two or three dozen villages were involved. Besides, the villagers would not be exiled to Siberia, just moved somewhere nearby.

The commission intended to locate launch test sites near the sea, as the Americans had done in Florida, with the headquarters and other support services built right on the shore, by the Sea of Azov's sandy beaches. It was true that the Americans, in trying to stay near open water, were thinking more of economics than comfort. Used rocket stages falling into the ocean did not present a threat to anything except the odd ship. Therefore, it wasn't necessary to create exclusion zones along the trajectory of the rockets, to purchase land or worry about other factors, all of which could cost a great deal.

In our case everything was the other way around. Obviously we couldn't launch toward Turkey. The test site would stretch across the Don steppes toward Stalingrad. A mass evacuation of the inhabitants would be required.

Father flew into a rage. As soon as his office door closed after the stubborn commission chairman, he grabbed his special phone and asked to be connected to Beria. Their relations had remained good and many even thought them to be friends. But in this case nothing helped. Beria thought Father was interfering in something that was none of his business and flatly refused to cooperate.

One last possibility remained: Stalin. For that, special skill was required. Choosing the right arguments was not enough; you had to pick the right moment to make them. If he spoke too soon, people would laugh. If he waited too long, then Beria would report to Stalin first. In that case, it would be better not to butt in.

Father had argued with Stalin more than once, and had sometimes managed to change his mind. But it was impossible to know how another display of independence might end. This time Father was lucky. He succeeded in convincing Stalin that densely populated areas of the Ukraine were not the ideal place for such things. The main argument he employed was the need for secrecy, not the problems that would be caused by dislocating thousands of people. Father argued that it would be impossible to move everyone, and because of that the rockets would fly over dozens of villages and possibly hundreds of unauthorized witnesses. Stalin agreed, and Beria received an order to look for a test site farther away from people's eyes. The choice fell on Kapustin Yar.

Father fell silent and looked inquiringly at Sergei Pavlovich—as if to ask, is that all or do you have something else we would enjoy looking at?

"I would like you to know about still another project." As he noticed that his visitors were about to leave, Korolyov added quickly: "It will only become feasible with the birth of the R-7. I wrote a report about it to the Central Committee and have had a positive response."

Sergei Pavlovich led us to a stand occupying a modest place in a corner, near the door. A model of some kind of apparatus lay on the stand. It looked unusual, to put it mildly. A flying machine should have a smooth surface, flowing shapes and clean-cut angles. But this one had some type of rods protruding on all sides and paneling swollen by projections.

Korolyov began his exposition far back, with Tsiolkovsky.[8] He recalled the latter's dream of escaping the bonds of earth.

"And now we can achieve that," exclaimed Korolyov rather emotionally. But he checked himself at once and continued in a businesslike tone to explain that if a flying apparatus attained a certain speed it would not return to the earth, but would turn into a small planet or something like the moon, and begin revolving around the earth.

"In the design bureau we have carried out computations," continued Korolyov, "showing that the R-7's speed must be increased by a few thousand kilometers per hour—and that is within our power. We have only to reduce the weight of the payload. We can then lift a satellite of the earth into orbit."

---

8. Konstantin Eduardovich Tsiolkovsky—a great prewar Russian rocket and space researcher. In 1895, he published *Dreams of Earth and Sky* (*Gryozy o zemle i nebe*), and the following year he published an article on communication with inhabitants of other planets.

Korolyov paused, while his listeners were silent. What would these scientists think of next? A satellite! Well then, let there be a satellite. His earlier demonstration of the intercontinental missile made an incomparably greater impression. Moreover, the objective it helped to solve seemed immeasurably more important.

Without waiting for a reaction, Korolyov said that the United States was working intensively on a project to launch an earth satellite. He pointed to a nearby display. It showed a very slim, pencil-like missile which had all the stages of the R-7 and was lifting a tiny sphere resembling a tennis ball into orbit.

Korolyov was convinced that we could outpace the Americans by launching a much larger satellite sooner than they could. Moreover, he continued, it would cost very little, since the main expense was for producing a vehicle, and we already had the rocket.

"Or *will* have," he corrected himself. The possibility of thumbing his nose at the Americans appealed to Father, who grew very animated and began quizzing Korolyov about whether any serious modifications would have to be made to the rocket. "Won't the pursuit of prestige have a negative effect on meeting the main challenge, which is to create a weapon vitally needed by this country?"

Korolyov looked at the display: "The Americans have taken a wrong turn. They are developing a special rocket and spending millions. We only have to remove the thermonuclear warhead and put a satellite in its place. And that's all."

Korolyov turned to Father, who was closely examining the model of the satellite. It seemed as if he were still debating the matter. In his life he had met many inventors who had promised golden treasures at low cost. You had only to agree, and the next thing you knew there were "unforeseen complications" that increased the expenses a hundred times over.

But he did not sense anything false here. The proposal felt solid. On the one hand, it was important to remind these scientists of our priorities, on the other it was important not to deprive them of their dreams.

That is more or less how Father remembered his reaction to Korolyov's demonstration. At the time he simply said: "If the main task will not be affected, go ahead."

Father had no idea at the time that the launch of our sputnik would stun the world. Neither did Korolyov, though he had dreamed of that moment his whole life.

Our visit came to an end. Everyone scattered to their cars.

Father was ecstatic about what he had seen at Korolyov's. Finally that accursed problem seemed to have found a solution. Resistance to the Americans, who with absolute impunity had surrounded our country with their bases, was becoming not only possible in principle but likely in the very near future. Let them think that today they can do whatever comes into their heads—send planes or balloons with intelligence-gathering equipment, or hold maneuvers dangerously close to our borders. We won't have to put up with it for long. We'll force them to treat us with respect, and then negotiations on disarmament will proceed on a different and far more serious basis. Negotiations between equals are incomparably more effective than those between the strong and the weak.

In Father's eyes, Korolyov had already won the competition. He had finally received an answer to the question that had bothered him for years. But the finish line was still ahead. Entirely new challenges had to be met. There were as many, if not more, economic and political problems to be solved as there were technical ones, before missiles could be introduced into military operations. Series production had to be organized and dozens—even hundreds—of military facilities would have to be built.

Accomplishment of all these tasks still lay ahead. In the meantime Korolyov, it seemed, had no rivals.

FATHER VISITS BRITAIN

Father's next major political move after the Twentieth Party Congress was to visit Britain. Three years after Stalin's death a trip abroad was still considered an unusual event. That was especially true for this kind of visit: for the first time since the Revolution there would be a state visit to the "cradle of imperialism."

Father was nervous. He was particularly worried about making a fool of himself. What if the Foreign Ministry wasn't being careful enough, and the Soviet delegation wasn't accorded the honors befitting its rank? He expected all kinds of underhanded tricks from the imperialists.

On the other hand, he wondered how working people would greet the delegation. At one time, in the 1920s, workers in the British Isles had risen in support of the young Soviet republic. Since then much had changed.

Father decided to arrange for a trial visit. International relations had become more cordial, and British officials in the electric power industry had invited their Soviet colleagues to visit. Shortly before this Malenkov had become the minister of the electric power industry.

The official reason for the appointment was the important, key role of this branch of industry. But in reality it was simply the need to find a job for the retired chairman of the Council of Ministers. Malenkov remained a member of the Presidium. If Malenkov were given an honorable reception in Britain, everything would be fine. If he were hissed, then there was no reason for Father and Bulganin to poke their noses in there; they would only be humiliated.

Malenkov hurried over to visit Father at the dacha the day after returning from London. Malenkov was enthusiastic and filled with impressions of his trip. At first he talked about how friendly the English were—both the leaders and the common people—and that he was sure the government delegation would receive a warm welcome. Then he began to talk about his visits to electric power stations. They had made the greatest impression on him.

It's hard to say which had the higher priority for Soviet leaders in those years, negotiations or discoveries. Discoveries made—not in museums, of course—but at factories and farms, at any place that might teach us something about what was being accomplished in the outside world.

Malenkov's hosts chuckled, but obligingly included in the program anything their guest wanted to see. They didn't understand what it meant to break out of isolation or how often our people's eyes were being opened by foreign marvels. At home, meanwhile, conferences were held, reports written, and decisions made to introduce their achievements into Soviet industry, into Soviet lives, as quickly as possible.

It's only today that people have become used to concentrating on only one thing, that government leaders focus on negotiations and specialists on technology. Father had a particular interest in new things. Unexpectedly, Malenkov talked about how the British were intensively developing nuclear energy: they had gone beyond experiments and were building the first industrial stations. It looked as if we, with our miniature, five-thousand kilowatt nuclear turbine, were beginning to lag far behind. Father was surprised. He himself thought that construction of nuclear power stations was a dubious proposition, at least for the present.

As early as a year or a year and a half earlier, when newspapers had reported the Obninsk experiment, he had requested information from engineers on the cost of kilowatts produced by the various types of stations. It turned out that nuclear electric power was the most expensive and that specialists could not promise to reduce its cost in the foreseeable future. With that, Father dismissed this branch of energetics from serious consideration. But now there was this unexpected development. Father questioned the specialists again; they reaffirmed their earlier conclusions and said that the high cost of imported oil was responsible for the British interest in this new type of fuel. Father was reassured and never returned to the subject of generating nuclear electric power.

Preparations for the visit continued. Father took an interest in everything, even the details.

How to get to London, seemingly a simple matter, became the subject of special discussions. After returning from Geneva, Father called together the airplane designers Tupolev, Ilyushin, and Antonov. He wanted to find out why we were flying in small planes, apparently economizing on everything, while the capitalists were building four-engine giants. It was hard to believe that they were doing so at a loss. Information supplied to the meeting showed that the cost of transporting each of two dozen passengers on the small IL was far higher than on the four-engine Constellation, not to speak of the latest turboprop airplanes being introduced abroad.

The designers did not arrive at the meeting with empty hands. Ilyushin proposed building a four-engine turboprop airliner in an unbelievably short time. He had preserved a great deal of the preliminary work for the IL-18, carried out before Stalin had canceled the plane's development. Father remembered that unfortunate history. Immediately after the war Sergei Vladimirovich had designed a new plane at his bureau. It looked no worse than the American equivalent: four powerful engines able to lift more than one hundred and fifty passengers. In those years everything required the leader's approval. Not one film or automobile, much less an airplane, could come into being without passing through Stalin's office in the Kremlin. On that particular occasion he was in a bad mood and said crossly: "What are you asking for! Who do you think you are? Two engines are good enough for you." No one dared object, so the IL-18 was not put into production and experimental models were dismantled. Now Ilyushin proposed to build a new airplane with the old name.

Antonov tried not to be outdone. He had never worked with passenger planes, but he thought that since his transport troop-carrier AN-8 was already in production, it could be transformed into a passenger plane without much extra cost. Father asked about the number of engines.

"Two," answered Oleg Konstantinovich.

Father wondered if such a plane would be safe. Would it be able to land if one engine shut down? "It's not for me to give you advice, but start working on a four-engine plane," he concluded.

Antonov didn't protest. In the past they had obeyed Stalin's dictum that four-engine planes were too much of a luxury. Now the situation had changed.

The proposals made by Antonov and Ilyushin were both impressive, but Tupolev was the hero of the day. He was preparing to make a jet passenger plane modeled on his TU-16 bomber. In our day it is almost impossible to imagine how fantastic his words sounded at the time. It was almost like someone today proposing to build a passenger rocket.

But Andrei Nikolayevich had thought through everything carefully: "We only need to widen the fuselage and keep everything else: engines, wings, landing gear, and equipment. That way you save time and money." Andrei Nikolayevich looked slyly at Father and continued: "It's true there are only two engines, but we were clever enough to locate them as close to the fuse-lage as possible. The result? The plane can make it to an airport and land, even on one engine."

The idea appealed to Father, but he wondered whether a jet-propelled plane would be economical, since jet engines use huge amounts of fuel.

"But it flies faster and carries more people, and we calculate fuel con-sumption on a per passenger and per kilometer basis," countered Tupolev. "The capitalists are starting to build such planes. At the moment Great Brit-ain is ahead, and they are already testing a new airliner, the Comet. Other countries are a little behind. However, they've found some defects in the Comet and there have been some accidents. So we have a chance to take the lead."

This last argument was a very persuasive one. Tupolev's proposal was adopted.

By the beginning of 1956 the new TU-104 was almost ready. It seemed to be both efficient and reliable. However, an extensive test flight program still lay ahead.

Father couldn't wait to surprise the English. After all, they were reputed to be the most inventive nation in Europe. And now here was an opportunity to show what a formerly backward Russia had achieved. The new Tupolev plane was perfectly suited for that. Father even thought of flying to London on the TU-104. When he mentioned this, the security service was aghast: the KGB chief, General Serov, argued that he didn't have the right to risk his life. Father wavered and decided to consult Tupolev. He invited him to the dacha to discuss the matter in an informal setting.

Andrei Nikolayevich had been warned not to agree to the flight under any circumstances. He was in a difficult position: on the one hand, why ruin his relations with the all-powerful "services"? On the other, he was even more eager than Father to show off his newest brainchild in London.

They didn't launch into the main subject right away. First, they took a walk along the snowy paths, then they had lunch. After that Father ushered his guest into the study. With Father's permission, I joined them.

Without beating around the bush, Father asked Tupolev what he thought about the idea. The designer hesitated.

"Of course, the plane has not flown the required hundreds of hours and thousands of kilometers yet, but its prototype, the TU-16, has been giving reliable service for years, and that's the best testimonial," began Andrei Ni-kolayevich.

Father started to interrupt, but Tupolev continued—he had finally made up his mind.

"As chief designer, I cannot accept the responsibility. The government delegation must not fly on the new plane at this time." Andrei Nikolayevich looked gloomy and his voice grew severe.

In answer, Father smiled.

"But you yourself would fly?" he asked craftily.

"I myself would fly, but you must not," answered Tupolev without smiling. "Aviation is not a joke. Anything can happen, and then I would be held responsible."

"So I shouldn't?" asked Father again.

"No," repeated Tupolev.

"If you feel that way, I will have to agree. But it's too bad," Father continued.

Tupolev didn't answer.

Father approached the matter from a different direction. The delegation would get to London a different way, but the plane could fly there without them. Tupolev perked up, pleased by this idea. He assured Father that as far as anything could be predicted, he would swear there would be no unpleasant surprises.

So it was decided. The TU-104 would make several flights to London while the high-ranking guests were there, and the delegation would travel to Britain on a warship. British seamen were bound to admire our achievements in that field. In its day the cruiser *Sverdlov* had produced a sensation in Portsmouth. Now it was decided to use an even more advanced ship, the cruiser *Ordzhonikidze*, for the state visit. It had only recently been commissioned, after escaping the fate of its counterparts sent to the scrap heap. The newest achievements in the science of shipbuilding had been used in its construction. Because of the new shape in the lines of its hull and propellers, the ship reached a speed its counterparts could not attain. It immediately attracted the attention of both specialists and intelligence agencies.

The TU-104 made a stunning impression, not only on the English but on the whole world. The power of its engines attracted particular attention. Photographs, articles, and descriptions began appearing regularly in newspapers, not to speak of professional publications. The English recognized that our plane was an enormous step forward—not even a step, but a leap forward, as a result of which Soviet aircraft builders outpaced their Western colleagues.

Throughout the visit the TU-104 regularly brought the delegation the latest mail from Moscow. The giant attracted an audience whenever it came in for a landing. Its flight path took it near the queen's palace, and she told Bulganin and Father that every time she heard that unusual rumble in the sky, she never failed to walk out onto her balcony to admire the Russian marvel.

Father was exultant. He had gotten his revenge for Geneva.

However, not everything went smoothly. Complications arose unexpectedly on the very eve of the visit. General Ivan Serov, the chairman of the KGB, left for London to work out arrangements with the British security service. He flew there on the TU-104, incidentally.

No one had foreseen any difficulties. Moreover, Serov had already been in Geneva, where no one had taken any interest in him. It turned out that Britain was not Switzerland. Moreover, rumors of Father's secret speech at the Twentieth Party Congress had really stirred up the atmosphere.

Serov was met at the airport by demonstrators carrying posters telling him unambiguously to leave. In London there was talk of the deportation of the peoples of the North Caucasus and a great many other things. The English people clearly did not want to receive him in their country. Father became uneasy. This was the first time he had run into such a reaction. Serov was ordered to return. Finishing up his business, he left abruptly for home.

There are reasons why we had not anticipated this reaction. In 1956 we still knew too little about the outside world and measured everything by our own yardstick. However, it was all repeated more than a decade later when trade union leader Aleksandr Nikolayevich Shelepin, a former KGB chief, had to cut short his stay in London because of noisy demonstrations.

Serov reported to Father without concealing anything. He showed him newspapers with huge headlines and photos of demonstrators. Father turned the papers around and around in his hands, then set them aside. They sat for a long time, thinking.

"You shouldn't go with us," said Father decisively. "I think the English will cope pretty well with security on their own. They have lots of experience. If anything were to happen, you wouldn't be able to intervene anyway."

Serov never went abroad again.

The time came to name the delegation. It was easy to pick the government officials who would go, but Father wanted an illustrious delegation, so he thought of including Academician Igor Vasilyevich Kurchatov.

Why Kurchatov in particular? In the first place, Malenkov had talked about how interested the English were in nuclear power, and we considered ourselves to be pioneers in that field. In the second place, at a recent meeting Kurchatov had inspired Father with the idea of a thermonuclear synthesis, a limitless source of energy. Kurchatov thought that not only were we coming close to exploiting thermonuclear energy, we had also left the West far behind.

Father was delighted. Not long before we had announced that the world's first nuclear power plant was on line. We were the first to build a hydrogen bomb, and now there would be a thermonuclear power plant.

Kurchatov explained that we were far from ready to build a plant; as yet there were only encouraging results. Father questioned Igor Vasilyevich in detail about whether the plants could be used to produce weapons. Kurchatov simply replied "no." Father was surprised: then why were they being kept secret?

I would like to note that Father was not just pursuing propaganda goals. He felt that the time had come to promote cooperation among scientists in various fields, including thermonuclear power. And not only among scientists. If we were not preparing to wage war, then we should make friends with our neighbors. And we should be the first to extend the hand of friendship.

Objections to including Kurchatov soon came thick and fast. Serov complained to Father: "I don't like it. He heads the project to build a nuclear weapon." In point of fact, even today in the new Russian republic such people are not allowed to go abroad.

Father disarmed Serov with a simple question: "Don't you trust him?"

After the Twentieth Congress that question could be answered in the negative only if you had substantial reasons. Kurchatov was added to the delegation list.

After some hesitation the British accepted our proposal. They arranged for a lecture to be delivered by Kurchatov at the British nuclear research center, Harwell. The Soviet side continued to be assailed by doubts. We would have to make a friendly reciprocal gesture and invite British scientists to visit our research centers. There was good reason to be alarmed. Security officials protested to Father, saying: they won't really show us anything, but they'll worm everything out of us.

Father took the problem seriously. It was a matter of the country's security, after all. This was the 1950s, and back then reciprocal military inspections did not feature in our worst nightmares.

Father summoned Kurchatov for a lengthy consultation. Kurchatov assured him that there was no danger.

"Of course they won't show us any secrets at Harwell, but that isn't necessary for us or the English scientists. There's enough to talk about without divulging military secrets. It's not secrets that are interesting, but the train of thought, the way problems are approached," said Igor Vasilyevich.

Kurchatov simply laughed at fears that the English would visit our secret sites.

"Of course everything there is secret, even outhouses. You can't do anything about that. But we know where and how to escort our guests. Everything will be done on a reciprocal basis. We won't show them any more than they show us."

So the matter was settled.

The triumph of the TU-104 prompted Father to include Andrei Nikolayevich Tupolev in the delegation. Along with Kurchatov, he would serve as a kind of calling card of the new Russia. Complications nevertheless arose. No one objected to Tupolev's candidacy. Father was informed that Tupolev always went abroad with his wife, and that he probably would not agree to go alone this time. Father saw no problem in that: so, let him go with his wife. Father's decision provoked a storm of objections. Perhaps "storm" is too strong a word, but there was talk: "Tupolev is going with his wife!" According to our warped customs, people were discouraged from taking their wives on official travel abroad.

Andrei Nikolayevich's wife, Yuliya Nikolayevna, was not able to accept the invitation. She was not well. As predicted, Tupolev refused to go alone, pleading advanced age and poor health. Father suggested that he take his daughter, Yuliya Andreyevna.

Naturally, a decision to include Yuliya Andreyevna in the delegation had to be discussed by the Presidium of the Central Committee. I don't know whether that occurred at an official session or during a break when, in Father's phrase, they often spent time kidding each other. At one point Mikoyan—who was considered their protocol expert—"tossed out," as Father put it, still another idea: the delegation head shouldn't travel alone. That was considered bad form in the world.

This put Bulganin in a difficult position. Because of his family problems he desperately wanted to avoid taking his wife. There was an oppressive silence.

Anastas Ivanovich broke it, commenting that etiquette did not exclude the possibility of taking other family members, especially if a wife could not accompany her husband. Seeing that Bulganin didn't like that idea either, Mikoyan turned to Father and said: "Maybe you should take your son or daughter?"

Father decided that I should go.

When Father told me about all this at home that evening, I was in seventh heaven. To go to England—no one dreamed of it in those days. The whole household was envious. With the exception of Rada's husband, Aleksei, none of them had ever been out of the country. He had been on *Komsomolskaya Pravda* assignments to Finland and Austria, if I remember correctly. Mama shook her head disapprovingly, but said nothing.

The question of a tailcoat unexpectedly popped up again, as it had before Geneva. Now Father rejected the proposal out of hand. Even a mention of the planned visit to the queen had no effect. Their hosts were consulted. The British replied that the conventional dress was a tailcoat, but if their guests were unhappy with the idea they could come in any proper attire, preferably of a dark color.

A black suit jacket was immediately made for Father and served him faithfully for years afterward, both during visits abroad and for receptions in Moscow.

At the last minute, almost on the eve of departure, still another problem arose. The British Embassy requested the Foreign Ministry's agreement to send their naval attaché on the cruiser, along with the delegation. That was the custom on state visits. Our protocol office confirmed that the request was a legitimate one.

The military were aghast. An English spy on the cruiser! They reported to Father. He ordered that international norms be observed, but that steps be taken to prevent our guest from poking his nose into secret places.

The day of departure finally arrived, April 14, 1956. The delegation left by train for Kaliningrad. Bulganin and Father settled into special salon cars, in which top Soviet leaders had been accustomed to travel since the civil war. They had lived and worked in the railroad cars. Another two cars were provided for other members of the delegation, as well as a large entourage. The British naval attaché was put there, along with a squad of the Navy's counter-intelligence officers.

The train arrived in Kaliningrad toward evening of the following day. The springtime sun was setting and the freezing air seemed to long for warmth. There was no wind, not even a breeze. At the station the delegation was met by a large crowd of local civilian, Merchant Marine, and Navy officials, as well as others, who had obviously just arrived from Moscow. Since there were still a few hours before the cruiser's scheduled departure, the regional party secretary and local Navy commander suggested a tour of the city and its environs.

We drove around the narrow streets in a ZIS limousine, with Father sitting in the front, Bulganin in the back. I squeezed in next to Bulganin, while a general sat on the jump seat. He talked about the history of the area, most of it relating to past battles. Father was silent, deep in his own thoughts. He had long since lost any interest in subjects like military assaults and attacks. They had, he hoped, receded irrevocably into the past.

After traveling around the city and passing through a gate, we drove onto the grounds of the naval base, where we were met by the Navy commander, an admiral, who was our host. The limousine stopped for a moment, and the admiral joined the general on the jump seat.

The base covered an enormous territory. An endless line of buildings and warehouses painted a dark gray color alternated with earthen embankments studded with ventilation pipes. I also remember an enormous circular concrete mass, which was a shore defense artillery tower. The sight was incredibly impressive. I suddenly thought: "The British attaché couldn't have missed it." Well, what can I say? We were trained to be vigilant.

We finally arrived at the cruiser, its tall gray side up against a wharf. They were waiting for us. Bulganin and Father boarded, the captain reported that the ship was ready to depart on its distant journey, requested permission to leave, and then hurried off to the bridge. Seizing the opportunity, I asked one of the guards I knew the question that had been bothering me during our entire tour: "What about the Englishman?"

"Everything's in order. He's in his cabin," my companion said, smiling.

That didn't satisfy me.

"But how did they take him through the base?"

"They brought him here, carried him on board, and put him to bed," the KGB guard laughed openly. "He probably doesn't even know what country he's in."

I was reassured and looked admiringly at the amused and muscular guard.

Father and Bulganin were given comfortable quarters. Father was put in the admiral's cabin and Bulganin in the captain's. The other delegation members occupied almost all the cabins meant for the ship's officers. As a result, the latter had to put up with that inconvenience, as well as with all the fuss caused by the presence of such high-level passengers.

The cruiser was accompanied by two destroyers, the *Smotryashchy* and the *Sovershenny*. Our small flotilla was commanded by Rear Admiral Kotov. The voyage enjoyed calm weather, aside from the rolling motion that suddenly began in the channel, causing the cruiser to begin swaying from side to side. It had no effect on Father, who settled down at a large table in the captain's stateroom to look over the voluminous materials he had brought. The others crawled away one by one to their cabins. But the wave motion soon died down.

The delegation was divided into two unequal groups. Most lapsed into idleness. Father and Bulganin were busy all day reading papers, the daily mail, which had been delivered by plane the day before in Kaliningrad, and memoranda about places they would visit and people they would meet. These contained meticulously detailed descriptions, not only of the professional careers of future interlocutors, but also about their habits, families, and sometimes even their friends.

Speeches received special attention. Protocol greetings several pages long and detailed speeches, written earlier in Moscow, lay in their separate folders. Bulganin would be the one to speak, but Father scrutinized every word typed on small half-sheet pages, which were to fit into the jacket pocket of the chairman of the Council of Ministers.

Naturally, reading papers didn't take up the entire day and there was time for strolling on deck. The wooden deck was a good hundred meters long from prow to stern. In the morning sailors scrubbed it until it shone like glass. Father didn't waste time during his walks; he talked over certain things with Kurchatov, had friendly chats with Tupolev.

Our voyage took several days. We had to take on fuel halfway along, in the straits, so we would have enough for the return trip. No consideration was given to refueling at our destination—not because we begrudged the foreign currency, but because we were wary. After all, we were not visiting friends and had to expect the worst.

Everyone knows from reading sea stories that the appearance of birds is a sure sign of approaching land. I don't remember any. However, small planes, rented by local newsreel companies, began to circle in the air above us as we neared our goal. They flew lower and lower, trying to get more interesting pictures and perhaps capture Father with Bulganin. Our cameramen had an advantage, since they were taking pictures right on the cruiser's deck.

Yachts, launches, and small ships circled the cruiser, now and again incautiously approaching it and then darting away. Their number increased as we got closer to shore.

After a brief welcoming ceremony the delegation boarded a train. Prime Minister Anthony Eden was to greet us at the London train station.

The special train traveled slowly. The delegation settled around a large square table in the salon, which was as big as a hall. The car was very similar to the one Father used in Moscow. British officials described the program for the visit. Father listened inattentively, since every point had been talked over and agreed on before we left Moscow. We were then invited to lunch. Foreign food, served by foreign hands. We were on our guard. And for good reason. Turtle soup was served as a first course. Is such a thing edible? Some kind of brown cubes floated in a cup of bouillon. Tupolev defused the awkward situation, observing that he had tried turtle soup when he visited England several times before the war, that it was nothing to be afraid of—it was even rather tasty. Father tried a spoonful, and praised it—then the rest of us "risked" it. I can't say that we liked it, but it was edible. Someone couldn't resist commenting that our borscht was better.

Finally we arrived in London. Father and Bulganin greeted Eden like old friends. When all the formalities for heads of government required by protocol were completed, we left for the Claridge Hotel, located in the very heart of London.

Father was concerned about the delegation's being lodged in a hotel and not in a special residence, as was our custom. Was this evidence of discrimination? As soon as we were left alone, Father asked me to call Gromyko. Andrei Andreyevich knew the local customs well from his time as ambassador in London and explained that there were no special residences in Britain. All guests of the government stayed in hotels, and in our luxury hotel the apartments given Father and Bulganin were designated the royal apartments. Father was pacified.

Work began the following morning, April 19. Naturally, I didn't take part in the negotiations, but I could see by the expressions on their faces and by their remarks that Father and Bulganin were pleased. Both sides were trying to preserve and build on the beginnings of mutual understanding generated in Geneva, and both emphasized their mutual good intentions.

For example, the day we arrived in Portsmouth it was announced on Moscow Radio that the Cominform, an organ created by Stalin in 1947 to coordinate communist activities, was terminated. Our hosts appreciated this gesture. On their part, they tried not to bring up issues their guests might consider sensitive.

The talks focused primarily on events far from our borders. The British were especially worried by developments in the Middle and Near East, which were slipping out of their control. They were very anxious not to have the Suez Canal, Iraqi oil, and a great deal else escape from their grasp.

A few years earlier the British government wouldn't have dreamed of consulting with Moscow. We were not involved in affairs in the Arab world. The coup carried out by a group of young officers in Egypt and events in far-off Yemen initially attracted no attention in Moscow. Father regarded them cautiously. He was in no hurry. In general, in those days that entire world of pyramids, camels, and sphinxes seemed so very distant.

Father changed after the meeting with Josip Broz Tito. The Yugoslavs had quickly established friendly relations with the new president of Egypt, Gamal Abdel Nasser. During Father's visit to Yugoslavia, Tito urged him to keep an eye on the young officers who had come to power.

At about that time the crown prince of Yemen, El' Badr, came knocking at our door. The kingdom needed arms for its struggle against the British. To buy them in Western Europe was out of the question, and the king decided to send his son to the communists. The arrival of an heir to a throne, even a relatively minor throne, aroused a great deal of talk. Father was informed of every step taken by our high-born guest. The prince was given some encouragement: we would help, since the struggle against colonialism was a sacred cause. The only question was: in what way?

Father gave it some serious thought. We had not traded in arms previously. Moreover, everything related to defense was held in the strictest secrecy. Kalashnikovs and T-55 tanks were not even shown to our allies. Never mind allies—not even every officer in our own army was given the opportunity to become familiar with new weapons. And now we would be selling them to God knows who! The military objected. Father insisted. He didn't believe that we would be at war any time soon and he felt a sacred obligation to show solidarity with people fighting for their independence. We had to help. If we did not, who would? Again the accursed question was—how? Father vacillated. He considered it too risky to enter the arms market himself and decided to look for an intermediary. His first thought was of Yugoslavia, of Tito, who had built the bridge between us and the

Arabs. Father was preparing to talk with him when he had second thoughts. The Yugoslavs did not enjoy our full confidence; they accepted U.S. military assistance and permitted Western advisers in their army. No one could be sure that our secrets wouldn't sail off across the ocean. Besides, Tito wouldn't accept such a mission. It's one thing to give advice, another to resell tanks. He cherished Yugoslavia's nonaligned status.

Father decided on Czechoslovakia, a highly developed, industrialized country that was itself an arms producer. Father thought that was especially important. He didn't want to leave any traces.

An agreement was quickly reached with Antonin Novotny, the president of Czechoslovakia, and the Arabs were advised to turn to the Czechs: we don't trade in arms, but they are old hands at it. The deal was struck. True, we didn't manage to keep it secret for very long.

Father loved to recall how he had adroitly avoided British attempts to sound him out:

> Lloyd[9] came with us. . . . There were just the two of us and, of course, Gromyko. We were driving along and Lloyd, who was very friendly and liked to joke, turned to me and said: "A little birdie perched on my shoulder the other day and chirped in my ear that you're selling arms to Yemen."
>
> I said: "Different birdies are flying around chirping different things. One perched on my shoulder too, and chirped that you're selling arms to Egypt, you're selling them to Iraq [at that time a very reactionary government was in power in Iraq], you're selling them to Iran—that you're selling arms to anyone who wants to buy them from you. And if they don't want to, the birdie says, then you foist them on them. So there are all sorts of birdies."
>
> He said: "It's true, there are all sorts of birdies, and some chirp in your ear and some in ours."
>
> I said: "Wouldn't it be nice if all the birdies started chirping that we should assume a mutually binding obligation not to sell arms to anyone? That would contribute to the cause of peace."
>
> . . . All the same, we did indeed hold negotiations . . . and agreed to supply a certain amount of arms to Yemen. . . . They were preparing to finish the war with Aden. We were interested in helping Yemen become a fully independent state.

The "birdie" didn't chirp in their ears the fact that exactly six months later our countries would clash head on, right there in the Middle East.

---

9. "Lloyd." This is a reference to Selwyn Lloyd, Eden's foreign secretary. See *Khrushchev Remembers* (New York: Little, Brown and Co., 1970), chap. 14, for the senior Khrushchev's account of this meeting and the London visit.

Father felt that he was ready for a trial of strength. After the February tests of the R-5, he had a club in his hand with which to threaten an intractable European interlocutor, if that proved necessary. Not use against, but simply threaten with.

He worked out a strategy: he preferred to use nuclear arms at the table, not on the battlefield. And since that was the case, why keep them secret? It wouldn't hurt to boast of them. In London he allowed himself to talk about them at various dinners.

Father pursued his line: we were now in the era of missiles, which relegated all previous types of weapons to the category of targets. The balance of forces, he asserted, had undergone a fundamental change. Who needs all these bombers if one, or perhaps several, missiles can accomplish more than a whole air armada? And the Soviet Union has enough missiles. His words gave his interlocutors a lot to think about.

I didn't understand what was going on, and worried: how can he treat secrets so casually? Once, alone with him at the hotel, I tried cautiously to bring up the subject, but he grimaced and pointed at the ceiling. He had no doubt that his room was bugged.

Father was constantly on the offensive. He sometimes showed a lack of tact. He would suddenly start asking the person he was talking to if they knew how many missiles it would take to destroy the country.

For example, this is what happened at Chequers, in Father's words:

> During dinner Eden's wife turned to us with a question: "What sort of missiles do you have? Can they fly a long way?"
>
> "Yes," I said, "they can. They can not only reach your British Isles, they can go farther."
>
> She held her tongue. It was a little rude of me and could have been construed as some kind of threat. . . . We did not mean to threaten, but wanted to show that we had not come as suppliants, that we were a powerful country.

From then on the subject of missiles began to dominate Father's diplomacy. He made use of it for six years, until the Caribbean Crisis. The method yielded rather good results, although in general the missiles Father referred to were sometimes still in the test stage. Who could tell where and how many missiles we had? If you look at estimates of Soviet missile potential made at that time and now declassified, you see a striking variation in numbers. Some are close to being accurate. But we only know that today. At the time, politicians preferred to overinsure themselves. All the more so, since the regular monitoring of tests by radar installed on Iranian territory and trained on the test sites confirmed Father's words—he did have missiles. But the Americans could only guess at their location and number.

On the evening of April 20 the Soviet delegation was invited to dinner at the Royal Naval College in Greenwich. Their guests had arrived in Britain on a cruiser, and the British sailors took on the role of gracious hosts. However, there was some awkwardness. Fleet Commander Lord Mountbatten refused to meet with communists. As Father was informed, Lord Mountbatten was related to the tsar's family, which had been shot in Sverdlovsk (Yekaterinburg). Father only grunted, but I noticed that he was stung by the news.

A festive evening was arranged in Greenwich. We were welcomed by the president of the College, an admiral, accompanied by young cadets in dress uniform. We were then escorted to a hall. Bulganin and Father were given places at the head table, on a stage, while the rest of us were seated evenly around the tables.

Our cruiser was attracting a lot of attention at the time. Aside from professional interest in the new elements in its construction, the cruiser acquired a certain fame because of a scandalous episode that occurred the previous evening: someone was seen swimming underwater by its side. Glimpsed on the surface, he disappeared in full view of the public, and now newspapers were carrying versions of the incident, each more fantastic than the next.

The speeches soon began. Our hosts spoke first, then it was the guests' turn. By rank, Bulganin should have been first, but Father seized the initiative.

In justification of his behavior, Father writes in his memoirs that Bulganin, because of his passivity, turned acrimonious discussions over to him, asking in a whisper that Father reply. Perhaps that was the case: as had happened a year earlier in Geneva, Bulganin read his speeches on official occasions and shrank from impromptu exchanges, confining himself to general phrases, whereas Father was never at a loss, but responded to an opponent immediately with a relevant and sharp—sometimes too sharp—answer.

However it was, this practice did not strengthen the friendship between the chairman of the Council of Ministers and the secretary of the Central Committee. Nikolai Aleksandrovich felt that he had been relegated to a secondary role and that perception bothered him constantly. He couldn't always restrain himself, and his irritation sometimes broke through in a reply, a gesture, or a glance. But only for a moment—a benevolent smile would immediately reappear on his face.

When the time came to make an answering toast in Greenwich, Bulganin, in Father's words, nudged him: "You speak."

There was no need to ask Father twice. He tore into battle.

After his stormy argument with Admiral Kuznetsov the previous year, one of his favorite topics of conversation was the role of the submarine and surface fleets in modern warfare. Here too Father couldn't wait to share his views on modern naval war strategy with British naval officers.

He spoke interestingly and at length, getting increasingly worked up and giving the impression that there was no question more important to him than the military readiness of the Royal Navy. The British sailors listened to Father attentively. You felt that they were not simply showing the respect due to a visiting guest, but were profoundly interested in the subject.

This is how Father recalled the "lecture":

> I spoke. It was a freewheeling meeting of free speech. I chose a subject which would display our country and its possibility of, to put it crudely, attacking the English.
>
> I said: "Gentlemen, you represent Great Britain. Great Britain was mistress of the seas, but that is all in the past. We must look at things realistically. Everything has changed, technology has changed and the status of a naval fleet has changed. It used to be a floating artillery base. It brought fear to the enemy. It blazed a trail for the marines. Now, when there are missiles and missile-carrying aircraft that can strike from a great distance, from a distance beyond the range of any ship's guns, a new situation has been created. One can therefore say that battleships and cruisers are now obsolete. They are just floating coffins.
>
> "We arrived here on a cruiser. Our cruiser is new, it's good, so I've heard from your specialists. They regard our cruiser highly. But . . . we can sell it. Sell it because it's obsolete and its armament is obsolete. In some future war it won't be cruisers or even bombers that decide the issue. Bombers are also obsolete. Not as much as the navy, but they are becoming obsolete. Submarines will be the main weapon on the sea, and missiles in the air—missiles which can deliver an attack from a great distance. In the future, from an unlimited distance."
>
> There were questions and answers. The conversation always revolved around this subject. We wanted to point out the decline in military possibilities available to the British fleet with respect to us. . . . These were not aggressive remarks with threats; everything was said with a smile. They also joked, asked questions, spoke ironically. . . . In a word, the conversation was rather frank and relaxed.

At the Greenwich Naval College Father spoke publicly for the first time about the change in our military doctrine and about the transition from the massive use of troops on the battlefield to a nuclear-missile confrontation.

Far from everyone in our country approved of Father's initiative. Behind his back, some people even accused him of giving away secrets. Father's opponents thought in the concepts of the imminent inevitability of war, whereas he had moved beyond the dogma. Why hide it, he thought—let everyone know that we are not just a land power.

The meeting ended, as all such occasions in Britain, with a toast to the queen. At first this grated on Father: how could they force him, a representative of the revolutionary proletariat, to drink a toast to a crowned head? He felt out of place. But only the first time, when he didn't expect it. At the next reception he rose promptly from his seat and respectfully observed the ceremony. That evening he justified himself with a laugh: "You don't bring your own rules to someone else's monastery."

Father awaited the reaction to his speech with interest. He didn't have to wait long.

> The next day we met with Eden. Eden asked, with a smile as usual, "How were our sailors?"
>
> I answered: "You have good sailors. They're known the world over."
>
> "Well, and the conversation?" he looked at me, smiling.
>
> "I see from your smile that you must already know."
>
> "Yes," he said. "It was reported to me."
>
> "And what did you think of my remarks?"
>
> "You know, I agree with you. But I, as prime minister, can't start to talk about this with our military. We have no other weapons besides our surface fleet and our bombers. They are our main means for waging war. I can't undermine their faith in those weapons," he said, smiling.

During the dinner I committed a serious indiscretion. I was seated next to a man in civilian dress, who had introduced himself as being from the Foreign Office. He quizzed me at length about life in Russia and told me humorous stories about English traditions. He didn't speak Russian, so I proudly showed off my rather limited knowledge of English. Toward the end of dinner he asked how our people were reacting to the recent unmasking of Stalin. My companion referred in passing to Father's speech, as if its existence were taken for granted. I completely lost sight of the fact that an official in the British service was not supposed to know about such matters, and I started talking about it. Of course, I knew how one should speak to foreigners, and I explained the matter "correctly." I said that everyone supported the basic theses of the speech, but that naturally a great deal would have to be reexamined, and such changes are always painful.

My companion nodded his head sympathetically, agreed, and continued to ask questions.

Next morning before breakfast I described—or, to be psychologically correct—reported this conversation to Father. I wanted very much to be useful in some way, and not simply included in the delegation because I was his son. I thought he would be interested in the Englishman's reaction to such a timely subject.

To my surprise, his reaction was unexpectedly somber.

"There's no reason for you to talk about such things," he said very quietly without turning toward me, his gaze fixed on the far corner of the enormous, luxurious living room of the royal apartment, and seeming to look through the wall to some far-off place. He looked upset. I understood that I had made a mistake, but couldn't understand what it was and began trying to defend myself or to explain: I didn't say anything like that, I only mentioned that students support the Congress's decision. Father scowled. I became completely flustered.

Still without turning around, Father reminded me that we had never mentioned the speech and had not admitted its authenticity. But now, through me, the British had received confirmation.

I wished the earth would swallow me up, since I now thought I'd allowed myself to be tricked by British intelligence.

"But what can we do?" I was thoroughly upset, and turned to Father for help.

He had already calmed down and headed for the bathroom to get a tie. I followed him.

"There's nothing to do." Father began trying to calm me. "In fact, there's nothing secret in the speech. It's simply a formality. But in the future behave more cautiously."

His finger pointed toward the ceiling, in a gesture already familiar. Father strictly observed a simple rule: don't carry on any conversations in the room which you don't want the British secret services to hear. He had a lot of experience in this area. In Moscow the KGB reported regularly on the conversations of visiting diplomats and accredited ambassadors and the contents of intercepted and deciphered telegrams.

I remember U.S. ambassador Llewellyn Thompson's insistent appeals to Father. On several occasions during visits to the dacha, he talked about the Embassy's lack of space and offered to pay almost any price for the buildings adjacent to it.

Father reluctantly refused. He really didn't want to disappoint his guest. But to agree would have been even more complicated.

The ambassador nodded in disappointment: "I understand perfectly. I suppose you listen to us from them?"

Father didn't reply, and they began talking about something else. The subject of those buildings came up more than once later on, but Father remained adamant.

But sometimes after returning from one of the ambassador's receptions, Father would mumble unhappily: "If he understands what the problem is, why does he keep insisting? He's not a stupid person." Then he fell silent. He understood that the ambassador wasn't acting on his own initiative, but on instructions from Washington. Finally, in Brezhnev's time, the Americans got their way. Leonid Ilyich couldn't refuse President Nixon.

And there's the famous story of the Great Seal of the United States, a wooden eagle presented to Ambassador Charles Bohlen by the Young Pioneers[10] on July 4, 1955.

I remember General Serov's delight as he described their success. The "specialists" who prepared the eagle had installed a microphone with a tiny antenna. It didn't even have a power unit, but was activated by a ray from a high-frequency narrow-directional electromagnetic beam projected from the National Hotel, located next to the Embassy. In those years the U.S. Embassy was located on Manezhnaya Square, across from the Kremlin.

The ambassador hung the eagle in his office and for quite a long time information directly from "the horse's mouth" arrived on Serov's desk. The Kremlin's surprising fund of information began to worry the Americans. Previously, Soviet secrets had flowed into Langley at about the same rate as American secrets into the Lubyanka.

A commission descended upon the U.S. Embassy in Moscow. Professionals climbed all over the building, from basement to attic, with sensors, checked all the walls and, as a result, discovered the uninvited guest.

Serov wasn't discouraged. Such are the rules of the game: one hides, the other searches—we'll see who is more clever.

Our polite hosts couldn't help but notice that I was often left behind at the hotel, and they suggested a trip to Oxford, apart from the delegation. At the time I was studying at the Electric Power Institute and the English assumed that I would enjoy some contact with students.

I very much wanted to go, but I was more afraid to be separated for even a short time from my own people and to be alone in a strange and hostile world. Not that I was afraid of anything specific. No. The danger appeared formless, like a fog crawling one dank evening out of a low-lying area. But it was all the more frightening because of that.

That evening, before the next scheduled official dinner, I took advantage of the chance to consult with Father. At first he was enthusiastic about the idea: "Go, see how people live."

The next morning his mood had changed.

"I advise you not to go," he began. "We are in a capitalist country, even if on a state visit. Anything can happen here. The papers write about people being kidnapped. Stay with the rest of us, out of danger."

So my trip to Oxford did not take place. I was eventually fortunate enough to get there, in 1989. No one kidnapped me.

Father learned quickly. Three years later, during his visit to the United States, such a thought would simply never have entered his head.

_____

10. Pioneers—the Soviet youth group for ten- to fifteen-year-olds, similar to the Boy Scouts.

The visit passed harmoniously, to the satisfaction of both sides. The only dissonant note was an unexpectedly acrimonious squabble with the Labourites. So much was written about it at the time that I won't go into details, but I can't omit the unpleasant episode entirely. It cast a bright light on both the irreconcilable attitude toward social democrats of all types which we inherited from Stalin, and on Father's own distrustfulness. He was constantly alert to make sure that any hint at interference in our affairs, even simple criticism, was rebuffed. He threw himself tooth-and-nail into battle. Then, having crushed his opponent, he still "pawed the ground," looking around to see if anyone was left standing. Good-natured and genial in everyday life, he was suddenly transformed into an irreconcilable orthodox communist. At the very first sign of a desire to tone down or smooth over the contradictions and confrontation between the two worlds—of socialism and capitalism—he pounced upon the "philistines." That word aroused his deep scorn for people who lacked a "class instinct," who were capable of submitting to pressure, of retreating. He himself fought to the finish, arguing the "indisputable" advantages of the socialist structure.

The meeting with the Labourites was held around a long table in one of the rooms in Parliament, and at first it proceeded according to the script. You couldn't have called the atmosphere in the hall friendly, but despite a certain feeling of strain there was nothing to foretell an approaching storm.

It all began when one of our hosts, named Brown, appealed to the Soviet government, in the person of Bulganin, to help free a number of prominent social democrats arrested in Eastern Europe during the Stalin era. He was supported by Hugh Gaitskell, the party leader. Initially Father's irritation was not caused by the questions from Brown and Gaitskell, but by "the apolitical position taken by Bulganin," as he phrased it.

In those years Father was psychologically incapable of responding positively to such a request. It was one thing to condemn Stalin's unjustified repressions of his brother communists, quite another to defend "socialist traitors." That was how, in our distorted world, the role of social democracy was treated: from the Mensheviks, who allegedly betrayed the Revolution, through the German Social Democrats, who allegedly brought Hitler to power, all the way to our Labourite hosts. But in the mid-1950s there was no "allegedly." Neither for me, nor for Father. The idea that no one was worse than the socialists had been pounded into us. In school, teachers explained that it was far easier to deal with owner-capitalists than with their lackeys from the "workers" parties.

Instead of replying sharply as Father expected, Bulganin hesitated for a moment, then accepted the lists held out to him. Promising almost inaudibly to look at them, he put them into his pocket. Father was seething, but still restrained himself. Possibly his indignation would not have burst into the open if Nikolai Aleksandrovich had not proposed a toast to friendship and cooperation. He did it in a way that was very homespun, I would even say, as if he were in a family circle. That was his way of trying to smooth over the awkwardness that had arisen. When Bulganin, smiling, reached out to clink glasses with Brown, Father exploded. He couldn't put up with that. Even many years later he would get nervous and excited when describing this contentious meeting, eager to reenter the fray.

In fact, that evening Father expressed himself unrestrainedly. The meeting broke up. However, the following day the proprieties were reestablished, with some assistance from the prime minister and after a mutual exchange of courtesies. But a bitter taste was left for many years. Unlike Stalin, Father was not at all intent on a total break with the social democrats. He was ready to cooperate with any movement opposed to war. But—without interference in our internal affairs and without intrusions into ideology, whether real or imaginary.

Here there is freedom for conjecture, for interpretation, especially if age-old cultures are very different from each other, if an impassable barrier has existed for many years between countries, peoples, and individuals. Some might say that to understand is not so very important. But Europe grew out of the democracy of the Roman Forum, of Roman law. Emerging from the troubled period of the Middle Ages, it embarked on reforms; constitutions followed revolutions. Human rights, obligations, guarantees, and presumption of innocence. We, with a culture whose sources were in the Byzantine empire, only quite recently even learned those words. The age-old immutable and absolute rule of princes, replaced by the autocracy of the tsars, naturally developed into the authority of the Leader. We read our constitution in school, but did not encounter it in real life.

It is incredibly difficult to understand each other under these conditions. Our ways of thinking are profoundly different. Sometimes even simple gestures are perceived differently. There were a great number of such examples in my own life, some funny, some sad, and some dreadful.

Here is one of them, the most simple one.

It happened the day after the scandal with the Labourites. Father was behaving guardedly. I don't remember if we were on our way from a meeting to a reception, or from lunch to a meeting. Our attention was attracted by an elderly man standing on the sidewalk of a London street with his fist raised to his ear in the greeting of Germany's Rote Front, a gesture already half-forgotten by that time. He flashed by and disappeared.

This scene could have been forgotten like so many others, but fate decreed otherwise. An agitated Father perceived the fist as a threat and immediately took up the challenge. He mentioned it for the first time immediately after returning to Moscow, accompanying it with an angry rebuke to anyone who would dare to threaten us. That fist imprinted itself in his head for the rest of his life. I tried in vain to correct the mistake. That fist migrated from one appearance to another, from one speech to another, threatening our well-being, becoming increasingly sinister. It lost its physical existence and turned into a fearsome political symbol, living a life of its own in the stormy clash between two systems. Just like the quick-tempered words "We will bury you," pronounced a year later. Today it's impossible to prove to generations of Americans, and not only Americans, that those words did not constitute a threat. It meant no such thing! The West also needed an enemy, not an abstract one but a specific, tangible enemy. And it got one. No matter how often you explain that this was a metaphor, that Father meant the burial of the outmoded capitalist structure and its replacement by a socialism that would benefit the people. He believed faithfully that the day was not far off when everyone, even the Americans, would ask to enter our paradise. He believed, he held the doors open, but wasn't prepared to chase anyone in by force. Friendly listeners smiled, nodded, and didn't change their opinions. Unfriendly listeners did not smile. That was the only difference. It's difficult to break out of stereotypes, change ways of thinking, change an image that has grown familiar and recognizable.

The visit was coming to an end, but the delegation hadn't decided how to return home. The underwater swimmer in a black diving suit, spotted by a vigilant watchman on board the destroyer *Sovershenny*, was found dead. Headless, it was said. Newspapers soon reported that the diver in the mask and flippers had been Commander Lionel Crabbe, an experienced and daring individual.

Our seamen were very concerned that our uninvited guest might have left some "presents."

A paradoxical situation arose. The problem of how to return home was discussed more than once in Father's room. On these occasions he took no precautions. When embassy officials began to insinuate that a mine might have been attached to the cruiser—and in the atmosphere of mutual distrust which prevailed at the time such a conjecture was taken seriously—and that if it exploded in the open sea, far from any coast, no accusation could be made against Britain, Father embarked on a tirade in a booming voice. He talked about the responsibility of the authorities, about how such an act of piracy would mean war. He didn't fail to mention how many missiles would be required to wipe the island off the face of the earth. His speech was incisive and militant, and his finger, pointing from time to time at the ceiling, left his listeners in no doubt for whose ears it was intended.

Nevertheless, he himself spoke in favor of returning home by plane. He was dying to try out the TU-104 jet. However, the security service continued to resist, and no one wanted to assume responsibility. Moreover, Bulganin objected. He didn't want to fly on the plane. In case of an accident on the cruiser you might be saved, the two destroyers would be nearby, whereas in the air . . .

The security service turned to Tupolev, demanding his support. Andrei Nikolayevich was again put in an awkward position. Tupolev resorted to the same argument: he was confident of the plane, but no one was entitled to violate proper procedures. Father gave in and decided to return on the *Ordzhonikidze*. Bulganin heaved a sigh of relief.

After a moment's pause, Tupolev began to complain that he was tired of traveling by sea, that such an adventure was not for his advanced age. "You must not fly, you are outsiders"—his eyes smiled at Father—"but I'm a designer, it's my business to test my machines. If I were afraid, then who would want to fly on my planes?"

Andrei Nikolayevich asked permission to leave the delegation and return home on the TU-104. No one objected. I asked to accompany him, using the approaching examination period as an excuse. Just like Father, I was eager to go for a ride on a jet.

Father nodded. Along with joyful anticipation of the flight, I was stung by the thought: "What if something happens?" But I chased it away: "After all, Tupolev's flying with us."

The flight came to a successful end, and it's hard to convey the delight evoked at the time by the roar of jet turbines, as well as by the absence of the bumps from air pockets which invariably accompanied flights on the IL-14 or Li-2! I felt as if I were in a fairy tale.

The plane was soon cleared for general use, and Father took the opportunity to fly on it during his first trip around the country. His enthusiasm was boundless.

The next time he met Tupolev Father couldn't resist asking if he really had doubts about his plane in London, or if it was a trick by the security service.

In reply, Andrei Nikolayevich burst out laughing.

"To tell you the truth, I wasn't worried about the plane. But I was in a difficult position. On the one hand, you were pressuring me, as you yourself know, and on the other, I was afraid. I'm a broken man. So I had to hide behind the instructions."

"That's what I thought"—Father supported him—"that's why I didn't insist. I didn't want to put you in a difficult position."

During the departure of the delegation, the security service became the "hero of the day." From the very beginning, they had run into a lack of mutual understanding in coordinating the security for the delegation in Britain. Their secret service was categorically opposed to our armed bodyguards. They claimed that it was international practice for the hosts to be responsible for the safety of their guests.

Serov insisted, referring to Geneva, where Moscow KGB agents had arrived fully equipped. The British objected, saying that an international conference was one thing; the Swiss were only, to put it crudely, providing a place for negotiations. A state visit is something else again. In London the KGB would have nothing to do. This wrangling threatened to develop into a serious clash. Serov consulted with Father, who sided with the British, saying they know the proper procedures better. In essence, Father thought that our guards would be powerless in a foreign country. What could three, five, or even ten people do? Nevertheless, Serov insisted on a compromise: the British agreed to accept a limited number of KGB agents, but without weapons. Ivan Aleksandrovich gave in, but ordered them to carry handguns, "concealed in such a way that nobody will suspect." They were all supplied with the new Makarovs, instead of the usual Walthers or Nagans. The Makarovs had just been introduced and were considered secret. Of course, the British weren't so naive as to believe that their guests would "travel light," without weapons. But they had achieved their main purpose—all the heavier guns were left at home. Their Soviet colleagues looked very unthreatening as they walked down the cruiser's gangway.

The services quickly established a mutual rapport, but our agents did not part with their Makarovs. During the day they kept them in their pockets, at night under their pillows. Until the very last day there were no incidents. Then, in the excitement of leaving, someone left his Makarov under the pillow. After the guests left the floor occupied by the Soviet delegation, a maid started to clean the room and discovered it. She was not surprised, having seen much worse. She hurried to return her find to its owner. Wrapping the gun in a napkin, the girl ran after them. At the hotel entrance, she sighed with relief. The guests were just getting into their cars. But how could she find the gun's owner in all the activity? She remembered what the room's occupant looked like, but there was such a crowd near the entrance. Then the maid took what she thought was the only right decision. Throwing off the napkin, she lifted the gun over her head and shouted: "Misters, you forgot something!!!"

For an instant everyone froze, but only for an instant. The owner was found. Feverishly putting the gun in his pocket, he said something incomprehensible. "Thank you" was all he said in English.

It's hard to imagine those idyllic times, when a stranger waving a gun could run up close to guests on state visits. Nowadays the unlucky maid would have been riddled with bullets the instant she'd lifted the gun. No one would have hesitated or taken the time to ask questions.

ANOTHER VISIT TO BRITAIN

Eight years later, in 1964, I happened to visit Britain again, this time with a delegation from the aircraft industry.

By the way, that trip would be my last for a long time. I was forbidden to travel to capitalist countries for many years. Brezhnev came to power in October of 1964, and the cage door slammed shut. From then on I was numbered among the "unreliables," and naturally, they were not allowed to travel abroad.

Just as in 1956, we arrived in London in the spring, at the end of April. The sun shone just as brightly. We visited most of the aviation construction companies. We also visited the famous Rolls-Royce factory. Among specialists it is better known for its airplane engines than for its cars. We were well received. I wouldn't say we were given a friendly reception, but it was a neighborly one. In the capital of airplane engine-construction, on the Avon River, the delegation was lodged in a comfortable cottage, a hotel belonging to the company. It had a small billiard room, which we made our club. In the evenings after dinner we would gather there, exchange impressions, indulge in reminiscences. Sometimes we would go to the billiard tables and set up the balls, but never managed to play a real game. Our specialists were of a different type. After striking a couple of balls, General Designer Chelomei would suddenly be distracted by a discussion on the fine points of the mechanics of elastic collisions. Academician Leonid Ivanovich Sedov behaved the same way. Artyom Ivanovich Mikoyan, also a general designer, never touched a cue. The more he refused, the more persistently we tried to draw him into a game. Finally, Artyom Ivanovich got fed up and proposed to satisfy their requests by telling a story connected with billiards.

"I *have* played billiards, and I've even won a very important game," he began intriguingly. "I won no more, no less than the future of our jet aviation, and for myself the MIG-15."

The players put away their cues; this was a promising start. A close circle of listeners drew around Mikoyan's armchair, in the corner of the room.

Artyom Ivanovich paused, his eyes glinted slyly. We were all ears.

"It's well known that we didn't have any good turbojet engines after the war. Of course, work was proceeding, but we were a long way from production." Since Mikoyan was talking about generally known facts, without naming names, I remembered that "they" were probably listening.

"You remember how much fuss there was about German jet fighters, which took part in military actions toward the end of the war. We received an urgent command: make the same plane as quickly as possible!"

His listeners nodded; they had received such instructions more than once. The head of our delegation, A. A. Kobzarev, deputy chairman of the State Committee on Aviation Technology, tried to put in a word. He knew a great deal about what went on during those years. But Mikoyan cut him off.

"What I'm talking about, even you don't know, Aleksandr Aleksandrovich," he said softly, and continued: "At that time we still had very good relations with the British and we quickly came to an agreement. They promised to sell us several of their newest engines. I was instructed to make the arrangements. I prepared to go to England, but by the time they arranged and coordinated everything at home and drew up the necessary documents, not only had the war ended, but our friendship showed signs of deteriorating. It wasn't yet the Cold War, but our welcome was lukewarm and lacked the cordiality shown earlier.

"We were alone in the hotel. There wasn't even anyone to talk to, except that occasionally one of the local people would drop in for a cocktail in the evening to show some hospitality. And we made frequent calls to the Embassy. You can't have much of a conversation with them." Artyom Ivanovich shrugged his shoulders.

"I went to the company every morning, as if I were going to work. I was received kindly and spent a lot of time discussing various unimportant details, but they didn't give me an answer. Just like in our country." Mikoyan smiled, glancing slyly at Kobzarev. "My host felt very uncomfortable. He called London every day, trying to get an agreement in the corridors of power on terms for the sale, but in vain. The government changed, the Labour Party replaced the Conservatives. They didn't exactly forget about earlier promises, but times had changed, relations were cooling off, but hadn't deteriorated to the point that they said a definite 'no.' At the beginning the English hid their problems from me, but finally admitted them.

"I understood that the mission was hanging by a thread and that every day of waiting worked to our disadvantage. But what was I to do? I had to wait. But I changed my tactics, and at every meeting I started to tease them: you only say you're in charge of the company, but actually you're just like us—you can't take a step without the ministry. The English frowned; they didn't take it as a joke. But apparently our conversations were noted." Artyom Ivanovich paused. No one moved, waiting for the denouement.

"Well, one evening ——— dropped in." Mikoyan mentioned the name of one of the top directors of Rolls-Royce (but after all these years I've forgotten it).

"Naturally, the conversation revolved around the engines. I started to press him and again taunted him about the ministry. My host laughed it off, but it was obvious that he was stung to the quick. We were talking right in this same place, sitting in armchairs in the corner, just like now. Finally, he decided to get back at me: 'Mr. Mikoyan, I am prepared to show you my independence, but you have to answer in the same coin.'

"I waited to hear what he was going to say.

"Then my host proposed a wager—a game of billiards: If I won he would sign the contract at once and send off the engines. If I lost, that meant that it was not meant to be, there would be no more negotiations and we should pack our bags and go home."

Mikoyan poured himself some water and, testing our self-control, slowly drained the glass.

"My position, as you already know, was not an easy one." Artyom Ivanovich said, smacking his lips. "I'm not even referring to the fact that I could hardly play billiards—and still can't. Maybe I had struck a ball once or twice. It would cost me nothing to lose. To win was another matter! I had to hope for a miracle.

"At stake were two of the best English engines, the 'Nin' and the 'Dervent.' I couldn't imagine appearing in Moscow without them. On the other hand, it was already clear that the government was not likely to approve the sale; they would drag things out, procrastinate, and finally refuse.

"The main thing was that I had no one to consult with, no one to ask for instructions. I couldn't get through to the Embassy, the game had to begin at once. Besides, I would have been embarrassed—I'd harangued *them* about being independent so many times. And the Embassy wouldn't tell me anything anyway.

"At least now there was a slight chance. I sensed that he would keep his word.

"So I made up my mind and tried to look nonchalant. 'Certainly,' I said, 'only I'm not much of a player.'

"It seemed to me that my host momentarily regretted his offer. He had been certain that I would refuse. He had studied our psychology very well and knew that we didn't make a move without orders. But now it was too late. We racked up the balls and began to play."

Mikoyan rose from his chair and walked around the table. "Yes, this is the very same table."

Returning to his chair, he settled into it more comfortably.

"I don't know what helped me, luck or God? Or maybe he decided to let me win, thinking that otherwise he'd be stuck with me forever? Most likely I was so afraid that it awakened whatever talent I had. I struck the balls one after another. The last one fell into that pocket over there."

He pointed to the far end of the table.

"We finished the game. My host looked a little upset. They brought in some champagne. We drank to our wager. The next day we signed the contract. I left with the engines. I didn't trust anyone." Artyom Ivanovich laughed suddenly. "At home everyone congratulated me. I didn't tell anyone how I'd managed to get them. Only now does it all come back. The samples were sent to Mikulin, Aleksandr Aleksandrovich, and not long after that we got our first Soviet jet engine. It was mounted on the MIG-15. And the other Mikulin engines emerged from it."

We listened to this story as if it were a fairy tale. Do such unlikely events occur in real life? What things our future depends on!

Artyom Ivanovich's acquisition really did enable our engine builders to skip several steps. The English engines served as prototypes for Soviet development. The Rolls-Royce "Dervent," with a 1600-kg thrust, became the Soviet RD-500, while its slightly more powerful counterpart "Nin," with a 2000-kg thrust, became the RD-45. Their numbers, 500 and 45, refer to the factories where they were copied.

The other branch of our engine construction grew from a graft of a German wilding.[11] The RD-10 was developed from the Junkers JUMO-004, while the BMW-003 served as prototype for the RD-20.

ANDREI ANTONOVICH GRECHKO

The search for foreign prototypes began under Stalin and continued after his death. Father recalled more than once how the future marshal, Andrei Antonovich Grechko, then commander of the Group of Soviet Forces in Germany, arranged to purchase an American missile. A real missile.

Father was skeptical about the plan. He didn't think Grechko was a shrewd dealmaker and suspected that he was being taken in. The whole negotiation went on for a long time and everything seemed to be going well except for some details, but still the object in question didn't show up. Grechko swore that the sellers were reliable people and wouldn't deceive him.

Finally, they bought the missile. The general simply beamed. The valuable cargo was delivered with all possible precautions to Moscow and moved to one of the design bureaus. It didn't take specialists long to examine it. The new American missile turned out to be homemade, and not very skillfully at that. The money had been wasted.

Grechko arrived at Father's dacha with head hanging. I should think so—he had made a fool of himself. But no explosion followed. Father thought that expenses were inevitable in such matters. Intelligence agencies existed in order to deceive each other. Furthermore, he regarded Andrei Antonovich with undisguised sympathy. He forgave him a great deal. They had gone through much of the war together. Father first met Major General Grechko when he was commander of a cavalry division, during the retreat of our forces. As the lanky general rose up the service ladder, commanding a division, then a corps, and finally an army, he served on the fronts under the supervision of Father, who was a member of the Front Military Council with the permanent rank of lieutenant general. For him, as a representative of Moscow's supreme power to the army in the field, the number of stars on someone's shoulder boards was not particularly important. By the time of

---

11. "A graft of a German wilding." An adaptation of a German (nondomestic) model.

the operation to force the Dnieper, Grechko had already surpassed Father in rank and was a colonel general and deputy front commander.

After 1945 Grechko again appeared in Kiev, now as commander of the Kiev Military District, one of our country's most prestigious ones. There he and Father became even closer and met outside business hours.

Father's friendly relations with Grechko continued even after fate again sent them in different directions. The general became the commander of the Soviet Occupation Forces in Germany, while our family moved to Moscow. After Stalin's death Grechko, now a full Army general, started visiting Father's dacha again.

That summer day Grechko tried in every possible way to save face, while Father observed with interest the general's attempts to extricate himself from his awkward position. Grechko recounted in comic detail the complications involved in obtaining the desired missile and the trouble expended to assure that nothing would happen on its way to Moscow. In his interpretation, the annoying episode took on an amusing note.

"It wouldn't matter if they'd sold me an old one, that wouldn't be so insulting. But to palm off some kind of rubbish for fun, for a laugh . . ." Grechko pretended to be distressed and repeated: "It was the devil's work, Nikita Sergeyevich. They cheated us, the devil take them."

His eyes glinted with humor as he said this. The general understood that the threat of a storm had passed. He had transformed his report on the operation's failure into a humorous adventure story.

Father allowed Grechko's even more foolish ideas to pass without consequences. For example, after returning from Germany and assuming the position of commander of ground forces, Grechko visited us at the dacha one Sunday. During a stroll along the meadow he began talking about conquering Western Europe.

Naturally, every self-respecting general staff has war plans for all possible contingencies, even those involving one's present allies. But it's one thing to have such plans and another to advocate implementing them, even in an informal setting.

At first I thought that Andrei Antonovich was joking. But no. His eyes were serious, without their usual cunning look. He was expressing his thoughts precisely, without hesitation, and it was obvious that he had gone over every point carefully with the staff of the ground forces.

I don't remember why he wanted to start a war. The political aspect didn't bother him particularly; the general juggled tanks, planes, and guns. There, in his opinion, the Americans couldn't cope with us.

Father's expression darkened as his guest held forth. But Grechko, taking his host's silence for approval, plunged into an outline of his battle plans.

According to Grechko's calculations, on the second day after the start of hostilities, he intended to force the Rhine River. His voice took on a triumphant ring. You could almost hear the roll of kettledrums. Father looked up with amazement at the general, who was well over six feet tall. He didn't expect such bragging, even from Grechko. Nevertheless, he kept silent, apparently deciding to see how far his companion's fantasy would stretch.

Grechko sang like a nightingale. On the fifth or sixth day he seized Paris and advanced unhindered to the Pyrenees, ignoring Britain. The mountains didn't stop him either; he leaped over them without pausing and halted only on the shores of the Atlantic Ocean. At this point the general fell silent, caught his breath and looked inquiringly at Father. He radiated the triumph of a conqueror.

Father didn't say a word. This silence lasted for, probably, about two minutes. Then he looked up.

"And then what?" he said dryly.

Grechko continued to smile.

"And then what do you plan to do?" Father was beginning to get angry.

"Then what?" Repeated the general uncertainly, and then replied: "That's all . . ."

He spread his hands.

"What do you mean, that's all?" Father continued emphatically. "What are your plans for further action? You are reporting to the chairman of the Council of Ministers!"

"There are no plans for further action," the general said, as if bringing his report to a conclusion.

Father simply exploded. He delivered a tremendous tongue-lashing. I walked off a bit, but even at a respectful distance every word was audible.

Father raged. He couldn't understand how, in this day and age, a general could entertain such thoughts. And even more, how he would dare express such wild ideas to the leader of the government.

"Haven't you ever heard of nuclear weapons?" Father exclaimed. "What advance? What do you mean, Paris? You think you're Napoleon? On the first day there would be nothing left of you but a wet spot!"

Grechko shifted from one foot to another, his face gradually taking on the expression of a guilty schoolboy.

"Moreover, our policies are now generally based on a defensive posture, while you're talking like a crude aggressor. Aren't you informed of the decisions made by the Defense Council?" Father was beginning to calm down.

"All in all, it's time we took a look at what's going on in your staff. Do you really have absolutely nothing else to do?" The last peals of thunder rumbled off into the distance.

Grechko immediately perceived that the storm was passing. On his face there appeared the smile of a mischief-maker who suddenly realizes that he won't be punished.

"Were you really preparing to fight?" asked Father again, now somewhat curious.

"Well, no," mumbled Grechko.

"So, yes or no?" Father persisted.

"No," Grechko enunciated clearly.

"Then don't let me hear about such projects again." Father frowned severely and, calming down even further, added: "So he'd reach the Atlantic."

Grechko got off with a rebuke. Such a fantasy would have cost someone else his position and possibly his rank.

After Father's resignation Grechko became the Soviet minister of defense.

He was already on friendly terms with Brezhnev, who unlike Father, couldn't refuse his friend anything. It was during Grechko's time in office that we flooded Europe with tens of thousands of tanks, guns, and planes, not to speak of missiles.

Did the sounds of the waves breaking on the coast of Spain echo at night in the dreams of the increasingly senile military commander?

Not long before 1964, when the eulogizing of Father was spreading uncontrollably, Grechko resolved to make his contribution. At the time Grechko was already a marshal of the Soviet Union. He conceived the idea of making Father happy. Father told the story of their encounter more than once. The marshal's arguments had a straightforward soldierly quality: Father began and ended the war as a lieutenant general. The situation had now changed fundamentally. He was first secretary of the Central Committee, chairman of the Council of Ministers, and commander in chief of the Armed Forces. The rank of lieutenant general did not correspond to his position. It was time to correct this oversight.

"We military people are peculiar," Grechko told Father. "We don't like it if someone subordinate to us in rank gives orders. But if you become a marshal, everything will be as it should be."

He stopped to wait for a reaction. It wasn't at all what he expected. The idea clearly didn't appeal to Father, who mumbled: "Don't waste your time with such foolishness. I should be a marshal! We're not preparing for war, and in peacetime I can handle you even though I'm just a general. If, God forbid, war breaks out, we can decide then. A rank isn't the most complicated thing."

This idea of Grechko's also passed without unpleasant consequences. It just became another subject for Father's jokes. But Grechko didn't forget his idea and returned to it after he became minister of defense. The new supreme commander in chief, Brezhnev, graciously acceded to the proposal.

IN THE SPIRIT OF GENEVA

Despite all the incidents, Father and Bulganin were satisfied with their visit to Britain. It had proceeded in the "Spirit of Geneva," and it seemed that European policies were truly turning toward peace.

On May 9, 1956, Victory Day, newspapers published a draft law on pensions. Father had been planning it for a long time, reworking the budget in the search for crumbs to make at least modest improvements in the impoverished lives of the elderly. But a great deal of money was needed, and it was not easy to dislodge it from powerful governmental departments. The defense ministries consumed astronomical sums.

The revision of our military doctrine made it possible to liberate funds that had been tied up in the military budget. Father put his hopes mainly on missiles. It was true that our missiles could be counted on your fingers, that their quality was not all one could hope for, and that the tasks they could perform were limited—but Father regarded the future with optimism. He prepared for a dramatic reduction in the armed forces. If the country were to straighten up, it was essential to remove that weight from its shoulders.

A reduction in the armed forces promised a great deal. But, as always, Father considered the main capital to be the working hands of healthy, industrious young people, able to accomplish much in both agriculture and industry. And if, in addition, you had the technology! Father asked for an accounting of how many trucks, tractors, and prime movers were standing idle in armories.

The numbers presented were simply staggering. The "emancipation" of the military became a priority. It was not the easiest task. In those days everything, even small items, was still designed for the military.

Father had to squeeze the specter of war out of the pores of the state organism, to shake it out of the cracks, a very difficult process. His attempts to reduce the army and the production of military equipment were viewed almost as treachery.

By the beginning of May the decree on a further reduction of the armed forces had become cluttered with details and transformed from a political declaration into a healthy bureaucratic document. It awaited a final decision. A great deal, if not everything, depended on the visit to Britain. The emissaries returned saying that peace would continue.

In his office on Staraya Square Father awaited the latest versions of the decree, which had been prepared in his absence. He thought they were too limited. The military complained. He had to revise them himself. At last, a final figure was decided on: one million two hundred thousand men, even slightly more than Father cited in January. But it had taken a lot of work. Together with the previous year's reductions, the armed forces were shrinking by more than two million men. However, the actual strength of the armed forces was not specified at the time.

They met to announce the decision on May 15, the day that the prime minister of the French Republic, Guy Mollet, arrived in Moscow on a state visit. For the first time since the start of the Cold War a Western political leader of that rank was welcomed in Moscow. The "Spirit of Geneva" warmed no less than did the spring sun.

In Geneva the invitation had been accepted by Prime Minister Edgar Faure, but in those years French premiers lasted in office only a few months. It was his successor who was greeted at Vnukovo Airport. The negotiations with Guy Mollet went well. Father described him as a reserved person and a sober statesman.

As in Britain, the main item on the agenda was the Middle East. The revolutions under way there worried the French as much as they did the British. It was only much later that Paris became reconciled to the inevitability of the process of decolonization. Blood had to be spilled in both Africa and Asia before the French reached a sober appreciation of developments.

Guy Mollet followed Anthony Eden's example in trying to convince the Soviet leadership to adopt at least a neutral policy. But there he ran into a brick wall. The Soviet-French declaration referred only to the balance of forces that had emerged in the region, calling for prudence and for solving disputes at the negotiating table, not by force of arms.

Meanwhile, events in the region were taking their course. Evacuation of British forces from Egypt was completed by the middle of June. Soviet leaders sent Colonel Gamal Abdel Nasser a telegram warmly congratulating him on his election as president of the Republic. Egypt was transformed from Farouk's kingdom into Nasser's republic. A high-ranking Soviet delegation, headed by newly appointed minister of foreign affairs Dmitry Trofimovich Shepilov, a rising star in Father's entourage, traveled to Cairo to take part in the national festivities.

TITO'S VISIT

Moscow was preparing for the arrival of Josip Broz Tito. He was expected in early summer. His visit put an end to the many years of confrontation, mutual recrimination, and even attempts to kill the strong-willed Partisan leader. A great deal had changed in Yugoslavia during the months following Father's first meeting with Tito. We recognized that a socialist society was being built there.

However, academicians of Marxism frowned: self-administration, workers' councils, the absence of a monopoly in foreign trade. None of these elements fit into the ossified framework of their concept of orthodoxy. They wrote notes to the Central Committee, but lacked the will to skirmish with Father openly. His reasoning was simple. Yugoslav property was nationalized and there were no capitalists, so that means they are "ours." The orthodox Marxists had strong support; far from all members of the Central Committee Presidium welcomed the rehabilitation of yesterday's "renegades." However, only Molotov argued with Father openly. In his heart he could not accept Yugoslav socialism and continued to view its leaders as traitors to the working class.

Tito's attitude toward Molotov was no better. He wanted nothing to do with him. Father's disagreements with Vyacheslav Mikhailovich also multiplied with every passing day. Their relations deteriorated sharply after the return of our delegation from London. In discussing the results of negotiations, Molotov attacked Father for relegating Bulganin to a subsidiary role, thereby, in his opinion, unjustifiably reducing the status of the chairman of the Council of Ministers. Besides, the Presidium had appointed Bulganin, and not Khrushchev, leader of the delegation. Father immediately went on the offensive: he had saved our position by defending our principles, and there could be no second thoughts based on protocol. The argument became heated and threatened to turn into a serious conflict until Bulganin himself calmed the situation. He said that he and Father had agreed on who and when each would speak. The storm subsided, but left its mark on Bulganin's mind.

Rumors of conflicts in the Kremlin leaked through its high walls, and for a long time "informed Moscow circles" gossiped about something unusual that had occurred.

And now, on top of that, a visit from Tito. Father proposed that the positions of first deputy chairman of the Council of Ministers and foreign minister be held by two different people. He nominated Shepilov as foreign minister. Father thought highly of him. He thought that Shepilov possessed initiative and ingenuity—important qualities in the field of diplomacy—and, in addition, Father respected his exceptional intellect and ability to carry out policies independently (in contrast to his predecessor), not just to follow instructions and directives. Father felt that Molotov completely lacked any independence of thought and that his main qualities were stubbornness and intransigence. Shepilov would probably have risen to high positions if not for his blunder in June of 1957, when he joined the "mighty" majority at the last moment, after it seemed that Father's fate had been decided. As it was, he has gone down in history as neither here nor there, as someone with the longest name: "Shepilov-who-sided-with-them."

Our own "orthodox" communists were echoed by the "real" communists who had emigrated to the Soviet Union from Yugoslavia after 1947. Some of them sincerely believed in Stalin; others hoped that if Soviet forces invaded Yugoslavia they could catch a big fish in the muddy waters. Such a development was considered far from fantastic at the time. Then they would seize power in Belgrade. Father's initiative undoubtedly threatened not only their ambitious plans, but their carefree existence under the Cominform's wing.

Father didn't know how to get rid of them. The Yugoslav émigrés had become a real headache for him. Over the years since the late 1940s they had grouped together and established an extensive propaganda network. A radio station broadcasting to Yugoslavia "exposed" the bloody crimes of the Tito-Rankovic "clique," while newspapers issued from Moscow calling for the overthrow of the "fascist regime." Now the hundreds of fighters working on this ideological front were irrelevant. They were not about to give up, and they demanded that the sacred struggle against Titoism continue. They found many sympathizers in Moscow. Father understood that relations with Belgrade would always be strained as long as this source of tension existed. But what to do?

He conceived the idea of reconciling the émigrés with Tito, of obtaining a pardon for them and sending them home peacefully. No doubt the project seemed a fantastic one, but Father believed in it and decided to carry it out. He immediately ran into difficulties, however. The émigrés didn't want to leave. Some of them were afraid, some resisted out of principle, and some simply enjoyed their carefree existence in Moscow. The "refuseniks" were headed by General Mihajlov. A few agreed to Father's plan, but then only in case of a complete pardon and assurance of safety at home. Tito was also not at all eager to be given such a present. He had no doubt that these people would remain faithful to Moscow's orders to the end of their days.

But Father still hoped for success. The day after his guest arrived in Moscow he raised the subject of General Mihajlov and his people. Tito categorically refused to meet them—if they wanted to return, that was their business. At home they would be prosecuted for treason. Father tried to persuade him, but none of his arguments had any effect. Tito was firm: they had committed crimes against the state and deserved punishment.

Father was in an untenable position: if these people remained in the USSR, trouble was inevitable. He tried repeatedly to obtain guarantees from Tito and to persuade him to meet with Mihajlov. All in vain.

Father then decided on one last effort. He ordered that a delegation of Yugoslav émigrés be sent to Kiev at the same time he was visiting the city with Tito. He had Tito run into them, literally face to face. There was no way to retreat, and the meeting took place. Father wrung agreement from Tito. Through clenched teeth, Tito promised that those who had not committed any crimes would not be prosecuted. Soon after his visit the Yugoslav émigrés lost their legal status in our country. Their newspapers and radio broadcasts had been banned for a long time, even before Father's first visit to Belgrade, and now their status as a "national group" was terminated. The émigrés were given the choice of returning home or becoming Soviet citizens. Most left reluctantly, knowing that at home they would not be greeted with bouquets of flowers. That's what happened. After crossing the border they were not arrested, but they were isolated, restricted in their movements, and subjected to nagging interrogations. Some were released, but many had to stand trial. Father tried unsuccessfully to intervene. However, he didn't want to cause additional complications with Tito, so he didn't really persist. In his heart he despised anyone who opposed his own country.

Those who remained free didn't have an easy time of it either. Traitors are not pitied anywhere.

Tito traveled to Moscow slowly by train from our western borders. At every stop he was greeted with bread and salt.[12] Yesterday's "fascist and murderer" was returning as a "true disciple of Lenin."

The Yugoslav delegation stayed for a long time—more than three weeks. At the time official visits were usually prolonged. Tito conducted negotiations unhurriedly and traveled extensively around the country. Father wanted to show him our achievements. Outwardly it seemed that relations not only between the two countries, but between the two parties—particular emphasis was laid on that aspect—were becoming almost idyllic.

But that was only outwardly. I was struck by some of Father's comments. Although he continued to speak of Tito very warmly and saw the restoration of friendship with Yugoslavia as another of his victories, I sensed that something was worrying him. Father reacted to my questions with unusual reluctance and answered unwillingly. I slowly realized that Father was coming more and more to the conclusion that Belgrade aspired to the role of some kind of alternative to Moscow as the center of the communist movement.

The Stalinists gloated. There were even some, still timid, hints that Father was an opportunist, an ominous charge in those times. He had reason to be depressed.

Father himself was not yet prepared to grasp views that differed from those held on Staraya Square. He had a long way to go before accepting pluralism. Democracy and openness had barely emerged from the cellars of the Lubyanka and were looking around cautiously, wondering if they would be sent back. Tito paraded his independence ostentatiously. His judgments of events taking place in the people's democracies not only differed considerably from ours, they were sometimes diametrically opposite. The two parties

---

12. "Greeted with bread and salt." A traditional welcome in Russia, Ukraine, and other Slavic countries.

were united by one belief alone: the world's future was socialism. But what kind of socialism? Until then the world had known only one indisputable, as people say today, model—the Soviet one. But now there was a Yugoslav one. To some people it seemed more attractive. Both the Poles and the Hungarians were at a crossroads and were examining the experience of their heretical neighbor closely.

In those years a breach of unity remained the most terrible thought-crime. Father clearly had not foreseen such a turn of events. He tried to talk openly with Tito. Though Tito assured Father of his total loyalty, he had no intention of repudiating his special path to socialism. This competition, sometimes hidden, sometimes breaking into the open, had a substantial influence on the crises brewing in Eastern Europe. More than once it brought our countries close to a break. So it was fated that Tito and Khrushchev would go down in history as both friends and competitors.

The question of Yugoslav membership in the Warsaw Pact was one of the thorniest problems in those years. At first Father had no doubt whatsoever that all socialist countries should stand together, sharing both victories and defeats. That would make it much easier to repel the enemy. However, when he expressed his ideas to Tito, he ran into a stone wall. Father was afraid of going too far and didn't try to press him. He hoped that Tito would eventually change his mind. They agreed that for the time being Yugoslavia would not join the Warsaw Pact, but that in case of war it would enter on the Soviet side. Father took Tito's caution to be a natural reaction to the unhappy events in our recent past. He judged soberly that Tito's position reflected the mood of his people. Father understood completely, but could not accept it in his heart.

I didn't understand Yugoslavia's attitude either. To my mind the world was clearly divided into two opposing camps and the choice seemed simple: you were either with us or against us. Father didn't answer my questions clearly, but I remember one of his explanations. He thought that the Americans had to some degree ensnared and bribed Tito with their assistance, especially their military assistance. Now Tito had to behave circumspectly. He might have agreed with our proposals, but then he would have had to break with the United States. So Tito was maneuvering, trying to cultivate friendship with the Soviet Union without spoiling the relationship he had established with America.

Father tried his utmost to show Tito who his true friends were. He traveled with Tito around the country and promised that he could see our latest achievements in the military field. Father was thereby emphasizing that Yugoslavia was still one of us, even though it did not want to enter into our defensive alliance. Father decided to display some new planes to Tito and his delegation at the Kubinka air base near Moscow. Until then those planes had only been seen in the air during air shows, not on the ground.

Everything we could boast of in those years was arrayed on the airfield: the 3M, TU-16, IL-28, fighters, and even the newest achievement, the TU-95 long-range bomber. I saw it for the first time. Viewers were always enthusiastic about the beautiful shape of the plane—its lean fuselage resting on long and well-proportioned landing gear, its graceful propeller blades rotating toward each other.

The day began with an air show. MIGs performed aerial acrobatics, spinning in loops, zooming low over the ground and then soaring up into the sky like candles. The program came to an end as the planes, without breaking formation, landed on the airfield. Some minutes later the pilots were introduced to their high-ranking guest.

Tito began to walk around, inspecting what was on display. Bombs and shells lay on the ground before each plane. Smartly dressed officers provided explanations. Tito listened attentively and asked questions. He didn't need an interpreter. He sized up the goods like a merchant, obviously comparing it with what the Americans had offered him. He chose. He pondered.

Father followed close behind, but didn't intrude into conversations, only smiling occasionally to himself.

Tito spent an especially long time in front of the TU-95. The bombload capacity, the flight range—all that was impressive, but did not surprise him. Other countries could boast of similar achievements. The briefing officer concluded without giving the plane's maximum operating speed. Tito asked him what it was. The officer hesitated. Tito looked inquiringly at Father: "Of course, if it's secret . . ." he began. Father interrupted him: "We have no secrets from friends." He nodded to the captain, who was standing quietly at attention: "Report." The captain drew in his breath, but said nothing. His gaze was fixed on a short, husky military officer standing behind Father, Marshal Zhigarev, commander of the Air Force. "Report," the marshal echoed. Only then did the officer say, "Its speed . . . ," but Father interrupted. He elbowed Tito and said with a laugh: "Discipline. Here I'm not in charge."

Tito laughed in turn: "We have the same situation. You and I are far away, but their commander is nearby." Those standing around laughed politely. Finally everyone quieted down. The captain, perspiring from tension, was able to continue his report: "Its speed is somewhat less than 900 kilometers an hour"—for a moment he again hesitated—"but more than 850."

The Yugoslav minister of defense, who was standing next to Tito, whispered something in his ear. Tito shook his head incredulously: you couldn't fool him. The maximum speed of turboprop planes is 650 kilometers an hour.

The officer did not respond. But Father, stung by his guest's distrust, intervened. Calling on the Air Force commander for support, he began trying to prove to Tito that they were not trying to trick him. In answer to his tirade, Tito nodded respectfully. Neither changed his opinion.

Soon afterward our guests departed. Tito and Father took their final leave of each other as friends.

THE SPY PLANES

According to tradition an impressive air show was always held at Moscow's Tushino airfield on Air Force Day, August 18, or on the nearest Sunday. Unfortunately, in August you can have rain or sun in Moscow. More than once the organizers had to postpone the show to the following Sunday, and sometimes it was postponed a second time or even canceled.

Father decided to change this arrangement. He left Air Force Day alone, but rescheduled the air show for June. As it turned out, the new arrangement didn't last long. When he tried to find money for housing and other urgent needs, Father thought of the air show. He decided that far too much money was spent preparing for it, for the numerous training flights of hundreds of planes. Although people tried to persuade him that Muscovites were used to the show, that hundreds of thousands of people came to Tushino Airfield every year, he wouldn't give in. "People will be even happier to get more city housing," he would say, parrying all objections. As a result, in the early 1960s the air shows were canceled.

But that year, 1956, the year of hope and the "Spirit of Geneva," Father proposed to invite delegations from foreign countries, including capitalist ones, to the celebration. The Americans were included.

Not everyone supported Father's proposal. His opponents, among them Zhukov, protested: "Of course, high-ranking guests won't be able to detect our secrets. They don't have the knowledge or experience. But each one will bring a whole entourage of professional and expertly trained intelligence officers. They won't miss the chance to film every detail and spread everything out for examination. And the devil is in the details."

From an intelligence standpoint they were undoubtedly correct. Americans themselves have supplied proof of that. In 1988 an American publishing house, Harper and Row, issued a book by historian Michael Beschloss titled *May Day: Eisenhower, Khrushchev and the U-2 Affair*. It investigates in detail the history of the evolution of America's postwar air espionage against the Soviet Union.

The author writes that General Nathan Twining, Curtis LeMay, and nine other Air Force officers in the U.S. delegation viewed their visit primarily as a way to obtain information on the actual state of Soviet military aviation.

President Eisenhower saw further ahead. He interpreted the invitation as a first step toward establishing mutual inspection. To be specific, he said at the time: "If they want to exchange military delegations and really see what's being done in the military field in other countries, they have to invite our officers. . . . I am very curious to find out how far the Soviets are prepared to go along the path of establishing friendly relations."

Father was thinking along very similar lines. However, he was ready to show, unlike the American president, who only wanted to look.

"We are not preparing to wage war. Let's extend our hand and demonstrate our power at the same time. We'll prove that we are equal partners, not supplicants," he declared emphatically.

The air show in Moscow on Sunday, June 23, was attended by delegations from many countries, including all the great powers, besides that of General Nathan Twining and his entourage.

It was customary for design bureaus to prepare some new aircraft for the shows, so that what appeared before the grandstands was sometimes the single experimental model of a fighter or bomber. That year the Soviet government decided to surprise foreign specialists by quantity as well as quality, especially of our heavy bombers. But Soviet heavy bombers could be counted on your fingers: about ten 3Ms and three or four TU-95s. Rather thin. So it was decided to use a trick known from ancient times.

The nine Myasishchev bombers that flew sedately over Tushino in formation of threes had hardly disappeared from view when, after gunning their motors and circling rapidly over Moscow, they reappeared over the grandstands. Over and over again. I don't know what impression the trick made on the Americans, but Father laughed infectiously when he described it that evening.

The delegations were not limited to sitting in the place of honor in the Tushino grandstands. They were able to examine the planes on the ground, as Father had intended. Afterward they fanned out to visit Moscow's various aviation clubs, schools, and factories. No particular secrets were divulged to them, but Russian cordiality and hospitality were fully on display. On June 30 they were given a farewell reception hosted by Chief Air Marshal Zhigarev, commander of the Soviet Air Force, at the House of the Soviet Army.

Father had not planned to attend, but toward evening he changed his mind. He wanted very much to satisfy his curiosity concerning the effect produced by his initiative. The reception was just getting under way, the tables groaning with refreshments, when he appeared in the spacious hall.

In those years, when we were being initiated into world civilization, we were only beginning to comprehend the complex science of etiquette. Our efforts were sometimes successful, but more often not. Hosts spared no effort to impress their guests by the size and extravagance of their receptions, especially since nothing was paid for out of their own pockets. Foreigners ridiculed the Russians, while doing full justice to the food and drink. Father decided to terminate this bacchanalia after he noticed guests efficiently whisking whole plates of appetizers and candies off tables and into large bags. Father scolded the protocol lovers at length: in the West they know what money is worth. After their receptions, the guests go home and eat dinner, but after our receptions they don't eat for three days. The amount spent on such events was sharply reduced, but resourceful officials were always looking for loopholes.

With Father's appearance the mood in the hall changed. People seemed to straighten up. Father behaved naturally, chatted with different people, joked, but kept his distance from the Americans.

When it came time to welcome the guests officially, he proposed a toast to his friend President Eisenhower, to peace and friendship. Later, although it seemed time to leave, Father lingered. He was waiting for an opportune moment to talk about missiles. Only the missiles could have been a surprise to the foreign generals. Planes wouldn't impress them, even if they performed acrobatic loops the entire day. American planes were just as good, and their array of bases was nestled right up against our borders. Missiles alone could change the balance of power. Plans called for the first tests of the R-7 to take place in about six months, but Father didn't intend to wait for the first launches. He wanted to make some use of the missile now. Leaning across the table—as far as his stomach permitted—he asked General Twining if he wouldn't like to familiarize himself with Soviet missiles.

The general was dumbfounded at this unexpected question, but quickly recovered and nodded.

"We have very good missiles," Father continued, "and we'll show them to you if you'll show us yours."

Father stopped, expecting some reaction. But the American didn't know what to say. No one in Washington had foreseen such a turn of events.

"But not now," Father continued, without waiting any longer for an answer. "It's a little early now! But we could agree on a time. And first you show us yours. We can't be the only ones to open our doors. In the meantime, you hold on to yours and we'll hold on to ours. Let's compete."

Father smiled contentedly. Now let his guests rack their brains and argue. What he said would be confirmed later on, when the R-7 was launched.

Father waited for questions. He counted on continuing the conversation, but General Twining didn't say anything. Father was a little offended by his guest's lack of response.

Returning home, Father complained about American arrogance and said they were flaunting their invulnerability.

"But it won't last long," he smiled.

Naturally optimistic, Father was not referring only to the regal missile, but to the superiority of our socialist system in general. It wouldn't be long before we would be talking with them as equals.

A few days later Father substantiated his claim. Speaking in Moscow, he announced that the Soviet Union was capable of launching a missile with a range of 8,000 kilometers. His official statement only stimulated American desire to find out what was concealed behind the "iron curtain."

The day after the reception the delegations left for home. Father's ruse with the bombers was only partially successful. American specialists rated the technical qualities of our planes rather highly, but they didn't see the Soviet bomber fleet as a worthy opponent.

As for the possibility of reciprocal acquaintance with missile and air bases in some indefinite future, the United States had other plans.

The Americans had decided that they could manage very well without Father's invitation. The U-2, a state-of-the-art, high-altitude reconnaissance plane, flying beyond the reach of planes, antiaircraft, or air-defense missiles, was awaiting authorization for its first flight over Soviet territory. The U-2 was no doubt invulnerable to guns and planes, but American claims that it was also invulnerable to antiaircraft missiles can be accepted only with reservations. The Lavochkin S-25 missile had been in service in the ring of antiaircraft installations around Moscow for several years. It possessed "an upper limit of performance of 23-24 kilometers altitude," as its technical manual stated. Work on it had been completed as early as 1952. The trouble was that a plane had literally to run into the missile. Attempts to move the missile from place to place were unsuccessful and launches were strictly limited to sites set in concrete in the ground. Furthermore, the plane had to be detected in time. So there were a lot of ifs.

The constant flights of spy planes along our coasts began right after the war. Every time the invisible line of the border was crossed, there would be another TASS protest reporting that, after the necessary measures were taken, "the plane withdrew in the direction of the sea." Everyone understood this ambiguous expression as meaning that it had been shot down. This dangerous game went on for years. Both sides got used to it.

At the end of the 1940s the Americans seized on a new idea. In those years research into the atmosphere was making considerable progress. Scientists had determined that at great heights the winds blew steadily from west to east. It was decided to put this newly discovered natural phenomenon to good use. On paper it all looked ridiculously simple: a balloon launched somewhere in Europe would fly over the Soviet Union and land in Japan or somewhere close by. Cameras, tape recorders for recording radio signals, instruments for taking air samples, and other equally essential and ingenious devices were suspended from the balloon. The balloons floated over Soviet territory. Not all these messengers reached their destinations, by any means. Leaking balloons lost altitude and landed, some in the taiga, others in fields.

Newspapers occasionally reported mysterious finds by lumberjacks or tractor drivers. Enthusiasts began looking in the woods for them, as if they were mushrooms. Some of the balloons were shot down by interceptors. But they were only, as the saying goes, "a drop in the ocean, which means very little."

Moscow reacted very sharply when this program began. The government tried everything. It arranged special exhibits of recovered equipment. Press conferences were held. It sent protest notes to countries connected in any way with launches of the balloons. It raised the question of assuring the safety of civil aviation. After all, if a plane collided with the heavy cargo of a balloon it would certainly crash and all its passengers would be killed. Nothing had any effect.

As time went on the launches stopped causing a sensation and became routine. Balloons continued to float over the Soviet Union. Sometimes Moscow protested, sometimes not. Sometimes the Americans launched a lot of them, sometimes only a few. One high point occurred during the Twentieth Party Congress, at the beginning of 1956.

Father didn't attribute much importance to flights of these balloons. He thought they were an expensive form of entertainment. Where would the wind carry a drifting balloon? Where would the camera shutters operate and what would they photograph? The taiga? Swamps? Clouds? Or an airfield? In his opinion, even photographs of military sites were unimportant. Such information is important before a war, when you are selecting targets, but in peacetime? Father didn't believe that war was on the horizon.

Although one can reason that way, the violations of Soviet borders were a painful wound to Soviet national pride. But U.S. intelligence services didn't doubt that they had the right to "peer through the keyhole"—one of Father's favorite phrases—"at what was happening in their neighbor's bedroom."

The development of a high-altitude spy plane began in the United States in 1954. By February 1955 an experimental model was ready. However, they were still a little afraid to use it.

They conceived the idea of linking it to the question of disarmament. In May 1955 the parties agreed that no arms reduction agreement was possible without effective control over its implementation. I mentioned earlier that this continued to be a stumbling block for many years. Soviet generals were outraged at the very idea of allowing foreigners into their secret sites.

Even Father didn't allow himself to go that far. He understood that inspection was necessary. But how to implement it without revealing military secrets? Father's greatest fear was that inspections would show Americans how much weaker the Soviet Union was and therefore might tempt them to launch a preemptive strike. Proposals to bomb the Soviet Union before it grew stronger had appeared more than once in the American press, and intelligence had reported corresponding Pentagon plans. Father thought that inspections should be put off until the possibility of mutual destruction would be, if not equal, then at least mutually unacceptable.

Max Millikan, of the CIA, proposed the "Open Skies" plan as one method of inspection. It would allow both parties to fly over each other's territory and photograph, if not everything they thought up, then a great deal of what we can't even imagine today. The plan seemingly offered equal opportunities to both sides. But one aspect was unclear: how would Soviet planes fly to the United States and how could the Soviet Union use any information they obtained?

The "Open Skies" plan was one of the basic proposals in a package that Eisenhower took with him to Geneva in July 1955.

The president, as always reading from a document, outlined his proposals during the daytime session on Thursday, July 19. Bulganin, inclined to compromise, offered no objection. According to him, the American plan had "certain merits" and was worthy of "further study." Father barely managed to restrain himself. He said nothing during the session, since he could hardly argue with his own prime minister in front of everybody. But the talk must have consequences: he had to make the president understand that he was dealing with representatives of a great power, not some minor state he could overawe or take liberties with.

Father decided to make use of the relaxed atmosphere of the bar where delegation members gathered during breaks in the sessions. During the cocktail hour he sought out the president. They often told each other jokes. The evening before, on Wednesday, Eisenhower had introduced him to David Rockefeller. Father embraced him with a laugh, captivated by the fact that the millionaire was a person like anyone else, and was even more modestly dressed than others who were present. Both Americans and Russians laughed heartily.

On that day Father again began in a joking tone: "You Americans think there's no democracy in the Soviet leadership, that everyone repeats the same thing. But in fact we don't always agree with each other and sometimes we even argue." He continued more seriously: "I cannot agree with my friend Bulganin, even though he's chairman of the Council of Ministers. Your proposal amounts to legalized espionage. I don't care what your motives are, but why are you trying to make fools of us? The plan is very advantageous to you. The American Air Force would get all the information it needs and we would get nothing."

Eisenhower tried to change Father's mind, but he remained adamant. We would not allow anyone to spy on us. This created a ticklish situation: the head of the delegation thought the plan deserved attention, while Father rejected it. Therefore, having become convinced that the president understood the gravity of his words, Father didn't try to argue when Eisenhower asked him, as they parted, "not to throw the idea out the window."

Father brought home an attractive yellow brochure advertising "Open Skies," which Eisenhower had given him in Geneva. Handing it to me to look over, he praised the achievements of modern technology. The photographs were indeed impressive. Taken from an altitude of ten kilometers, the first photograph showed the overall plan of a city; in the next you could distinguish houses, and in the next, cars. Finally, in the last you could make out the rather murky figure of a man reclining on a lounge chair and holding a newspaper in the courtyard of his home.

The capabilities of American photo technology made Father more certain than ever that we could not allow American planes in our skies. A reply was delayed until the end of the year, but on November 25, 1955, Bulganin sent a message to President Eisenhower rejecting the "Open Skies" plan as unacceptable and as violating the sovereign rights of the Soviet Union.

When he decided to send the U-2 over Soviet territory, President Eisenhower raised espionage to a new level. Henceforth such actions would be of concern, not only to the CIA and the KGB, which were created to oppose each other, but to the political leaders of the two countries. Any mistake or failure of nerve could lead both countries to the brink of danger.

However, in Washington they did not expect a scandal, much less a confrontation. They thought that the plane would fly invisibly, like a phantom, over the territory of the Soviet Union. The Americans were making a simple miscalculation. They thought that the Russians were not capable of making a breakthrough in the field of radar and that the most they would succeed in doing in the postwar years was to slightly improve the American and British radars sent to them during the war. Those radars were not capable of detecting targets higher than forty-five to fifty thousand feet. Surprisingly, this was the basis of the entire concept of using the U-2 in Soviet airspace. Where did I get this information? In August 1995 I, as a veteran of Soviet space intelligence, was invited to visit a small and until recently highly classified company called Itek, located in Massachusetts, which had produced and still produces cameras for planes and intelligence satellites. A conference held there was devoted to American achievements in this field: forty years have passed and long-standing secrets have lost their security classification. During the conference I talked with one of the founders of American aerial photo-intelligence (I won't mention his name), who, after recounting this history, complained about how dangerous it is to underestimate an opponent's technical capabilities.

Either because of a fondness for external effect or some other reason, the Americans timed the U-2's first flight to coincide with their national holiday, July 4, the 180th anniversary of the establishment of the United States of America. Charles Bohlen, the U.S. Ambassador in Moscow, had some general knowledge of the project, but didn't suspect that the first flight would occur at the moment when Khrushchev, as the Embassy's guest at a holiday reception, was proposing a toast to Eisenhower's health.

Of course, that's not to be taken literally, since the plane crossed the Soviet border early in the morning. Father was immediately informed, but didn't hurry to do anything. Who knew what might happen? First we needed to investigate, to weigh our actions. Therefore he, like Bohlen, revealed nothing at the reception, joked and chatted, even though he was fuming inside.

The "Spirit of Geneva" had appeared to give hope for a gradual (Father didn't nourish any illusions) transition from armed confrontation to, if not cooperation, then peaceful coexistence. Therefore such a demonstrative violation of international rules of propriety stunned Father. He said over and over again: how would President Eisenhower, a distinguished general and reputedly a man of honor, have felt if we had sent our planes over Washington or New York?

"It would have meant war," Father exclaimed heatedly.

He saw the flight as an insult to our national pride, as the demonstrative reluctance of a rich "uncle" to respect the sovereignty of a poor "nephew." He had used just that comparison in Geneva when he talked about "Open Skies" with the president. Now it seemed that the polite, smiling Eisenhower had shown his true attitude toward his partner in negotiations. Father thirsted for revenge.

The U-2 flights, particularly that first flight, produced more than shock in the Soviet leadership. They had a profound influence on subsequent Soviet policy. In Father, they exacerbated a crisis of confidence in his negotiating partner and confirmed the idea that it was pointless to negotiate with the United States, because they only understood strength. Just the week before he had proposed to General Twining that they agree on mutual inspections of missiles and air bases. And now, they deliver this slap in the face.

For a long time I was unsure whether the U-2 really flew over Moscow. If it did, it must have overcome the antiaircraft defense ring or, more likely, slipped through undetected. Otherwise Semyon Lavochkin's missiles, the Twenty-fives, which were arrayed like a solid fence around the capital and could reach an altitude of twenty-four kilometers, would have shot down the intruder. What happened? Did they miss their chance? Or did the U-2 slip through at its maximum altitude between two positions? When I asked Father, who was usually loquacious, it was like pulling teeth to get him to say anything. He only reluctantly confirmed that a plane had indeed flown over our territory, and as to where—that was now being investigated. Interceptors had not been able to reach it. Father grunted with chagrin: "The American, or whoever it was, just flew too high." In fact, no one knew which country had sent the intruder. But who, besides the Americans, would dare to do such a thing?

Heading off further conversation, Father said that nothing could be done. It was not within our power to "punch the culprit in the mug" and we would have to put up with it.

"We have to create air defenses capable of reaching that altitude—but in the meantime . . ." He let the phrase trail off.

Officers who participated in the events of those years—and are now generals—unanimously assert that the flight over Moscow was a fabrication. The intruder really did fly toward the capital, an alarm had already sounded on the air-defense ring and crews had scrambled, but the pilot didn't commit himself and turned back. A last attempt to reach it, in the area of Smolensk, was made by MIG-19s, the newest, most advanced Soviet fighters. Only a few had been built for the recent air show. Now they should prove their capabilities. But even they couldn't reach that altitude. The intruder escaped.

Some Americans say that, relying on the element of surprise, they did fly over Moscow on July 4, 1956, while others claim that there was indeed a flight over Moscow, but it was the fifth, not the first.

Grigory Vasilyevich Kisunko, one of the creators of the radar guidance system for the antiaircraft missiles installed around Moscow, thinks that radars tracked the intruder only near the border and then lost him. Soviet Air Defense could only guess what course the mysterious plane took. It was not until a few hours later that the picture of an air target again appeared on radar screens of the Moscow antiaircraft defense ring, but it was somehow fragmented. The plane was flying at the extreme range of the radars. The captain on duty reported the signal, but by the time he got through to his superiors the target had left the operational zone of the detection station. Possibly they wouldn't even have believed the duty officer, but instructions required him to photograph the radar screen. The developed film was evidence of the fact that the intruder had been there, and they had missed him.

When the country's air defense commander informed Father of the unpleasant incident, it turned out that the S-25 missile system was not yet fully operational and that the military had accepted it for, so to speak, experimental trials. In other words, the missiles in launch positions were not armed and their warheads had been replaced by blanks.

The American pilot was lucky—just as, thirty years later, a German kid was lucky. Matthias Rust,[13] the aerial hooligan, not only flew to Moscow but landed his small plane in the very center of the capital, on the Vasilyev slope

---

13. On May 27, 1987, USSR Border Guards' Day, the young German adventurer Matthias Rust violated Soviet state airspace in a Cessna light sports plane, with impunity covered a distance of about 900 miles—from the Baltic Sea coast to Moscow—and landed at the walls of the Kremlin. His flight caused a tremendous scandal and resulted in the firing and retirement of USSR Defense Minister Sokolov and the Air Defense Commander in Chief Marshal Koldunov.

of Red Square at the base of Saint Basil's Cathedral. It is very probable that U-2 flights over the Soviet Union would have ended in 1956 if there had not been such carelessness, if the air-defense forces throughout the European part of the country had been put on alert. If . . . Father was exasperated. He didn't want to listen to the marshal's excuse, that they still had to solve problems with the antijamming system. He ordered them to end interdepartmental wrangling and make the missiles operational. But the target did not reappear over Moscow. The Americans did not dare to fly there, nor over Leningrad, where the U-2 had turned on the way home during its first flight.

After interpreting the photographs made, evidently the CIA properly evaluated the military capabilities of the air-defense ring around Moscow, as well as the one then being constructed around Leningrad, and decided not to take the risk.

Probably Kisunko has finally revealed the truth. Unlike the military, he wasn't concerned with the "honor of the service." Furthermore, "his" radar detected the target.[14]

What I remember most in connection with that U-2 flight is how reluctant Father was to send a protest note to the U.S. government. All his injured pride resisted this, as he thought, humiliating act. He thought that something like this couldn't have happened by chance and that the Americans were now chortling over our impotence. A protest note would only add to their pleasure.

On the other hand, he understood that we couldn't act as if nothing had happened.

Before the ink on the note was even dry, before it had been handed to the U.S. ambassador, the flight was repeated. On the next day.

The note had to be rewritten to provide new details. It was not delivered until July 10. It noted in particular: "According to fully confirmed data, on July 4 of this year, at 8:18 A.M. Moscow time, a twin-engine medium bomber of the American Air Force departed from the American occupation zone in West Germany, flew over the territory of the German Democratic Republic and entered Soviet air space at 9:35 A.M. in the area of Grodno from the direction of the Polish People's Republic. The plane violated the air space of the Soviet Union, following a course which took it over Minsk, Vilnius, Kaunas, and Kaliningrad, penetrating up to 320 kilometers into Soviet territory and spending one hour and thirty-two minutes over it.

"On July 5 of this year, at 7:41 A.M. Moscow time, a twin-engine medium bomber of the United States Air Force appeared . . . and at 8:54 A.M., it entered the air space of the Soviet Union in the region of Brest from the

---

14. G. V. Kisunko, *The Secret Zone* (Moscow: Sovremennik Publishing House, 1996), pp. 379–81.

direction of the Polish People's Republic. The plane violated Soviet air space, following a course which took it over Brest, Minsk, Baranovichi, Kaunas, and Kaliningrad, penetrating 150 kilometers into the territory of the Soviet Union and spending one hour and twenty minutes over it. That same day another twin-engine bomber of the U.S. Air Force encroached upon Soviet airspace and flew a considerable distance into the Soviet Union. On July 9 of this year there were still more intrusions by American planes into the airspace of the USSR."

This was followed by grave warnings. They were the reason for Father's bad mood. He was imagining the smug smiles on the faces of officials reading these words, who probably knew there was nothing we could do. No mention was made of Moscow or Leningrad. It was bad enough without admitting that the enemy's plane had flown over both capitals!

On July 12 the Soviet government submitted a protest to the U.N. Security Council concerning the violation of its sovereignty.

President Eisenhower became concerned about the growing activity of the CIA. He seems not to have been very happy about these flights. He summoned Allen Dulles and forbade further flights over Soviet territory without his personal permission. Though reluctant, he repeatedly yielded to pressure. The CIA couldn't seem to live without new photographs taken over Soviet territory.

In November 1957 Eisenhower authorized another flight. At the time it was indistinguishable from previous or later ones. It acquired importance only afterward. On this occasion Francis Gary Powers took off on his first reconnaissance mission. He needs no introduction. His flight path took him over airfields of the Soviet strategic air forces and the secret test site of Kapustin Yar. Then, after circling over the Ukraine, he was to return home. The flight proceeded without incident until it was over Kiev, when antiaircraft artillery fired at the plane, but without effect. The shells, their charges set to go off at maximum height, exploded far below the plane.

This barrage, which reminded people of the recent war, caused a lot of talk in Kiev. Rumors, gradually acquiring new and improbable details, spread throughout the country like circles in the water. When Father was told of what had happened, he strictly prohibited opening useless antiaircraft fire.

"So as not to disgrace ourselves and not to cause panic," he explained morosely.

Meanwhile, everything possible was being done to bring down the insolent intruder. Father considered it a matter of honor.

Immediately after the confusion that occurred on July 4, 1956, Father summoned everyone who might be able to do something: Mikoyan, Pyotr Dmitriyevich Grushin, Tupolev, Pavel Osipovich Sukhoi, and other designers of interceptors and antiaircraft missiles. The meeting was devoted to one subject: how to deal with this misfortune. All these years we had said repeatedly that our borders were inviolable, and now see what's happening! They fly as they want, where they want and when they want! What most worried Father was whether the intruder could carry an atomic bomb. If that were the case, we were virtually defenseless. Specialists categorically rejected that idea. Tupolev explained that although he had not seen a silhouette of the plane and had no data aside from the plane's altitude, speed, and to some extent the duration of its flight, we could be certain that we were dealing with a structure built at the very edge of what was possible. In such a case, carrying capacity was calculated in grams and even the slightest excess weight would come at a high cost, primarily in altitude. Therefore it could not carry any substantial payload. In his opinion, the plane was reminiscent of his prewar monoplane, the ANT-25, built specially to set a record for nonstop flight. That was the plane that made the sensational flight from Moscow across the North Pole to America in the 1930s. At the time the plane had to have very long wings in order to stay in the air, in the style of a glider, leaning into the wind.

In technology there are no miracles; the American plane must resemble a dragonfly: a very narrow fuselage and long, thin wings. The maximum weight it could lift would be a camera, and not a big one at that. Tupolev thought that the military were also mistaken in thinking that the plane had two engines—a second engine would be an inexcusable luxury, superfluous weight. It had only one engine, asserted Andrei Nikolayevich. When we saw the actual U-2, it turned out to be exactly like the picture drawn by this great designer.

The entire Soviet air-defense system was geared to shooting down massproduced bombers flying at about the speed of sound and at an altitude of ten to twelve kilometers. Interceptors and antiaircraft missiles were planned with these parameters in mind. Now reference points had changed, or, rather, new ones had been added. Artyom Ivanovich Mikoyan and Pavel Osipovich Sukhoi, both designers of interceptors, were optimistic, and thought the challenge could be met. But it would take time: three to four years of intense work. Engine-builders confirmed their predictions.

This didn't satisfy Father. To put up with this humiliation for four more years! He asked them to try to find a faster solution to the problem.

Several weeks later Mikoyan suggested trying to reach the intruder by means of an acrobatic trick. Planes would fly at their maximum speed and then launch themselves upward by utilizing their accumulated energy. In aviation this maneuver is called exit onto a dynamic ceiling and is not considered especially difficult. However, no one had ever tried to use it in air combat. Luck would be more important than skill in this case, since a fighter plane is almost unmaneuverable in the stratosphere. Two grains of sand would have to meet in the infinite skies. Since there could be only a single attempt, the likelihood of success was judged to be low.

Marshal Yevgeny Yakovlevich Savitsky, commander of air-defense aviation, became enthusiastic about this breath-taking maneuver—about such a battle in empty air, where wings barely support a plane. A dashing fighter pilot, whose daring and courage had made him famous during the war, Savitsky was convinced that this fantastic plan would work and persuaded Father that it was feasible.

Father grasped at this straw. They mapped out a program for making a corrective adjustment on interceptors. The best pilots started training. The maneuver was performed several times, but without achieving its goal. U-2 pilots apparently failed to notice the acrobatic tricks being performed below them. The method I've described did result in setting altitude records. These were widely publicized, perhaps with the hope of frightening those insolent Americans.

At the meeting described above, the most confident speaker was Grushin, a general designer of antiaircraft missiles. His design bureau already had plans to build a mobile missile that could reach that altitude. However, the problem was that the higher the altitude, the more accurate the hunter had to be to reach the intruder.

The U-2 flights did a great deal of harm, most importantly by casting doubt on hopes for speedy and effective disarmament negotiations and by seriously undermining any initial confidence in our partner. The "Spirit of Geneva" lasted only one year. Mutual distrust revived. A freeze set in.

TESTING

THE AFTEREFFECTS OF THE SECRET SPEECH

The subject of Stalin gradually disappeared from the press after the Twentieth Party Congress. Not much earlier, on March 5 and December 21, special articles about the leader, signed by academicians, had been published in all the newspapers. Now a sinister silence surrounded his name, but forces awakened by the Congress began to work.

At Home

They erupted in Georgia. Although the Georgians had suffered as much as anyone under Stalin, they perceived Father's speech as a personal insult. On March 5 their displeasure spilled onto the streets, a reaction to the total silence on the anniversary of the leader's death. Students were the first to act. They decided to correct the authorities' "omission." Thousands of demonstrators carrying flowers headed toward the monument to Stalin in the center of Tbilisi. In reply to the panicky call from local authorities, Father advised restraint. He hoped that the students would, as he put it, "kick up a row and then calm down." They didn't. Demonstrations continued the next day. Encountering no resistance, they gradually gained strength. On March 8 about ten thousand people gathered around the Georgian Central Committee building. They demanded that flags and portraits of Stalin be hung in the city and that newspapers publish articles appropriate to a day of mourning. Father again decided to retreat, but that only added fuel to the fire. On March 9 the crowds grew to eighteen thousand people. A meeting began. Speakers demanded that the decision of the Congress be revised and that Stalin be put back on his pedestal. But one of them, Revaz Kipiani, went even further, proposing that Beria be rehabilitated and Khrushchev replaced. Some called for Georgia to leave the USSR. No action was taken against the meeting's participants.

Some of them headed for the House of Communications, where the radio center was located, to broadcast their appeals.

Another group went to the railroad station, where they threw rocks at the departing Moscow Express, broke windows in the train cars, and shouted, "Russian dogs!"

The demonstrators were not allowed into the radio station, which was guarded by a reinforced KGB unit. Seven people were killed and fifteen wounded. The attack halted.

When Father was informed of the tragedy, he realized that the use of force had been unavoidable. Tanks were sent to the city, followed by motorized infantry and units of the Ministry of Internal Affairs. Two more people were killed while order was being imposed. The KGB arrested thirty-eight of the most active instigators of the disorders, as Serov described them in his report. Twenty were sentenced, some for "hooliganism," some for "participation in mass disorders" and "igniting interethnic dissension." The sentences were mild compared to those under Stalin. Kipiani received the maximum, ten years imprisonment.

Naturally, at the time I didn't know all of this. I only heard echoes of the tragedy being played out. When I pestered Father with questions, he reluctantly confirmed: "The students in Tbilisi didn't go to classes, attacked a train, broke windows." He got some photographs out of a folder and showed them to me. They had been sent by Serov. I remembered the train that had arrived in Moscow the previous day, with jagged glass fragments in its gaping windows. He didn't want to discuss what had happened and said only that such upheavals don't subside easily, that we had to show self-control and determination and not allow emotions to run wild. He thought that, with time, Georgia would return to normalcy. For that, he very much counted on the newly appointed first secretary of the Georgian Central Committee, Vasily Pavlovich Mzhevanadze, a former general and commissar. Father knew him well from the front and considered him a Georgian in name only and therefore not infected by nationalism.

In addition, the Presidium of the Central Committee decided to appoint a Georgian to a prominent, though not key, position in Moscow. The choice fell on the Presidium of the Supreme Soviet, and Mikhail Porfiryevich Georgadze, who had worked as deputy chairman of the Georgian government, replaced Nikolai Mikhailovich Pegov as secretary.

In the Near Abroad

Father's speech also propelled forces outside the Soviet Union into motion. While the West saw only a sensational piece of news, the words spoken about the tyrant's crimes meant just as much in the people's democracies as they did in the Soviet Union. There too, despicable trials, similar to the Moscow trials of 1937, had taken place.[1] Some leaders, such as László Rajk and Rudolf Slánsky, had perished and others, like Władysław Gomułka and János Kádár, had landed in prison. Their places had been taken by their accusers. Now events were taking another turn. Changes proceeded differently in each country: in some the tension was relieved by confessional speeches and a relatively peaceful replacement of leaders who had compromised themselves, while in others there were grave crises.

Father followed events closely. He was most worried about Poland and Hungary. The situation in Poland became increasingly unstable after Bolesław Bierut's death.[2]

In Poland Stalin's name was associated with many bitter memories. These included the Ribbentrop-Molotov Pact, signed on the eve of the invasion of Poland, the anonymous graves of Katyn, and the crushing of the Polish Communist Party, whose leaders perished in Soviet torture chambers. In those years I heard about Katyn for the first time.

I was staggered by the monstrous accusations, and of course I didn't believe them. However, I soon realized they were true.

I happened to hear confirmation of them from General Serov, an authoritative source who had very vehemently denied the accusations. It was a topic he didn't mention in Father's presence, but for some reason he dropped in one day while Father was away. At the time everyone was disturbed about Katyn. Rada's husband, Aleksei, in some connection I no longer recall, asked the general how they could have missed it.

Ivan Aleksandrovich reacted angrily, I would even say painfully, to the question. He started to make caustic remarks about the Belorussian Chekists,[3] who in his opinion, had been unforgivably careless.

---

1. The reference here is to the period of "Stalinist consolidation" in the Soviet bloc, as communist leaders perceived as having "nationalist" leanings were purged by those more faithful to Stalin's Soviet Union. Thus, in Hungary László Rajk was executed on questionable charges in October 1949, and his chief adherents were similarly executed or imprisoned in 1950. János Kádár came into conflict with the Stalinists and consequently was expelled from the party, jailed (1951–53), and allegedly tortured. In Czechoslovakia, Rudolf Slánsky and thirteen others were arrested on fabricated charges (of being Zionist agents—Slánsky and most of his codefendants were Jewish), and tried before a party kangaroo court in November 1952. Eleven of them, including Slánsky, were sentenced to death and executed. In Poland, Władysław Gomułka was—on Stalin's orders—accused of a "nationalist deviation" in 1948 and eventually he was arrested and imprisoned in July 1951. Both Gomułka and Kádár were rehabilitated in 1954.

2. Bolesław Bierut, the Stalinist who was among Gomułka's chief accusers—and who replaced him as party secretary.

3. "Belorussian Chekists." A "Chekist" is an agent of the political police (NKVD, MGB, KGB), so named after the acronym of the Bolsheviks' first secret police organization the *Chrezvechanaia komissia*, CheKa. The NKVD massacred some five thousand Polish officers (who had been Soviet prisoners of war during the period of the Hitler-Stalin pact) in the Katyn forest, near Smolensk, in western Russia.

"They couldn't cope with such a small matter"—in a fit of anger Serov let the cat out of the bag. "There was a lot more in the Ukraine when I was there. But not a thing was said about it, nobody found even a trace."

He broke off and started talking about something else. No matter how hard Aleksei Ivanovich tried to return to the "hot" topic, the general said nothing else.

What I heard wouldn't sink in. "So it's true," I thought, my head throbbing.

I didn't try to question Father. The secret I had learned by chance seemed so terrible that I was instinctively afraid to mention it.

All this information, which had been concealed for years, came out into the open and lay between our countries like a stone.

Immediately after the Twentieth Party Congress Father was confronted by the first crisis provoked by his revelations. During the last ten days of March the Central Committee of the Polish United Workers' Party held a plenary session in Warsaw to elect a new party leadership and set out landmarks for the future.

Father writes:

> After the Twentieth Congress clouds began to gather over Poland. Hungary followed Poland. After Bierut's death I went to Warsaw, where a Central Committee Plenum was being held, as the authorized representative of the Central Committee of the Communist Party of the Soviet Union.
>
> I myself was not present at this plenum, so that the Soviet Union would not be blamed for interfering in the internal affairs of the Polish United Workers' Party. The sessions were very stormy, and during them Central Committee members expressed dissatisfaction with the Soviet Union. I heard this from my closest contacts in the party central committee.[4] We weren't happy about it, but we viewed this display of democracy as a positive sign. However, some time later there were more and more events that caused us serious concern.
>
> The plenum . . . elected Comrade Ochab to be first secretary of the Polish United Workers' Party.

Father described him as an honest person, but weak and incapable of making the basic changes in policy that now seemed unavoidable.

Then, on March 21, 1956, Alexander Zawadski became chairman of the State Council and Jozef Cyrankiewicz became chairman of the Council of Ministers.

> We had very good personal relations with Ochab. I respected him, and by his external qualities he deserved that respect. He was an old communist, who

---

4. NSK is probably referring here to Alexander Zawadski.

had passed through the school of Polish prison. He was himself, it seems, from the working class. At first we thought that he was a person worthy of trust.

After his election as first secretary we talked with him, and during our conversation I asked: "Why are you keeping Gomułka in prison? When I talked with Bierut about it, he said that he didn't know why he was in prison or what crimes he was accused of. Perhaps you've considered releasing him?"

When Father said this the Twentieth Congress was already in the past. But those who had signed arrest warrants yesterday were in no hurry to change. Ochab hoped that he could get by with cosmetic changes. That was his chief mistake. Either he simply didn't grow into his position, or else he was too worried about his own fate—not without cause, as the future would soon show.

Ochab began to argue that that was impossible. And Gomułka wasn't the only one sitting in prison—Spychalski was there, Loga-Sovinsky was there, and Klishko also, I think.[5] A lot of people were in prison. That bothered me, and I couldn't for the life of me understand why they were being held. I talked with almost all members of the leadership of the Polish United Workers' Party, and they all argued that . . . these people must not be released.

I remember those days well: both the anxious departure for Warsaw and Father's gloomy mood when he returned. He couldn't understand how they could keep innocent people in prison. The longer it took for justice to triumph, the more painful the process would be for society, and it could simply turn into a tragedy for the leadership.

He tried very hard to make Ochab understand. Unfortunately, without result. Father writes:

Some time later Ochab left with a delegation for China. . . . When they returned from China via Moscow I had another talk with Comrade Ochab. By that time Comrade Gomułka had already been released from prison. They had released him only under the pressure of circumstances. Ochab wasn't in control of the process that had begun in Poland; he was lagging behind. I asked Comrade Ochab whether he would object to our inviting Comrade Gomułka to come to the Soviet Union for a rest on the Black Sea coast, either in the Crimea or in the Caucasus. The climate there is better for a rest than in Poland. He said something unintelligible and left for Warsaw. I wasn't reassured by this, but was even somewhat worried.

---

5. Marian Spychalski, Zenon Kliszko (note Polish spelling), and Loga-Sovinski—Polish communists, and allies of Gomułka.

Father met Gomułka for the first time in 1944, when Stalin sent him to Poland to help restore Warsaw's devastated economy. Gomułka wasn't getting along with the republic's leadership even then and stood in opposition, as it were. He made a favorable impression on Father. Now Father wanted to revive their old acquaintance. He understood that once out of prison, Gomułka would not be in the shadows for long. Ochab justifiably viewed Gomułka as a competitor, a leader stronger than he was. For that reason he both delayed releasing Gomułka and then did everything he could to prevent him from resuming his relationship with Father. Their meeting took place only at the height of the crisis, under dramatic circumstances.

Hungary followed Poland.

I've spent some time thinking over how I should write about the stormy events of the second half of 1956. A substantial reappraisal has occurred. At the time people spoke of counterrevolution in Hungary, but today we refer to a national uprising and missed opportunities. We thought then that we were helping the people of Hungary overcome their enemies. Now our interference in the bloody events in Budapest is called the crushing of a national movement. Imre Nagy has been transformed from a counterrevolutionary leader into a national hero. I decided to leave everything as it was in my notes. My intention is not to investigate the processes as they actually occurred, but to attempt to describe the events as I understood them then and as they were understood then by those on the Soviet side who participated in them.

And so, about Hungary. The struggle for power, for influence in the party and the country, between Mátyás Rákóczy and Imre Nagy had its roots deep in the past. Father frankly acknowledged that he didn't understand the sources of their conflict, and he was skeptical of the labels Rákóczy applied to Imre Nagy. Both had been party members for some decades and both had worked in Moscow, in the Comintern. The sources of their rivalry lay somewhere there. They had both enjoyed Stalin's confidence, but no one knew which one he had preferred.

Father spoke of how Rákóczy had vehemently resisted Stalin's pressure to expose "enemies" in Hungary. Although no one absolves Rákóczy of responsibility for the unlawful acts that occurred, since the highest-ranking official is responsible for everything, Father pointed to the minister of defense, Mihály Farkas,[6] as the one who really inspired and carried out the

---

6. Among the leaders of the Hungarian Socialist Workers Party, Mihály Farkas was known for his accurate interpretation and zealous implementation of the Moscow party line. He became head of the secret police under Mátyás Rákóczy's Stalinist party leadership, and is usually portrayed exactly as the senior Khrushchev saw him: Beria-like in his clinging servility to the top leader and brutal in his implementation of the leader's policies. However, by most accounts, fingering him ahead of Rákóczy as the real inspiration of the Stalinist repressions of 1948–53 in Hungary would be something of a stretch.

crimes committed during Rákóczy's rule. He considered him the "Hungarian Beria." Other incidents, even though minor, indicated that Rákóczy had not been close to Stalin. Once, for example, MGB agents reported to Stalin that Rákóczy was telling people that the all-night dinners that Stalin gave at his dacha, a few of which Rákóczy had attended, were little more than drinking bouts in which Stalin not only drank heavily but forced others to as well. The Great Leader could not forgive Rákóczy for rashly describing his way of passing the time as drunkenness. Stalin took characteristic revenge. When Rákóczy visited Stalin in Georgia, Stalin forced him to drink until he passed out.

After March 1953 events in Hungary developed by fits and starts. Imre Nagy rose to power in 1953, only to be crushed less than two years later, in April 1955, when a plenum of the Hungarian Workers' Party Central Committee, under pressure from Rákóczy, removed him from all his posts and expelled him from the Politburo and the Central Committee on a pretext typical for those times: "because his views diverged from those of the Central Committee." Then, after the Twentieth Party Congress, it was Rákóczy's turn. No one cared to remember whether he had participated in or resisted the excesses of Stalinism. He was in charge. He was responsible.

Power slipped increasingly from Rákóczy's hands. Prisoners were released from jail. They described soul-chilling insults and tortures endured by prominent communists like János Kádár, as well as by people with no connection to politics and government.

In Budapest numerous large and small groups began to form, mainly among the intelligentsia, where people discussed what had happened and tried to explore sources and reasons and find out who was guilty. These groups coalesced to form the so-called Petofi Circle. The best men of letters, truly the intellectuals of the Hungarian capital, named their organization after the revolutionary poet who had given his life and talent to his homeland. The Petofi Circle's influence grew by the hour. The most frequently heard questions were: Who is guilty? What is to be done?

The authorities were unprepared for this turn of events. On July 7 the party central committee passed a decree condemning the Petofi Circle's activities. Once upon a time that would have been sufficient, but given the temper of the times, it did little more than arouse general indignation. People openly demanded an accounting from Rákóczy and those close to him.

It's always difficult to talk honestly about one's sins, and a hundred times more difficult if you've considered yourself to be without sin as recently as yesterday. The Central Committee plenum that convened on July 18 in Budapest tried to save face. They discussed the further democratization of political life. Most of all, they talked about holding elections. They acknowledged that it was essential to vote for individuals, in election districts, and not by list. They admitted mistakes had been made with respect to the National Front. There was talk of the third five-year plan, about miscalculations, about reforming the planning process. And then they finally took up the real reason for their meeting—and voted to dismiss Comrade Mátyás Rákóczy from all his posts. However, the reasons they gave had nothing to do with past misdeeds, but rather his age and the state of his health. They did mention that he had made mistakes associated with the cult of personality, but only vaguely. Mikoyan was present at this plenum, just as invisibly behind the scenes as Father had been that spring in Poland. However, witnesses, in particular Vladimir Kryuchkov,[7] who was working at the Embassy under Andropov, claim that Rákóczy was not even in Budapest that July, and so of course was not present at the plenum. In June, on "the strong recommendation of Moscow," he had asked for a six-month leave and had left for "rest and medical treatment" in the Soviet Union. As it turned out, he never came back.

Rákóczy was not allowed to take up residence in Moscow, but was told that he could go to Krasnodar Territory. "The climate there is better for you," the newly declared refugee was informed.

Father gave me a different explanation. He didn't want to meet with this political figure, who had compromised himself. The less he was around, the better for everyone.

At the July plenum they elected a new Politburo, which included those who had suffered under Stalin, Rákóczy, and Farkas. Among them was János Kádár, just released from prison. Erno Gero replaced Rákóczy. He suited everybody. A balance of forces was established between the members of the old politburo, who were really too weak to keep power, and the newcomers, who were still too weak to take it.

In his description of Gero, Father writes: "The theoretical work of political education of the masses was his main interest. Both by inclination and character, he was most suited for theoretical work. . . . Gero headed the Central Committee . . . but such a tumultuous time began that Gero couldn't cope any longer. They didn't recognize him as the leader."

The advent to power of such a weak figure largely determined the dramatic development of further events. Gero's first report to the plenum as first secretary included a reference to the Petofi Circle, which was the subject of particular concern. It was justifiably viewed as a kind of center that was attracting opposition to the Central Committee. Everyone was talking about the Petofi Circle in those days, some people hopefully and others with fear and anger. Its appearance was evidence of the birth of new forces and new relationships. However, new times had not yet arrived. The opinions ex-

---

7. Vladimir Kryuchov, "KGB SSR. Lichnoye delo," p. 46. Moscow, "Olymp" AST, 1996. Vladimir Kryuchov, Chairman of the KGB during the Gorbachev era, was a close colleague of Yury Andropov and in 1956 was working at the Soviet embassy in Budapest.

pressed at meetings of the Circle had a seditious ring. The Soviet ambassador in Budapest, Yury Vladimirovich Andropov, had strong misgivings about its activities, as did departments of the CPSU Central Committee.

Father agreed with them, but he thought that prohibitions would not achieve very much: it was up to the Hungarian Central Committee itself to seize the initiative and lead the process of renewal. Whether or not the new leaders could do so would quickly become apparent. And events quickly proved that they could not. They did not have the strength to ban the Petofi Circle outright, and because they had forgotten how to communicate, they failed to attract the popular support they needed. Their slogans were out-dated, their credibility was nonexistent.

The plenum decided to place all blame for their crimes on Farkas. His extreme cruelty was common knowledge. Men whom he had only recently tortured with his own hands were returning to government positions.

While they had merely shown Rákóczy the door, they expelled Farkas from the Central Committee and asked the party presidium to strip him of all responsibilities and titles. The main accusation against him was involve-ment in the persecution of old communists. A week later a session of the Republic's National Assembly voted to remove Farkas as minister of defense.

However, these belated decisions had virtually no effect on further devel-opments. The party didn't manage to buy itself off with one sacrifice. New crimes were being uncovered, one after another. The party was not ready for a dialogue. On the contrary, it closed ranks and began to defend the security services, with their bloody past. By doing so, the party accepted joint respon-sibility for the tortures, murders, and other crimes.

Could they have acted differently in Budapest? It's hard to say. Too much was interwoven: the security services, the Central Committee, and the gov-ernment. And each one was dreadfully afraid of exposure.

Even today, more than thirty years later, the inhumanity of that period causes one to shudder. Then, the blood was still wet. Victims and butchers faced each other. Yesterday's prisoner, now rehabilitated, could simply run into his jailer on a Budapest street. People thirsted for revenge.

Much of what happened at the July Central Committee plenum had never happened before. For the first time they dismissed a first secretary without accusing him of being an enemy of the people, without putting him behind bars.

For the first time men released from prison, yesterday's enemies of the people, joined the highest echelons of the party. This decision received a cautious reaction in Moscow—after all, these people had been humiliated and who knows what they might think up. But again it was decided not to interfere.

Imre Nagy had not yet appeared on the scene, but his influence was felt everywhere.

All these developments caused surprise and concern in the CPSU Central Committee. It was proposed that Mikoyan, who was in Hungary at Father's suggestion (his visit there was now announced officially), continue on to Yugoslavia. In Moscow no one doubted that even though Tito was not directing developments in Hungary, he knew exactly what was going on there. They hoped to work out a joint policy with him. If that were possible, of course.

Father counted heavily on relations with Tito. After their recent meetings, our apologies and their friendly embraces, he felt fully justified in counting on reciprocity. Father's personal relations with Yugoslav leaders had their ups and downs. He felt enormous respect for Tito and considered him wise, though somewhat haughty and self-indulgent. Father had even warmer feelings for Aleksandar Rankovic, whom he valued as an honest and open comrade. On the other hand, he had a guarded opinion of Koca Popovic, the state secretary for foreign affairs.

After a final meeting at the Yugoslav Central Committee, where he received assurances of their firm friendship with our country, Mikoyan traveled to Brioni to meet Tito, but he did not succeed in reaching an agreement with him.

Father was increasingly worried about the way the situation was developing. The quiet after the storms of June was unlikely to continue. He decided to meet with Tito himself. At home we were totally unprepared for this decision and learned of it only a few days before he left. At the end of October newspapers reported that N. S. Khrushchev was leaving for a vacation in Yugoslavia.

Father took none of the family with him, not even Mama. He said that the situation in the world was not favorable for traveling and that anything could happen. His words caused even greater concern. Trouble seemed to hang in the air.

Each day Father's secretariat told us the latest news. The next day these reports appeared in newspapers. They were reassuring: meetings, talks, even invitations to go hunting. The talks with Tito went well and left nothing to be desired. Mutual understanding seemed complete: "Our common goal is the building of a communist society. . . . We must preserve monolithic unity." It all ended on that note.

Wishing to thank Tito for his hospitality and continue political contacts, Father invited him to spend a few days in the Crimea. By chance the Hungarian leaders were to vacation there at the same time. Tito and they flew to the Crimea together, as old friends. At the end of September Father and Tito met with the Hungarians: Erno Gero, János Kádár, and Istvan Hidas. Surprising as it may seem, they really were in the Crimea on vacation and spent a rather long time there. They seemed not to have noticed the ominous developments in their country. The meeting left an unfavorable impression on Father.

Before returning home the Hungarian leaders visited Moscow and met with Suslov and Mikoyan. On behalf of the Central Committee Presidium, Suslov and Mikoyan had been concentrating on Hungarian party problems for some time. The Hungarians assured them that they were fully in control of the situation and there was nothing to worry about.

Though a great deal is vague after all these years, I remember well Father's words to the effect that Gero didn't entirely understand the complexity of the situation, that he saw what he wanted to see, rather than what really existed, and that he was too good-natured.

Father considered the situation in Budapest very dangerous and he expressed his opinion to the Hungarian comrades frankly. Tito supported him. But Father didn't know what Tito said to the Hungarians behind his back.

During those days I continued to ask him about the situation in Budapest. October was approaching. The sense of menace grew stronger. Father often didn't reply. It seemed that he simply didn't know what to say. When he did answer, his words were not encouraging. He was extremely worried that Gero would not succeed in maintaining control over developments. Even so, Father didn't expect the situation to deteriorate so rapidly or so badly. Perhaps he had been misled by his own hopes for a favorable outcome.

THE SUEZ CRISIS BEGINS

A crisis developed in the Mediterranean at almost the same time as those in Poland and Hungary. Clouds gathered around an Egypt that was no longer obedient to the West. On July 15 Egyptian president Nasser visited Yugoslavia. He and Tito had formed a special relationship. Both were pursuing a policy independent of those of the world's most powerful leaders.

Father had not yet fully defined his relations with the new Egyptian leaders. Their nationalistic slogans struck him as very questionable. On the other hand, Father understood that the liberation movement in the Middle East was only beginning and that it was gaining strength. He was very much interested in seeing who would come to power and which regimes would be established near our borders. For the time being, Britain and France, with their military bases, were dominant in the region. If they were "smoked out," as Father put it, the situation to the south would change radically. Moreover, if the Arabs were to lean in our direction, we would no longer need such a large army in the Caucasus and there would be a real opportunity to reduce defense expenditures even further.

The West began to rock the boat. On July 21 the United States withdrew its promise to help Egypt build the Aswan Dam. So much hope rested on that grandiose project that the threat of cancellation could not fail to bring even the most refractory government to its knees.

However, only a month earlier, during Shepilov's visit to Egypt, Nasser had secured a promise in principle of Soviet economic assistance. Because of our years of experience in the construction of hydroelectric installations, Father thought that we were capable of building any dam. Moreover, he reasoned, the dividends to be expected would far outweigh the expense. Our help was not a present. Like any merchant's, our money would earn interest. Our assistance would be of immense value politically. In addition, we would show the world what we had achieved in the science and technology of construction. The capitalists would be displaced. Most important of all, the peoples of the Middle East would see with their own eyes who their real friends were. I heard him reason this way more than once that summer.

On July 27, after returning from Yugoslavia, where Tito had conveyed our additional assurances of support, Nasser announced to a vast gathering in Alexandria that the Suez Canal would be nationalized, a step that would change the country's history. Revenues from the canal would henceforth be earmarked for construction of the dam. More than that: in answer to the West's refusal to extend credit, he made public the Soviet Union's promise of economic assistance. Everything was turned on its head. Both they and we had to reformulate our policies without delay. The West looked feverishly for a way to hold on to its position, while Moscow was unsure how to support the ally that had unexpectedly fallen into its hands.

Initially Father was cautious. When I asked why we were doing nothing to help oppressed peoples in their struggle against the imperialists, he replied that we could not offer them direct military assistance. We had no common borders. Besides, we were not sure about the true position of the Egyptian leadership. Perhaps they were simply posturing in an effort to extract even more money from the West.

Meanwhile, our government decided to support the Egyptians morally by issuing a statement about the nationalization of the Suez Canal. In it we condemned the aggressive and colonialist position of the Western powers. We proclaimed that people fighting for their freedom could rely on the Soviet Union. Holding similar instructions, Shepilov left for a large international conference on the Suez Canal that convened in London on August 16. It was attended by all the principal countries interested in assuring normal navigation through the canal.

The week of negotiations ended without result. The (now former) Suez Canal Company decided to exert some pressure on the Egyptians: it recalled all its harbor pilots who worked there. All but one or two left, and almost no one was left to steer oceangoing ships through the narrow and complex waterway, so traffic came to a halt.

In August Father left as usual, with the family, for a rest in the Crimea, at the government dacha near Livadiya. Days were spent on the beach from morning to night, except for meals. His aides spread out any papers that required immediate attention on a round wicker table, under a cloth umbrella. A white telephone for long-distance government communications, the so-called VCh (high-frequency) phone, lay nearby. After reading a document, Father often picked up the phone and asked to be connected with Moscow. At the time there was no automatic long-distance dialing. After discussing some problem, he sometimes made a decision on the spot.

It was there, at the beach, that Father received reports from Shepilov at the London conference, as well as word that ship traffic in the Suez Canal had come to a halt. At first Father didn't react. But the next day, after reading TASS dispatches about the Egyptians' problems, he conceived the idea of sending our specialists, Black Sea pilots from Odessa, to Egypt. He telephoned First Secretary of the CC Ukranian Communist Party Aleksei Illarionovich Kirichenko in Kiev. Kirichenko had been the Odessa provincial committee secretary for a long time, and Father expected that he could offer qualified advice. In those years Father thought of Kirichenko as his devoted supporter and had high hopes for him. Aleksei Illarionovich enthusiastically endorsed the idea and said he was prepared to send all the Black Sea pilots to Port Said and Suez, even by the next day.

Father was fired up, as the saying goes, and immediately set out to implement his idea. He called the Merchant Marine Ministry and spoke with the minister, who agreed that we could send our pilots and said they were fully as qualified as the British and French. Though they were not familiar with the Canal, he was confident that they would quickly master its features. Father talked to Bulganin, along with some others whose names I no longer remember. There were no objections. They decided to send the Egyptian government a proposal and begin the operation at once if the reply was positive, which Father did not doubt.

Father thought that, aside from everything else, our pilots would not only display their ability, training, and skill, but would show the whole world that our country no longer intended to stay in its shell. The Soviet Union would demonstrate that it was ready to play an active part in world politics. Cautiously, to be sure.

The pilots, Father emphasized, must go as private individuals employed by the Egyptian department in charge of the canal. Officially, the Soviet government would not be involved, although Father was confident that no one would have any doubts about its position.

The pilots of Odessa, Nikolayev, and Kherson soon left for their distant destination. Father followed their activities attentively and often talked about them. He took a childish glee in our success in "thwarting" the imperialists.

The Suez Canal administration demonstratively fired all of its employees as of September 14. Dulles resumed consultations with his British and French colleagues on September 20.

Father was in Yugoslavia at the time. The Suez crisis was one of the "burning" questions the two leaders discussed. Tito urged Father to support Nasser. The chance to acquire a favorably disposed partner to our south was undoubtedly tempting, but there was considerable risk of being drawn into armed conflict. While appreciating his host's reasoning, Father did not commit himself during their meeting on Brioni.

POWER STRUGGLES IN POLAND

For Father, events in the Mediterranean increasingly receded into the background as, virtually at the same time, the situation in Poland and Hungary became more dramatic.

Poland was the first to show signs of instability. During the previous month the power struggle had absorbed all of Ochab's attention. He was unsuccessful in fighting off the supporters of Gomułka, whose position had strengthened. A crisis was inevitable and imminent.

Resentments that had accumulated over the years finally came to a head. Father tried to lower the pressure. He made a proposal designed to alleviate Poland's economic situation: Polish payments to the Soviet Union for credits granted earlier would be postponed for four to five years. This was not an easy decision to make, since in those days we were counting every kopeck. However, the Poles paid no attention to the bilateral agreement signed on September 23. Passions were running too high, and the skirmishing in Warsaw was approaching a showdown.

Father had regarded Ochab with obvious mistrust since their brief meeting that summer, when Ochab awkwardly avoided, if not fled from, discussing the question of inviting Gomułka to our country. Not a trace remained of his former warmth. At home the change did not go unremarked. Every report from Warsaw received special attention. Only echoes of the disturbing news reached me. Father himself later described some details of the events of those days. Other facts came to light during his friendly chats with Władysław Gomułka and Josef Cyrankiewicz when our families met on vacation in the Crimea.

The Soviet Embassy in Warsaw was the source of most of Father's information on the situation in Poland. By the middle of October its reports sounded quite alarming. In his memoirs, Father writes as follows: "We learned through our ambassador that tumultuous events were taking place in Poland, that the Poles were vilifying the Soviet Union and were all but preparing a coup to put people with anti-Soviet tendencies in power."

On October 16, the same day Anthony Eden and Selwyn Lloyd arrived in Paris, a session of the Politburo of the Polish United Workers' Party was held in Warsaw. It was devoted to the convocation of the party central committee's Eighth Plenum. There was an unusual postscript to the official report on the session which provoked a storm in Moscow: "Comrade Władysław Gomułka took part in the Politburo session." That could only mean that power was passing into other hands. It was not the change that angered Father. He favored having a strong individual in the top position. However, he was extremely upset that for once Moscow had not been consulted on a "personnel matter" and that everything had been done, as it were, in secret.

A report from the Embassy poured fuel on the fire. It concerned an article by E. Forgan in *New Culture*, the Polish Writers' Union newspaper, where the author speculated that the slogan "Proletarians of the world, unite!" might be out of date. By the standards of the time that sounded more than seditious. Father flew into a rage. On top of everything, he received panicky embassy reports about a wild outburst of anti-Soviet emotions in Warsaw. Father decided it was time to, in present-day terminology, send the Poles a message. On October 19 *Pravda* published an article unambiguously titled "Anti-Socialist Articles in the Polish Press" and entirely devoted to the ill-starred slogan.

The Polish party plenum convened that same day. That was a coincidence, but a significant and somber one. According to information obtained by our Embassy, the session began with speeches sharply critical of the CPSU Central Committee, of the Soviet Union, and of its policy toward Poland in general. Speakers demanded that Ochab resign and Gomułka replace him. This report was credible, since it came from Alexander Zawadski, chairman of the State Council of Poland. He asked that it be relayed to Moscow, personally to Comrade Khrushchev, as quickly as possible. Father reacted at once:

> I called Warsaw and spoke with Ochab. I asked whether the information we received from our Embassy was correct.
>
> "Yes, a stormy session of the Central Committee is going on and these matters are under discussion."
>
> Our Embassy reported that anti-Soviet feeling was growing rapidly in Poland and that Gomułka's rise to power was being supported by anti-Soviet forces.
>
> I told Ochab that we were very concerned about what was happening (the Presidium of the Central Committee of the CPSU was meeting at the time and we had already talked over the situation). . . .
>
> I said: "We would like to come and talk with you."
>
> Ochab replied: "And we would like to consult with you. Let me suggest it and call you back."
>
> Ochab soon called back and said: "We would ask you not to come until our Central Committee session is over."

That might seem to be the right answer, if you trusted your interlocutor. At the time we didn't trust Ochab. Naturally, if we had trusted each other, it would have been better not to go, not to exert pressure. But since we didn't trust Ochab, when he turned down our request we were only more disturbed—it reinforced our suspicion that an anti-Soviet mood was growing and that it might spill over into actions. Then the situation would be very difficult to put right.

We told Ochab that we wanted to come anyway, and we said openly that Poland was of great strategic importance to us. A peace treaty with Germany had not yet been signed, so our troops were stationed in Poland on the basis of provisions resulting from the Potsdam Agreement. They guarded communication lines that crossed Polish territory. We said all this to Ochab and told him that we would be arriving in Warsaw.

We talked things over and then selected a delegation, which consisted of me, Mikoyan, Bulganin, and someone else.

It happened October 19, 1956. Father's unexpected departure for Poland produced a real shock at home. In the first place, during those years any trip abroad, even to a friendly socialist country, was unusual. It usually coincided with some important date, was announced ahead of time, and accompanied by thorough preparations.

This time Father called from his office at the Central Committee: "Collect my things, I'm flying to Warsaw." No explanations. His things were quickly collected, since the process of preparing Father for business trips had been perfected over the years until it was automatic. A special small suitcase stood in a specially assigned place, where it would be filled with enough white shirts for a daily change, underwear, an electric shaver, and slippers. That was practically everything. An extra suit was put in a garment bag bought for this purpose in Geneva, so that it wouldn't get wrinkled.

Furthermore, Father wasn't going alone, but was accompanying Molotov and Bulganin. Or were they accompanying him? The combination undoubtedly pointed to one thing: there was a calamity, a major one.

Father came home for only a moment. Without replying to questions, he just muttered: "We have business there" and went upstairs to change.

He didn't touch the glass of tea with lemon that had been set out for him. He came downstairs, went immediately into the hall, put on his dark gray topcoat and matching hat, glanced at us with a distracted air, nodded in farewell and left. All his thoughts were already on Warsaw.

A tense silence prevailed in the house. A few hours later his aides called from the Central Committee: "He arrived safely and has started work." No details. What could have happened there to cause such a hurried departure?

We were dying of curiosity.

Both the preparations and flight were hurried, nervous. Father later described his emotions: they had not obtained Ochab's agreement to the flight to Warsaw or received permission to fly over the Polish border. As far as they knew, they were departing at their own risk. And risk causes apprehension. According to reports from our Embassy, which could not be dismissed after the unpleasant telephone conversation with Ochab, a counterrevolutionary state coup was possible. In that case, uninvited and unauthorized guests crossing the border might be met by interceptors. Father thought such a development unlikely, but in view of the panicky reports he could not entirely exclude it.

Fortunately, events developed in a way far different from that imagined from the Embassy's windows. The meeting couldn't be called friendly, but talks proceeded in a businesslike manner. However, both sides had to demonstrate restraint and composure in order not to allow . . . what? Something that the panicky reports sent to Moscow might have provoked. They might have cost dearly. Many years later Father recalled:

> We flew to Poland. When we landed, we were met at the airport by Ochab, Gomułka, Cyrankiewicz, and other comrades. The atmosphere was very chilly. We were really quite worked up, and right after saying hello at the airport I told them that we were dissatisfied with what had happened:
>
> "Why is all this going on in the name of anti-Sovietism? What is the reason for that? We—both I personally, and other comrades—always stood for freeing Gomułka." When I had talked with Ochab earlier, I intended that Gomułka visit the Crimea and we could talk there. He would get medical treatment, and we would clarify our position in the matter of his release at the same time.
>
> Ochab flared up and said: "Why are you complaining to me? I'm no longer secretary of the Central Committee. Ask them."
>
> Pointing to Comrade Gomułka, he made no effort to hide his displeasure.
>
> I think that what I said when Ochab was on his way back from China had put him on guard. Maybe he thought that we wanted to overthrow him and put Gomułka in his place. In our hearts we were not Ochab's opponents, but by then he had proved to be a weak leader and Gomułka was a better choice. We thought highly of Gomułka.
>
> From the airport we went to the Central Committee. . . . The discussion was very stormy. . . . The conversation was crude, undiplomatic.

Mutual distrust had grown very deep. Moscow's envoys suspected the Poles of plotting somehow to leave the socialist community. By the standards of the time, that automatically meant joining the hostile, imperialist, pro-American camp. In those difficult years a small country could not remain independent in the stormy area between the two blocs. The shaky balance of power would be disrupted. A weakening of one camp automatically meant the strengthening of the other. The simple diplomatic rules followed at that time simply would not allow it. Father's memoirs continue:

> We . . . demanded an explanation of the actions we felt were directed against the Soviet Union. At the time the Polish armed forces were commanded by Marshal Rokossovsky. . . . When we arrived, during dinner, we received word from Rokossovsky that troops under the Ministry of Internal Affairs had been deployed and were assembling near Warsaw. . . . This increased our distrust and even caused us to suspect that the actions of the Poles were deliberately directed against the Soviet Union. Demands were already openly being made that Rokossovsky be sent away to the Soviet Union, since you couldn't trust him; he is not a Pole and is pursuing an anti-Polish policy.

A decision had to be made, but the wrong move could cost dearly. His associates pushed Father to take the simplest way out: to take decisive actions, to use force. He hesitated and resisted, but he was gradually beginning to lose confidence that the matter could be solved within the framework of consultations and inter-party negotiations.

The Poles, for their part, didn't trust our so-called delegation. Every move by the Muscovites provoked suspicion and seemed full of sinister meaning. Why did they come here? Why are they constantly whispering with the minister of national defense? What are they plotting?

Marshal Rokossovsky, "recommended" by Stalin for the top military position, irritated the Poles. He was like a red rag to the bull. They were correct in supposing that at a moment of decision he would follow Khrushchev's orders, not Gomułka's, that he would serve Russia, and not Poland.

"I'm being shadowed, and I can't take a step without its being reported to the minister of internal affairs," Rokossovsky complained to Father.

Father said that Alexander Zawadski played a positive role at the time. Father trusted him, and he served as a connecting link in those troubled days between the members of the Polish Central Committee, with their turbulent emotions, and the members of the high-ranking Soviet delegation, who were prey to dire forebodings. After each session he visited Father, discussed what had happened, and persuaded him that there was not, and could not be, any basis for concern that Poland was going to repudiate the alliance with our country.

Father wanted to believe him and agreed with him about some things. But then he would again be assailed by doubts.

> The wave of anti-Soviet feeling had an effect on us, although we thought that it was a residue from Stalin's incorrect policy.
>
> The stationing of our troops in Poland was a more complex problem. However, our right to station them originated in the Potsdam Agreement

and was therefore sanctioned by the authority of international law. We had to maintain troops in Poland to secure rail and road communications with our troops in Germany. We decided to defend that right.

I asked Rokossovsky:

"Tell me, Rokossovsky, how are the troops behaving?"

This was a time when something irrevocable could have happened. Therefore, it is particularly useful to examine how, in 1956, we approached the brink and how we stopped at its very edge.

In answer to Father's question, Konstantin Konstantinovich Rokossovsky, Marshal of the Soviet Union and Marshal of the Polish Armed Forces, former Stalinist prisoner and war hero, replied: "Not all Polish troops obey my orders now, but . . . there are units which would fulfill them.

"I am a citizen of the Soviet Union, and I think that steps have to be taken against those anti-Soviet forces which are elbowing their way into the leadership. It is vitally important to preserve our communications with Germany across Poland."

Indeed, the Poles had every reason to distrust Rokossovsky.

How did events unfold? Father described what happened: "Our forces in Poland were not large. Konev had come to Warsaw with us. At the time he commanded the Warsaw Pact forces and we needed him. Through Marshal Konev we ordered that Soviet troops in Poland be put on the alert. Some time later we ordered one tank division to move toward Warsaw. Konev gave the order and reported that the troops had left and the tank division was moving in the direction of Warsaw."

Marshal Rokossovsky issued similar orders to the troops who were still faithful to him.

Naturally this did not remain unnoticed by the Poles. Warsaw undertook feverish preparations for defense. The job of trying to avert the blow fell to Gomułka.

> There was a stormy, nervous session. We were arguing with the Poles. I saw Gomułka coming toward me. He said, very nervously: "Comrade Khrushchev, your tank division is moving toward Warsaw. I ask that you order it to stop and not enter the city. In fact, it would be better if it did not approach Warsaw. I'm afraid that something irreparable could happen."
>
> Gomułka both asked and demanded in a very nervous manner. Gomułka is an emotional man, and bubbles of saliva even appeared at the corners of his mouth. He spoke very sharply.
>
> . . . Zawadski informed us that anti-Soviet agitation was being carried on among the workers in Warsaw. . . . Factory workers were arming. . . . A very bad situation was developing.
>
> We were, in reality, prisoners.

It's awful to think of what might have happened if someone else had been in Father's place, someone with a different character, someone who would have preferred to stay in peaceful Moscow, not push into the thick of things, who would make decisions based on information reaching him through various channels. And that information was unequivocal: in Warsaw anti-Soviet (therefore, in the logic of those days, and not those days alone, antisocialist) forces were thirsting for power. Measures had to be taken before it was too late.

A great deal has changed since that time, and the Soviet Union has sunk into oblivion, but measures have stayed the same—tanks. Who would ever have pardoned us for spilling still more Polish blood? Fortunately, God was merciful.

At last Father and Gomułka found a way to bring the conflict to an end:

Gomułka again took the floor, and he really won me over with his speech. He spoke passionately:

"Comrade Khrushchev, I ask you to stop the movement of your forces. Something irreparable will happen! Do you suppose you're the only one in need of friendship, in this case of the Polish people? I declare, as a Pole and a communist, that Poland has a still greater need of friendship with the Russians. . . . Do you think we don't understand that, without you, we could not exist as an independent state? Everything will be all right. Just don't allow your troops to enter Warsaw. Then it would be hard to control the situation."

We took a recess. Our delegation, along with Rokossovsky, met and talked things over. I was convinced that we could have confidence in Gomułka. I had believed him earlier. Despite his hot temper and abruptness, his words were sincere. . . .

I said: "Comrades, I trust Gomułka. I trust him as a communist. It's difficult for him. But if we express confidence in Gomułka, if we withdraw our troops and give him time, then he will gradually be able to cope with those forces which are now taking the wrong positions."

Everyone agreed, and we ordered Konev to halt the advance of Soviet troops on Warsaw. Then we explained that those troops had not been moving toward Warsaw but were performing military maneuvers and, having completed them, had now halted at the designated point. Of course, no one believed our explanation, but they were pleased that the troops had stopped. . . . The Poles understood that we could reach an agreement. The entry of our troops into Warsaw could really have been irreparable. It would have caused such problems that it's hard to imagine where we would have found ourselves.

I think that Gomułka saved the situation. . . . The rest was of secondary importance. We had no objection to Gomułka's being appointed first secretary.

There was no further need for us to stay in Warsaw. We said our farewells and flew home.

Father returned home extremely tired and drawn, but in an elated mood. All he said at home was: "Gomułka has replaced Ochab. He is a true communist and it looks like matters in Poland are on the mend."

THE HUNGARIAN CRISIS

On October 16 newspapers published a letter from Imre Nagy and a decree of the Politburo of the Central Committee of the Hungarian Workers' Party reinstating Imre Nagy in the party "because, although he did commit some political mistakes, they did not justify his expulsion." The November 1955 decree expelling Imre Nagy from the party was annulled. Then Rákóczy was on top, but now times had changed.

Personally, Father had nothing against Imre Nagy. They had known each other for a long time. He remembered ferocious arguments between Rákóczy and Nagy on the peasant question back in Stalin's day. Even then Nagy was considered a "revisionist." He opposed general forced collectivization, favored a limited amount of freedom for the peasant and was inclined toward the NEP. It reached the point of insults, and Rákóczy accused Nagy of being a traitor, but Stalin only laughed. Apparently he had his motives: quarrels inside the Hungarian leadership suited him and he didn't believe in Imre Nagy's "apostasy."

Probably there were reasons why Imre Nagy was not among those who caused Stalin apprehension. He didn't want to have Nagy executed along with the Hungarian leaders who had displeased him, including László Rajk and many, many others. However, Stalin didn't openly come to Nagy's defense when he was expelled from the Politburo in 1949 for right deviation. Stalin didn't say anything, but he didn't allow Nagy to be touched.

When Stalin died, Imre Nagy delivered an emotional speech about the Great Leader. He continued to quote him loyally, and when Nagy was expelled from the party in 1955 he accused his opponents of conducting an anti-Stalinist policy.

In those years Father proclaimed a policy of "nonintervention" in the course of events in friendly countries. Of course, this "nonintervention" was of a special kind and bore the stamp of its time. It was viewed as a major step forward when Moscow no longer had to approve every appointment considered even slightly important. Father was inordinately proud of that achievement. He also tried, often unsuccessfully, to avoid getting involved in internal quarrels. The losing side would run to Moscow for help, while the winners tried to consolidate their successes there as well.

Of course, any instance of "grave ideological apostasy" provoked a harsh response. No one had the right to transgress orthodox doctrine. A step to the left or the right, especially to the right, meant someone was planning to desert the socialist fold. That left no room for sentiment. But still the train creaked ahead, the rusty wheels turned. The first step is the most difficult, although not the most obvious.

Imre Nagy had a lot of spare time after he was expelled from the party, which he devoted to literature. Nagy writes that unreasonable, dogmatic, excessively harsh and inflexible policies of leaders alienate and estrange people from the party, thereby doing immeasurable harm to the entire communist movement. Of course, you can clearly see here an element of personal resentment over what had happened to him, as well as to others.

Nagy continued to look for ways to improve conditions for the peasants. But within the framework of the prevailing dogmas, he did not dare take a decisive step. He reminds me somewhat of Father in that respect. They were also alike in their search for an economic structure that would reconcile the proletariat and the peasantry and would ensure harmonious and mutually advantageous progress, i.e., put an end to a system whereby cities robbed the countryside for the sake of industrialization and the peasants suffered from hunger as a result. And Father, despite all his zigzags and retreats, was moving in the same direction. For example, in 1955, while he was in disgrace, Imre Nagy called for humanizing our society. Father wrote that to surround "paradise" with barbed wire was at the very least unreasonable. However, his words date from the 1960s, when he was in retirement.

A communist by conviction, a decent man, and a realistic politician, Imre Nagy welcomed Father's decision to visit Tito first to make peace, thereby recognizing the right of various forms of socialist development to coexist.

There are other examples of similarity between policies pursued by Father and ideas advanced by Imre Nagy. One thing is apparent: in the middle of October 1956, Father did not yet consider Nagy an enemy.

On the other hand, Father saw Nagy as a person oriented toward Tito. That bothered him. In Father's eyes, the Yugoslav path to socialism seemed very dubious. There was nothing to be done about Yugoslavia, but he didn't want their experience, and Tito's influence along with it, to spread to other countries.

Father was taken by surprise when student demonstrations began in Budapest on October 23. The demonstrators paraded under slogans calling for the resignation of the Hungarian leadership and the appointment of Imre Nagy. The clap of thunder certainly did not come out of the blue. The clouds had been gathering on the horizon for a long time, but Moscow didn't expect a storm. The situation was considered tense, but no more so than in previous days.

Father came home at the usual time. He looked preoccupied, but not grim. As always, we went for a stroll. Father walked beside me silently. On our second circuit I broke the silence. I wondered how could such a thing happen in our extremely just society? I didn't define the word "just" in any specific way. It was a universal term. And what would happen next? I asked.

Father answered with annoyance: "This is all because of Gero's indecisive policies, his effort to satisfy everybody. They need a strong person, capable of taking events into his own hands."

According to an embassy report, "Nagy Imre"—Father put his last name first, in the Hungarian style—had just been appointed to head the government. In Father's opinion, he might be able to cope with the storm. All the more so, since the demonstrators had demanded his appointment. More than a decade later, Father wrote: "Nagy Imre acceded to the leadership. We hoped that if Nagy Imre became the leader he would preserve communist leadership over the Hungarian people."

Although Erno Gero was reelected first secretary of the Hungarian People's Party on October 24, the same day that Nagy was appointed, Gero was considered a political corpse.

To my question, Father replied that he was not going to fly to Budapest. "Mikoyan and Suslov are going," he said, without giving any explanation, and added: "And our ambassador there is a strong one."

Looking back, it's hard to say whether there was still a chance to save the situation and avoid bloodshed, or if events, already out of the central government's control, were following their own laws. There are as many opinions on the subject as there are commentators. It seems to me that such an opportunity still existed on the day that the delegation headed by M. A. Suslov and A. I. Mikoyan arrived in Budapest. Furthermore, if Father himself had gone, a great deal might have turned out differently. Somehow I think he would have tried to find the rope that, if pulled, would have stopped the slide toward the brink. It was very important to mark that brink clearly—the brink beyond which blood would inevitably be spilled. Father had found a common language with Gomułka, and he would have found one with Imre Nagy. So much depends on the individual at such crucial moments. Still, what's past cannot be undone.

Mikoyan and Suslov arrived late. The conflict had already spilled out onto the streets. Apparently the Embassy had not foreseen this.

Father's hopes were not realized. Imre Nagy did not act decisively and could not control the situation. Perhaps he didn't want to? In my opinion, he could not. An intelligent and gentle person by nature, Nagy tried to reconcile the irreconcilable and rejected the very possibility of using force. One has to remember that he had very little time. He did not come to power on the threshold of events, as Gomułka did, but at their crest. To a great extent, he could only record what was happening.

As Father says in his memoirs: "Nagy Imre. This man looked to the crowd and relied mainly on young kids. . . . That's what our people reported. Then Mikoyan and Suslov went there, along with some of our other officials."

Father also recorded what Mikoyan told him: "I went to see Nagy Imre. We began to talk. Suddenly a group of young boys, gymnasium students, rushed in. They were all armed. They reported to Nagy that they were doing such-and-such, had done such-and-such, and would do such-and-such. Others also came in to get arms. In a word, Nagy's support consisted of young people from secondary schools." That is what Father remembered about the events of those days.

He was probably right. It was just those young people, as Father said, who brought the new prime minister to power and they counted on him to follow them.

I don't rule out the possibility that in the first few hours and days Anastas Ivanovich was not sufficiently firm and decisive. He simply couldn't master the situation. After all, vacillation and doubt were so characteristic of him as well.

Suslov could not be relied on at all. He disliked encounters with real life, so different from theoretical diagrams. He had long before disassociated himself from organizational matters. His last active involvement in real politics had been when Stalin ordered him to organize the destruction of bourgeois nationalists in the postwar Baltic republics. He was sent there by the Central Committee as an observer—more precisely, a provincial governor—and given extraordinary powers. He was backed up by the Army, the MVD, and the MGB. He relied on them. Who knows, perhaps the experience he gained in Lithuania revealed itself in Hungary. The plan of action was generally similar.

In Budapest Suslov insisted on implementing a right-wing policy. His opinion, given to Father over the telephone, was that immediate and ruthless intervention was necessary.

I have often asked myself why Father rushed off to Warsaw at the first sign of trouble, but did not go to Hungary. It's possible that he was trying to share responsibility for any decisions more widely in view of the complex balance of forces established in the Central Committee Presidium after the Twentieth Party Congress. That would both prevent his being accused of seeking undue prominence and keep all sins from descending onto his shoulders. But I think he simply underestimated the danger in the way events were developing. Reports from Budapest, unlike the alarmed summons from our ambassador in Warsaw, did not presage such terrible shocks. At first it seemed that Imre Nagy's government, having established close touch with the Soviet emissaries, would be able to cope with the situation.

During the night of October 24–25 the Soviet Army finally intervened, but it acted together with the Hungarians, not alone. There was still a chance to control the course of events and send them in a safe direction. Just that, safe. At a time of sharp confrontation between two camps, of two forces thinking in terms of victory and defeat, only political adventurers could talk of a neutral Hungary standing outside pacts, much less of a Hungary going over to the West, to NATO. That time was still to come.

How were these events presented to the Soviet people? *Pravda* reported:

> By order of the Central Committee of the Hungarian People's Republic, the Hungarian Army, internal troops, and armed worker brigades, with the help of Soviet forces, liquidated a counterrevolutionary putsch on the night of October 24–25.
>
> The counterrevolutionary forces were defeated! However, small armed groups are continuing to operate in certain places.

That same day János Kádár replaced Erno Gero as first secretary of the Central Committee of the Hungarian Workers' Party.

In his statement, Premier Imre Nagy promised the people that after order was restored he would convene a session of the National Assembly to examine a program "encompassing important questions of interest to the nation."

Though Father sighed with relief, he was not certain the worst was over. His reading was not confined to the newspapers. So in response to my delight that the confrontation was over, he only laughed bitterly and mumbled that no one knew how events would turn out. During those days the Embassy sent Moscow an album filled with photographs of people armed with rifles and machine guns running through Budapest streets, of broken glass and bricks on the pavement and smashed store windows. Father brought the album home to show anyone who was interested, but made no comments. There was no need for explanations.

In Budapest events swept out of control—out of Imre Nagy's control, as well. Today it's hard to say which had a greater influence: the tense situation and destructive impulses of the masses, who rejected the old order and wanted revenge for its crimes and offenses, or attempts by bloodstained officials of the state security apparatus to provoke a clash with Soviet troops, to cause a bloody slaughter and then hide their responsibility behind it.

At any rate, the fraternization of Hungarians with Soviet soldiers on Budapest streets on October 25, which ended tragically, points to the latter explanation. Shots rang out near the Parliament. People were killed and wounded. It's not clear who began the shooting, which was said to have originated from the windows of homes. Father was informed that counterrevolutionaries had committed an armed act. A rumor spread among Hungarians that Russians had started it, that they had decided to use trickery, to weaken the vigilance of a rebellious people and then reveal their true face.

The next day all Budapest was out on the streets. Sympathies were changing. Hungarian troops began to join the demonstrators and new government organs began to take shape: revolutionary committees in the cities, workers' councils, on the Yugoslav model, in factories. Not a trace was left of the previous day's embraces with Soviet soldiers. The people demanded that occupation forces withdraw from the city.[8]

Father's worried look did not go away despite optimistic reports in the Soviet press that by October 25 the situation in Budapest was returning to normal, that the quiet was interrupted only by occasional forays of armed individuals, and that on the twenty-seventh the Hungarian government, reorganized under the leadership of Imre Nagy, had declared an amnesty and rebels were surrendering en masse to the authorities as a result.

Father came home from work at the usual time, not late, but on our walks he was silent and answered questions reluctantly. It was only long afterward that he talked about how he had vacillated. He brooded about more than what was happening—he was also struggling vainly to find a reason for it. First Poland, now Hungary. Of course one could blame it all on Stalin. He had violated explicit Leninist norms. If we return to them, everything will be all right. Father avoided looking any deeper.

The situation was developing unfavorably. The Hungarian government could not bring the city under control. Events were unfolding rapidly and decrees issued with Imre Nagy's signature simply registered changes that were occurring spontaneously. On the day it was formed, the new leadership stated that Soviet military units in Budapest were taking part in the struggle at the request of the government. The very next day Imre Nagy declared a ceasefire, promised to dissolve state security agencies, and demanded that Soviet troops withdraw from Budapest.

Father reluctantly agreed to the proposal to use occupation forces to bring about order. He was still counting on the Hungarian working class itself to deal with the actions of what were viewed as "a few counterrevolutionary elements." Mikoyan held the same opinion. But Suslov insisted that use of the Soviet Army could not be avoided. The initial prevailing opinion about using force changed. Though military units left the city, they halted not far away, at the military airfield being used by the Soviet Army, in full battle readiness. Moscow's emissaries moved there. Mikoyan and Suslov spent nights in military quarters and traveled into Budapest during the day.

---

8. Hungary, like Germany and Austria, belonged to the coalition of states defeated in the Second World War.

However, the Army's withdrawal from Budapest did not stabilize the situation in the least; events moved even more rapidly.

On October 30, the day after Soviet tanks withdrew, the building of the Budapest City Party Committee was looted. The hated members of state security, who so recently had inspired fear throughout the country, began to be hunted down on the streets of Budapest. In reports to Moscow they were described as political activists and innocent victims.

Ruined buildings with doors torn off and windows shattered, traces of fires, corpses lying on the streets—all were photographed. New pictures were quickly sent off to Moscow. Dispatches, coded messages, telephone calls from Budapest, all sounded increasingly alarmed. They left the impression that although "neither workers nor peasants are taking part in the clashes—they are remaining neutral," the course of events would change only if Soviet military forces intervened.

The Kremlin was almost completely in the dark about what was going on in Imre Nagy's circle. Father grew increasingly morose and began coming home late. Once we waited almost until morning for him.

In his memoirs Father painstakingly emphasizes that all decisions were made only after collective discussions in the Presidium of the Central Committee. In the aftermath of Stalin's despotism, collective leadership was considered the panacea for all evils, the symbol of a new, genuinely Leninist approach to governing the country. There is no reason to doubt that decisions were indeed made that way. However, every collective leadership has to have ideas and proposals. And there, Father was unquestionably the initiator.

He decided to act in two directions. On the one hand, officials quickly prepared a Declaration of the Government of the USSR on the bases for developing and further strengthening friendship and cooperation between the Soviet Union and other socialist countries. No one even thought it necessary to discuss this document with our allies. Besides, there wasn't time to hold discussions. In Budapest the situation was reaching a crisis. In the Declaration Father tried to dispose of Stalinist hegemonic aspirations and lay the basis for cooperation between parties possessing equal rights. Five fundamental principles were enunciated in the document, some of a general nature and others referring to a resolution of the current Hungarian situation.

Echoing the debates with Gomułka, the first point solemnly affirmed the principle of mutual benefit and equality of the partners in economic relations. Further, it proclaimed that the USSR was committed to recalling the advisers who had been planted by Stalin at all key points in allied countries: in the economy, the army, and the police. They interfered in everything. In fact, not a single decision of the slightest importance could be made without their approval. Third, the Declaration stated that the government was prepared to discuss the question of the stationing of Soviet forces on the territory of friendly countries.

I would like to add some explanations at this point. Throughout his entire career Father remained firmly opposed to stationing our troops on foreign territory. Now he felt that if our army withdrew, it would demonstrate the superiority of socialist foreign policy over the aggressive policy of the imperialists. As for the economic aspect, Father always tried to save money on everything and didn't like the fact that it cost several times more to keep our troops abroad than in the Soviet Union.

He thought that the appearance of nuclear weapons had reduced the importance of deploying ground forces into forward positions.

Plans were being made to withdraw our forces from Romania. Hungary was to be next. Plans called for a drastic reduction in the Soviet contingent there. Father was considering a substantial reduction in Soviet forces in Germany, as well as withdrawing almost all troops from Polish territory except those concerned with maintaining communications. Not everyone approved of Father's intentions. The military were especially uneasy. These projects went nowhere from the very beginning. The Hungarian uprising disrupted Father's plans. Far from leaving, our forces increased in number. Father's attempts to return to this question in subsequent years ran into his colleagues' friendly opposition. Their argument amounted to one sentence: "We must not forget what happened in 1956." However, our forces did finally withdraw from Romania in 1958.

And one other factor. In one of his meetings with Gomułka, during a vacation in the Crimea, Father brought up the subject of withdrawing our forces from Poland. He thought that after the tumultuous events that had prompted Soviet tanks to advance toward Warsaw, the Poles would be glad to get rid of Soviet divisions. Gomułka unexpectedly disagreed. He insisted that the Soviet Army remain. Father was extremely surprised. He thought long and hard about what led the Polish leadership to take this position, and finally concluded that economic considerations were paramount. The presence of our troops provided the Poles with a substantial income. In any case, the Hungarian uprising delayed the withdrawal of Soviet forces from Eastern Europe for decades.

The last two points of the Declaration related to specific questions concerning the situation in Hungary. On the one hand, we announced that we were prepared to withdraw our forces from Budapest upon the first request by the existing Hungarian government. This point was overtaken by events, since our divisions had already left the capital.

In another move, the Soviet Union agreed to negotiate the withdrawal of Soviet forces from the country, but only with the *lawful* government of Hungary.

The Soviet leadership, which had by now lost confidence in Imre Nagy, advanced the thesis (I don't know whether the idea was Father's or one of

Nikita Sergeyevich Khrushchev and the author, Sergei Nikitich Khrushchev,
in Livadiya in the Crimea, 1959.

Rada, Father, Mother with Yuliya, and Lenya. Kiev, 1929.

Father and Stalin
on the rostrum
of the Lenin
Mausoleum.
Moscow, 1935.

Father posting a list of the
foremost collective farms in the
Moscow *oblast* on the Board of
Honor. Moscow, 1936.

Father and two others break for lunch in the shade of a haystack.
Kherson *oblast*, summer 1940.

General Rodion Yakovlevich Malinovsky, an unidentified individual, and Father. Southern Front, February 1943.

General Georgy Konstantinovich Zhukov (left) and Father (center). Kiev, November 6, 1943, the day that the Soviet Army liberated Kiev from the Germans.

Father and I. Father had just returned from the front. Moscow, 1944.

Father at the oars, with Mikhayl Sergeyevich Grechukha (left) and Vasily Fyodorovich Starchenko and their wives, in an American-made inflatable boat. Kiev, 1944.

Nina Petrovna Khrushcheva, at her desk. Kiev, summer 1945.

Father, Lazar Moiseyevich Kaganovich, and Dmitry Zakharovich Manuilsky, the Ukrainian foreign minister. Kiev, 1947.

Father with Starchenko (left) and Ivan Aleksandrovich Serov. Kiev, 1948.

A polar bear cub at the dacha in Ogaryovo. Moscow, 1951.

Nikolai Aleksandrovich Bulganin (left), Father, and Admiral Nikolai Gerasimovich Kuznetsov. Port Arthur, 1954.

The state visit to China. Bulganin, Mao Zedong, and Father. Beijing, 1954.

Father and Bulganin at the railway station in Moscow, departing for the state visit to the United Kingdom. I am immediately behind Father to the left. Moscow, 1956.

Father, Kaganovich, and Bulganin. Moscow, 1956.

Father and the aircraft designer Andrei Nikolayevich Tupolev
on the train en route to Kaliningrad. 1956.

Father and Bulganin boarding the cruiser *Ordzhonikidze*
for the United Kingdom. Kaliningrad, 1956.

Sergei Khrushchev, Nikolai Aleksandrovich Mikhailov (Soviet minister of culture), Yakov Malik (Soviet ambassador to the United Kingdom), and Anthony Eden. London, 1956. It was Malik who in 1960 told Mr. Sulman, the Swedish diplomat, about the American pilot Francis Gary Powers.

Father with Aleksandr Trifonovich Tvardovsky, poet and editor-in-chief of the journal *Novy Mir*, at a reception in the Kremlin for writers. Moscow, 1958.

Father and Walter Ulbricht. Berlin, 1957.

Mao Zedong and Father.
The individual in the center is Fedorenko, the interpreter. Beijing, 1958.

Kliment Efremovich Voroshilov and Father. Behind them, Aleksei Illarionovich Kirichenko and Marshal Kirill Semyonovich Moskalenko. Crimea, 1958.

Father and Aleksei Nikolayevich Kosygin. Moscow, 1958.

Father, Marshal Malinovsky, Leonid Ilyich Brezhnev,
Mikhail Andreyevich Suslov, Averky Borisovich Aristov, Nuritdin Akramovich
Mukhitdinov, and Kirichenko. Moscow, Kremlin, c. 1957.

Father, in the uniform of a lieutenant general, and I.
The Fortieth Anniversary of the Soviet Armed Forces, 1958.

Father and Ambassador Llewellyn Thompson (the man in black without a hat to Father's left) at the site of the unfinished American exhibition. Moscow, 1959.

Father and Richard Nixon at the dacha after the opening of the American exhibition. Moscow, 1959.

Nikolai Viktorovich Podgorny (first secretary of the
Ukrainian Central Committee) and Father. 1959.

Father and Mother at the dacha, just before the visit to the United States. 1959.

On the balcony at the dacha, from left to right:
Sergei, Father, Mother, Rada, Yelena, and Aleksei Ivanovich Adzhubei. 1959.

Sergei and Yuliya Khrushchev reading on the plane during the visit to the United States. In the background from left to right: Foreign policy aide Oleg Aleksandrovich Troyanovsky, Soviet ambassador to the United States Menshikov, Akolovsky, Henry Cabot Lodge, and Father. 1959.

President Dwight D. Eisenhower and Father. 1959.

Father presents President Eisenhower with a replica of the "Lunnik" sphere
deposited on the moon in September. From left to right: Ambassador Thompson,
Vice President Nixon, Henry Cabot Lodge, Eisenhower, and Father.
The man standing directly behind Eisenhower is Secretary of State Herter.
The White House, Washington, D.C., 1959.

Father and his aide Grigory Trofimovich Shuisky, catching up on
paperwork at the Blair House. Washington, D.C., 1959.

Mother and Eleanor Roosevelt. Washington, D.C., 1959.

Mother and Mamie Eisenhower in evening gowns.
The White House, Washington, D.C., 1959. Photo courtesy of the Dalmas Agency.

A reception at the Soviet Embassy in Washington, D.C. Father is shaking hands
with the pianist Van Cliburn. Standing directly behind them are Ambassador
Menshikov and Troyanovsky. Mother is standing on the far right. September 1959.

The train to San Francisco. To Father's left are Ambassador Menshikov
and the interpreter Viktor Sukodrev. September 1959.

Father examines milk cartons in a supermarket near San Francisco. 1959.

In the cafeteria at the IBM plant. Father and Thomas Watson carrying their own trays. San Jose, 1959. After Father returned to the Soviet Union, self-service appeared in stores and dining halls.

Father at Roswell Garst's farm. Garst is standing to Father's immediate left.
Iowa, 1959. Photo courtesy of the Dalmas Agency.

Mother and Father bidding farewell in Des Moines, Iowa. 1959.

An unidentified admiral, Admiral Sergei Georgiyevich Gorshkov
(who succeeded Kuznetsov), and Father. The Black Sea, 1959.

Marshal Moskalenko, Marshal Malinovsky, Manolis Glezos, Father, and
Ivan Semyonovich Senin (the deputy prime minister of the Ukraine). I am on the left
in the white shirt with my back to the camera. Crimea, 1959.

Father, a foreign visitor, and Marshal Vasily Danilovich Sokolovsky
(chief of the general staff), in the Kremlin. Moscow, 1959.

Testing a hydrofoil on the Volga. From left to right: Father,
Frol Romanovich Kozlov, the designer of the craft (standing behind Kozlov)
R. Alekseyev, Mikhail Andreevich Suslov and Nikolai Grigoriyevich Ignatov. 1959.

Red Square, with the Kremlin in the background. Anastas Ivanovich Mikoyan,
Father, and Aleksey Illarionovich Kirichenko. Moscow, 1959.

his colleague's) that since the existing Hungarian government had not been approved by the National Assembly it could not be considered the lawful government of the Hungarian people.

This ambivalence with respect to Imre Nagy—at one point he headed the lawful government, at another only the existing government—mirrored Father's vacillations. He simply could not make up his mind whether Moscow should intervene or should allow the Hungarians to solve their problems independently. We have no evidence of serious disagreements in the Central Committee Presidium. One gets the impression that Father was given the heavy responsibility of making the final decision.

The harrowing photographs of the aftermath of the city committee's storming by the insurgents; the incipient restoration of bourgeois parties and reorganization of the cabinet on the basis of a coalition; and finally, the release from prison of Cardinal Mindszenty, who had an extremely bad reputation in Moscow—all these factors impelled Father to come to the defense of socialism.

In those days only two colors were recognized, white for allies and black for enemies. There was nothing in between. By the canons of the time, actions taken in Budapest meant that Imre Nagy's government was moving over to the hostile camp. From that time on, Father could see him only as a counterrevolutionary, an enemy. However, I have always been bothered by the thought that Father was struggling with his double, with his reflection in the mirror of history. With himself, only somewhat ahead of his time.

This is how he described his feelings at the moment decisions were made:

> Active party members and especially Chekists were being hunted down. Party committees and Chekist organizations were being crushed. People were being hanged and murdered. People were hanged by their feet, and there were also other outrages.
>
> Nevertheless, we decided it was possible to withdraw our troops from Budapest in response to the demand of Imre Nagy's government. They were relocated at the airfield. . . . But our people and ambassador were still in Budapest. We knew what was going on there.
>
> We discussed the situation in the Presidium of the Central Committee and decided that it would be inexcusable for us to stay neutral and not help the working class of Budapest in its struggle against counterrevolution. Counterrevolution was visible in many ways. Hungarian émigrés were returning, mainly through Vienna. Planes were arriving at the Budapest airport from Vienna. NATO countries were insinuating themselves, doing everything in their power to stir up trouble, begin a civil war, overthrow the revolutionary government, liquidate revolutionary achievements, and return Hungary to capitalism. Not surprisingly, that was the goal of the imperialist states. Our

aim was to support progressive movements, to help people in the transition from capitalism to socialism. But the enemies of socialism had the opposite goal, which was to liquidate socialist systems, push back the working class, strengthen capitalist elements, and have capitalism in every country.

We adopted a unanimous decision on this matter, except that Mikoyan and Suslov were absent. They were in Budapest at the time.

We wanted all countries to understand us properly, to understand that we were pursuing only international goals, not egotistical ones. Therefore, we thought it absolutely essential to consult with other parties, and primarily with the fraternal Chinese party.

From that moment on the initiative was in Father's hands. He was faced with carrying on all negotiations up until the final hour of decision. He bore the responsibility for making decisions, as well as for their consequences.

The Chinese responded quickly and sent a representative delegation to Moscow. It was headed by Liu Shaoqi, the country's second most important figure after Mao Zedong. A meeting was held the night of October 31–November 1 in Stalin's former dacha at Volynskoye. Father headed the CPSU delegation. That night he had not yet made a final decision and still hoped to avoid ordering Soviet forces to intervene.

Father gives the best account of his vacillation:

> We met throughout the night, weighing the pros and cons of whether or not we should apply armed force. We kept changing our positions. At first Liu Shao-chi said we should wait and let the working class in Hungary grow stronger. They would realize that this was a counterrevolutionary uprising and could deal with it themselves. We agreed with that. But when our talks resumed, the discussion turned to the fact that it would be difficult for the working class to deal with the problem in Budapest since some elements of it, especially young workers, had been drawn into counterrevolution. . . .
>
> We began to talk things over again, and this time we came to the conclusion that we had to provide some assistance. I don't remember how many times we changed our positions. Every time we arrived, independently, at a joint decision to use or not to use armed force, Liu Shao-chi would consult with Mao Zedong. . . . It was easy for him to call Mao on the telephone. Mao Zedong approved whatever Liu Shao-chi recommended. We finished this all-night session with a decision not to use military force. I went home.

At home Father could not go to sleep. He was tormented by doubts. He kept thinking of the photographs sent by Andropov, showing people hanged by their feet and corpses dragged through the streets. He writes:

> It was a historic moment. Should we move our forces and crush the counterrevolution, or wait for internal forces to rouse themselves and deal with the situation?

It could happen that counterrevolution would win temporarily, and then a great deal of proletarian blood would be spilled. And another factor . . . if counterrevolution wins and NATO takes root in the region of socialist countries, i.e., if it reaches into Hungarian territory, then this will be difficult for Czechoslovakia, Yugoslavia, Romania, and the Soviet Union. Nothing good will come from having a border with a country that might join NATO.

There was a lot to think over. . . . In the morning the Presidium met to talk over the subject again. I told them about our discussion with the Chinese delegation, how we had changed our position a number of times and had finally reached a decision not to use military force. However, I then talked of the possible consequences if we didn't lend a helping hand to the Hungarian working class. . . . We talked for a long time and finally decided that it would be unforgivable if we did not help. . . .

We summoned Marshal Konev, who was in command of the Warsaw Pact forces at the time. We asked him how much time he would need if ordered to crush counterrevolutionary forces and restore order.

He thought for a moment and replied, "Three days, no longer."

We then told him: Make preparations. We will inform you when to begin.

The Chinese delegation returned home on November 1. The entire Central Committee Presidium saw them off at Vnukovo Airport, where they were told of the decision to use force. Liu Shao-chi did not object. His behavior was indicative of the fact that Mao Zedong didn't want to get mixed up in European affairs. News came that same day that the Hungarian government had decided to leave the Warsaw Pact and had appealed to the United Nations for protection. This information only hardened the resolve of the Soviet leadership. The three days requested by Marshal Konev to prepare for the operation were up on November 4. Father thought that before beginning to move it was essential to gain the support of the other socialist countries allied with us. Unlike China, they were directly affected by events in Hungary. A great deal depended on their attitude, even though the decision to intervene militarily had in fact already been made.

Father believed implicitly in his obligation to help the Hungarian working class defend its socialist choice. But armed intervention was an extreme measure. It required the agreement, if not the approval, of neighboring countries. I would even say that Father wanted to clear his conscience. In this case he felt he had no choice but to intervene, unlike in Poland, where he was bluffing rather than really intending to act.

Could Father have doubted that the socialist choice was the only correct one? Who could have had such a thought? If someone could, that person was not Father. The time for doubts was still in the future. Father had devoted his whole life to the construction of a new life and now he didn't waver. He could not remain on the sidelines when the imperialists were rearing their ugly heads and threatening once again to oppress the people, the workers and peasants. And Father wasn't the only one who thought that way. I felt the same, and the people I happened to talk with did too. I can't speak for everyone. Of course, today we judge the events in Budapest differently (of course, the Hungarians judged them differently at the time). But that is today. We should not forget that no one knows how we ourselves will be judged by our descendants.

There was virtually no time left for consultation. Father had only a day and a half, at most two days. The easiest solution would have been to convene a conference in Moscow, but Father dismissed that idea out of hand. He considered it unethical to hold talks in Moscow about the intervention of our forces in the internal affairs of a neighboring state. He also rejected a proposal to meet in some other capital. While it was fairly easy to predict the attitude of Czechoslovakia, Bulgaria, Romania, and Albania, at the time Gomułka's reaction was unpredictable.

Yugoslavia's position was even less certain. It had not joined the Warsaw Pact organization and, most important, had always firmly supported Imre Nagy in the many years of conflict between him and Mátyás Rákóczy. Father counted on one factor: the new Hungarian government's sharp turn to the right and its appeal to NATO for help must have shaken Tito's faith in Nagy.

If everyone met together, the discussion would threaten to drag on. But there were only two days left! No one except the members of the Presidium of the Central Committee knew that the order had been issued and the troops had begun to move.

Father decided to hold talks separately. First he would meet with Gomułka and try to persuade him. If the Poles were obstinate, at least they would be neutralized. In any case, our actions would not come as a surprise to the Poles. That was the important thing.

It was decided to meet them at a Soviet airfield near the border, in the vicinity of Brest. There was no time to spare. Every minute was precious.

The next stop was to be Bucharest. Antonin Novotny, president of Czechoslovakia, and Todor Zhivkov, the first secretary of the Bulgarian Communist Party, agreed to travel there. The Romanian side was represented by Gheorghe Gheorghiu-Dej. The Albanians were absent. I don't know why. Perhaps in the haste they were simply forgotten.

After securing the support of his allies in Bucharest, Father intended to take the most difficult step—to try to win Josip Broz Tito over to his side. Tito was then vacationing on the island of Brioni.

Their flight left Moscow in the early morning of November 2. It was shrouded in the same secrecy as the recent flight to Warsaw. As before, the duty officer called after lunch from the Central Committee and laconically passed on Father's request to collect his things for a business trip. Again there were no details about where he was going or for how long.

Of course, we guessed the reason for the hasty departure. Father came home late, nervous and exhausted. He spent the rest of the day on the telephone, making calls to our allies. He didn't feel that he could entrust that delicate task to anyone else. Luckily, the phone connections worked smoothly.

That evening a session of the Presidium, the second of the day, approved instructions for the delegation and its composition. Father was appointed delegation leader. Molotov and Malenkov went with him, along with the usual entourage.

Bulganin had accompanied Father on the earlier visit to Poland. During their stormy meeting with Gomułka, Bulganin said hardly anything, only making brief rejoinders from time to time. Father was not pleased with him. He was not a fighter. In the new delegation, he counted on Molotov's stubbornness, if not his authority, on his position as the senior member in our party leadership. After the meeting with the Poles, Molotov was to return to Moscow and report its results to the Presidium.

Father was to continue on by plane with Malenkov, regardless of the results of the Polish-Soviet negotiations. There would be no time to rest up.

That evening Father was brief: "I'm not leaving for long, just a couple of days. First to Brest, and then to Bucharest. We have to consult with the comrades." That was all he wanted to tell us. He didn't mention Yugoslavia.

Some time before midnight, just after Father had fallen asleep, he was awakened by a call on the special telephone. Aroused, he quickly grabbed the phone. During those nerve-wracking days a call at night could mean almost anything.

Mikoyan was on the line. He and Suslov had just returned from Budapest. Anastas Ivanovich began to describe what he had seen there. Though events had become increasingly awful and unpredictable, Mikoyan still had faith in Imre Nagy and thought that a turning point might soon be reached.

Anastas Ivanovich had nothing to say that would have justified such a late night call. Events in Budapest were developing according to their inner logic. Furthermore, the decision had already been made.

Father prepared to thank Mikoyan and put an end to the lengthy conversation. As if sensing the change in mood at the other end of the line, Anastas Ivanovich began to speak faster. From emotion, his Armenian accent became more noticeable and he began talking rapidly and swallowing words. Mikoyan asserted that military intervention would be a terrible mistake, that it was premature. The decision made that day by the Presidium should be reversed or, at the very least, the Presidium should meet again and listen to him and Suslov.

"Suslov has not called me," Father interrupted, with just the faintest note of irritation in his voice. "And we've already decided."

Mikoyan continued to insist.

"It's begun," flashed through Father's mind.

He was preparing to persuade Gomułka, and now he had to start here in Moscow, with Mikoyan. He had no intention of changing his mind. There was no more room for doubts. They belonged to the past, to his previous sleepless night. Now they were part of history. The time had come to act, and every additional discussion would only result in delay and inflame the situation still further, resulting in new and unnecessary victims.

Mikoyan continued to talk. He seemed afraid to stop.

"Anastas, we won't get anywhere now, it's late," Father interrupted again. "Last night I didn't get any sleep, I was meeting with the Chinese. And tomorrow promises to be a difficult day. If you want, let's meet before my departure for the airport. We'll talk then, with clearer minds. In the meantime, calm down, think it over."

Mikoyan reluctantly agreed and said he would come by in the morning. Fortunately he lived in the house next to Father's.

After hanging up Father tossed and turned, unable to fall asleep for a long time.

It was dark when Father got up in the morning. The usual breakfast was waiting for him in the dining room. He pushed aside the plate and swallowed some tea with lemon. Without finishing the tea, he got up and, going into the next room, picked up the telephone connecting him with the chief guard on duty. The usual answer was heard: "This is Captain ———," followed by his name.

"This is Khrushchev." Father's voice was muffled. "Tell Mikoyan that I'm coming outside."

"Yes, sir," answered the Captain.

Mikoyan didn't keep him waiting. They greeted each other not coldly, but without the usual warmth. It was early, and the subject of their forthcoming discussion didn't lend itself to lightheartedness.

They decided not to go into the house and began to walk on a path along the fence. Anastas Ivanovich spoke first, repeating what he had said over the phone: "All is not yet lost. We should wait and see how events develop. But we must in no case send troops into the situation."

Father had an extremely high opinion of Mikoyan's intellect, or more precisely, his wisdom and ability to negotiate. But when it came to taking action, you needed someone with a different mindset.

Time was running out. The gates opened with a rumble and a cumbersome ZIS-110 limousine drove slowly into the courtyard. It was time to go. But Mikoyan kept talking.

"So what are you trying to achieve, Anastas?" interrupted Father.

"They're hanging and killing communists there, and you want us to sit with our arms folded and wait until American tanks show up at our border? We have to help the Hungarian workers. They are our class brothers. History won't forgive us if we are timid and indecisive."

Mikoyan didn't reply.

"Furthermore, the decision has already been made," continued Father. "We discussed everything and could arrive at no other conclusion. Do you think it's any easier for me?"

Father was silent for a moment, sighed deeply and added: "We have to act; we have no other course."

He left the path and headed toward the car, but Anastas Ivanovich drew him back.

"If there's bloodshed, I don't know what I'll do to myself!" he almost shouted.

Father looked at Mikoyan with amazement. He had never seen him like this before. But what could he say? Trying to persuade him was useless, and there was no more time. Malenkov and Molotov were waiting for him at the airport.

"Anastas, you're a reasonable person. Think it over, take all the factors into consideration and you will see that we've made the only right decision. Even if there is bloodshed, it will spare us greater bloodshed later." Father tried to reason with and calm his friend. "Think it over and you'll understand."

Father didn't finish the sentence and walked with determination toward the car. A depressed-looking Anastas Ivanovich trudged to the gate.

Father's heart ached all the way to the airport, but he had no doubt that he and the others were right. He didn't say anything to Malenkov or Molotov about the conversation. He wasn't afraid they would be influenced by Mikoyan's opinion, but he didn't want to "betray" his friend, who had opposed the collective decision of the Presidium. If he wanted to, Mikoyan could tell them himself.

In the plane Father kept thinking of Anastas Ivanovich's last despairing words. "He won't do anything," he reassured himself. In fact, Mikoyan did nothing. He accepted the party's decision.

Suslov never did call Father.

As the host, Father arrived first at the meeting place with the Poles. The session was held in the recreation and reading room of the Air Force unit stationed at the air base.

I return to Father's reminiscences:

Comrades Gomułka and Cyrankiewicz arrived. . . . We explained our point of view. . . . They listened without saying anything. We asked: What do you think should be done?

Gomułka said that he thought that military force should not be employed, even though the situation was very complex. I asked:

"But then what should we do? Now Imre Nagy is demanding that Soviet forces withdraw from Hungary."

"Don't withdraw them!"

"But then what? Hungarian communists are being exterminated. They are being killed and hanged. Should our forces just look on? . . . We have to consider carefully where this is going!"

"We still think that your forces should not be withdrawn, but neither should you order them to intervene," Gomułka continued. "You have to leave time for the government, which is taking a counterrevolutionary position, to show its true colors. Then the Hungarian working class will rise up and overthrow it."

"But how much time should we leave?" I said. "How much time will pass before it has the strength to fight back? They are killing party activists who advocate the right policies. Destroying them physically!"

After explaining our positions, we said good-bye to each other. They left for Warsaw immediately.

Unfortunately, Malenkov and Molotov are not mentioned in Father's memoirs about the negotiations. Were they silent? I never thought of asking when Father used to talk about the subject. Now there's no one left to ask.

As I've already written, Father didn't expect the Poles to directly favor armed intervention. But they didn't oppose it, they didn't categorically object to it. Actually, Father had been rather worried that Gomułka and Cyrankiewicz would to some degree support Imre Nagy's demand that Soviet troops be withdrawn. So the position taken by the Poles was a pleasant surprise. After everything that had happened, they did not reject the principles of internationalism. It was proletarian internationalism, the illusory shadow of world revolution, which provided the moral basis for the right to intervene.

That same day the Polish leaders, in the name of the Central Committee of the United Polish Workers' Party, appealed to the Hungarians to display prudence and good sense.

Father and Malenkov flew on to Bucharest, arriving in the middle of the day. The others were already there. They met, according to plan. The participants were in an anxious and nervous state of mind. Hungary's neighbors were particularly worried about their borders. Border violations had become frequent. Not everyone in Hungary welcomed what was going on in Budapest. Some people were worried about their fate and were fleeing the country. Others were looking for weapons.

Participants in the meeting were unanimously in favor of acting, and acting at once.

Todor Zhivkov, followed by Gheorghe Gheorghiu-Dej, proposed that their military units take part in the operation. Father refused: Soviet divisions would manage on their own. They were in Hungary under terms of the Potsdam Agreement and, as occupation forces, they were responsible for maintaining order, so their intervention would have at least some legal basis.

The atmosphere in Bucharest was relaxed and friendly, in contrast to the strained encounter with the Poles. Father even allowed himself to joke that in offering their forces the Romanians were following a familiar path. After all, in 1919 they had taken an active role in crushing the Hungarian uprising led by Bela Kun. The day passed in conversation. They had to fly on to Yugoslavia during the night. The weather forecast along their flight path was bad. Thunderstorms were predicted. Father was informed that they could not fly.

He asked to see the plane's pilot. A few minutes later Colonel Tsybin entered the room. He had been waiting nearby for instructions.

Father trusted Tsybin implicitly, having had many opportunities to witness his skill as a pilot.

Tsybin came in and stood by the door. Drawing himself up as far as his corpulent figure would allow and employing not quite the standard military phrase, he said: "I ask permission . . ."

Father smiled: "I hear the weather is bad? They don't want us to fly?"

"Quite right, we shouldn't fly." Tsybin broke into a smile.

"But if we have to?" continued Father.

Tsybin smiled even more broadly. "If we have to, we'll fly, Nikita Sergeyevich." Approaching, he concluded in a stern voice: "Do you order us to get ready?"

"Let's go," Father answered.

Tsybin answered briefly: "Yes, sir!" and left.

Father knew that this wasn't bravado. The pilot was simply sure of his skill. Whenever Tsybin said no, Father did not insist, knowing that it really was inadvisable.

This is how Father remembered the flight:

The weather was awful. Mountains below us. Night. A storm began. There were storm clouds all around us and lightning flashes. I couldn't sleep and just sat by the window. I have flown a lot during and after the war, but never in such terrible conditions. . . .

Malenkov turned as pale as a ghost from all the turbulence. He gets motion sickness even driving on a good road.

Their successful landing near Dubrovnik[9] didn't bring an end to the trip. They had to head out to the island of Brioni. The sea was very rough. "We

---

9. At the same airport where, half a century later, the plane carrying U.S. Secretary of Commerce Ron Brown crashed on its approach during the conflict in Bosnia.

climbed into a small boat. Malenkov lay down and closed his eyes. I became very worried about how we would get to Brioni and what shape Malenkov would be in. But there was nothing else to do."

Of course, it wasn't the sea's motion but the upcoming conversation with Tito that was making Father nervous. He always saw Tito's shadow behind Imre Nagy's back. Events in Budapest were rehearsed in Belgrade. As the crisis developed, whatever confidence Soviet leaders had in the Yugoslavs gradually waned and relations became strained and nervous. Those who had earlier "exposed" the "Tito-Rankovic clique" (and who had been quiet for some time) now raised their voices, saying "we warned you." However, as yet that was only said in an undertone in the corridors of the gray Central Committee building on Staraya Square.

"I expected that we would have to resist a more complex attack from Tito. More complex compared to our discussion with the Polish comrades." Father was worried.

They arrived at the island and docked. "Tito was waiting for us on the pier. He welcomed us very cordially. We embraced and kissed each other, to my surprise and pleasure."

Negotiations began immediately. Neither hosts nor guests paid any attention to the fact that it was getting late. Malenkov was in bad shape, but tried his best to hold up. Bouts of nausea almost prevented him from taking any active part in the conversation. For the third time in twenty-four hours Father presented our position and prepared to discuss it. However, the Yugoslavs offered no objections.

"Tito said: 'You're absolutely right. You must send in troops at once and help Hungary crush the counterrevolution.'

"He began to speak eloquently about the necessity for this action. All the arguments we had prepared, expecting him to object, went unsaid. We had even thought that we might have to leave without reaching an agreement. That would have complicated our situation even more. But now we suddenly received so much support. I would even say he urged us to act more quickly and decisively."

Apparently Tito was also worried about how events would develop. Any hope of preserving power in the hands of the indecisive Imre Nagy had become increasingly illusory. Tito never expected that communists would be removed from power, much less become the target for other measures. In that he agreed with Father. The struggle had gone beyond the framework of a conflict between supporters and opponents of Mátyás Rákóczy. Yesterday's, or more precisely the day before yesterday's (the hands on the clock in Tito's residence showed that it was past midnight), Hungarian government declaration that it intended to leave the Warsaw Pact organization had an unambiguous sound. Furthermore, Tito understood that they had come for support of a decision already made. Father had not really concealed that fact.

Father spent the rest of the night talking with Tito. Then it was time to leave. Their flight was scheduled for the morning of November 3, the last day allotted to prepare for the military operation. Father had already been informed in Bucharest that János Kádár and Ferenc Munnich had left Budapest to join the Soviet forces, as agreed earlier. They were now en route to Moscow to "discuss" a plan of action. They had not yet been told that our troops were about to intervene.

Father managed to have a nap in the plane. They flew into Moscow in late afternoon, almost evening. Father went straight to the Kremlin without coming home.

During the day and a half that Father was away from Moscow important events took place in Budapest. The government was again reorganized. It now included people openly opposed to the alliance with Moscow. It issued a stiff demand that Soviet troops withdraw from Hungary. In the meantime Konev reported that the troops were moving to their assigned positions. They had already begun to surround airports, transportation centers, and other strategically important points. The operation could start the following day. On November 3 János Kádár, now in Moscow, was becoming worried. He, a member of the government, had not been seen in Budapest since November 1. They might already be searching for him. But there was nothing he could do. To all his questions, the athletic young men accompanying him answered respectfully: "Wait, please." They themselves didn't know anything.

Finally, late that evening, the Hungarians were invited to the Kremlin. A session of the Presidium, which began when Father returned, was in progress. It was time to tell the Hungarians what had been decided. They did not oppose it. Both the Presidium and the Hungarians agreed that a new, revolutionary government would be headed by János Kádár, who had proclaimed the creation of a new Hungarian Socialist Workers' Party before his disappearance from Budapest.

However, the decision was not made painlessly. Molotov opposed Kádár's candidacy. He didn't trust the Hungarian, who had been in prison, then had joined Imre Nagy's government. Molotov preferred Ferenc Munnich, a man of proven worth who had spent half his life in the Soviet Union.

Father disagreed with Molotov. He had known Munnich well since the 1930s. Father objected precisely because he knew Munnich to be straightforward but inflexible, while from their first meeting Kádár had impressed Father as being intelligent, flexible, and articulate. Moreover, to have served time in Rákóczy's prisons didn't have the same connotation to Father as it did to Molotov.

That evening I waited for Father even more impatiently than usual. I no longer understood what was going on. The world seemed to be poised on the brink of an abyss. According to newspaper reports, Hungary was becoming a real slaughterhouse. Yesterday we had heard about the excesses of counter-revolutionary bands hunting down communists forced into hiding. Those they captured were killed right on the streets. Fascists, Horthyites, and heaven knows who else, people who had fled after the war, were returning to Budapest on planes coming from Austria.

That day's newspapers carried even worse news. Budapest radio had announced that all former members of the disbanded state security service should surrender to the authorities immediately. A little lower down on the same page there were reports of violence against communists, again accompanied by photographs. It was reported that enterprises had stopped working and the government was being reorganized. Right-wing bourgeois figures returning from the West were replacing the dismissed communists.

I kept wondering how we could put up with this and why we were not doing something. A real betrayal was going on!

I simply couldn't keep quiet. I began obliquely, asking Father where he had been. We still didn't know.

Father made no mystery of it. He said he had been in Bucharest and then continued on to see Tito, but said nothing about the purpose of the trip.

"What's going to happen?" I asked apprehensively. Weighing his words for a moment, Father snapped: "Wait until tomorrow." I could only guess what would happen "tomorrow."

I said nothing to anyone about the "secret" entrusted to me. Something would happen tomorrow. The following day everything did indeed take place. The military intervened and events took a whole different turn. Blood was spilled, a great deal of it. Konev stormed Budapest. Stormed is a high-sounding way to put it. He seized Budapest. He and Serov, the chairman of the KGB, who was with him the whole time, were awarded the highest military decorations for the operation, the Order of Suvorov, I believe. Others received medals. All participants in the operation, who were fulfilling their "internationalist duty," were for the first time equated with those who fought the Hitlerite Fascists. In my eyes they were heroes, saviors.

I sincerely approved of the intervention. It seemed to me that truth and justice were entirely on our side, that our tanks were bringing freedom, peace, and prosperity to Hungary and defending it from the forces of evil.

Serov sent Father another album containing photographs of Budapest's deserted streets: the walls of buildings pitted and cratered by bullets and shells, windows gaping or covered by boards.

The Embassy reported that the majority of the people supported the operation. Judging by Andropov's coded messages, only a handful of anticommunist intellectuals had taken an active part in the uprising. They had managed to attract some of the students to their side. The working class, especially outside Budapest, had not responded to the counterrevolutionary appeals. In some places they were neutral, in others they had been preparing to resist.

In the Embassy's opinion, the peasantry resisted being drawn into the armed struggle and had not responded to appeals to leave the collective farms. They were continuing to work peacefully.

Its conclusion: the uprising had no support among the people and its suppression would draw a positive response from a substantial portion of the Hungarian population.

The crises in Poland and Hungary exerted an enormous influence on democratic processes, not only in those countries, but in the Soviet Union as well. I can say without reservation that the rumbling salvos of weapons in Budapest constantly reverberated in the heads of the members of the Presidium of the Central Committee when they made decisions, all the way up to 1964 (after that I simply don't know).

Andropov, who was in Budapest that entire time; Suslov and Mikoyan, who bivouacked with our troops at the airfield; and Kirichenko, Kozlov, Ilyichev, and many of our other leaders, who had not been there—they were all simply traumatized by Hungary. The mere mention of 1956 often allowed them to place still another obstacle in the path toward democratizing our society.

Unfortunately, specific words and phrases have faded in my memory. But I remember that on the occasion of the strike in Karaganda, at the beginning of the 1960s, they all kept saying that harsh measures had to be adopted. Father had a different opinion. I remember vividly the sharp objections they raised whenever he spoke in favor of a further, even if only very modest, liberalization of our society. They vied with each other in scolding him: "How can you say that, Nikita Sergeyevich? Remember, in Hungary it all began with the 'Petofi Circle.' And how did it end? With bloodshed."

Father would give in. Those arguments had their effect. He would retreat. The specter of the "Petofi Circle" and its probable tragic consequences can also be seen in the notorious criticisms of the intelligentsia in the early 1960s. It provoked a natural demand that sedition be crushed in its cradle. They crushed it, and not without success. But without any benefit either.

A few words about Father's role in Imre Nagy's fate. Nagy had sought refuge in the Yugoslav Embassy, which he thought was safe and the only embassy appropriate for a communist. He did not consider it possible to appeal for assistance to the Americans, as Cardinal Mindszenty had.

The Yugoslav decision to extend its protection to the former premier put a great strain on Father's relations with Tito. Father felt himself to be deceived and betrayed, and thought Tito was playing a double game. "After all, he supported intervention, and not only supported it but urged us on," Father complained. Edward Kardelj's speech sharply condemning Soviet actions poured fuel on the fire. After that Father viewed Tito with ill-concealed distrust and hostility.

Imre Nagy's stay in the Yugoslav Embassy was a problem for Tito. He had no intention of disrupting his newly improved relations with Moscow. He therefore gratefully accepted János Kádár's assurances that Hungarian authorities would not arrest Nagy if he left the Embassy. Their assurances did not extend to guarantees of his safety and inviolability, and the Soviet side assumed no obligations whatsoever. Though they knew that a Soviet commandant was in charge of the city, the Yugoslavs did not set any other conditions. Father immediately authorized Nagy's arrest. Now Tito was the one who'd been deceived.

When I asked Father about it, he explained: "Imre Nagy presents too great a danger to be left free in Budapest. Disaffected people would inevitably begin to gather around him, and the present leadership has enough worries without that. Let him live in Romania until the situation stabilizes and the government becomes stronger and more stable. The same way Rákóczy lives here with us."

There was no talk of the possibility of a trial, much less of Nagy's physical extermination. "Time will pass, then we'll see," Father said vaguely.

Time did pass. The situation in Hungary stabilized. The people who had come out on the streets met various fates. Some were put on trial, others pardoned, many were shot in the streets in the heat of the moment. Many fled abroad. Fortunately, in the first few days there was no real control over the borders. Cardinal Mindszenty continued to hide in the U.S. Embassy. In Romania, Imre Nagy awaited his fate. For the time being they seemed to have forgotten about him. But that was an illusion. The new government couldn't settle the score once and for all without prosecuting—or rather, convicting—the former head of government. They had to confirm, even if after the fact, that the seizure of power was legal and that their predecessor, Imre Nagy's government, had been illegal, even criminal. Kádár asked the Soviet Union to intercede with Romania and ask that Imre Nagy be handed over.

Father was disheartened by the request. The first time he talked with his friend János over the telephone, he tried to dissuade him. He pointed out that the Hungarians had promised not to arrest Nagy. But Kádár insisted.

As a politician, Father could not underrate the arguments advanced by Hungarian leaders. Besides, good relations with them outweighed Tito's inevitably negative reaction. Relations with him were extremely strained in any event.

Father gave in, and Imre Nagy found himself in a Hungarian prison. His old foe Mátyás Rákóczy continued to live in the Soviet Union, in Krasnodar Territory. He no longer thought of returning to his homeland, and the Hungarian government did not demand his extradition.

Imre Nagy was put on trial. The court passed an unexpectedly harsh sentence. It decided to put to death the former chairman of the Council of Ministers. This was the first such sentence in the political process since Stalin's death, if you don't count Beria's execution.

Father called Kádár to express his doubt that such a harsh sentence was expedient. He thought that Imre Nagy did not present a real danger, since the government was in total control of the situation in Hungary. If worst came to worst, he could always be expelled, back to Romania for example. But Kádár insisted. He also rejected Father's proposal that Imre Nagy be pardoned after the verdict and exiled.

Father replaced the receiver in its cradle with a heavy heart. On April 17, 1958, Father's birthday, Imre Nagy was executed. That deed brought shame not only on János Kádár, but on Father as well.

When I asked Father about that decision, he justified or, more accurately, explained, Kádár's motives. He said that if Nagy had remained alive, he would have been a force attracting opponents of the new government. They would have coalesced around him. Nagy's punishment, harsh as it was, at least solved that problem.

From that day on Nagy cast a shadow over relations between Father and Tito.

THE SUEZ CRISIS ERUPTS

Let us return to Egypt, to the Suez crisis. On October 30 it was reported on the radio that Israeli forces had begun an offensive in the Sinai peninsula. Some sources say that the attacking forces advanced eighty kilometers, others that they were only twenty kilometers from the city of Suez. The Egyptian army was equipped with Soviet tanks and armored personnel carriers, not to speak of all the other equipment. And to suffer such a defeat on the very first day! I was extremely upset about the Egyptians, and still more about our armaments. I tried to find out from Father what had happened, but the crisis in Hungary had begun. He was preparing for the Chinese delegation's arrival.

A general mobilization was announced in Cairo.

Until then the Soviet Union had had little time to think about Nasser. Britain and France had taken on the role of "peacemakers." They had sent a joint ultimatum to both their ally Israel and to an Egypt under attack, which demanded that they both withdraw their forces ten kilometers from the Suez

Canal. At the same time, they demanded that Nasser agree to the occupation, of course temporary, of Port Said, Ismailia, and Suez. The terms were harsh, the deadline even more so—only twelve hours. After that, the allies would use force. The deadline expired on October 31 at 4:30 A.M., Greenwich Mean Time.

That was about when the Chinese were due in Moscow. The Ministry of Foreign Affairs was urgently instructed to prepare a Declaration of the Soviet Government on the armed aggression against Egypt. Written in the standard boilerplate, it vilified imperialism, placed entire responsibility for any consequences on the aggressors, and reserved freedom of action for the Soviet Union. Analysts in the British Foreign Office could draw the conclusion that Moscow was not in the mood for thinking about the Suez Canal and that the Soviet Union's reaction would be limited to words. Moreover, the Declaration did not appear until November 1. It was brought to Father at the dacha where he was holding talks with the Chinese. He glanced over the document mechanically, his mind elsewhere. He made no corrections and only nodded in approval. By the time our Declaration appeared, a great deal had changed. Nasser had categorically rejected the ultimatum. British and French planes, which had been massed in advance at bases in the region, had begun to bomb Egyptian ports and Cairo, the country's capital.

Nasser sent messages appealing for assistance to Eisenhower; the chairman of the Council of Ministers, Nikolai Bulganin; Indian prime minister Jawaharlal Nehru; and Indonesian president Sukarno. The former as leaders of great powers capable of acting against the aggressors, the latter as leaders of the nonaligned movement.

President Eisenhower issued a wide-ranging appeal to the opposing sides, and to all states and peoples, outlining his position. I will mention only the main points. He condemned the use of force in resolving conflicts between countries and stated that Britain and France had not consulted the United States in making the decision to intervene militarily. Further, he solemnly stated that his country would not take part in the war on either side, but that his condemnation of the aggression of Britain and France would not in any way affect the bonds of friendship between North Atlantic Treaty allies. In conclusion, he proclaimed that the goal of U.S. policy was to localize the fighting and end the armed conflict.

Father learned of Eisenhower's appeal just before flying to meet Gomułka in Brest. He had only enough time to scan the text, not study it carefully. Even from a cursory examination, it was clear that the American president had seized the initiative. On the one hand, he appeared in the role of peacemaker; but on the other, his announcement that the United States would not be helping the French and the British meant little or nothing, for who could possibly imagine that those two great powers needed any help against the

Egyptians, who had only recently shifted from sitting on camels to sitting in tanks.

The statement prepared by our Foreign Ministry couldn't compete. A more peppery dish was called for, but Father had neither the time nor the strength to prepare it. He threw up his hands; we had set out our position, and as for what might happen further on, we would see. Father did not return to the Suez problem until the night of November 2–3, in conversing with President Tito. They had already exhausted the subject of Hungary and Father was hoping for a few hours' sleep before leaving early the next morning. Instead, an obviously nervous Tito persuaded him to sit and talk.

Father touched on the conflict in the Mediterranean. He asked if it wasn't dangerous for Tito to stay on the island at such a time. As he put it, too many bombers were flying around and one or two could easily drop their loads "by mistake" on the residence of Nasser's friend. It would later be impossible to determine the truth.

Tito urged Father to support the weakened leadership of Egypt by every means at the Soviet Union's disposal. In his opinion, Hungary would not draw off large numbers of troops.

Father was dubious. He was afraid of being drawn into the war. He didn't even want to hear about it. To intimidate the aggressors was one thing, but it all depended on how the situation developed in Hungary.

They talked until morning. Father made no promises. He wanted to think everything over carefully. But a plan was already beginning to take shape in his mind. It might not be a bad idea to threaten Eden and Guy Mollet with missiles. That spring in London he had talked about missiles in detail and at great length. He had juggled figures exultantly: how many it would take to destroy Britain, how many France. Father knew perfectly well that we had far fewer missiles than we would need to carry out such threats and that those we had were not armed with nuclear warheads. In his opinion, that was not important. The intelligence agencies of the Western powers would surely confirm the fact that we had missiles capable of reaching either country, since they had to have detected the R-5M launches at Kapustin Yar; but they could not know how many we had or how they were armed. At any rate, they shouldn't know. The goal was worth the risk.

It seemed to me that all was lost. After reading Eisenhower's appeal, I came to the conclusion that the pieces were in place, the basic moves had been made, the game was under way. It remained only to finish the match. And that was a matter of technology. The professionals, face to face, would quickly show the obstinate Colonel Nasser what was what.

I was really upset. At the time we considered the liberation of Africa from colonial dependence to be in our vital interest. Perhaps not everyone felt as I did, but I took these events very much to heart. And now—we faced defeat!

I didn't manage to talk with Father about Egypt until November 4, when the situation in Hungary had become clearer. He looked noticeably more cheerful and started coming home earlier, so we resumed our walks. To my exclamation, "What's going on with Egypt?!" Father replied that we would make every effort to help the Egyptians.

"But how?" I asked in surprise. "We don't have a fleet there, and our ships are locked into the Black Sea. They won't be allowed through the Straits."

"Why force our way through the Straits?" Father said. "We can go much more directly, from the Caucasus."

"But that would have to be across Turkey or Iran," I said, even more surprised.

"We could ask them to let our forces pass through, or we could fly over them. They're not going to shoot down our planes. The Turks and Persians would think twice before they would refuse a neighbor," Father retorted. "But I'm talking about possibilities. I hope it won't come to war."

When he talked that way, it meant that certain plans had already taken shape in his mind.

I asked a question that had been bothering me for several days: "Why haven't the Americans sent their forces into Hungary?"

"Everything happened so fast they may simply not have had time. Moreover, they weren't invited. Of course, since they only respect force you can't trust them. But they have assured us unofficially that they would not intervene with their armed forces or with direct shipments of weapons. They consider Hungary to be in our sphere of interest," Father replied.

I persisted: "If that was the American interpretation, then do we have the right now to intervene in Egypt?"

Father replied that in a formal sense in Egypt we were on the same side as the United States. They were also in favor of the speediest possible resolution of the conflict. "In words. So we will act together." Father began to smile. "We'll see who is only talking and who is really ready to help."

On November 5 newspapers reported that parachute troops had landed in Egypt, at Port Said, Port Fuad, Gabana, and the airport at El Gamalia. This time no denials were forthcoming from either London or Paris. No one was deceived by the optimistic bulletins issued by the Egyptian army's press service about the annihilation of the enemy.

An appeal signed by Nikolai Aleksandrovich Bulganin, head of the Soviet government, was published the same day. It was addressed to the leaders of the aggressor states: Anthony Eden, Guy Mollet, and David Ben-Gurion. Unlike the previous declaration, this document was written in its entirety by Father. Harsh in tone, it warned that what had seemed a local conflict could develop into a third world war. The Soviet Union proposed a joint deployment of forces, with the United States in the first instance and together with other member states of the United Nations, to put a stop to the bloodletting. For our part, we announced, we were prepared to use force no matter what anyone else decided.

Father didn't like making ultimatums. It was easy to make mistakes when you used them. On this occasion he displayed toughness. But the most important part of his message was contained in instructions sent to Soviet ambassadors. As Father described it more than once, when the ambassadors presented the appeal to its addressees they were instructed to add verbally that it was not Moscow's intention to make jokes—that the missiles Father had mentioned to Eden were in place and ready to be launched. We were not prepared to wait indefinitely. A deadline for a response was set. I don't remember now whether it was twenty-four hours or forty-eight.

An appeal was sent simultaneously to the president of the United States. The Soviet Union urgently, I would even say officiously, proposed joint military action against the aggressors, with the Second World War as a model. But now action would be directed against U.S. allies. Father hoped to force Eisenhower into a corner.

Father did not forget the United Nations. Shepilov presented Djelal Abdokhu, the chairman of the Security Council, with a proposal that the U.N. give the aggressors an ultimatum demanding an end to military actions within twelve hours.

In this case there was no need to conceal the deadline. Shepilov informed the chairman that the Soviet Union was ready to put its air and naval forces at the U.N.'s disposal in the event of noncompliance with a Security Council demand.

All these documents originated in Father's head. They were simply signed by the minister of foreign affairs and the chairman of the Council of Ministers. The fact that Shepilov's signature was on them didn't bother Father particularly—he was the minister, the executive. Besides, in general they worked well together. But the fact that Bulganin's signature was appended to messages sent to heads of government and states did make him jealous. The whole world was talking about the Bulganin initiative. It was a trifle, of course, but it bothered him on more than one occasion.

Father decided to employ a form of pressure that was highly unusual for us. Demonstrations were organized in front of the embassies of Britain, France, and Israel. In Moscow demonstrators shouted: "Hands off Egypt." Nevertheless, the fighting in the Suez continued.

Father fretted, waiting for an answer to his message. He wasn't at all sure that his threats would work. The deployment of parachute units to the region was a possible next step.

There was no response from London and Paris. Zhukov called and reported that the General Staff had been studying the feasibility of an airborne operation. The findings were not encouraging. Even if Turkey and Iran did not interfere with our flights, we did not have the planes to send enough troops and weapons and to arrange for their supply. The IL-12 could carry barely two dozen men, not to speak of heavy equipment. We would be defeated in any conflict with the expeditionary forces of the allies, who were supplied with everything they needed by the Anglo-French fleet, which ruled the Mediterranean.

Father agreed with Zhukov. Whatever he said could be trusted. They knew each other well. Though their relationship did not amount to friendship, it *was* a friendly one. They had known each other for almost twenty years.

During the long years of war they had met often, at Stalingrad and in the Kursk salient. Zhukov represented the Supreme High Command, while Father occupied his regular position as political commissar and member of the Front Military Council.

Zhukov replaced General Vatutin as commander of the First Ukrainian Front where Father was serving, after Vatutin was killed by submachine gun fire in a chance ambush. That was after the liberation of Kiev.

In 1945 Father and Zhukov met briefly in Kiev as Zhukov was on his way to his new post as commander of the First Belorussian Front, which was to take Berlin. Anticipating victory, Zhukov promised to send the captured Adolf Hitler in an iron cage through Kiev on his way to Moscow; however, the Führer had anticipated the fate prepared for him and took poison, and Zhukov was not able to fulfill his promise.

After the war they both fell out of favor. The marshal was sent back to the Ukraine, where he commanded the Odessa Military District. Father, no longer the first secretary of the Ukrainian Central Committee, often went to Odessa in his new position as chairman of the Ukrainian Council of Ministers.

After Stalin's death Zhukov, on Father's initiative, became minister of defense.

Now both of them—Central Committee first secretary and head of the military—tried fruitlessly to think of a way to help an Egypt that, though not that distant, was nevertheless very difficult to reach. The idea of an airborne landing was discarded. They couldn't think of anything else.

The appeal sent to London, Paris, and Tel-Aviv remained their only hope. The waiting became intolerable.

It's not for me to judge what was actually going on at the time in Western capitals. I am describing what happened through Father's eyes. As he expected, Washington paid no attention to his proposal for joint military action.

In London and Paris, however, his message had an explosive effect. Prime Minister Guy Mollet, as Father described it, rose from his bed. After reading the official text, and particularly the associated notes listing the number of nuclear warheads required to destroy France, Mollet didn't take time to get dressed and hastily phoned London in his bathrobe. The same nervous atmosphere reigned in the British capital. I could only guess how Father heard about such private details.

Consultations continued through the night. How real was the threat of Soviet intervention, and would they really employ nuclear weapons? After Washington's declaration of noninterference, they stood alone. Eden recalled Father's boastful accounts of new Soviet missiles and was inclined to think that the risk was not justified. Guy Mollet allowed himself to be persuaded. They decided to make a simultaneous announcement in London and Paris that a cease-fire would begin on November 6, before the deadline set by Moscow expired.

On November 6, the eve of the thirty-ninth anniversary of the Great October Socialist Revolution, Father was still pacing up and down in his office. The torment of not knowing was finally replaced by relief. A report of British prime minister Anthony Eden's speech to the House of Commons came in. Eden announced that the British forces in the Suez Canal zone had largely achieved their goals. Therefore, in order to avoid further bloodshed, Her Majesty's Government had decided to call a cease-fire, which was to begin at midnight on November 7, 1956. French prime minister Guy Mollet issued a similar statement. These reports were the best possible holiday present Father could have received.

Without going into details, one thing is indisputable—the cease-fire resulting from our message made an enormous impression on Father. He was extraordinarily proud of his victory. He had a way to influence the course of international affairs and would return to it more than once. He resorted to similar arguments when tensions arose around Syria, Iran, Jordan, and Iraq. Fortunately, none of these crises was on such a scale. Most are remembered only by professional historians.

And one other thing. Father became convinced that the mere mention of nuclear-armed missiles had a powerful effect. That led him to these two conclusions: intensive development of missiles was necessary, but extensive production of them was not. He realized that he had only remind the world that we had such missiles to exert the pressure he needed to accomplish his goal.

The effectiveness of such a tactic—a bluff cannot be called a strategy— depended on concealing the number and location of the missiles we had. No "Open Skies" program! That was why Father was especially worried by flights of the high-altitude spy plane, as yet unidentified, over our territory. The consequences of Suez were felt throughout the years to come. Its echo could even be heard in the diplomatic cannonade that reverberated during the Cuban Missile Crisis.

However, when I've talked with Western political analysts about what went on during those years, I have not found any comprehension or confirmation of Father's words. They credit Eisenhower with restoring peace in the Middle East. I don't presume to judge.[10]

Despite the cease-fire announcement, the fighting did not end in Port Said on November 7. There were even a few tank battles after the deadline. The expeditionary forces were trying to seize more advantageous positions—after all, they did not know how long they would have to hold those positions before they were permitted to return home. Firing did not die down until the following day.

Israel celebrated victory: it had defeated a numerically superior Egyptian army, acquired new territory on the Sinai Peninsula, and taken an enormous number of war trophies. There were so many that even the well-schooled Soviet press couldn't ignore them. The Egyptian army lost a large part of the heavy armament supplied by Czechoslovakia and the USSR, including all its tanks and armored personnel carriers. Egyptian soldiers had simply abandoned them and fled.

American experts estimate the value of the equipment seized by the Israeli army at fifty million dollars, an enormous figure in those days. The Egyptians tried to put the best face they could on it and, without denying their losses, agreed that thirty T-34 tanks and fifty armored personnel carriers could not be repaired and were unfit for further use. So, they would become scrap metal.

A rumor circulated in Moscow that, when the fighting ended, the Israelis asked the Soviet government to sign an agreement to supply spare tank parts. Perhaps that wasn't a joke. Our relations had not been totally cut off at the time.

Father took Nasser's defeat more calmly than I did. He explained that the Egyptians were only beginning to learn how to use tanks and were unfamiliar

---

10. "They credit Eisenhower . . ." Historians do credit the Eisenhower administration with securing the Anglo-French pullback, as well as the subsequent Israeli withdrawal from the Sinai. The president essentially ordered his allies to disengage and used intense economic pressure to make them comply. Documents suggest that Khrushchev's ploy was seen in Western capitals as dangerous but probably empty bluster. Eisenhower's ultimatum was private, however, while Bulganin's warning was very public. While most accounts maintain that the warning played little role, they tend to accept that Khrushchev sincerely believed in the effectiveness of his policy of nuclear threats from a position of nuclear inferiority. Sergei Khrushchev indicates both in this book and in interviews that the origins of his father's subsequent missile diplomacy lie at least in part in his belief that he had employed it successfully in Suez.

with them both technically and tactically. It was no wonder that they panicked and fled under the first blows from a well-trained and modern Israeli army, many of whose officers and men had served in Allied armies during the war against the Fascists.

"They have to be taught. In time they'll also master the latest weapons. Then Israel won't be able to cope with them. After all, there are fifty million Arabs," continued Father. "Now we'll have to help them again and replace their losses. There's no way to avoid it."

Father was mistaken: neither long training nor modern equipment have taught the Arabs how to conduct modern warfare.

All through November and into early December Father pressured the British and French to withdraw their expeditionary forces from the region along the Suez Canal.

He thought of threatening to send "volunteers," as happened in Spain during the war against Franco. The occupiers were ignoring Egyptian forces, who presented no threat. But they might have second thoughts at the prospect of a third, trained Soviet "volunteer" force in the region. TASS was instructed to publish a suitable statement.

The statement declared that, if the aggressors did not withdraw their forces from occupied areas, appropriate Soviet agencies would not stand in the way of "volunteers" wishing to help a friendly people in their struggle against the colonizers.

When I asked Father how such volunteers would get there, Father answered, rather flippantly, "by sea." Apparently he hadn't thought about it seriously, and after a moment's thought he added: "They don't need many people there, just specialists: pilots, tank crews. But . . . I don't really think it will come to that."

The TASS announcement was taken seriously at home. A register was set up for those who wanted to teach the greedy imperialists a lesson and help our brother Arabs. Volunteers were even to be found in our Institute.

The crisis, drained of its energy, fizzled out. On December 22, reports came that the evacuation of British and French troops was complete. Egypt exulted and celebrated victory. In London they added up the results. Immediately after the beginning of 1957 Anthony Eden submitted his resignation. Harold Macmillan replaced him as head of the Cabinet.

THE POWER STRUGGLE IN POLAND—A POSTSCRIPT

On November 13, Polish Defense Minister and Marshal of the Polish Armed Forces Konstantin Rokossovsky resigned from all his posts. The Polish government gave him their highest military medal and promptly sent him back to the Soviet Union. In his place they appointed Marian Spychalski, who had only recently been released from prison. Father was not surprised by such a turn of events, but he reacted guardedly to news of Spychalski's appointment. Of course, Spychalski was Gomułka's man but, thought Father, his lengthy imprisonment could hardly have deepened his love for the Soviet Union. How would he behave, with the power of a large and well-armed army at his disposal? Doubts were soon dispelled. More than any intelligence reports, the friendship with Gomułka showed that there was nothing to worry about.

Although uninvited, a representative delegation consisting of Władysław Gomułka, Josef Cyrankiewicz, and Alexander Zawadski flew to Moscow in November as if to answer the October Warsaw visit by Bulganin and Father. They were greeted with unimaginable pomp and heartfelt cordiality. The negotiations, lasting three days, ended to the guests' complete satisfaction. A joint declaration solemnly declared that the Soviet Union had agreed to cancel the debt (a large one) of the Polish People's Republic as it stood on November 1, 1956. At the same time, it announced that the Soviet Union would no longer request a discounted price for Silesian coal. The discount had been imposed in Stalin's day, as if in compensation for the blood of Soviet soldiers spilled during the liberation of Poland.

A RETURN TO CALM

Even very profound upheavals cannot last forever. The political storms that had agitated the whole world and brought opposing groups to the brink of conflict gradually subsided.

At the beginning of 1957 Father could finally return to what he considered his main goals: propelling our ponderous economy forward and forcing the wheels and connecting rods of the rusty machinery of state to move faster. He had long planned to revamp the clumsy, centralized administrative structure, where for every small detail managers at all levels had to take themselves off to Moscow and spend weeks beating down doors, coordinating arrangements, and looking for departmental partners around the whole country. I recall that in those days Father would tell anyone willing to listen that the belts for coal conveyors made in the Donbas were shipped all the way from Vladivostok. That suited the ministry, for some reason. This was reported in the movie documentary *Science and Technology*, which Father watched regularly, absorbing new ideas with childish enthusiasm and often telephoning the pertinent ministry afterward. This particular report acted like salt on a wound. The announcer was exasperated: how much money would be saved if the belts were produced nearby, in the same region. But Moscow wouldn't allow it. Father couldn't have agreed more. The methods of those days—administering from the center through a multitude of ministries—seemed to him completely unsuited to a dynamically growing economy. Father's reasoning was simple: in order to administer, you had to know; in order to know, you had to be in touch with things personally, to be aware of the complexities of everyday problems and to experience them along with everybody else.

It was no accident that he thought trips around the country were essential. He tried to see through the varnish to the real state of affairs. After his long years at the summit of power, Father was used to window dressing. He fought against it as much as he could, but admitted that it was beyond his power to eliminate. He adopted a simple rule: window dressing embellished reality, but could not change it. If you learned to adjust how you looked at things, you could discern something. This was sometimes, but not always, successful.

He had no doubt that it was impossible for anyone sitting in a Moscow office to imagine the needs of distant factories and mines and to understand the spiderweb of interconnections in the regions. In general, he didn't like bureaucrats. He tried to move managers closer to producers and force them to immerse themselves in real life. So a time of transfers and reassignments began. Father thought he had found the solution. He was very much attracted to the idea of returning to the old Leninist system of *sovnarkhozy*, or regional economic councils, with the center retaining only oversight functions. The "return to Leninist norms" began that year, and the expression sounded strange.

Father worked on a reform plan throughout the winter. He discussed it with scientists and economists, factory directors, and collective farm chairmen, all the while transforming previously vague thoughts into language suitable for the provisions of a decree.

By the end of March work was complete and the finished document was sent to the Presidium of the Central Committee for discussion. Not all of its members supported Father's ideas.

Representatives from the central agencies, primarily Gosplan[11] and the ministries, resisted in a variety of ways. Some simply grumbled. Others predicted that the national economy would collapse into chaos. In the localities, where both economic managers and party administrators favored the innovation, the reaction was different. They would gain real power.

Father prevailed, and on March 30 newspapers published a decree of the Central Committee of the CPSU and the Council of Ministers of the Soviet Union offering for nationwide discussion a detailed document of many pages entitled "Theses of a Report by N. S. Khrushchev. On Further Improving the Organization of the Management of Industry and Construction." The theses were to become law at the next session of the Supreme Soviet, held at

---

11. "Gosplan." The Soviet central state planning committee.

the beginning of May. The fact that Nikolai Baibakov was dismissed from his position as chairman of Gosplan on the eve of the session shows how turbulent discussions had been. He was prominent among those who opposed Father's innovations. Despite Baibakov's opposition, Father thought highly of him as an experienced economic manager and knowledgeable oil industry executive. Baibakov soon left to become chairman of one of the largest regional economic councils. In 1965 he got his revenge when, after signing documents consigning regional councils to the historical archives, he returned to Moscow and took up his old post. In 1957 no one suspected that everything comes around full circle. It seemed as if Father had won and that the tentacles of the Moscow octopus were lopped off for good. The reorganization began. It proceeded painfully. I won't go into that in this book. It would be a separate investigation and take us far afield.

THE DECENTRALIZATION OF MISSILE RESEARCH

However, I would like to consider one aspect of the reorganization that began then: survival in the event of nuclear war. That question was taken seriously at the time.

Father thought that decentralization, the delegation of administrative functions to localities, would not only have a beneficial effect on operations of the national economy in peacetime, but would also make it more stable in case of nuclear attack.

"If Moscow were destroyed today, which wouldn't be difficult," Father reasoned, "everything would collapse, since every small detail is decided in the center. For each and every nail they come to the capital. If there were several administrative centers, some would survive and recover, and the whole infrastructure could be resurrected on their basis."

Father had been mulling over this subject for a long time, from around the end of 1953. At the time he was not thinking about the entire economy. He was concerned that our foremost intellects, the people who determined our progress, were vulnerable. The main scientific and design organizations related to defense were located in Moscow and its environs. Father decided to relocate and disperse them throughout the country. The decentralization of scientific centers would, he thought, not only increase their survivability in the event of nuclear war but promote development in the regions to which they were sent. As examples, he cited those cities in the Urals, Siberia, and Central Asia that had sheltered factories evacuated at the beginning of the war. They were transformed in a few years from backwater towns into important industrial centers.

Missiles were Father's main concern. He thought that the future belonged to them and that planes, tanks, and artillery would gradually become obsolete and disappear from the scene. Perhaps he also had other goals in mind, and wanted to put an end to Korolyov's emerging monopoly in the field. He was the only major designer of ballistic missiles.

Father handed Ustinov the job of developing a proposal. Ustinov rolled up his sleeves and went to work. A man of great energy and initiative, Dmitry Fyodorovich saw this assignment from the first secretary as an opportunity to greatly expand and strengthen the missile industry over which he presided.

A rough draft was submitted to Father at the beginning of 1954. It provided for creating two independent groups (in addition to Moscow)—one in the south, in the Ukraine, and another in the east, in the Urals, with a possible future additional advance into Siberia. The structures to be created were to be able to function autonomously, from planning to manufacturing all missile components. Cities were selected and recommendations were made about where scientific-research institutes, design bureaus, and experimental bases should be built. Substantial sums would be needed to carry out the project. Estimates ran to tens of billions of rubles and considerably more than a year of intensive work.

Ustinov generally had a hard time wringing additional capital investments from Father for military requirements. But this time, once he approved the plans Father didn't ask for scaled-down variants.

He telephoned Korolyov personally and invited him to visit the Central Committee at a convenient time to talk over an important matter. Korolyov knew what the subject would be. Sergei Pavlovich thought that the fastest way to create new enterprises would be to use existing Moscow organizations as nuclei and establish branches of them on the periphery. Experienced specialists sent to those branch organizations would help shorten the transitional period and progress would be more rapid. Collectives would form around the Moscow "luminaries." People would learn more and work would prosper. He proposed that special missile technology faculties be established at local higher educational establishments, so that personnel could be trained locally. We should not send young specialists from Moscow, since each would require an apartment and not everyone would be willing to go. He described the disposition of new design bureaus and factories the way a commander in chief deploys his armies and corps before a decisive battle. There was something reminiscent of Zhukov about him. It wasn't just that he was short and stocky. Perhaps it was mainly his eyes, which reflected an indomitable self-assurance, decisiveness, and the sense that it was his destiny to command.

Father admired Sergei Pavlovich's drive and powers of concentration, but didn't agree with him in everything. He objected to the idea of branches. He thought that the newly created organizations should be fully independent, both financially and in their research.

"I know you. You'll give them some minor jobs and they'll wind up spending their lives as assistants. We want to create competitors for you, so they'll keep you awake," joked Father.

Korolyov didn't argue. He was already aware of Father's opinion, but thought it worth putting up a trial balloon.

Ustinov recommended that Mikhail Kuzmich Yangel be appointed director of the Southern Complex. Yangel was an experienced designer who had been in the aviation field for many years. He and Korolyov had worked together for a while after the war, but they did better working separately.

Yangel found Ustinov's proposal that he leave Moscow and head a new center appealing. He would be his own boss, work without interference, and pursue "his own line" of research. For a long time he'd been itching to get his hands on something big. He agreed without hesitation.

Father asked for Korolyov's opinion of Yangel as designer and scientist. And, of course, his personal qualities were not the least important factor. Korolyov undoubtedly saw Yangel as a future rival. Since he was naturally straightforward—and not just honest and fair, but punctilious—Korolyov did not consider dissembling. He agreed that Yangel would be a suitable candidate.

For the Eastern Complex, Korolyov recommended Viktor Petrovich Makeyev,[12] who was young but, he thought, had showed promise; however, after finishing the institute he had devoted himself primarily to Komsomol work. He had first become secretary of the Komsomol organization at Korolyov's design bureau and had then moved to the position of instructor in the All-Union Komsomol Central Committee. There he had no connection with missiles, but kept an eye on metallurgical plants and coal mines. He had traveled to the Olympic Games in Helsinki, where he carried on political work with the athletes. In 1954 Makeyev returned to Korolyov. In Father's eyes, the candidate's youth was not a handicap. On the contrary, he thought it a considerable advantage. When everything is ahead of you, nothing is too difficult and you feel capable of anything. Father asked Korolyov to work out a proposal with Ustinov. If they both agreed, the nomination could go ahead.

Korolyov made no comment. He had already discussed the candidacy with Dmitry Fyodorovich, who kept a tight grip on personnel matters and wouldn't have forgiven any initiative on his part. Both Father and Korolyov were pleased with their talk.

In the summer of 1955 Makeyev became the chief designer at a new missile enterprise in Miass, in the southern Urals.

In July of 1954 Yangel was appointed head of a new design bureau and

---

12. Makeyev later became the chief designer of submarine ballistic missiles.

put in charge of a large plant in the Ukraine. The plant's equipment had been shipped as reparations from Germany, where it had been used to manufacture cars—the famous BMWs and Porsches. At first plans called for the plant to produce cars in the Ukraine as well, but then it was decided that tractors were more urgently needed. Now missiles were added to tractors. Cars were forgotten.

Yangel was ordered to work on medium-range (in today's terminology) missiles. Father was not the only one who thought that the R-5, with a flight range of 1200 kilometers, was a good missile. However, its range had to be increased to avoid positioning launchers right at our borders. They had to be spread over a large area and made less vulnerable to air attack.

Father talked about this when Yangel called on him before being appointed chief designer. They had never met and Father wanted to take his measure.

Yangel said the task was feasible and that he had some ideas for designs. It would be possible to build a missile with about a 2000-kilometer range rather quickly.

Korolyov built his missiles using the traditional components, liquid oxygen and alcohol, which the Germans used for the V-2. Kerosene later replaced alcohol.

When he talked to Father, Yangel insisted that liquid oxygen was not practical for battlefield missiles because troops could not become skilled at using them.

He thought that a battlefield weapon should employ something less exotic. He planned to use nitric acid (to be precise, red fuming nitric acid) in his missiles. Though volatile and toxic, it could be used if safety measures were strictly observed.

The first product of the young collective was designated the R-12. Initial flight tests were scheduled for the middle of 1957. Korolyov couldn't keep Yangel on a leash. From his first days on the job, the newly appointed chief designer made it clear that he wouldn't put up with any oversight. They soon became keen rivals.

Things were different with Viktor Petrovich Makeyev. After growing up in Korolyov's design bureau, the young man (jokingly referred to as the "Pioneer" by the chief designer's colleagues) naturally viewed Korolyov as his teacher and mentor. Sergei Pavlovich gave him as much assistance as possible. He gave Makeyev some of his own work—not the most prestigious part, but short-range ballistic missiles, with a range of two to three hundred kilometers, so-called operational-tactical missiles. They only distracted Korolyov from his more interesting work on intercontinental missiles and from his main preoccupation: a breakthrough into space.

It takes as much work to develop a small missile as a large one. It may not be prestigious, but that doesn't mean it isn't important. The prototype of this type of missile, the mobile self-propelled launch system R-11— awarded like a dowry to the young design bureau—was to become one of the Army's main missiles of this class. Over the course of many years it was modified, improved, and altered, but always remained in service.

New missiles followed, at first along lines set by his teacher and utilizing Korolyov's experience, but later on independently. Among them was the R-17, later unhappily familiar to the world under the NATO designation "Scud." It was the only Soviet ballistic missile to be used. Iraq attacked Israel and Saudi Arabia with R-17 missiles in the 1991 war. Fortunately, the attacks were not very successful.

However, Makeyev made his name in submarine ballistic missiles, not ground-based missiles.

SETBACKS WITH THE R-7

While Father was preparing for one of the most severe tests of his career, the creation of the regional economic councils, Korolyov completed arrangements for the first launch of the R-7. Both events occurred in May of 1957. The launch of the R-7 had been repeatedly postponed because defects kept appearing. At last a final, absolutely definite date was set. One evening Father mentioned casually that an intercontinental missile test was tentatively set for the first few days of May. I waited impatiently from then on to hear when it would happen. Worried and excited, I kept pestering Father with questions.

Father wasn't sure himself how things were going. He thought that too much attention from above during test preparations would do nothing but harm. Telephone calls from higher-ups make people nervous. Even if you are told not to hurry, you can overlook something when you're in a rush, and in this matter every detail is vital. Any minor mistake or carelessness can be catastrophic. Furthermore, how could he help? It was a matter for engineers, for specialists.

"If necessary Korolyov will call me himself. We agreed to that," Father said, fending me off.

He understood my impatience and didn't get angry. He himself was impatient to hear good news. But he had to wait for Korolyov's call. I couldn't resist asking Father repeatedly. Suppose Korolyov had already called, and Father had forgotten to tell me?

He did not forget. On May 15 he returned from work looking gloomy. We headed out for our usual walk, but he was deep in thought and didn't seem to notice me. I didn't dare ask, although I realized that something must have happened. Father finally broke the silence.

"Korolyov called. They launched the R-7 this evening," he said. "Unfortunately, it was unsuccessful. One of the boosters caught fire and it exploded in the air."

For some reason I felt this was really tragic news. Today my despair seems to me a little amusing and extremely naive. An unsuccessful launch is an event that can't be avoided in the work of a designer.

At the time I was so upset that I foolishly asked: "What will happen now?"

Father was surprised. He hadn't noticed my distress.

"What will happen? They'll look into the reasons for the failure, eliminate the defects, and launch the next one. After all, they have more than one missile. The main thing is that the launch site is undamaged. If it had been destroyed, we'd be in for a long delay."

Father fell silent, making it clear that the subject was exhausted and there was nothing more to talk about.

Six years after that memorable launch of the R-7, I came to Tyura-Tam for the first time to participate in launching a Polet-1 satellite, developed in Chelomei's design bureau. On my day off one of the drivers, a sergeant, found us an old Pobeda car and took me to see the local sights, among them the famous Korolyov launch site No. 2. There he told me the following story:

Many generals had arrived from Moscow to watch the first launch of the R-7. It was impossible to fit them all in the command bunker. Korolyov ordered workers to build a wooden platform with a roof of narrow boards to protect them from the warm May sun. It was about one kilometer from the launch site. A narrow dugout was located nearby—just in case.

The generals watched as the rocket began to zigzag in the air. The four strap-on boosters separated from the main body like fireworks and flew in different directions. One of them headed toward the test assembly building, where the next rocket was being assembled. Another seemed to the observers to be coming directly at them, a fiery ball falling on them from the sky. This frightened even the battle-hardened generals. Shoving one another out of the way, they rushed toward the dugout. As they tried to squeeze through the narrow doors a brief scuffle broke out. Fortunately, everything ended well. The rocket flew over the platform and exploded several hundred meters away. A brown mushroom-shaped cloud of smoke formed over the steppe. Seeing that the danger was past, the generals resumed the staid appearance appropriate to their rank and, pretending nothing had happened, moved back under the roof. During the days after the accident, soldiers picked up as souvenirs the shiny buttons with emblems torn off the generals' uniforms during the scuffle.

In fact the first R-7 accident happened more prosaically: the rocket broke into pieces not at the launch site, but almost one hundred seconds into flight. Its fragments fell far off, in the desert. The fireworks described by the sergeant occurred considerably later, in 1960, also in the spring, but on April 19, when one of the Lunniks was launched. And no generals were present—at most a couple of colonels, because by then R-7 launches had become routine. Nevertheless, I decided to give his account without any changes. This is the way legends are born, legends which then sometimes become "history."

After an investigation into the causes of the accident, the next launch was set for June 11. This time everything ended before launch. During the countdown a light on the control panel went on, indicating an engine malfunction. It turned out that the fuel valve in the manifold had been installed upside down. Tests were delayed for another month.

Father waited patiently, not hurrying Korolyov even though he was counting very much on success. It would mean that the missile worked, would "learn to fly," and that preparations could begin to install it in launch positions. Even if a great deal of work remained, specialists would cope with it. The important thing was to make certain that the designer had not made a mistake in principle, that he hadn't misled himself and others.

In the meantime, there were only promises. Of course, Father trusted Korolyov, but you need more than an inventor's assurance. However, there was nothing to do but wait.

The May launch did not go unobserved by the Americans. Radars detected the fact that the missile was launched from a new location. In the United States they had known about the existence of the test site at Kapustin Yar since 1949, almost from the start. This unusual launch was located much farther east and considerably farther south.

American intelligence services burrowed like ticks, trying desperately to find out everything they could about the secret site. It was never possible to get much information from agents—tidbits at best. The U-2 was their only hope.

A plane took off from the Peshawar air base in Pakistan and landed in Bodo, Norway. It was the same flight path attempted by Francis Gary Powers on that beautiful May day in 1960. The 1957 flight was highly successful. The photographs even enabled the CIA to build a three-dimensional model of the test site, with all its installations. The secret was revealed. But perhaps only the United States knew about it. I never once heard, then or later, from Father, his entourage, or my numerous friends in the military, about a reconnaissance flight over Tyura-Tam.

It's possible they simply missed it and the airborne secret agent crossed our country "from the southern mountains to the northern seas" without interference.

There was no problem keeping the test site secret until man flew into space. Here we should note the fact that our American competitors trumpeted the news of their launch site in all the newspapers. Neither Ustinov nor Malinovsky wanted to take the responsibility for lifting secrecy and they appealed to Father. He shrugged his shoulders in amazement: "Well, you're saying that the launch took place from a test site, so what do you call it? You yourself reported that American radars from Iran and somewhere else plot our missiles, follow them and calculate exactly the location of the launch site by their trajectory." But such a decision seemed too simple. In order to confuse the "adversary," Ustinov found a small place on the map of Kazakhstan named Baikonur, which was located considerably north of the test site. Since that time the cosmodrome has been known around the world as Baikonur. In those years the only ones who knew its real name were on the staff of the strategic missile forces or in the CIA.

No failures could shake Father's faith in missile technology. The new weapon (at the time people weren't thinking about peaceful space, or even about space in general) belonged not simply to the future, but would very soon assume a dominant position in the present. It would restrict the role of traditional planes and guns and revolutionize strategic thinking about how to wage war. Father thought the development of homing and guidance missile systems made the effectiveness of aviation doubtful. The Suez crisis played an important (psychological, at any rate) role here. Father was convinced of the value of missiles, especially if they were put into the equation at the right time. No bombers or attack aircraft would have caused London and Paris to act so hastily.

I keep returning to this subject. That is unavoidable, since it occupied Father's thoughts constantly during those years. The ideas generated by the film of the Kometa destroying naval ships had developed, matured, and now demanded expression. Father decided that his thinking had "ripened." At the beginning of 1957 he presented his seditious ideas to the country's top military leaders during a session of the Defense Council. Father didn't propose putting an end to military aviation, for in many cases no automatic equipment could substitute for human beings. It was a question of working out a new strategic approach. Where should limited resources be invested? Where would we get the biggest return? Should we follow the American example and invest billions in Tupolev and Myasishchev bombers or, after evaluating the situation, develop our own approach and surprise the adversary? Not chase directly after them, but weave to the side and unexpectedly appear ahead? That would require both audacity and wisdom, since a well-worn road would be replaced by an untrodden path. Father was insistent. He proposed the immediate approval of a program requiring the gradual replacement of long-range bombers with ballistic missiles and a shift in the emphasis in air defense systems from interceptor aircraft to antiaircraft missile complexes. When a new concept is adopted, it invariably entails redistributing capital investments, revamping factories, and retraining officers. Father fully understood the complexity of such a decision, but he felt that avoiding it and leaving the status quo would expose the country to the danger of defeat in case of war, besides spending money on unneeded and outmoded "toys."

When he was meeting Korolyov during the winter of 1956, Father asked him the ritual question: who owns the future? Can missiles replace bombers? Naturally, Sergei Pavlovich agreed with Father. But he was not a disinterested party.

At the Defense Council session, Father proposed that no time should be wasted. As soon as we were sure that the R-7 would fly, construction of launch sites should begin. Even if certain things had to be redone later, we would save several years by not waiting until tests were completed.

Father certainly presented them with a difficult decision. A mistake would be costly to the country. He wanted to weigh the advantages and disadvantages of the new weapon carefully and reassure himself that he was correct. Unfortunately, the discussion was not a success. Yes, the high-ranking generals supported Father, but he alone would be responsible for failure, even if only to his own conscience, an even greater burden. Not even Zhukov, with his direct and decisive nature, took an unequivocal stance. Not that he held the opposite viewpoint. If he had, he would not have hesitated to express it. After all, who was Khrushchev? In his day, Zhukov had argued even with Stalin! It was just that such novel gadgets didn't really appeal to him. Yes, during the war the Katyusha rockets had been a good complement to artillery, but only a complement. And the Germans hadn't won anything with their V-2; they had just dug up parts of London. On the other hand, Father's proposal would provide an answer to the question: how do we strike targets in the United States? Zhukov voted in favor, but he never became a genuinely enthusiastic proponent of the new direction in military technology. And what can be said of the other famous generals and marshals, who had lived through the war? Military leaders lived with their old baggage. The traditional, tested methods of carrying out operations counted heavily with them. When Father turned to them with his ideas about creating a new military strategy, one based on missile power, they did not hear him—they were simply unable to hear him.

In the 1930s Marshal Tukhachevsky had predicted a great future for missile weaponry and rocket-propelled artillery. Most of his colleagues thought it was a fantasy. After his arrest and death, his ideas about using rocket weapons were considered treasonable and the engineers who were developing them followed the marshal into the Lubyanka and Lefortovo prisons.

The Army's reliance on traditional barrel artillery seemed to have paid off, since it performed well during the war.

Father's argument in favor of a transition to new types of armaments didn't stimulate an open discussion. Military officers either had no arguments to put forward or they didn't want to get involved, which is more likely. Who knows what epithets they applied to Father at home, "over a shot glass of tea" (a phrase the military were fond of using when they didn't want to mention vodka). Tukhachevsky was surely not forgotten, but he was remembered quite differently. Many still considered him a controversial figure, if not an enemy of the people. Generals who had received their ranks and medals from Stalin's hands remained faithful to him, regardless of Father's report at the Twentieth Party Congress. No support for missiles could be expected from that direction.

Moreover, habits are not easily broken. Missiles seemed supernatural and incomprehensible to the old warriors. Even the unconventional appearance of the new weapon tended to make them skeptical.

The Military Council approved Father's initiative, but it did so reluctantly. Ustinov and his staff were ordered to prepare proposals. Now it remained to be seen if the R-7 would fly. Its initial failures depressed one camp and provoked spiteful laughter in the other.

THE OLD GENERALS

Zhukov was the first to bring up the need to revitalize the Ministry of Defense's personnel. After assuming the post of minister, he carried out a review of the command staff and was extremely dissatisfied with the results. The Army had aged catastrophically. Generals who had commanded fronts and armies during the war now headed up military districts and arms of the service and occupied other key positions. Most of them were well over the age of fifty. After making a careful study of personnel matters, Zhukov came to Father.

"In case of war I don't need front and army commanders who count on having field hospitals with them," said the marshal, with the rather crude frankness so typical of him. "In wartime you need people who are physically strong and healthy, whose morale is high, who can go nights without sleep and set the soldiers an example. But these types will spend more time thinking about a warm bed."

Father later recounted their conversation more than once, so Zhukov's words remain imprinted in my memory. Georgy Konstantinovich placed a list in front of Father of the old men he recommended for retirement. Another one contained the names of young generals he wanted to promote. Putting on his glasses, Father pored over the first list. All the names were very familiar. With many he had shared the bitterness of defeat and the joys of victory. He thought about how much resentment such a decision would provoke and how many lives it would shorten. It's very difficult to stop suddenly, in full stride, and switch to fussing over your grandchildren.

Leaving emotion aside, Father essentially agreed with Zhukov. He also thought that it would be better if more young people were at the top. After reading the page again carefully, he made no changes to the list. He only asked: "Try to do this as tactfully and carefully as possible. There's no need to humiliate people." Zhukov nodded.

The paper circulated. A few days later the Central Committee Secretariat took the appropriate decision, without which any transfers in the Army were unthinkable. Coded telegrams with similar contents were sent out to military districts: "You are relieved of the duties of commander of the district (or army) in connection with your retirement. I order you to hand over command to so-and-so (usually the deputy, until appointment of a new commander) and come to Moscow." And the curt signature: Zhukov. Georgy Konstantinovich paid no attention to Father's call for tact. Tact was simply not part of his style.

Recipients reacted in various ways. Some grunted and, after giving full vent to their emotions, went to pack their bags. Others started to call everyone they could think of in the Ministry, the Council of Ministers, and the Central Committee to find out what was going on, to complain, to "get at the truth."

The most drastic reaction came from Army General Andrei Ivanovich Yeremenko, an ambitious and emotional man, commander of the Baltic Military District.

Clearly inferior in culture and education, Yeremenko was not the most intelligent, the cleverest, or even the most sensible man who ever served the Soviet Union as a general. His groveling before the powers that be particularly grated on those around him. Yeremenko's messages to Stalin from the front were sometimes simply embarrassing to read. Is it possible that a fighting general, one of the victors in the battle of Stalingrad, could write those servile appeals? However, said Father, a different person would suddenly emerge in the complex situations that arose at the front, one who made bold, original and, most important, correct decisions.

Yeremenko didn't have the slightest intention of handing over his district. Locking the door to his office, he made it known through his adjutant that he would shoot anyone who dared to break in by force. He kept a pistol and a supply of cartridges in his personal safe. Everyone knew that. No one doubted that the general would carry out his threat, and no one wanted to risk his life. The generals who gathered in the office of the military district discussed what to do. A report had to be sent to Moscow, but about what?

About a military coup carried out personally by the commander in his office? They decided to wait.

From his voluntary confinement, Yeremenko ordered over the telephone that a coded telegram be sent to Khrushchev, Bulganin, and Zhukov. He said that he refused to carry out Zhukov's "treacherous" order and that he would defend himself to the last bullet. However, at the end of the telegram he agreed to hand over his district in exchange for being appointed deputy minister of defense. The contradictory nature of this hero of Stalingrad was transparently clear in this bizarre hodgepodge of a message.

The telegram caused consternation in Moscow. No one wanted to arrest the mutinous general. They decided that Zhukov should visit Father in person to explain the situation. After listening attentively to the marshal, Father suddenly started to laugh. He detected the eccentric personality of Yeremenko, with whom he had shared a mess kit on the Stalingrad front. His amusement was short-lived. Something had to be done. He didn't think it was fair to humiliate the general, but his escapade couldn't be ignored. All the others would mutiny at any sign of weakness.

"What should we do? The situation was a stalemate. Zhukov wouldn't rescind his order. He's not that kind of man. Besides, he was right," Father later described his thinking. "But Yeremenko's hysterical telegram, his outcry, reflected the general resentment felt by the dismissed heroes of the last war."

Father turned to Zhukov: "What should we do? Couldn't we storm him in his office?"

Zhukov looked glum and didn't answer. In his opinion, once the general had disobeyed the order, he could be seized and court-martialed. Father thought it over.

Finally, Father thought that he had found a compromise. High-ranking military commanders who had distinguished themselves in the war and were particularly deserving would not be retired, but found some honorary and undemanding duty appropriate to their rank. Something that would keep them from interfering in operations and even, where possible, be beneficial. Such a sinecure was not a new concept, of course.

Zhukov didn't object. He proposed establishing a special group of inspectors attached to the Ministry of Defense. Father worried: Won't they make a mess of things? Zhukov explained that the existing corps of inspectors, with its staff, would remain and continue to verify the Army's military readiness, while the new inspectors general could be given ceremonial duties. That would please them, and the arrival of a marshal or general of the army, a war hero, at military units would be good for morale.

Father agreed, but suggested: "As an added incentive, let's increase the rank of generals transferred to the newly created inspectorate as a sign of appreciation for their service during the war. Not all of them, but selectively, depending on their record."

Zhukov didn't argue, though he muttered that ranks were awarded for greater military proficiency, not in appreciation. Father made no comment but, summoning his secretary, asked to be put through to Yeremenko.

A minute later the secretary reported that Yeremenko was on the line.

Father greeted the general warmly, without revealing that he knew what had happened. He asked how things were going, how was his health. Yeremenko answered in detail, without showing his cards. An old and experienced hand, he had no doubt that Father knew about the scandal. Now it behooved him to wait and see what would be offered in exchange for his obedience.

Father finally came to the point. He said that the Central Committee attributed great importance to strengthening the fighting efficiency of the Soviet Army and would like to make greater use of the exceedingly rich experience gained by military leaders during the war. Consequently, they were creating a General Corps of Inspectors to which the most experienced generals and marshals would be transferred. They would be directly subordinate to the Minister of Defense and, of course, to the Central Committee. These last words displeased Zhukov, who frowned. The marshal didn't put up with any interference in his business and regarded the political organs in the Army with undisguised hostility.

In conclusion, Father said that the Central Committee had chosen him, Yeremenko, to be one of the inspectors general. Yeremenko began to complain that he had received notice of his retirement from Zhukov. "That was a misunderstanding," Father assured him. Zhukov again frowned. He didn't tolerate cancellation of his orders either. The pragmatic Yeremenko, realizing that he couldn't count on anything better, expressed his thanks and promised to justify the party's confidence in him. The incident was resolved peacefully.

In the Ministry of Defense the inspectors general were dubbed "the heavenly group."

THE COUP D'ETAT IN THE PRESIDIUM

Immersed in his daily concerns, Father didn't suspect that a new crisis, one of the gravest in his career, was imminent.

I was wrapped up in my own affairs, preparing to get married. The wedding was set for early June, immediately after the end of exams at the Institute. My future wife and I studied in the same group. After the wedding we were to leave, not on a trip, but to work at one of the instrument-building plants located in Zagorsk, near Moscow.

In my memory these circumstances, seemingly unrelated to the theme of my narrative, are closely bound up with the political skirmish in the Presidium between Father and the Stalinists, who were later called the "Anti-Party Group of Malenkov, Kaganovich, Molotov, and Shepilov-who-joined-them."[13]

The reasons for the crisis are obvious: the position taken by Father in judging Stalin, against the wishes of Molotov, Voroshilov, and Kaganovich; the radical changes in domestic and foreign affairs he initiated; and the relegation of first Malenkov, and then Bulganin, to secondary roles. Father's opponents, experienced politicians, couldn't help but see that the way things were going, their political careers would soon draw to a close. They joined forces and decided to strike first.

The former harmony they had achieved before Beria's arrest had long since disintegrated. The gradual turn from confrontation and isolation to peaceful coexistence and the promotion of trade and other ties were viewed by Father's opponents, primarily Molotov, as ideological treason. In these matters Malenkov stood apart from his confederates. He never had a reputation as an orthodox thinker and in some ways went even further than Father. But not in his company.

There was no unanimity on domestic policy either. Molotov didn't agree with the grandiose project to develop the virgin lands. He thought it would be better to invest money in the peasant economy in the European part of the country. He would have found many adherents in today's arguments over the virgin lands. Father demonstrated that to upgrade the failing agriculture of the non-black earth zone, the central belt, would not only be terribly expensive, but time-consuming and difficult as well in view of the complete lack of fertilizer production. It was urgently necessary to obtain grain literally within a year, or at most two, in order to eliminate the lines forming at daybreak in front of bakeries, even in relatively well supplied Moscow. Grain could be produced quickly only by plowing up the new lands. "We'll make up the shortage," thought Father, "and then we can focus on agriculture in European Russia. In time, after crop yields increase, the need for the virgin lands, with their unpredictable droughts, will decline. Or, more precisely, the land will revert to pasture, of course on a new and more modern level." It didn't turn out that way, but that is what he thought.

Nothing is so permanent as what is temporary. Those five-story buildings planned to last twenty years are still standing over forty years later. The housing problem was supposed to be solved during that twenty-year period

---

13. The "Anti-Party Group" was Khrushchev's term for the leadership coalition that sought to oust him in June 1957. Its main leaders were Molotov, Malenkov, Kaganovich, Bulganin, and Voroshilov. Shepilov joined the group at the last moment, which is why he received this title. Though outvoted in the Presidium, Khrushchev prevailed by taking the matter to the Central Committee, to which the Presidium was formally responsible. These struggles are recounted by the author below.

and everyone would move into high-quality, well-built homes of "heightened convenience," as people say these days. It's the same with the former virgin lands, which the country can't do without. Moreover, the one-time purchase of foreign grain associated with the harvest failure of 1963 became standard practice and has persisted to this day.

The somewhat earlier decision about shifting to regional economic councils further inflamed the atmosphere in the Presidium. Father managed to get his plan through the Supreme Soviet, but Baibakov's dismissal did not put an end to resistance. Pervukhin, Saburov, and the other ministers appointed by Stalin had no intention of relinquishing power. They readily joined the coalition of Father's opponents.

Father himself pushed Bulganin into the camp of his enemies. They had stood together through all the previous years, both at the time of Stalin's death and during preparations for Beria's arrest. When he thought over suitable candidates to replace Malenkov as chairman of the Council of Ministers, Father naturally picked Bulganin. It seemed that he could trust Bulganin in everything. I have already described what happened during the visits to Geneva and Britain, when—either deliberately or inadvertently, because of his personality—Father crowded Bulganin off stage and seized the initiative, sometimes preventing Bulganin from even opening his mouth. That continued in Moscow. At first Bulganin tolerated it, but then he began to take offense and his displeasure with Father increased.

And then, during Tito's visit to Moscow, in a burst of friendly feeling, Bulganin made the unfortunate mistake of calling him a "true Marxist-Leninist." At the time, that was a serious transgression. The Central Committee circulated a special letter censuring Bulganin and issued a reprimand.

Colleagues in the Presidium poured gasoline on the fire. Some whispered sympathetically, others tauntingly: "Nikita doesn't give two cents for you!"

Finally Bulganin decided not to take it any more. He couldn't stand the role of supernumerary. He would show who was first. So he joined Father's opponents.

On May 20, Kaganovich, Malenkov, Molotov, Bulganin, and Pervukhin agreed in principle that the time had come to get rid of Father. They decided to appoint him minister of agriculture, to make Suslov minister of culture, and to have Bulganin assume a second position as head of the KGB, replacing Serov. A little later Voroshilov and Saburov joined the "initiative group." They conducted cautious negotiations with Zhukov, but he didn't give yes or no as an answer.[14]

Father's fate seemed to be sealed. They planned to make Molotov first

14. R. Pikhoya, *The Soviet Union: A History of Power, 1945–1991* (Moscow: RAGS Publishing House, 1998), 172–83.

secretary of the Central Committee. Later they developed another variant, which called for completely discarding the "Boss," as Stalin had done after the Nineteenth Party Congress.

Father still had no idea what was going on. Preparations were being made in the greatest secrecy.

Father unexpectedly invited a mass of people to my wedding, in addition to my friends and relatives. He was such a sociable person that when he talked with people he couldn't resist boasting that his son was getting married. Then he was obliged to invite them, to honor the ceremony by their presence, in accordance with the Russian custom.

Among those invited were Bulganin, Malenkov, Voroshilov, and Kaganovich. There were also other oppositionists, or representatives of the majority in the Presidium—I don't know which to call them. Father also invited Zhukov and KGB chairman Serov.

Mama silently counted the steadily increasing number of guests, wondering how to seat such a mob. We decided to hold the ceremony at the dacha. It had a large dining room, but it wasn't big enough to hold everyone, so another table was set up on the verandah.

The wedding celebration was merry, as called for by the occasion. Our guests split up into two groups—young and old—who didn't get in each other's way. They drank moderately. Father didn't like drunks. I've forgotten much of what happened that evening, but some incidents stand out. I'll mention a few that were in some way related to subsequent events.

Zhukov and Serov spent the whole time whispering to each other. As soon as the official toasts were over, they went out to the garden and spent a long time walking along its paths. I don't know whether that had any relation to subsequent events. Perhaps they simply hadn't had a chance for a quiet talk previously.

The Malenkovs, who arrived somewhat late, came as neighbors, informally. Though Georgy Maksimiliyanovich normally had a pleasant smile on his face, that day he looked gloomy. I remember something incongruous which my wife called to my attention the next day, when she was looking over the wedding presents. Some were expensive, others less so, depending on the situation of the giver. Some were conventional, others more personal, depending on the person's attitude toward the bride and groom.

"But what's this?" said my wife in surprise. She was holding a small, shabby woman's suede bag in a dark green color (sometimes called marsh green).

With some difficulty I remembered that Valeriya Alekseyevna, Malenkov's wife, had slipped it into my hands. Then, without lingering to congratulate us, they had hurried over to the group of older people. The bag turned out to contain a cheap alarm clock with a picture of an elephant on its face—

the stores were full of them at the time. It didn't look new either, but as if it was picked up in passing from a bedside table. I wouldn't have remembered this episode, since I didn't attribute much importance to presents and still less to their price. But what surprised me was the psychological disparity between the gift and my conscious image of the Malenkovs. They loved to give presents, often for no special reason, and they always tried to choose something unusual that would be remembered and cherished. In this they differed from most of Father's friends. When I began studying at the Institute they gave me a marvelous Faber case of drawing instruments in a polished wooden box. It looked genuinely valuable, and I never risked using it. Another time, on no particular occasion, I received from them a set of magnifying glasses, also very beautiful. And now this.

These thoughts flickered through my mind that day, or perhaps simply remained in my subconscious. I only recalled them later, when I came to the conclusion that on that day the Malenkovs must have thought that everything was decided. The figures on the chessboard were standing in new positions, and no place was assigned to Father in the game that lay ahead.

I also remember an altercation at the table. By then the group of older people had long been immersed in their own conversations and had almost forgotten the younger members of the party. I've mentioned that almost no one got drunk, but that doesn't mean that people didn't drink at the table. Bulganin got a little tight, though his associates only sipped their drinks and behaved cautiously.

Father was in a fine holiday mood, joking and teasing people. When Bulganin started to propose a toast, Father interrupted and cracked a good-natured joke. Bulganin reacted with fury. He simply exploded. He started to shout that he wouldn't let anyone shut him up and order him around, and all that was soon going to end. They had a hard time calming him down. Father tried to persuade his friend that he had no thought whatsoever of offending him. They managed to quell the unpleasant and inappropriate outburst.

The next morning I accompanied Father as usual on his morning stroll, before he left for work. The sun was bright, the grass green, and the birds were singing. There was no sign of the approaching storm.

A few days later my wife and I left for Zagorsk.

It all began on Tuesday, June 18, which was unusual, since the Presidium of the Central Committee customarily met on Thursdays. Apparently they counted on finishing the business by Sunday.

They had prepared thoroughly and their arrangements seemed likely to preclude any unpleasantness. On one side, I repeat, there were Malenkov,

Molotov, Kaganovich, Voroshilov, Bulganin, Pervukhin, and Saburov, seven members of the Central Committee Presidium, who were, moreover, the senior members. On the other was Khrushchev himself, and with him Suslov, Mikoyan, and the newcomer Kirichenko. However, the candidate members of the Presidium elected during the previous few years—Zhukov, Shepilov, Brezhnev, Nikolai Shvernik, Mukhitdinov, and Furtseva—came out on Father's side. Another of Father's potential allies, Frol Romanovich Kozlov, Leningrad provincial committee secretary and candidate member of the Presidium, was absent. They hadn't called him, and he was up to his ears in preparations for the city's 250th anniversary celebration. In any case, candidate members were not taken seriously, since they did not have the right to vote.

Not much information has survived about those days. Snippets of information have to be put together. Most of the firsthand evidence is to be found in the diary of the Yugoslav ambassador to Moscow, Veljko Micunovic.[15]

Father was trying to reach an understanding with Tito and counted on bringing him back into the family of socialist countries. But he wasn't very successful. Actually, he was totally unsuccessful. Tito kept his distance. Father tried in every possible way to persuade the Yugoslavs. But, convinced that little would be gained by writing letters, he preferred personal conversations. His interlocutor became the Yugoslav ambassador, who was a member of Tito's inner circle. At diplomatic receptions Father would corner Micunovic and talk for hours one-on-one. Once, when they hadn't finished their conversation, he offered to drive the ambassador home to his residence on Khelbny Street. They arrived quickly, but sat in Father's limousine "finishing" their talk until long past midnight, with a ten-degree frost outside. The ambassador's wife finally lost patience (she had gone inside as soon as they reached the residence) and invited them in to drink tea and warm up.

As time went on, Father developed friendly, as well as trusting, relations with Micunovic. He was the only person Father told what had happened. As an ambassador should, Micunovic immediately wrote everything down and sent a report to Tito. He included this report in his book.

Father told Micunovic that he had already sensed something was wrong during a recent trip to Finland with Bulganin, but didn't think it was important.

That day, June 18, Father had lunch at home from one to two o'clock, as usual. Lunch was interrupted by a phone call. It was Bulganin.

"Nikita, come here, to the Kremlin. We're having a session of the Central Committee Presidium," he began.

---

15. Veljko Micunovic, *Moscow Diary* (Garden City, N.Y.: Doubleday, 1980), 210, 252–85.

Bulganin spoke with uncharacteristic brevity and constraint, almost as if afraid of something.

"Nikolai, what's the hurry?" Father said in surprise.

"We have to discuss the speech in Leningrad" (on the 250th anniversary of the city's founding), answered Bulganin.

"Well, we can do that on Thursday, especially since right after lunch today I have a meeting with a delegation of Hungarian journalists, and then some Japanese are coming for an interview," Father continued, puzzled.

But Bulganin continued to insist, saying that they were all gathered in the Kremlin dining room and everyone thought it essential to meet.

"Who's there?" Father asked.

"Everyone who's having lunch," answered Bulganin.

"But people having lunch in the Kremlin are not the same thing as the Central Committee Presidium," said Father, beginning to get angry.

Bulganin continued to insist and Father gave in, saying that he would come to the Kremlin. There, since the meeting was so sudden, he found that eight members and three candidate members of the Presidium were present. Absent were Kirichenko (he had left for the Ukraine), Suslov, Saburov (he was in Warsaw for a meeting of the Comecon Executive Committee), Shvernik, Mukhitdinov, Kozlov, and Central Committee secretaries Aristov, Belyayev, and Pospelov. The session began literally at the lunch table, though Father tried to postpone the session, referring again to his meeting with Hungarian journalists.

The others pounced on him: "Why are you meeting journalists alone?"

"But everything was discussed earlier at the Presidium," parried Father. "And wouldn't it be funny if the entire Central Committee Presidium went to give an interview with journalists."

That attempt at humor didn't help. All of them, including the candidate members, went to meet the Hungarians. After this group interview everyone returned to the hall. They started arguing again. Now Malenkov and Molotov voiced displeasure over the fact that Father was the only one who presided over meetings. He objected that he had suggested more than once that they should rotate the chair. Finally, they agreed that this time Bulganin would assume the role of chairman (that was unfortunate for Father's opponents, since he was a mild and indecisive person). They would decide later about who should preside at future sessions. Father and they agreed on only one thing. Those members and candidate members who were away must be informed of the meeting and asked to return to Moscow immediately.

I've already discussed Father's principal "mistakes." Now a whole slew of petty complaints, some farfetched and others laughable, accompanied them. For example, Kaganovich said that when Father was still working at the

Donetzk Coal Basin, in the early 1920s, he had supported Trotsky, and Malenkov said that Khrushchev "was wrong to equate, in the manner of Grigoriy Zinoviev, the dictatorship of the proletariat and the dictatorship of the party" and incorrectly understood the relationship between the party and the state. This was clearly an echo of the usual 1930s pattern of accusations.

Bulganin, referring to their visit to Finland, "accused" Father of having gone to the sauna with Urho Kekkonen after the president's reception, thereby demeaning the dignity of a Soviet leader.

"You can't be serious, Nikolai," said Father, looking at Bulganin in surprise. "I didn't go there to wash, but to hold confidential negotiations with the president of Finland—what is more, in such heat."

Father's joke fell flat. Those present unanimously condemned his visit to the sauna.

A few weeks after these events, Urho Kekkonen telephoned Father and said that he wanted to give him a real Finnish sauna. He would send his specialists, and they would assemble it wherever Father wanted. This provoked a nervous reaction from the KGB. Let foreigners visit the "object," Khrushchev's dacha?

The Finns arrived in Moscow with logs, boards, and wash basins—everything, down to the last nail. And with that, things came to a halt. They were not allowed onto the dacha grounds. Kekkonen had to call Father, who flew into a rage and summoned Serov.

"Do you think that I roasted in that hellhole in Finland for pleasure?" he said harshly. "I was trying to establish good personal relations with the leader of a neighboring country, which may be small but is very important to us. And now you're ruining everything. Let the Finns get to work immediately."

"I will order it," said Serov, having listened to Father's tirade in silence.

Soon a small resinous log hut, with a large clear window and small terrace, framed by a heavy beam resting on low supports (in Finland they usually tie horses to such a structure) rose under the pines at the ninth dacha (now Gorky-9), not far from the main entrance.

Inside, the sauna gleamed, the walls were paneled with smooth boards (something we had never seen before), and there was even a fireplace in the room where people relaxed after taking a sauna—an unheard-of luxury at the time.

Father carefully examined the present, sent Kekkonen his thanks, but never again entered the sauna. When he had worked at the mines, he had gone to the banya (a Russian version of the sauna) to wash, but afterward he had acquired a bathtub. The banya/sauna remained to him a symbol of poverty and disorder.

My friends and I took over the sauna. On weekends we often used to steam ourselves. Adzhubei sometimes dropped in, but didn't linger. Our "engineering" company was of little interest to him.

But I have digressed. Let's return to the Kremlin, to the Central Committee Presidium session.

Father defended himself fiercely. He didn't admit to a single one of the main charges, but called his actions correct. He agreed with only some of the minor criticisms. For example, he admitted his Trotskyite "delusions," but reminded Kaganovich that in 1937 even Stalin, who was aware of the episode, had not considered it worthy of attention. Furthermore, when Kaganovich heard all about it from Khrushchev himself, he had advised him on how to avoid trouble. So why was Kaganovich now dragging this moth-eaten "history" into the discussion?

The winners had counted on persuading Father to compromise. In exchange for giving in, the majority proposed, as already mentioned, that he become minister of agriculture. Here they were following a well-worn path. After being removed from the position of premier, Malenkov became minister of the power industry. Now it was Father's turn. Otherwise . . . Well, they didn't say what would happen otherwise. Father's opponents had a wealth of experience in such matters.

The battle dragged on for days. They sat late into the evenings. Worn out, they then went home, to resume wrangling the next morning. Each member and candidate member spoke more than once. Some might have preferred not to say anything, but that wasn't possible—they had to make a choice. And so they talked and talked and talked. Father's supporters were inconsistent. Some backed him throughout, while others occasionally gave in to pressure from the majority.

Zhukov held firm. He was well aware of each person's true character. He had seen enough during the war, especially in 1941. And not just in the Kremlin. He had clashed with Voroshilov in Leningrad, where Zhukov was sent to rescue the front from the bungling of the "First Marshal." Moreover, he had not forgotten Voroshilov's behavior near Moscow. Sent by Stalin to discover the reasons for our most recent defeats, Voroshilov hysterically accused Front Commander General Konev of treachery. All in all, Zhukov had no respect for the man who had been the People's Commissar for Defense before the war and who had succeeded only in ruining his own armed forces during the 1930s.

Nor had Zhukov forgotten Molotov's telephone calls to the staff at the Front during the most difficult days in the defense of Moscow. Molotov could think of nothing better than to threaten officers with execution.

At the time Bulganin was a member of Zhukov's Front Military Council.

Nothing good or bad could be said about him; he was neither fish nor fowl. Later they worked together at the Ministry of Defense. They were not close there either, and had not become either friends or confederates.

Zhukov didn't know the others as well, but he had no intention of linking his fate with theirs. He had chosen his side carefully and was determined to keep to it no matter what happened. He had been in seemingly hopeless situations more than once, but had always emerged victorious.

Rumor had it that Zhukov said at the time: "Not a single tank will move unless I order it." I never heard that. I also never heard anything to support the later legend that when tanks were rushing toward Moscow in Father's support and couldn't find the right road, they demolished whole villages in their path. Father never considered the Army to be an arbiter in political arguments and he did not appeal to it. He chose a different strategy. Since the exposure of Stalin's crimes and mistakes, the only way to resolve an argument was the democratic way. A fight for the votes of Central Committee members was the only engagement in which he would participate.

Brezhnev's performance at the Presidium was unfortunate. He had been elected to the enlarged Central Committee Presidium and Secretariat at the Nineteenth Party Congress. He seemed poised for rapid advancement, but everything changed radically after Stalin's death. Both the Presidium and the Secretariat were drastically reduced in size. There was no need for Brezhnev, and they found him a job as head of the Navy's Political Department (PUR), a position vacant at the time. As time passed, his situation improved. Father liked Brezhnev. Although his pliancy and dependent nature were not the best recommendations, Brezhnev enjoyed a reputation as a shrewd administrator. In 1957 he returned to the Central Committee and again became a secretary and candidate member, though not full member, of the Presidium.

In the complex circumstances of the June crisis there was no need for Brezhnev to choose. He saw no future for himself without Khrushchev. When it was time for Brezhnev to speak, emotions were running high and everyone was shouting and interrupting each other. Leonid Ilyich barely managed to utter the first words he had prepared in Father's defense, when Kaganovich, his mustache bristling, loomed over him and rudely interrupted. The last words Brezhnev heard were something like: "You like to talk. You've forgotten how you were relegated to the PUR—we'll chase you back there soon enough." Leonid Ilyich faltered, started to clutch the back of his chair and sank slowly to the floor. A doctor was summoned. Guards carried the unconscious and unfortunate warrior to an adjacent room, where he revived. Brezhnev soon returned to the hall, but didn't ask to speak again. He sat looking pale and dejected.

Kirichenko behaved quite differently. The senior members didn't consider Ukrainian Central Committee secretary their equal. But Aleksei

Illarionovich had a different view of his role. He had no intention of giving in. Kirichenko gruffly and flatly rejected all the accusations, without bothering to make distinctions among any particular arguments. He knew he had nothing to lose, since without Father he had no future.

Mikoyan took a deeply reasoned and sound position. A convinced anti-Stalinist, he supported Father out of conviction. Or, more correctly, it wasn't so much support of Father as the fact that they fought for the same idea and would either win together or perish together.

I simply don't know what Suslov said. That information never reached me.

As the confrontation began, Shepilov took Father's side. They had recently begun pulling together, as the saying goes. Both at home and abroad Shepilov made a point of his devotion to Father. Sometimes people were surprised by his behavior. Micunovic cites the following in his book: "One time, at Tito's dacha (this was during the Soviet delegation's visit to Yugoslavia in 1955), with fewer than ten people present, including Shepilov, Khrushchev began to reminisce about various events in his life. Every once in a while he turned to Shepilov for confirmation. Each time Shepilov picked up his napkin from his lap, pushed back his chair, rose and, standing at attention, answered: 'Just so, Nikita Sergeyevich.'" That was in 1955, but everything was different in 1957. Shepilov had to choose. Toward evening of that day, June 18, it seemed more and more apparent to Shepilov that he had bet on the wrong horse. He became increasingly nervous and finally, just before the vote—when Father's position looked utterly hopeless—Shepilov decided to change his bet, to switch to the winning side and vote to dismiss Khrushchev as first secretary. His whole life would have been different if he had just held his ground and not panicked. He would not have been among those "joining," but would be found on some (God knows what) iconostasis. But he didn't stand fast. Like a duck, he flapped his wings and took flight when he sensed the hunter's approach.

At the end of the session the Presidium voted to dismiss Father from his duties as member and Secretary of the Central Committee. Seven votes were cast against him, four votes in his favor, including his own.

The opposing camp celebrated victory. However, Father had no intention of giving in. He obstinately stuck to his guns, declaring that the decision was illegal, that he, like the others, had been elected by a plenum of the Central Committee and that it alone could decide who should remain in the Presidium and who should leave.

These were not just empty words. Father sensed that he was in a strong position, for he had not been idle during those days. He knew he could count on support at a Central Committee plenum. Provincial committee secretaries and officials with various ranks and titles—who were a majority in the Central Committee—wanted stability. They were not at all pleased with the idea of returning to Stalinist procedures. They vividly remembered those times, not that long ago, when you shuddered at every footfall on the stairs. More important, they were fed up with being subservient. They wanted to be the ones in charge. They thought that Father was capable of understanding them and defending their interests.

Personal connections played an important role. Father was well known to many of those who would decide his fate in the next few days, and not only because they had served on presidiums at various meetings. He had fought beside some in the war; others he had met often during his travels around the country, on visits to factories and collective farms. He seemed to be one of them. They could understand him.

In order to win, he had to bring together Central Committee members scattered around the country before the opposition could do so. He had to move very quickly, in hours, not days.

A person of proven ability was needed for this purpose. Father's choice fell on KGB chairman General Serov. Actually, there was no alternative. All the lines of communication were either in the hands of the KGB or controlled by it. To bypass the KGB when calling a provincial committee by the special phone or sending an official letter was unthinkable. Each provincial committee secretary had a bodyguard-informer who watched his every step. Special departments attached to troop commanders performed the same function.

Father trusted Serov. He had promoted him to that important position, and Serov wouldn't have lasted a day in Moscow without Father. At one session Molotov had openly stated that Serov should be replaced. Serov knew that. Father invited Serov to the dacha to talk to him in person. They went for a walk in the woods, where they couldn't be overheard. Since Serov knew everything that was going on, he had a good idea of why he had been called. He assured Father of his loyalty, swore allegiance to the line declared by the Twentieth Party Congress, and said that he was prepared to carry out all orders given by the Central Committee first secretary.

The intricate web woven over the entire country by the Committee of State Security turned out to be very useful. It enabled Father to contact all the people he needed both quickly and confidentially.

Father was in an ambiguous position. During the preceding years he had demanded that the KGB be excluded from the country's political life and that its functions be limited to the fight against hostile intelligence services, agents, and spies. He thought that neither the state security agencies nor the Army had the right to interfere in politics. Their task was to carry out the decisions of political leaders, the Presidium of the Central Committee. As he elaborated on this principle, Father would later formulate the policy that the defense minister, foreign affairs minister, and the KGB chairman should never be members of the Presidium, so that when making decisions Presidium members would not feel pressure from the so-called power departments.

Now, however, he had to use the services of this organization. There was no alternative. Father consoled himself with the fact that Serov was entrusted with purely logistical tasks. But "one claw snared—and the bird is lost." Who could tell in such a situation where logistical functions end and important policy matters begin? It was extremely naive to hope that with one stroke of the pen you could exclude such an organization from making policy, remove it from power, and deprive it of its former might. Still, Father believed, or wanted to believe, in the limitless power of Central Committee decisions.

In any case, Father asked Serov to contact Central Committee members and, after explaining the situation, find out their point of view. It was most important, he thought, to inform Kozlov, the first secretary of the Leningrad provincial committee. Father counted heavily on support from Leningrad, the city of the Revolution.

Serov understood at once. He asked permission to leave and begin carrying out his assignment immediately. He would report the results right away. Naturally, the anti-Khrushchev majority of the Presidium didn't learn of this meeting. The only person who could have informed them was Serov. Their isolation was increasing with every day that passed. Serov kept track of every step taken by the "majority."

In the Kremlin stormy discussions continued, with lengthy speeches enumerating Father's real and imaginary sins, followed by rebuttals. Time and again furious skirmishes flared up. One day passed in this manner, then a second and a third. Meanwhile Serov telephoned, explained, described, persuaded. The majority of Central Committee members quickly grasped what was going on and asked what they should do.

The answer was brief and to the point: "Come to Moscow as soon as possible and convene a plenum of the Central Committee."

Some made their own way. Others, especially those in distant regions, were brought by military aircraft. Zhukov helped arrange that.

Today it's hard to imagine how difficult it was in those years to get to Moscow from Siberia. There were few civilian flights. The slow IL-12 hopped from airport to airport, from city to city. It moved only a little faster than a train, over distances measuring many thousands of kilometers. Provincial committee secretaries and other Central Committee members from far-off places were flown to Moscow on jet bombers.

First to arrive in Moscow was Kozlov, who hurried there from Leningrad. Nikolai Grigoryevich Ignatov arrived from Gorky at almost the same time.

Immediately after landing he joined in the fray, receiving information from Serov and talking with all of the incoming members of the Central Committee. Thanks to his energy, Ignatov became the focal point for many of them and something like an "alternative" Presidium formed around him.

Preparations for the plenum necessitated dealing with organizational questions. For the first time a plenum was convening on its own initiative and not by order of the Presidium. It was organized by the so-called Twenty, an initiative group of twenty activist Central Committee members.

Ignatov called Khrushchev on their behalf and asked for an appointment. Father invited him to the dacha that evening, since the entire day was taken up by a nonstop session of the Presidium. Ignatov has said that for the sake of secrecy he came with Vladimir Pavlovich Mylarshchikov, head of the Central Committee agriculture department, supposedly to look at the corn crop.

Every spring Father planted a new crop at the dacha and experimented, sometimes with cereal grains, sometimes with millet. Now the entire area was under corn. He derived obvious satisfaction from fussing over the plants and he liked to relax in the garden after a day of intensive work in the office.

According to Ignatov, after taking a cursory look at the rows of corn he casually asked Mylarshchikov to leave them alone for a serious conversation. Ignatov reported that the initiative group (the "Twenty") planned to insist on meeting with members of the Presidium the next day. Their purpose was to demand the immediate convocation of an emergency plenum of the Central Committee. Father had already heard about this from Serov. He supported Ignatov and said that any further delay would simply be dangerous.

Despite the fact that a majority of the Central Committee members were already in Moscow, the "Twenty" had decided not to convene a session of the plenum without permission from the Presidium. But the Presidium had not been able to implement its decision to dismiss Father. For the first time in the previous two decades, if not longer, it faced opposition from the Central Committee. It had been a long time since anyone had taken the Central Committee into consideration.

However, it would take a little more time for the "Twenty" to become conscious of their strength and assert themselves. At first, sensing that they were masters of the situation, the previously mute *apparatchiki* demanded that their representatives be admitted to the Presidium session. They had Nikolay A. Romanov, head of the Central Committee's General Department and one of the few with access to the meeting hall, deliver a note that had the ring of an ultimatum: "To the Presidium of the Central Committee. We, the members of the CPSU Central Committee, have learned that you are discussing the question of the leadership of the Central Committee and the Secretariat. Questions of such importance to the party must not be concealed from members of the Central Committee. In this connection we, members of the Central Committee, cannot stand aloof from questions of our party's leadership."

The Presidium had no idea how to react to this message. What should they do? The slow-witted Molotov couldn't even imagine that such a thing was possible. The clever and shrewd Kaganovich understood that all was lost and that they could only hope for a miracle.

Time passed. There was no word from the Presidium. The "Twenty" didn't want to wait any longer. A new message was sent requesting that the initiative group be admitted to the session immediately. Again there was no answer. The majority of the Presidium, which only yesterday had seemed omnipotent, felt as if it were in a trap.

After a third reminder that Central Committee members, representatives of the "Twenty"—Ignatov, Marshal Konev, and someone else—were waiting outside the door, it was obvious that no further delay was possible. Observing the long drawn-out struggle, Father poured fuel on the fire by declaring that he was ready to meet with "the people."

Voroshilov, chairman of the Supreme Soviet Presidium, and Bulganin, chairman of the Council of Ministers, were appointed to negotiate with the "Twenty." The choice was an unfortunate one, since neither possessed the power of persuasion. Apparently they relied on the "magic" of their titles; mostly, they just did not fully realize what was going on. They thought it would be enough to raise their voices and everything would return to its proper place. That was an unforgivable error, characteristic of all rulers facing a revolution, great or small. They don't notice the moment when power escapes from their hands, leaving behind only an empty and brittle shell.

At that moment power shifted definitively into the hands of the Central Committee apparatus. It agreed, of course, to observe the old rules of the game and preserve the appearance of an all-powerful Presidium or Politburo, but only when the latter respected its interests. It would strike back at anyone who tried to infringe on them.

Neither Bulganin nor Voroshilov had the slightest suspicion of this.

Bulganin began swearing at the "Twenty" as soon as he entered the room. He seemed like a serf-owning landlord scolding his rebellious slaves. Voroshilov behaved more or less the same way.

The Presidium had to suspend its session while these negotiations were going on. Taking advantage of the pause, Father also left the hall and looked in on the meeting. He didn't intervene and was simply an interested observer of the furious row.

The two sides parted in anger. However, although a certain degree of crisis and uncertainty was evident in the Presidium session, the "majority" didn't know what to do next. The "Twenty," which soon became "Thirty," and by the last, fourth day of the Central Committee Presidium session, July

22, had grown to eighty-three, became all the more determined. The threats from Voroshilov and Bulganin did not produce their expected effect and only inflamed passions. The "Parliamentarians" were sent away with a final message: either the Presidium immediately convened a Central Committee plenum, or the plenum would open its session independently and invite members of the Presidium to report in the Sverdlov Hall of the Kremlin.

This was effectively the end of the crisis. The plenum, which convened on Saturday, June 22, only summarized the results. Father delivered a report. I suspect that it amounted to more than a dry recital of the facts.

Molotov spoke in defense of his position. He remained firm, in contrast to his recent allies, who were lost in terrified speculations about their fate. Later Father often referred to that with respect. The remaining "representatives of the majority" repented with alacrity.

Central Committee members spoke very harshly. The plenum gradually began to follow the usual pattern. Each person tried to throw his share of mud on the "oppositionists." The sessions lasted an entire week, until June 29. Anyone who wanted to speak was given the floor.

In early July I finished my internship in Zagorsk, near Moscow, and returned home, completely unaware of what had happened. The plenum was already over, but no official reports had been published. Father didn't say anything to me about it. I found out what had happened from the newspapers.

For some reason I remember that sunny summer morning at Father's dacha. The mail had just been delivered: multicolored envelopes sealed with wax, and the newspapers. Father signed receipts for the courier items and, piling the documents in a heap on a round wicker table, began to read the newspapers. I sat next to him and over his shoulder noticed the official report on the plenum, which was on the first page of *Pravda*. As usual, my eyes slid down the lines printed in bold-faced type to the end, which always had the important news, i.e., organizational questions: who was elected, who was dismissed. This time the list of names took up an entire paragraph. Among those dismissed I saw such names . . . I couldn't believe my eyes—top leaders. Moreover, these were friends. Quite recently, we had all been sitting together at my wedding. I couldn't believe my eyes! When Father was working, he was not to be disturbed. That was a long established and sacredly observed custom. That day I couldn't resist and deluged him with questions. He wouldn't go into details, and said only that his former colleagues had taken an incorrect position, so the plenum had to straighten them out.

"They admitted their error and voted to condemn themselves." There was a tinge of scorn in Father's voice. "Molotov was the only one who held firm to the end."

The only thing I learned from him that morning was that the four named in the newspaper—"Malenkov, Molotov, Kaganovich, and Shepilov-who-joined-them"—were not the only ones voting against Father, but were joined by several other members of the Central Committee Presidium, including Bulganin and Voroshilov.

"We decided not to include their names," Father added. "They repented at the plenum. What happened will be a good lesson to them. And it looks better to the outside world this way," he concluded, going back to his papers.

Those not listed in the official report as Father's opponents gradually left the Presidium, one after another. Some, like Saburov and Pervukhin, immediately; others were kept on a little while longer.

The June plenum expanded the Presidium's membership. There were now fifteen members and nine candidate members. Father made up the list, from among his supporters, naturally. Ignatov soon joined the Presidium.

Father was extremely proud that for the first time in decades no repressions followed a political defeat, although proposals of that sort were made.

He had demonstrated to his opponents the realities of the Twentieth Congress, against which they had rebelled. "Law alone must rule," Father said repeatedly. It turned out to be far more difficult to carry out this promise than to enunciate it, unfortunately. But at the time it seemed as if the main obstacles had been overcome.

Members of the "Anti-Party Group" waited helplessly to learn their fate. Only Kaganovich couldn't hold out and telephoned Father.

Several years later Father recalled this telephone conversation as he spoke to the Twenty-second Party Congress. Here is some of the stenographic account of the conversation, although from what I remember Father telling me, they actually spoke much more simply, without fervor or pomposity.

"Comrade Khrushchev! I have known you for many years. I ask you not to allow them to treat me the way people were treated under Stalin." These are Kaganovich's words in Father's interpretation.

Father's reply: "Comrade Kaganovich! What you say is another indication of the methods you were ready to use to achieve your vile aims. You wanted to return the country to the practices that prevailed during the cult of personality. You wanted to carry out reprisals against people. You measure others by your own yardstick. But you are wrong. We firmly adhere to Leninist principles and will continue to do so. You will be given work, and you can live and work in peace, provided you work honestly, like all Soviet citizens."

Father decided that his opponents should not remain in Moscow. When I asked about the fate of members of the "Anti-Party Group," he said that work would be found for them, but far from the capital. It would be not dangerous, but awkward, to have them in Moscow. That was how he gradually squeezed Stalinism out of himself.

It has to be said that at the time everyone considered this decision to be progressive and humane. No one was shot, no one was put in prison. Moreover, an attempt was made to assign them work that suited their tastes and, so to speak, their professions.

Kaganovich had the reputation of being an energetic general manager, though not in any particular field. He had no specific profession except that of shoemaker. He was sent to the Urals, as director of the Solikamsk Potassium Combine. An important position.

Malenkov, a former minister of electric power, was appointed director of the large Ust-Kamenogorsk Electric Power Station on the Irtysh River.

"Shepilov-who-joined-them" was sent to teach Marxism-Leninism to students in the south, in Central Asia.

Molotov presented the most difficult problem. It was decided to appoint him to an ambassadorship. A suitable country was selected. It was not among the dozen or so most important ones and not a country with which the Soviet Union expected to have any special dealings. A request for accreditation was sent, but it was denied. Another country had to be found. Another rejection. This time they not only refused, but reproached us for lack of respect: how can you nominate as ambassador a person who does not enjoy his government's confidence?

Foreign Minister Gromyko came to Father for instructions. At first Father laughed: "So they all refuse?" He seemed amused by the situation, but not for long.

"Their thinking is correct," he said, either to himself or to Gromyko. "We should have foreseen their reaction. It really is annoying to receive an ambassador already known not to enjoy any respect and unlikely to be able to communicate with his leaders."

Father said that he would give it some thought. Not, of course, about leaving Molotov in Moscow. He decided to have a personal chat with one of the leaders of the socialist countries and try to persuade him to accept Molotov as ambassador.

Father first called Novotny in Prague, thinking that he would agree. A huge monument to Stalin had recently been erected on a hill overlooking the Vltava River and seemed to signify certain friendly feelings in the Czechoslovak leadership. But Novotny categorically refused. Father had to knock on other doors. All without success. He finally managed to persuade Yumzhagiin Tsedenbal of Mongolia, but only with difficulty and as a personal favor. The *agrement* for the new Soviet ambassador soon arrived, and Molotov left for Ulan-Bator.

The first time you weed a garden you never succeed in eradicating all the weeds. The roots remain, and when you look a week or two later they have emerged from the soil. It's the same with politics. Bad habits are the most tenacious. Although members of the "Anti-Party Group" avoided the usual "refuge" of oppositionists—prison—in other respects they were subjected to the old, traditional humiliations.

For many years Molotov was an honorary member of the Academy of Sciences. No one knew what services he had performed, but no one asked. It was decided to deprive him of that title, now described as undeserved. I don't know who took the initiative in this matter, but someone can always be found in such cases. When Father was informed, he didn't object.

"What kind of scientist is he, anyway? Stalin invented all that," said Father indignantly when he came home.

No sooner said than done. Shepilov was expelled as a corresponding member of the Academy at the same time as Molotov.

In June of 1957 Father, it seemed, had won a final victory in the Central Committee Presidium. No opponents or rivals were left in the leadership. Or so it seemed.

In fact, in June 1957 a completely new balance of forces was formed. For the first time in many years the *apparat*—and it was precisely representatives of the apparat who comprised the members of the Central Committee—was transformed from a bit player into an active performer determining the distribution of power, including that at the very top, in the Presidium. It is undoubtedly true that even earlier no one, including Stalin, could act without considering the interests of this powerful element of the government. But in the past the mystery of power had been preserved. Now everything became simpler. The members of the Presidium of the Central Committee, who had previously been enveloped in some halo of inaccessibility, suddenly came down into the hall and turned out to be ordinary people. It was possible to support them, and it was also possible to oppose them successfully. Thus was revealed what was perhaps one of the most vital lessons of the Twentieth Party Congress. Gradually, with experience, the apparat grew in strength and real power flowed increasingly toward the middle echelon of the party.

I recall a very characteristic conversation with Ignatov. One autumn day, probably in 1958, a large group came to visit the dacha. They hadn't finished discussing some subject at the Kremlin. We went for a walk. Father was ahead. I brought up the rear of the procession. By chance Ignatov fell in along with me. He had just moved to Moscow and I barely knew him. It was the first time he had visited Father at the dacha. For a while we walked in silence. Then Ignatov started to talk about how I shouldn't worry, they would not let Father be insulted, they had already proven that . . .

At first I didn't entirely grasp what he was talking about. It was only afterward that I guessed he was referring to the events of that memorable June. I didn't respond. I simply didn't know what to say. Ignatov said a few more words and then moved forward and joined the main group. I probably wouldn't have remembered these few phrases if I had not been amazed by his patronizing tone about Father.

The era of the apparat had truly begun. It lasted from 1957 until October of 1964 and then, naturally, evolved into the period when administration by the apparat flourished, which for some reason we call the "period of stagnation." One particular comment: when we think over the personnel changes at the very top occurring in subsequent years, we should always keep 1957 in mind. A great deal can be traced back to the events of that year.

SYRIA, A CRISIS PREVENTED

After his "debut" in the Middle East, ending with the expulsion of British and French expeditionary forces from the Suez Canal zone, Father followed events in the region with a great deal of interest.

He developed a special attitude toward Syria. In his opinion, most of the regimes in the Arab countries were strikingly reactionary in character: those who came to power were either protégés of the colonial powers or nothing more than local feudal rulers. In contrast, Syria was distinguished by both democratic governmental institutions and a legal communist party, which was playing an important role in society. Father could therefore not remain neutral when an anti-Syrian campaign began in neighboring Jordan and Turkey under the banner of the struggle against communism and with American participation. Negotiations, conferences, and a demonstrative exchange of visits, among them military visits, began.

Father hinted to Western diplomats that the Soviet Union would not remain neutral in case of conflict. He explained that in this case geography would favor us, which was not true during the Suez crisis. Turkey should not forget about its common border with the Soviet Union. We would find a way to help our friends.

Father reacted decisively in response to the deployment of Turkish troops along the Syrian border. The Georgian newspaper *Zarya Vostoka* reported that Marshal Rokossovsky had arrived to take command of the Caucasian Military District. Such appointments did not usually appear in our newspapers and the appearance there of such a high-ranking military leader, who had so much experience in the recent war, was open to only one interpretation. At the same time troops began to move toward the Turkish border. The Turks took the hint. There was no intervention. Father's belief that you could gain a great deal by threats was reinforced. But you had to know your limits.

THE R-7, SUCCESS AT LAST

The next test of the R-7, on July 11, was another failure. This time it was the guidance system. There seemed to be no end to disappointments. When one defect was eliminated, a new one appeared.

I began to worry that it would never fly. Father also became less optimistic, but he had faith in Korolyov and thought that sooner or later the engineers would manage to eliminate the defects and make progress.

News from the test sites that summer was not all bad. Yangel began to test his R-12. Father was almost childishly delighted at the successes of the young team. Three years before he had given them his blessing, and now they were not disappointing him and were fulfilling their promises.

Father met with Yangel during the summer. They had a long talk. The designer proposed taking the next step: more than doubling the range of a missile, to 4500 kilometers. According to him, a new missile could be produced quickly. Father agreed. The R-14, as it was designated, would make it possible to disperse launch positions still further and locate them deep inside our territory. Secrecy would be enhanced, and it would be harder for enemy bombers to reach them. Father thought that was particularly important.

During their talk Father brought up a subject that always concerned him—an intercontinental missile. Yangel reacted with interest and proposed cautiously that he work to develop one. Father didn't hurry to answer, and then advised him to think it over carefully. They would talk about it the next time they met. He was afraid that an untested team might collapse if given such a hugely difficult assignment. Then we would have neither an intercontinental nor a medium-range, "European" missile. Furthermore, when could they succeed in carrying out such a project? Korolyov had spent many years working on his concepts. How many more years would the country have to wait for Yangel?

Still, Father didn't forget their conversation. In the meantime he could only wait until the R-7 managed to fly the hoped-for seven thousand kilometers from Tyura-Tam to Kamchatka.

I found out from Father that he had heard from Korolyov, who reported that they had eliminated the defects that caused the first test failures. The next tests were scheduled for the second half of August, probably sometime after August 20. At the beginning of August my wife and I left by car for a vacation in the Caucasus. Since I was traveling far from Father at the time, I wasn't aware of what was going on at the test site. In those years neither missile launches nor nuclear explosions were made public.

Three weeks, or even a little more, went by. I waited impatiently to meet Father—not just to learn the test results, of course. I simply missed him very much. We were not usually apart for that long. Summer was drawing to a close, and it came time to return to the Institute in Moscow. I had to defend my thesis, get my diploma, and start working in March of the following year.

On August 27, turning on the radio somewhere in the North Caucasus not far from Tuapse, I heard Levitan's voice, sounding triumphant. He was reading a TASS report about the successful tests of an intercontinental ballistic missile in the Soviet Union. The announcer sounded especially animated when he said emphatically that we could now reach any point on the globe without resorting to airplanes, which were vulnerable to modern methods of air defense. The same report referred to the successful completion of a series of tests of nuclear and thermonuclear warheads. It concluded by expressing thanks, on behalf of the government, to all who took part in the tests, as well as sincere congratulations and wishes for new successes.

In fact, the missile had been fired on August 21. After receiving confirmation that the warhead had reached the target area on the Kamchatka peninsula, Korolyov immediately called Father by special telephone. Unlike previous calls, this one delighted both parties. After listening to Father's congratulations, Sergei Pavlovich proposed that an artificial earth satellite be launched without delay. In his words, the Americans had almost reached their goal, their rocket was virtually ready, but now we had a real chance to outstrip them. Father wasn't averse to thumbing our nose at the Americans, but he was afraid that the sputnik would distract the team from its main task, testing an intercontinental missile.

Korolyov assured him that one would not interfere with the other, and that the next launch of a missile would take place in September. The satellite could be ready to launch by the beginning of October. Father wished him every success.

Father called Ustinov immediately after being informed of the successful launch and asked him to speed up preparation of proposals to deploy the R-7 to launch positions. Father had no further doubt that construction should begin as soon as possible. The successful September launch of the R-7 only made him more certain that he was right. Father was not deterred by the fact that in both the first and second launches the high temperature generated when the warhead entered the atmosphere caused it to burn up before reaching the ground. Korolyov knew his business and would solve that problem.

THE FALL OF ZHUKOV

Zhukov, who along with the other candidate members of the Presidium had supported Father at the June plenum, became a full member of the Presidium. That summer he appeared several times at the dacha. By all external signs, relations between him and Father seemed cloudless. They took long walks along paths in the park, talked things over, laughed together.

Then Father and I were apart for a long time. First I was away, traveling in the Caucasus. Father was detained by business and couldn't leave for vacation until the beginning of September. We met in Moscow for literally only a few days before he left for a month in the Crimea.

In September Zhukov left on an official visit to Yugoslavia. A great deal of planning had gone into this trip: he sailed from Sevastopol on the heavy cruiser *Kuibyshev*. Many years later its captain recalled that Zhukov was in a good mood, joked, spoke warmly about Father, and during one dinner proposed a toast to his health. The visit began auspiciously. The Yugoslavs, who remembered the recent war very well, made a point of showing their respect for the man at whose feet Berlin had fallen. Neighboring Albania wanted to imitate Yugoslavia and invite the high-ranking guest. Zhukov asked the Soviet government to agree. Moscow decided it would be useful for Zhukov to visit Albania also.

Suddenly, like a bolt from the blue, an item appeared on the last page of *Pravda* under the heading "Chronicle of Events." (At that time *Pravda* put its controversial and sensational stories on the last page of an edition, never the first.) It reported that the Supreme Soviet Presidium had appointed Rodion Yakovlevich Malinovsky minister of defense.

A little further down, in small print, it said that Marshal of the Soviet Union Georgy Konstantinovich Zhukov was relieved of his duties as minister of defense. And no comments! Neither on the first or last page. As if this were an ordinary occurrence!

When I tried to ask Father about it that evening, he only muttered that the comrades had made this decision in light of various circumstances.

"It will be better this way," he said vaguely.

I couldn't understand it at all, but Father's tone and behavior showed clearly that further questions would be useless.

The following Sunday morning at the dacha I happened to overhear what was, apparently, the last conversation they ever had.

I was coming into the house when the telephone rang. I recognized the sound of the Kremlin line. I hurried to answer it, but then saw that Father was coming out of the dining room and heading toward the phone. He waved me off. As I was removing my jacket, I overheard Father say in a muffled voice, "Hello, Georgy."

That caught my attention and I lingered in the hall. There were only two people Father called Georgy: Malenkov and Zhukov. In October 1957 it could not be Malenkov on the phone, so it must be Zhukov. He had returned quickly to Moscow. After the greeting there was a pause, then Father said in an annoyed tone of voice: "But do friends act the way you did?"

There was another silence. It was awkward to stay in the hall any longer. Father could scold me for eavesdropping. I went into the dining room. The whole family gradually drifted in for breakfast. A few minutes later Father joined us. I looked at him inquiringly.

"Zhukov called," Father said to no one in particular.

On November 3 *Pravda* and all the other papers reported that in October (no date was given) a Central Committee plenum had convened to discuss the question of improving party and political work in the Soviet Army and Navy. Readers were informed that a decree would appear in the press. The last paragraph stated: "The plenum removed Comrade G. K. Zhukov from the Central Committee Presidium and from party ranks."

No explanation was given, either then or later. The decree was studied in party organizations, especially in the armed forces. There was unanimous approval of the decisions made. Party educational work was raised to a new level. No one was accustomed to ask questions in those days. The leadership itself knew what should and should not be discussed.

Marshal Zhukov was sent off to retirement and a pension at the age of just under sixty-one. In our country the life of a disgraced pensioner is very far from an easy one. The only consolation was that in Stalin's day it was incomparably worse. Not much of a consolation. It wasn't pleasant for Zhukov to live under Khrushchev, just as it wasn't pleasant for Khrushchev to live under Brezhnev. It's not for me to describe the marshal's life.

Time passed and almost no one remembered Zhukov. I once overheard a conversation between Father and one of the KGB heads at the dacha. I don't remember now whether it was General Serov or one of the "Komsomol members" who replaced him. However, the substance of the conversation has stuck in my memory. It concerned Zhukov.

Father was informed that Zhukov had begun writing notes and was apparently composing his memoirs. The KGB kept a sharp eye on the marshal.

Father listened, walking silently along the path. After finishing his report, his visitor didn't say anything else. I was walking on Father's other side. The silence continued, while the visitor waited for a reaction. Finally he couldn't wait and asked a direct question: "What should we do?" following this up by saying loyally: "We could remove the materials unofficially." Father suddenly blew up. He began with the rhetorical questions he typically asked in such circumstances: "Don't you have enough to keep you busy?" Finally, having spoken his piece, he concluded: "Don't interfere. Zhukov is retired, and what can a pensioner do but write his memoirs? He has a lot to remember." His visitor was obviously taken aback at this reaction, but didn't object.

I don't know whether the marshal was working on his book at the time or on something else. There were no other references to the subject in my presence.

After Father himself was pensioned off and we were working on his memoirs, I asked several times why Zhukov had been dismissed. This is what

Father told me: from the end of July on, compromising information about Zhukov began coming into the Central Committee from the KGB and Army political offices. In brief, it amounted to the following: special sabotage and assault units were being formed in the Soviet Army at the marshal's order. Schools for saboteurs were being set up. These special units were allegedly concentrated in the Moscow area. They were all under the direction of Army general Sergei Matveyevich Shtemenko, head of the Chief Intelligence Directorate of the General Staff. Everything was being kept secret from the Central Committee. The conclusion: Zhukov may be involved in a conspiracy.

An investigation confirmed the information. Such units did in fact exist. Furthermore, they were located not only near Moscow, but in other regions as well, such as the Ukraine.

More and more complaints about Zhukov were coming into the Central Committee. Some of his fellow marshals complained about his impatience and rudeness and whispered the frightening word "Bonapartism."[16]

Finally, there was Zhukov's well-known aversion to "empty talk," as he called political work. An endless stream of complaints issued from the Political Directorate about how the marshal underrated political workers. There were rumors that Zhukov had threatened to teach commissars how to fight, to make them stop talking so much and force them instead to assume command of units. And that he was carrying out this threat with his usual determination. Many grumbled, considering this to be a violation of their special status. With the marshal's position undermined, they were getting even with him for things, some real and some imaginary. The official reason for replacing the minister of defense was that he didn't pay enough attention to political work. That reason was a warning to others: better keep your nose clean.

Father talked of an occasion when Zhukov himself attended a meeting held soon after the plenum, during the period when it was customary to study and discuss its decisions. Marshal Moskalenko, head of the country's antiaircraft defenses and someone recently close to Zhukov, was especially zealous in criticizing the former minister. Moskalenko's choleric nature was notorious in military circles. In the space of half an hour he could heap dirt on a person, then kiss him, then go back to cursing him.

This time he exposed, unmasked, and vilified Zhukov's mistakes with great fervor. For a long time Zhukov put up with it. Then he lost patience and asked venomously how he should interpret today's speech, since Moskalenko had quite recently and with equal conviction advised Zhukov to seize

---

16. "Bonapartism"—terminology for military officers who aspire to take power from a revolutionary government.

power. Moskalenko was disconcerted and sat down. Father was quickly informed of what happened.

If not for the June insurgency, I am positive that Father would have reacted differently to the information he was receiving about Zhukov. Now he was afraid to take risks. Recent events forced him to be cautious. Instead of carrying out a careful and critical investigation, which would inevitably alert Zhukov and possibly prompt him to take decisive action, Father preferred to make a preemptive strike.

Father drew far-reaching conclusions from what had happened, or rather what hadn't been permitted to happen: from now on the minister of defense should not be included in the top party leadership, in order to avoid concentrating too much power, both legislative and executive, in the same hands. This principle was violated under Brezhnev, when Grechko replaced Malinovsky as minister of defense and became a member of the Politburo.

The rest of his life Zhukov denied having had any Bonapartist intentions or even the possibility of such. A careful study of archival documents should make it possible someday to determine the truth. But perhaps we will never know. Right now the picture is not very clear. Such schools for saboteurs could certainly be organized to meet the Army's requirements, and Zhukov thought he was entitled to deal with his own military bailiwick independently, without asking permission from either the Central Committee or Father. That was quite in keeping with his character.

But it's possible to conjure up the opposite picture. A person with Zhukov's character might develop an involuntary urge to impose order in his domain. We hear enough nostalgic calls now for an iron hand, one which would supposedly solve all the country's problems with one stroke. No doubt they'll be heard in the future as well.

I won't hide the fact that I would prefer that Father was mistaken in this case. I have a great deal of respect for Zhukov.

Father returns to the subject of Zhukov numerous times in his memoirs. He never openly doubts that the information he received and the conclusions drawn from it were correct.

There were many times when I pestered Father with questions, trying to find out more. One time, when I was especially persistent in asking whether the denunciations could be entirely trusted, Father replied that he did have certain doubts at the time, but that he had been forced to act because there was so much at stake.

In any case, the personal relationship between these two extraordinary people was ruined from then on.

Zhukov makes very little mention of Father in his book, *Memories and Reflections*, except where he can't avoid it. And he writes without warmth, to put it mildly. One can certainly understand him.

Father didn't read Zhukov's book. When I suggested getting it, he replied with irritation that someone (he didn't say who) had described the contents to him. He thought that a great deal was presented in a way which Zhukov himself would never have written, especially concerning Stalin's role in directing the war effort. That's what he asked Zhukov to be told when the latter tried to find out, in a roundabout way through relatives, what Father thought of his memoirs.

What can you say?

That is everything I know about this sad history. Only fragments, but I hope they will prove useful to meticulous historians.

The stenographic record of the Central Committee plenum that dismissed Zhukov has now been published. Suslov delivered the report. I think that Father couldn't compose himself and entrusted that unpleasant job to the "chief ideologist." After all, the meeting was formally called to discuss political work in the armed forces. "The Central Committee Presidium has recently learned that Comrade Zhukov, without the knowledge of the Central Committee, decided to organize a school of saboteurs with more than two thousand students," Suslov stated. "Comrade Zhukov did not even consider it necessary to inform the Central Committee of this school. Only three people were supposed to know of it: Zhukov, Shtemenko, and General Mamsurov, who was appointed head of the school. But General Mamsurov felt it was his duty as a communist to inform the Central Committee of this illegal action by the minister."

The plot unraveled, beginning with General Mamsurov. Father was especially concerned by the complicity of Army general Shtemenko. Father had had a low opinion of him ever since the war, when they often presented their reports to Stalin at the same time. In Father's opinion, Shtemenko leaned toward intrigue. Lacking direct proofs, I would not want to use a stronger expression.

Somewhat before the events I have described, Zhukov had put considerable effort into persuading Father to appoint Shtemenko to the responsible position of director of the GRU (Main Intelligence Directorate of the General Staff). After General Mamsurov's report, the marshal's insistence looked sinister indeed. Especially considering recent and somewhat earlier events. Father did not hide his concern when he spoke to the plenum.

"As far as the school of saboteurs is concerned," he said,

> Zhukov and Shtemenko were the only ones who knew that this school had been set up. I think that the fact that Zhukov brought Shtemenko back to the intelligence department was not an accident. He obviously needed Shtemenko for some shady business. . . . Why would anyone bring these saboteurs together without the knowledge of the Central Committee? Can you imagine

such a thing? And this was done by the minister of defense, with his type of personality. Beria also had a sabotage group. Before we arrested him, Beria had summoned the group of cutthroats and they were in Moscow. If he had not been exposed, who knows what heads would have rolled.

I leave the reference to Beria on Father's conscience. In connection with Zhukov it grates on the ear. However, Father saw more clearly. The marshal was known to have sacrificed the lives of others without too much thought at critical moments, when it was necessary. However, that was in wartime. But you can't remake someone's character.

How justified was Father's alarm, in view of what we know today? I find very interesting the opinion expressed by the writer Vladimir Karpov, a World War II hero and frontline intelligence agent, who has written a book on Marshal Zhukov. It seems that General Trusov, Shtemenko's deputy and the former chief of intelligence of the First Belorussian Front (which Zhukov had commanded), offered Karpov, an experienced intelligence agent, the position of Mamsurov's deputy.

Both Suslov and Father were mistaken, or else the top leadership simply didn't know the whole truth. It wasn't a school that was organized, but an entire special-operations division. Special brigades were formed in military districts to support the division. What was their purpose? Here I can only quote the article Karpov published in *Pravda* in August 1991: "The special units recently [in 1990] formed under the Ministry of Internal Affairs are microscopic in size compared to those well-organized 'forces for special operations.' " That comment does make one think, especially since the rules of those days dictated that the creation of a regiment, much less a division, had to be approved by the relevant Central Committee department and often required a special decision by the Presidium. But that didn't happen in this case. It would seem that Father had good reason for concern.

And he probably did not know that, as Karpov writes: "After the war came to an end . . . General Trusov, on orders from Stalin and Zhukov, arrested the government of Admiral Dönitz, Hitler's successor; moreover, he carried out that breath-taking operation in the city of Flensburg, which was located in the British occupation zone."

One last thing. Preparations for removing Zhukov, who was in Yugoslavia, were made in the strictest secrecy. They were afraid of a counterstrike. Communication with the delegation virtually ceased. Nevertheless, Shtemenko took the risk of sending a warning to the marshal "through his totally secure line." Was that a sign of military solidarity? Or was the head of military intelligence trying to warn his boss of something far more important? Army general Shtemenko was not known for being reckless.

That is about all I know. People have to draw their own conclusions.

Mine are diametrically opposed to those of the intelligence agent and writer Karpov. Unfortunately, my former certainty, or rather continuing effort, to view the accusations leveled against Marshal Zhukov as slander has been severely shaken.

There is one last piece of evidence—a letter Zhukov wrote in March of 1965 to Brezhnev. In it, Zhukov writes:

> In the summer of 1964, Khrushchev called me. In the course of our conversation about the plenum of October 1957, he said: "You know, at the time it was hard for me to figure out what you were thinking. There were people coming to me and saying that Zhukov is a dangerous man; he's ignoring you and he can do whatever he wants at any time. He enjoys too much authority in the army. Apparently he's obsessed with the 'Crown' of Eisenhower."
>
> I replied: "How could you decide someone's fate on the basis of suppositions like that?" Khrushchev said: "I'm awfully busy right now. When I get back from vacation, let's meet and have a friendly talk."[17]

In *The Life and Military Exploits of Marshal G. K. Zhukov* (Khabarovsk, 1992), the journalist Svetlishin quotes Zhukov's words in greater detail:

> At the end of August 1964, Khrushchev called me at the dacha. After inquiring about my health and frame of mind, he asked what I was doing. I replied that I was writing my memoirs.
>
> "Well, how far have you gotten?" he asked.
>
> I said that the work was essentially finished and that a thousand-page manuscript was ready, but that it needed careful editing.
>
> "That's very interesting," observed Khrushchev, and added: "You have a lot to tell people. It's important to tell the whole truth about the war."
>
> After a brief pause, he said literally the following: "It's too bad, but I have to admit with all frankness that a great injustice was done to you in October 1957, and I am also guilty of what happened. They slandered you and I believed them. Now it's clear to me that this mistake must be corrected. I'm leaving for vacation in a few days. As soon as I return to Moscow, I will get back to this matter and, I hope, rectify everything." (245–46)

We can only guess what Father was thinking and what he wanted to rectify. Furthermore, the conversation itself is recounted only from the perspective of one interested party.

However, the fact that the conversation took place is indisputable. I don't think that Father changed his opinion about Zhukov's former "Bonapartism." He probably wanted to explain himself in human terms to a man who

---

17. Russian State Military Archives, F.41107, Op. 2, D. 3, pp. 24–28, typewritten copy.

was no longer a political rival but an old comrade from the front of the Second World War.

Their talk over the phone had no sequel. After he returned from vacation, Father, dismissed from all his posts in October of 1964, could only follow in Zhukov's footsteps and write his memoirs. In them he repeated: "It was with great and heartfelt regret that we—and especially I—had to part with Zhukov, but the interests of the Party required it."

BREAKTHROUGH

In early October 1957, Father decided to make a detour through Kiev on his way back to Moscow from his vacation in the Crimea. In Kiev he could relax. He enjoyed everything there: the ancient monastery, the hills over the Dnieper, and the ravine of Kreshchatik. I flew from Moscow to meet him.

During his visit maneuvers were held on October 5 in the Dnieper area. The Army wanted to show off something new: tanks capable of crossing a river on the bottom. Father was extremely interested in this innovation. He vividly remembered what it had cost to force the Dnieper during the war. Now he wanted to see with his own eyes how a tank could move under water.

On October 4, the day the first sputnik was launched, the Ukrainian leadership and their Moscow guests gathered in the large dining hall of the Mariinsky Palace: First Secretary of the Ukrainian Central Committee Kirichenko, Chairman of the Presidium of the Supreme Soviet Presidium Korotchenko, Chairman of the Council of Ministers Kalchenko, and Central Committee secretaries. Secretary of the Party Central Committee Brezhnev, who dealt with matters of defense, and Malinovsky, first deputy minister of defense and commander of ground forces, had come to see the maneuvers and were also present in the hall. The defense minister, Marshal Zhukov, was visiting Yugoslavia. Perhaps he was no longer minister of defense, but neither he nor the Army knew that yet. Conversation at the table followed the usual pattern. What do they talk about on such occasions? About the harvest, the inadequacy of capital investments, about new factories and obsolete equipment. Their purpose was transparent: the hosts want to elicit funds, while the distinguished guest weighs their remarks and decides whether he should agree or refuse. It was the usual and customary game in that style of governing, which we now call the command-administrative system. Father understood his companions very well. Until quite recently he had also solicited handouts from the center.

The conversation dragged on. It was almost eleven when an aide came into the hall and whispered something in Father's ear. He nodded, said, "I'll be back," and went to the next room, where there was a telephone. I guessed what the call had to be about and became very tense. The launch had probably taken place. Was it a success or another failure? The odds were obviously not in our favor: only two out of five attempts had been successful. When Father returned after only a few minutes and appeared in the door with a broad smile, I was relieved. If that was Korolyov on the phone, the launch had obviously been a success.

Father took his place without comment, but was in no hurry to resume the conversation. He looked unhurriedly around the group, his face shining.

He finally couldn't resist saying: "I can tell you some very pleasant and important news. Korolyov just called [at this point he acquired a secretive look]. He's one of our missile designers. Remember not to mention his name—it's classified. So, Korolyov has just reported that today, a little while ago, an artificial satellite of the earth was launched."

Father looked triumphantly around at those present. Everyone smiled politely, without understanding just what had happened.

The earlier conversation forgotten, Father began to talk about missiles. He spoke of how the appearance of ballistic missiles had radically altered the balance of forces in the world. His audience listened in silence. They seemed completely immersed in his account, but their faces revealed their indifference. They were used to listening to Father, regardless of the subject. The Kiev officials were hearing about missiles for the first time and didn't clearly understand what they were. But if Father was talking about them, that meant they were important.

Father referred to the satellite as an extremely significant and prestigious offshoot of the intercontinental missile. He emphasized that here we had succeeded in surpassing America. He dreamed of demonstrating the advantages of socialism in actual practice. And now there was such an opportunity.

"The Americans have proclaimed to the whole world that they are getting ready to launch a satellite of the earth. Theirs is only the size of an orange," Father continued excitedly. "We, on the other hand, have kept quiet, but we now have a satellite circling the planet. And not a little one, but one weighing eighty kilos."

He went on talking about missiles awhile before returning to the earlier conversation. His aide reappeared to announce that signals relayed from the satellite were now being broadcast on the radio. He turned on a radio in the corner of the room and everyone listened curiously to the squeaky staccato of the first communication from space.

Korolyov had not labored in vain to be the first to launch a sputnik. Now his hour of worldwide but anonymous celebration had arrived. He had stolen a march on everyone else on the planet.

Upon returning to Moscow, Father immediately called Korolyov. He was eager to hear all the details and find out everything that had happened.

Today it's impossible to say who brought up the possibility of launching a second satellite on the anniversary of the Revolution. Historians in the rocket field ascribe it to Father, and even say that he ordered it. I find that very unlikely. Father understood that as far as technical matters were concerned, he was not in charge. Everything depended on the chief designer, and not even on him, but on the degree of readiness for launch. Orders could only give rise to haste and cause harm. For that reason Father usually expressed his wishes in the form of questions.

My sense is that Father asked Sergei Pavlovich whether it would be possible to schedule another launch to brighten the holiday and Korolyov quickly seized on the remark. He returned Father's call a few days later, saying that the launch would take place and that, for the first time ever, a living being would fly into space—a dog. New launches would follow this second one.

Success lent wings to Korolyov. He planned to make the engines more powerful and begin launching super-heavy satellites and even interplanetary probes on an improved version of the R-7.

Such urgency put Father on guard. He wondered if such a program wouldn't hurt the testing of the missile for which the military had been waiting a long time. Propaganda was all very well and science was all very well, but defense was of the utmost importance. Korolyov assured him that that would not happen. The tests would be completed in a year, possibly a little longer. He misjudged his abilities. He was either mistaken or unrealistic, because the R-7 did not come into service until the beginning of 1960, more than three years later.

Work on the second satellite went on day and night. The November 7 deadline was less than a month away. A hundred times more than anything else, Korolyov wanted to launch a second satellite for the holiday, to demonstrate his (even if only anonymous) supremacy to the whole world. However, everyone in his design bureau knew that, in not sparing themselves, they were carrying out a personal order from the "Boss," and that the chief designer was keeping the Kremlin informed of their progress on a daily basis.

Sergei Pavlovich wasn't the only one to employ this simple method. When I began working, our chief designer also often referred to Father's orders and to the fact that Nikita Sergeyevich was personally keeping track of what we were doing. It must be said that this tactic was effective. People felt that their work was important, so they labored untiringly and accomplished "the impossible."

At any rate, the deadline was met and a satellite weighing 508 kilograms, with the dog Laika on board, was launched into orbit on November 3. Father was ecstatic. I was too, although I couldn't help thinking of the fate awaiting the likable mongrel. I tried to discuss that with Father, but although he loved animals, he just dismissed the subject: "The scientists know what they're doing." Laika cigarettes, bearing the image of a sympathetic, shaggy, smiling dog on their packs, became a memorial to the dog-cosmonaut.

Korolyov began to enjoy himself and proposed launching another, even heavier satellite, weighing 1327 kilograms, for the May 1 holiday. The launch date was set for April 27, 1958. It ended in failure and the satellite was lost. A reserve second model was not launched into orbit until May 15.

Father drew his own conclusions, and when manned flights began he was adamant. Proposals to have the launch of a cosmonaut coincide with any important holiday were rejected out of hand and prohibited.

His reasoning was simple: "The joy of success can turn in a moment into a funeral march. Risk, losses, are inevitable in this new field. Therefore it doesn't do to tempt fate." He added, with a smile: "Haste makes waste." If you look through the calendar, you'll see that no manned launches occurred on holidays until the end of 1964.

Father's hostility to potentially deadly aerial, and later space, theatrical stunts had its roots in the 1930s and the tragedy of the *Maksim Gorkiy*. That was the name of the largest Soviet plane, designed by Tupolev. Only one was built, and it was claimed that the *Maksim Gorkiy* had no equal in the world. I wouldn't swear to that, since too many things that we considered our unsurpassed achievements turned out in reality to be far from unequaled.

One fact is beyond question: people were justifiably proud of it. Such a plane had never been seen in our country before. It became identified in people's minds with the country's might and with the indisputable merits of socialism. It was shown off on every suitable occasion. For one of the May Day celebrations someone conceived the idea of giving outstanding industrial workers a ride in it over Moscow. Everyone had such a good time that the "rides" were continued during the next few days. To show off its size, they sent up one of Polykarpov's agile I-153 fighter planes. Organizers thought that the comparison would make the giant look even more impressive. The fighter circled the *Maksim Gorkiy* like a bee circling a jar of honey— until on May 19 the pilot miscalculated and one of his wings struck the plane. Both aircraft plunged to earth. All the passengers and crew were killed.

The tragedy had a crushing effect on Father, who was secretary of the Moscow City Party Committee at the time. People were killed. Moreover, Stalin blamed Father and Bulganin, who was the chairman of the Moscow Soviet at the time, for indulging in a dangerous escapade. The bravura holiday music was replaced by a funeral dirge. Father and Bulganin joined others in carrying urns of what could be scraped together from the wreckage.

THE MISSILE RACE

Tests of the R-7 continued in parallel with the satellite launches. There were mixed results. Successes alternated with whole sequences of explosions, crashes, and breakdowns. It's not my job to describe them, and it would take a large book to do so. But I do think it essential to mention one episode.

On that particular day Father returned home in a state of agitation. A nightmare scenario had unfolded. After an R-7 was launched there was a failure in the instrument controlling the flight range. The missile overflew Kamchatka, left our territory, and continued in the direction of the United States. Fortunately, its fuel ran out and the last stage, along with its test reentry vehicle, fell into the Pacific Ocean. No one knew whether or not the Americans had plotted its trajectory. Father was upset. Such an incident could have started a war.

It was around that time that Father first talked about the usefulness of establishing a special communications link with Washington. It could be used to warn of mistakes and eliminate the possibility that one might cause a nuclear war.

The rapidly increasing weight of Soviet satellites gave rise to a legend that spread around the world of some secret Soviet fuel. In fact, both sides were at about the same level of development. The Americans were even somewhat ahead of us in avionics and guidance systems, while we were ahead in engines.

In the 1950s the rockets developed in both countries were very similar. The intercontinental Atlas, which used oxygen and kerosene, was prepared for testing in the United States. The Soviet R-7 used the same components. The other American rocket of that class, the Titan, employed nitric acid, so-called fluid oxidizers, and fuel. These rockets didn't require complicated cryogenic equipment, but they had other disadvantages. The vapor they emitted was truly poisonous. In those years no special attention was paid to that fact. Nitric oxidizer, with its rust-colored fumes, was a pervasive presence in the lives of those who worked with engines. Few of them managed to avoid "professional emblems"—burns on the face and hands. Soviet medium-range rockets, the R-12 and R-14, also used acid. American rockets of similar range, and therefore purpose, were the Jupiter and the Thor. They used kerosene and oxygen. As we can see, there was not a wide range of choices.

Our countries did not differ significantly in rocket technology either. We both danced to the same original tune, Wernher von Braun's V-2.

What gave rise to the legend that the Soviets were ahead and the United States was lagging behind? We actually were the first to begin testing intercontinental missiles. We were twelve to eighteen months ahead there and several months ahead in medium-range missiles. The reason is very simple: we were in a great hurry, while they were not.

The intercontinental ballistic missile was the Soviet Union's last hope for parity in the arms race. The government and Central Committee intently followed the work being done on it. It was given the highest priority for resources. At a call from the chief designer, the seemingly impossible could be accomplished.

The Americans were making progress without hurrying. According to their strategic concept, missiles, no matter what their range, only supplemented aviation. Of course, ballistic missiles had advantages, primarily their invulnerability to air defense. The merits of the new weapon were counterbalanced by its shortcomings: a lower degree of accuracy in hitting targets and, most important of all, the need for scrupulous attention to geographic reference points. That necessitated an enormous amount of geodesic research. The same problem did not exist for airplanes, since navigators could always correct any mistakes. Previously no one had paid much attention to kilometers or hundreds of meters in determining the location of such large objects as cities. Where could they escape? But when the subject began to be examined more closely, problems emerged that previously had been of interest only to scientists: no one knew exact relative positions, even of continents. So our imperfect knowledge of the location of launch sites and very approximate information about the coordinates of targets were added to flaws in the missiles themselves. In other words, it was like firing at a penny tossed into the air. The Americans counted on the U-2 to help define precise coordinates on our territory. We didn't even dream of such a possibility. The problem could only be solved by satellites. They would link continents and determine the exact location of targets, large and small.

It was characteristic of the time that the military didn't bother the leadership with such "trifles." When he brandished missiles, Father had no idea that the military simply didn't know where to shoot.

Still, Father had achieved his purpose. We appeared to be a menacing opponent, having outstripped the mightiest country in the world, even if not by very much. Father simply beamed. He was not, of course, getting ready to fight, but now at least he had something to brandish. The balance of forces in the world seemed to be shifting radically. Father intended to continue his successful policy of missile pressure, blackmail if you like, in the future. Over and over again he recalled the previous year's events in Suez, the phenomenal effect produced by the mere mention of the R-5. Now we didn't have to prove we were powerful. All anyone had to do was lift up his head and see a star crossing the firmament. Our satellite. Or turn on the radio and hear its signals.

The number of missiles actually ready for launching was a different matter. There was no way for anyone to find that out. The important thing was not how many missiles we had but that we had any missiles at all.

The kilograms and tons lifted into orbit were impressive and provoked a great deal of speculation. Complicated conclusions were drawn. Intelligence agents risked their lives trying to ferret out the secret of this astonishing success. The answer was in plain sight: the backwardness of our technology, especially our instruments. They were heavy and bulky. Because they were unreliable, they required one or two backup systems. And all this added more and more weight. The poor degree of accuracy made a more powerful explosion necessary. The R-7 was the first Soviet missile adapted to a 5.5-ton thermonuclear warhead.

How could the Americans compete with us! The takeoff weight of the R-7 was almost two hundred and eighty tons. The American intercontinental Atlas rocket, which was designed to perform the same type of tasks, weighed one-third of that. It therefore lifted a much lighter load.

The saying "every cloud has a silver lining" comes to mind here. The power we were forced to put into the R-7 enabled the Soviet Union to stay ahead of the competition for many years. A whole decade passed before the Saturn broke all existing records, but then quickly dropped out of the race, whereas the R-7 continues to toil on into its fifth decade. An unimaginable length of time for a flying apparatus.

Did Father know all this? Yes and no. He followed the development of rocket technology with great interest and soberly evaluated its real battlefield capabilities. On the other hand, when Korolyov and Valentin Ivanovich Glushko talked about how they had managed to leave America behind, it was balm for his soul.

All the publicity about our country's superiority in the rocket field was a boon to American rocket scientists, and they viewed it as such. Without it, they couldn't have dreamed of receiving appropriations for their projects without arguments and red tape. The cost of the moon landing program alone was astronomical! If not for our "help," a manned flight to the moon would probably have remained in the realm of science fiction to this very day.

In this context, I should cite a conversation between Father and President Dwight Eisenhower two years later, at Camp David.

Eisenhower brought up the following subject: "Tell me, Mr. Khrushchev, how do you make decisions on financing military projects?"

Before I had a chance to say anything, he continued, "Perhaps first I should tell you how it's done here."

"Good, how is it done?"

He smiled, and I smiled back. I guessed what he was going to say.

"It's usually like this. Our military leaders come to me and say, we need such and such sums for such and such programs. If we don't get what we need, we'll fall behind the Soviet Union. I'm forced to give it to them. That's how they squeeze money out of me. Then they ask for more, and I give it to them. Now tell me, how does it happen with you?"

"It's exactly the same. People come from the Defense Ministry and say: Comrade Khrushchev, look at this! The Americans are developing such and such a system. We could develop the same one, but it will cost such and such. I tell them that there is no money. It's all been allocated already. Then they say: If you don't give us the money and war breaks out, the enemy will have the advantage. The conversation continues, I resist as much as I can but finally have to give the military what they want. Then I put the matter to the government, and we adopt the decision recommended by the military."

"Yes," he said, "that's what I thought. You know, we really should conclude some kind of agreement so we could stop these useless and really empty expenditures."

"That's our dream! We're prepared to devote every effort to reaching such an agreement with you, in order to curb military expenditures.

"One of the reasons for my coming to the United States was the search for mutual understanding. But how can we reach agreement? On what basis?"

That was the main problem: we could not agree then, and we can't agree now.

Fortunately, times have changed.

Father was ready to share even the most important secrets with friends. The Soviet government decided to give the Chinese People's Republic the technology for manufacturing nuclear warheads. Father promised that as soon as testing was completed on the R-12,[1] the Chinese would receive blueprints of this missile. Plans called for starting production almost simultaneously in both countries. The R-12 wasn't the only thing we gave the Chinese. We sent prototypes of cruise missiles equipped with homing systems—the ship-based P-15 and the shore defense Sopka. They were going to be produced at new factories being built with our help. The list is endless. Unfortunately, this idyll soon came to an end.

The history of our conflict with China goes far beyond the framework of my memoirs. Moreover, I simply don't know what was going on behind the scenes. I will mention only a few episodes.

Having thrown open the gates of our arsenals to our friends, Father sin-

---

1. Literature describing the Chinese acquisition of missile technology mentions the transfer in 1957 of documentation and two models of Korolyov's R-2 to China, but makes no mention of Yangel's R-12. However, I am not mistaken—in the late 1950s the R-2 was not considered a weapon, and when I talked with Father the subject was weapons. Documentation on the R-2 was given to China in 1958, whereas I remember the subject of the R-12 being discussed in 1959 and subsequent years. As I indicate somewhat further on, the intention was to transfer documentation on the R-12, but that may not have been carried out, so it is not reflected in the documents published by historians. Archival evidence may perhaps appear in the future.

cerely counted on reciprocity. After all, we had the same adversary, U.S. imperialism. In reality, everything turned out differently.

I have described the squabbles over the type of navy we should have. Now oceangoing submarines were being riveted, welded, and assembled at western, eastern, northern, and southern shipyards, in accordance with newly adopted strategic concepts. The first were diesel powered. Maximum use was made of experience gained during the last German submarine construction projects.

Design and construction work was being completed on the very latest nuclear submarines, armed with traditional torpedoes, and new ones armed with ballistic and cruise missiles.

The submarine fleet was becoming an oceangoing fleet, liberated from the land, ensuring our menacing presence in all of the planet's oceans. Reliable communications were needed to manage the numerous boats. At the time no one dreamed of satellite systems. To secure a reliable communication link to all the oceans from our own territory would be very difficult, as well as costing many billions of rubles—and, as usual, there wasn't enough money.

The problem was discussed at length by the Navy's Supreme Command staff. One option after another was rejected. Proposals were laboriously put together and presented to the Defense Council for discussion. The first, most expensive and least effective option envisaged using only our own territory. The second provided for basing radio transmitters as close to shorelines as possible. It called for basing one on the Chinese island of Hainan to cover the south Pacific region and one at the tip of the Hindustan peninsula for the Indian Ocean.

Father rejected the Indian option out of hand. He felt it was quite impossible to make such a request of Nehru: Father was afraid that such a proposal could disrupt the friendly relations between our countries. How could we ask for a military base only a few years after they had chased out the British colonizers?

"What interests do you have in the Indian Ocean?" Father inquired of Admiral Gorshkov, the Navy's commander in chief. "Who are you planning to fight there?"

Gorshkov did not let himself be baited. He explained that the proposals were designed to establish a communications network over the entire globe. There were no plans to deploy a large submarine force in the Indian Ocean. It was therefore possible to postpone any use of Indian territory, but Gorshkov insisted on establishing a station on the island of Hainan. That was an extremely important zone, in view of the U.S. naval bases in the Hawaiian Islands and on the island of Midway, not to speak of the Philippines and Taiwan. We also wanted at the same time to bring up the possibility of basing and repairing ships in Chinese ports if the international situation became threatening. That would drastically reduce the time spent on ship movement and markedly improve the Navy's military effectiveness. Because their bases were located so far away, almost one-third of Soviet ships were always on their way either to or from their home base.

Father didn't foresee any difficulties. Friendly China, engaged in building socialism, would agree, particularly since the Chinese themselves were beginning to build submarines. According to our blueprints and with our help, of course. Therefore, Gorshkov's proposal seemed likely to appeal to both sides: Chinese seamen could also use both the radio station and the repair bases. Furthermore, our presence in Chinese ports would tie the hands of any aggressor. Someone attacking China would have to deal with Soviet armed forces as well. Father proposed giving the Chinese navy the right to use bases on Soviet territory if necessary, on the basis of reciprocity. Father asked that specific proposals be drawn up for him to sign and send to Mao Zedong.

The Chinese were in no hurry to agree. Then Father decided to meet personally with Mao. He thought that perhaps the Chinese didn't fully understand the proposals and that a talk would overcome any obstacle. With this in mind, he traveled to Beijing with Marshal Malinovsky at the end of July 1958.

Historians have written a great deal about these negotiations. Father has also referred to them in his memoirs. I will mention only that the Chinese tried to get assurances of military support for their attempts to conquer Taiwan. Or, more precisely, to control the waters off the Chinese coast. Father dodged this request. He thought that joint efforts should be coordinated and directed toward repelling aggression, not provoking the Americans to an unnecessary confrontation. In Father's opinion, the principal goal should be to stimulate China's economy and raise the people's standard of living.

He viewed the liberation of Taiwan as important politically, but quite unattainable militarily. Father convinced his negotiating partners that, lacking a navy, China could not solve the Taiwan problem by force. We could not help in any way, since our Pacific Fleet was not capable of fighting the U.S. Seventh Fleet. Such an adventure, Father felt, could lead to a world war. He therefore flatly refused to participate in military actions in the Taiwan Strait. The Chinese declared that they intended to act independently. Father assured them that they could count on our political support.

Father got nowhere with his proposals concerning a radio station and submarine bases. The negotiations left him with an unpleasant taste. The almost barefaced attempts to drag us into armed conflict with the Americans, the refusal of our request—none of that matched Father's understanding of the principles of proletarian solidarity.

The USSR fully supported the Chinese in the conflict over the offshore islands, which flared up after Father's visit to Beijing.[2] Newspapers fulminated in condemnation of the aggressors. But Father left it at that, and there was not the slightest hint that the Soviet Union might intervene. However, in one of his public statements he warned the Americans that we would not stand aside in case of an invasion of friendly China.

The Chinese themselves were not spoiling for a fight either. After noisy declarations about arming their people, they switched to innumerable grave warnings about violations by U.S. planes and ships of their recently established twelve-mile offshore zone. These warnings were counted carefully and soon reached the impressive number of almost one thousand.

During one of those violations, either at the end of 1958 or early 1959, an American pilot lost the Sidewinder air-to-air missile suspended under his fighter plane. The incident was reported in Moscow newspapers, with a reference to Chinese sources. Father took an interest, and our ambassador in Beijing was told to ask our friends to send us the missile for study. Father promised that we would share the results of the analysis and any blueprints made of the missile.

Time passed and there was no response from Beijing. Father asked that they be reminded. Again nothing. After a third reminder, the Chinese replied that they were searching for the missile. Father became angry and reproachful: we had transferred our knowledge, our blueprints, and our technology to our friends without asking for payment. We had shared everything openly, and here it was a matter of U.S. secrets, not Chinese ones.

Reproaches had no effect. For the first time Father sensed the deep fissures that had appeared in our "fraternal friendship." For the first time he wondered whether it made sense to transfer the newest military technology and teach the Chinese how to build missiles and nuclear warheads.

In the winter of 1959, evidently in February, he decided to exert pressure for the first time. In response to the delay over the Sidewinder, he held up transfer of instructions for the R-12. It did the trick. The missile was immediately found.

A few days later it was being examined in Moscow. The missile had broken in two when it hit the ground, but there were no other signs of breakage. Unfortunately, an important part was missing, the sensing element of the infrared homing system. By then Soviet specialists had acquired some experience with this element and they were very interested in finding out what had been developed across the ocean.

---

2. "Offshore islands." This is known in the literature as the "Quemoy-Matsu" crisis, which took place August 1958 when Chinese artillery began an intense bombardment of the Nationalist-held islands of Quemoy and Matsu. The U.S. Seventh Fleet resupplied Chiang's Nationalist forces, while Khrushchev pledged to defend mainland China. Both superpowers discouraged offensive action on the part of their allies.

After the missile had been thoroughly examined, we discovered that it had been taken apart more than once and was given to us only after being reassembled. That was what they were doing while they were "searching." Whether the Chinese got any benefit from their examination is hard to say. They still knew very little and were able to do still less. But they kept stubbornly trying.

A Soviet naval officer who was teaching his Chinese colleagues about the P-15 told me that one morning he came to the hangar and found the missile completely dismantled. During the night local specialists, either distrusting their Russian teachers or for some other reason, had decided to investigate on their own. They managed to take it apart, but couldn't put it back together. The situation was rather awkward. Our people pretended that nothing had happened. That was friendship. It took them two days to reassemble and adjust the missile before it was back in workable condition. The Chinese smiled politely and gave no explanations. And this wasn't the only such occasion.

The same thing happened with the Sidewinder. The Chinese wanted to understand everything themselves, without relying on their friends. Since the sensing element could not be removed from the homing system, it was not sent. The Chinese obviously thought that they needed that part the most. Father was informed. He ordered that a new request be made. Beijing assured us that they had sent everything. Negotiations went on for several weeks before Father finally got angry and ordered an end to the unproductive squabbling.

The missile incident played a rather important role when Father reassessed our attitude toward China. It was a key factor in the change.

It was during that time that I first heard of the agreement to give nuclear secrets to China. Father was beginning to worry that we had acted too hastily. A few days later he returned to the subject during one of our walks and said that he had consulted with Yefim Pavlovich Slavsky. The latter reassured him that the technology had not yet been transferred and the documents were still being prepared.

"Let them have the R-12," he added thoughtfully, as if mulling it over. "Two thousand kilometers is not such a huge distance."

He fell silent. Perhaps he thought of the possibility that they could turn this weapon against us?

After a pause, Father continued. He was concerned that the Chinese would interpret a violation of the agreement we had signed in 1957 as an unfriendly act.

"That's the way it actually works out." He sighed, and repeated: "Let them have the R-12. The rest too. But as for the atomic bomb, we have to give it more thought."

A few days later he said that the Presidium of the Central Committee had given careful thought to the question of transferring nuclear technology and had ordered Slavsky to slow down the process.

Now it was China's turn to send inquiries, and ours to give evasive answers.

I once expressed my doubts and asked Father whether the decision made any sense. Nuclear secrets, as such, did not exist and the Chinese would eventually make their bomb without us.

Father essentially agreed, but said that the nuclear weapon was such a terrible force that we didn't have the right to take the slightest risk. Of course, the Chinese would eventually make their own bomb, but it would take time—a lot of time.

"Everything in the world changes quickly, and we can hope that by then the clouds will have dispersed." Father was always an optimist. "But if not, then the later they master the mysteries of the atom, the better."

In those days Father still hoped for an improvement in international relations. But as relations with the United States grew warmer, the frost to the East hardened.

As spring came to an end, Soviet officials apologetically informed the Chinese that because of technical difficulties we could not fulfill the obligations we had assumed. Beijing was simply furious. Although they did not descend to the level of insulting us, relations grew strained and shrill notes began to appear in correspondence.

Father was more upset than angry. After all, the agreement had provided for our unilateral obligation to transfer modern technology. The Chinese could not respond in kind. China's reaction only confirmed that our doubts were well founded.

"We have shared so many secrets—the only problem was the bomb," said Father regretfully.

By May Father had made up his mind: nuclear secrets must not be shared under any circumstances. The Presidium of the Central Committee voted in favor of that policy, and on June 20, 1959, the Soviet government unilaterally annulled the agreement providing for the transfer to China of the latest technical achievements, primarily in the military field.

China did not receive Soviet nuclear technology. For many years, and still to this day, Father's decision was seen as a sign of an unfriendly policy that had a grave impact on the worsening of relations between the two countries. But if the Chinese had received an atomic bomb in 1959, would those relations have improved?

It was decided to replicate the U.S. Sidewinder air-to-air missile. Father made that decision after familiarizing himself with the conclusions of experts. They said that the Sidewinder was substantially superior to Soviet designs, primarily because it weighed far less. Our designers resisted and disputed the conclusions drawn by experts. The decision damaged their prestige.

It didn't help. A new design bureau was created, provided with blueprints and what was left of the missile, and began work. The deadline was a very short one. The major problem was that infamous sensing element of the homing system. The principle of its function was not a secret, but the factory ran into extraordinary difficulties in technology. Defects were found in more than ninety-nine percent of the parts produced. They struggled with it for a long time, but without success. It was decided to create a committee of competent scientists, manufacturers, and administrators. The committee was instructed to investigate and find a solution to the crisis. Father's reasoning was simple: "Since they've organized mass production in America, they work without producing defective parts. What's keeping us from doing the same?"

The committee met for a long time, made a thorough investigation of the technology, and listened to dozens of proposals and hundreds of complaints. Electronics experts blamed machine builders for the lack of the equipment they required. When the machine builders were asked for their explanation, they complained about the poor quality of metal. They couldn't do any better with the metal they were given. Metallurgists simply threw up their hands. The quality of ore they were given was so bad that the machine builders should be thankful for what they got. The mining industry in turn referred to the poor quality of equipment supplied by the machine-building industry for processing ores. That closed the circle.

Everyone gradually got used to the unbelievable percentage of defective parts, which slowly decreased as people mastered production techniques. The situation was considered satisfactory, so the committee disbanded itself and was soon forgotten.

The Soviet Sidewinder was tested with good results and, under the designation K-13, became a part of our arsenal. It saw service for a long time. On both sides.

VLADIMIR NIKOLAYEVICH CHELOMEI

That spring Bulganin, another member of the "Anti-Party Group," departed from the scene, and on April 1, 1958, Father became chairman of the Council of Ministers. His first step in his new capacity was to appeal to all nuclear powers to stop testing. Without waiting for a response, Father announced a unilateral moratorium on nuclear tests, to begin on January 1 of the following year.

His decision was like a bolt from the blue. Neither Ustinov nor Slavsky, not to speak of the designers, knew about it ahead of time. They found out at the last moment, just before it appeared in the newspapers. Needless to say, the military were quite cool to the idea of a moratorium. Soviet warheads were still very heavy and imperfect. The military wanted opportunities to improve them.

I was also surprised. I was afraid that we would fall behind in the race and turn out to look foolish. I expressed my concerns to Father. His reasoning was simple: we already had nuclear and hydrogen bombs. We had tested thermonuclear warheads for missiles. Tests of the missiles themselves would soon be concluded. It was time to stop. What we already had was enough to ensure our security, and the improvement of weapons could go on interminably. It was a waste of money. Missiles could now reach any part of the world. That meant that no one would want to start a war.

I didn't give up. Could you possibly trust them? While we were doing nothing, across the ocean they would be making warheads that we hadn't even dreamed of. We would turn out to be the fools.

Father reassured me that work would continue. We had to give our rivals the opportunity to think things over, to evaluate the situation. They were not, after all, suicidal. Well, and if the Americans didn't follow our example, we would resume testing. If we could come to an agreement, the new designs would remain on the shelf. Father wanted to believe that would happen.

Father chose the moment carefully. It was precisely in 1958 that it became possible to freeze Soviet and U.S. nuclear arsenals in a state of the least inequality, if not at full parity. We had just finished a series of tests. The Americans, with a five-year head start, were only preparing new tests. This was the most appropriate time, Father thought—if, of course, there was good will. We had not caught up with the Americans, but that was not so terrible as long as they did not try to increase the gap. Now it was up to our competitors to respond.

Unfortunately, Father's appeal did not receive a positive reply. His messages about banning tests, which had been sent to the United States, France, and Britain, were answered by the Americans on behalf of all three. On April 27 a thermonuclear explosion was set off on the Pacific atoll of Eniwetok.

Father began a difficult and prolonged period of struggle on two fronts. On the one hand, with the Americans, whom he tried unsuccessfully to convince that a continuation of tests would have devastating effects. And, on the other hand, with his opponents at home, both military and civilian, who asserted that a unilateral moratorium would be ruinous, and in case of a military conflict could result in defeat. Meanwhile, the Americans reinforced their arguments and undermined Father's by continuing to set off nuclear explosions.

Reports on an increasing number of R&D projects lay on Father's desk. The warheads were becoming more powerful and at the same time lighter, smaller, and cheaper. However, because they weren't tested, we had no way of knowing whether they would work. Father was becoming tense. New appeals, accompanied by threats to end the moratorium, were sent to the West. The appeals went unanswered. The warnings were not effective.

Meanwhile, I was finishing work for my degree in engineering. It was time to think about the future. In those years the nonmilitary branches of industry seemed somehow of secondary importance, unworthy of attention.

The solution appeared unexpectedly of itself. Vladimir Chelomei, the chief designer of cruise missiles for submarines, invited me to come work for him. I went there to introduce myself. What I saw in the design bureau amazed me. It seemed that they were designing things that the Americans had not yet even dreamed of—cruise missiles launched underwater capable of destroying targets hundreds of kilometers away. Chelomei proposed that I join his firm to work on guidance systems.

I was absolutely delighted. That was exactly what I had dreamed of doing and I agreed without hesitation. Vladimir Nikolayevich checked my enthusiasm somewhat: "Better talk it over at home first."

The moment Father appeared, I began eagerly telling him about receiving the offer to work on submarines armed with cruise missiles with wings that opened up after launch and about other marvels. I expected to surprise him, but it turned out that he knew about everything. Three years earlier Chelomei had visited him at the Central Committee and shown him a model of his remarkable missile. Father was enthusiastic about this innovation. He had asked Chelomei to keep him informed about his progress and urged him to call him if he needed to.

Father then told me about the background of my new acquaintance. Chelomei had become a chief designer at the end of the war, when he was still quite young, barely thirty. Since his student years he had been passionately interested in the study of various vibration processes.[3] He was especially attracted to the study of unexplained phenomena. Chelomei had worked in an institute that developed airplane engines. On the eve of the war he had gotten the idea that a flying apparatus could rise into the air with the help of vibration. The combination of a pipe and the dampers that blocked it in a very complex way became known as a pulse-jet engine. It was put into development.

By 1944 the experimental model came increasingly to resemble something capable of flying. But what to mount the engine on? The answer came

---

3. Vibration in a missile could devastate performance, either by upsetting the gyro and destroying accuracy or even causing spontaneous explosion. Hence the need for expertise on "vibration processes."

from the front lines. V-1 cruise missiles began bombing London. They were sent off by a German double of Chelomei's invention.

Vladimir Nikolayevich didn't know whether to be pleased or chagrined. On the one hand, this was clear proof of his vision. But it was annoying to see what you thought was yours in someone else's hands! His misgivings turned out to be fully justified. In the years that followed even specialists assumed that the pulse-jet engine had come to us from the Germans.

The V-1 made a suitable impression in Moscow. When Nikolai Nikolayevich Polikarpov, the designer of the I-15, the I-153, and the I-16, died of cancer in 1944, Chelomei was given his design bureau. The bureau worked night and day. The combination of German experience and our own initial efforts produced a whole series of land, sea, and air cruise missiles. They received the index number 10X, and a subsequent model, which was far more advanced than the German one, was designated the 16X.

Unfortunately, Chelomei's period of success soon ended. The pulse-jet engine exhausted its possibilities when barely out of the laboratory. It turned out that it was impossible in principle to achieve a speed in excess of one thousand kilometers an hour. But in those years everyone's goal was to break the sound barrier.

Troubles don't come singly. A powerful rival of Chelomei appeared on the scene. Artyom Ivanovich Mikoyan conceived the idea of transforming the MIG-15 jet fighter into a cruise missile. That became the Kometa, which had made such an impression on Father. It was designed to attack ships. Experienced fighter aircraft designers, Mikoyan and his colleagues were able to make a glider, so there was no problem with engines.

Now a third, possibly most important, partner was added for development of a guidance system. On cruise missiles everything done previously by a human being was taken over by instruments. This project had to start practically from scratch. Construction of a giant complex began on the Leningrad Highway. Sergo Lavrentyevich Beria,[4] a twenty-four-year-old colonel and recent graduate of a military academy, was appointed chief engineer of the new Design Bureau N1.

Work proceeded on a grand scale. Lavrenty Beria himself was in charge of missile research and development, and he was an expert in large-scale projects. When the laboratories and production buildings were planned, they included an internal prison. Plans called for German scientists to be housed

---

4. Sergo Lavrentyevich Beria—son of the NKVD/MGB chief Lavrenty Beria. For four decades after his father's execution in 1953, Sergo Beria went by the name Sergei Alekseyevich Gegechkori. He published his own memoir—highly controversial, to put it mildly—in 1996. Artyom Ivanovich Mikoyan (1905–70), who designed several famous MIG aircraft (MIG-1, -9, -15, and -21) with M. I. Gurevich, was the brother of CPSU Presidium member Anastas Ivanovich Mikoyan.

there—those whom they could find in Germany. And perhaps not Germans alone.

Chelomei was not included in this newly formed alliance. In fact, he became a rival of the powerful Artyom Mikoyan (the younger brother of Anastas) and Sergo Beria. The "Xs" of Vladimir Nikolayevich and Artyom Ivanovich's Kometa belonged to the same class of weapons and occupied a common "ecological niche." Therefore the struggle between them for support and funds was a matter of life and death. Mikoyan proposed to Lavrenty Beria that the two organizations, his and Chelomei's, merge their work, naturally under his leadership. Together they would squeeze out their rival.

Mikoyan had all the advantages. And it wasn't just a question of having the backing of two powerful families. Mikoyan promised that after the Kometa, he would develop new supersonic missiles.

A decree to merge Mikoyan's and Chelomei's design bureaus, signed by Stalin, appeared in February of 1953. Vladimir Nikolayevich found out about it when it was a fait accompli and he was asked to vacate the building. He began knocking on doors. He tried angrily and desperately to phone the elder Beria. Without success. His secretary said that if Chelomei were needed, they would find him.

"But how will you know how to find me? May I give you my home telephone number?" asked Vladimir Nikolayevich in dismay. The secretary only mumbled: "We can easily find people we want." They never called back. Soon Beria was gone.

Chelomei became a professor at the Moscow Technical University, the so-called Bauman Institute. Professors as well as students came to hear his lectures. But the peaceful life didn't satisfy Vladimir Nikolayevich. He unexpectedly conceived the idea of wings opening in flight while on a business trip, to Leningrad I think. He was given a room on the top floor of a hotel, under the roof. By an architectural whim, above the window in the room was a round porthole, like those on ships. There Chelomei suddenly had a vision of a rocket darting like a bird from its nest in a tree trunk through a round hole and, now free, spreading its wings in flight. This revelation occurred sometime in 1954.

This idea solved the problem of placing missiles in submarines. Six, eight, ten, or more cruise missiles could be inserted into tubes and easily concealed under the deck.

Now the design work, some intensive drafting, had to be done. But where, and with whom?

Vladimir Nikolayevich began knocking on doors. He managed with great difficulty to get an appointment with Bulganin, who was then the minister of defense. The conversation went badly. Bulganin listened to him inattentively and was obviously bored. Chelomei left without achieving anything.

When Chelomei heard about Father's remarks at the Pacific Fleet's maneuvers in 1954 and his enthusiasm for the unprecedented possibilities of the Kometa, Vladimir Nikolayevich focused his attention on the Central Committee.

It turned out to be easy to arrange a meeting with Father. I've already mentioned that they impressed each other favorably. However, Father didn't commit himself, saying that he had to consult with the Presidium. His visitor didn't know whether to be encouraged or dismayed.

Father shared his impressions with Bulganin. Bulganin's reaction was very negative and, to Father's surprise, aggressive. His assistants favored Chelomei's rival Mikoyan and had influenced their patron accordingly. Bulganin relied totally on their conclusions.

"Send him to the devil," he advised Father. "Stalin got rid of him."

By then, references to Stalin no longer impressed Father. They argued a bit. Father persuaded his friend, then still his ally, to support the designer.

In reality Bulganin couldn't have cared less about Chelomei and his proposals, so he gave in to Father's prodding. In August 1955 the Central Committee and the Council of Ministers issued a decree establishing a new design bureau, No. 52, under the Ministry of Aviation Technology, and assigned it the job of developing a submarine-based cruise missile for attacking strategic targets on the territory of a potential foreign adversary.

Father consequently knew a great deal about my new acquaintance. He was not excited by the news that I was invited to work at Chelomei's bureau: "I asked Kalmykov [minister of radio technology] about you, and he suggested that you go to Pilyugin. He's designing guidance systems for Korolyov. Kalmykov was going to call there. But then, do what you want. It's your life." I had already made up my mind, and I didn't want to work for Pilyugin.

I must say that I never regretted that decision, despite the various vicissitudes that befell me. I worked with Chelomei for ten years, from March 8, 1958, to July of 1968. During those years I learned a great deal.

Chelomei did not restrict himself to cruise missiles. After they went into production he came down with space fever and wanted to start working on new boosters for intercontinental ballistic missiles. When he began to work in the field of space and ballistics, however, Vladimir Nikolayevich was encroaching onto territory divided between two powerful departments. To understand why this is so we need to compare the origins of the postwar rocket industry in the Soviet Union and in the United States. In the United States rockets were quickly assigned to their proper place—aviation companies. Specialists quickly mastered the new production. Plants did not have to be retooled. Changing over to rocket production cost about the same as changing from one type of airplane to another.

In the Soviet Union, on the other hand, cruise and antiaircraft missiles were assigned to the aviation industry, since by all criteria they were like airplanes. But there was another claimant for ballistic missiles. The energetic and ambitious young minister of defense technology, Dmitry Fyodorovich Ustinov, was not satisfied with being in charge only of artillery, which had brought his department renown during the war.

What was the main function of artillery? To hurl shells as far as possible, after loading them with as destructive a charge as possible. To that end designers increased calibers, lengthened barrels, and resorted to other devices. But there was a high price to pay for that, and not in money alone. Cannons began to weigh tens and hundreds of tons. It was almost impossible to move them from place to place; weeks were spent on mounting and installing the weapons. They required special trains and hundreds of men to service them. Ustinov understood that heavy artillery was approaching its limits. He found a solution in the ballistic missile. It was simply a greatly enlarged artillery shell that did not need a barrel. Moreover, arms builders had already made missiles: the Katyushas, which became famous during the war.

As a result, Soviet ballistic missiles were assigned to the artillery. This false first step brought fantastic expenses in its wake. It necessitated the creation of an entire parallel branch of industry from virtually the ground up: research institutes, engine building, instrument building, design bureaus, and factories without number. The cost rose into the tens and hundreds of billions of rubles. Former master gunners learned unfamiliar, aviation-related technological processes, studied, made mistakes, and rediscovered painfully and expensively what was already known. It was not until the beginning of the 1960s that this new missile branch of industry effectively took shape.

Chelomei's proposals for a space and missile program brought these two departments together again. Passions seemingly long dead were reignited. Vladimir Nikolayevich's ideas met with a hostile reception in the Military-Industrial Commission of the Council of Ministers, whose chairman was then Dmitry Ustinov. Ustinov and his colleagues were ready to destroy Chelomei, and I think would have destroyed him if not for Father. Vladimir Nikolayevich's relations with Ustinov became extremely tense, and he had to work around him, through the Central Committee's defense department. In extreme cases, he appealed directly to Father.

Chelomei introduced modern aviation technology into missile production. Parts became lighter, and at the same time stronger. The so-called tank fuel and oxidizer support structures made their appearance. With Father's backing, aviation plants began series production of missiles. It was Chelomei who made our first mass-produced intercontinental ballistic missile.

Vladimir Nikolayevich remained on good terms with Brezhnev after Father's retirement, but his star began to fade nevertheless. He made just as many proposals and his energy did not flag. Indeed, he was at the peak of his powers. It was just that Ustinov under Leonid Ilyich was a completely different person from Ustinov in the time of Stalin or Khrushchev. He changed from being an active manager into a despotic little tsar, who sensed that the heavy hand from above had finally disappeared.

Chelomei's projects on space and ballistic missiles were doomed, one after another. To be sure, Vladimir Nikolayevich took advantage of every opportunity. For a time he enjoyed the support of the new defense minister, Grechko. He modernized his intercontinental missile and was the first in our country to install Multiple Independently targetable Reentry Vehicles (MIRVs). But all this activity resembled death throes. It was soon taking years to obtain government decrees on new projects. Sometimes more time was spent getting signatures than producing blueprints. Ustinov had previously resolved such matters in the space of a week. Moreover, the fact that a decree was issued didn't necessarily mean anything. An experienced hand could always "cut off the air" and stop the financing. The situation became quite clear after Ustinov became defense minister. The newly appointed Marshal Ustinov ordered his generals not to associate with Chelomei—not to visit him and not to receive him. Of course, it was impossible to isolate him completely. His UR-500 Proton was the only booster capable of lifting Korolyov's orbital station. But Chelomei himself couldn't get a foot in the door.

It took almost a decade to obtain approval to launch the Almaz orbital station. In the 1970s it was ten years ahead of its competition. The station was built on orders from the military. It enabled observers to see the slightest suspicious movement on earth, even through a cloud cover. It was equipped with a special radar for this purpose. But Ustinov rejected it. The hundreds of millions spent on it were wasted.

When Chelomei contrived to deliver the Almaz to a test site and that was reported to the defense minister, Ustinov ordered angrily: "Cancel the launch. Destroy the station!"

The general in charge of the test site couldn't bear to carry out that terrible order. He took the responsibility for hiding the satellite until better times. Of course, the general was taking a risk: if Ustinov had found out, he would have been demoted. The minister wouldn't forgive such disobedience. But he was not told.

Almaz was launched only after Ustinov's death. Chelomei never saw it. He passed away at the same time as Ustinov, in December of 1984.

KOROLYOV LOSES HIS MONOPOLY

Launches of the R-7 continued all that year at the Tyura-Tam test site. There were ups and downs, successes and failures, but progress was being made.

On March 29, 1958, the missile warhead finally overcome the atmospheric resistance encountered during reentry and hit the ground. That was the day that the R-7 became a weapon. However, its accuracy left something to be desired. Deviation from the target amounted to fifty or more kilometers, but in the overall picture that was considered an unfortunate detail.

At the beginning of May Ustinov and Mitrofan Ivanovich Nedelin[5] gave Father a report on their plan for mass production of the R-7 and for adding it to the military arsenal. Problems surfaced immediately. The defense industry didn't have factories capable of producing such large objects. Two years previously, on a visit to Korolyov's design bureau, Father had promised the chief designer to consider the possibility of transferring aviation plants to his jurisdiction. Now it was time to decide.

Father proposed converting the giant Kuibyshev Airplane Plant to missile production. Until then it had been producing Tupolev bombers. This caused quite a storm! Protests came from all sides. Father ignored the objections of Pyotr Vasilyevich Dementyev, chairman of the State Committee on Aviation Technology. Then Tupolev asked for a meeting. Their discussion didn't satisfy Tupolev. Father joked and avoided serious subjects. But before they parted, he referred to an earlier conversation during which Andrei Nikolayevich had admitted frankly that no airplane could penetrate U.S. air defenses. So Tupolev had himself passed the verdict on bombers. Now we had found a weapon that was no more threatened by all those antiaircraft missiles than it would be by the crossbows of the Middle Ages. "You have to squeeze over a little," Father tried to joke. But Tupolev didn't respond. They parted with an unusual degree of coldness.

New customers appeared at the Kuibyshev plant.

Father seemed closer to achieving his goal than ever before. But that was only an illusion. The plan to deploy new divisions of strategic missile forces had been carefully prepared. Military geodesic specialists had identified several dozen launch sites in various regions of the country. Timetables for construction, supply, and missile installation had been compiled. Everything had been thought of except the cost. It should have been taken into account originally, but at that time the goal of achieving seven thousand kilometers "at any cost" was dominant.

One evening Father came home from the Kremlin looking preoccupied and, I would say, sad. It had seemed as if the finish line was just ahead, you had only to reach out your hand and—suddenly it was all a mirage. Nothing Father described was new. It simply all came together to form a whole picture. Flaws were revealed that some people had failed to see and others tried to avoid noticing. An enormous missile required a massive launch pad. It

---

5. Nedelin was marshal of artillery. He was in charge of the military application of missiles and later became commander in chief of Strategic Missile Forces.

would necessitate removing many thousands of cubic meters of earth, pouring enormous quantities of concrete and building railroads, all this in inaccessible, sparsely populated places. Plans called for installing the new missiles in such places, far from the eyes of outsiders, for reasons of secrecy.

Just as many problems were foreseen when construction was completed. Missiles had to be kept armed, ready to be launched quickly—if not in minutes, then in only a few hours. But at the time it took days to prepare a missile for launching. Liquid oxygen, used as an oxidizer, caused the most problems.

According to directions set down by the General Staff, missiles should always be kept fueled. To handle liquid oxygen and cool it in tanks was impossible; it evaporated constantly and was vented through special valves. Additional tons of liquid oxygen, dozens of tons, had to be pumped in to replace it—day after day, month after month, year after year.

Still another important detail: radar control stations had to be "set down" onto the impassable taiga, on marshy bogs. Hundreds, if not thousands, of kilometers of roads would have to be built and electricity brought in.

A missile's range was controlled by an instrument that operated like a battery. It was called an electronic integrator. Charged up to a certain point on earth, it ran down in proportion to the missile's acceleration and at a given moment gave the signal: "We've arrived." It could be kept on the missile in working condition for only a very short time, after which it had to be removed, recharged, and calibrated.

According to estimates presented to Father, each launch site, with all its auxiliary servicing, would cost half a billion rubles.

Toward the end of his recital, Father complained that the half billion was only the beginning. In fact, each project would cost several times the initial estimates. Father wavered: we could not appropriate that amount of money. The country would be ruined.

"If we're forced into doing this, we'll all lose our pants," Father joked sadly. When I asked what we could do, he said that he had asked Korolyov to come in for a talk. Father was somewhat hopeful.

But here Father ran into a stone wall. Korolyov insisted that they had found the only possible engineering solution for the R-7. He categorically rejected the possibility of creating an intercontinental missile using nitric acid instead of oxygen. It all depended on making an engine that could develop enough thrust. "It's impossible to build such an engine. Acid is for such trifles as the R-11. You could increase its range another ten times. Yangel is trying to do that with the R-12, but acid won't work for an intercontinental missile. Besides, it's impossible to work with acid. It will corrode everything: the joints, the pipelines. It will turn the tanks into dust. It's not even worth trying," said Korolyov, disappointing Father with his summary.

However, Korolyov yielded somewhat, promising that they would eliminate remote radar guidance stations, that the missile could be controlled automatically, without radar assistance. Father gasped in surprise: "Then why did we pour so much money into building a new test site in Tyura-Tam? An autonomic 'R-7' could have been launched from Kapustin Yar, which already existed," he said reproachfully.

Korolyov didn't argue the point. He simply said that when the new test site was set up he had not even dreamed of an autonomic guidance system.

In everything else Korolyov remained adamant. In his opinion, the government had no choice but to spend whatever was required and begin to implement plans for including his missiles in the military arsenal. Father commented sadly that the country would wind up as world beggars. Then the imperialists wouldn't have to fight us.

Father persisted in trying to explore other options. Korolyov said that the Americans were doing research in solid fuel and special powders. But we would not be able to solve this problem easily. A whole industrial branch for new chemical products would have to be organized. We would have to spend many billions, fully as much as to equip launch sites for the R-7. And it would take much more than a year. Furthermore, we didn't know whether we would find anything better.

Korolyov said, with a shade of resentment in his voice, that Father should consult Glushko if his word was not good enough. In contrast to previous meetings, they parted, if not unhappy with each other, at least with a feeling of dissatisfaction.

That evening Father complained that Korolyov was apparently more interested in setting records in space than working on defense.

Talk was all very well, but the decision whether or not to add missiles to our military arsenal had to be made without delay. Father rejected the grandiose plan for deploying the R-7 submitted to him. The country could not afford it.

He had no doubt that a totally different situation would be created in the world as soon as the United States realized we were capable of delivering a nuclear strike against it. The threat that even a few cities could be destroyed would force the United States to wonder whether it was worth paying such a price for the dubious satisfaction of far greater destruction in the Soviet Union. Father's words did not yet amount to a concept. They simply justified an unavoidable decision. Nevertheless, his idea is worth remembering. Father never supported the doctrine of one hundred percent nuclear parity and thought such a competition would be fatal for our country.

After all the reductions and cancellations of plans only three R-7 bases remained, effectively those already being built. One additional launch site was proposed, in Tyura-Tam/Baikonur, not far from the experimental base. Naturally, it would be the least expensive of all.

The second cluster was to be near Arkhangelsk, not far from the Plesetsk railroad station. Two first-phase launch sites were completed in 1959. The first launch took place on July 30, and the two missile sites were accepted into service on December 15, 1959. Two more sites were ready in 1961. They were in use until the middle of 1964, when it was decided to convert the base into a cosmodrome. It is now called *Zvezdny* (Star).

The third cluster was designated for the east, for the Krasnoyarsk region. There, everything would have to be built from the ground up. I have never been able to find any information about this project. It was probably not built.

One of the missiles was aimed at New York, another at Washington. Two more were supposed to be aimed at Chicago and Los Angeles. I have never seen a map showing the targets, but at the time there was much talk in missile circles about the primary hostage-cities on the territory of the United States. Father also mentioned them.

As far as I remember, those missiles were armed only once, in the final days of the Cuban Missile Crisis.

Father didn't forget Korolyov's advice. Literally on the following day, he called Glushko. Valentin Petrovich already knew why he was calling. Secret rumors travel even faster than non-secret ones. He therefore answered Father's question without hesitation. Yes, he would tackle the design of an engine with acid. As far as the missile itself was concerned, he advised Father to talk to Yangel. Anyway, there was no real choice: it was Korolyov or Yangel, Yangel or Korolyov. Makeyev was not yet taken very seriously.

Father invited Yangel to come to his office. At first they talked about tests of the R-12, which were in their final stage. Father received reports about the circumstances surrounding every launch. Regardless of the outcome, the chief designer called the first secretary from the test site on the special phone. That was customary. The designer would listen to the usual dose of congratulations or words of sympathy. Father didn't berate anyone for failures. He felt that designers didn't deserve such treatment, which would be counterproductive in any case.

I had many occasions to observe the procedure. In case of success, a radiant Chelomei would hurry to the test site communications unit—with a light, almost winged step. In case of failure, he didn't hurry, preferred to wait for the first decoding of the telemetry and look for excuses. Only then would he head to the phone. Before reaching for it he would pause briefly, as if preparing to dive into cold water. Then he would pick it up, be quickly connected, and deliver the mournful report: "Nikita Sergeyevich, this is Chelomei. Unfortunately . . ."

I think other chief designers behaved more or less the same way.

So Father knew everything about the R-12 tests. The results were now being studied. Yangel talked about the technology of missile construction. It was now possible to introduce a conveyor belt and eject finished missiles "like sausages," as he put it. Father was pleased by the comparison. He promised to make use of his first chance to visit the factory. He had never seen mass production of missiles.

Then they turned to the main subject. Mikhail Kuzmich repeated what he had said at their previous meeting: he could build an intercontinental missile using new components. As fuel, instead of kerosene he would employ the more efficient asymmetrical dimethyl hydrazine, while as oxidizer he would continue to use nitric acid, which had already proven itself. Unlike liquid oxygen, it did not evaporate under normal temperatures, so the rocket did not require refueling and could remain ready for launch for a rather long time.

There were, of course, serious technical problems, and not only with the engine. Korolyov was right. Acid was very toxic and corrosive. With the slightest mistake, it could turn the rocket into dust.

Father was delighted. After Korolyov's categorical "no," he had prepared himself for the worst.

In general, Yangel thought that he was equal to the task. He told Father that the Americans had considered a similar missile.

They agreed to meet again in a few weeks.

Yangel's proposals were based on a solid foundation. His team had been working on developing its own intercontinental missile for several years, virtually from the day it gained independence from Korolyov. As Boris Yevseyevich Chertok writes in his marvelous book *Missiles and People: The Hot Days of the Cold War* (Moscow: Mashinostroyeniye, 1997, p. 22), at the very end of 1956 Mikhail Kuzmich had even managed to obtain a decree from the Central Committee and the Council of Ministers sanctioning, or more precisely, authorizing, work on a new intercontinental missile. At that time the R-7 had not yet flown, and Father thought it was essential to have a second option. But after the R-7 enjoyed its first successes, Yangel's proposal was virtually forgotten. Far from being given the highest priority, both relations with his suppliers and work at the factory proceeded with only indifferent success.

Appearance of the decree certainly did not give the work a green light. A great number of such papers were issued, and as Mikhail Pavlovich Petelin, the very experienced director of the NII-10, told me—a young engineer at the time—it was simply physically impossible to carry out all government decrees. A director would have to choose which to implement and which to put aside, to judge according to circumstances when nonfulfillment might get you "killed," when you might be "severely beaten," and when you would only get a scolding. Yangel's intercontinental R&D fell into that last category, and all the power and resources were given to Korolyov.

Until then Yangel, despite all his efforts, had not managed to emerge from Korolyov's shadow. Now such an opportunity presented itself.

This time Yangel came with Glushko. The two designers agreed that they could build the missile, and rather quickly too. Tests were expected to begin as early as 1960.

Father kept thinking about his talk with Korolyov. He, a specialist who had made his reputation with both the R-7 and satellites, had claimed that it was impossible to make a missile that used acid. Now Yangel was embarking on such a project. Could he and Glushko have overlooked something? Or were they simply being presumptuous? Father decided to call Korolyov and discuss it with him again.

However, Korolyov preempted Father by asking for a meeting. It was not an easy conversation. This time the usually straightforward Sergei Pavlovich beat around the bush.

He talked about the new oxygen-fueled R-9, but Father already knew about his proposals. Then he talked about tests of the R-7 and about launches. That too was old news.

Father began to wonder why Korolyov had asked for an appointment if he was going to waste their time.

Korolyov finally brought himself to the point. He asked Father to change the order to build an intercontinental missile with acid and transfer the responsibility to him.

Father gasped: "So that's it!" he thought.

Sergei Pavlovich explained that he was not retracting his words—acid was inferior to oxygen—but that since the government did not agree with him, he felt that he could not stand aside. His design bureau was far more experienced than Yangel's. It would therefore make a better missile and make it faster.

Father was dumbstruck. He finally recovered himself somewhat.

"But you said yourself that it was impossible to make such a missile," he began somewhat uncertainly.

"Not impossible," Korolyov interrupted. "But it would be far inferior to an oxygen one."

"Well, all right," Father said, recovering from his surprise. "You make a missile with oxygen, and let Yangel compete with you. Why hurt his feelings?"

Father was trying to joke, but Korolyov wouldn't play along with him. He continued to insist.

Father began getting angry. He had not expected this of Korolyov.

"We made a decision, Comrade Korolyov," Father said in a severe official tone of voice. "You were assigned the oxygen version and Yangel was entrusted with the acid missile. That decision will not be canceled by the government. We'll see who wins."

As Father described it that evening, he thought Korolyov was going to hit him. But he only glared at Father and then looked down glumly. He realized it was useless to argue any further with the chairman of the Council of Ministers.

They parted with unusual coldness and formality. Father could forgive a great deal in the way of mistakes and delusions, but in this case Korolyov was simply trying by every means he could think of to preserve his monopoly, to "sink" a rival.

Father didn't forgive anyone for that, even those people he sincerely liked, such as Sergei Pavlovich. However, he didn't reveal his feelings. Father never brought up the painful subject in subsequent conversations with Korolyov. But on our walks he sometimes returned to the conversation, even as it gradually receded into the past. It was the ethical aspect, not the difference in technology, that bothered him. When he knew what it would cost the country to deploy the R-7, how could Sergei Pavlovich still insist on "his variant" and reject a proposal from Yangel that was far more advantageous to the country? Father couldn't understand it.

It soon became known (and did not escape Father's ears) that after Yangel and Glushko visited Father together there was a stormy scene between Glushko and Sergei Pavlovich.

Korolyov and Glushko were linked by many years of joint work, if not by friendship (I don't presume to judge). They had started working together at the Rocket Research Institute in the 1930s. They wound up in "those awful places" in 1937, were released at the same time, and went back to work on their main interests in life, Korolyov to rockets, Glushko to rocket engines.

Now Korolyov felt that Glushko had betrayed him. He felt that Glushko should have refused to work with Yangel on an intercontinental missile.

Reacting to this accusation, Glushko flew into a rage. He was far from convinced that Korolyov should have priority in Soviet missile technology and space science. He had long been sick and tired of playing second fiddle on Korolyov's postwar "team." He was dying to be independent. Yangel's proposal seemed a good escape from his current situation. Moreover, he saw no obstacles to building the proposed engine. It would finally make clear to everyone who was the sleigh and who the horse. You don't put engines on missiles, but they are used to hurl missiles into space, into orbit, into a trajectory. Glushko was not Korolyov's property, and Yangel was not the last missile designer who would turn to him for help. Others would come, and

Glushko would decide himself which designers he preferred, whose orders were worthy of his attention and whose he could ignore.

Their conversation ended in a complete rupture. Korolyov called Glushko a "traitor" and swore never to have anything more to do with him. None of his engines would ever be used for Korolyov's missiles.

Here Sergei Pavlovich had gone too far, in view of the fact that Glushko and his engines were irreplaceable and that Korolyov would have to work with him for a long time to come. But Sergei Pavlovich would carry out his threat at the first opportunity.

I feel a little uncomfortable commenting on the personal relations of two outstanding designers, people for whom I felt a genuine liking. But just as the trivial clash between Ivan Ivanovich and Ivan Nikiforovich near a puddle of water in Mirgorod led to tragic consequences,[6] in the same way the quarrel between Korolyov from Zhitomir and Glushko from Odessa left a perceptible mark on the history of Soviet missile technology and space science. It is visible even today.

At first the clash between the two titans didn't seem that important. It was felt that though they had quarreled, they would make up. That was the only result possible, considering the joint work they had to do. When time didn't heal the wound, Father ordered Ustinov to impose peace on the warring sides. But Korolyov wouldn't even listen to Dmitry Fyodorovich. Attempts by Kozlov, and later by Brezhnev, were also unsuccessful.

Far from setting, Korolyov's star burned even more brightly, but he had to leave a little more room in the firmament. At the end of 1958 and beginning of 1959 Yangel's position became more and more solid. He began to squeeze Korolyov out of military missile construction for good. Sergei Pavlovich's attempts to regain lost ground proved futile. Neither the oxygen R-9A, which somewhat resembled the Atlas, nor the solid fuel RT-1, was widely adopted by the armed forces. Rivals forced them onto the shoulder of the road.

But the successful R-7 serves faithfully, lifts satellites into orbit, takes cosmonauts for rides. From that time on, missile technology divided into two branches, space and military.

Father had almost no doubt that missiles would play the key role in modern warfare. But they seemed to him like very vulnerable pencils, protruding helplessly from the earth. He thought constantly about how they could be protected. The problem became an obsession and wouldn't let him sleep.

---

6. Reference here is to N. V. Gogol's *The Tale of How Ivan Ivanovich Quarreled with Ivan Niki-forovich (The Two Ivans)* in his cycle of short stories, *Mirgorod* (1835–37). In the comic mock-epic tale, familiar to educated Russians, an all-consuming feud begins when the two Ivans quarrel over geese in a pond.

In his youth Father had dreamed of a career as an engineer. At the end of the 1920s he managed to persuade the Kiev leadership to let him go to Moscow to study at the Industrial Academy. But fate had something else in store for him. He had not completed the course when Stalin remembered him and made him first secretary of the Bauman District Party Committee in Moscow. So Father never worked with technology, but he never lost his attraction to engineering. He loved to be with engineers, and their ideas aroused his enthusiasm. He sometimes offered advice and made suggestions.

In the summer of 1958 Father thought he had discovered how to protect missiles from enemy attack. They should be hidden underground. He first shared this idea with Korolyov, I think in the Crimea. Sergei Pavlovich was vacationing at the Lower Oreanda Sanatorium, which was not far from Father's dacha.

Father was often a guest at the sanatorium, where ministers, provincial committee secretaries, designers, and scientists vacationed. A circle would form around Father, and everyone would begin discussing the issues of the day. When the talk eventually began to sound something like a session of the Council of Ministers, he would break off, and smiling and pointing to the empty volleyball and shuffleboard court, apologize for distracting them all from their "work." Waving farewell, Father would continue on his walk.

Father outlined his idea to Korolyov cautiously. Every inventor, even if he is chairman of the Council of Ministers, is affected by timidity before the authority of an expert. Korolyov wasn't thrilled by Father's proposal, but promised to think it over and give an opinion after a few days.

A week later Sergei Pavlovich regretfully informed Father that his proposal would not work. One of the objections Korolyov raised was that the hot gases from the engine nozzles would ignite and burn up the missile in a shaft. Father did not agree. In response to Korolyov's criticism, he proposed placing a steel cylinder with a smaller diameter inside the shaft, and putting the missile in it. Then the gases could escape through the gap between the cylinder and the wall of the shaft, leaving the missile intact.

Korolyov insisted he was right. It was impossible to launch a missile from a shaft, and not even worth trying. It's hard to say why he didn't think much of the idea. Perhaps he was always measuring everything against his R-7. It was certainly true that cramming such a monster into the ground would not be an easy job. But Father didn't give in. He decided to consult Vladimir Pavlovich Barmin, who designed the launch sites and the launchers for all Korolyov's missiles, as well as others.

A few days later Barmin flew in from Moscow. Father invited Yangel, who was also vacationing at the Lower Oreanda, to come over together with Korolyov.

They all gathered around a large table on the terrace off the second floor of the big, white stone house occupied by Father. Father again described his idea.

Barmin was not enthusiastic either. He offered politely to look it over and make some calculations. You don't simply dismiss the ideas of such a person. However, he gave every sign of thinking it was a waste of time. On this occasion Korolyov said nothing. Yangel didn't say a word either. He kept revolving an unlit cigarette in his fingers. He obviously wanted very much to smoke, but couldn't make up his mind to light up in Father's presence, even on the open terrace. Father didn't smoke and couldn't stand the smell of tobacco.

Father grasped the general mood and retreated, saying that of course he was not an engineer, not a specialist. It wasn't up to him to pronounce the final verdict. They would have the last word. Barmin promised he would think it over some more.

The conversation turned to other subjects. They sat until it grew dark. Personally, I was sorry that Father had proposed his technical solution to the designers. It wasn't his specialty and had therefore caused some awkwardness.

When his guests left, Father accompanied them to the next corner, where they headed for home and the two of us turned back toward the dacha.

"Apparently nothing will come of my idea," said Father sadly. "Well, they know better."

I felt bad for him and wanted to help. But how? I sincerely thought that he had meddled in what wasn't his business.

The vacation flew by quickly. Father returned to Moscow and we went with him. Leafing through the scientific journals and news bulletins that had piled up during the month, I found a brief report in one of them about a new method proposed by the Americans to protect ballistic missiles from nuclear strikes. It was accompanied by a small drawing, which showed a vertical shaft enclosing a cylinder, and in the cylinder a missile.

Arrows were drawn to indicate how hot gases from the engines escaped into the space between the shaft wall and the cylinder, then were ejected up and away into the air, exactly as Father had proposed.

I put the leaflet aside to bring home that evening and show Father, to give him a pleasant surprise.

When I told him about my find and showed him the picture, Father was as gleeful as a child. He spent a long time looking at the sketch and then during our walk he talked on and on about how even good engineers sometimes make mistakes and don't immediately recognize a valuable idea.

INTERLUDE: THE IRAQ CRISIS

According to my concept of events, what took place in the summer of 1958 was the last in the series of shocks set off by the Suez "explosion" in October and November of 1956. For the last time U.S. Marines, British gunners, and

Soviet divisions faced each other. This time they were separated by the territory of Iraq.

In Father's opinion, Iraq remained a land of colonialism and Nuri Said's government the embodiment of corruption and reaction. It was not by chance, he felt, that the military alliance directed against our country was called the Baghdad Pact.

A military coup occurred unexpectedly in Baghdad on the night of July 13, 1958. A division of the Iraqi army marched through Baghdad. When its commander, Abdel Kerim Kasem, burst into the royal palace, he could simply grasp the power relinquished by Nuri Said.

The new government's first action was to denounce the Baghdad Pact. According to the standards of the time, that meant Iraq became automatically "ours," "like us." There was an immediate reaction. By the next day, July 15, the Americans had already begun landing Marines in Jordan. They had every pretext for intervening, since armed clashes had been going on in Jordan for four months.

Father was not in Moscow on July 15. On Walter Ulbricht's invitation, he had left for Berlin to attend a congress of the SED (Socialist Unity Party of Germany) on July 12, the eve of the coup. He had asked me to go with him when I returned home from the test site some time earlier. Getting time off from work was not difficult.

As I understand it, Father acted in accordance with the pattern set down during previous crises in that region. Before the morning session of the Congress on July 14, an aide informed him of what had happened and read a draft Soviet Government Declaration drawn up by the Foreign Ministry. Father changed the wording and inserted a paragraph that made it very clear that the USSR would support the anticolonial revolution not simply in words, but by armed force if necessary.

After hearing of the U.S. Marine landing, he telephoned Moscow and ordered a Soviet military show of force, like the recent one in support of Syria but on a larger scale, along the border with Turkey and Iran. He thought that there might very well be military intervention by the United States and Turkey. Especially by Turkey. Father believed that it was assigned the principal role in this "show." Turkish forces would fire the first shot, and the Americans and British would then rush in to assist them.

The word "believed" is not really appropriate here. Father knew. He had received virtually firsthand information about what was planned across the ocean. The intelligence reports containing disposition of forces, proposals for surprise diplomatic and other moves, as well as other important papers sent to the White House and No. 10 Downing Street, arrived punctually at the Kremlin and lay on Father's desk in modest, gray-blue paper folders. Father proposed that maneuvers begin immediately, and that in addition to moving local forces toward our borders there begin a demonstrative transfer of Army units from deep within the country. Air units should move first. He considered them to be the key factor. Ground forces assembled in the border region would have to rebuff any intention by Iran and Turkey to link up with the Americans.

On July 17 Soviet newspapers prominently featured an announcement that ground and air forces would begin carrying out military exercises in the Transcaucasus and Turkestan, with the participation of ships of the Black Sea Fleet. In those years the Soviet press never announced maneuvers, so this information alone should have been seen as a serious warning. In order to emphasize the significance of these measures even further, Father proposed publicizing the fact that First Deputy Defense Minister Marshal Grechko was leaving for the Transcaucasus as commander in chief of ground forces, and that Marshal Meretskov, hero of the defense of Leningrad, was to secure his left flank.

The armies sprang into motion, tanks and armored personnel carriers began raising clouds of dust on the roads, and planes filled the sky.

Father began to get nervous: our troops should have moved sooner, but bureaucratic red tape had delayed them. The British might have hesitated to barge in earlier. Now British forces were already landing in Jordan. Both sides began to exert more pressure.

Father returned to Moscow. I found out what was going on only during our evening walks. When I asked him about what was happening in Lebanon and Jordan and whether American and British units were moving toward the Iraqi border or remaining in place,[7] Father couldn't give a definite answer. He didn't know himself. In his opinion, the situation was complicated and the pendulum could swing toward war at any moment.

Father said he had called Zhivkov and they had agreed on combined operations. The Bulgarians would announce the next day that their army was going on maneuvers. He added: "So that it will appear more convincing to the Turks. Without the Turks, the Americans won't stick their noses into Iraq. We'll send our planes to Bulgaria and appoint Air Marshal Skripko as their commander." Father grinned. "American intelligence is well aware of the fact that he's in charge of strategic aviation. Let them think that one over." This information appeared in our newspapers on July 18. An unstable equilibrium was established.

In those days Father often referred to the Suez crisis, when his appeal to the governments concerned had brought about the desired solution. Now he decided to repeat that maneuver.

On July 19, after a second statement by the Soviet government (this one

---

7. The U.S. Marines landed in Lebanon, and the British landed in Jordan, as noted below.

concerning U.S. and British aggression in the Middle East), he dictated messages to Dwight Eisenhower, Harold Macmillan, Charles de Gaulle, and Jawaharlal Nehru calling for an urgent meeting at any appropriate place in the world to determine what steps to take to end the aggression.

He was ready to fly anywhere, but thought that wouldn't be necessary. "It wouldn't pay the imperialists to have a meeting," said Father with exasperation during our walk that evening. "What do they have to say? Nothing! They want to strangle Iraq stealthily, and we're trying to get in their way. They won't agree to a conference. Just as well! They'll look like the aggressors."

The reply came three days later. NATO did not consider such a meeting to be useful. The U.N. Security Council existed to hear such conflicts. Let it take up the subject of Iraq. Father reacted to this reply with what I might call delight. That very day he dictated a new message. While agreeing to examine the question in the Security Council, he made it a condition that the leaders of the states and governments concerned be present. And he immediately set a specific date—July 28, five days hence.

That evening he rubbed his hands together with satisfaction. Immersed in a dispute, Father felt in his element. He again waited impatiently. How would his opponents respond this time? Father had no doubt that they would try by whatever means possible to postpone the start of discussions. That would be to their advantage. Time worked against the Iraqis in this confrontation. Armed clashes had broken out, and Kasem's precarious hold on power seemed less secure. A little while longer and he would fall without any interference by British and U.S. forces.

Father pressed ahead. The opponent must not be allowed a respite or time to adjust to the situation.

In his reply, Eisenhower said that the date proposed by Father for government leaders to assemble in New York could not be met. Without delaying a single day, Father sent a new message asking him to suggest a suitable date. He did not receive an answer. A lull ensued. On July 28 a conference of Baghdad Pact members was to convene in London, instead of the U.N. Security Council session in New York that Father had proposed. Father had ascertained that the conference agenda would preclude discussion of military actions on the borders of Iraq, so he decided not to change his plans. On July 31, Father was in Beijing, accompanied by Defense Minister Marshal Malinovsky. Let them speculate in London about what was being discussed beside the swimming pool at Mao Zedong's residence. Now we know that the Chinese had very little interest in the Middle East, and that Father was being cautious. He did not want to be drawn into the conflict unfolding in the Taiwan Strait.

In Beijing Father finally received a belated answer from Washington: Eisenhower wrote that he could not attend a Security Council session or any other meeting, but thought that a special session of the U.N. General Assembly on this question could be convened no later than August 12. Similar messages came from Britain and France.

On August 5, after returning to Moscow, Father agreed to a meeting at the U.N. He was pleased, feeling that the crisis and the threat of an attack on Iraq had passed. Now he had only to "help" the Western powers withdraw from the conflict.

Father celebrated a victory. His mood during those days was serene, and he allowed himself to relax a little. When I asked what would happen now, he mumbled good-naturedly that it was time to ease the tension. He had already ordered an announcement to be made that maneuvers were concluded and Grechko and Meretskov were returning to their regular duties.

Newspapers reported the completion of military exercises on August 7, and a special session of the U.N. General Assembly convened on August 9. Foreign Minister Andrei Andreyevich Gromyko went to New York, while Father headed to Kuibyshev for the opening of the Volzhskoye Hydroelectric Station.

There, he spoke at a meeting and publicly proclaimed his victory. He thought we had succeeded in forcing the aggressors to abandon their plans to attack Iraq.

Contrary to Father's expectations, the question of withdrawing expeditionary forces from Lebanon and Jordan was decided briskly. By the end of August all participants in the U.N. session had reached overall agreement.

These events still further reinforced Father in his belief that diplomacy was effective in relations with the imperialists only when backed by real power.[8]

MISSILES AND THE RESTRUCTURING OF THE MILITARY

The first generation of missiles, a serious weapon and not just a trump card in the game of diplomacy, was undergoing tests. The results were encouraging. But there were problems with warheads for them.

The Americans did not respond to Father's announcement of a morato-

---

8. "diplomacy . . . backed by real power." Here we have an echo of the Suez crisis both in contemporary policy and perceptions as well as in later historical accounts. Most recent treatments still maintain that the Marines landed in response to the Lebanese government's request, based on its reported fears that the new Iraqi regime might intervene. The U.S. withdrawal in October is usually thought to result from acknowledgment that there was no threat, that the Americans had been called in for domestic political purposes, and most important, that the whole effort to build up a Middle Eastern alliance against communism (the Baghdad Pact) had run afoul of Arab nationalism. Again, the Soviet military threat is discounted, although as in the case of Suez, analysts agree that Khrushchev might have seen the crisis as another successful application of his policy of bluff.

rium on nuclear weapons' tests. They continued testing methodically and successfully. One explosion followed another. And each explosion meant an addition to the arsenal of our adversary. We, on the other hand, were marking time. By the end of summer Father was starting to get nervous. There were very few who consistently supported his decision for a unilateral end to testing. No one spoke against it in the Presidium, but generals and missile designers grumbled in quiet corners. Naturally, no one said anything out loud. Not in those days.

Although the Soviet Union was the first to explode a hydrogen bomb, the construction of warheads left something to be desired. Of course, designers had progressed far beyond the five-and-a-half-ton monster of a thermonuclear warhead planned for the R-7, but everything we had belonged (at best) to the technology of yesterday. The devices of tomorrow, and even today, promised to bring steadily increasing explosive power, along with a sharp decrease in weight and size. Without tests, all designs either went into the wastebasket or lay on the shelf.

The pressure on Father grew. Sometimes designers telephoned, but more often they submitted the results of their work in writing, including comparative data on old and new products and hypothetical computational parameters of analogous devices tested in the Pacific by the United States. Minister Yefim Pavlovich Slavsky often brought Father memoranda asking "whether factories should make the new or old products?" It was far more expensive to manufacture the old warheads. Dmitry Fyodorovich Ustinov proved that warhead miniaturization would reduce the weight of the ballistic missile many times over, and not just that of the missile, but the entire complex. In the absence of testing and new warheads, more work to perfect missile technology would be meaningless.

Father's old friend Rodion Yakovlevich Malinovsky, the minister of defense, was also a frequent visitor. He didn't write memoranda, but growled: "If we want to create a modern army, we have to have the right weapons, but we won't get them without testing."

I've already mentioned that on this occasion I did not support Father. Every American explosion sounded an alarm: we will fall behind. What if war broke out? I often asked Father such questions. He didn't answer and only became irritated.

Now I understand how difficult it was for him. His initiative was ignored in America, and he had invested so much in his proposal. Not because he considered that we were leading in the nuclear race. He was quite well aware of the true state of affairs. He knew how far ahead the Americans were. That was the very reason he counted on a favorable response from Eisenhower. And it was all the more bitter for him to admit that he was mistaken.

Only now, decades later, is it becoming clear how much his view of the world differed from that of other people. We all—I, our military, and the Americans—essentially occupied the same position. We all proceeded from the simple supposition that a country can try to win a nuclear war! It would be horrible, losses would be enormous, but victory would make up for everything. For victory you need modern weapons, of course nuclear ones. So you can't avoid testing.

Father was alone in opposing this overwhelming pressure. He had no doubt that victory was impossible, that it was a mirage, that the next world war would have no winner.

What we already possessed was enough to deter an aggressor. Perhaps the seeds of what we now refer to as "nuclear sufficiency" were already germinating in his mind.

No one understood him. Even his closest associates viewed the moratorium as a diplomatic maneuver. The reaction across the ocean was no better. There we were considered crafty Asiatics and they searched for a hidden meaning in every word, a deeply concealed threat in every proposal. At their recent meeting Father had tried to convert Mao Zedong to his viewpoint. Nothing came of it. I can imagine the bitter aftertaste those conversations left in Father's mouth.

Newspapers continued methodically recording American explosions. By the end of July more than thirty tests had been carried out.

Father faltered. He hadn't given in yet, but he retreated a step, perhaps only half a step. He decided to make one more, possibly final, appeal. At the same time, he issued the order to begin preparing for our own tests. It would be easy to stop the process if a political solution were achieved, but if not, we would have saved time. Slavsky and Malinovsky greeted Father's decision with a sigh of relief. For them there was no "if." On August 30 Father gave an interview to *Pravda*. He wrote both the questions and the answers himself. Father proposed that negotiations to end nuclear testing begin on October 31. He thought that if negotiations went on for a long time, even years, we would be at a disadvantage if we observed a unilateral moratorium. Negotiations could serve as a cover for our opponents to continue testing. Father therefore proposed setting a time limit for the negotiations.

The proposal hung in the air.

In 1958 Father attempted to carry out a radical reorganization of the armed forces, on land, at sea, and in the air.

At first seen as expensive toys, missiles had rapidly assumed an important role and had been introduced into all branches of the armed forces. Ballistic and cruise, antiaircraft and antitank, suspended under the wings of planes and attached to the decks of ships, missiles could destroy any target with unprecedented accuracy and at distances unimaginable only shortly before.

Their possibilities appeared limitless to Father. Aviation, with its problems of penetrating air defenses; field artillery, with its limited range and accuracy; not to speak of antiaircraft artillery, which was even less effective—all seemed hopelessly obsolete when compared with missiles. It was almost like what happened to cavalry in the period between the First and Second World Wars. Father remembered vividly that people didn't listen when Tukhachevsky fought to replace horses with motors. They had given in to Voroshilov and Budyonny, and paid the price in blood in 1941. Father could not allow a repetition of that tragedy. Now, when he had the final word, he stood at the forefront of those in favor of reequipping the Army with nuclear missiles and reviewing military doctrine. There was a split in the Army. Most generals refused to change. Many high-ranking military officers, even some of Father's recent friends, were among his opponents. To some extent, Father overestimated missiles. They could not fully replace either planes or antiaircraft guns.

In the early 1950s Father still felt like a student. He could not visualize modern weapons. But he wanted to learn about them, so he began visiting one design bureau after another and talked with virtually all the leading chief designers.

Even after acquiring a certain amount of information and learning a considerable amount, Father felt that he didn't grasp the whole picture: what *was* a modern army? And Father found out something else that simply horrified him: he knew much more about the new technology than the military commanders who would have to employ it in the event of war.

More than one authorization was necessary before anyone could gain access to nuclear or missile weaponry. Very few were given that authorization. As a result, most district commanders had never even seen a missile. That was even more true of republic central committee and provincial committee secretaries. The newest weapons may have been produced in their regions, but they were not allowed to see them. The picture was almost the same in the central apparatus of the Ministry of Defense. Father was horrified. He convened a conference of top Ministry of Defense officials and heads of defense branches of industry. The agenda consisted of a single item: how to familiarize the Army in a short time with the modern means of waging war. How to teach troops to handle those weapons and to fight against them.

Father thought it would take a long time before new weapons were provided to frontline units. By then they would already be growing obsolete. The latest weapons should become familiar from the very beginning, when production was just getting under way. It was decided to start at the top.

Father proposed holding a demonstration of our achievements in the military field. The new weapons should be seen in action, with live firing and missile launches, not on the parade ground. The Kapustin Yar missile test site was selected for the first demonstration. The plan was to put all generals, plus party and government officials associated with defense, through this school of modern military science.

The demonstration was held in 1958, during the second half of September.

I met Father at the airfield as one of his hosts.

After greeting everyone, Father drew me after him. There was hardly any room for me in the car. Father sat in front, while Kirichenko, Malinovsky, Brezhnev, and Presidium member and Central Committee secretary Andrei Pavlovich Kirilenko, squeezed into the back seats. I perched on the small jump seat.

Two parlor cars had been brought to the test site rail siding, close to the test area, for the use of Father and other important officials. That was where Father was headed. I lived at my own test site. Therefore, I went with Father as a guest.

The railroad car assigned to Father had an air conditioner, a great rarity in those days, so it was cool and comfortable.

Father didn't like to rest after traveling. He had no complaints about his health. So, after washing up quickly, he walked into the part of the car arranged for meetings. All the participants, military and civilian, were already there. Malinovsky was to deliver a report on the training exercise, which was the official name for the demonstration. There were posters on the walls, a diagram of the test site, charts showing features of missiles, planes, and other weapons. The lights were on because all the windows were covered by thick blinds, despite the fact that no one could have approached the carefully guarded car.

After Malinovsky's report everybody started talking at the same time. All the participants, especially the civilians, tried to show off their knowledge of missiles—sometimes successfully, but more often inappropriately. Finally, Father and I were left alone. Father wanted to rest after having read the evening mail. As I was leaving, he asked me if I could find the information about silos I had shown him in Moscow. I nodded, since I had brought it with me. Knowing Father, I didn't doubt that at the first convenient occasion he would return to the subject of the silos, so I had put the newsletter in my suitcase. "When do you want it? Now?" I asked Father. "Tomorrow," he said. "Bring it with you."

While the group was touring Yangel's site the following day, Father asked someone to find me. As a junior member of the group, I was standing toward the back. I made my way to where there was a little open space around Father. Yangel was next to him and, as his host, was giving explanations.

"Did you bring it?" asked Father softly. I handed him the newsletter, open to the right page. Yangel followed our movements in some perplexity. Father folded the newsletter and stuck it into his pocket without saying anything.

Some time later, as we approached the R-12, which protruded from the steppe like a candlestick on a holiday table, Father drew the paper out of his pocket and, calling over Barmin, pointed to the open page. He was obviously showing him the drawing of the American missile being launched from a silo. They started discussing something animatedly. Yangel joined them. Then Korolyov walked over. I didn't hear what was being said, but it was easy to guess. When I visited the car that evening, Father was sitting alone drinking tea. As soon as I walked in, Father triumphantly announced that they had decided to build an experimental silo for the R-12. This time Yangel supported him, and even Barmin gave in after seeing the information from America.

"I scolded him for not keeping up with the technical journals," Father added suddenly. I frowned. He shouldn't have said that. But the unpleasant sensation soon gave way to a feeling of satisfaction. I was sincerely happy for Father. His idea had turned out to be a valid one. But the most important thing was that we would have a reliable way to conceal our missiles.

One year later, in September of 1959, the R-12 was launched from its silo. Everything went well. I very much regretted being in Moscow at the time and missing the incredible spectacle.

At the very beginning Yangel employed both the "normal" and silo methods for tests. Later he switched entirely to silos.

Korolyov had to catch up with him. The R-9 also had to be concealed in the ground.

There is a tremendous gap between testing a theory and making it a reality. The work was only completed toward the middle of 1963 and beginning of 1964. It was only after Father's retirement that silos were really added to the military arsenal.

Father had even more respect for Yangel after the episode with silos. However, that was not to Korolyov's detriment. To the end of his life, Father thought that Korolyov was a very great designer. He felt that arguments, disagreements, and even quarrels were normal. Without them you couldn't achieve anything important in life. On the other hand, he saw that Korolyov had totally lost interest in military matters and viewed them as a burden. At first such an attitude by our chief rocket designer toward defense matters grieved Father. Then he came to accept it. Space was no less important.

The September demonstration was very successful. Viewers saw a magical spectacle. Ballistic missiles were launched one after another, raising very tall clouds of dust. Korolyov began the parade by launching the R-5, then the R-2, and finally the R-1. The R-7 was only described. They had decided that transporting such a monster to this test site was not useful. On the other hand, a whole family of geophysical research rockets was lined up on the ground. During the past few years they had lifted various instruments into the upper layer of the atmosphere. Father listened politely to the explanations of the scientists. He nodded from time to time, but was not really interested.

His interest revived when we approached Yangel's R-12, which was standing at a distance. It impressed everyone with its simple design and absence of any aerodynamic forms. It even lacked the rudimentary tail stabilizers, which had been preserved on the R-5. The atmosphere was only a brief obstacle for it, since most of its flight took place in airless space.

All the launches were successful. When the loudspeakers announced the destruction of targets, giving the highly classified number of meters, or to be more precise, kilometers, of deviation from the target, Father smiled broadly, shook hands with the designers and congratulated them. He was simply ecstatic about what he had seen, turning every now and then to nudge Kirichenko and Malinovsky, who were sitting next to him.

The first day ended with our P-5, as the schedule dictated. Everything went well. After being ejected from a tube-launching container by the multiton force of powder accelerators, the P-5, opening its wings and ejecting the now unnecessary boosters, stayed close to the ground as it took off toward the east in the direction of the target. The guests began to disperse without waiting for the results.

Father was tired after the hectic day and left for his parlor car, accompanied by Kirichenko and Brezhnev, with only Malinovsky representing the military. I was some way behind and barely managed to jump into the car. I was interested in hearing their reactions to today's demonstration, mainly what they said about our cruise missile, since I was already rooting for my design bureau.

Father went into the parlor car and I followed him, while the entourage waited outside to be invited in. After washing his hands, Father ordered some tea. While we were taking our seats, he summoned his aide and asked him to invite in, as he put it, "all the rest." Soon Kirichenko, Brezhnev, Kirilenko, Ustinov, Marshals Malinovsky and Sokolovsky, and Father's aide Grigory Trofimovich Shuisky were sitting around the table. I sat down next to Shuisky at the very end of the table.

Father was loudly enthusiastic about what he had seen. He had heard so much about missiles, but this was the first time he'd seen them in action. En masse, they produced a powerful impression and amazed people with their destructive force. The separate fragments came together to produce a whole picture of a new army, one totally different from the army Father had known during the war.

Father was already excited, even though there were many things still to come—the firing of antiaircraft missiles, aircraft, and tactical missiles. He had no doubt that if there were to be a war it would be a war of missiles.

It was time to take an inventory, to see whether we were investing money in the right place or were wasting it on obsolete weapons. Father thought we should focus on the most important thing, missiles. We could afford to reduce both aviation and artillery. There still wouldn't be enough money for everything. If it were done intelligently, the army could make a quick transition to missiles; with them as a shield, we could concentrate on peaceful matters.

His listeners were obstinately silent. The only sound was their spoons rattling in tea glasses.

Father began to elaborate on his thoughts. He felt that there should be only a minimum of strategic aviation. We shouldn't waste money on new airplanes. Ballistic missiles could perform all of their functions. Air defense against enemy aviation was also, in his opinion, a job for missiles. Neither interceptors nor antiaircraft guns could compete with them. Long-range artillery, with its clumsy, heavy cannons, able to fire no more than a dozen shells without changing the barrel, were not worth taking into consideration. They couldn't compete with missiles. Only tactical bombers and fighter-bombers were still irreplaceable. The time had not yet arrived when missiles could compete with them.

The more Father talked, the louder Malinovsky grumbled, while staring at the table. No one voiced objections when Father concluded his lengthy monologue, but no one supported him either. Father sensed the heavy silence hanging over the table and added: "Of course, we have to think everything over, make the proper calculations, and only then decide."

With that, everyone left.

When Father began to carry out his ideas, he met wordless resistance. People of all ranks in the field of aviation, from scientists and designers to generals and line officers, now rallied together, even though they had been tearing each other apart only the day before. Artillery officers joined them. So did naval officers. Father was accused of everything: illiteracy, shortsightedness, criminal suppression of the army, disarming in the face of the enemy. Such conversations were held surreptitiously. No one argued with him openly. For the time being. Father knew what they were saying, but stood firm. In his opinion, if you gave the military their way they would impoverish the country and say at the end: "This is still not enough."

Father's "mistakes" in underestimating the role of aviation, artillery, a surface fleet, tanks, and much else began to be "corrected" in 1964, immediately after his removal from power. Now they have built enough of everything.

At the test site they persuaded Father to resume nuclear testing. Neither Washington nor London had answered his August appeal. Here he was being shown new planes and missiles, but without what was most important—new warheads and new bombs.

Father gave in. However, he insisted there should be a limited number of tests and they should be carried out only when absolutely necessary. Furthermore, he wanted to wait until October 31. Deep in his heart, he hoped that the West would suddenly change its mind. Well, and if no answer came—then it was fate.

While waiting for an answer, Father took an additional step. By then the number of American explosions had reached forty. In order not to tie his hands, he chose the form of a TASS statement. Everyone in the world knew that TASS statements were written in the Kremlin and reacted to them accordingly. TASS warned: "The USSR cannot permit the security of the country to be put at risk and is obliged to resume testing." Again he waited for a reaction. Meanwhile, intensive preparations for tests were being made by various departments. They were only waiting for a go-ahead from the top.

The Americans finally completed their series of explosions. There had been about fifty by the end of October. Father received messages from the president of the United States and the prime minister of Britain. They offered to suspend tests for one year, and after that to resume discussions of the issue.

"They take us for fools," was Father's succinct comment on the messages.

When he had calmed down, Father explained that specialists thought one year to be the optimal interval between two series of tests. It was the length of time needed to examine and interpret the results and put the finishing touches on designs. Therefore in a year the West would be a step forward, while we remained just where we were. Of course, such an agreement would be to their advantage.

My opinion remained as before. I remarked cautiously that in response to such an obvious tactic, we should carry out our own tests and begin negotiating as equals. Father only nodded.

I soon found out that Father had finally made up his mind and that tests would resume in a few weeks. One evening he said that he had overestimated American willingness to reach an agreement. But Father didn't lose his optimism. A decision would have to be made sooner or later, but for now we would test only what was absolutely necessary.

The tests were carried out successfully. The R-12 gained a warhead with an explosive force of about one megaton, a colossal charge in those days. We also got some good news: the equivalent of the P-5 warhead charge more than tripled, from two hundred to six hundred and fifty kilotons.

I'm not sure what else was tested. Tests continued for a little more than a month. Moreover, there was a great deal I didn't know at the time. Then it grew quiet again. Neither we nor the Americans were carrying out tests, but negotiations to stop them limped along. No end seemed to be in sight. Father became nervous: since we could not reach an agreement, across the ocean they're plotting, waiting for a suitable time, preparing. Our nuclear scientists were working day and night. Therefore, it was impossible not to resume testing. The question was: whose nerves would give out first?

THE OPEN CITY

The autumn of 1958 brought a new crisis or, to be precise, greater tension. The situation in Germany grew feverish. The political temperature rose; then fell somewhat. Father kept trying to link together two incompatible things: a peace treaty with a unified Germany with the existence of two German states: the capitalist FRG in the West and the GDR, building socialism, in the East.

And he was trying to do all this while living in a besieged fortress, at a time when only unremitting vigilance kept the enemy at bay. Despite all the talk about peaceful coexistence and calls for peace and friendship, neither the Kremlin nor the people ever lost the sense of threat. The socialist camp, besieged camp, armed camp—that was the terminology of those years. Therefore, to ensure security, we had strong borders, preventing penetration into our territory of both hostile forces and spies trying to learn our secrets.

When he ordered the partial opening of the Soviet borders, Father was not thinking in terms of living together, but of achieving peaceful coexistence. They are two entirely different things. The new term—peaceful coexistence—represented a first step and suggested that war no longer be considered the only way to solve international problems. It meant no more than that.

We tried in our world to prove our superiority, our very great superiority. On the horizon we imagined victorious peaks and a vanquished capitalism in its death throes. Father had already put aside a spade to bury it. We imagined a great many other things.

We maintained our defense as a monolithic socialist camp. The GDR, which inherited our share from the division (temporary, of course) of a defeated Fascist Germany, had recently become a part of the camp. But now we ran into some bad luck. An outpost of the enemy—West Berlin—was wedged into its territory. This created more problems with communications, since anybody and everybody could travel freely within the territory of the

GDR. The absence of borders between East and West Berlin complicated the situation. People could cross the demarcation line without showing their documents, presenting a free field for intelligence agents and political provocateurs. That was how Father reasoned, and how Stalin reasoned before him. To be objective—the West thought that way too.

Stalin tried to solve the problem with military simplicity: he announced the Berlin blockade. He adhered to a gulag-style logic: when they get hungry they'll crawl back. They didn't go hungry and they didn't crawl back. They organized an air bridge. Relations with the allies deteriorated completely. It almost came to war. A new agreement providing rules for Western access to West Berlin had to be reached urgently. For the Soviet Union this agreement was to a large extent more rigid than the Potsdam protocols. Learning from bitter experience, the Western allies were cautious about every point, every small detail.

Father was now bothered by essentially the same problem that had troubled Stalin. Since a foreign entity existed on the territory of the socialist camp, it had to be assimilated, or at least neutralized.

The goal was the same, although Father chose different methods to achieve it. He did not plan to threaten starvation. Fortunately, those days were gone forever. Father hoped to tempt West Berliners with a crisis-free and prosperous socialist economy.

He thought that their trade ties with the West would be replaced, one after another, by a stable Eastern partnership. Life would become better and more attractive and West Berlin would gradually change from a political opponent into, if not an ally, a benevolent neutral. Father cautiously expressed these ideas for the first time in an interview with West German journalists at the beginning of the year. They didn't attract any special attention in the world.

Here is how he describes his reasoning in his memoirs:

The GDR could not conclude an agreement with West Germany; and West Germany, if it had to choose, would not agree to create a united Germany on a socialist basis. It was necessary to work out proposals to strengthen the status quo. We thought that the capitalist part of Germany and the socialist part could each be recognized as independent, which would be recorded in a document. Each would sign a peace treaty. West Berlin now exists separately, with a special status. It was proposed to give West Berlin the status of an open city.

I advanced a proposal to solve the problem. I spoke on the phone with Comrade Ulbricht and described my proposals. . . . Comrade Ulbricht expressed some skepticism about them, especially about my proposal for an open city. I replied that I also thought this was a very difficult condition, and perhaps it would not be accepted during peace negotiations, but that we had no other proposal. We could not retreat, renounce our gains and create a unified Germany on a capitalist basis. The other side would not accept socialism. We had to think realistically and, together with the West, take existing circumstances into account. They would be sensible to conclude a peace treaty with us and not create hostile clashes, not violate peaceful coexistence.

Comrade Ulbricht said: "There is a precedent. At one time Danzig was an open city, and what came of that?"

I replied: "Something has to come of it! Perhaps not right away. Perhaps we won't reach an agreement on our conditions with our former Western allies. But we have to look for a reasonable solution. We should guarantee the independence of West Berlin, include that in a treaty and get United Nations approval. West Berlin will become an open city with social and political conditions decided by its inhabitants. Both sides should guarantee total noninterference in the internal affairs of the open city."

Father was as concerned by the prospect of the nuclear arming of West Germany, the installation on its territory of missiles aimed at Soviet cities, as by a peace treaty. The more people able to press the nuclear button and the closer nuclear bases came to our borders, the less confident we were of our own security.

In this light, West Berlin was particularly worrisome. Weapons could be fired from it in any direction. Nuclear weapons would be, not near our borders, but quite simply on our territory.

One of Father's initiatives at the time was a proposal to hold negotiations on averting the possibility of surprise attack. For this purpose, he proposed banning flights of planes with nuclear weapons on board over other countries and over the open ocean. The greater the separation, the wider the neutral zone between offensive forces, the more secure both sides would be. Father didn't expect the Americans to agree easily. He was not in a hurry, but hoped for future results.

On November 27, 1958, the Soviet government sent official notes to its former allies in the anti-Hitler coalition, and also to both Germanys, which stated that six months hence it would transfer all its rights with respect to relations with West Berlin and the communications of allied forces in the Soviet occupation zone to the government of the GDR. It proposed that West Berlin be given the status of an open and demilitarized city. The Soviet government assumed the obligation of providing orders to its industry and assuring a supply of raw materials and food for its residents.

The West regarded these Notes as an ultimatum. In effect, that's what they were. A countdown began. It was the start of the so-called First Berlin Crisis.

I thought that the Americans would never accept the proposed conditions. And what then? Father laughed at my fears. He said that nobody would start a war over Berlin. On the other hand, it was time to clarify the situation and put in writing the balance of forces that had emerged after the war. In his opinion, there was no reason for the West to hold on to Berlin. It was an organic part of the Eastern group, whether or not it preserved capitalist customs or a new socialist system emerged. He left that entirely to the city's residents.

I was trying to get a clear idea of what we would do after May 27 of the following year if Soviet proposals were rejected and the deadline for the ultimatum expired. Father didn't have a simple answer. He intended to act according to circumstances, depending on the reaction of his partners. He hoped to intimidate them into agreeing to sit down at the negotiating table.

Father said that if he had not set a specific date, the exchange of notes, letters, appeals, and statements would go on forever. A deadline would force both sides into action and make them look for a compromise.

"What if a compromise is not reached?" I insisted.

"Then we'll look for another solution. There's always something," answered Father with a note of irritation in his voice.

I was not satisfied. His explanations even frightened me a little. If we didn't carry out our promises or threats—our statement could have different interpretations—they would stop taking us seriously. If we displayed determination, then the course of events threatened to have unpredictable consequences. I chased away the word "war."

Father proved to be correct. His ultimatum forced a reaction. The world reacted. Calls for army mobilization were heard in the U.S. Congress. Military units began redeploying in Europe. At the beginning of January 1959, a draft peace treaty with Germany was published in Moscow. That was how Father showed that his intentions were serious. At the same time, a Note was sent to the United States. It stated that the Potsdam Agreement on Berlin was of a temporary nature. Almost a decade and a half had passed since the war, new conditions had arisen in the world, and we could not ignore them.

Father put steadily increasing pressure on the West. He forced the West to guess what would happen when the six months were up. He himself wasn't yet able to answer that question. Or rather, he realized that if the Americans didn't give in and agree, then *he* would have to give in. After all, we didn't want a war.

Father displayed prudence and caution. Not only were no preparations made for a potential conflict, he even refrained from his favorite ploy, a demonstration of force. Germany was not the Middle East.

What additions were made to our military arsenal? Could Father really threaten Washington then, or at least in the future? No. By the beginning of

1959 no changes had taken place in the nuclear missile game. Yes, we had launched three satellites into orbit, one heavier than the other. Yes, we had worked hard and sent a probe carrying spheres to the moon. However, there was no end in sight for tests of the military missile, the R-7.

Launches of the R-12 were completed in December. Father received triumphant reports from Yangel and Major General Semyonov, chairman of the commission. However, before the missile would become a real weapon, we needed to begin series production and equip launch sites. There were no particular changes to the basic design of the R-12, and its use was still restricted to European targets. In those years Asian border regions were not considered of primary importance for missile deployment.

So Father actually had only that same R-5 which he had threatened to use two years previously, during the Suez crisis.

What did Washington know about Soviet capabilities? It's hard to say. Father thought that they knew very little. I'm inclined to agree with him, even now. I think that the West greatly exaggerates American knowledge gained from the U-2 flights. On the other hand, it would not be reasonable or logical to suppose that significant forces were deployed only a year after the first launch of an intercontinental missile. However, the threat of even one single warhead would make them think.[9]

At this decisive moment both leaders, Father and President Dwight Eisenhower, tried to guard against a false step and acted with extreme caution.

Father replied with a categorical "no" to the military's proposal for a demonstrative concentration of several divisions around Berlin. That could provoke the Americans. The president did not grant the CIA's request for permission to carry out U-2 flights. He considered such a step at this moment of crisis to be a provocation that might lead directly to war.

Father grew nervous. One-third of the time until expiration of the deadline had passed and nothing had changed. He tried to find a solution. He thought that a summit might resolve the matter. Discussion of the Berlin problem at a summit, even if it didn't achieve results, would allow the dead-

---

9. The U-2 intelligence did help to dispel earlier fears of a "bomber gap" in favor of the Soviet Union, but failed to turn up evidence of a large Soviet ICBM deployment (partly, of course, for the excellent reason that there was no such deployment). As a result of this uncertainty, Eisenhower faced intense pressure to continue U-2 flights. Today, the standard view is that many U.S. decision makers—most importantly Eisenhower himself—discounted Khrushchev's missile bluffs, but the government as a whole could not be sure of the real balance of forces until after satellite reconnaissance began late in 1960. It was only in September 1961 that the CIA downgraded its official estimate of Soviet missiles. Thus, many historians believe President Eisenhower had an assessment of the strategic balance that approaches what we now know to have been reality, but that the larger U.S. government was indeed fooled—or at the very least made uncertain—by Khrushchev's ploy. As a consequence, determining the actual impact of the missile deception is a complicated task.

line of the ultimatum to be extended, even if the ultimatum was not disavowed.

He decided not to inform Eisenhower of his proposal officially, but to make it as if by chance. He needed a special messenger for this purpose. His choice fell on Anastas Ivanovich Mikoyan. Father thought that if there was any possibility of agreement, no one was better than Mikoyan. Also, in those days the fact that Mikoyan had traveled abroad more than once was considered important. "He's made many acquaintances there," joked Father. Father decided to take advantage of that fact. Anastas Ivanovich could not count on an official invitation from the U.S. government. He left for the United States as a guest of the business community.

On January 19, 1959, the president received Mikoyan at the White House. Of course they spoke about Berlin. Of course their viewpoints were different about everything, except that the crisis must not lead to war. Mikoyan proposed a meeting at the highest level, as in Geneva. When ministers meet, even very clever ones, they have to adhere strictly to their instructions. An adversary's opinions often reach top leaders only after being digested and reworked by the departments dealing with foreign policy and colored by their likes and dislikes. A summit can accomplish in one day what diplomats cannot achieve even in the course of a year.

Eisenhower reacted negatively. In his opinion, the Geneva meeting had not brought any results. He didn't feel the need for direct discussions. If Father wanted a meeting, then let the foreign ministers meet. As for Berlin, there was nothing to talk about. The Western allies would not retreat one iota from the Potsdam Agreement.

The answer not only disappointed Father, it left him somewhat vulnerable. However, he remained optimistic. He recounted Mikoyan's stories about meetings in the United States with a smile. The Americans would agree to sit down at the negotiating table.

Now Father counted on the visit of British prime minister Harold Macmillan to our country. He hoped that, after sober consideration, Eisenhower would respond to his proposal after all. Moreover, attitudes toward the threat of war arising from this dispute over Berlin differed markedly on the two sides of the ocean.

What threatened the United States? Destruction of one, or at most two, cities. Terrible! Unimaginably terrible! But incomparably less than the possible response: dozens of Soviet cities disappearing from the face of the earth.

A war over Berlin would threaten Europeans with ruin. Macmillan remembered Father's estimates when they were sitting by the fireplace at Chequers. Not many nuclear bombs would be needed to destroy his country. British experts agreed with his estimate. In the autumn of 1956 his predecessor did not withstand the pressure, and now he was also inclined to reach an agreement.

Father prepared a warm reception for his guest. He tried by a show of hospitality to thank him for the reception given him and Bulganin in April 1956. Besides, foreign visitors were still a rarity in the Kremlin. Father tried to establish informal, personal contacts and to go beyond the boundaries of official protocol. He accompanied Macmillan everywhere.

One day Father took Macmillan to a horse farm near Moscow. There they had a ride in a real Russian-style sleigh drawn by a troika, like the ones in old prints. Horses reminded Father of his childhood. He was absolutely ecstatic about the ride, while his guest only thanked him rather coolly.

However, Father miscalculated. Before Macmillan left for Moscow, Eisenhower warned him that he should not even dream of retreating on Berlin, that the most America would agree to was a meeting of foreign ministers. The British prime minister was also in a political vacuum in Europe. De Gaulle did not intend to yield to pressure. Moreover, France was preparing to become a nuclear power. A date for the first test of a nuclear bomb in the Sahara desert was already set.

The warm reception had no effect on the negotiations.

Father became angry. He announced that he was unable to accompany his guest to Kiev and Leningrad. For days he had been describing all the wonders of Kievan hospitality, the beauty of the Dnieper River—and then, he suddenly refused, saying that he was busy and had to have the dentist replace a filling! Macmillan was insulted and even thought of cutting short his visit and returning home, but decided not to exacerbate the tense situation. He made it clear that the possibility of a summit was not excluded if the course of events developed satisfactorily. He took a chance in saying that, since he had not agreed on it with his allies.

Father took immediate advantage of this opportunity and publicly stated that if the ministers of foreign affairs made progress in negotiations, he would not tie adoption of a final decision on Berlin to the May 27 deadline. "The important thing is to make progress, and whether it's on July 27 or August 27 doesn't matter very much"—that was how he tried to weaken the force of the ultimatum, with its ominously approaching deadline.

Of course he retreated. The whole world saw him retreat. It showed the West the effectiveness of their rigid and uncompromising stance. Did Father lose? Yes, he bluffed, he miscalculated. West Berlin never became an open city. But it was also not worth a war. In the final analysis, it was an episode in big-power politics. Father's main mistake lay elsewhere: he didn't realize that bluffing no longer worked and that any new attempt at missile pressure would run into a brick wall.

Did Father think he'd won? I think that deep in his heart he did not, but he tried hard to convince himself and his associates that he had.

After saying farewell to Macmillan, Father left that same day, March 4, for the German Democratic Republic. He wanted to discuss the current situation with Walter Ulbricht, as well as visit the Leipzig Fair. He had wanted to see it for years. Father very much enjoyed visiting exhibits. He didn't miss a single one in Moscow, especially the international ones. He was attracted to new things, whether they were locomotives, trucks, combines, fabrics, or new strains of wheat.

Ulbricht met Father and remained at his side the entire time. He was Father's guide at the exhibit pavilions. Evenings were spent talking. From the very beginning Ulbricht was extremely dubious about Father's hopes for a summit. In his opinion, the West's consent to a foreign ministers' meeting was already a great achievement. The German problem would take years, perhaps decades, to solve. Father insisted that it would not be solved at all if the interested parties sat with their hands folded.

Ulbricht told Father that his contacts with the West German Social Democrats begun last summer were now on a solid basis, and that they were asking to meet with Khrushchev. If Father agreed, he would arrange a meeting with their party chairman, Erich Ollenhauer. Father had no objection.

Late that evening they left for Berlin. They went by car. Not a long trip, by our standards. Father preferred cars to trains. He felt more at ease in a car.

Father was pleased with his meeting with Ollenhauer, for whom he summarized all his arguments in favor of an open city. Father sincerely believed that the only obstacle was a stubborn disinclination to admit the existence of an East German state. If that were overcome, then transit procedures, border crossings, and other practical matters could easily be resolved. They would be essentially unchanged, except that German officials would replace Soviet officers.

But he met with a lack of understanding. The Western position remained negative and monolithic. Father did not sense much understanding in his meeting with the Social Democrats either, though he noted their positive reaction to the progress that had been made in the GDR in the building of socialism.

In a speech delivered in Berlin, Father repeated his warning that a separate peace treaty would be concluded with the GDR, though he did not give a date. President Dwight Eisenhower responded the following day, stating that if the Soviet Union signed a unilateral agreement with the GDR on the status of West Berlin, the United States would use military force to ensure its rights.

"There will be war," he warned unambiguously.

On March 11 *Pravda* (on Father's instructions, sent from Berlin) published the president's words.

Meanwhile the Soviet Union increasingly shifted its focus from conclusion of a peace treaty with the GDR to convening a conference that would discuss, not only the Berlin question, but also questions of disarmament and peaceful coexistence. Father thought that a shift of focus in the Soviet press would push the Western allies to react.

Father returned to Moscow on March 12, and Macmillan arrived in Washington on March 20. The conversations with Father had made an impression. Macmillan had persuaded Eisenhower to agree to a conference of foreign ministers. This created a useful escape route for Father from a difficult position. The May 27 date, when the ultimatum expired, no longer marked the boundary between peace and war. Father declared the already existing negotiations to be his victory.

Nevertheless, the world awaited the expiration date fearfully. When I asked what would happen after May 27, Father laughed and said, "May 28." His goal was achieved, negotiations were in progress. Here he was being sly. His words had had a different ring earlier.

In April and May Father was involved in intense diplomatic activity. He demonstrated a constructive approach to the issues planned for discussion in Geneva. He forwarded proposals to ban nuclear weapons' tests. However, he remained firmly against inspections, which he called camouflaged espionage. Find out what you can by national means on your own territory, was his view.

Personal contacts expanded. Father thought they were more important than any messages. Trust would come gradually. To foster it, you have to make contacts.

On May 4 Father, accompanied by Ambassador Thompson, visited the construction site for an American exhibit in Sokolniki Park. It was an unprecedented event, even for countries with the warmest of relations. However, it had nothing to do with politics. Father wanted very much to see an American construction site, to see what machines were being used and how they worked. But under other circumstances, he would have restrained his curiosity.

On May 9, Victory Day, Father received a group of American war veterans. In talking with them he emphasized our common front in the struggle against Fascism, not the existing confrontation in Berlin. And he made no mention of the ultimatum.

Father viewed the foreign ministers' conference as a real opportunity to work for world peace. He hated war with his whole heart and did not see it as a way to solve world problems. It was not just that he understood the impossibility of winning a nuclear war. Father personally rejected war on the grounds of humanity. He had seen enough blood in the trenches during the civil war. At that time he felt it, so to speak, with his own hands. During the Second World War the horrors were multiplied many times over. Not as a battalion commissar but as a general, a member of the front Military Council, Father had ridden in a jeep back and forth, from the Soviet border to the Volga and from the Volga back to the border. Father never tried to describe what he saw, and to his last days could not watch films about the war or read books on the subject.

He thought that Eisenhower, who had also suffered during the war, shared his convictions. In the long run, they would find common ground.

The parties had agreed that the Geneva conference would be attended by representatives of both Germanys, and not only by the foreign ministers of the great powers. Heinrich von Brentano and Lothar Boltz, who were directly involved in the matters under discussion, joined Selwyn Lloyd, Couve de Murville, U.S. Secretary of State Christian Herter (who had replaced John Foster Dulles), and Andrei Gromyko.

The first complication arose at the very opening of the conference: Brentano refused to be in the same room as Boltz. He undoubtedly had instructions from Adenauer to torpedo any hope of achieving an agreement, even before negotiations began. Brentano stayed at his hotel the whole time, and Wilhelm Greve, a lower-ranking official, represented the Federal Republic.

The Western allies took a rigid position from the very start. They proposed that Germany be united, but of course within the framework of the FRG, or under its auspices. Gromyko rebutted the proposal: the question of German reunification was not even on the agenda, and proposals would have to be worked out by the two Germanys. A solution could be found only on the basis of mutual goodwill. The victorious great powers would only be involved in whether or not to approve such an agreement, based on the highest considerations of preserving peace and stability both in Europe and the world. The usual diplomatic game commenced.

Seeing that the idea of demilitarizing West Berlin would not be accepted, Father modified his position and now proposed that symbolic contingents of allied forces remain there. He thought that might serve as the basis for agreement. His reasoning was simple: if they are not planning to attack us, why should they keep a large military force in Berlin? It was expensive, to begin with, since they have to bring everything from West Germany, and capitalists know how to count their money. If they're afraid of us, it doesn't matter whether there is a division or a platoon. Our forces in the area are so superior that they would be wiped out instantly. Father saw only one reason why the Americans would want to keep a large force in Berlin: they intended to base strategic missiles there. Then everything would make sense. Missiles required service personnel and security staffs. The increased costs of maintaining troops would therefore be justified.

Father didn't overlook espionage, subversive activity, and propaganda, but though he protested vigorously, he considered the whole package to be an unavoidable evil.

Therefore the categorical "no" to his proposals, which seemed to ensure the security of both sides, not only disappointed him but put him on guard.

The West stood firm: if the USSR did not agree to preserve the occupied status of Berlin, they did not even want to consider the question of holding a summit.

At that point the conference, which had barely begun, broke up. The death of John Foster Dulles was announced. It occurred on the eve of the ultimatum's expiration. Western delegation heads prepared to leave for the funeral of their colleague in Washington.

Gromyko sent a telegram to Moscow asking for instructions. He expressed doubt of the usefulness of sending high-level representatives to the funeral of our devoted enemy and proposed that the Soviet ambassador attend. Father simply blew up. I don't know what he said in the Kremlin, but he was still outraged when he came home—how could we behave in such a formal way?

Father was distressed. A diplomat has the duty of using every opportunity to establish contacts and strengthen ties. But his main concern by far was that it was easy to predict how our participation or nonparticipation in the funeral would be interpreted. If we took part, it would show loyalty, and if we did not, Father thought it would demonstrate stupidity.

"And how would it look?" he fumed. "Everyone goes to Washington and our minister remains strolling around Geneva? Even the chickens would laugh at us."

Simple human emotion also lay behind Father's reasoning. We had worked with Dulles for so many years, and now we would not even pay our respects? Yes, he was an enemy. But that was due to his class and his status. He couldn't have taken any other position.

A coded message was sent to Gromyko instructing him to participate in the funeral ceremony and to express the most sincere condolences.

Meanwhile the ultimatum expired. May 27 passed and nothing changed in the world. U.S. convoys moved unhindered across East German territory, just as before.

At the beginning of June 1959, Walter Ulbricht and Otto Grotewohl arrived in Moscow. Father decided to make one more attempt to work out proposals acceptable to all sides. On June 10 the Soviet side announced a four-point proposal that would not infringe on the rights of the allies. Father agreed to confirm that Western forces had the right to be stationed in Berlin. They were already there and they were not planning to leave. But he proposed to our negotiating partners that they assume obligations that would improve the existence of West Berlin within the GDR and lay the foundation for good neighborliness. Soviet and East German joint proposals called for an end to hostile propaganda. However, there was no clear definition of hostile propaganda. Anyone could interpret it as he wished. Therefore, we were demanding an end to all broadcasting.

Two other conditions were easier to accept, in my opinion: an end to espionage and subversive activity emanating from the territory of West Berlin, and a pledge not to deploy nuclear weapons or missiles there.

The answer was a categorical "no." The conference was deadlocked. An announcement was made that it would recess until July 13.

Father thought that everything was not yet lost. He continued to show loyalty. On June 24, after the foreign ministers had left Geneva, he received Averell Harriman warmly. He even invited him to the dacha. However, not to his family dacha, but to the special official one in Novo-Ogaryovo. They spent almost the whole day together, walking, dining, and talking. The host wanted to convince his guest of his sincere desire for peace and peaceful coexistence. People themselves should choose the economic system that suited them, and they'll manage that without intermediaries. Of course, Father couldn't help emphasizing his belief in the victory of socialism.

On July 4, the American national holiday, Ambassador Thompson spoke on Moscow television. Three days later Father received a group of American governors. Kozlov left for the United States. That year he became the second member of the Presidium to visit faraway America.

Father thought that actions were better than words. We should not be exchanging threats over the radio and in newspapers, but establishing personal contacts. It seemed that his work was beginning to bear fruit.

THE MISSILE PROGRAM CONTINUES

Tests of the R-7 continued, but interest in it waned noticeably. In the confrontation with America the focus had now shifted to the next generation of intercontinental missiles.

On May 13, 1959, the government issued two almost identical government decrees on missile development. One related to the R-16 intercontinental missile of Mikhail Kuzmich Yangel's design bureau. It placed Yangel's work in the first rank and gave him a special status, perhaps even higher than that of Korolyov. The other decree concerned the R-9 of Korolyov's design bureau. The two missiles differed in more than the type of fuel they used. For the R-16 Yangel decided to use a self-contained, inertial guidance system, which would deliver the missile to its target without any connection with the earth. We had never attempted anything like that, although the United States already had a lot of experience in using such systems.

Korolyov did not particularly like new things. He had a certain degree of skepticism toward instruments in general, especially unproven ones. For his R-9 he modernized the guidance system with radio corrections that had been used for the R-7. An intriguing situation developed: Glushko was making the engines for both missiles. His relationship with Korolyov hit rock bottom. Sergei Pavlovich thought that Glushko preferred his rival and became angry and nervous.

Glushko carried out his obligation to make engines for both missiles. Flight tests of both began almost simultaneously. Yangel finished two years before Korolyov and won the competition.

That summer Father decided to travel in the Ukraine before taking his vacation. As he had promised that winter, he intended to visit Yangel's factory along the way and see if they were really turning out missiles like sausages. But he was primarily interested in the R-16.

During their last previous meeting, Yangel had promised that it would take very little time to develop it. The new missile would be based on the already tested R-12 and the planned R-14. They were both one-stage, but the new one would be two-stage—as if the R-12 were mounted on the R-14. The successful conclusion of work on the R-12 had given Father complete confidence in Yangel.

Now Father wanted to see with his own eyes how work was going. The factory made a stunning impression on him: kilometers of shops, huge engine-construction buildings, design bureaus, gigantic test platforms. It was hard to see it all by car, much less on foot.

Father was first taken around to see the shops. Sausages aside, thick cylinders many meters long were indeed lying close to each other and being moved from one shop to another. All security regulations were observed as the products were being transported between shops. Missile parts were carefully wrapped in tarpaulin, which was stretched on square frames to hide their slender shapes.

Father was very pleased with his visit. For the first time he could actually see how missiles were made, and not just hear about it. They were on a conveyor—really, almost like sausages. He liked that comparison very much. He could see with his own eyes that this was no impractical scheme, that work was really progressing.

A meeting was held after the tour of inspection. Several thousand people gathered in a large open area between the shops. Father spoke with emotion, thanking the workers, exulting in their successes, and repeating Yangel's words, saying that he had become convinced that they were really turning out missiles like sausages. The next day every newspaper published his remarks. The comparison of missiles with sausages grated on my ear. The following day, I complained to Father that he had gotten carried away, that his enthusiasm over what he had seen had pushed him too far. After all, since the R-5 no new weapon had appeared. Tests of the R-7 were going on and on, while Yangel's promises were still nothing but promises.

Father just laughed. According to him, the number of missiles we really had wasn't so important. We were not planning to start a war. The important thing was that Americans believed in our power. That in itself would reduce the likelihood of war. "So don't get upset," he said, clapping me on the shoulder.

Leonid Vasilyevich Smirnov was the director of the factory. He would soon take the post of deputy chairman of the Council of Ministers responsible for coordinating the work of the defense industries, replacing his boss, Dmitry Fyodorovich Ustinov. Excited by the successful organization of missile production, Father appointed Ustinov chairman of the Supreme Council of the National Economy, responsible for coordinating the work of the regional economic councils, which were trying to evade control from the center. A few years later both Smirnov and Ustinov took an active role in chasing Father from all his positions.

After inspecting production areas and meeting factory workers, they went to the design bureau to talk over the future. A model of the planned intercontinental missile was standing on a table in the large room. The R-16 looked like an old-style rifle cartridge. The thick base of the first stage was surmounted by a second stage slightly smaller in diameter. At the very top of the structure was a warhead shaped like the cone of a bullet. Just like a cartridge, except that the band where the two stages were joined was not solid, but was similar to a truss-like ring. On the lower edge of the first stage there was something like a narrow, flared ring, and nothing else—neither rudder nor stabilizers.

After examining the model intently, Father sat down at the head of the table and prepared to listen. The others arranged themselves down the table: Ustinov; chairman of the State Committee of Defense Technology, Konstantin Nikolayevich Rudnev; chairman of the State Committee of Radio Technology, Valery Dmitriyevich Kalmykov; director of the Central Committee's Defense Department, Ivan Dmitriyevich Serbin; Marshal of Artillery Mitrofan Ivanovich Nedelin; Ukrainian Central Committee Secretary Nikolai Viktorovich Podgorny, and officials of the Council of Ministers concerned with the work of the defense branches of industry. The chief designers arranged themselves along both sides of the table. They were to deliver reports.

The discussion began with Yangel's description of work on the R-16. Mikhail Kuzmich picked up two small models of the R-14 and R-12 which I only then noticed lying on the table next to him, and placed one on top of the other to demonstrate how the R-16 was formed from them. Actually, it did look as if the slim R-12 were perching comfortably on the pudgy R-14. Let us leave this oversimplification to the chief designer's conscience; there was much more to building the R-16 than simply stacking two missiles. He then talked about how the R-14 was planned and produced, concluding with a description of how mass production of the R-12 was organized. The report sounded excellent and well organized, with every step following cogently from the one before. Yangel also described his problems with supply and construction, subjects no such conference could avoid. Father made decisions on the spot. He rejected almost nothing, and the ministers recorded his instructions in their notebooks. That was unusual, since as a rule Father criticized and only reluctantly agreed to the appropriation of additional resources.

Yangel then turned to the subject of missile launches from silos. He reported that a launch site was under construction and the launch complex was being equipped. He thought they would be able to follow the schedule already set, and a trial launch could be carried out in September. Father's face lit up. I had not seen him in such an elated and celebratory mood in a long time.

In concluding remarks Father could not restrain his feelings. "These are real miracles," he exclaimed with almost childish glee.

He went on to say that the ground forces were not really the proper place for missiles. The fact that they were subordinated to the artillery was an anachronism. Father proposed that consideration be given to organizing special missile forces with a strategic function. This proposal was unexpected for all, both juniors and seniors. The matter had not previously been discussed anywhere. Apparently Father got the idea at that very moment, under the influence of what he had seen at the factory. There was a restrained buzz from those present.

"The Americans have assigned strategic missiles to aviation, since the missions they perform and their technical servicing are similar," said Pyotr Vasilyevich Dementyev, chairman of the State Committee on Aviation Technology, not so much objecting as providing information. He had the privileges of a guest at the meeting, since his ministry only supplied special instruments for missiles.

Father thought for a moment and then objected: "American experience doesn't relate to us," and then began to explain that heavy strategic bombers were traditionally favored by Americans. Their targets were the most important sites on an enemy's territory. Missiles performed the same tasks. The Americans assigned missiles to planes, though only bombers would fly along certain routes and missiles would take different trajectories. A unified command was therefore expedient and justified, since you could not make decisions on the same mission in two different places.

"We simply do not possess strategic aviation in the American sense," said Father emphatically. "If we assign missiles to the Air Force, it will begin adapting them to its own customs and structures. They will take forever to organize the operation, and we have no time to lose. For this project we need new people, enthusiastic people not constrained by their previous history."

Father glanced around the table and stopped at Nedelin.

"Let's entrust Comrade Nedelin with this matter. He's in love with missiles, has been working on them practically since childhood, and knows a lot about them." Turning directly to him, Father said: "Take your time over this, Comrade Nedelin. Don't be in a rush. It's an important matter. Discuss it with anyone you need to, and first of all with Comrade Malinovsky, and report to us in the autumn. Meanwhile, think of what I've said as a working proposal."

Nedelin enthusiastically tackled the mission of organizing a new branch of the armed forces. By early autumn the basic estimates lay on Malinovsky's desk. They met with no objections. On the one hand, no one at the Ministry of Defense except Nedelin had any interest in advancing these new-style Khrushchevian ideas, but on the other, no one there was eager to argue with Father.

During that autumn all documents were written, agreed upon, stamped, and signed. On December 17, 1959, the Strategic Missile Forces came into being. Marshal of Artillery Nedelin was appointed its first commander. He was destined to occupy the position for a little less than a year.

Reassured, Father continued on to the Crimea. Progress was being made. We now had more than the R-7 to rely on.

Father planned to do more in the Crimea than rest. He wanted to check up on the Navy and see what had changed during the four years since his stormy encounter with Admiral Kuznetsov. In Sevastopol there would be a demonstration of the latest achievements.

THE NEW NAVY

The so-called small demonstration of naval armament was held in the summer of 1959 in Sevastopol. Father came by car from Yalta at the appointed time. It was the middle of July. He arrived in the front seat of an open ZIS, looking tanned and rested. Brezhnev and Malinovsky were sitting in back.

The warships were at the stations assigned them by the program. Spectators were invited to watch the naval exercises from the deck of the *Angara*, a comfortable yacht.

The lighthearted whiteness of its sides and superstructure stood out among the dark gray silhouettes of the cruisers and destroyers positioned in the bay. The yacht had formerly belonged to Admiral Dönitz, commander in chief of the German navy, and had passed to us when the allies divided up captured German vessels. After refitting, the *Angara* and a somewhat smaller yacht named the *Rioni* (which had belonged to former King Michael of Romania) were docked near the Grafskaya Pier in Sevastopol to wait until Stalin might be seized by a desire to sail around in the Black Sea. As far as I know, such a trip had occurred only once. Soon after the war, in the late 1940s, Stalin decided to travel by sea from Yalta to Sochi. The trip was not a success. He became seasick along the way. No one used the yachts after that, so they lay idle at the pier for many years, a whole decade, although prepared to accept guests at any moment. But no guests appeared. In vain the crew polished brass fittings, painted the sides, and scraped the wooden deck with pieces of glass.

That day the yacht was all spruced up for its outing, and a clear, thin, almost invisible column of smoke issued from its funnel. The absence of smoke at sea was considered evidence that the ship's machinists possessed the highest degree of skill.

I won't try to describe the endless artillery and missile barrages, the attack by a submarine on our yacht, and subsequent pursuit of the submarine from the air by planes and helicopters and on the surface by antisubmarine ships. It all looked extraordinarily effective. Missile launches brought the day's full program to a close. Our part in it went successfully. A beaming Chelomei accepted congratulations.

Father was satisfied with the changes in the Navy that had occurred during the previous few years. Missiles had replaced large-caliber gun turrets on the decks of those cruisers and destroyers which remained after the program for building a surface fleet was curtailed. Submarine striking power exceeded that of battleships many times over. Father congratulated Gorshkov on the Navy's great achievements. Breaking into a smile, the commander in chief bemoaned the fact that there was a lot he had not been able to show. The Black Sea was too small to deploy submarines armed with ballistic missiles. They were concentrated in the Northern and Pacific Fleets.

Father joked: "You don't want to show us everything at once. Leave something for the future. Otherwise you won't have anything left to brag about." But then, growing serious, he proposed having the next demonstration in the North. When? They decided to agree on the date later on.

The intervals between exercises, while moving from one position to another, were not wasted. Designers of ships and weapons talked about their ideas, one diagram after another was hung on the bulkheads with kaleidoscopic speed: submarines, torpedoes, antisubmarine helicopters, and planes. It seemed as if almost nothing was missing!

Chelomei's turn came. He spoke in tandem with Pavel Petrovich Pustyntsev, a submarine designer. Pustyntsev had supported Vladimir Nikolayevich during his difficult days, believed in his crazy idea of unfolding a wing in flight, and—despite a torrent of ridicule—accepted the job of designing a submarine armed with the new and still very hypothetical weapon.

Since then they had worked together for many years, had shared failures and rejoiced in victories. Now they celebrated the first recognition of their achievements.

Chelomei felt himself to be in the saddle. He didn't report, he sang. And it really was true that the year had gone successfully. Tests of a new antiship missile, the P-6, had begun. It was launched from submarines. Its guidance system seemed fantastic for that time. After flying hundreds of kilometers and locating a large group of enemy ships, the missile would choose the most tempting target and, arming itself, destroy it on the spot. Chelomei promised in the near future to create a large family of missiles capable of neutralizing actions by aircraft carrier flotillas of any, even the most improbable, adversary.

The exercises came to an end. Father left for Yalta, where he still had a few days of vacation left.

NIXON VISITS THE SOVIET UNION

By the beginning of July Father had virtually no hope of reaching agreement at the conference of foreign ministers, which was to reconvene on July 13. The positions taken by the parties were irreconcilable. The ministers seemed incapable of constructive ideas, but his Western partners were obviously against a higher-level meeting and set unacceptable preliminary conditions to prevent one from taking place. Father was distressed.

Apparently, the American president was also troubled by somber thoughts as the Geneva meeting was set to resume. And he looked for a way out. Otherwise, why, on the eve of July 13, would he have had the idea of inviting Father to visit the United States for personal negotiations?

Kozlov flew home after attending the opening ceremony at the very first Soviet exhibit ever held in the United States. On instructions from Dwight Eisenhower, State Department representative Robert Murphy gave Kozlov an invitation to pass on to Father. Father received it with enormous satisfaction, I would even say joy. He considered it a sign that our socialist state was finally recognized. He was the first Soviet leader to be invited to the United States on an official visit. This is how Father described it:

> When the program for our delegation ended and they were preparing to depart, a courier arrived unexpectedly from the president and handed Kozlov an envelope to be given to Khrushchev.
>
> After returning to Moscow on a Sunday, Kozlov called me at the dacha

and said: "I have an envelope from Mr. Eisenhower, president of the United States."

He then came to the dacha and handed over the envelope. We looked through its contents. The document was very brief. It was an invitation from the president to the chairman of the Council of Ministers to make a friendly visit to the United States. It was addressed personally to me.

I must admit that I could hardly believe it, it was such a surprise. We weren't prepared for it, because our relations were so strained that an invitation for a friendly visit by the chairman of the Council of Ministers and secretary of the Central Committee seemed unlikely. Still, a fact is a fact. . . .

It was unexpected, but it was also both pleasing and interesting. By that time I had already been abroad several times, but America occupied a special place in our minds and our imaginations. It couldn't have been otherwise. America was our strongest opponent among the capitalist countries: their leader was the one who set the anti-Soviet tone in the capitalist world.

Who led the way for the economic blockade of the Soviet Union?—the United States!

Its other partners made certain economic contracts. . . . We bought some equipment and sold some things abroad, mostly raw materials. . . .

America boycotted us completely. They announced a special ban on purchases of crabmeat! They gave as the reason that Russians used slave labor to harvest crabs from the sea. It was absurd, but that's the argument they used in their "law." They even refused to buy our caviar and vodka. . . .

And all of a sudden—to send an invitation! What did it mean? Did it indicate a change in policy? That was hard to imagine! With no forewarning—a letter from the president!

The Central Committee Presidium met in the Kremlin, read the document, and decided to thank the president and accept the invitation.

As a politician, Father could see the opportunities that might present themselves as a result of the meeting. Perhaps not immediately. Time would pass. But they would be sure to come eventually. Furthermore, in purely human terms he was very flattered by the invitation.

There was a lull in Geneva in the period before the Washington meeting.

Further progress depended entirely on the result of negotiations between Father and the president of the United States. The future of the world depended on the wisdom of the two leaders, on their moods, on the degree of care put into preparations for the meetings, on the spontaneous manifestations of mutual sympathy or antipathy, the weighing of decisions, and the state of their personal well-being.

Meanwhile, Moscow was expecting an important American guest. For the first time since the Second World War an American vice president, Richard

Nixon, was coming to open an American exhibit. Father considered the exhibit in Sokolniki to be of the utmost importance. And he was not alone in that. The exhibit was a big event. For the first time, I repeat, Americans were allowed, not without some trepidation on our part, to appeal directly to Muscovites. Father disregarded warnings from ideologues about the danger of exposing us to infection from bourgeois ideology.

We were completely ignorant of each other. We made mistakes at every step. After all, mutual understanding is only gained through contacts, and we had missed that for the decade and a half since the war.

As an example, I will give my version of the American vice president's widely publicized first morning in Moscow. Nixon woke up early. No one remains unaffected by flying across eight time zones. The American organism experienced our morning as if it were the previous evening.

Our guest expressed the desire to meet ordinary native Russians, not officials of the Ministry of Foreign Affairs and employees of special services. U.S. embassy officials with years of experience in Moscow suggested a visit to a market, since markets were the only places in the country where private enterprise was permitted.

They set out around seven o'clock in the morning, when the market opened. Their Soviet hosts were not told the destination until everyone was seated in their cars. For some reason, the Danilovsky Market was selected. At the time its rows of stalls stretched for almost a kilometer in the open air and were surrounded by a board fence dark with age.

Since the market visit was not included in the official program, no preparations had been made. Only a few Soviet and American bodyguards bustled around Nixon as he strolled along the stalls. A crowd started to gather. Nixon decided to chat with an ordinary Russian before he left. He enjoyed spontaneous conversations with people and was good at them. Nixon chose a man wearing work clothes, walked over to him and, holding out his hand, introduced himself. The Embassy's interpreter immediately translated. He had a strong foreign accent, not the best recommendation in those days.

The Russian, whose name was Pyote Smakhtin, turned out to be the man who checked weights at the market. He was preparing to accept products and wasn't thinking about the American vice president, or about America in general. Like all Soviet citizens, he had no doubt that he should avoid foreigners. He should give the impression of being very busy and disappear. But that didn't work out in this case. A crowd gathered and someone, apparently one of "ours," pushed Smakhtin firmly toward Nixon and whispered or hissed something unintelligible. Since he hadn't managed to slip away, Smakhtin decided to uphold the dignity of a Soviet citizen and show the foreigners that we had everything we wanted and nothing would surprise us. Smakhtin was ready to give the American a proper rebuff. After all, later he would have to answer for every word.

Nixon's initial questions were easy to answer: What's your name? What do you do? Do you have a family?

Then it got more complicated, but Smakhtin gave the right answers: he was satisfied with his apartment, he was paid very well, and was happy with his life in general.

The man standing next to him, who had pushed him toward the foreigner, gave barely perceptible nods of approval.

Smakhtin didn't know how he should answer the question of whether he had heard of the American exhibit and intended to visit it.

To say that he didn't know about it would be insulting to the high-ranking guest and show disrespect: everyone knows about it but him.

To say that he was planning to visit Sokolniki might be seen, in Soviet eyes, as admiration for the West. Anyway, why would he bother going?

He arrived at a compromise: he knew about the exhibit, but was not planning to go there since he couldn't "find" a ticket.

At this point mutual understanding broke down. The Soviet concept of "find" doesn't exist in America and consequently there is no proper translation for the Russian word. Only now, with the help of television, have Americans become rather familiar with the fact that we had some empty shelves. The interpreter therefore translated "find" as "buy," and Nixon concluded that he was speaking with a poor man who could not afford a ticket. A newcomer from across the ocean was hardly likely to know that a weight checker at one of our markets could not possibly be poor.

Richard Nixon decided to make a gesture—not a grand one, but within the boundaries permitted by American proprieties. He had some Soviet money in his pocket, but wasn't sure what the various colors signified. How much could a ticket to the exhibit cost? Thinking quickly, he took out the largest gray bill, worth one hundred rubles (ten rubles after the 1961 reform), and held it out to Smakhtin. The interpreter hastily explained that the vice president was asking him to take the money and use it to buy a ticket for the exhibit.

"What does money have to do with it, if you can't 'find' a ticket?" Now Smakhtin failed to understand Nixon. Mutual misunderstanding, a different interpretation of facts and intentions, is one of the important causes, if not of conflicts, then of serious discord, including international discord.

Smakhtin thought that the hundred-ruble note offered him was a political provocation. If he took it, he would be a lackey of American imperialism. He had to give a "worthy" answer.

Meanwhile, Richard Nixon was holding out the money. Smakhtin roughly pushed aside the vice president's hand and retorted that Soviet citizens were in no need of handouts. They were able to buy whatever they needed with their own, earned money.

Nixon listened to the translation and understood that he had made a mistake, but didn't understand why. He only understood that this man, despite his dirty appearance, was rich enough to buy a ticket with his own money. Nixon put the bill back in his pocket and headed for the exit. But the feeling of having made an mistake remained with him, and he apparently lost any desire to become acquainted with the lives of the ordinary citizens of Moscow.

As soon as Father woke up he was handed a report of the episode. How did it look in our interpretation?

In those days even the slightest detail was noted, and every word spoken by a guest was recorded. We weren't the only ones to do that. When Father went to the United States he was observed just as closely.

It was reported to Father that at seven o'clock in the morning Richard Nixon demanded to be taken to a market. According to our concept of things, a market is not a suitable place for a high-ranking state guest to visit. Why did he go there? Not to buy young potatoes. As for a stroll, he could have found better places. Father made up his mind that this wasn't so simple, that Nixon wanted somehow to make fun of his hosts. After a detailed description of Nixon's walk around the market, the report went on to say that the vice president tried to hand a hundred-ruble note to a market worker (biographical data attached), but the latter refused to take it.

Father didn't understand any of it. Laughing, he read the report out loud to those of us sitting at breakfast. In Father's opinion, Nixon obviously thought that he had arrived in a colonial country and wanted to bribe or win over people and gain authority by distributing tips. In addition, Father suggested that that was just what people did in America to buy up votes during elections. Father folded the pages of the report in half, as he always did with information he wanted to look at again later on.

"Let Satyukov[10] publish it in *Pravda*. Our people will get a laugh. How could such a person occupy the position of vice president?" said Father thoughtfully and in some perplexity.

This mysterious episode continued to trouble Father in subsequent days. How could a guest of the government conceive of distributing money on the street? Father thought that his guest's reputation was seriously tarnished. He now expected almost any escapade from Nixon and was on his guard, ready to retaliate in kind.

He didn't have long to wait. The world-famous "kitchen debate" took place that same day. Several decades have gone by, so I don't suppose every-

---

10. Pavel Alekseyevich Satyukov, editor-in-chief of *Pravda* and one of Father's close aides.—S.K.

one remembers that episode in the history of Soviet-American relations, however scandalous it was.

Nixon felt himself to be the host of the exhibit. He told Father about each display at great length and kept pointing out how great Americans were and how far ahead of the rest of the world. His tone irritated Father, who delivered rejoinders whenever possible. The conversation resembled a squabble between two friends who, unable to agree about anything, constantly show off their "uniqueness." Father gradually got hot under the collar. He couldn't muster many arguments—the exhibits spoke for themselves. He searched for something to find fault with, to expose the propaganda essence of this entire project, an advertisement for the pretty facade of capitalist America. Nixon sang like a nightingale.

It was in that mood that they approached the interior of an American home. The exhibit was entitled "A Typical American Home." The entire display was attractive, but the kitchen was simply a housewife's dream. Father lingered in the kitchen, sensing that was where he could engage in battle. Noticing an electric lemon squeezer, he began to talk about how unnecessary it was. Father loved to seize on such a detail and then go on to generalize. A sweeping discussion ensued—each tried to prove his point, to convince the other of the superiority of his system and the correctness of his worldview. Each emerged from the debate pleased with himself and convinced that he had devastated his opponent.

Father decided to build on his success and at the same time show off our openness to his guest. He proposed showing the kitchen debate on television in both countries and in full. Let viewers decide who was right. Nixon had no objection. In any case, it depended far less on him than on Father. American television isn't controlled by the president. That evening Father watched the chronicle of the day's adventure with great satisfaction. But he really felt triumphant the next day, when the Soviet ambassador in Washington reported that local television had muted Father's voice and replaced it with remarks by a commentator. At the first opportunity he reproached Nixon: "Where is the much vaunted American freedom of speech? We weren't afraid to bring your arguments to Soviet viewers, but you, the American vice president, didn't keep your word, you were afraid."

Nixon cited the independence of American television. Father didn't bother arguing and only smiled "knowingly."

The next few days Father tried to smooth over any negative impressions from the previous day's spat. He behaved toward his guest with special benevolence. Emotions should not predominate over reason, especially in the prelude to such important negotiations. However, in conversations with his own people Father emphasized the positive side to the pugnacity he had displayed: "Let the president know with whom he has to deal."

Events, meetings, and conversations related to the exhibit were now seen in a new context. Every gesture was viewed in light of the forthcoming meeting in the United States. The future partners scrutinized each other and took each other's measure.

On the weekend Father brought Nixon to the Novo-Ogaryovo guest dacha in Usovo. In the morning he mentioned that he would not return home for lunch, since he would be spending the whole day with his guest.

After eating breakfast and glancing at the morning's papers, he headed down the path to the house where Nixon was staying. I accompanied him to the gate in the fence, secretly counting on permission to accompany him further. My hopes were not realized.

"There will be serious negotiations. You would be in the way," explained Father.

I returned home. I learned what happened next from Father's own account.

During the day's meeting Father was amiability personified. They walked and then took a cruise along the Moscow River. Seeing groups of people on the bank, Father took his guest over to them, introduced him, and appealed to them to persuade Nixon that free people, and not "slaves of communism," lived in our country.

People greeted Nixon warmly, shook his hand, and spoke of our joint fight against Fascism. Our guest wasn't the only one surprised by such a meeting—even a year earlier we ourselves could not even have imagined anything similar.

Nixon was shown whatever he wanted to see. Except for missile installations. Nothing of the kind was as yet in existence.

When the Americans proposed taking Kozlov to Cape Canaveral, Father advised him to decline politely.

"They're doing it in order to demand reciprocity. We can't show them anything, and there's nothing for Kozlov to do there," he said, summarizing the discussion about a coded message sent from the Soviet Embassy in Washington, D.C., and asking for instructions.

Father proved to be right. Nixon persistently displayed an undiplomatic desire to see missiles. At one point in the conversation Nixon kept asking Father what type of rocket fuel we used. Father didn't reply. And when he related this episode at home, Father even became indignant: "He's not a vice president, he's some kind of spy. How can he fail to understand that ferreting out that kind of information is a job for special services. It's not fitting for a government figure of his rank. He doesn't work for the CIA!"

So Nixon didn't succeed in seeing our "rocket miracle." They just teased him by publishing, on the very eve of his visit, newspaper reports on the launch of high-altitude geophysical rockets with dogs on board. Father would soon present a puppy of one of these dogs to President Eisenhower.

There were virtually no real negotiations. During talks at the dacha Father frightened his guest about missiles, while Nixon tried to extract concessions over Berlin.

KHRUSHCHEV VISITS AMERICA

Preparations

Father's vacation, spent first in the Crimea and then in the Caucasus, was taken up with preparations for the trip. Gromyko flew back and forth between Moscow and the shores of the Black Sea. There was one meeting after another. Offices on Lubyanka and Smolensk Squares prepared detailed papers and sent them to Father in carefully sealed envelopes.[11]

Right there on the beach Father's aides, supplemented by a writing fraternity from major central newspapers, prepared rough drafts of speeches to be given on arrival and departure, at breakfasts and lunches, before business people and before journalists. Such a ferment accompanies the preparations for all state visits. But they were not the main thing.

How should the talks with the president be structured? Where would it be possible to retreat? And where should he be firm? Father had to decide these questions himself. He thought constantly about the future negotiations while he was sunning himself on the beach, floating in the sea on an inner tube, and most of all during evening walks.

After returning from a walk he would summon a stenographer and begin to work. Father's positions gradually took shape in this manner. He thought it was first of all essential to make it clear that we wouldn't let anyone hurry us, that we wouldn't allow anyone to live at our expense. On the other hand, by proceeding from the principle of peaceful coexistence, Father wanted to try to find possible approaches to solving disputes. He understood how difficult it was to combine these two concepts, but wanted from the outset to indicate clearly the boundaries beyond which our principles would not let us retreat. A clear position marked out today would make it easier to achieve constructive solutions tomorrow.

In preparing for the trip to the United States Father again immersed himself in studying the subtleties of protocol and again imagined that the Americans intended to humiliate our country and its representative. He involved himself in every trivial detail and sent constant queries to our Embassy. He became fault-finding and distrustful.

He thought, not without reason, that those "capitalists and aristocrats"

---

11. "Offices on Lubyanka and Smolensk Squares." The KGB headquarters were on Lubyanka Square; those of the Foreign Ministry on Smolensk Square.

viewed him, a former worker, as an inferior, and condescended to sit down with him at the same table only because of extreme necessity.

> We agreed on times and procedures. We were somewhat concerned about the arrival ceremony, whether there would be some kind of discrimination. They could ostentatiously omit something due to a head of government. That had happened before, to some degree. . . . On what level had they invited us? On the level of head of government or head of state?
>
> They made a point to our ambassador that it was at the level of head of government. That corresponded to my rank. . . . There was talk about how, in response to my arrival in Washington, Eisenhower would accept an invitation to visit us. We instructed our ambassador to say that, in working out procedures and the arrival ceremony for the Soviet delegation, he . . . should notify officials that the exact same ceremony would be arranged for Eisenhower.
>
> It's true that if you look carefully into the matter, our demands were somewhat exaggerated. Still, we wanted to be emphatic in order to prevent the slightest discrimination. We knew that they inclined toward that, and that temptation was even greater than desire.

One document referred to negotiations with President Dwight Eisenhower at Camp David. Father didn't have the slightest idea what Camp David was and started to worry.

I remember that day. They were working on the beach, sitting in a circle under cloth tents. Gromyko, who had flown in from Moscow, read aloud the program for the trip. Hearing this unfamiliar name, Father drawled: "C-a-m-p David? What is that?"

No one said anything, and then Andrei Andreyevich said uncertainly: "Camp David . . ."

"But what kind of camp is it?" persisted Father. Everything interested him: where the place was located, why negotiations would be held in some kind of camp and not in the capital, Washington.

None of those present could answer the question. Even Gromyko. They called Moscow, but the Foreign Ministry had no information about Camp David. They had to call Washington.

"Now it seems funny and even a little embarrassing," Father admitted later. "They discovered that it was the president's residence outside the city. . . . Well, you see how afraid we were that they could humiliate us."

After receiving this explanation Father was reassured, but the episode always stuck in his memory as an example of how poorly we knew each other. And it was precisely on the basis of this knowledge or lack of it that decisions were being made that could change the fate of the world. The process of acquiring knowledge continues to this day.

Father wanted to fly to America only on the TU-114. Other planes would have to stop and refuel en route, but the TU-114 could make the trip non-stop.

The plane had not yet completed all the tests required by regulations. It made its first long-distance flight, which was successful, only at the end of May, to Khabarovsk. However, microscopic cracks were found in parts of the engine after the flight.

Everyone tried to dissuade Father, including Malinovsky and Father's pilot Nikolai Ivanovich Tsybin, as well as his colleagues in the Presidium. But Father often referred to the TU-104's triumph in Britain and wanted to repeat it across the ocean. The fact that the TU-104's tests had not been completed had prevented him from becoming one of its first passengers. This time he was determined to get his way.

Father asked Tupolev to visit and began to ask him about how safe it would be to fly on the new airliner. Tupolev should have refused to permit it. According to both our rules and international regulations, passenger flights are not allowed until a plane has been certified. Anything can happen during tests—and not only during tests. Structures that have worked reliably a thousand times sometimes suddenly manifest defects resulting in the destruction of machines and people's deaths.

Those who sign a certificate of formal acceptance bear the responsibility for such incidents once the machine is put into service, whereas now Tupolev alone would be responsible. According to the law, Tupolev should have refused, acting as he did in 1956, when he categorically forbade Father to fly on the TU-104.

But this was a different Tupolev. The old fear left over from Stalin's camps no longer constrained him. Tupolev's legendary habit of assuming all the responsibility, not looking over his shoulder at higher authority, of being guided, not by orders but by his own knowledge, experience, and finally, intuition, had returned. He gave his "OK" and guaranteed the safety of the flight.

Tupolev joked in parting: "So you'll feel safer, take my son Alyosha along with you on the trip." Aleksei Tupolev, himself an aviation designer, was his father's deputy at the time. Father burst out laughing: "Let's have it your way. We went to England with you, and we'll fly to America with your son." So the delegation added another person.

However, Father was not the first government leader to try out the TU-114. Kozlov traveled on the plane first, on his way to open the Soviet exhibit in the United States. He personally would have preferred the inconvenience of landings on the well-tested IL-18, but Father insisted. He watched attentively for any reaction to the new air giant in the American press and was as pleased as a child when they couldn't find steps high enough to reach the door of the plane.

"Look at us! See what we can do," exulted Father.

All those present agreed with him. No one explained to Father that the high stairway was necessary because of messy conditions on the country's runways. Designers tried to place engines higher, further away from the rubbish, stones, and other debris that should not have been on runways, but were always there anyway. The giant vacuum cleaners of the engines sucked in everything they passed across, and if a very hard stone flew into the outside engine it could pass through the nozzle and into the turbine blades. The giant propeller blades also added to the height of the TU-114. It was therefore the tallest plane in the world.

I didn't want to disappoint Father either. He was so childishly joyful that I couldn't rob him of that pleasure.

Father said that not only would Mother accompany him, but he would take my sisters and me also. For the second time, after Britain, I was to go "there." Now it was not just going abroad, it was going to America, in our imaginations a fantastic country which had gripped our curiosity all through the preceding years. Now I was to see everything with my own eyes.

We took off on September 15, at seven in the morning. The hour was dictated by diplomatic protocol, which was beginning to influence our schedule. President Dwight Eisenhower was to meet us at Andrews Air Force Base near Washington at exactly twelve noon. A round of meetings, receptions, and interviews, scheduled minute by minute, would follow. Father made special note of the fact that the Washington airport was a little too small for the TU-114. Its runways were too short for our giant to land. There could be only one conclusion: we were ahead of them again. Let them envy us. This time I completely supported Father.

We flew for a long time, half a day. We ate, slept, and ate again. Father read his papers. He enjoyed exchanging telegrams with the prime ministers of the countries we flew over. There were many of them, since we flew over half the world. A few people who had nothing to do with the delegation or the crew sat in a closed off area in the middle of the salon, where the wings joined the fuselage. They consisted of a whole team of engine specialists sent by Nikolai Dmitriyevich Kuznetsov, chief designer from Kuibyshev. They listened throughout the flight to the regular hum of the engines through some little pipes that resembled stethoscopes. They sat in front of complicated control boards and panels with a multitude of blinking green lights. Two lights, green and red, protruded next to each tumbler and each switch. The red ones stayed reassuringly dark, while the green ones next to them remained encouragingly lit. Nevertheless, the presence of these people and the unusual equipment installed in the passenger salon caused some nervousness. We were drawn, as if by magnets, to their boxes, checking to make sure that no red lights went on. We couldn't forget those microscopic cracks.

The passengers weren't the only ones nervous about the unusual flight across the ocean on an experimental plane. The security service had taken all possible precautions well before the flight. They had agreed with the Navy that their ships would come immediately to the location of any possible accident. But how many Soviet military ships were in that enormous expanse of ocean? One or two submarines? The surface fleet stayed close to its own shores. The KGB wanted to send a special expedition to the Atlantic Ocean and station cruisers and destroyers along the flight path of the plane. But when they came to Father, without whose permission no one would dare to take such a step, he categorically forbade it. He thought it would be a waste of money. If there were an accident they wouldn't find anyone, and there probably wouldn't be anyone to find, while it would cost millions and cause embarrassment. American journalists would surely give lurid descriptions of such a plan in their newspapers. He was persuaded to take halfway measures. Our cargo ships and fishing vessels located in the Atlantic were instructed to maintain constant contact with the plane in case of need. If forced to ditch, the pilots were told to head toward the nearest ship. Father didn't object to that, but asked that people not be distracted from their work and that ships remain on their normal course.

In fact, fishing boats did stop working and line up with cargo ships and tankers to form a chain from Iceland to New York.

Fortunately, the plan worked out in such detail on paper did not have to be implemented.

The Reception

The greeting in Washington dispelled Father's apprehension. He was met with a red carpet, crowds of welcomers, groups of journalists, and even a "presidential" twenty-one-gun artillery salute. And most important of all, President Dwight Eisenhower greeted him personally at the plane. I will not describe all the meetings and receptions. Special accounts are devoted to them. I will mention only a few episodes, some important and some not so important, which I think deserve attention. We parted with our TU-114 at Andrews Air Force Base. Father was to travel around the country on the president's Boeing 707. This had been agreed upon in advance, though not without difficulty. Our hosts insisted that a Soviet plane should not fly in American air space. They were mortally afraid of cameras that might be concealed in the fuselage of the TU-114. The wise men of the CIA thought that the Russians could use them to precisely locate targets for their missiles, even if they did not fly directly over any areas of interest.

Theoretically, they were undoubtedly right. But in practice it would have been difficult. As far as I know, there had been no plans to install the necessary equipment, and perhaps it wasn't even possible. It was an experimental plane, and to install cameras we would have had to make new holes in the fuselage and then camouflage them well enough to fool the sharp eyes of professionals. I don't think Father would have agreed to that. If they discovered that the chairman of the Council of Ministers was engaged in espionage it would not only cause embarrassment, it would ruin the efforts to build bridges which had been pursued for many years. Besides, he didn't favor intelligence work.

Our people did not agree with the Americans: how would they provide security on their plane? What if our crafty hosts decided to explode it in the air? Or thought of something else sinister? Negotiations became deadlocked. They appealed to Father, who snapped: "Don't fantasize. Agree. Do you think they're crazy? Who would decide to cause a crash during a visit?" Father thought for a minute and then added, in a different tone of voice: "However, you can't guard against everything. Then it would be easier to stay home and not go anywhere, like Stalin." Then he again spoke sharply: "Agree."

The Americans insisted that their own navigators—or rather, one from the United States and another from Canada—accompany us, since the flight crossed over both countries on its way to Washington. Their mission was to assist in following the flight path, but mainly to keep an eye on the Soviet crew to see if there were some trick switches and knobs on the control panel. Here too, it took time to reach agreement. Our pilots were indignant: "We'll fly there by ourselves." They sensed an element of professional distrust in the American proposal. Diplomats explained that such a request was in accordance with accepted practice.

They again appealed to Father. "If they want to fly, let them fly," he said unhesitatingly. "It will give them a chance to admire our TU-114 and see that our planes are as good as theirs."

During the flight Father showed his goodwill. When we crossed the Canadian border, he went forward to shake hands with the Canadian navigator. The same thing happened with the American. Everyone was pleased.

From his first steps on American soil, Father made an effort to meet the people. Arrogant diplomats, ministers, and bankers were one thing—he was a stranger to them—but he expected to find a common language with ordinary people on the street in the course of personal encounters.

This was not something that happened only in America. He behaved the same way in Moscow and in other Soviet cities, and often conducted similar experiments in foreign countries.

Confusion sometimes followed. Once, during Tito's first visit to our country, Father stopped the official motorcade on Gorky Street and suggested to his guest that they walk to the Kremlin on foot, talking to people along the way. The street in summertime looked festive and beautiful. They had hardly walked half a block when they came upon a stall selling beer. Father asked if Tito was thirsty. It was very hot. His guest looked suspiciously at the murky mugs, but didn't dare refuse. Father was already handing him a heavy mug holding half a liter of beer with a cap of white foam. Father drank one himself. Then it was time to pay, but neither Father nor Tito had any money. They never handled money in everyday life. The head of security came to the rescue. Later Father often used to joke about how he'd made a fool of himself.

So now again, on the way from the airport to his residence, he looked searchingly at the crowds of people welcoming him, or simply gazed at the strange Washingtonians. People behaved with unusual indifference. They didn't cheer, as in other countries, but didn't seem hostile. Father was surprised. After arriving at his residence, Blair House, he began asking people from the Embassy: Is that the usual behavior here?

The ambassador hastened to expose the "machinations" of the local government. It seems that all along the route the motorcade was preceded by a car with a large banner calling on Americans to act with restraint, not to display any emotions, either positive or negative.

Our hosts later apologized, saying that they were trying to prevent unpleasant incidents, because Russians were not regarded with much favor. Decades later, in 1990, the mayor of San Francisco at the time, Mr. Christopher, told me that on the eve of the delegation's visit he had to give several speeches urging the city's population to show hospitality to the president's guests and not spoil their stay on the West Coast.

Father tolerated official efforts to insulate him from the crowds during his stay in Washington, D.C., and New York, but his patience was finite. It was only after arriving in California on the drive from the airport into Los Angeles, that he finally became infuriated. The motorcade had left the planned route and was driving aimlessly around the outskirts, even turning away from the city. The ambassador reported that they were driving along completely different streets from those listed in the program along which, of course, people would be waiting. Father pounced on Henry Cabot Lodge, who was accompanying him, but Lodge couldn't shed any light on the matter and only repeated that local authorities chose the route for reasons of security. Father could barely restrain himself and only hissed: "In that case it would be better not to go anywhere and just sit inside the hotel." However, he quickly mastered himself and, already smiling, said that he was not a coward, and that if Lodge and Mayor Paulson feared for their lives, he could put them in a safe place. The joke fell flat. After wasting two hours driving along the highways, we headed for Disneyland. Father was told that an especially large number of people had gathered there. Halfway there our hosts suddenly had an attack of nerves. Now it seemed that we would not manage to see Disneyland. The crowd there was hostile, and a tomato had been thrown at a local police officer checking the route.

"A fresh one, I hope," said Father sarcastically. He flew into a rage and said that he would go alone. The proper Lodge retorted, "In that case, the state government cannot be responsible for your security." That was a serious consideration, and Father gave in. At the reception that evening he gave Mayor Poulson a piece of his mind.

For unknown reasons related to human psychology, that episode with Disneyland has stayed in people's memories and to this day is practically the only thing Americans remember about the visit. According to the legend, to his dying day Father wanted to see the famous attractions of the park. When he was not allowed to go there, he was so angry that he couldn't repress his emotions. Well, this version appeals to the American sense of humor. I would accept it if it bore the slightest relation to reality. However, Father had only a very vague idea of what a "Disney country" consisted of and what made it so famous.

Father's attempts to carry on a direct dialogue with Americans over the heads of the administration caused a great deal of trouble to both parties throughout the trip. Father took offense and suspected that they wanted to erect a barrier between him and the ordinary people of America. Sometimes his fears were well founded, but sometimes he simply didn't want to understand that far from all Americans were ready to give him a friendly handshake. It was there, in California, that Father had the occasion to visit the IBM computer plant in San Jose. Thirty years later Ambassador Thomas Watson, Jr., the company's president at the time, told me that he was especially worried about what kind of "warm" welcome might be organized by the Hungarian refugees who worked at the plant. The State Department had given him two pieces of "advice." First, on the day of the visit he was to give his Hungarian workers a day off and ask them to stay home. This he did. Second, he was to behave in an official manner with Father and smile as little as possible. This he tried to do but failed. "Your Father told various stories with such genuine humor that I simply couldn't hold back. My lips parted in a smile all by themselves and after that they wouldn't go back to the mask prescribed by Washington," Watson recalled to me. He added: "Before meeting him I knew only one other person who could so easily find the right tone with any audience, and that was my father. Now your father joins him." From Tom Watson's lips, those words sounded like the highest praise.

I have found an old photograph showing a short, round Father and a thin, lanky, crane-like Watson walking side by side and smiling, carrying trays piled with food from the cafeteria.

I should note that at the time Father, and Soviet specialists as well, had only the vaguest idea of what IBM was. Father did not pay any particular attention to the computers during his visit—only that expected from a guest, and no more. He didn't fail to observe that we also had computers, no worse than these. His host didn't argue, he just laughed.

Father was staggered by the IBM cafeteria much more than by its computers. In 1959 the idea of self-service had not reached our country. Father was enthusiastic about the self-service counter along which trays were moved, and by the dishes and platters set out for general inspection. He was amazed by the shiny plastic surface of the tables. It turned out that table-cloths, eternally dirty and spotted, were unnecessary.

"You brush off the crumbs, wipe it with a cloth, and everything's clean," he said admiringly.

Father pushed his tray along the cases with enthusiasm. Gromyko imitated his example. The rest of the delegation followed. They picked up their trays uncertainly, lowered them warily onto the cafeteria service counter and slowly began sliding them forward, expecting some dirty trick at any moment. Most of them had not moved food from stove to table in a good many years. Waiters, maids, or at worst, secretaries existed for that purpose.

They didn't have long to wait. For some reason there was a small opening in the counter, about the width of a tray. Father, following after Watson, negotiated it successfully, although he noticed it only at the last moment. Gromyko also coped with the gap, but Vyacheslav Petrovich Yelutin, the minister for higher education, dropped his tray with a crash and stood staring at it. The incident attracted everyone's attention. Father joked that the minister would have to go into training, since his arms were not used to work. The embarrassed Yelutin tried to brush off some cabbage that had stuck to his trousers.

After returning to Moscow, Father ordered that food service be organized on the IBM model. Without tablecloths and without waiters. That innovation alone would save a great deal of money if applied country-wide. However, the food—well, the food selection simply could not be compared with what was available in America at the time. But Father firmly believed that ours would improve, that abundance was just around the corner.

The supermarket surprised Father as much as the cafeteria. We stopped at one in Stonetown on our way back from San Jose. It's hard to say whether the supermarket was on our schedule, or if Father showed a "lack of discipline." I don't see this stop listed in the official program, which I happen to have saved. Father was surprised not so much by the abundance and variety of goods, which we had already become used to during the week, as by the absence of salespeople. At that time we didn't know the word "self-service." In the Soviet Union everything was sold only over the counter. After returning home Father began enthusiastically to introduce this foreign innovation.

Roswell Garst

On September 22, Father flew from San Francisco to Des Moines, the capital of Iowa and the corn supplier of the United States. Heads of state and government did not usually visit that city, which is located far off the itinerary of official delegations. An exception was made for Father. The corn-loving millionaire farmer Roswell Garst lived there. They had met during the first post-Stalin years, in either 1954 or 1955. It all began with the publication of an article in an Iowa newspaper, the *Des Moines Register*, which challenged the Soviet Union to compete on farmers' and collective farm fields, instead of spending billions on an arms race. The winner would prove the superiority of its social system by peacefully sowing corn and wheat in the earth, not by disfiguring it with explosions. For his part, the newspaper's editor promised Soviet guests a warm reception and assured his readers that Iowans would share their agricultural secrets with them, without hiding anything. Today it's hard to say whether the editor counted on his message reaching Khrushchev or if it was simply a journalistic ploy. Father read a translation of the article, published in the American heartland, the very next day. Intelligence agents serving in the Soviet Embassy subscribed to many local publications, hoping—and not without some basis—to glean snippets of information from them. The U.S. Embassy in Moscow did the same. However, not always with success. The KGB exerted great effort to prevent them from subscribing to the local press, especially to district newspapers, from which it was possible for professionals to pick up many valuable details.

Father responded eagerly to the newspaper's invitation. A few months later a delegation of Soviet scientists, headed by Agriculture Minister Vladimir Matskevich, left for Iowa. When they returned they were to give Father a detailed report on the reasons for American successes and how we could catch up with the United States in the output of food products.

All his life Father closely followed innovations in agricultural production. During the 1940s he literally exhausted designers of potato and corn seeding machines, forcing them to carry out the American idea of planting corn and potatoes by the square-cluster method, i.e., at precise intervals, so that they could then be cultivated and weeds could be destroyed by tractors operating in the fields transversely as well as up and down parallel rows. In order to set the proper distance, they would stretch a wire along a field with knots tied into it at regular intervals. Catching on these knots, seeding machines were supposed to drop seeds into the furrows. More than one spring, Father tramped around in the muddy or dusty fields near Moscow during tests of the newest models of such machines. But they were not successful. Tractors would pull out the wire and turn the square into a rhombus. And in general the scheme turned out to be too complicated. Herbicides came along just in time and promised to make destroying weeds remarkably easy. The square-cluster method was discarded.

The Americans gave Matskevich and his group a cordial welcome, drove them around the fields tirelessly, showed them everything without concealing anything, and supplied them with a whole mountain of literature. When they returned to Moscow, the scientists presented Father with a fat report and upon meeting with him they described marvels unheard of in our country. One of them particularly amazed Father—the clever Yankees sort corn seeds at special plants and sow only the very best, which substantially increases the harvest. Not only that, they don't just sow corn, they sow special hybrid seeds, which increases the yield even further. However, in talking with Father about hybrids, his guests became flustered. This idea contradicted assertions by Trofim Lysenko, who had recently regained influence and was increasingly supported by Father, and smacked of "bourgeois idealism in biology" and "Weismannism-Morganism."[12] People had been put into prison for such "scientific heresy" during the recent Stalin era. Now other winds were blowing, but the speaker felt he had to emphasize the ideological inconsistency of hybridization. Father wasn't particularly interested in whether or not the American hybrids contradicted Lysenko's theories. Results were what was important.

Father was intrigued by what he heard. He wanted very much to talk personally with the people who had achieved such results, which were unheard of in our country. An invitation was sent to the United States, to the farmers of Iowa, to make an answering visit to the Soviet Union. It was received with a notable lack of enthusiasm. Distant, hostile Russia did not attract tourists. Furthermore, absolutely everyone was forbidden to trade with the Soviet Union.

Roswell Garst, who had so amazed his Soviet guests with stories about corn hybrids, turned out to be an exception. He decided to go, and not just as a tourist. He planned to sell Khrushchev hybrid corn seeds and a seed grading plant—and, if things went well, then "the devil take it," he would establish long-term trade relations with the Soviet Union. But U.S. authorities were opposed. Trade with the Soviet Union? Only a madman would dream of such a thing! The correspondence, or more correctly the squabble, with Washington went on for a long time. Garst argued that his seeds and equipment would not in the least strengthen the Soviet Union's military machine, while opposition to private trade contradicts American principles of free enterprise. In the end the central authorities gave in and a reply came

---

12. "Weismannism-Morganism." In other words, the American practices assumed the truth of the chromosome theory of heredity—established by Thomas Hunt Morgan—and contradicted the neo-Lamarckism of Trofim Lysenko, which had achieved the status of "Marxist-Leninist" genetics.

from the State Department: "You can ship your promotional materials and commodity samples to Moscow. Khrushchev won't buy anything from you anyway."

After Garst's arrival in Moscow Father met with him on October 6, 1955, in Yalta, Crimea, where he was on vacation. They liked each other—both idolized the earth and could talk for hours about corn and soybeans. When he returned home, Garst boasted triumphantly that "Khrushchev bought everything that I took with me to Moscow and ordered more." That was the start of their friendship, an unusual one in the 1950s. Garst traveled to Moscow several times, meeting with Father and signing deals with the Ministry of Agriculture. Father became increasingly fond of the American farmer, appreciated his skill, and listened attentively to his advice. Garst returned the favor. During one of their meetings Father asked Garst to go to Kazakhstan, to the virgin lands; perhaps he could explain why we were losing almost half of the crops planted there. When Garst returned, they talked for almost an entire day. Garst advised Father to concentrate on roads, which in autumn became almost impassable, with the result that crops lay in the fields until the onset of frost. Soon after, the government issued a decree on developing the road network in the virgin lands. However, the roads were never built. And after Father was sent into retirement, Garst's advice was forgotten.

Another time, during a trip one spring around fields in Krasnodar Territory, Garst saw collective farmers sowing corn, while the fertilizer delivered earlier was left lying at the side of the field. Furious at this blatant incompetence, the American found the collective farm brigade leader and began through his interpreter to drive home the point that this must not happen and that without fertilizer they would lose a good half of the harvest. The brigade leader couldn't comprehend what this peculiar American was trying to say. Growing angry, he told Garst to "bug off." Garst got even more angry and threatened to complain to Khrushchev. This had an effect, and the brigade leader ordered a halt to the sowing while his assistant went for the fertilizer spreader.

When Garst told him about the incident, Father lamented: "An American capitalist cares more about our harvest than the collective farmers themselves." After this their relations grew into a genuine friendship.

To this day, when Father's name is mentioned in Russia, people think of corn, and then of the state of Iowa.

I have digressed. To return to the year 1959: Garst, like Father, couldn't stand protocol. He wanted to do a thorough job of showing his guest his fields, farm, and seed-grading plant, which allowed him to select the very best grains from among a vast variety. But there was one restriction after another: don't go there, don't step here. Furthermore, they were surrounded by hordes of journalists blocking out the light. Garst finally proposed to

Father that they simply leave. He would pick Father up with his own car at sunrise the next morning. Garst knew that Father got up early. They would be able to look at the farm while the pack of journalists slept.

Father imagined for a moment what a fuss would be made in both countries if the chairman of the Council of Ministers disappeared, even for a short time. Frankly, he wanted to play that game and accept the proposal, but his schedule called for him to leave at nine in the morning on September 23. During the whole day Garst struggled with nosy reporters, pushing them away with corn stalks, throwing manure at them, and even threatening to loose a fierce bull on them. The angrier he became, the more pleasure it gave his "enemies." Newspaper reports contained juicy details, to say nothing of the photographs. They traveled all over the world. Perhaps Garst played up to it, since it's not every day you can get such publicity. That isn't important. The main thing is that the day was successful and both Garst and Father were pleased. Father often reminisced about the American farmer, citing him as an example to our agricultural specialists. Garst and his sons produced more than any of our collective farms.

Security

During the evening of September 22 Father visited a meat processing plant in Des Moines. He saw both the sausage producing section and the automated production line which stuffed hot dogs. After sampling some, Father praised the product, though he promised that we would soon surpass our hosts. He mentioned that he had recently seen such a production line at one of our plants, but it was turning out missiles. This went over his listeners' heads, since missiles didn't enter their sphere of interests. Only the interpreter from the State Department, Mr. Alexander Akalovsky, wrote what Father said in his notebook. His job was to note down every word Father uttered. For internal analysis.

Now these notes have been declassified and are available. What can't you find there! Father's comment when he noticed an aircraft carrier in San Francisco Bay—that we would not have a surface fleet because it could not resist attacks by submarine-launched cruise missiles. And his comment on the vulnerability of modern bombers. And his mention of our AN-10 airliner, capable of landing at unequipped airports with hundreds of passengers on board. And a great deal else.

One of the reports mentions me as well. Akalovsky writes that during the landing at the Des Moines airport, the premier's son filmed jet fighters parked near the runway.

I remember that I did commit such a sin. During the whole trip I competed with professionals and used eight-millimeter film to capture everything that caught my eye. The result was a long and boring film, though it was successful among my Moscow friends. The door to the outside world had just opened a crack and any information from outside caused surprise and admiration.

However, the fighters attracted no one's interest except Mr. Akalovsky's, even though I showed the film at Chelomei's design bureau and to some other aviation professionals. The planes were old and of no interest to them.

I refer to this episode not because I want to offend anyone or took offense myself, but because it perfectly illustrates the mutual suspicions that accompanied us at every step, at every move. We were watched every single minute.

Another story comes to mind in this connection. In the first half of 1959 Chelomei's first cruise missile, the P-5, was added to the military arsenal. That was done then by a government decree, which describes in detail where it will be produced and stored and to whom delivered. The sweeteners are saved for the very end: orders, medals, and prizes. All of this was, naturally, "secret" and sometimes "top secret, of special importance." Vladimir Nikolayevich became a "Hero of Socialist Labor" and was awarded a Lenin Prize. Eleven people from the design bureau received Lenin Prizes in addition to him.

Naturally, secret prizes were awarded separately from others, to avoid revealing the identities of the winners. Our prizewinners received their medals in the conference halls of the Moscow Soviet. I was among those invited. The ceremony took place sometime in July or August. After receiving a pass, I folded the invitation, which looked like an induction notice, and put it in the breast pocket of my only black dress suit. And forgot about it.

For some reason I reached into my pocket in Washington and found this invitation. Although it wasn't secret, I had not followed proper procedures. At first I wanted to tear it up and throw it away, but then I changed my mind. I knew from detective stories that specialists can easily decipher even burned paper. I turned the piece of paper over and over again in my hands, and then put it back in my pocket. And, of course, in all the excitement I forgot about it. In New York I remembered the invitation again. A maid took my suit to iron it before one of the receptions. When I got it back I mechanically went through the pockets. Something seemed wrong, but I couldn't remember what. The pockets, naturally, were empty. It was only on the following day that I realized what was bothering me—the invitation had disappeared.

I didn't tell Father about this occurrence, and a few days later forgot about it. However, what happened in the New York hotel had consequences. The sequel occurred the following winter. Returning home one day, Father grimly asked me if I hadn't talked too much in America. In particular, if I had told someone about my work.

I was genuinely indignant: how could he think such a thing? I was not a child, and I had my instructions about maintaining secrecy.

Father didn't probe. He said nothing for a bit, and then reluctantly added: "We have caught an American agent here. During questioning he said that one of his assignments was to find out which project earned Chelomei a Lenin Prize and what Khrushchev's son Sergei was doing in his design bureau."

Father said nothing more. He found the conversation unpleasant. Obviously, the KGB didn't want to question me themselves and, deciding to act in a roundabout way, sent the report from the spy's interrogation to Father.

It ran through me like an electric shock, and the vanished invitation flashed through my mind: that was what happened, a CIA intrigue! I had to tell Father about everything. He became even more grim, although he didn't attribute any particular importance to the lost paper. "Be more careful in the future," he mumbled. He never returned to the subject, either that day or later. Feeling guilty, I didn't ask him about the fate of the foreign intelligence agent.

It's hard to say what role the paper which disappeared from my pocket played, but I've never forgotten the incident. Every agency carries out its duty. I refer to these details in order to show the degree of tension in our relations in everything, even minor matters.

The Visit Comes to a Close

Father was in the United States for fifteen days—an enormous amount of time by today's standards. Today a day or two are spent on negotiations and then the parties split up. Time is precious. Then, when we were still getting to know each other, it's hard to say which was more important in the long run: negotiations with the president or learning about an unfamiliar country. In those days each trip abroad resembled a landing on an unknown planet. Our contacts with the outside world were just beginning.

On the last day of the visit, Father was to speak on television—and for the first time in his life. Of course, special sessions, meetings, and celebrations were televised in our country, but leaders had never appeared one-on-one with the camera. For a long time Father couldn't make up his mind. He wanted very much to speak to Americans, but that would automatically incur an obligation for the American president to appear on Soviet television the following year. In Moscow they were especially fearful of that. They weren't particularly worried that viewers would instantly change their allegiance, but official circles were horrified at the very concept of broadcasting "foreign" ideas over our media. Father rejected that, saying that if we don't trust our people and fear that they would follow an American president as soon as he opens his mouth, then we, the leadership, aren't worth anything and aren't needed by anyone. They didn't all agree with Father, but no one argued.

Now Father prepared—or, rather, worried—as he waited for the broadcast to begin. Not about the substance of what he would tell the American people. Father had a clear idea of what he would say, about peace, about coexistence, and of course about the advantages of socialism and its approaching universal triumph. Father was worried about how they would show him on television screens, whether they would think up some trick. He behaved cautiously and categorically refused the services of a makeup artist. In his mind, makeup was associated with some kind of humiliation and even provocation. People would talk later about how the Soviet premier was made up. They were unable to persuade him that under the floodlights his nose and his bald head would look shiny and red. Father remained firm. After the broadcast he proudly described how he'd fought off all the director's requests.

Father left for the studio by himself, while we waited nervously at Blair House for him to appear on the screen of the color television set, which was rare even in the States in those days. But everything worked out well. Father said everything that he wanted to say and then, saying good-bye in broken English, disappeared from the screen. The only problem was that his face appeared unusually red and his bald head gleamed with every movement.

Apparently Father's appearance before television viewers created as much apprehension as the prospect of Eisenhower's did in the Kremlin. As soon as he finished he was replaced by three commentators, who began to explain, refute, and clarify.

Father was disturbed by this tactic, but not angered. We were not in a friendly camp, so what could you expect? Smiling, he advised our propagandists to learn from the Americans and take this lesson into account for the future.

Father was pleased by what he had seen in the United States. He was especially taken with the people, with their openness, spontaneity, and friendliness.

He and President Eisenhower had talked about many subjects. On certain questions no rapprochement was apparent, while on others the sides seemed close to agreeing but then, as if in alarm, retreated to their initial positions. Both sides were obviously afraid to trust each other.

What was the principal question before us? The principal question was to agree on disarmament.

I saw that this troubled Eisenhower, and troubled him greatly. I sensed that he was not posing but really wanted to reach an agreement to prevent war. . . . In the negotiations—or, rather, in conversation—he said: "Mr. Khrushchev, I am a military man. I've spent my whole life in military service.

I took part in war, but I'm very much afraid of war. I would like to do every-thing to avoid war. Mainly, to arrive at an agreement with you. That is most important. . . ."

I answered: "Mr. President, nothing could make me happier than if we could come to an agreement and exclude the possibility of war between our countries. . . . But how can we come to an agreement?"

This question greatly preoccupied both Eisenhower and our side. That was the main question. The others were, as they say, derivative: how to im-prove our relations, develop trade, and promote economic, scientific, and cul-tural ties.

We knew their position, they knew ours. I didn't see that anything had changed in this matter. I didn't hope that we would be able to reach agree-ment.

Both sides understood that war must be excluded. The specific question was—banning thermonuclear weapons.

The American side stuck to its position that international supervision must be established. At the time we were absolutely unable to agree on interna-tional supervision. I stress the phrase, at that time.

We therefore wanted to agree on banning nuclear weapons tests, which we considered possible without international supervision.

Every explosion was detectable by technical means. It was possible to en-sure supervision without setting up equipment on the territory of another country, but simply from one's own territory or that of one's allies.

The Americans had surrounded us with their military bases. They could watch everything and listen to everything, so they had established that over-sight long before. They obtained reports of inspectors, not necessarily from the United States of America. International supervision was possible, but we could not accept it.

Even now, while a pensioner, I have thought over this question. I think that today such inspection is possible. It would not damage our defenses. Now this inspection would be mutual.

But at that time we were far behind in the accumulation of nuclear weap-ons. We did not have enough nuclear missiles. We could not reach the terri-tory of the United States with our bombers. We were weaker.

We could blow U.S. allies in Europe and Asia to smithereens, but the American economic potential was located at too great a distance for our weapons.

Naturally, we could not agree, because inspection would not have been to our advantage. They would simply have been given the opportunity to count our weapons and see that we were weak! At that point it would have been to their advantage to finish us off by means of war. . . .

We took along specific proposals: to specify certain border regions in the

Soviet Union and in the western NATO countries, where it would be possible to carry out mutual inspections, both from the air and, I think, ground inspections. I don't remember now which regions, but I think that we proposed large territories near our western borders. Mainly on our own territory and of course on the territory of the GDR, where our troops were stationed.

The first negotiations between Father and President Eisenhower look childishly naive, childishly straightforward, permeated with ideology and ambition, when seen from the vantage point of the knowledge and experience we have gained in the years since. Nevertheless, in my opinion these first steps were notable for the sincerity shown by both parties. Both leaders wanted to achieve peace; they both knew the cost of war. These were the first steps, and because they were the first, without them no subsequent ones would have been possible. Our path to a new world, to the peaceful coexistence of two political systems, began then, more than thirty years ago, and only now, toward the end of the century, has a real possibility of freeing ourselves from the threat of war become visible.

In September 1959, while preparing for the negotiations with Eisenhower, Father soberly evaluated the possibility of reaching agreements. He didn't nourish any particular illusions, and therefore did not experience any disillusionment. This is what he wrote in an article published in September in the magazine *Foreign Affairs*: "The main thing is to keep from policies of ideological struggle, not to use weapons to achieve one's objectives." This balancing on the border between ideological struggle and peaceful coexistence seriously complicated the achievement of agreements. But such were the realities of those years.

The problems seemed simpler to the president than they were in reality. He hoped that an open exchange of opinions would melt the ice. He underestimated its thickness, which joint efforts had increased over the course of many years.

To return to Father's reminiscences:

When we began to examine matters which were of interest to both parties and which had to be solved, we ran into obstacles. They prevented our moving closer, but we could not remove them.

I felt at once that Eisenhower had grown flabby. He had the look of a man who has been pulled out of an ice-hole: "He was worn to a shred, and water was running off him." Apparently I looked no better than Eisenhower. Though perhaps I looked better, because we had no illusions. We didn't hope that all the obstacles on the path to better economic relations with the United States were going to be removed on our first visit. . . .

We wanted to be seen and to see the United States of America. We wanted to demonstrate our resoluteness: we were not going to make any of the unilateral concessions which America was demanding. The situation therefore distressed us. We wanted to smooth over disputes, but we saw that conditions were not yet favorable. . . . It came time for dinner. . . . The dinner was not a festive one. The atmosphere at the table resembled one in a house where someone lay gravely ill. That emotion predominated on our side, and still more with the president of the United States.

Agreement was possible, but only if realistic and sensible steps were taken. To reach an agreement without making any concessions would mean that the other side was forced to capitulate. It was impossible for the United States to achieve that.

By inviting us, they showed initiative after the many years of ideological warfare which we had been conducting. But that invitation did not confer on them any hope of forcing us to capitulate. Quite the opposite! We were strengthened in our policies; we were unassailable—we stood, as the saying goes, like a rock.

In short, we dined. . . . The dinner was somber. Not celebratory. Just . . . contacts. Neither a wedding nor a funeral. We got into the car. I returned to Washington in the same car as Eisenhower. I don't remember how many words we exchanged during the whole trip—very few, very infrequently. The conversation didn't take off.

Both sides stood firm. The negotiations were tough, uncompromising—and fruitless. Conversations outside the formal meetings were completely different. Whatever the subject, they conversed with sympathy and good humor. They talked about a variety of things: about golf and relations with the military, about the president's bulls and ways to preserve peace, about cowboy movies and the future of Europe. It was this human communication, common interests or, rather, inclinations, concern about what kind of future our children and grandchildren would inherit—and not arguments over payment of the remaining debts for lend-lease deliveries during the war or stubborn disagreements over the German question—which were, in my opinion, the main result of the visit, opening many possibilities for the future.

The president expected Father to protest the U-2 flights over Soviet territory. Father, however, talked about all sorts of things, but not about that. Eisenhower decided that he had reconciled himself to the inevitable. But Father said nothing about it because he didn't want to give his hosts the satisfaction, didn't want to demonstrate his weakness and inability to punish the offender by begging overly curious neighbors "not to peer into his bedroom." When we shot down the first U-2—then we would talk as equals, he thought.

At home Father explained his position by saying: "You have to use your fist to teach insolent people a lesson. We now have a very powerful fist. Just let them try to barge in again." He was mistaken. The American president interpreted Father's silence as a sign that he was resigned to the situation. Perhaps a vehement protest would have made the White House hesitate, if not put an end to the flights.

But Father was silent on the subject.

The "Spirit of Geneva" was resurrected, although for only a short time. However, now it was called the "Spirit of Camp David." These two old men, without resolving a single specific question, made a lot of progress in the most important area, the sphere of human understanding of each other. The first glimmers of trust became visible. I don't believe there were any lost opportunities for achieving agreement in those years. Objectively speaking, our countries were not yet ready. Even in strictly military matters, the might of the United States loomed over us. The United States was aware of its might and we were aware of our weakness and, clenching our teeth, we were building missiles. Agreement is attainable only between equals.

We had to move away from the "image of an enemy." It seems that this first attempt succeeded. Father produced a rather good impression on Americans. He personally believed in the American president's desire to achieve peace and a good-neighborly relationship. The image of Eisenhower as an evil instigator of war was finally dissipated and what remained was a clever, kind, somewhat tired person who had seen a great deal in his life.

After his conversations with the American president, Father regretfully concluded that his proposal to make West Berlin a free city was not realistic. A new solution, a new way, had to be found that might lead to a peace treaty without relinquishing the foundation of socialism in East Germany. He abandoned his original idea with regret.

I am profoundly convinced that the Berlin Crisis cannot be considered a real crisis. It should instead be called a sophisticated imitation of a crisis. Neither the Soviets nor the Americans took any steps that might have provoked a flare-up or a conflict. Both sides limited themselves to striking military poses and making loud statements and cautious threats. But if you consider it a crisis, then the First Berlin Crisis came to an end at Camp David. The air went out of the sails of the movement toward a separate peace treaty, though Father decided not to dismiss the idea entirely. Someday it might come in handy.

"The struggle to achieve a peace treaty with the two Germanys continued," wrote Father. "When the deadline we set for concluding a peace treaty arrived, we realized that nothing would come of it. We had wanted to create a strong basis for peaceful coexistence, but this way we were even heading toward a possible military conflict. I should say that I did not expect a military clash, even if we did sign a unilateral peace treaty with the German

Democratic Republic. . . . There was no sense in signing a unilateral peace treaty unless we wanted to put an unbearable strain on our relations with the West. After mutual consultations, we decided to postpone the signing of a peace treaty indefinitely."

Now the question of a free city seldom came up. At home Father joked—and later loudly announced—that he saw West Berlin as the tail of the Western cat. It had fallen by chance into his hands, and he could yank it any time he wished.

A shortage of workers, as well as the departure and flight of qualified specialists, was the principal source of the GDR's woes. Father thought that the situation would soon change: life would improve, the stream of people leaving through West Berlin would stop, and the inhabitants of the FRG would even want to move to the GDR. The important thing was to get through the crisis and hold out until better times.

INTERLUDE: FATHER'S LAST VISIT TO CHINA

After landing in Moscow on September 29, and with barely time to change his shirt and speak to the public in the covered hockey stadium in Luzhniki about his famous trip, Father left with Suslov on September 30 for Beijing to attend the celebration of the tenth anniversary of the founding of the Chinese People's Republic. It was his last visit to that "fraternal" country, the last, desperate personal attempt to repair the increasingly large rift in relations between the two nations.

I allow myself to express the supposition—based on my personal impressions—that the warm reception given Father in the United States, his great success there, and the prospect for improved world relations had inclined Father toward euphoria. It seemed to Father that talks with Mao Zedong in Beijing would enable him to resolve any disagreements. He was bitterly disappointed. On October 11 Father returned to Moscow.

THE ARMS RACE CONTINUES

Father regarded our country's first successful launch of the R-12 missile from a silo as his personal triumph. He immediately made a special decision: we would add only silo-based, not aboveground, strategic ballistic missiles to our military arsenal. However, it would take time to carry out this decision. The first R-16 was not lowered into its silo until the middle of 1963. A year later the medium-range R-12 and R-14 missiles followed.

The decision to make it compulsory to install missiles in silos created additional difficulties for both Yangel and Korolyov. Now poisonous acidic vapors and potentially explosive oxygen fumes accumulated in the closed, underground wells. The problem of missile pressurization was aggravated.

In the acid version the problem was difficult, but solvable. The oxygen version created even more serious problems.

Father continued to doubt that liquid oxygen could be tamed, but Korolyov insisted that he could do it. Work on the R-9 continued. The engines for it were made by that same Glushko, and Korolyov was increasingly bothered by his dependence on the "traitor." He very much wanted to have "his own" engine designer, one who wouldn't have to please two masters at the same time. Fate brought him to Nikolai Dmitriyevich Kuznetsov, designer of turbojet engines for the Tupolev bomber TU-95 and its passenger version, the TU-114.

In 1959 no nuclear explosions were carried out by the USSR, the United States, or Britain. The countries in the nuclear pool eyed each other cautiously, without for a moment halting their research and design work. If one of them broke the moratorium and upset the unstable balance, which was not sustained by any treaty, then the other two countries could resume testing immediately.

Our tests carried out at the end of 1958 did not solve all our technical problems. The most serious of them was raised during Father's visit to Yangel. What warhead should be used for the R-16? Should we use the megaton warhead recently tested for the R-12, or plan to use a very promising new one that was two to three times more powerful?

They expected Father to make this decision. Kirichenko, Brezhnev, and Ustinov, to say nothing of officials one rank lower, such as ministers and state committee chairmen, favored the new one. They had no doubt that tests were necessary and considered our commitment to discontinue explosions as nothing more than a political maneuver, a piece of paper vulnerable to "the demands of real life."

Father made a Solomonic decision: plan to use the old warhead, but retain the option of using the newly developed one. He simply couldn't adopt a more rigid position. The Americans had obligated themselves for only a year, which had almost expired. The French, who had not joined the nuclear club, were ignoring the campaign and preparing for their first test. That first test caused Father a great deal of concern. After all, the Americans could be carrying out their explosions under a French guise. How could you check on them?

For the time being, however, he stood firm. And as if to support Father, the U.S. State Department announced on July 26, soon after the meeting at Yangel's bureau, that the American moratorium would be extended until the end of the year. This was not a big step, just a small one, since it was only a question of two months—the expiration date moved from October 31 to December 31—but Father took the announcement as a good sign. Moscow immediately responded: as long as Western countries did not test, the USSR would not resume testing. The United States held back until December 29, when almost simultaneously with the announcement that agreement on a summit in Paris on May 16, 1960, had been reached, President Eisenhower stated that as of the new year the United States would no longer feel bound by its voluntary promise to observe a moratorium on nuclear testing. Any explosions would be announced well in advance.

Father considered this to be a concession by the president to the demands of the military. However, he himself did not follow the president's example, although both Slavsky and Ustinov proposed planning a new series of explosions immediately. They did not yet succeed in shaking Father's determination. Only an insane individual would decide to take such a step immediately before a summit meeting.

He was also unmoved by the news that the first French bomb had exploded at seven o'clock in the morning at their test site in the Sahara Desert.

Father was in India on a state visit at the time. I accompanied him and was present when this unpleasant news arrived. A proposal came from Moscow that we respond unequivocally to this violation of our unilateral condition for ending tests: until the first explosion carried out by the West. Not just by the United States, but by the West.

When that phrase was written, Father had in mind both British and French preparations for an explosion. Kirichenko and Slavsky thought that our policy would not be adversely affected at all if we were to carry out at least a limited series of explosions, to be completed before the opening of the Paris summit. The Soviet position would thereby be strengthened, and we would be able to negotiate with the Americans as equals, or almost equals.

Father disagreed. The arguments of the "Muscovites" made the opposite impression on him: how could they fail to understand that after the first explosion there would be nothing to talk about? In his opinion, the military balance remained unchanged. France had simply satisfied its ambitions by joining the other nuclear powers. Father believed in the American president's sincere desire for peace and hoped to reach an agreement. He decided "not to notice" the explosion in the Sahara.

KOROLYOV HITS THE MOON

Beginning in the autumn of 1958 Korolyov desperately tried to maintain his lead in the conquest of space. Now he fought to be the first to reach the moon. Ignoring the expense and the utter exhaustion of those who worked for him, he sent up one rocket after another. He launched a frontal attack, like Marshal Zhukov in May 1945 when he threw division after division into reinforcing the Seelow heights, sacrificing thousands and thousands of soldiers for the sole purpose of being the first to enter Berlin and beating his "neighbor" on the left, Marshal Konev. As I mentioned earlier, Korolyov resembled Zhukov physically, as well as in his style—just as short, sturdily built, and just as ruthlessly uncompromising in achieving his goals.

The first three launches, on September 23, October 12, and December 4, 1958, ended in failures of the rocket. Then, on January 2, 1959, the guidance system failed and the space vehicle flew past the moon. The launch on June 18, 1959, again saw a failure of the rocket's second stage. By September two more rockets were ready.

Father invested great hopes in this launch. He asked Korolyov to schedule it for the start of his visit to the United States. However, Father warned that the launch should not occur if he had any doubt of its success. We must not be disgraced at such a moment. Korolyov assured him that we would not be embarrassed.

He himself was far from sure of success and put his hopes on his lucky star. The launch of the next lunar rocket, the sixth in number, was set for September 6. Despite frantic efforts by the launch team, it failed to lift off—in the rush someone forgot to plug in one of the connector assemblies. The second and third attempts again ended in failure—water of unknown origin froze in the pipelines. On the fourth try the engines started up, but did not develop thrust. Korolyov decided not to tempt fate any longer and switched to the backup rocket. It brought the long-awaited success.

On September 14 a Soviet rocket carrying a sphere slammed into the moon. Korolyov presented Father with a copy of the sphere, which upon hitting the moon, was designed to split open into a rain of glittering pentagons, each with our country's coat of arms, the launch date of September 1959, and the four letters "USSR." One of these pentagons, which I keep in a box lined with dark blue velvet, is among my most cherished mementos.

Father asked them to make another copy of the sphere. It would make a good souvenir to give the American president. Father wanted passionately to show the leader of the world's most advanced country what our technology could do. He always remembered how Leskov's Levsha amazed the ingenious wise men of England by shoeing their mechanical flea.[13]

---

13. *Levsha* means "left-handed person" in Russian. Reference is to the Russian novelist N. S. Leskov's popular short story, "The Tale of the Cross-eyed Lefty from Tula and the Steel Flea" ("Skaz o Tulskom kosom Levshe i o stalnoy Blokhe," 1881). The story, which would be familiar to any educated Russian, features an illiterate smith from Tula who outwits the skill of the most advanced British craftsman. The hero and his fellow craftsmen of Tula save the honor of Russia by shoeing the tiny feet of a mechanical flea—a gift of the English to the tsar which had symbolized England's technical superiority.

Sergei Pavlovich adopted Father's idea enthusiastically. His sphere in the White House! Korolyov said that his design bureau had already made several such spheres, and that he would send one of them to the Kremlin immediately.

Father reminded him: "Just make sure that they put it into an attractive box." Korolyov assured him again that he would not be embarrassed.

Indeed, there was no cause for embarrassment. The spacecraft fulfilled its planned program, and after arriving in Washington on September 15 Father presented the sphere to Dwight Eisenhower with a triumphant smile. Photos marking the momentous occasion flashed around the whole world.

Father enjoyed giving the spheres as presents and repeatedly asked Korolyov for copies. He presented them during his visits to the leaders of various countries: Indian prime minister Nehru, French president de Gaulle, Indonesian president Sukarno, and King Zakhir Shah of Afghanistan. They were also given to high-ranking guests arriving in our country.

THE R-7 PASSES ITS LAST TESTS

Military versions of the R-7 were also being developed successfully. Tests were drawing to a close after slightly more than two and a half years, during which scientists tasted both the bitterness of catastrophe and the joy of achievement. The missile still had to be tested at eight thousand kilometers. That was possible only if it landed outside our territory, as even the Soviet Union's enormous expanse was inadequate.

Korolyov decided to draw on American experience and proposed launching the missile toward the waters of the Pacific Ocean. His idea initially provoked a storm of protests: launch an extremely secret reentry vehicle prototype toward unguarded territory, where it could be seized by hostile agents? Korolyov assured doubters that we would meet the requirements of secrecy by equipping the prototype with explosive devices. In his opinion, there was simply no other solution to the problem. There was no point in wasting time.

Ustinov came to give Father a report. He brought along Minister Rudnev and, of course, Korolyov.

After they had decided the question in principle, a new problem arose: at home launch dates and targets were held in the strictest secrecy. But what should the procedure be in this case? They decided to consult the Ministry of Foreign Affairs. The ministry replied unequivocally that if there were any potential threat to shipping in international waters, advance notice must be provided to interested countries.

Ustinov and Rudnev argued that after such an announcement, intelligence agents from around the globe would assemble in the designated area.

By analyzing its fiery track, the Americans could tell what materials were used in the warhead, calculate any deviation from the target, and in general, obtain a mass of data not intended for them. "Perhaps we should not take that risk."

Father listened to their fears—and did not agree. He favored the publication of warnings in the press. Launches could not be concealed in any case, and a violation of international law would provoke false rumors and friction. Besides, it was even a good thing that Americans be convinced we had missiles capable of reaching them, if necessary.

"What are you afraid of when you say that their intelligence agents will learn how accurate the missiles are?" Father asked Ustinov. "You *did* report that they have a high degree of accuracy. Or is that not the case?"

Ustinov reaffirmed that the degree of accuracy was very high.

"So let them be convinced of that," continued Father, and added: "But how will they know what you are aiming at? You don't drive a pole into the ocean."

Korolyov explained that the target point could be calculated by the results of several launches.

"Then let them calculate it," Father summed up the discussion.

On January 10, 1960, newspapers published a report that the Soviet Foreign Ministry had sent the governments of all countries, through diplomatic channels, a TASS statement about forthcoming missile launches to a central part of the Pacific Ocean in connection with scientific research projects.

Ten days later a report on the successful completion of tests appeared in *Pravda*. It described not reentry vehicles, but a mythical last stage of the rockets, specially adapted to penetrate dense layers of the atmosphere and therefore successfully reaching the target area.

On January 20, 1960, the R-7 ICBM was officially added to the arsenal of the Soviet Army.

THE FUTURE BRIGHTENS

Now Father associated all his hopes with the forthcoming summit meeting, and still more with President Eisenhower's visit to the Soviet Union. An especially warm welcome was being prepared.

Father demonstrated his desire to achieve agreement in every way possible. Not, of course, by abandoning principles. Categorical statements, threats, and accusations disappeared from newspaper pages. Not entirely, however: the skirmishing over Berlin continued, but without its former ardor and malice.

Pravda began to publish excerpts from a book by Averell Harriman, considered until quite recently one of the warmongers. On January 15, 1960, a session of the Supreme Soviet declared that it viewed disarmament as the only way to strengthen peace and assure friendship among peoples. Father proposed that we reduce our armed forces for the fourth time, by one million, two hundred thousand men. Total reductions during those years amounted to about three and a half million. There remained 2,423,000 men in the armed forces.

I have made careful attempts to sum up all reductions in the armed forces, beginning with 1953. The numbers don't add up. Apparently not all plans were fulfilled and some adjustments were made in the process. But the trend was consistent. The Army shrank steadily and rapidly.

On January 18, *Pravda* reported that President Eisenhower's visit to our country would occur in June of 1960, from the tenth to the twentieth of the month. You could sense an elated mood in Moscow. It was like the atmosphere in a home which awaits the arrival of a dear and hoped-for guest. The city was tidied up, decorated, and in general, made ready.

Everyone knew how hard it was to get any money from Father for anything except housing. In those years no one even breathed a word about putting up government office buildings. Such a suggestion could have cost the person his job. If an official took advantage of Father's absence and managed to push through such a project, heaven forbid that Father saw it. It would be stopped immediately. That is what happened to the white stone, wedding-cake style building of the Russian Council of Ministers on the banks of the Moscow River. Noticing walls emerging from the ground, Father asked what was being built. Work was halted on the huge structure until the end of 1964. After Father's retirement they quickly resumed construction of the building.

But now, in preparation for the visit, Father acquiesced without argument to the building of special villas in various parts of the country to receive his high-ranking guest. One was located on the picturesque shores of the celebrated Lake Baikal, in Siberia.

Father was also concerned about where to organize one-on-one, confidential talks, in the style of Camp David: at his dacha in Gorky II or at the guest house in Novo-Ogaryovo, where Nixon was lodged. He decided on the latter, since at Gorky II it was not possible to provide the conveniences to which guests were accustomed. For example, there was only one toilet for everyone, located at the end of the hall. The bath was there, too. By American standards, only people in the slums lived in such conditions.

I can't say that Father counted on eliminating all the obstacles in Moscow that they had not managed to overcome in Washington and Camp David, especially since Eisenhower was coming to the end of his second term and elections were approaching. Father hoped more to establish a sound foundation for the future. The world seemed finally to have begun moving from dead center. Exhibits in our countries, exchanges of visits, and finally, the planned summit meeting appeared to give some hope for an improvement in the international climate, for a turn toward contacts, agreements, and as mutual trust grew, to irreversible changes. It was extremely important not to stumble, especially at the beginning, when nerves were on edge. One wrong or wrongly interpreted step, and all their efforts would turn to dust.

The first half of 1960 was filled with various international contacts, meetings, and visits. It was as if a dam had broken. Father was incredibly busy.

At the beginning of February Father conducted negotiations in Moscow with the president of the Italian Republic, Giovanni Gronchi. They were held in a warm and relaxed atmosphere. On a day off Father even invited his guests to his private dacha. They strolled in the winter woods around Moscow and threw snowballs. It was as if good friends had dropped in for the day. Serious talk alternated with trivia. The president's wife disconcerted Father by suddenly asking where his suits were made.

Father had read more than one critical comment about his suits in the foreign press, which described them as baggy and carelessly cut. Father never dressed stylishly, even as a young man. In those postwar years a lack of attention to one's appearance was considered chic. Though he still paid little attention to tailors, those comments hurt his pride. He ordered his suits from a special sewing workshop attached to the KGB, as did the other members of the Presidium. The tailors there tried their best, especially after Father mumbled something about how their work was rated by the foreign press. Because of all this, the question about clothes both confused and offended him.

In answer, he just muttered: "They're made here, in Moscow. There's a workshop. But why do you ask?"

"Your suit fits extremely well. I thought that you ordered it from abroad. The cut looks Italian. So I thought that perhaps it was from Italy. We have very good tailors," she answered effusively.

She prattled on a bit longer about suits and tailors, about the wonderful master tailors in Italy. Father listened without interrupting. I was laughing to myself. Father couldn't stand conversations about clothes. He considered them petty and was quite capable of interrupting anyone. Now he managed to keep a hospitable smile on his face. Perhaps it was after the walk with the Italian president and his wife that rumors of Father ordering his clothes exclusively from Italian tailors traveled around the world.

In February and March Father visited India, Burma, Indonesia, Afghanistan, and France. He spoke everywhere about peace, disarmament, and peaceful coexistence. He attached particular importance to the negotiations with General de Gaulle. They had not really met before.

Father thought that the world situation encouraged hope for a successful summit—if nothing went wrong, naturally. But what could happen? Despite the substantial problems in relations among countries, which could not be ignored, we should not be afraid to make a beginning, thought Father, as he looked toward the future with optimism.

Throughout 1959 Chelomei's design bureau worked with great intensity. Tests of the first cruise missiles were finally completed and some were installed on refitted diesel submarines. New, modern nuclear-powered submarines slid down their slips into the water.

Toward the summer of 1959 Chelomei caught space fever. The earth became too small for him. Naval matters receded into the background.

More than anything, Chelomei wanted to build a manned cruise-type spaceship. It must be highly maneuverable. He continued research on this idea to the very end of his life. At first the spaceship received the rather unoriginal name *Raketoplan* (Rocketglider). The military did not support his project. They thought it was one of his wild fantasies. Research was very poorly financed, and sometimes given nothing at all. The General Staff always kept track of what was being done across the ocean. There it was announced that research into the possibility of creating a cruise space plane, dubbed Dyna-Soar, was being carried out. This was some time after Chelomei came up with the idea. Occasionally we had the impression that our projects were directed more from the Pentagon than from Frunze Street. When funds for Dyna-Soar were cut, we were immediately accused of wasting money. When we heard that the American military had renewed interest in the project, we were given extra money again.

Two specific projects emerged from these space dreams.

One proposal called for launching a phased system of satellites into the low orbit then available, satellites capable of receiving, processing, and transmitting radar and other information (these were called "US" for *upravlyaye-myi sputnik*). That was to be carried out within the next few years. The satellites were supposed to maintain position in orbit on commands from earth. When their service life expired they would automatically move to a higher orbit and turn into space junk. Such a system would allow continuous and uninterrupted observation of the whole surface of the earth, both land and water, and give warning of catastrophes or relocations of enemy military units or ships. That would be up to the customer. In the West it later received the name RORSAT.

Another satellite was even more exotic. In those years specialists argued until they were hoarse about the possibility of space docking, about whether two spaceships were capable of finding each other. People disagreed about whether it would be possible. Chelomei was one of those who not only had faith, but resolved to prove his faith in action.

A new satellite, later known by its unclassified name Polyot, was conceived as a rolling stone in space. It was designed to learn how to change its orbit by precisely assigned magnitudes, not only its altitude—difficult enough in itself—but also its orbital inclination. That would take an enormous effort, comparable to the cost of launching an object into orbit. Receiving only hints from earth, the satellite would independently find its brother or enemy in space, recognize it, and then move to the assigned distance.

If the Polyot carried a bomb, however, it could attack an enemy satellite, like a "kamikaze," destroying both itself and the enemy. Polyots so equipped were secretly designated "IS" (*istrebitel' sputnikov*, "satellite destroyer").

CHELOMEI DREAMS OF SPACE

Father worried about the possible appearance of American spy satellites. First we had the problem of the U-2 planes and now there was a new danger, this time from space. However, for the time being the danger of observers appearing in orbit was a theoretical one, whereas real American spy planes flew over our territory regularly, and thinking about them kept him awake at night. Fortunately, they had not appeared during the previous few months. Father considered this a good sign from the American president. In the same way, Father refrained from making the caustic remarks common in those years. Neither he nor, he thought, Eisenhower wanted to disturb the growing trust in our relations.

By 1960 a great deal had changed in antiaircraft defense. Along with the new Grushin S-75s,[14] there were also the Sukhoi T-3 interceptors,[15] which were capable of climbing to the desired altitude of more than twenty kilometers. Not to speak of the new MIG-21, which could fly even higher. Father brought up the subject of the U-2 constantly. But his tone had changed: now the intruder would not escape punishment.

But what could be done about satellites? Father asked chief designers and the military, but without result. It was more a question of international law than of technology. However, international law had not yet confronted the problems of space.

Because of the laws of mechanics, satellites—of course—do not respect national borders. The entire planet is their home. That needed no explanation. After Korolyov's launches, concepts like orbit, trajectory, and orbital period became part of every housewife's vocabulary. No one could distinguish peaceful satellites from intrusive spy satellites without flying near them

---

14. S-75—"System 75" (called the SA-2 in the West)—an antiaircraft "ground-to-air" missile designed by the bureaus of Pyotr Dmitriyevich Grushin and Aleksandr Andreyevich Raspletin.

15. High-altitude fighter-interceptor, designed by the bureau of Pavel Osipovich Sukhoi, now registered as SU-9.

and examining them closely. No instruments from the earth's surface could identify spy satellites. During one of our talks I suggested that we should put up with this, since there seemed to be no other course. Father was furious: How could we allow foreign satellites to fly over our country without permission and stick their noses wherever they wanted? Intellectually he realized that my view was a valid one, but he hoped and wanted to believe that our scientists would find a solution. Chelomei's maneuverable space interceptor might help to solve the problem.

At the beginning of April, Father left for a vacation in the Crimea. Those demanding international visits were all behind him. He was just back from France and a still more exacting summit meeting lay ahead.

Chelomei had been asking for a meeting with Father for a long time. He wanted to tell Father about his plans and report the latest achievements, but Chelomei's priority was to receive authorization for his participation in space research. The meeting had been postponed repeatedly. It was easier to find time during a vacation, and Father invited Dementyev, Butoma, Chelomei, Admiral Gorshkov, and our main specialist on gyro systems, Viktor Ivanovich Kuznetsov.

Aside from problems related to the development of naval armaments, Father wanted to talk about improving missile accuracy. That depended directly on gyro technology. Specialists thought that it would require several billion rubles to create a modern gyro industry. Father wanted to consult specialists one more time before making a final decision. A huge sum of money was involved, and we would have to sweat blood to get it.

Learning that Chelomei was leaving for the Crimea, I asked to come along. By that time I had joined the circle of Chelomei's closest colleagues and participated in developing all his new ideas. Therefore my request did not seem too impertinent, especially since it was my Father he was flying to see. Vladimir Nikolayevich did not object; however it was Father who had to make the final decision. I called him in the Crimea and received his approval.

The Crimea welcomed us with a warm bright sun, flower-covered mountains, and a blue sea—quite a contrast to Moscow, with its dirty, melting snow.

First of all, Father took us all for a walk to admire the surrounding area and especially his pride and joy, the cherry trees in bloom on the mountainside near the house.

After lunch we proceeded to business. It was too cool to sit outside, besides which the wind was getting stronger and would make it hard to keep papers on the table. We settled down on the first floor, in a room off a large terrace open to the sea.

Chelomei began with his usual report: he talked about various successful projects. He emphasized that the first of the new submarines for the P-5 were ready to be launched. Tests of homing missiles capable of hitting enemy ships were continuing.

At that point Father looked interested and interrupted the speaker. He referred once again to the Kometa and asked how much better the new missiles were. Chelomei became emotional—according to him, it couldn't hold a candle to our P series. Father smiled: "Every cook praises his own broth."

After a short break we continued the meeting.

Father waited until everyone was seated, then spoke first. He began by talking about Korolyov's achievements in space. He called him our magician. Then he moved on to military missiles. "Korolyov is not so successful in that field. He doesn't have the resources. We brought Yangel in at the right time." Father moved on to his favorite subject and talked for a long time about tests of the R-16, which were to be held in the autumn, and about the need to put all missiles in silos. He also mentioned that specialists had laughed at first at his proposal to put missiles underground, but that he had turned out to be right. Father often went off onto one of these digressions. He sometimes got carried away and talked for hours, following his own peculiar logic and deviating more and more from the original subject. That day he spoke for half an hour before finally stopping. As if just noticing Chelomei, who was fiddling nervously with some small pieces of drawing paper, Father returned to the subject of our meeting: "Let's hear what innovation Comrade Chelomei wants to talk about. He has proven himself in developing cruise missiles, but in space he's a novice. However, sometimes a fresh eye will notice what old experts might overlook." Father waved his hand vaguely, inviting Vladimir Nikolayevich to talk.

Chelomei began with what was most important. The era of single launches into space would soon end, no matter how powerful the rockets were. A single launch could not send into orbit everything necessary for a long-term project. In his opinion, the future belonged to complex, guided space systems, consisting of many components, manned spaceships, automatic satellites, and devices designed to communicate with earth. They would have to cooperate with each other, meeting and separating, exchanging loads and information. In a word, functioning as a single integrated mechanism or, more precisely, organism.

Chelomei handed Father one drawing after another. Father looked at them attentively and silently passed them around. Vladimir Nikolayevich drew a picture of enormous orbital factory-home space complexes. Space factories could produce things not possible to manufacture on earth. Special spaceships capable of lifting heavy payloads would be needed to link them with earth. He said emphatically: "They must be winged spaceships—the wings, by relying on the atmosphere, will help to deliver heavy payloads into orbit and perform the maneuvers necessary to return to earth. Of course, there are many technical problems. The primary one is work under extremely high temperatures. We should begin with that problem."

Concluding his discussion of the peaceful uses of space, Vladimir Nikolayevich passed on to military matters. In his opinion, future military operations would inevitably involve space. Whoever controlled space would be able to dictate conditions on earth. If we were not able to confront our adversary in space, we could not avoid defeat.

The next series of drawings showed military operations in space. One drawing depicted a huge orbital station, a whole city, surrounded by round, saucer-like missiles. Some were contained in special niches, waiting to be used, while others raced toward enemy spaceships, some of which were hidden by the blinding flashes of nuclear explosions.

One picture showed a drum that looked like a crab, with a multitude of arms that had grabbed hold of a foreign body and was pulling it into the opening of its mother ship.

Father asked how long it would take to create a system to fight against American spy satellites. Chelomei took only a minute to think it over. "By 1962—or 1963," he answered, but immediately warned: "It's much easier to knock down a satellite than to find out whether it's a spy or not. Especially since it's easy to camouflage a spy as an innocent research object."

"The question of whether it's possible to determine a satellite's purpose from the earth's surface is one for radar specialists," said Chelomei. He added regretfully that it was very unlikely that we could, within the next few years, identify a spy satellite and prove that it belonged to an intelligence agency.

Father looked through the drawings, then put them down on the table and asked: "Does that mean that today—or more likely tomorrow—we won't be able to do anything if the Americans launch spy satellites into space?"

There was silence. No one had a quick answer.

"We'll work on it," said Chelomei finally.

"All right, what else do you have?" said Father, realizing that further questions would be useless.

Chelomei moved on to the next subject. He thought it was possible to create a space system to intercept ballistic missiles. Space, in Vladimir Nikolayevich's words, could also serve as a base for deploying counterstrike weapons. Nuclear warheads located on space stations or simply turning in orbit—global missiles, as he called them—could wait for decades to be used. If they were surrounded by multiple false targets, it would be easy to render any counteraction ineffective. When needed, they would race down on command. An adversary would have far less time to activate a defensive system and it would not be clear where the strike had originated.

That was approximately how Chelomei described our not too distant future. Those present, looking depressed, made no comment.

"Whether the development of space technology will take a military or a peaceful direction depends on politicians. In any case, the future belongs to controlled systems. We have to set to work creating them now," Chelomei said, concluding the first part of his report. He moved on to specific tasks.

"We propose to begin working on a controlled multi-satellite space flight," said Chelomei. "For that we will need a unified system, composed of a rocket and a series of satellites."

Aside from everything else, Chelomei very much wanted to avoid being dependent on either Korolyov or Yangel—at present they could send something into orbit if they wanted to, and they could hold it back if they wanted to.

There was still another reason. Chelomei planned to encroach on "someone else's" territory through space, to make his intercontinental ballistic missile better than those of his rivals. He was simply itching to do it. He was still afraid to talk about it openly. He knew that would cause an uproar: everyone, from Ustinov to Korolyov and Yangel, would begin attacking him and accuse him of squandering money. He was most concerned about the latter accusation. It would be easier, he thought, to obtain approval for the whole package. By the time they understood everything that was involved, it would be too late. He had brought along materials on components of the rocket in a separate folder. Chelomei intended to produce them only if the meeting went well.

Father asked about the rocket. This was the point at which Chelomei was most vulnerable. Why couldn't the satellites be launched by an existing rocket? The R-7, for example. Chelomei had an answer ready: The R-7 was too powerful and too expensive a carrier for the multiple launches proposed in his project. A balanced "rocket-spaceship" system was needed. Experience had shown that boosters of various classes and degrees of power were required—each with its particular task.

Chelomei confidently described the need for an organic fusion of all components of the system, presented his arguments against using the R-7, and then described the technology, without mentioning a ballistic variant. He repeated his main thesis: from the very beginning, the aviation industry had higher standards and better equipment. Chelomei promised to build a rocket that would be both lighter and stronger by the application of welding, cellular structures, and other innovative technologies developed for the production of supersonic aircraft.

The engine would operate with a new oxidizer—nitrogen tetroxide. Like nitric acid, it did not require cooling, and it was substantially more efficient. Chelomei didn't mention the fact that nitrogen tetroxide was extraordinarily toxic—to assure safety was his problem. The fuel would remain the same as with the R-16—asymmetrical dimethyl hydrazine.

Dementyev nodded approvingly, but said nothing. No one knew better than he what Ustinov was capable of! When they were equals, he could compete, but now Ustinov was on top, a deputy chairman of the Council of Ministers! In his heart Dementyev supported Chelomei, but wanted him to win the initial fight by himself. If he succeeded, Dementyev would support him with all his production might.

Vladimir Nikolayevich mentioned as yet another reason to support his program: the question, which had recently become acute, of providing work for aircraft plants, especially those making bombers. He proposed putting them to work making his rocket. This idea couldn't help but appeal to Father. Here Chelomei was sure of success. He was also sure of Dementyev's support. The minister would naturally prefer to have his designs produced at his own plants. It would be easier to administer, and there was no danger that if you didn't act quickly, the plants might "drift off" and you'd never get them back.

Father looked with interest at the drawing, as if thinking something over, and finally asked: "Wouldn't it be possible to use the booster as a ballistic missile?"

Chelomei beamed. He had been steering toward this moment like an experienced fisherman landing a large pike.

Retrieving a sketch from the sacred folder, he placed it in front of Father.

"Nikita Sergeyevich, without making any changes, you have a missile able to hurl a warhead weighing several megatons to an intercontinental distance. We've even named it the universal missile, the UR-200."

"He's a sly one!" said Father, turning to his companions. "He wants to horn in on Korolyov and Yangel. Well, competition is a good thing, especially since we'll get an intercontinental missile out of it. Let him try."

Father began talking about how important the proposed program seemed to him. If war reached into space—he thought Chelomei's arguments were very convincing—then we must not allow ourselves to be caught unprepared.

"We have to find the money for it," said Father with a sigh.

Chelomei was triumphant. Now Ustinov could not interfere because Khrushchev was on his side. The future would show that his joy was premature.

The discussion continued. Father asked Dementyev what he thought of these new ideas.

"Vladimir Nikolayevich and I have talked everything over in detail," responded Pyotr Vasilyevich. "We have already drawn up plans to put the rocket into production. We'll be able to do it."

"But what about engines?" asked Father. "Yangel can't share Glushko even with Korolyov, and now how are you going to fit in?"

There was a note of caution in his voice. The growing conflict between the chief designers was beginning to worry him considerably.

"We'll solve everything ourselves, using aviation facilities," said Dementyev. "We can work with an expert engine designer, Semyon Ariyevich Kosberg, from the Voronezh Aviation Engine Factory. He'll tackle the problem."

"O.K., that's good. The less monopoly there is the better," Father said uncertainly. He had never heard of Kosberg.

In conclusion, Chelomei brought up a delicate question: his design bureau had too much to do. If an aviation team that was not doing such vital work were joined to it, the new tasks could be solved more quickly. Vladimir Nikolayevich didn't mention any particular team. If his idea was approved, let the minister have the last word. Father didn't object.

"Well, what does the committee chairman think?" he said, turning to Dementyev.

The question did not catch Pyotr Vasilyevich by surprise. He and Chelomei had been talking it over for a long time, weighing all the pros and cons. Nevertheless, Dementyev started from the beginning. Mikoyan, Lavochkin, Sukhoi—they could not be touched, their field was front-line aviation, which we could not do without. Father nodded in agreement. Passenger aviation depended on Ilyushin and Antonov. Tupolev was out of the question.

In the minister's opinion, that left only Myasishchev. He had an outstanding facility in Fili: a large factory and an extremely modern design bureau. If the proposal were accepted, there would not only be a place to design the new rocket, but its production could be organized right there, on the spot.

Myasishchev was presently completing work on a new supersonic strategic bomber, the M-50. If the design bureau were reoriented toward rockets, he would have to abandon work on the bomber.

I had heard about this proposal earlier and was very sorry to hear about the beautiful M-50. Just before this meeting I had even mentioned this to Chelomei, but he just brushed me aside—bombers had outlived their day.

Father wanted to make sure that the M-50's range did not extend beyond Europe and that its maximum altitude would not allow it to fly over borders defended by antiaircraft missiles. Dementyev confirmed those facts, and only added that a lot of money had been spent on the plane's development. His last words caught Father's attention.

He held the minister's gaze and, not so much asking as confirming, said: "And if we begin production of the M-50, we'll be spending a great deal more?"

"That's true, Nikita Sergeyevich," agreed Dementyev.

"And we won't have gained anything!" exclaimed Father.

Those present were silent. Father thought for a bit longer, and then gave his approval to preparing the appropriate government decree. The M-50 made its last flight during the air show at Tushino Airport on July 9, 1961, impressing the audience with the perfection of its form and generating a host of conjectures abroad. It was then sent to its eternal resting place in the aviation museum.

That was how the decision was made to merge the largest scientific-production facility with Chelomei's design bureau. It would be hard to overestimate its role in carrying out the country's rocket and space program. Famous missiles, the heavy space booster Proton and the manned space station Salyut, all originated at this facility.

After the Crimean conference, a third participant appeared in the space rocket field, one who simultaneously competed in space with Korolyov and in rockets with Yangel.

Both Ustinov's apparat in the Kremlin and Nedelin's in the Ministry of Defense gave Chelomei a hostile reception. The flock refused to accept this "ugly duckling" from someone else's Ministry of Aviation.

PART TWO

CHAPTER FIVE

THE RACE

THE INTRUDERS

When our group arrived in the Crimea to visit Father, he already knew that an unidentified aircraft was violating our airspace. His guests also knew about the unpleasant incident. However, aside from the time and track of the flight, he had no reliable information. The plane had crossed the border on April 9, 1960, from the direction of Pakistan. It was not detected until 4:47 A.M., when it was already deep inside Soviet territory and 250 kilometers from the Soviet-Afghan border. Our aircraft had not been able to shoot it down.

T-3 (SU-9) interceptors were beginning to arrive at Air Force units, but only those in the border areas in the east and west. Within the country's interior, they were known mostly by hearsay. Meanwhile the intruder was approaching Semipalatinsk without interference. A MIG-19, piloted by Captain Vladimir Karachevsky, was sent to Semipalatinsk from Perm. Karachevsky was supposed to land at an airfield near Orsk to refuel and then resume the chase. For some reason he was flying alone, although normally two planes would have been assigned this mission. He did not even reach Orsk. On his approach to Sverdlovsk he began to lose altitude over a forest. He ejected, but too late and too low. He was killed.

When they issued the order, the local military command knew very well that a MIG-19 could not reach an altitude of 70,000 to 75,000 feet, much less try to shoot down what they knew to be a U-2. They therefore ordered two "transit" T-3s equipped with air-to-air missiles—the planes just happened to be at the Perm antiaircraft base—to prepare quickly for takeoff.

The fighters were being moved from the factory to a border region and had landed in Perm to refuel. They were quite capable of intercepting the intruder, but would not have enough fuel to return "home."

The Semipalatinsk test site had its own airfield, but ordinary Air Force pilots were not permitted to land there. A special "atomic" pass was required. The local military headquarters sent a request to Moscow. Since it was the middle of the night, naturally only the air defense duty officer was there. He was already aware of the border violation.

The duty officer followed regulations. He woke up the Air Defense commander, Marshal Sergei Biryuzov. Biryuzov informed the defense minister, Marshal Rodion Malinovsky, of the intruder. Malinovsky telephoned Yefim Slavsky, the minister of medium machine building. He was the only one who could take responsibility for allowing "uncertified" pilots to land at his airfield. While all this telephoning was going on, time passed and it was 7 A.M. before the unit finally received permission to land at Semipalatinsk. By then the U-2 had finished photographing the nuclear test site and was heading toward Lake Balkhash, where the pilot was interested in the Air Defense missile test site located near the village of Sary-Shagan on Lake Balkhash. The T-3s tried to catch him, but without success.

On the way to Lake Balkhash the U-2 deviated from its course to film a strategic bomber base and the TU-95s parked on it.

No antiaircraft defenses awaited the test site's guest. It had neither duty officers nor antiaircraft missiles ready for launching. No antiaircraft defense personnel were stationed at test sites to protect them. However, tests of new antiaircraft rockets capable of hitting a plane at a great height were nearing completion at one of the launch pads. But the rockets were equipped with mechanisms to measure the degree of error in firing—not warheads. The workers at the test site had not succeeded in installing the warheads, which were stored a hundred kilometers away. Those in charge of carrying out the tests had the daring idea of firing at the intruder anyway, but quickly rejected it: there was absolutely no possibility of hitting the target, and they couldn't bring themselves to waste expensive hardware and disrupt the tests.

After filming the new air defense installations, the U-2 headed for the ballistic missile test site at Tyura-Tam. There, it turned out, they were equally unprepared for the encounter. Having successfully carried out its entire mission, the pilot turned back on a course that took him across the Turkmenian town of Mary and toward the Iranian border.

The Air Defense command made a last desperate attempt to shoot down the intruder. Technically, it was possible. An air defense regiment in the area had just received new T-3s, although they were not equipped with missiles. Inventive technicians coped with that problem; they somehow mounted missiles from a MIG-19 on Senior Lieutenant Kudel's T-3, and he was ordered to take off. However, there was no chance to test the effectiveness of the quickly equipped hybrid, since the U-2 was at the interceptor's extreme range and outside the operational zone of the regiment's radar stations. A neighboring battery was asked to assist. Unfortunately, their radar personnel had never worked with T-3s. As a result, they lost the target.

A second pilot, Captain Doroshenko, was also unsuccessful, but for a different reason. There wasn't time to rearm a second plane, so he took off without missiles, on the off-chance that he could do something. He had some difficulty in flying the new plane. After reaching an altitude of seventeen and a half thousand meters, he was amazed to see the American. The foreign plane was flying about three kilometers higher than Doroshenko. The pilot, who had not mastered flying the T-3, couldn't manage to climb those three kilometers. He had to return home empty-handed. With that the pursuit ended. From that point to the country's borders there was simply nothing available that could intercept the U-2.

The conference with Chelomei couldn't be squeezed into one day. As the sun began to set, Father proposed postponing its conclusion until the following day. His guests said their farewells. I stayed at the dacha with Father.

We accompanied the visitors to their car and then set out on a walk.

We walked for a half hour without speaking.

I took the opportunity to ask: "How could Air Defense have missed the plane?"

"They overslept," said Father, though he used a cruder expression.

He didn't bother to give any details, preferring to avoid the unpleasant subject. I told him about the telemetric missiles at Balkhash and complained that such an important and secret site had now been entirely revealed to the Americans. Father shared my concern, saying that the Air Defense system must be extended to firing ranges; antiaircraft missiles and planes must be based at them too.

"This should all have been done before. Now that they've accomplished their objectives, when will they poke their noses in again?" said Father, sounding more annoyed than sorry.

He was eager to teach the insolent Americans a lesson—and now, when the opportunity was there, Air Defense had botched it. He had to swallow another bitter pill. I asked if the Foreign Ministry was preparing to send an official protest. It seemed to me that an official note should no longer be considered a sign of weakness, since we were now capable of downing an intruder.

Father didn't answer directly, but began to talk about how he was at a loss to explain why the Americans had sent a spy plane over our country at such a time, after his successful visit to the United States and before the conference in Paris. He would not concede the possibility that the president had approved the flight. What use would it be to him?

Father thought that Allen Dulles had given a green light for the flight without asking the president. He assumed that the Dulles brothers didn't give special consideration to the president. Father referred again to those unfortunate notes that John Foster Dulles had passed to Eisenhower in Geneva.

Father grew agitated: then he stopped to catch his breath and in a different, calmer tone of voice observed that none of this was accidental. It wasn't just a case of irrepressible curiosity on the part of intelligence agents. Someone wanted to expose our weakness to the world on the eve of the conference.

"Gromyko prepared a protest note, just as the situation called for," Father continued, "but we put it aside. Why give our enemies the satisfaction?"

In his opinion, a protest note would not play a positive role. The unavoidably acrimonious words would only draw us into contentious arguments, rather than contributing to a calm search for solutions in Paris. He thought that a protest note would push the Americans toward taking a position of strength, which would inevitably lead to a confrontation. That would be a loss all around.

Father thought that the provocation would not be repeated. Allen Dulles would not dare to hide from the president the fact that the intelligence flight had taken place. Father had no doubt that Eisenhower would not approve another such flight.

In general, the Presidium of the Central Committee agreed with Father's proposal not to send diplomatic démarches. At the same time, Marshal Malinovsky was given a strong reprimand. A directive went out to heighten vigilance: Air Defense missile units were put on the alert, rockets were armed with warheads, and Air Defense fighters were put on round-the-clock duty at airfields. As usual, we were preparing after the fact, not before.

Much is still unclear about these U-2 flights in April and in May of 1960.

It is said that the purpose of the April 9 flight was to photograph the launch installations for the first Soviet intercontinental missile at Tyura-Tam. Who was threatened by this single launch site? Why was it necessary to photograph it before the summit meeting?

U.S. Secretary of State Christian Herter was also asking himself that question: "Like everyone else, I was thinking constantly about the summit in those days. The real question was: how urgently was the information needed and what time of the year was preferable to obtain it? From the technical aspect, the period selected was better than any other. From the diplomatic viewpoint, I thought that complications would arise in connection with the president's intention to visit Russia later on."

For the May 1 flight (it was the twenty-fourth U-2 intrusion into Soviet air space), the Americans chose the route already tested in May of 1957. From Peshawar (in Pakistan) the U-2 headed toward Tyura-Tam. From there its path lay toward Sverdlovsk, or more precisely, toward Chelyabinsk-40 (Kyshtym), a nuclear industrial center. Several military airfields were supposed to be photographed along the way. The next main target was Plesetsk. According to CIA information, a launch site for intercontinental missiles was being built there. (I remind the reader that two launch sites for the R-7 were activated in December 1959 and another two were planned for 1961.)

From Plesetsk it was a stone's throw to Norway, to the air base at Bodo.

I simply cannot agree that a survey of these rather interesting sites was so necessary that it was worth the risk of disrupting the summit conference. Of course, intelligence lives in its own world and by its own rules, which are often unintelligible to the uninitiated. Field operatives risk life and limb for a few more map reference points and a bit more data.

The fact that the operation was carried out on May Day shows it was not undertaken by chance. It seemed to have been arranged to goad Father into responding irrationally.

Of course, it's possible to take a different view: on a holiday it's easier to sneak in without being noticed. However, that's only true on the first attempt. It wouldn't be reasonable for the Americans to expect our Air Defense system to go back to sleep so quickly.

May 1 dawned pleasantly warm and sunny. After breakfast we were to leave for Red Square. Father would be on the Mausoleum, while the rest of us had passes to one of the side stands on the left. That had been the custom since Stalin's day.

Father came downstairs right after eight o'clock, looking gloomy. He was obviously not in a holiday mood. He sat down silently at the table. There was only the sound of the spoon clinking against the sides of his glass of tea. We also fell silent, somehow subdued. No one asked: "What happened?" He would tell us himself, if it were possible. A great deal could happen in our vast country that we were not supposed to know at home.

Father drank his tea quickly. He wanted to get to the Kremlin, where the members of the Presidium had already gathered.

So something serious had happened! But what?

I got up to accompany Father to the car. You could hear music beyond the high stone wall of the residence. Loudspeakers on Vorobyovskoye Highway were on at full blast. Father usually drove everyone to the Kremlin on a holiday, but this time we had to get there on our own.

At the gate Father finally shared the news.

"They flew over again," he said with annoyance.

"How many?" I asked.

"Like before—one. It's flying at a great height. This time it was detected at the border, at the same place. Malinovsky called me at dawn, around six o'clock." That was all Father himself knew.

The U-2 had crossed the Soviet border at 5:36 A.M.

During the night Father switched the "Kremlin line" to the bedroom. The phone lay on a bedside table near his head. Just in case.

We approached the car.

"Will they shoot it down?" I asked.

"That's a silly question," retorted Father. "Malinovsky said that they're sending up planes and preparing to launch the Grushin S-75s. They claim that they'll shoot it down—unless they miss. You know perfectly well that we have only a few T-3s there and that missiles have a small operational radius at that altitude. It's all up to chance: whether it runs into a missile, whether they don't miss it," he said, repeating the defense minister's words. "If they hit it . . ."

"But where is it now?" I hurried to get in one last question, since Father was already getting ready to jump into the ZIL limousine, whose door was being held open by the head of the guard unit.

"In the area of Tyura-Tam. He took a direct course there after the border, but who knows where he'll go after that," concluded Father as he got into the front seat of the limousine.

The car took off, and I returned to the house, discouraged. "Giving away the secret" to the rest of the family was out of the question. I was tormented by the thought that the intruder might escape.

We arrived at Red Square at about nine-thirty. The stands quickly filled up. The same people gathered there every year: generals, aviation and other defense designers, officials from the Council of Ministers and the Central Committee. I looked for Ivan Dmitriyevich Serbin, head of the Central Committee's Department of Defense Technology.

He told me the following: the intruder reached Tyura-Tam without interference, maneuvered to obtain the best camera angles, and then flew further north. He was apparently heading toward Sverdlovsk. Serbin thought he was probably not planning to return to Pakistan as before, but intended to fly directly across the entire country to Norway or Britain. That way he could take in Plesetsk, Arkhangelsk, Severodvinsk, and Severomorsk.

As a result, in one flight the spy would uncover a multitude of secrets.

"But why wasn't he shot down over Tyura-Tam?" I asked.

Serbin just waved his hand: "Something always happens in our Air Defense system. This time, I suppose, they'll use the holiday as their excuse."

But this is what happened: three S-75 batteries were guarding the test site, not many for such a large area. There were no fighters based there.

The U.S. pilot, Francis Gary Powers, was lucky. I was wrong. In a mere three weeks the Air Defense system had indeed gone back to sleep. One of the missile battalions was taken off duty before the May 1 holiday: that was called for by the schedule. Naturally, no one was working on a holiday. The soldiers were sitting in their barracks, and the officers had scattered in various directions. The plane passed over their position and flew peacefully onward. The other two missile battalions were located in distant corners of the test site. They had been placed on alert status, and one could only hope that they had been successful. But fate was watching over the American. He approached the outer limits of engageability. They had him on their radar.

In a few seconds they would have fired, but at the last moment he turned away.

"If he moves toward Sverdlovsk," Serbin continued, "he'll be faced by antiaircraft missiles—several batteries of S-75s were deployed there recently—and interceptors. MIG-19s have been transferred there from Perm. But not much can be expected from them. Fortunately, a pair of T-3s are at the Sverdlovsk airfield, but without their pilots. The planes were on their way from their Siberian factory to their unit in Baranovichi, in Belorussia, and were delayed by bad weather in the capital of the Urals.

"They're looking for the pilots, but will they be found on a holiday? If the spy gets past Sverdlovsk, there won't be another chance to intercept him before Arkhangelsk, and then Severomorsk. There's nothing in between. However, in Plesetsk there is a battery of S-75s, but no one knows if the men have been placed on alert status or are also off duty."

"So he could escape," I lamented.

"He could," responded Ivan Dmitriyevich.

"But how will we know?" I said impatiently.

"Biryuzov is at his command center. After Sverdlovsk he'll come and let us know," Serbin said, trying to calm me.

That couldn't calm me! I felt as if they were all reconciled to the fact that the intruder would escape.

The country's Air Defense command center was located near the Kremlin, outside the Ministry of Defense on the Frunzensky Embankment. It had been tracking the intruder since it had crossed the border—so far without result. Biryuzov was sitting behind a large table, facing a map of the whole country on a lighted screen, which covered the entire wall. The small and hated plane moved across it in spurts. A sergeant sitting behind the screen moved the image of the plane. Every few minutes he was given new data on the coordinates, speed, and altitude of the intruder. In the pauses between reports the sergeant moved the foreign spy plane intuitively, so that sometimes it had to be moved back. That meant that Powers had changed course.

To Biryuzov's left sat Marshal Yevgeny Savitsky, the commander of Air Defense Aviation. That day his code name, "Dragon," sounded ominous. To his right was Colonel-General Pavel Kuleshov, in charge of antiaircraft artillery and missiles. Staff officers milled around behind the commanders.

The small plane, drawing away from Tyura-Tam, turned toward the north and slightly west. The U-2 was heading toward Sverdlovsk.

Having been alerted, the missile batteries around Sverdlovsk were waiting for their target, but aircraft were to begin the operation.

Savitsky had been unable to find out from his subordinates what was going on. They reported that the MIG-19s flown from Perm were being quickly refueled, but the T-3 pilots had not yet been found.

Finally they reported that one of the pilots, Captain Igor Mentyukov, had been caught at the last minute at the bus stop. He was brought to headquarters on the double. There he was stunned to hear that Moscow had ordered him to take off at once. The enemy plane was approaching at an altitude of more than twenty kilometers. The only hope rested on the T-3 and on him, Mentyukov.

The pilot tried to explain—the plane was not armed and he himself was not ready to fly. The target would fly over the city before he could be suited up.

The general reported this to Moscow. A categorical order came back from Savitsky: take off at once in whatever you're wearing, ram the intruder. It meant certain death to ram at an altitude of twenty kilometers, where there's no air to breathe and internal pressure would blow a man up into a balloon in an instant.

But you don't argue with orders. Moreover Mentyukov didn't know what was on board the intruder, a harmless camera or a nuclear bomb.

"Take care of my wife and mother," he exclaimed. His wife was expecting a baby.

"Don't worry, we'll take care of everything," answered someone Mentyukov couldn't make out. He ran to the plane in the dress uniform he had put on for the holiday. A few minutes later he took off. The U-2 was already in the intercept zone. Now it was being tracked by ground-based Air Force and missile radars. However, the latter could only look at the target, since the plane was outside their range.

On orders from ground control, Mentyukov began to maneuver: he reached the same altitude as the U-2 and approached from the rear. The radar control officer reported his distance from the target to be fifteen and a half miles. The pilot engaged his radar, but it did not function properly. There was such a mess on the screen that it was impossible to see the target. The interceptor was racing forward on its afterburner at a speed of two thousand kilometers an hour when a shouted order came from ground control: "The target is ahead! Look out!" But how can someone see a target when he's approaching at a one-third of a mile a second? And when he can see it, he doesn't have time to carry out a maneuver to ram the enemy. The T-3 overflew the U-2, but neither pilot saw the other. I think Mentyukov must have sighed with relief. He didn't have enough fuel for a second approach. He was ordered to turn off the afterburner, and the plane, losing speed, plunged downward and came in for a landing.

In 1996 the former captain, now retired lieutenant colonel, Igor Mentyukov gave an interview to the Moscow paper *Trud* in which he said that he saw the intruder plane: at the instant of attack the U-2 went into a right turn and changed course. Mentyukov didn't manage to turn after him and missed.

In the same interview Mentyukov claims that he carried out Savitsky's order, that Powers's plane flew through the exhaust from his fighter and broke apart. It's conceivable that Mentyukov saw the U-2—that's certainly not impossible—but the second part of his statement is a fabrication of the first water. The pilot of a fighter flying at two thousand kilometers an hour is hardly able to see what's happening far behind him. Moreover, Powers flew several tens of kilometers further on before the fateful moment.

SUCCESS

The missile radar operators saw on their screens that the pursuer had disappeared, the target was again alone, but still outside range. The missile battalion's chief of staff, Major Mikhail Voronov, counted off the seconds to himself: "One, one more, now the intruder will enter within firing range."

Powers did not suspect the drama that was unfolding around him in the air and on the ground, in Sverdlovsk and in Moscow. Noting the assigned reference point on the map, he turned toward Kyshtym. He still had to photograph Chelyabinsk-40.

"The target is moving away," reported the operator.

"The target is moving away," Major Voronov transmitted to the next level of command.

"The target is moving away," they informed Biryuzov in Moscow.

The pilot assiduously avoided dangerous places, as if he knew and saw where missiles were based. Kuleshov suggested that perhaps the spy was equipped with a special receiver that reacted to signals from the Air Defense radar detection system. The situation was becoming catastrophic. There was no opportunity to send up another T-3. Savitsky ordered a formation of four MIG-19s into the air. Biryuzov didn't believe that the interceptors could catch the intruder, but he had to do something.

At that moment Major Voronov was informed that the target was returning and would be within range in a few seconds.

Instructions called for firing two missiles, but they decided to launch three, to be on the safe side.

The launch crew proceeded automatically, just as during training. But after the button was pressed only one missile ejected. The other two didn't move.

Voronov felt his heart grow cold: "Failure." It seemed that fate was really protecting Powers. What happened was that at the moment of launch the truck carrying the guidance cabin blocked the path of two of the missiles as they revolved toward the target. The launches were automatically aborted. The lone missile now approaching the target was the only hope. Operators had already guided it into the strike zone.

Finally a fiery point appeared in the sky. Several seconds later came the faint sound of an explosion. This occurred at 8:53 in the morning, Moscow time. The target disappeared from the radar screens, which were covered with greenish flakes of "snow." That was the way passive interference would look if chaff were ejected from a plane in order to confuse radar operators. It would also look that way if the plane had been hit and was breaking up. Neither Voronov in the battalion nor people in the regiment could believe they had been successful.

At this point, as if fate took a hand, a radar officer, Senior Lieutenant Eduard Feldblum, reported distinctly: "The target has discharged chaff and is performing an evasive maneuver."

"After the missile launch, the target released chaff and performed an evasive maneuver" reported Voronov to his command post in Sverdlovsk. The information didn't go any further. They decided not to forward it to Moscow until the situation was clarified—especially since the target had reappeared on the commander's radar plotting board. In the absence of new information, the sergeant-major in Sverdlovsk acted just like his colleague in Moscow and intuitively moved the marker on the screen.

At that moment Voronov's neighboring battery, under the command of Captain Nikolai Sheludko, fired its three missiles at the disintegrating plane.

As reported later by experts, Voronov's missile did not hit the plane but exploded a little behind it. Powers was lucky. The plane shook, the U-2's long wings folded, then tore off and fluttered slowly down to earth. Of course, the pilot could not see this. He saw only the sky, the boundless sky, revolving before his eyes. He also felt that his seat was shoved forward from the force of the explosion and realized that his legs were pinned against the instrument panel. It was impossible for him to eject and to destroy the plane. But again Powers was lucky. He was saved by one of Captain Sheludko's missiles, which hit fragments of the plane at a height of six thousand meters, relatively close to the ground. The pilot's legs were freed by this new explosion and he threw himself awkwardly over the side of the fuselage. His parachute worked perfectly.

On the ground they couldn't believe that the target had been destroyed. They reported to Moscow that military actions were continuing. The imaginary intruder discharged chaff and changed altitude, but didn't succeed in leaving. However, they couldn't shoot him down. He turned into a mirage. God only knows what was going on in the sky for the following half hour.

Missile radar operators scoured the sky, hunting for the target. They kept finding and losing it. Sometimes there even seemed to be several targets, but no one asked himself the question: "Where did the others come from? Only one was tracked from the border." People were gripped by a kind of nervous frenetic activity.

Meanwhile, the MIG-19s took off, carrying out Savitsky's orders. Captain Boris Ayvazian was the first to take off, followed by his wingman, Senior Lieutenant Sergei Safronov.

They had to accelerate and then, making use of their great speed, jump up to the U-2's altitude and try to hit the intruder. I have already referred to this innovative maneuver conceived by Artyom Mikoyan and Marshal Savitsky. The pilots had only a few seconds to accomplish the maneuver. Moreover, what would be the relative positions of the fighter and its target? The maneuver had been performed many times previously, but none of the pilots had ever even seen the target. Nevertheless, for want of anything better, they continued to "jump up."

In the air the pilots could not find the intruder. Only somewhere far off Ayvazian noticed an inverted trace of something falling toward the earth. Command headquarters relayed: "Radar operators report that the target has released chaff and has descended to an altitude of twelve thousand meters. Find it!"

They didn't succeed. Ayvazian and Safronov were alone at an altitude of twelve kilometers—but not for long. A few minutes later they were approached by two MIGs and Captain Ayvazian heard over his radio: "Look sharp! Target ahead." This was directed to the pilot of the interceptor that had scrambled after him. Fortunately, it was flown by an experienced pilot, Captain Gusev, who possessed a sense of humor. Approaching Ayvazian from the rear, he realized that the plane was from his squadron and, without reporting anything to ground control, he started playing a game. For a few minutes he followed orders precisely and chased Ayvazian, who had no choice but to take part in an aerial ballet. However, Ayvazian flew warily. In his role of "mouse," he expected to get a round into his tail at any moment. Finally they separated. It was time to land, since they were running out of fuel.

Voronov was the first in all of the missile units to realize what was happening. The radar screen lit up and fragments of the U-2 drifted down from the sky. What other proof did they need? But the generals in Sverdlovsk insisted on continuing the search. Then the radars of the neighboring battery detected two objects. At first its commander, Major Shugayev, was dubious: "Why two? And at a lower altitude?" He called staff headquarters. But General Solodovnikov, the commander of the Air Defense forces, snapped back: "We have no planes in the air." Still another puzzling statement, since Ayvazian had just been playing a game of tag with Gusev in the sky.

There was no time to think: if we had no planes in the air, then the enemy planes must be destroyed at once. Radar operators began tracking them. The radars first locked on to Ayvazian's plane, but then it suddenly disappeared. Deciding to show off, the pilot had put his plane into a steep dive toward the airfield.

The lead plane piloted by Ayvazyan was replaced on the less crowded radar screen by its partner. The radars of Shugayev's battery locked onto this new target. Still another parachute opened up in the air—this time Safronov's.

When Voronov saw the U.S. parachute, about thirty minutes had elapsed since the first missile was fired. He automatically noted several more missile bursts at a high altitude. "They're just shooting aimlessly," he thought, then became absolutely certain that the intruder had been hit, and hit by his battery. Now they just had to capture the pilot alive and finish the job.

Voronov ordered one of his officers, Captain Kazantsev, to take his men, rush to the spot where the parachute landed and capture the pilot. Precious minutes passed while the men were assembled and issued submachine guns and cartridges. The parachutist was not at the place he had landed. Some excited peasants milling in a field next to the road explained: "The spy has been taken to the state farm."

The meeting between two civilizations was surprisingly calm and pedestrian. It was only subsequently that newspapers described the anger and indignation of Soviet citizens. But this is what actually happened. The driver of a car, who was taking friends to the neighboring village of Povarnya for the holiday, heard an explosion somewhere high up in the sky. Curious to see what was going on, he stopped the car. Patches of clear blue sky were visible through cumulus clouds. They decided the bang must have come from a fighter plane breaking the sound barrier. People in the area were already used to such sound effects. Then, in the shafts of sunlight they noticed some glittering dots, with a parachute visible among them. A few minutes later the friends were helping the pilot to his feet and disentangling him from the parachute's shroud lines. They had no idea who he was, but marveled at the pilot's equipment. After all, it's not every day that supersonic pilots eject. They were totally confused when they asked the survivor how he felt and his reply was incomprehensible—clearly not in Russian.

"Are you Bulgarian?" asked the driver of the car. The whole district knew that pilots from Warsaw Pact countries were training at the neighboring airfield. The parachutist shook his head and spoke rapidly in his own language. His rescuers were baffled, then one of the passengers, who was smarter and had been in the Navy, wrote "USA" on one of the car's dusty windows. Powers nodded. They slapped him on the shoulder and pointed to the front seat of the Moskvich. They decided to drive the captured spy—they had no doubt that was what he was—to the office of the state farm. There Powers was also received quite calmly. They helped him to take off his flight suit and he was left in his leather jacket. They sat him down at a table, and barely refrained from offering him a glass of vodka in honor of the holiday. This was the almost idyllic scene that greeted the group sent by Major Voronov to capture him and presented itself to the local KGB men hurriedly following them. They took Powers away to Sverdlovsk.

For a long time I couldn't understand why Powers was taken to be a Bulgarian and not, for example, a Czech or German, and thought the report was an invention. But I was mistaken. I had an opportunity, in October of 1995, to visit the air base in Bodo, Norway. Powers didn't reach it on that May Day in 1960. Now, thirty-five years later, a conference devoted to the Cold War was held in the local aviation museum. I was invited to give a talk, since I was, if not a witness, at least a contemporary of the events in May 1960. In Bodo I met the son of the U-2's pilot, Francis Gary Powers Jr., an engaging and smiling young man. He had a dark complexion and black wavy hair, the very image of a Bulgarian. When I talked about his father's first meeting with the people of Sverdlovsk, he told me his family history. It seems that the Powers family is descended from a small, originally Muslim, nationality—the Melungeon—that originated in Asia Minor, but moved from there to North Africa, and in the twelfth century from North Africa to Catalonia. They were forced out of Catalonia by the Spanish Inquisition, eventually settling in Illinois. Mountains, bright sun—everything there resembles nature in fertile Bulgaria. It's no wonder that the peoples resemble each other.

HISTORY AND OFFICIAL HISTORY

The MIG-19 fell near the village of Degtyarka, to the west of Sverdlovsk. Safronov's parachute was seen by local residents. When they ran up to him, the pilot was no longer breathing and blood was flowing from a deep wound in his side.

Missile command was the first to report to Marshal Biryuzov: "The intruder has been shot down." Sergei Semyonovich was relieved: Then came new information. The local fighter aircraft commander, Major General Vovk, reported to "Dragon" from Sverdlovsk: "One pilot has been caught, we are looking for the second." Biryuzov decided to wait for confirmation of the second spy's capture before reporting to Father personally about what had happened.

The marshal was debating whether to go home to change his clothes or go straight to Red Square as he was, straight from the "battlefield," when there was another call from Sverdlovsk on the special phone. The general haltingly reported that they had found the second parachutist and that unfortunately he turned out to be one of ours, Senior Lieutenant Safronov.

"What do you mean, one of ours?" The marshal barely repressed a shout. "How many planes did you shoot down? Can't you tell the difference between ours and theirs?"

"His transponder wasn't working," lied the general.

This lie was repeated later, although pilots attested otherwise. The matter was cleared up by Igor Mentyukov: the transponders were operating, but not with the new code for May. They still had the one for April. In the pre-holiday flurry of activities, personnel servicing the planes had not changed it. So it was not surprising that the radars perceived "friendly" as "foe."

"How many missiles did you fire?" said Biryuzov, gradually calming down.

"One, three, and then two more," the general in Sverdlovsk began counting uncertainly. "Fourteen in all," he continued, sounding depressed. "And which one brought down the American?" asked the marshal.

"The first," he heard in a hollow voice from the other end of the phone.

"Why the hell . . . !" For the next few minutes the usually calm Biryuzov employed nothing but unprintable expressions and then angrily slammed down the phone.

His joyful sensation of victory vanished in a moment. In this form, his report did not promise to be a triumphant one.

"Find out which plane they shot down, the T-3 or the MIG," the marshal ordered Savitsky.

Savitsky called Sverdlovsk again.

"A MIG-19," he reported succinctly after a few minutes of vigorous conversation. "First I sent the T-3 and ordered it to ram, but the pilot missed and flew above the target. Then they sent up a MIG-19, since the target seemed to be lower."

"Good." Biryuzov stopped listening to his deputy.

He was struck by the fact that the interceptor had flown over the high-altitude spy plane. That was an achievement in itself. But how should he report it? And then he thought of a helpful idea. The marshal summoned his deputies.

"This was what happened," he began in a calm and confident voice. "The intruder only brushed the edge of the missile range. We expected that and sent a T-3 to intercept it. No—better a pair of T-3s," he corrected himself. "There were two of them. They had already reached the target when it entered missile range. At its extreme limit. It was decided to launch. The interceptor was ordered to leave the firing area, but only shouted in reply: 'I am attacking.' Two missiles were launched, as called for. The planes were so close together that they could not be distinguished from the ground. Signals on the radar merged. Therefore one missile hit the spy plane, while the other one went after our plane. Unfortunately, it also hit the target. What was the lieutenant's name?"

"Senior Lieutenant Safronov," said Savitsky.

"Yes, the Lieutenant," the marshal said, "died a hero. And that's the end of the story! There were never any other missiles!" He continued sarcastically: "You just kept shooting wildly! Chaff—a likely story!"

The marshal looked searchingly at his deputies. He read agreement in their faces. This version suited everyone, first of all Central Command.

"You"—Biryuzov turned to Kuleshov—"fly there immediately. Investigate thoroughly, but the main thing is that everyone must give the same account of things. Is that clear?"

"Yes," replied Colonel-General Kuleshov.

Savitsky simply nodded.

The marshal's version was the one reported to Father. What really happened when Powers was shot down was completely "forgotten" by the participants for a long time. I was also unaware of the truth. It was only with the coming of Mikhail Gorbachev's glasnost that those who have retired and were one rank lower—Voronov, Ayvazyan, and a few others—began to talk about what happened. Their accounts were published in the Soviet and Russian press.[1] It seems to me that this story is very instructive. What disinformation can be provided to top officials under conditions of secrecy! And it was on the basis of such reports that Father, and not Father alone, made decisions that affected the fate of the world!

Biryuzov shook hands with Kuleshov and Savitsky, loudly congratulated those present in the headquarters on the victory, and strode resolutely to his car. He had decided to go to Red Square in his field uniform.

On Red Square the columns of troops had already marched by and the civilian parade was in progress. Father was waiting for a report, but no one had called from antiaircraft headquarters. He himself didn't want to make people nervous for no reason. As soon as the plane was shot down they would report it immediately, and if they missed—they would report that also.

The appearance at the edge of the grandstand of Marshal Biryuzov striding purposefully toward the Mausoleum did not go unnoticed. Foreigners wondered what was going on. Officials in the know immediately drew the right conclusion: they'd shot it down! The marshal's field uniform made the right impression; everyone remembers it. Biryuzov mounted the Mausoleum, leaned down toward Father's ear and whispered the news of the victory, ac-

---

1. See *Novoye vremya*, January 1991, pp. 38–40; correspondence from Colonel A. Dokuchayev, in *Krasnaya zvezda*, May 1990; "That Memorable Day," *Pravda*, April 30, 1990; Igor Mentyukov, interview by Nikolai Kulin, *Trud*, October 1996; and Anatoly Dokuchayev, "A Nocturnal Call to Khrushchev. Who Shot Down Powers and How Did He Do It?" *Krasnaya zvezda*, November 16, 1996. They are all trustworthy to the extent that memories of onlookers are trustworthy after the passage of decades. They agree in their description of most facts.

cepted the well-deserved congratulations, and walked with dignity to the right side of the tribunal, where military officers stood.

Within minutes the news had traveled from the Mausoleum down to the stands and the phrase "They shot it down" circulated, accompanied by sighs of relief and mutual congratulations. Pyotr Dmitriyevich Grushin, who designed the S-75, and Aleksandr Andreyevich Raspletin, who designed its guidance system, broke out in smiles and were besieged by people wanting to shake their hands.

Father was extraordinarily pleased when he returned home after the celebration. He felt that he had finally gotten his revenge on the people who had been offending him for such a long time.

I found out from him that the pilot was alive, was being interrogated in Sverdlovsk, and was talking freely about everything. Father repeated with relish Powers's account of how U.S. specialists had assured him that it was impossible to shoot down the U-2. He talked about the espionage equipment, which had been captured almost intact. The film in the camera was now being developed.

Father told me right away of his plan. He had decided to play hide-and-seek with the Americans and not report immediately that the plane had been destroyed. He would wait until they began to concoct a story and only then expose them, to pay them back for all those years of humiliation.

He thought that, just as on April 9, the initiative for that day's flight came from unauthorized military officers and the CIA, not from the president. Father didn't even mention the summit conference. I specifically asked him about it. Father reacted calmly: intelligence was intelligence, but diplomacy was diplomacy.

At the time Father didn't feel that it was useful to cancel the visit to the United States planned for May 14 by Marshal Vershinin, commander in chief of the Soviet Air Force. His trip was in exchange for General Twining's recent visit to attend the air show in Moscow.

Father thought that when he proved that the U-2 had violated our borders, the president would be forced to apologize for his subordinates. In the scenario devised by Father, the finale would be a public trial of U.S. spy Francis Gary Powers, publicized around the world.

The Paris crisis is an example of how a mistake in predicting a partner's behavior leads to an inadequate response. Both sides misjudged the situation—unless people in Langley intended from the start to disrupt the negotiations. Somehow I can't rid myself of that suspicion.

General de Gaulle, president of the French Republic, conducted himself in the most far-sighted manner. He instructed his ambassador in Moscow, Maurice Desjean, who had developed almost confidential relations with Father, to find out unofficially whether Father had changed his intentions with respect to the Paris meeting. Father assured him that he wanted to strengthen peaceful coexistence and that he regarded the forthcoming conference with hope. Father said the same thing in his report to the fifth session of the Supreme Soviet. And although the report was titled "On Abolishing Taxes on Workers and Employees and Other Measures to Improve the Well-Being of the Soviet People," Father devoted considerable attention to matters relating to the Paris conference. He expressed his misgivings, but stated firmly that we were going to Paris with a pure heart and would spare no effort to achieve a mutually acceptable agreement.

However, Father was gravely offended by President Eisenhower's warning that he could not spend more than a week in Paris. Father perceived the reference to a previously scheduled visit to Portugal as insulting and humiliating. Negotiations on disarmament, peace in Europe, and the fate of Germany were put on the same level as a protocol visit to a country whose policies had absolutely no effect on world affairs. To this was added the hostility that Salazar had inspired in our country from the very start.

Meanwhile, events connected with the mysterious disappearance of the U-2 were being played out in accordance with the scenario conceived by Father. In his speech before the Supreme Soviet, he only reported the fact of the violation of our borders and the downing of the plane by Soviet antiaircraft fire. Where this happened, whether near the border or deep inside Soviet territory, the fate of the pilot, captured espionage equipment and other details—about all that he was silent. "Let them worry about it," repeated Father. "Let's see what the State Department dreams up. When they've become completely enmeshed in lies we'll show them the living pilot. But in the meantime—not a word!" The Supreme Soviet greeted the sensational news of the intrusion with indignation. The information flashed immediately around the world.

The Americans had to start playing a game, make an answering move. The State Department's report, subsequently added to and elaborated on by NASA, stated that "a plane of the U-2 type . . . , designed for scientific-research purposes and being used since 1956 to study atmospheric conditions and wind bursts at high altitudes, disappeared on May 1 at 9 A.M. (local time) after its pilot reported that he was experiencing problems with oxygen and was located over the Lake Van region of Turkey." Some technical details followed.

I completely fail to understand why the Americans brought Turkey into the picture, when they knew that the plane had flown out of Peshawar and was lost in an entirely different place. Perhaps they were afraid of problems in their relations with Pakistan?

Whatever the reason, their awkward lie was grist to Father's mill. He waited to see what would happen next; he was simply enjoying the game. It's hard to say how long Father could have kept the secret. I think that he himself had no definite plan. But fate took the matter out of his hands. Soon after Father's speech—the next day, I think—Rolf Sulman, the ambassador of Sweden and dean of the diplomatic corps, met our deputy foreign minister, Yakov Malik, at a reception. It was later said that Malik had allowed himself to drink too much cognac, but no one knows for sure. In any event, he behaved extremely incautiously. When the Swedish ambassador "casually" asked about the fate of the pilot of the U.S. spy plane, Malik answered artlessly: "I don't know exactly. He's being questioned." A moment later Malik suddenly realized what he had done, but words have wings and cannot be recalled. He could only hope that the ambassador would not pass on the information to the Americans. Sweden was a neutral country. Sulman thought differently. He hurried to his embassy and immediately called the U.S. ambassador.

An hour later the chairman of the KGB called Father and reported the content of the conversation between the two diplomats. Father was angry and upset. The next day the unfortunate diplomat was summoned to the Central Committee, given a dressing-down, sacked as deputy minister, and even expelled from the party. But not for long. A few days later he was forgiven.

There was no longer any point in keeping silent about Powers's capture, and Father, taking the floor on the final day of the session, gave a detailed account of the U.S. version of the U-2 flight and then disproved it point by point, while mocking the clumsiness of the liars. He read excerpts from Powers's interrogations, described the plane's route, and enumerated with relish all the espionage equipment found in the plane's wreckage. His report culminated with a demonstration of the developed film, showing airfields, nuclear storage sites, factories. Father triumphantly presented the packet of photographs to the session chairman, Pavel Pavlovich Lobanov.

Father brought copies of the pictures to the dacha. I looked at them closely. They were of outstanding quality: you could see fighter planes, spread in a chain along the landing strip, and in another picture there were fuel tanks and headquarters buildings.

Father was pleased. He had won the first round. Meanwhile he ordered the wreckage of the plane to be exhibited in Gorky Park, at the same place where captured German military equipment was put on display during the war. Father was one of the first visitors to this unusual exhibit. I went with him. The twisted pile of metal (which showed no evidence of fire), the instruments, and the spy apparatus were impressive. Foreign correspondents milled around Father. The sensation was just beginning to build. Upon leaving the pavilion that held the exhibit, Father answered their questions willingly and delivered a lively speech. It made the point that from now on anyone who violated our borders would be dealt with in similar fashion. The Americans should take note, unless they wanted to start a world war.

The visit to the exhibit took place on May 11, toward evening. But two days earlier the next (the fourth in number) statement by the State Department on the U-2 question, asserted that the president had in principle approved espionage flights over Soviet territory in order to prevent surprise attack and that he reserved the right to do this in future, until such time as the USSR opened its borders to inspection.

After reading this statement in his Kremlin office, Father simply flew into a rage. If its authors' purpose was to infuriate him, they achieved their wish.

That evening Father restrained himself. He had decided to wait and see whether Eisenhower would extricate himself from this situation with dignity.

On May 9, the fifteenth anniversary of the victory over Fascist Germany, newspapers published a decree of the Presidium of the Supreme Soviet presenting awards to the antiaircraft defense officers who shot down Powers. Battalion chief of staff Major Voronov was awarded the Order of the Red Banner. Senior Lieutenant S. N. Safronov and Captain N. I. Sheludko were given the same decoration. Other participants in the operation were given either less important orders or medals. Neither the decree nor numerous subsequent publications made any mention of the fact that Sergei Safronov was killed. Just who he was remained totally unclear. And the role of Captain Sheludko, who had fired his missiles at an already downed U-2, was also left unexplained. But almost all newspapers wrote about Major Voronov and his crew.

THE CRISIS IN PARIS

Some Western authors who write about the Paris crisis argue that there were serious differences in the Soviet leadership at the time and that pressure on Father from the right led to the breakup of the conference. This viewpoint strikes me as profoundly mistaken.

Of course there were people in the Soviet leadership who were cool toward Father's policy of improving relations with the United States, but they kept their opinions to themselves. In that period the eulogizing of Father was intensifying and multiplying. He was in complete command of the situation and made the decisions in both foreign and domestic policy.

The reduction in the armed forces announced at the beginning of the year did not, naturally enough, arouse enthusiasm in the Army. Not all military leaders supported Father's announcement of the need to minimize the traditional branches of the military and convert to missiles. But that was not manifested in the form of protests, open arguments, or even simple objections. They only complained to their families at home in the evening.

Top figures in the Ministry of Defense were no longer in the Presidium of the Central Committee. They had no direct influence on political decision-making. Furthermore, in 1960 both Malinovsky and Grechko were on good, even friendly terms with Father.

As far as the top echelon is concerned, it is enough to recall the Central Committee plenum held in the first few days of May, on the eve of the opening of the session of the Supreme Soviet. On Father's initiative, it produced significant personnel changes in the Presidium. For some time, Father had been expressing dissatisfaction with his protégé, Aleksandr Illarionovich Kirichenko. He was clearly not qualified for the role of second secretary of the Central Committee. He had only a superficial knowledge of the national economy and made no effort to learn more, while, on the other hand, he was notorious for being crude and boastful. He lacked a breadth of viewpoint and the capacity to grasp a problem on the all-Union scale, much less on a world scale. He could not rise above the level of a postwar provincial committee secretary.

Father decided to replace him with Frol Romanovich Kozlov. Father was increasingly pleased with him. Kozlov stood out among his colleagues by his ability to grasp the essence of any subject. Furthermore, he had acquired a great deal of experience in both party work and the economy. That played no small part in Father's eyes in choosing a person to perform the exacting duties of the second-ranking person in the party, and consequently in the country.

Kozlov's political views were not radical, but at that time he followed Father's line faithfully, step by step, even in small matters. Anyway, what differences could there be at the time he was selected? If there had been, his candidacy would simply not have been considered.

Three more new members who followed Father unquestioningly were elected to the Presidium of the Central Committee: Aleksei Nikolayevich Kosygin, his first deputy in the Council of Ministers; Nikolai Viktorovich Podgorny, from Kiev; and Dmitri Stepanovich Polyansky. These personnel changes did not, in Father's view, result from a political struggle, but were necessitated by the incompetence of new members brought into the Central Committee Secretariat in the wake of the fight against the "Anti-Party Group." Various reasons and excuses were given, but they had not the slightest connection with the forthcoming meeting in Paris.

More than once I heard Father refer to Averky Borisovich Aristov with disappointment: you start talking to him about business and he always changes the subject to fishing. He also expressed dissatisfaction with the inefficiency of Ignatov and Furtseva, who were close to him previously.

Pyotr Nikolayevich Pospelov and Nikolai Ivanovich Belyayev, who also lost their positions as secretaries of the Central Committee, were somewhat farther removed from Father. Belyayev was also expelled from the presidium of the Central Committee. Pospelov was accused of dogmatism and adherence to old Stalinist stereotypical thinking. Belyayev was charged with being responsible for the slow pace of agricultural development. He was replaced by Polyansky.

One further change took place on May 7, at the final session of the Supreme Soviet. Kliment Yefremovich Voroshilov, the last member of the "Anti-Party Group," was removed from the position of Presidium chairman.

His retirement was not the result of adherence to the Stalinist opposition—after June of 1957 he showed fidelity and devotion to Father. But age was taking its toll, and it had simply become dangerous to leave Voroshilov in such a high position. Father received complaints about the old man for a long time, but he kept delaying a decision. Until there was a scandal.

Kliment Yefremovich received the ambassador of Iran when he presented his credentials. Everything proceeded properly, in accordance with protocol. The procedure is not complicated. It is prescribed down to the smallest detail and, it would seem, held no surprises. The audience is supposed to conclude with a brief conversation. After thanking the ambassador for inquiring about the chairman's health, Voroshilov suddenly grew animated.

"Why are you still putting up with the shah?" He clapped the ambassador on the shoulder. "We got rid of the tsar, and it's about time you did the same."

The shocked diplomat mumbled something unintelligible and quickly took his leave.

News of this incident remained within the Presidium apparatus. They decided to protect their chief. I'm sure such things still happen. Officials everywhere quickly learn to adapt to the vagaries of their bosses.

The ambassador was more upset. He had no idea how to assess the attitude of the head of a powerful neighboring state to the head of his own country. He decided to write Teheran and describe everything just as it happened. A short time later a copy of his report, deciphered by the KGB, lay on Father's desk. He clutched his head, and then called Voroshilov. Voroshilov didn't deny it. He was distressed: "The devil got into me." Father flared up: "Yes, next time you might declare war!"

Voroshilov was replaced by the young and energetic Brezhnev. With the exception of Kirichenko and Belyayev, the changes didn't look particularly significant. Aristov and Pospelov were transferred to the Central Committee Bureau for the RSFSR. Nikolai Grigoryevich Ignatov was appointed deputy chairman of the Council of Ministers and Yekaterina Alekseyevna Furtseva became the minister of culture.

Father's struggle was not against the opposition but within himself, between his natural human striving to improve international relations and reduce the danger of war and a caution instilled for decades about relations with the imperialists. Moreover, he was constantly on the alert to see if any disrespect was shown to our country. Father tried to clarify the situation at a reception in the Czechoslovak Embassy on the occasion of their May 9 national holiday.

Father's remarks at the reception were extraordinarily conciliatory. He emphasized that the door remained open despite the U-2 incident and that he was prepared to search jointly for a reasonable way out of the situation that had been created. But only a reasonable one, not one that would hurt the national dignity of either party. Further, Father appealed directly to Americans and to the president of the United States. He said: "Today I state once again that we want to live in peace and friendship with the American people. . . . I respect the U.S. ambassador, who is present here, and I am confident that he had nothing to do with this intrusion. . . . I am sure of his high moral qualities. . . . I believe that he is not in favor of such incidents, either as a person or as a representative of his country." It would seem that there was nothing more to say. But Father did say more. He really trusted Ambassador Thompson and sincerely believed that he was trying to improve relations between the two countries.

In those days I knew nothing and would never have been told about Father's confidential talk with Ambassador Thompson. It took place there, in the Embassy. Father thought that an appeal through Thompson to the president would make it possible to establish confidential, unofficial contacts and would help in the search for a mutually acceptable solution.

Thompson assured Father that he would do everything he could. Unfortunately, the ambassador was too late. In Washington the State Department already announced that Eisenhower had personally approved the flights.

Even then the door didn't slam shut. I have already mentioned that at the exhibit on May 11 Father did not exclude the possibility of searching for a joint solution. Of course, the situation had become more complicated. But if both parties wished it, there was still a chance to undertake something, especially since the initiative was being taken by the party that had suffered an injury to its national pride.

Eisenhower did not rule out such a possibility either. In the Oval Office he told Secretary of State Herter that it would make sense to meet Khrushchev in Paris before sessions began and try to clear the air. Eisenhower asked Herter to arrange for "Khrushchev to drop by the U.S. ambassador's residence in Paris on the first day, let's say at about four o'clock." Herter objected, saying that Khrushchev might take that as a "sign of weakness."

Father never received this invitation. But with reference to a visit by Eisenhower to our country, he said openly at a May 11 press conference that "he would settle the matter of the visit with the president in Paris. We still wish to look for ways to improve relations with the United States."

After all, Father left early for Paris in hopes of meeting with the president. He was accompanied by Gromyko and, at the last minute, Malinovsky. Father was attentively following everything done by the Americans. When he heard that the secretary of defense would participate on their side, he responded immediately: why should we do any less? His colleagues in the Presidium of the Central Committee had no objection.

I remember a conversation with Father that occurred just before he left. We were taking our evening stroll at the dacha. Father suddenly began talking about Eisenhower's farm and said it would be a good idea to invite him to the dacha, show him the crops, and take a boat ride on the Moscow River. There was no indication that the visit might be canceled.

The same was true of official preparations for the summit. References, preparation of speeches, suggestions, neatly arranged in file folders, were waiting for their hour of use. They mentioned the U-2—but only in passing. Although most of the papers were dictated by Father, in the days preceding his departure he began to feel vaguely uneasy and dissatisfied. It seemed as if we were going to the conference as petitioners.

Father kept the door open until the last moment. It was the Americans, he thought, who rudely slammed it shut by declaring that they had the right to continue intelligence flights over our territory. What difference did it make that the statement was issued by the State Department? Enough time had passed so that the president could have made changes if he so desired.

Father made his final decisions in the plane while flying to Paris.[2] He recalled later:

> During the flight . . . I felt a keener sense of my responsibility. People think better under pressure. I thought: Here we are flying to a meeting. We have already met more than once, and there is little hope of reaching some kind of agreement. I couldn't forget that the United States sent its U-2 spy plane just before this meeting.

---

2. Oleg Troyanovsky, Father's foreign policy aide, claims that the decision was made before the flight, under the plane's wing, at the moment of farewell at Vnukovo Airport. As soon as the plane had taken off, Father summoned his aides to the rear cabin, announced his decision, and together they began to rewrite his speeches. The two versions are essentially the same, if you disregard technical details. Troyanovsky also recalls that as early as May 1, the day Powers was shot down, Father called and ordered him to convene the press group to prepare a speech on the violation of our country's borders by a foreign plane. During their conversation Father observed that the incident could wreck the Paris meeting. In other words, he did not exclude that possibility, although at that time he was still far from determining a final position. In my account I rely on Father's memoirs.—S.K.

The question is, what can we expect? Is it possible that the most powerful country in the world, the United States, would come to an agreement under these conditions? Or, to put it more properly, can you expect a sensible agreement from such a government when it tries to undermine the meeting ahead of time by launching a spy plane?

This thought kept running through my mind. I was increasingly convinced that we would look rather unimpressive. They present us with this pill just before the conference, but we pretend that we don't understand anything; we go to this conference as if nothing had happened. The conference will break up, and these powers will undoubtedly try to make our delegation, our country, responsible. We are, in fact, the injured party; our dignity was insulted, but we are still going to this conference.

I began to think that we had to review the content of our papers, especially the first—the declaration which we would make at the opening of the conference. I thought that we had to set conditions, an ultimatum to the United States of America: they must apologize for insulting our country by sending a spy plane. We must demand that the president of the United States retract his statement that they have the right to send intelligence flights over our territory, i.e., to unilaterally allow oneself to fly over the territories of other countries when you don't permit anyone to fly over your own country.

I dictated my thoughts. Andrei Andreyevich and his Foreign Ministry staff sat down to rework the documents. Everything had to be entirely rewritten. We wrote new papers . . . , but these had not been examined by the leadership of the party and government. . . .

By the time we arrived in Paris we had received complete approval of our new position from Moscow. Thus, we departed with documents containing one position and when we landed in Paris their content was quite different. I view this change in our position as completely justified.

It was decided at the same time to cancel the trip to the United States of a Soviet Air Force delegation headed by Marshal Vershinin, scheduled to leave that day.

Having taken the first step, Father could not and did not want to stop: "When we arrived in Paris I thought: Well, good, we are making such a statement, but the president will not apologize and will not cancel the flights. In Washington he has already said that they will continue intelligence flights. Well, and then what?"

Father's change in policy could not help but affect Eisenhower's visit to Moscow, which was, as it were, a continuation of the summit meeting. Father only remembered the visit when he arrived in Paris:

Naturally, under these conditions he (Eisenhower) could not come to Moscow, and we could not put up with his presence. How could we greet him on our territory? . . . That would be an intolerable situation! It would be offensive! The country would be humiliated! . . .

It occurred to me that we should include a point in the declaration we were preparing to read at the opening session, that if there were no apology we would retract our invitation to the president to visit our country.

Everyone agreed. We quickly sent this additional point to Moscow to get their agreement. We immediately received a positive response. We therefore had all the documents ready and we were stuffed with arguments of an explosive nature. They better not touch us, as the saying goes, or it would set off a spark.

Father, who arrived in Paris earlier, made one more attempt in Paris to meet with the president before the conference opened. He chose Harold Macmillan as an intermediary. He felt that the British prime minister had the most sober assessment of the situation and would be genuinely interested. Macmillan accepted the role of intermediary and made every effort to achieve results, but the Americans refused.

If the two leaders had met, a great deal of what happened in the world might have been quite different.

When Father made absolutely sure that Eisenhower was not going to meet him halfway, he changed. Now he was also not prepared to reach an agreement and he decided to pay Eisenhower back in the same coin. "On the first day," recalled Father,

I read the declaration. Precisely that: I read it, because under such circumstances ad-libbing is not allowed. When you ad lib you can come out with superfluous words and use phrases that distort your meaning. They would all be written down and would be hard to correct later on. . . . An opportunity might be created for a different interpretation, which would favor our adversaries. I therefore read the declaration and then sat down.

There was some confusion. Especially after the phrase that stated that we were withdrawing our invitation if there were no apology on the part of the United States of America, that the president could not be our guest after what he allowed with respect to our country.

Eisenhower and his delegation stood up, and we parted. . . . Our declaration was like a bomb which swept everything away . . . the round table, which should have united us, was shattered.

In reality, the conference ended then and there. Father burned the last bridges. The leaders of both superpowers dug in their heels: one demanded an apology, the other refused to make it.

De Gaulle and Macmillan made serious attempts to reconcile the parties. In talking with Father, de Gaulle angrily observed that a new Soviet satellite launched on May 15 had already flown over France sixteen times. Who knows, perhaps it was also taking photographs? Father vigorously denied that, saying that we were not engaged in such practices. De Gaulle's words rubbed salt in fresh wounds. The Americans had recently announced that they planned to launch spy satellites within the near future. With their help, the Americans could photograph any region on earth. After the destruction of the U-2, Father particularly wanted to prevent that as well. But how? He resolved to have another talk with missile designers after returning home.

The situation could not be saved. Two days later, after an unsuccessful attempt to open the conference, the delegations left for home. Father stopped in Berlin on his way to Moscow. The German question, which had subsided, flared up again and was threatening to develop into a serious crisis.

The matter of Berlin was not the only casualty of the U-2 affair. The roar of the U-2 engine and the thunderous explosion of Soviet antiaircraft missiles would be reflected in the harshness of Father's position in Vienna in 1961 and would also largely determine Soviet conduct during the deployment of Soviet missiles in Cuba.

Father's wounds never healed. The deception on the part of his "friend" General Eisenhower, who had gone on walks with him at Camp David and agreed that nothing was more terrible than war, struck Father to the heart. He forgave neither Eisenhower the president nor Eisenhower the man for the U-2.

From then on, when engaging in negotiations with the new president or receiving the U.S. ambassador, Father never allowed himself to forget that before him was not simply a person trying to survive on this earth, but a treacherous, irreconcilable foe, capable of anything. It was only after the Cuban Missile Crisis, when he began to trust John Kennedy, that he calmed down somewhat.

From then on Father wanted nothing to do with Eisenhower. But Khrushchev the politician also saw no reason to aggravate world tensions. He had no intention of renewing the dispute over Germany and counted on reaching agreement with the new president.

During the May 20 meeting in Berlin Father said that of course it was possible to sign a peace treaty unilaterally, but why hurry? That solution to the problem would not disappear, and it was better to give the situation time to mature. Two German states existed and were developing. The economy would show which system was superior. In the meantime, we could wait six to eight months and then convene a new summit meeting—with the new U.S. president.

Eisenhower's second term in office ended half a year later. His place in the White House was contested by Vice President Nixon and Senator John Kennedy, who was virtually unknown to Father. Father now simply couldn't stand to hear about the Republican candidate. That was when he began to call him, for some reason, the "shopkeeper." Half a year earlier, in Camp David, he had tried to find out from Eisenhower whether he would run for office a third time. Father thought that Eisenhower was an experienced and honest person with whom you could do business, irrespective of political convictions.

I think that when Father asked about a third term he was not interested simply in the fate of the U.S. office of the presidency, but was trying to compare the U.S. system for change and continuity of power to that in our own country, to what were our own customs. Could that have been the origin of his proposal that there be two terms of membership in the Presidium of the Central Committee and in the government? However, he suggested five-year terms, not four, relating them to the five-year plans.

Returning to Moscow, Father described with a twinkle in his eye the commotion he had stirred up in Paris. But at times his eyes took on a guarded expression and turned from brown to almost black. It became clear that Father was really not in a joking mood.

TENSIONS RISE

The failure in Paris and the episode with Powers radically affected the psychological climate in our country. Only the day before everyone was living in hopes of change, of concluding agreements with the United States, if not in the next few months, then in the near future, of the arrival of a time of mutual respect, if not friendship. At the end of May everything was back in its familiar round and newspapers were filled with harsh calls for vigilance and readiness to rebuff the aggressors.

An order was issued to the armed forces: repel all intrusions into the skies over the USSR or our allies. In the past the leadership had to give its approval before an intruder was fired upon. Now this approval was given in advance. Pilots patrolling the air and on ground alert, missile crews scanning the skies with radars, all dreamed of distinguishing themselves if an intruder dared to appear.

Whereas before May 1 antiaircraft defense units lived according to peacetime rules and pilots on duty, though in flight suits, could relax in specially equipped huts, now they took turns sitting in the cockpits of interceptors waiting for orders to take off. Missile antiaircraft units were ready for action. Missiles were no longer kept in storage sites. Equipped with warheads, they awaited the appearance of any uninvited guest over launch installations.

Naturally, there was an increase in the number of air incidents. As early as May 24 fighters attacked a U.S. plane in the Rostock region of the GDR when it violated the rules of movement within the air corridor. The pilot decided not to risk his life and landed at the airfield indicated to him. The incident ended without any casualties.

Americans became worried, and that was especially true of U.S. allies with air bases from which intelligence flights originated. Father's threat, voiced in Paris, that he reserved the right to carry out a retaliatory strike on such bases if a spy plane appeared over the Soviet Union, was having an effect. Only de Gaulle, showing a certain skepticism, muttered that "missiles fly in both directions." There were no such bases on French territory. Neither the British nor the Norwegians, Turks, or Pakistanis wanted to tempt fate, to test the seriousness of Father's intentions on their own skin.

Father understood as well as de Gaulle did that missiles fly in both directions, and his plans did not call for confirming that fact in practice. He no longer believed in the real possibility of war with the West. Once they understood that we could retaliate for a strike, who would decide to carry one out? Even if the number of Soviet ICBMs in firing position could be counted on the fingers of one hand, there were enough to destroy the major cities on the other side of the ocean. War had turned into an escapade equally dangerous to both sides. Father did not consider his opponents to be reckless adventurers. It was precisely his conviction that both sides were rational which allowed him to keep calm during times of greatest tension. Even during those difficult days, he thought that domestic matters were of primary importance. During the previous few years he was constantly bothered by the fact that hope for substantial progress was not being met. Soviet industrial production could not be compared to that of the West, nor could we even dream of such an advanced economy. Father decided to approach the problem from another direction. He thought that if we bought samples of modern products abroad, we would be able to improve domestic models. After gaining some experience, we could not only catch up with our teachers, but surpass them. However, lack of hard currency frustrated Father's plans.

At that point he decided to take a bite out of the emergency gold reserves. Its expenditure had been under a rigid taboo since Stalin's time. The gold was being saved in case of war.

It was at this time that Father began to talk about selling gold. I was shocked by his words.

"But how could you? What if there's a war?" I caught my breath and couldn't even finish the sentence.

"War?" drawled Father uncertainly. "But who would decide to start a war? Now we have missiles, and we can give even the Americans a punch in the jaw."

He fell silent, as if judging what he had said. As usual, our conversation was taking place during a walk. There was a lengthy pause. We walked silently along the path.

"Yes, war"—Father returned to the subject—"how can we view war as we used to? In the past, after a defeat you still had both time and territory. But now? No one would be left after nuclear strikes. Why should we sit, like the stingy knight,[3] on a trunk of gold, waiting for who knows what? We'd do better to spend it—not all of it, of course—in a good cause and buy what will improve the lives of people and the country. You can't cook kasha out of gold."

Father talked at length about how, once we sold the gold, we could move our national economy off dead center and infuse both industry and agriculture with fresh blood. He had no doubt that, once that push was given, we would make progress. We have always had people with initiative. Father grew more and more enthusiastic about the prospects opening up before the country. He went on at length about the subject, calculating and considering what to buy first. Once having made up his mind, he was afraid of underselling the gold and tossing our treasure into the wind.

I kept a dispirited silence. I frankly regretted the fact that gold would leak out of the Treasury. The prospect that we would be left with nothing in case of war was a frightening one.

Unfortunately, the gold that we sold didn't bring abundance to our country. Just like the two hundred billion dollars that we got for Siberian oil a few decades later. It didn't help either that Father meticulously kept track of every million dollars at each step, supervised every detail of purchasing and visited new construction sites where foreign equipment was being installed. It was all in vain. As hard as we tried, it didn't work the way it did "there." The products that emerged from factories looked unattractive, had many defects, and didn't resemble their foreign samples in the least. Hogs and poultry fed foreign rations stubbornly refused to fatten.

Meanwhile the situation in the world continued to grow more tense. There was a new incident on July 1. A U.S. RB-47, specially equipped to make observations of the Soviet interior from neutral waters, took off from a U.S. military base in Britain and set a course for the Kola Peninsula. Soviet air and naval bases were concentrated in that area. The plane's mission was to record the frequencies and operational procedures of radar stations, intercept radio conversations, and in general, collect all the information it could, all the while remaining outside the country's borders.

Such flights had long become routine for both us and the Americans. As soon as the "guest" appeared near Soviet borders, it would be followed diligently by Air Defense fighters. They watched and waited for the moment it might cross the forbidden line.

---

3. Father is referring here to "hero" of Pushkin's poem *Skupoi rytsar'*, who died sitting on six trunks full of gold that he refused to spend. —S.K.

It's not easy to identify a border, which over water is little more than an abstraction, especially one that is defined as twelve miles from an irregular shoreline. Therefore, the spy planes occasionally found themselves over our waters when they were pursuing something especially interesting—either by mistake or because of pilot fatigue. Then the interceptors would pounce on them. Depending on the political situation, they were given various instructions: to show their presence without using weapons when relations were calm, or to shoot down the intruder during especially tense periods. The opposite mistake could also occur. It sometimes happened that Soviet fighters flew outside the limits of Soviet territory. On both sides, almost everything depended on the skill of the pilots.

Today it's not possible to determine how the RB-47 encroached over our territorial waters at Cape Svyatoy Nos on the Kola Peninsula. The Americans rejected and still reject the fact of a border violation. Just as on May 1 they denied it in the case of the U-2.

Whatever happened, Soviet fighters shot down the plane and it sank into the sea. Six crew members were killed. Soviet sailors hurried to the scene, rescued two men who were in the water and took them into custody. For a long time U.S. ships searched the disputed region near the border looking for fragments of the plane, but found nothing.

Similar incidents happened more than once. They were usually accompanied by an exchange of angry diplomatic notes, then a return of bodies of the dead, and quiet was restored until the next occasion. After the U-2, the RB-47 violation seemed like an open challenge. Everyone waited to see if Father would carry out his threat. Everyone knew where the RB-47 flights originated. Of course, Father didn't think seriously about carrying out a missile strike on the bases. He understood perfectly well that "missiles can fly in both directions." But on the other side of the border, people didn't know what was on his mind, and to many he seemed unpredictable and inclined to be impulsive.

Eisenhower received word of the incident over the Barents Sea during a celebration in Gettysburg of his forty-fourth wedding anniversary. According to his son, John, the president looked like a deflated balloon. All he said was: "Is it possible that Khrushchev will carry out his threat to destroy Western bases?" Both leaders were hostage to mutual threats. Macmillan felt just as worried.

The missiles remained on their launch pads, but Father used the incident to assail "the aggressive essence of U.S. imperialism."

U.S. generals were given strict orders from the president to avoid possible conflicts. The commander of the U.S. forces in Germany issued an official order prohibiting their planes from flying within fifty kilometers of the East German border.

THE NEXT STEP IN THE SPACE PROGRAM

Turbulent events in the spring and summer of 1960 were not limited to politics. General Designer of Aviation Technology Semyon Alekseyevich Lavochkin died on June 10. That day saw not only the death of the scientist and designer, but the end of his swan song, the Burya, an enormous intercontinental cruise missile equipped with a ramjet engine. By the middle of 1960 the Burya was flying rather reliably, but its fate hung in the balance.

Korolyov had no respect for cruise missiles, "cruises," as he scornfully called them. He thought that they were hopelessly outdated. They would only divert resources, "spend money in a useless cause, money that was needed for the main direction," namely, his direction. Why bother with them when you had ballistic missiles, which were invulnerable to any enemy?

Sergei Pavlovich tried to bring both military and civilian authorities around to his viewpoint. It must be said, not without results. There was an increasing number of supporters in his camp. Marshal Malinovsky, the minister of defense, was one of them. However, Father held back. He thought that there was no hurry to make a definitive decision. After all, Chelomei and Lavochkin had disagreed with Korolyov.

In June there was another discussion about the fate of the Burya in the Presidium of the Central Committee. Some days before the meeting Sergei Pavlovich had gone to Kozlov to convince him to oppose the Burya. In those years Frol Romanovich was responsible for defense and he had to prepare a draft decision. Korolyov persuaded Kozlov, and together they persuaded Father; no one with influence remained to defend the Burya.

In those days Korolyov was concerned with other problems. He was preparing to launch a man into space. The additional third stage of the R-7 could now lift a payload of up to five tons into an orbit of 200 kilometers. The launch of a 4.5 ton sputnik on May 15 began a new stage in the space race. Korolyov was going all out, and now he meant to be first!

Korolyov understood that the R-7 was reaching the limit of its possibilities. He was thinking of building a fundamentally new booster with a payload capacity ten times greater. Such a monster could have no military use. Korolyov first talked with Father about this in 1958, soon after launching the first sputnik. At the time Father threw cold water on Sergei Pavlovich's enthusiasm, advising him not to scatter his forces and to limit himself to research: the R-7 was of paramount importance.

Nevertheless, on June 30, 1958, the government issued a decree calling for the development of a heavy booster with nuclear rocket engines. In those years designers in both the Soviet Union and the United States were obsessed by the idea of developing nuclear engines. The technology seemed almost within their grasp. But one problem after another cropped up as more and more research was carried out.

Korolyov decided to give the rocket a new name, rather than adding it to the "R" series. He dreamed of building the forerunner of a new family of heavy space boosters. A new index appeared—*N* for "booster" (*nositel'* in Russian). The new rocket was called the N-1, since it was the first of its kind.

Korolyov didn't have the slightest idea what its weight would have to be for it to perform missions in orbit. Sizes from 35 to 150 tons were mentioned. By 1960 a great deal had been established. Now nuclear engines were mentioned only in passing, and liquid hydrogen was in fashion.

That year, 1960, Korolyov decided that the time had come to bring up the subject again. He asked for an interview with Father. They talked about the brand-new N-1: with a weight on the ground of one to two thousand tons, Korolyov planned to lift sixty to eighty tons into orbit, and he promised to begin launches by the end of 1963—if, of course, the design bureau were given the resources immediately. Father asked what would be gained by spending such enormous sums. Sergei Pavlovich began talking—purely in general terms—about building semipermanent orbital stations, of expeditions to the moon, Mars, and Venus.

Father allowed himself to be persuaded. However, once again only funds for preliminary research would be appropriated.

From that time on manned space flight and then the moon program became virtually the only project of the Korolyov design bureau's team and its subcontractors.

MISSILES

The next regular show of military equipment was due in 1960. I flew to the test site a few weeks before the arrival of top officials. The efficiency and orderliness of the Kapustin Yar test site was impressive. Rows of interceptors were ranged on the airfield, which had not seen a military plane since the war. Antiaircraft missile batteries were located to the left and right of the highway at intervals of several dozen kilometers. They were exactly like the ones that shot down Powers. The military installations looked strong and well built: launch sites themselves were surrounded by earthen walls, with open dugouts a short distance away. President Eisenhower's statement that the United States reserved the right to conduct aerial espionage over the territory of the Soviet Union was taken seriously here, and commanders were fully armed and prepared to greet any uninvited guest.

The day for the show approached. Just as before, I attached myself to the main group. Its nucleus consisted of Father, with Kozlov next to him, and Brezhnev, Kirilenko, Ustinov, and Malinovsky behind them. The ministers, commanders in chief, and designers followed us somewhat further back. There were about forty people in all. I won't describe the missile launches, weapons firing, attacks of positions by airplanes, and other similarly impressive exercises. The program was essentially the same as before, only the armaments had changed. There was increased accuracy, range, and speed.

But what had really changed was the Army's attitude toward this new type of weapon—or not so much its attitude, as its practice. The Army had grown familiar with missiles. From bizarre toys provoking a certain degree of apprehension, they had become standard tools for waging war.

Now military personnel were in charge, whereas previously the people servicing launch installations had been mainly civilian engineers, the weapons designers, dressed in military overalls.

Strategic missile regiments assigned for combat duty arrived at the test site. The soldiers knew what to do with the R-5 and R-12. It was only the newest missile, the R-14, that Yangel's team launched themselves. Nedelin, the chief marshal of artillery, reported to Father that tests of the R-16 would begin that autumn.

Father was extremely pleased. Progress was being made. Generals had shifted from talking about missiles to working with them, even if there were not yet any noticeable structural changes in the Army. Although previously Father had used nonexistent missiles in his political maneuvering, they were now gradually becoming a reality.

Nuclear warheads were exhibited in a separate hangar. A moratorium on nuclear tests had already been in effect for a year and a half, virtually since the previous show. No new warheads had been added.

Enormous bombs and extremely heavy missile warheads lay on raised platforms. Next to them were displays of new designs, which were elegant, compact, and light. The new models had as much, if not more, destructive power.

Just as last time, exhibit organizers proved that further progress in developing missiles without testing warheads would be difficult, to put it mildly. Every extra kilogram of warhead load caused a multiple increase in launch weight.

Father listened attentively, without interrupting, to the arguments in favor of resuming experimental explosions. He was clearly impressed by their calculations.

When the last exhibit had been seen, Yefim Pavlovich Slavsky, the minister of medium machine building, joined in the conversation. He began talking about production, about technology, and, most important, about the economy. If the new designs were produced at factories, their cost would be reduced by many tens, and even hundreds, of millions. At the same time, he cited figures that described U.S. achievements from the latest series of explosions. The numbers looked not only impressive, but frightening. Slavsky reminded his audience that the Americans had announced an end to the moratorium as of January 1, 1960. They were preparing to begin testing as soon as they received the next generation of warheads. In that case we would inevitably be not one but two steps behind, if not more. In his opinion, we had to resume testing. If we wanted to rely on our nuclear missile strength, then we had to test.

Everyone waited for Father's reaction. He collected his thoughts, was silent for a moment, and suddenly began to describe his recent meeting in Paris. He talked about how he would not succeed in reaching agreements with Eisenhower and that it was hardly worth trying. Father talked emotionally and at length. Here, among his own people, he didn't think it necessary to hold back. We had to wait for a change in the occupant of the White House. Perhaps the president's successor would have a more sober approach to matters of war and peace.

Father praised the innovative designs, saying that they caught his imagination, but that it was not yet time to test them. He said that we now have almost two years of a moratorium to our credit, and with those we will go to meet the new U.S. president. We will thereby demonstrate our peaceful intentions in deeds, not words.

Frankly speaking, Father's words did not convince most of those present. Both the military and designers favored an early resumption of tests. "The stronger we become, the more they will listen to us," repeated Slavsky.

Father promised to give it more thought, but in general he was adamant. Until relations with the new U.S. administration were clarified, not a word should be said about testing until the following year. Neither side changed its opinion.

After lunch the next day Father met with designers, military officers, and ministers; they were all connected in some way with air defense. He wanted to discuss how to defend our sovereign airspace against the threat of intrusion from the air and violations of the state borders by spy satellites.

Planes did not present any particular problem, and the program for the design, production, and deployment of ground-to-air missiles was going well.

But space was altogether different! Designers threw up their hands. It was, of course, possible to shoot down a satellite. Chelomei outlined his ideas. In essence, he repeated what he had said to Father in the Crimea that April.

Many of those present listened to Chelomei and smiled condescendingly. Some frowned: he was just wasting their valuable time with his fairy tales. Back in those days the pictures drawn by Chelomei really did seem fantastic. He concluded by saying that all the preliminary work had been done, the basic design models had been selected, and a draft government decree was approved. That June the Central Committee of the CPSU and the Council of Ministers of the USSR issued a decree giving Chelomei's design bureau the job of developing systems of maneuverable space interceptors with stages and the UR-200 booster rocket to lift them into orbit.

The problem under discussion that day was not that of destroying an object in space, but of recognizing it for what it was.

Father, who had been silent for a long time, joined in. He talked about his brief conversation with de Gaulle concerning our spaceship. He conceded that the French president had an understandable interest in knowing whether or not the satellite was gathering intelligence information.

"And tomorrow we will be in the same position. Will we also be looking into the sky and making guesses?" he exclaimed heatedly. "What can we do?"

No one answered.

After a pause Father continued: "Today's remarks have confirmed a sad truth that we already knew. Well, we'll just have to wait and hope that someone—Chelomei, Grushin, or Mikoyan—finds an answer. Meanwhile we shouldn't sit with our hands folded; let's get ready for visits from uninvited U.S. spies."

Father turned to Malinovsky: "Rodion Yakovlevich, we will have to think back to our experience at the front, how we built false airfields and erected plywood tanks and planes. The Germans fell for it more than once, and they were flying near the ground."

"We'll think about it," Malinovsky nodded in agreement.

"Good." Father even seemed to be pleased. "We can prop up some missiles. From space you can't examine things closely. Let them guess whether they're real missiles or not."

They agreed to start camouflaging real missiles and begin building fake ones. Some time later they even adopted a special program and began building wooden launch pads with rubber missiles. Huge rubber submarines, blown up like children's balloons, were floated at naval bases. The idea appealed to Father. He thought that it was possible to produce the necessary impression without spending a lot of money.

By the end of the 1960s this scheme finally petered out. By then newly developed technologies probably made it possible to differentiate from space false platforms from real ones. Besides, the Soviet Union had made more than enough missiles, planes, and submarines. The opposite problem had emerged: not how to make the Americans believe that we had them, but how to hide them and keep them from being counted.

The problem of identifying and destroying hostile spies in space continued to concern Father for some time. He finally became convinced that it was impossible to establish national borders in space, just as it was impossible to judge which satellite was a threat to our security and which was simply carrying out peaceful research.

By November 1, 1963, when Chelomei began his experiments with space interceptors (IS) in orbit, the question of violating state sovereignty outside the atmosphere was removed from the agenda. In 1963 the United Nations adopted a resolution stating that national borders did not extend to space and that space belonged to everyone.

ESPIONAGE IN SPACE

Father's fears of space espionage were not without foundation. At the beginning of 1960 America tried to blast spy satellites into orbit, one after another. Both Father and I, as well as other specialists involved in rocket matters, followed the launches with something like the mystical horror of the condemned, and every report of a failure caused us to sigh with relief. But sooner or later, success was inevitable. After the data from the top-secret Corona project was disclosed, the world knew that the successful launch in August of 1960 was preceded by twelve failures, either of the rocket, the camera, or some other vitally important piece of equipment. But beginning in August the territory of the Soviet Union was photographed regularly and comprehensively, something the U-2 had never been able to accomplish.

Ray Cline and Raymond Garthoff are former high-ranking CIA officials whom I have encountered over the past few years at conferences devoted to the Cuban Crisis. They both turned out to be very nice gentlemen, and we became quite cordial. Cline and Garthoff both say that the CIA was able, with the help of intelligence from space, to ascertain that we had no more than seventy-five ICBMs.

This number was then reduced to fifty. By January of 1961 there was already talk of forty-four missiles. This shows that when Father talked about our country being literally studded with missiles, the satellites proved it was disinformation. Still, it was not yet possible to count them with the help of space spies. Of course, that would come.

The first successful launch of a U.S. spy satellite came as a real shock to Moscow. Father fumed and conceived the idea of writing a protest, but, after cooling off, remembered the first U-2 flights and discarded the futile idea. The next launch was seen as an unavoidable irritant. We gradually got used to the presence of spies in the sky, as you adjust to everything in life. It simply came to resemble somewhat the life of lizards in a glass terrarium, where anyone who wanted to could peer in.

The Americans went through a long and agonizing process in developing their system of space intelligence.

The successful launch of a spy satellite into orbit and even the photographing of a particular region did not put an end to problems. The information had to be delivered back to earth. If it was transmitted by radio, you lost a crucial element—the details, the specific information for which the expensive project was organized. The only alternative was a module with tape sent back to earth for further processing and study. It had to be dropped within a strictly defined area. For some reason those attempts were unsuccessful for a long time. The return modules fell anywhere but where they were expected. In the 1960s they were even found in our country.

Apparently the first time this happened was in the winter of 1960 or 1961. Loggers in the backwoods near Kalinin (now Tver), a city about 120 miles north of Moscow, found an apparatus ejected from a Discovery satellite. They were intrigued by this strange toy, but couldn't manage to open it. Without wasting any time thinking it over, they hacked the satellite into two pieces. Inside they found nothing valuable, just wires and a cluster of transistors. They took everything home and threw it into a shed. Some time later rumors of the strange find reached the authorities. Summoned to the village Soviet and then to the regional KGB office, the unfortunate villagers didn't deny that they had found something, but they didn't know what it was. Some kids had already stolen a few of the curious little components, but the villagers brought in what was left.

It was all sent off to Moscow. Then the find was transferred from the KGB to the Academy of Sciences. Finally, after many peregrinations, the priceless collection arrived in Korolyov's design bureau. People there could only say with regret that it was from a U.S. satellite—but in what condition!

An expedition was dispatched to the Kalinin woods, which were thoroughly searched without finding anything. A few small items were recovered in the homes of the villagers, some electric relays and scraps of wire. No useful information could be gleaned from this refuse.

In all likelihood, this was the Discovery satellite the Americans lost track of in 1959, after it fell unexpectedly from orbit. For some reason they searched for the satellite on the island of Spitzbergen, in the Arctic. This incident has served as the basis for numerous detective stories and films. In them the famous James Bond and other heroes and villains live through incredible adventures in order to gain possession of extremely desirable U.S. space secrets. In real life everything was far more prosaic.

Another U.S. satellite was found in the spring of 1961 by tractor drivers in the virgin lands, during sowing. They found a return capsule. In those years we thought that it belonged to a SAMOS, another U.S. spy satellite. The tractor drivers belonged to a higher class of specialists and didn't try to open it with an ax. They used a screwdriver to take the strange object apart. Inside they found nothing of interest except a miniature battery, a generally useful object. Large reels holding wide opaque film took up most of the container. Wedged in next to them was an unusual type of photographic gadget, as well as some kind of electronic gear. The film seemed unusually strong. Two of the strongest fellows couldn't tear it. Such resistance provoked the tractor brigade. What kind of snake was this, not to give in! They brought their find to a field camp, tied it to two tractors, and stepped on the gas—the film couldn't stand the pressure and tore apart with a crackling sound. Satisfied by the capitulation of the offender, they began to wonder if some kind of use might be made of this nonsensical object. They thought of something. The field station was located in the steppe. There wasn't a tree or a small hill anywhere in sight. Water for drinking and washing was brought in a tank, and the brigade members themselves had to devise all other conveniences. They had dug a pit for a toilet, but couldn't provide it any privacy. There was no wood available to construct walls. Now they found a solution: they hammered four stakes into the ground and wound the film around them. The installation looked elegant and modern. However, it didn't last long. The state farm director who came to check on their work immediately noticed the new structure.

When asked where they got such an unusual material, the men answered simply: "We found it in a furrow in the field." The director swore at the tractor drivers for not reporting it. Who knows what might have been hidden in the container? They shouldn't have opened it but should have given their find to the proper authorities. But what was done, was done. The director set out for home. He remembered their find only several days later, when he drove to the district center in connection with the sowing. With a chuckle, he described the unusual toilet to the district committee secretary, who immediately telephoned the local KGB office and described what had happened.

That started the ball rolling. Specialists called to the place ascertained that both the container and the film had come from space. They carefully rewound it and thoroughly examined the area where it was found, but there was nothing else. They collected everything that was still available: both the discarded remnants of film and the half-dismantled module.

Again results were poor; everything was broken and half the parts had disappeared. Intelligence analysts were particularly upset. They had very much wanted to learn what the Americans could see from orbit.

Father first heard about this occurrence from me. He ordered them to take measures. An instruction was sent out ordering people to turn over any unusual finds to the authorities. It went to all local offices, including those in the very interior of the country. Finders were promised a considerable reward, naturally after the object was examined.

The order was too late. Apparently the Americans perfected a system for dropping the exposed film. It now landed where it was supposed to land. I didn't hear of any more such finds.

In 1998 Lev Golovin published an article that provided some details about these U.S. satellites. According to him, the first satellite (he did not see it himself but read a report about it) was a "small spherical module with a diameter of 12 inches, made from an aluminum alloy, polished and gilded on the outside. Electronic and other devices were located inside the module. After careful study by various specialists and the writing of a report, it was destroyed. No features worth borrowing were found, although certain things might have been worth copying." The reason for destroying the satellite is unclear. We leave that to the author's conscience. The article states that the satellite descended by parachute into the Kalinin woods and was found in the winter of 1959. However, it's not clear whether that was in January 1959 or December 1959.

Golovin himself took part in examining the second satellite. Discovered in the spring of 1961 by

> . . . farm workers in the virgin lands steppe, it was several meters in size. Inside the satellite was a camera with an objective 12-inch lens, protected by a transparent aperture with an orange light filter. Reel-shaped canisters held hundreds of meters of four-inch-wide film. Inside the body of the pear-shaped module, covered in several places by heat-resistant fiberglass laminate, was an inertial orientation system driving a rather powerful electric motor, which in turn rotated the camera. That was where the electronic devices were found.
>
> Unfortunately, when examined, the satellite was incomplete and extensively damaged: the optics had suffered, a large part was missing, the film was unwound from the cameras and had been exposed, making it impossible to develop what had been photographed. Part of the equipment had been stolen—specifically, sources of electric power to the satellite were missing. We were not able to establish whether this apparatus was a prototype of a spy satellite, such as the SAMOS.
>
> Technological aspects: welding of aluminum alloy and heat-resistant fiberglass laminate were not novelties, but it would have been useful to copy smaller parts. Equipment within the apparatus had not been very carefully installed. Later on, spy satellites were improved and film could be dropped from orbit in a capsule after being partially exposed.[4]

THE BATTLE AGAINST COLONIALISM

After Paris Father was finally disenchanted with the possibility of achieving real results in negotiations with the United States, Britain, and France. But

---

4. Lev Golovin, "American Arrivals from Space in the USSR," *NG Nauka*, supplement to *Nezavisimaya gazeta*, October 7, 1998.

he thought that the pressure of public opinion might force the West to meet him halfway.

On June 3 Father sent the heads of all the world's governments a message outlining a plan for universal and complete disarmament. This proposal appeared rather utopian, but it would affect everyone. He proposed that the document be discussed at the next session of the U.N. General Assembly, which was convening on September 18.

For the first time Father thought seriously of going in person to the General Assembly in New York. He very much hoped that his example would be followed by the heads of other states, and primarily Asian and African leaders. In that case, he thought, Western governments would be put in a position where they simply could not ignore the session. By convening a high-level meeting without prior arrangement, Father would then have his revenge, as it were, for Paris. The time was favorable. The authority of the United States was in decline after the failure of the U-2 and the breakup of the Paris conference. Eisenhower's trip to the countries of Asia—Japan, South Korea, and Taiwan—was practically ruined by protests and demonstrations.

In the meantime Father was simply thinking things over and, while waiting for a response to his message, preparing new ones. Typists and aides worked nonstop. Father considered the question of decolonization to be no less important than that of disarmament. For him, the struggle for freedom in Africa, Asia, and Latin America was of deep personal concern.

Kwame Nkrumah in Ghana and Sekou Toure in Guinea announced that they were followers of Marxism. There, in the colonies, the almost forgotten dream of world revolution was reborn. It seemed to Father that the world was beginning to stir, that with only a small effort there would be progress. His duty was to support these new revolutionary movements. He saw it as up to him to ensure that the imperialists did not stamp out these shoots of a new socialist organism. However, this endeavor ran into increasing difficulties. Although power was transferred peacefully in many cases, in others the situation threatened to turn into a world crisis.

The prolonged war in the Congo, where a young, impulsive, and naive prime minister, Patrice Lumumba, was fighting simultaneously with the former colonizers, his own President Kasavubu, local separatists, and even the United Nations troops sent to ensure peace and tranquillity, had the effect of polarizing the international situation. The Soviet Union backed Lumumba. Our support was mainly of a moral nature. As far as real assistance was concerned, there were insuperable obstacles. Nevertheless, Father tried to do everything he could. Three Soviet IL-18s delivered food supplies to starving Leopoldville. They were supplemented by the ship *Leninogorsk*, which left Odessa with a cargo of wheat, sugar, and condensed milk. Other ships followed. They brought doctors, GAZ-67 cross-country vehicles, and of course, food.

In addition, two IL-18s, chartered by neighboring Ghana, transported Ghanaian military units to the Congo. It was all only a drop in the ocean. Father was nervous. The news from the Congo didn't make him feel any better. What irritated and alarmed him most was that all U.N. business in the Congo was administered by Americans. Four-fifths of the hundred and fifty U.N. personnel in the Congo were American, and not one was from our country. U.N. representatives used American planes to move around the country. Father became absolutely convinced that Dag Hammarskjöld didn't dare make a move without Eisenhower's approval.

The world press poured oil on the fire. Newspapers bristled with headlines: Khrushchev is suffering one defeat after another in the Congo.

Father tried to turn the situation around by taking another approach. On August 21 he advanced a proposal to the U.N. and the Great Powers to join forces to provide aid to the Congo. There was no response. Father became increasingly nervous. He was depressed by his own impotence and irritated by the arrogance of the West.

It was then that he thought of a new initiative: a U.N. declaration on the granting of independence to colonial countries and peoples. This is where you have to look for the roots of his demand that executive power in the U.N. be divided between representatives of capitalist, socialist, and developing countries.

On July 9, speaking at the All-Russian Congress of Teachers, Father announced to the whole world that, in answer to Eisenhower's announcement of an economic blockade of Cuba, we would extend a helping hand to that country. He predicted that this small country, located in a favorable climatic zone and freed from the exploitation of imperialists, would begin in a few years to flourish and would become the window on a new life in the Western hemisphere.

Nine days later Father was especially cordial when he received Raul Castro, brother of the revolution's leader and the second-ranking person in Cuba. That day can probably be considered the beginning of the special relationship between the two countries. It all began with sugar. Eisenhower had imposed an embargo on trade with Cuba. Since America was Cuba's largest customer for sugar, this one executive order cost Cuba most of its foreign trade. Fidel Castro was in urgent need of a new buyer. At first Father couldn't imagine buying Cuban sugar. Russia had never bought sugar, since it produced enough of its own. After the blockade was announced, world prices for sugar escalated and Father hoped that the Cubans could sell their sugar. He even poked fun at the Americans, who would now have to be satisfied with unsweetened tea. However, fate decreed otherwise: Cuba's neighbors in the Caribbean basin increased plantings of sugar cane and the Americans didn't have to do without. Castro asked for help. New friends had to come to the rescue. Father reluctantly agreed to the temporary purchase of Cuban sugar. Time passed, new buyers did not appear, and the agreement was extended. At the same time, sugar prices fell and our friends were threatened with serious losses. At Cuba's request the Soviet Union established fixed prices.

Only one year earlier the Soviet leadership couldn't have imagined that fate would link Moscow and Havana. Father, as well as foreign affairs "specialists" in the Central Committee, knew very little about Latin America. And they were even less interested. They had closed the Soviet Embassy in Cuba back in 1952, as unnecessary. Therefore Father didn't pay much attention to Batista's flight or to the speech given in Havana on January 1, 1959, by the guerrilla leader Fidel Castro.

When Father asked for information on Cuba, it turned out that there was nothing to give him. Neither the international department of the Central Committee nor KGB intelligence, nor military intelligence had any idea who Fidel was, what he was fighting for, or what he was trying to achieve. Grigory Pushkin, head of the international department of the Central Committee, had to take the blame. Father advised him to ask the Cuban communists. They explained that Castro was a representative of the haute bourgeoisie, moreover an agent of the CIA, and that there wasn't much difference between him and Batista. This is how it was reported to Father.

However, the KGB decided to investigate, and they sent Aleksandr Alekseyev, a "TASS correspondent" to Havana. He proved to be both smart and efficient. From his reports Father began to get a somewhat different picture, and he started to follow events on the island more closely. He gradually formed the opinion that the Cuban communists were mistaken (in fact, internal disputes were the reason for their comments). Fidel himself had not revealed his sympathies, but his brother openly called himself a Marxist. Father was simply delighted. A socialist revolution was taking place right near the United States. Here was yet another confirmation of the truth of Marxism and Leninism. But Father couldn't quite believe it; he had his doubts. And so did others. They decided to make sure. In February 1960, Anastas Ivanovich Mikoyan prepared to visit Cuba.

On the eve of his departure Mikoyan came to see Father at the dacha. I remember the following small episode. A group of us went for a walk. Anastas Ivanovich had brought his son Sergo, and my brother-in-law Adzhubei joined us. Aleksei Ivanovich talked about Fidel Castro's recent trip to Washington, where he had met with Vice President Nixon. No one knew what they had talked about, but such a meeting worried Father very much. Adzhubei cited reports in the American press and tried to persuade us that Castro was a U.S. agent and could not be trusted. And even if he's not an agent, he will still dance to the tune of the White House.

Anastas Ivanovich returned from Cuba in an enthusiastic mood. He described in minute detail his meetings with the brothers Castro, with Che Guevara, and with other Cubans. In his opinion, they were undoubtedly honorable fighters for freedom. Their ideology was rapidly evolving toward Marxism. Mikoyan thought that Cuba must be helped, but after taking every imaginable precaution. If people in Washington guessed where Castro was heading before the new regime had a chance to grow stronger, they would destroy it in a flash.

Father continued to watch Castro closely for some time longer, but already as a potential friend and congenial thinker. He found more and more to confirm Anastas Ivanovich's opinion and admired the heroism of the Cuban people. He no longer had doubts; we, as internationalists, must help Cuba. We will not allow the revolution to be choked.

That was easy to say, but what could we do? The United States had a powerful navy, and only ninety miles of water separated it from Cuba. And what did we have? Virtually no fleet, at least not one that, after sailing eleven thousand kilometers, could confront a powerful adversary. All we could do was provide economic assistance and political support.

After his meeting on June 3 with the head of an economic mission led by Antonio Nuñez Ximenez, director of the Cuban National Institute of Agrarian Reform, Father decided to make his attitude public.

On August 22, 1960, the first Soviet ambassador to Cuba, M. S. Kudryavtsev, handed his credentials to President Oswaldo Dorticos.

This gave Father yet another potential source for a headache. The subject of the borders of the GDR remained constantly on his mind, and now he had to think about guarding Cuba against U.S. aggression.

Even before meeting him, Father was enamored with the image of Fidel Castro. He simply couldn't wait to meet the "bearded one," but there were no plans for that as yet.

KHRUSHCHEV AT THE UNITED NATIONS

In the middle of July Father finally made a definite decision—he himself, at the head of the Soviet delegation, would go to New York for the General Assembly session. This was announced officially on August 10. However, the cautious Gromyko recommended leaving some room for maneuver. The announcement should say only that Father might participate in the work of the session. Gromyko was afraid that other countries would not follow

Father. In that case, Father might be, if not alone, then in the rather small circle of allies from the Warsaw Pact.

Father was given yet another folder, this one containing reports coming in about other government leaders who had decided to go to New York. It grew noticeably thicker with every day. Father was triumphant—the world was responding to his call. Leaders of the European countries, not just Indian leader Jawaharlal Nehru and Indonesian president Sukarno, would be coming to New York to discuss the problems of decolonization and disarmament. Even the prime minister of Japan, Norosiki Kese, announced his intention of taking part in the discussions. Father felt that he had won the confrontation with Eisenhower. Now Eisenhower could not ignore such an important meeting; he would have to respond to Father's initiative, and respond positively. Father hoped to drive his Western partners into a corner over the question of decolonization—let them try to object in front of the whole world. He thought that votes would tend to go in his favor. The call for universal disarmament, however, he considered to be more of a propaganda move. He didn't expect quick results there. It was a matter of taking the first step and preparing for a long journey.

Father loved to call himself an agitator and believed that a sincere word would find its way to a person's heart, even if not immediately. He thought it was very important that everyone would have to speak at the General Assembly: there the peoples of the world would see what the leaders of different countries stood for and what they were really worth.

With respect to reforming the U.N.'s executive power, Father had fewer supporters, even at home. The cautious Gromyko was worried about losing contact with our partners, and not only those in the West. Three secretaries general instead of one could only make that body even less decisive. However, Father didn't hide his purpose. He dreamed of destroying the automatic pro-Western majority in voting. Though his goal was understandable, he pursued it awkwardly. But Father would not accept anyone's advice in this matter. Here he took the bit in his teeth, as the saying goes. As soon as those around him sensed that he had no intention of changing his mind, his opponents vanished. They all became his fervent supporters. I refer, naturally, to the Soviet delegation.

Father decided to travel by ship. Leaving from the port of Kaliningrad, the trip would take ten days, but Father optimistically supposed that the time could be spent preparing speeches, polishing documents, and arriving at a final determination of delegations' positions. Accompanying him on the voyage to New York were not only delegations from the Ukraine and Belorussia, but representatives from most of the socialist countries as well. Only the Romanians turned down Father's invitation and decided to go by plane.

Apart from anything else, Father very much wanted to cross the ocean on a ship, just like the first settlers in America, whose adventures he had read about in his youth. He thought there would never be another such opportunity. Father was increasingly preoccupied by the thought of death. It all began with his general's uniform. He had it made for the fortieth anniversary of the Soviet Army. Returning home after the gala ceremony, he suggested rather diffidently: "Let's take some pictures. I'll probably never put it on again." His words really upset me. I started arguing with him, but he gently stopped my torrent of reassurances by repeating: "Let's take some pictures; you'll have them to remind you of me." As I write these lines, I'm sitting in a room where this photograph is hanging on the wall: Father in the uniform of a lieutenant-general with a row of medals on his jacket, and I, his son, looking very young, next to him.

The ship, the *Baltika*, cast off on September 9. Aside from Father, the Soviet delegation consisted of Andrei Andreyevich Gromyko and his two deputies, Zorin and Soldatov. Autumn weather in the Atlantic is changeable. The smooth and peaceful surface of the ocean soon gave way to large waves and the ship began to rock. Father was especially proud of his immunity to seasickness. He greeted his fellow voyagers with jokes when they crawled out of their cabins, looking green about the gills, to inhale some fresh air. He spent almost all of his time on deck, where he worked, chatted with colleagues, or simply relaxed.

The confrontation between Eisenhower and Father that started in Paris continued. Sometimes it would have seemed rather childish and even amusing, if not for the enormous concentrations of power involved. This time, on the eve of Father's arrival in New York, U.S. authorities announced that the Soviet delegation was forbidden to travel, not only about the country, but even around New York outside Manhattan without asking permission from the police.

This pinprick only emboldened Father. He became even more convinced that the only way to restore the U.N.'s ability to function and its authority in the world was to reorganize its structure and perhaps move its headquarters outside the United States.

Father launched himself into a battle to expose the aggressive nature of the United States and its president. He planned to start with the most painful and pressing matters. By the opening of the General Assembly session, the situation in the Congo had become extremely critical. Everyone was shooting at everyone else. Prime Minister Patrice Lumumba and his supporters were losing one position after another and their days were undoubtedly numbered. The U.N. forces were unable to do anything. At the General Assembly Father planned to raise the question of the situation in the Congo immediately. The discussion promised to be an unpleasant one. In the

Congo the United States and USSR had staked their prestige on opposite sides.

Another no less painful matter was the acceptance of new members by the U.N. The USSR regularly raised the question of replacing the representative from Taiwan with a delegate from the Chinese People's Republic and the United States just as persistently voted against the proposal. People in the White House became nervous. Father could seize the initiative and attract third world countries to his side. Eisenhower, playing by the rules of military art, decided to deliver a preemptive strike and remove Father from the game. The *Baltika* was to arrive September 19, on the eve of the opening session, scheduled for the twentieth. No power on earth could get Father to New York any sooner.

So the Americans proposed holding a preliminary, extraordinary session, with the following agenda: the acceptance of new members by the U.N. and the situation in the Congo. It was decided to convene it on September 17.

Delegations traveling to the U.N. in a less exotic fashion than Father could easily change their plane tickets. But the *Baltika*'s passengers fell into the trap. They were left to follow the course of discussion on the radio. However, Father was not discouraged. He took every opportunity to comment on how the Americans were frightened by his very appearance. Father spoke about the Congo and China at subsequent sessions, without paying much attention to what was on the agenda.

And so, on September 19 the *Baltika* approached the port of New York. The ship docked at one of the less fashionable berths. It's hard for me to say now whether Father had a choice. He said that he himself preferred an inexpensive berth.

The reception was not like that of the previous year: there was no red carpet, no podium with microphones, no officials to greet him, not even minor ones. At the boarding ramp stood members of the Soviet U.N. delegation and other residents of the Soviet community. In front were children with bouquets of flowers, just as if this were some small provincial town. And, naturally, a crowd of reporters.

The slim, neat figure of Cyrus Eaton was prominent among the welcomers. His gray head was uncovered and he held his hat in his hand. This Canadian-American millionaire allowed himself to have an independent point of view on relations between our two countries and on the proper way to greet Khrushchev.

This unfriendly welcome put Father in a fighting mood. He thought that this reaction by the imperialists showed that he was adopting the right policies. The main thing was not to panic, not to rush. It would all gradually work out. We couldn't get away from each other; sooner or later it would be necessary to face reality and reach agreement. We must be patient.

Meanwhile Father, who was usually sociable in any case, redoubled his energy. He talked, expounded his views, and tried to persuade people. His days were filled with visits and discussions, and not just with representatives of the third world. The Europeans could also not allow themselves to ignore Father. But one meeting left a really strong impression on him. Barely off the ship, Father asked where Fidel Castro was staying. He was told that Castro was living in a run-down little hotel in Black Harlem. Other hotels had simply refused to accept him. That made Father angry, and he decided to visit Castro at once. There was barely time to phone the Cubans. Fidel was a little taken aback and said that he would come himself. Father wouldn't hear of it. He felt that he was simply obliged to show respect to the representative of a small, fearless, and freedom-loving people.

Father understood that their meeting would be seen as a challenge and tried to arrange it to produce the greatest effect. However, that took no particular effort: Harlem, Khrushchev, Castro. A huge crowd of journalists rushed to the spot.

Father and Fidel Castro met in the lobby of the hotel. They hugged each other and kissed. Father recalled later that he felt as if a bear hugged him. He was captivated by Castro's sincerity, his unwavering determination to win or to die for the cause of his people's liberation. This meeting in New York completely convinced Father of the need to help Cuba in its struggle by every possible means, economic, political, and military. However, they didn't rush to talk about military assistance; they were cautious, since both parties were afraid of provoking the United States.

In New York Father looked for and found Americans who regarded him favorably: some waved, others smiled. Later he always remembered the concern shown by one of the many journalists who waited constantly under the windows of the building where he was staying. Father would get bored; in the intervals between sessions and meetings he was cooped up inside four walls. He couldn't walk along the streets and was forbidden to leave the city. The only outlet for diversion was a small balcony, from which he would chat with reporters and amuse himself. One time he was handed a note from a journalist, who wrote that New York was not Moscow and with today's situation Father was risking his life by standing on the balcony, which was exposed to thousands of windows in buildings on either side of the street. No one knew who was behind those windows or what they were thinking, and anyone could buy a gun. Father was touched and took the warning into consideration, but he didn't stop going out on the balcony. He didn't want to be suspected of cowardice.

At the General Assembly, Father wasted no time. He participated actively in the discussions, which went on for two weeks. He made statements, took the floor on procedural matters, raised objections. In his opinion, he conducted himself like a true Western parliamentarian. I don't want to describe the discussions, since a great deal has been written about them. However, still more has been written about the shoe. It has become a symbol of Father's stay in New York and in the United States in general. It eclipsed both Disneyland and Camp David. It might seem that there is nothing to add to the story. Why should I justify it? It's better to pass over it in silence. At first that was what I thought—that it would be a thankless and hopeless task to retouch that fixed image. Then I changed my mind. And this is why. "Look before you leap," advises the proverb. That's true in everyday life. But in politics, if you don't know your partner's way of thinking, his habits and customs can mislead you. But what has the shoe got to do with it? I will try to explain. Although Father was a sincerely emotional person, he exerted firm control over his actions. Otherwise how could he have become a politician?

A rebellious streak sometimes surfaced when Father was speaking off the cuff. Then, "winding himself up," he could overstep the boundaries he had set himself. That did happen. Newspapers from those years sometimes carried explanations of what the chairman of the Council of Ministers meant, and did not mean, to say in a recent speech. Sometimes he used this method deliberately, in order to see its effect somewhere in the West or East.

But in parliamentary discussions Father felt himself to be a novice—or more precisely, a student. He didn't have the chance to practice. When Father first began to speak from the Supreme Soviet rostrum, the most important part of any speech was considered to be the number of references to Stalin's name and the quality of the adjectives and hyperbole that accompanied them.

And what happened abroad, in foreign parliaments? Newspaper descriptions we read took our breath away. We believed that fights and mutual insults were normal conduct among Western legislators. During the visit to Britain, this belief was even reinforced during the delegation's tour of Parliament. We were shown two stripes painted on the floor of the Chamber which separated representatives of the ruling and opposition parties. It was strictly forbidden to step over them. Our guide explained that the space between the two lines must by law exceed a sword length, so as to ensure the personal safety of the debaters. At the time Father joked that such rules had also existed in the Russian State Duma when he was a young man.

After attending a session of the General Assembly, he was amazed: "It was the first time that I participated in such an organization. . . . Representatives of bourgeois countries used methods accepted in bourgeois parliaments: they talked loudly, banged on their desks, talked back and forth. In a word, they obstructed a speaker if they didn't like what he was saying. We began—I speak for myself—to repay them in the same coin. We made a racket, stamped our feet, etc."

We can also not ignore a certain sense of mischief, epitomized by the motto: "We'll show you." All that, along with his emotional nature, resulted in Father's surpassing the most vehement parliamentary troublemaker who furiously slams his fist on the table.

It wasn't the first time he put on such a show. During his previous year's visit to the United States, Father was extremely displeased by the reception shown him in Los Angeles. It all ended in a squabble or, more precisely, in the harsh response he delivered at a dinner given by the city's mayor, Norris Poulson. In reply to the mayor's reference to his unfortunate remark "We will bury you," Father exploded: "I have already said in New York that I was not referring to Americans, but to capitalism, the economic formation that will not withstand competition from socialism. Don't mayors read newspapers in America? I think they do, but deliberately throw this dead cat at me, hoping to make me quarrel with people. It won't work." Father went on to say that he was the representative of a great power and had a right to expect the respect he was due. If that were not the case, he would collect his bags and head back to Moscow immediately.

This whole show appeared spontaneous—an outburst of emotion from a not very self-controlled person. After the official dinner the delegation, aides, and others gathered in the spacious living room of the Premier's apartment. Everyone looked distraught and upset. Father took off his jacket and sat down on a stool. The others found places on couches and chairs.

Father looked intently at everyone. His expression was severe, but there were glints of humor in his eyes. He broke the silence and said that we, representatives of a great power, would not put up with people ordering us about. He spent the next half hour, without mincing words, expressing his attitude concerning the manner in which our delegation was being received. He practically shouted. His rage seemed infinite. But his eyes sparkled mischievously. Every now and then Father raised an arm and pointed to the ceiling, as if to say that his words were not intended for those present, but for those who were eavesdropping.

The monologue finally came to an end.

One minute passed, then another, while those present maintained a perplexed silence. Father wiped perspiration from his bald head—the performance had demanded an extraordinary effort—and turned to Gromyko: "Comrade Gromyko, go and tell Lodge[5] everything that I've said."

Andrei Andreyevich stood up, cleared his throat and headed for the door. A somber determination was visible on his usually unsmiling face. His hand

---

5. Henry Cabot Lodge, formerly the U.S. ambassador to the United Nations, accompanied Khrushchev on his trip around the country on behalf of the president.

was already on the handle of the door when his wife, Lidiya Dmitriyevna, couldn't restrain herself. "Andryusha, be more polite!" she implored.

Andrei Andreyevich didn't react to this dramatic appeal and the door closed silently behind him.

I glanced at Father.

He was openly exultant. Lidiya Dmitriyevna's reaction was proof that he had played the part successfully.

The next day we arrived in San Francisco. It seemed as if our hosts had changed: friendly faces and not one offensive word.

I don't doubt that Father would have responded immediately if one of our diplomats accompanying him at the U.N. had told him how his conduct was actually received by the delegates. Naturally, Father would not have been transformed into a dignified Macmillan, with his melancholy eyes, or a de Gaulle, who rigidly controlled every single gesture. He would have remained himself, but he would have discarded the mask of troublemaker. Unfortunately, it's not our custom to reprimand people in power. That is postponed until later, after the funeral or, less often, after retirement.

This is how Father remembered the incident:

It so happened that the Spanish delegation sat in front of us. The delegation was led by a middle-aged man with a large bald spot, framed by gray hair. He was thin, his face was wrinkled and his pointed nose protruded from a long face. If our two countries had been on good terms, I would have said, well, all right, quite a nice man. But our relations couldn't have been worse, and he made the appropriately negative impression on me. The feeling was mutual.

I should add a few words about meeting with Dolores Ibarrura, before our departure.[6] We were on very good terms.

She said: "Comrade Khrushchev, when you speak at the U.N. it would be good if you used the occasion to condemn the Franco regime in Spain."

So I was thinking about how to do that. We sat a little above the Spanish delegation, and the bald head of the Spanish representative was right in front of me. As I looked at him I suddenly remembered Dolores Ibarrura's request.

When the subject turned to the liquidation of colonialism, I decided to take the opportunity to carry out her mission. I spoke very harshly against Franco, naturally without mentioning his name. I spoke about a reactionary, bloody regime and used other expressions which we communists employ in the press to denounce the Franco regime.

Then the Spanish representative got up to reply.

Father categorically disagreed with the words coming from the rostrum and decided to show how indignant he was. Such a little devil always lurked

---

6. Dolores Ibarrura—"La Pasionarra." Among the founders and leaders of the Spanish Communist Party and famous civil war orator.

inside him. It peeped out now and pushed Father into some minor hooliganism. With a cunning expression, Father looked around and then leaned down toward the floor. Gromyko, who was sitting next to him, watched Father curiously. A quiet member of the Soviet delegation, called Georgy Mikhailovich Zhivotovsky, was sitting not far away. He may have had a different name at the time. He had been assigned by his agency to observe everything that happened. I will try to reproduce his account verbatim, as far as possible:

> Nikita Sergeyevich continued to fiddle with something under his desk and finally, beet red, straightened up in his chair. He was holding his boot, or rather his loafer. [Father couldn't stand laces.—S.K.]
>
> Looking around and smiling, he began to tap the bottom of the shoe on his desk, at first softly. No one paid him any attention, with the exception of Andrei Andreyevich, who followed his every movement as if mesmerized.
>
> Khrushchev gradually increased the tempo. He needed to attract people's attention. Finally he got his way as, one after another, the delegates turned their heads in surprise toward the Soviet delegation. A stir ran through the hall. The speaker, unaware of the cause, began to grow nervous. Then Khrushchev started banging the heel of his shoe on the desk as hard as he could.

According to Georgy Mikhailovich, it was then that a grimace of determination passed over Gromyko's face, as if he were about to jump into cold water. He leaned down, took off his shoe and began quietly to tap it on his desk in time with Father. While doing that, he managed to turn in such a way that only Father saw what he was doing. The rhythmic movements of the Soviet foreign minister's right hand didn't convey anything to those sitting in the hall. It looked as if he were shaking something off the lapel of his suit jacket. So the only other person who noticed was the man whose job it was to observe everything.

Father described how the altercation ended:

> The Spaniard returned to his seat. When he sat down we exchanged words, without understanding each other's language. We both employed gestures to express our displeasure.
>
> Suddenly a big tall policeman came up and stood like a statue in the space between us and the Spanish delegation. Apparently his job was to make sure that we didn't get into a fight. There were times when delegates disagreed and got into fights.[7]

---

7. Father was in error. In fact, his shoe was "bestowed" on a delegate from the Philippines, not the Spaniard. So Dolores Ibarrura had nothing to do with it. I decided not to correct Father. What difference does it make? And he described his foe so vividly. Perhaps when the Spaniard spoke Father pounded the desk with his fist, and no less energetically. But a fist doesn't exceed the bounds of propriety.—S.K.

When the session was over the members of the Soviet delegation rushed to congratulate Father.

Father recalled during his retirement that the only person who reacted negatively to his action at the time was Indian prime minister Jawaharlal Nehru. He thought that it was not the way to act.

The Soviet delegation was fined for improper behavior. I was informed of this many times—naturally, after Father retired. Of course, everyone was interested in the size of the fine. One million dollars, or even more, was mentioned. I tried to discover the truth. The most reliable sources said ten thousand. Still a sizable sum.

At the end of October 1964, after Father was ousted from power, Gromyko, speaking at a Foreign Ministry meeting, sharply condemned Father's behavior.

This essentially insignificant incident went down in history inextricably linked to Father's name. For many, especially Americans, Khrushchev is "the one who banged his shoe on his desk at the U.N."

Father returned to Moscow on October 14, by plane. He felt that he had won, that the unprecedentedly high level of representatives at the General Assembly session, as well as the importance of the subjects discussed there, compensated for the failure of the conference in Paris.

THE CATASTROPHE AT TYURA-TAM

Yangel enjoyed a remarkably successful year in 1960. The R-12, which had brought recognition to himself and his design bureau, was deployed by the military. Launch sites were located in the Ukraine, Belorussia, and the Baltics. The military reported that it was much easier to handle than the R-5. Designers had provided both large and small hatches, so that instruments and equipment could be reached easily; you didn't have to display acrobatic agility and "Russian native wit" to get to them.

Then it was the R-16's turn. Final preparations for the first launch, scheduled for the end of October (half a year earlier than Korolyov's R-9), were being made at Tyura-Tam.

Father referred to Yangel everywhere, making him an example to other designers, even Korolyov. He was childishly delighted at the successful choice he had made some years earlier. The new chief designer surpassed all expectations. One last step remained for his final triumph—the launch of an intercontinental missile.

Korolyov, who was used to being in the lead, was fiercely jealous of his rival. He claimed that Yangel managed to test first only because of the priority given to Glushko's design bureau to develop an engine fueled with acid.

When Father got back from New York, Nedelin informed him that the launch was planned for October 23.

No information came from the test site on October 23. Design bureaus were immediately aware of launches, even those of neighbors. On this occasion there was dead silence. That did not cause any special concern—the launch must have been postponed, which had happened more than once. That evening Father confirmed our guess. Nedelin had called and reported various bugs, which were being eliminated. Father advised them not to hurry. A day or two wouldn't make any difference.

The following day there were rumors in our design bureau of an accident at Tyura-Tam. No one knew exactly what happened. Not even Chelomei. The incident was held in the strictest secrecy. Only a little information leaked out: the launch site was destroyed and there were casualties.

That evening Father came home in a black mood. Getting out of the car, he started walking along the narrow paved path next to the stone fence surrounding the residence. I joined him. I was very eager to ask a question, but Father's scowling face discouraged me. I decided to let him begin.

It grew quite dark and the lamps were casting faint circles of light on the pavement. Fallen leaves rustled underfoot.

Finally Father broke the painful silence.

"The R-16 blew up at the launch site," he said in a muffled voice. "People were killed. Many people. They can't find Nedelin. Probably he also . . ."

Father didn't finish the sentence and fell silent. I simply froze with horror.

Until then accidents during our missile tests had not resulted in any casualties, much less many of them. God had spared us. During the recent accident involving the R-7, which occurred as the engines were starting, the launch pad was destroyed and the structure and parts were turned into twisted fragments, but no one was injured. Everyone not directly involved in launch preparations had been evacuated in advance to a safe place, in accordance with regulations, while the launch team and State Commission members were protected by a deep and safe concrete bunker.

In general, accidents had become rare, especially with Yangel. What could have happened? Naturally, I couldn't hold back and asked, "What about Mikhail Kuzmich?"

"It's hard to say. Something unimaginable went on there." Father was not able to reassure me. "They're investigating and will report. We've decided to send Brezhnev to the test site, along with specialists. We can only wait for their report. Such a tragedy."

The next day Father knew more: Seventy-four people had died, including Nedelin. Nothing was left of him, not even a handful of ashes. They found only half of his shoulder strap and the half-melted keys from his office safe.

These were later buried in an urn in Red Square, in the Kremlin wall. Yangel survived purely by chance. At the moment of the explosion he was in the area designated for smoking.

What had happened at the test site?

I will try to describe what I managed to learn from Father, Brezhnev, and those who survived the tragic event.

As I have already mentioned, the launch was scheduled for October 23, a Sunday. In those years it was considered bad form to take weekends off. Pre-launch preparations went forward normally. There were the usual defects that appear in the course of testing. According to the reports by specialists, Chief Designer Yangel decided to eliminate them, and his decision was confirmed by State Commission Chairman Nedelin.

Nedelin and Yangel had known each other for a long time. They had grown especially close during the previous few years. After all, the R-12 had become virtually the only important weapon of the military's new branch, the Strategic Missile Forces. The R-5 was obviously becoming obsolete, while the R-7 had only four launch sites.

The marshal and the chief designer had become, if not friends, then close colleagues.

Two launch sites were prepared for tests of the R-16, in order to avoid any delays in case of anything "unexpected." This word was a superstitious code for the possibility that an accident might occur. As a matter of simplicity and convenience, the sites were designated right and left.

Preparations for the first launch began early in the morning of October 21. Work went according to schedule. The rocket was lifted onto the launch pad and checks were begun, as called for by the launch protocol. They continued until October 23. With that phase completed, it was decided to start fueling, the most important and dangerous part of the operation. It was necessary to pour almost one hundred and fifty tons of fuel and oxidizer, which were not only deadly poisonous but would ignite at the slightest contact with each other.

The protocol called for a minimum number of people to be present during fueling. The rest were supposed to leave, some to conceal themselves underground and others to move further away. But neither Nedelin nor Yangel doubted the reliability of the new rocket, and they ignored the protocol. They felt that the rocket was their own, even that it was something tame and domesticated.

Nothing is more dangerous than when people begin to treat complex machinery with familiarity, when they lose a sense of distance. Machinery must be treated with respect, for it takes a terrible revenge for any "liberties." At that time, the first years of the rocket boom, many people believed that rockets no longer contained anything unknown. Everything had been researched, studied, understood—launches had become routine. Of course, you couldn't prevent defects, which were inevitable, but they tried not to think about them. Experience seemed to confirm that their confidence was justified. The series of failures with the R-7s had receded into the past. Yangel had never had any serious accidents. The R-12 and R-14 were launched one after another, proving that they were well designed. People had developed an illusion of being in total control.

When Nedelin was asked for permission to begin fueling the rocket, he merely nodded and reached into his pocket for a pen. They needed his signature. The launch site director, waiting nearby with the papers, began looking around for a table or chair to rest them on. Seeing nothing, he held out his thick and top-secret leatherette portfolio with the brown patch of the plastic seal near its lock. Without looking, Nedelin signed the protocol.

The launch director did not leave, but stood hesitating. He finally made up his mind to invite the marshal to go to the bunker. One of his duties was to make sure that regulations were enforced. Nedelin took a step toward the heavy green metal door hiding the steeply descending narrow stairs leading to the bunker, but changed his mind at the last moment. He waved his hand: "Begin," and walked about ten steps away from the rocket. The commission members followed his example. A large number of "industrialists"— representatives of numerous design bureaus and factories taking part in building the rockets—followed them.

Among those present was Major General Konstantin Vasilyevich Gerchik, the test site commander. It was his duty to enforce the rules and regulations in the territory entrusted to him. He knew that he was supposed to make sure that all outsiders, regardless of rank, left the launch area. But this was the marshal, his supreme commander. And he was only a major general. Gerchik ordered that chairs and a small table be brought from the staff office.

The commission members stood around under the rocket being fueled. There were at least an additional hundred and fifty observers: officials of all ranks. The fueling was completed without incident. It proceeded normally, up to that point. Then things began to go wrong. At the last minute, at six in the evening of that same day, October 23, during testing of the ignition circuits of the pyromembranes of the second stage's oxidizer ducts, the signal causing ignition of the pyrocartridges of the first stage's fuel duct was generated instead of the expected instruction, due to an undetected error in the electrical circuit controlling the engine.[8] It should be noted that, although the second stage's pyrocartridges were disconnected from the circuit and

---

8. Pyromembranes and pyrocartridges. These devices serve as fuel valves on liquid-fueled missiles. When the missile is to be fired, the pyrocartridge explodes the membrane that blocks each fuel passage, initiating a full fuel flow instantly.

replaced by simulators so they would not fire, those on the first stage were left in place. As a result, the first stage's pump became filled with the deadly poisonous and volatile liquid.

Moreover, for some reason the pyrocartridges of the blocking valves of the first block's gas generator of the first stage's main engine went out spontaneously. But that wasn't the final mishap: electrical engineers reported a broken main programming current distributor on the onboard cable network. These defects had to be corrected first of all. Both the regulations and common sense categorically forbade any work on the rocket's electrical system when the tanks were full. Fuel components must be drained, tanks deactivated, and only then should workers go inside to solder. But that was according to regulations. Draining fuel is an extremely unpleasant and lengthy procedure. Test personnel hate it and try in every possible way to avoid doing it. At this point the project chief proposed deviating from the regulations in order to save time. Otherwise, the launch would be delayed for weeks. The chief designer assumed the responsibility and allowed the electrical technicians to start working. The marshal didn't object. He sat silently on a stool under the fueled rocket and watched how the small figures of mechanics bustled about on the service tower, towering many meters high.

Time pressed. Then another unforeseen problem: once filled with the components of fuel and oxidizer, the pump could last for only twenty-four hours and then had to be replaced. The acid not only ruthlessly corroded gaskets, it dissolved metal. According to regulations, the membranes are to be opened by pyrocartridges immediately before launch, when it took tens of minutes to pump acid along the arteries of pipes. But now the pump had to last for many hours. They had to hurry. Haste added to the nervous tension. A mistake was only a short step away.

For the time being all problems had been dealt with. The circuit was re-soldered. The main current distributor was replaced. It was already late at night when the hatches were closed. The State Commission held a meeting right there, under the rocket, and decided to postpone the launch until the following day. People were exhausted. It was decided to let them rest and sleep. On the morning of October 24 they began testing all the systems from the beginning. They started with checks that were allowed only on an empty rocket. Now they had to ignore safety measures. All they did was disconnect the connectors of the pyrocartridges which blew up the membranes opening the path for components into the engine. The components ignite without any help when they meet in the combustion chamber.

Again, everything worked out. When the engine's ignition circuits were tested, several sharp bangs sounding like pistol shots were heard—they were caused by the pyrocartridges, which were hanging on the service tower brackets, simulating launch. The chief of the launch position sighed with relief and allowed the connections to be restored.

There was hardly any time left. According to tradition and operative instructions developed over the previous decade, the checks all had to be carried out in a strict order, one after another, and only with the permission of the "conductor"—the head of the launch team. He can permit the next step to be taken only after he is convinced that everything corresponds to the instructions. The instructions are equivalent to the score for a symphony. They show what should be done and what is categorically forbidden. Any false note can lead to disaster. Every performer watches the conductor attentively; no one moves without his permission. It appears that he, like a real conductor waving his baton, is doing nothing meaningful: "Set switch 4 in position 6," and only after that report ("Switch 4 is in position 6"), which precludes any error, does he move to: "Open valve 22." And so on, point by point, a very boring procedure for onlookers.

However, try to work without a conductor. Or try to rewrite the score as you go.

But the chief engineer, in charge of launch preparations, hurried to the chief designer with just such a proposition. Time was short. He therefore asked to be allowed to conduct checks on the various systems simultaneously, not sequentially, as prescribed by the "Talmud" of the launch team leader. Permission was given. The score was being rewritten on the run; actually, the pages of the score were being torn out and mixed up. The conducting now had to proceed by intuition. People were swarming over the rocket like ants. Underneath, in their chairs, sat the members of the State Commission and their entourages, waiting to hear that the launch was ready. They had no other business to transact at that point.

Evidently this gross violation of the regulations disturbed the test site commander, but he did not dare exert his authority in face of the marshal. It's possible that Gerchik suggested to Nedelin that he move to a safe place, but we don't know what he replied. One of the site's officers later described how Gerchik said to him, in a tone totally uncharacteristic of a general: "Perhaps *you* will listen to me? Take your officers and evacuate the site at once. There's nothing more for you to do here." They obeyed the order and survived.

But time was passing. And the less time remained, the more hectic the activity around the launch site. Each service thought only about its own work, almost no one thought about the "conductor," and the orchestra fell apart. The launch was doomed, although no one knew it yet.

Official documents show that a thirty-minute alert was announced. At that time, no one, neither directors nor workers, should have been on the ground near the launch site. But there is a system of delays, stopping time as it were, which stretch seconds into hours for carrying out procedures not foreseen in the regulations. "An hour-long delay in the one-minute alert" is a favorite joke among test personnel. That is the only possible explanation for the crowd of people at the launch site. And, of course, the total lack of control.

As mentioned earlier, a program current distributor was mounted on the rocket. From the moment the "Start" button is pressed, it issues a sequence of instructions for turning on different systems. Among them are instructions to start engines, beginning with the first stage, and then, after its operational period is finished and it separates, new contacts close and the second stage begins to operate.

Cables to the pyrocartridges that start the engines are not connected until all checks are completed and the program current distributor is reset to zero. Otherwise a catastrophe is inevitable. The "conductor" must be on his guard for that.

The first to occupy the control board were electrical and guidance system technicians. They checked the flight cyclogram and "drove" the current distributor forward.[9] Everything appeared to be in order and all commands— from igniting the first stage engines to the final one, detaching the head section—were issued correctly. Then, apparently because something distracted them or for some other reason, they left the distributor at the "tail end" and did not return it to its initial position. Nothing was reported to the "conductor." Meanwhile the engine technicians hooked up their connectors to the engine's pyrocartridges, charged the batteries supplying the electric signal that fired up those cartridges, and prepared for launch—all this without asking the "conductor."

At that point a third service unit intervened. The telemetrists had certain doubts. We will never know exactly what troubled them, but they requested additional testing. That necessitated starting the program over from the beginning. Then it was discovered that the program current distributor (PCD in jargon) was not in the proper position. In the confusion no one remembered the engines—another service unit was responsible for them.

One of the few witnesses who survived told me that as he went off for a smoke he overheard someone say: "So I should drive the PCD to zero?" And someone's reply: "Go ahead."

That was the decisive moment. Those near the rocket must have heard the bang of pyrocartridges somewhere above and seen a dazzling flash of flame shooting out of the engine nozzles. That would have been the last thing they heard, the last thing they saw.

A jet of fire instantly burned through the tanks of the first stage and almost one hundred and sixty tons of fuel and oxidizer—nitric acid—poured

---

9. The cyclogram initiated and timed the sequence of operations necessary to launch and control the missile.

down on the heads of the people directly under the rocket so quickly that they could not have understood what was happening. Flames blazed up wherever the liquids touched each other. The first stage fell into pieces. The second stage collapsed from above, completing the destruction.

Those who were with Nedelin, directly under the rocket, were killed instantly. Those who were to the side tried to save themselves by rushing toward the shelter to the right of the launch pad. That way led to a painful death. Tar had been poured over the space between the two positions before the arrival of the top brass. It melted instantaneously and people stuck to it like flies on flypaper. A few moments later the tar burst into flame. All that remained of those who had tried to flee were the outlines of their bodies on the ground.

The men working on the upper stages of the service tower fell toward the raging fire from a height of many meters, but never reached it. They burst into flames in the air.

Those running to the left from the launch site were halted by a high barbed-wire fence separating the supersecret launch site from the less secret zone. People threw themselves on the barbed wire and tried to climb it. They were cooked alive.

The chief designer was lucky. A few minutes before the disaster he had left to have a cigarette. One thing they didn't allow that day was to smoke under the fueled rocket.

Yangel had just managed to light up when there was a blinding flash, followed immediately by a deafening roar and a wave of heat from the direction of the launch pad. A suffocating stench invaded people's lungs and made them cough. Brown wisps of oxidizer vapor floated in the air. Mikhail Kuzmich was transfixed, looking at a scene resembling the end of the world. That lasted for several seconds. Then he rushed toward the launch area.

"People are there. I must . . . ," he shouted almost incoherently.

Bystanders tried to hold him back. Yangel tore himself away. He was almost out of his mind. His friends and his colleagues, his deputies Berlin and Kontsevoy were there, writhing and burning in the three-thousand-degree flames. Yangel tried to reach them. It's not clear whether he hoped to save them or share their fate.

In all, fifty-seven military personnel and twenty-five civilians perished.

An extremely secret echo of this extremely secret explosion spread through all Moscow offices, up to the very top. A government commission was appointed to investigate the causes of the accident. In bidding farewell to the commission members before they left for the test site, Father warned them against excessive zeal in looking for culprits. He didn't thirst for blood and was inclined to think that a tragedy had occurred and there was no reason to look in vain for some malicious intent. He knew that if the commission members were given free rein, they would find "culprits" and obtain "confessions."

The commission to investigate the R-16 accident was headed by Brezhnev. It included representatives of the most important departments: Ivan Dmitriyevich Serbin, director of the department of defense technology of the Central Committee of the CPSU; First Deputy Minister of Defense Andrei Antonovich Grechko, and Minister Konstantin Nikolayevich Rudnev, chairman of the State Committee on Defense Technology.

They flew to Tyura-Tam on the morning of October 26. Moscow's emissaries were met at the airport by the range site's deputy commander. The commander, General Gerchik, was in the hospital. He had survived, but was terribly burned and had lost his sight. Since Brezhnev refused to rest after the flight, they all went directly to the scene of the accident. It made a very sad impression on them all, even Grechko and Brezhnev, who had seen a great deal during the war. Their investigation began at once, on the spot. They were meticulous. They interviewed military personnel and civilians. They leafed through documents, carefully read maintenance logs, and closely examined whatever remains of the rocket had been collected. They found no structural defects that might have caused the accident or anyone directly at fault. Although Yangel insisted on his guilt, Brezhnev remembered the instructions he had been given in Moscow and was in no hurry to draw any conclusions.

Upon returning to Moscow, Brezhnev reported to Father that the disaster was an accident caused by a tragic combination of circumstances.

The dead were buried, some in a common grave at the test site, while the remains of others were sent to relatives in various cities of the Soviet Union. What remains were there? Handfuls of ash, mixed with burnt soil.

At a meeting with Father soon after the tragedy, Yangel demanded that he be punished. He considered himself to be the only one responsible. Father's attempts to calm him were in vain. Mikhail Kuzmich knew better than anyone what he had not done, what he had allowed, and what he had not prohibited in time.

A feeling of guilt, of responsibility, does not arise because of a judicial sentence or a government decree. It is born and dies along with a person. It was that pain, which he could not share with anyone else, for the irreparable tragedy which he could have prevented, if only . . . which had impelled Yangel to rush toward the fire.

That feeling of guilt was with him until the end of his life.

It was decided not to make public what had happened at the test site. Not simply because we were not yet ready for such openness: Father was afraid that the explosion would dispel the myth of our missile superiority. Satellites, publicity around the world—and suddenly this . . .

But this plan was complicated by Nedelin's death. The others could sink silently into oblivion, but it was necessary to explain what had happened to a marshal, the commander in chief of the Strategic Missile Forces. Newspapers carried a statement from the Central Committee of the CPSU, the Presidium of the Supreme Soviet, and the Council of Ministers of the USSR that Chief Marshal of Artillery Mitrofan Ivanovich Nedelin had died on October 24 as a result of an airplane crash.

Surviving victims of the accident were given strict instructions about the circumstances of their "plane crash." The necessary entries were made in their medical records and certificates of disability. The tragedy of the thirty-seventh launch site of the Tyura-Tam test site, i.e., the Baikonur cosmodrome, ceased to exist.

Launches resumed in January of 1961. The second—or rather, the first—launch of the R-16 was scheduled for February 2. This time the guidance system failed to operate in flight. The third attempt was successful. All subsequent tests proceeded without incident.

The last tests of the R-14 were completed at virtually the same time as the second launch of the R-16, in February of 1961, in the aboveground variant. Work continued on silos, but they weren't expected to be operational any time soon.

THE U.S. ELECTIONS

The main political event in the autumn of 1960 was the November 4 election of John Fitzgerald Kennedy as president of the United States. Father radiated delight. He joked that Kennedy's victory was his present to the celebration of the October Revolution, and thought of himself as something of a participant in the election.

Father knew very little about Kennedy, but reports from both diplomats and journalists were favorable, and the intelligence service considered him to be a sober and independent politician. If he were elected, Father counted on their finding a common language, especially on the German question. In general, beginning that summer Father had begun to "root" for Kennedy. Of course he could not endorse him. Father understood perfectly well that it would cost the candidate a large number of votes if it were known in the United States that he favored Kennedy. But he also wanted to participate in some way, so he decided to take action behind the scenes.

First of all, Father refused to play up to the Republicans. Not long before the election he received Henry Cabot Lodge, who was running for vice president on the ticket with Nixon. Nixon decided to take advantage of the friendly relations that had developed between Father and Lodge during their travels around the United States to assure a favorable attitude on Father's part. Nixon was very eager to get back—before the election—the Americans who were in Soviet prisons: the U-2 pilot Powers and the two survivors of the RB-47 crew.

Father didn't even want to hear a word about Powers. The trial was just over and his sentence had been passed. As he put it, the Americans should have thought of the humanitarian angle before they sent the plane deep inside our territory. But Father didn't intend to keep Powers in prison for very long.

"What use is he to us," he commented once during a walk at the dacha. "We just have to feed him. Let a little time pass and we'll release him."

He added, after a moment: "In exchange . . ." He didn't mention Colonel Abel. At the time I had no idea of his existence.[10]

Father intended to wait for the new administration before resolving the matter of the RB-47 crew members, who were being held in custody for violating Soviet borders. Of course, he didn't know who would win the election. If Kennedy were defeated, the pilots would be returned to Nixon. But after the election, not before. Meanwhile, Father and Lodge had a friendly talk, reminisced about the previous year's trip and parted. I would note that Father thought that the question of exchanging the imprisoned U.S. pilots was extremely important, almost decisive. I don't know if this plan had any influence on the outcome of the election, but he often brought up the subject in conversation. In addition, he did not fail to mention it during his private meeting with President Kennedy in Vienna. As Father put it, Kennedy thanked him for trying to support him in the campaign fight.

Immediately after the Inauguration, on January 26, 1961, the Soviet government returned the imprisoned U.S. RB-47 crew members. In reporting this event, the newspaper *Pravda* noted that the U.S. president had issued an order forbidding U.S. planes from violating Soviet airspace, thereby turning a new page, as it were, in relations between the two countries. Unfortunately, mutual understanding was subjected to a serious test before it was born. The United States, implementing a decision taken by the Republican administration, was actively preparing to invade Cuba.

Truly fatal bad luck! Each time a meeting was planned and there was hope of reaching agreement, some unforeseen "complication" appeared.

MOSKALENKO TAKES COMMAND OF THE STRATEGIC MISSILE FORCES

The R-16 catastrophe in October did not affect either the plans to launch a man into space or the program for installing missiles.

---

10. Colonel Rudolf Abel, the legendary Soviet spy, entered the United States from Canada in 1948 under the name Martin Collins. He was arrested in 1957 and exchanged for Powers in 1962. It was not Abel, but Feklisov (using the name Fomin), who ran the "atomic spies" Julius and Ethel Rosenberg in the 1940s. He will appear in my account of the Cuban Missile Crisis.

But what did we actually have? In 1961 regiments and divisions with the R-12 continued deploying along the western borders of our country. There were already several dozen missiles there. As they were installed, the R-5 was gradually withdrawn from use. The deployment of R-14s at launch sites was not expected any earlier than the following year. As before, only the R-7s could reach the United States. If you included the experimental launch site, there were now six of them. Father therefore did not hesitate to accept the military's proposal to begin deploying R-16 launch positions in April 1961, without waiting for tests to be completed.

After the death of Nedelin, Malinovsky recommended that Marshal Kirill Semyonovich Moskalenko be appointed commander in chief of the Strategic Missile Forces. At first Father was dubious. Nedelin had been a missile professional to the core, while Moskalenko had only seen them from a distance. But Father knew no one in the Army who was Nedelin's equal, so he agreed. Moskalenko was energetic; he would learn.

Father had met Moskalenko in the very first days of the war. At the time Moskalenko was commanding an antitank brigade. His brigade was surrounded near Kiev, but he fought his way out. By the end of the war he was commanding an army. As a person, he had the reputation of being restless and meticulous, of trying to probe into everything, and of possessing audacious courage. As the commander of an army, he retained the habit of siting his observation post near the front lines. Once, when Father was visiting his "household" with Zhukov, Georgy Konstantinovich looked around and asked: "And where are the Germans?"

"Over there. Behind that hill," answered Moskalenko, pointing to higher ground half a kilometer away.

Zhukov couldn't believe it at first, and then muttered: "What are you up to? Do you want to surrender us to the Germans?" Turning to Father, he added: "Let's get out of here."

His quick temper and explosive nature had gotten in the way of his promotions. But Father decided that his energetic character would be an advantage. He wouldn't just sit in his office or allow others to do so.

The new commander in chief got right to work. He toured missile installations and looked into every detail. His reports to Father were thorough and specific. Father couldn't stand generalities. Space launches were also under Moskalenko's authority. The last experimental Vostok, with the dog Zvezdochka on board, was launched on March 25 and landed that same day. A month earlier, on February 12, an R-7 had launched an interplanetary spaceship toward Venus. It was time for a manned flight.

Every Soviet launch hurt President Kennedy's pride. He didn't want to accept the fact that the United States was behind in the space race. In order to regain the lead America would have to accomplish something unusual, something beyond the power of anyone else.

THE SITUATION IN THE GERMAN DEMOCRATIC REPUBLIC

Father was pursued by other nightmares. The problem of Germany gave him no peace. He had not managed to force the Western powers to recognize the GDR. And that meant that the republic's security was always under threat.

Of course, for the time being no one thought of infringing on the sovereignty of the GDR. Soviet forces were still there. But they couldn't stay forever. Father thought that an agreement on the German question would stabilize the political situation in the center of Europe, as well as save a great deal of money.

However, the situation in Germany was steadily deteriorating. Ulbricht continued to complain about the absence of borders and the crucial lack of a work force. He even mentioned the possibility of recruiting workers from the Soviet Union. Father simply blew up in response. He recalled how the Fascists had taken away our people to work in Germany. Those were Fascists, but now Ulbricht was proposing something similar. Father came home seething with indignation.

"How could he even think of such a thing?" he repeated several times.

Father replied in the negative, but the problem of the East German exodus was a constant irritant. Father could get rid of it only by finding a solution. A decision had to be made, and time would show whether it was the correct one. His nature didn't allow him to distance himself from the problem. Father considered it natural to assume the initiative and the responsibility.

Father also remembered that Ulbricht told him about how the West Germans, known for being thrifty people quite capable of counting their money, were not too lazy to travel to the GDR to buy food, since the border was open and subsidies kept prices lower there. Total losses from these unexpected exports were very substantial. This particularly concerned Father, since a large proportion of food products in the GDR was supplied by the Soviet Union. From time to time the Soviet government simply forgave and wrote off the GDR's debts, which were rising steeply during those years.

It seemed to Ulbricht, and also to Father, that the situation would quickly stabilize if the flood of people and goods leaving the GDR could be cut off. Then living standards in the GDR would surpass those in West Germany. It was simply necessary to take the first step to stop the flood. But how?

Father placed considerable hope in future negotiations with the new U.S. president. If an agreement were reached, the peace treaty would legalize the existence of two Germanys and establish borders. The question of unification, put off to the indefinite future, would become the subject of negotiations between the sovereign GDR and FRG.

On February 17 Father renewed pressure on the West. An aide-mémoire was sent to the FRG explaining yet again the need for a peace treaty. In the expectation of future negotiations, the text was couched in a very agreeable tone. Specifically, it referred to positive changes becoming apparent in the world. This was a clear reference to the expected dialogue with the new U.S. president.

Everything now depended on negotiations with John Kennedy, on whether the partners would have sufficient wisdom and whether reason would prevail over ambition.

DAVID AND GOLIATH

His trip to the U.N. revolutionized Father's attitude toward Cuba. Now he did not see it as simply another country developing socialism. Father thought of Cuba as a David confronting mighty Goliath. He thought that it was our country's international duty, his personal duty, to do everything possible to preserve the Cuban revolution. In his opinion, events taking place around Cuba would determine the course of revolutionary processes in the world for many years to come. He developed a special attitude toward Cuba and paid very close attention to the development of events. One also cannot dismiss Fidel Castro's personal charm. Castro's ardor reminded him of his own revolutionary youth.

In those days, I often asked Father how we could help Cuba. He thought that all we could do was to supply weapons. Agreement to ship them had been reached during the visit by Raul Castro. As for the rest, we had to rely on the beneficence of fate and the courage of the Cuban people. I asked him if we shouldn't have a mutual assistance treaty with Cuba, like the one we had with our neighbors. Father thought the idea was useless and dangerous. If Americans landed on the island, how could we help the Cubans? Start a third world war? That would be insane. Besides, we couldn't know what Castro might do at some critical moment. Too much was unclear. Father preferred not to take the risk.

He decided to speed up deliveries of small arms, tanks, and artillery. There were problems with aviation, since Cuba did not have enough pilots. Father thought that to send our pilots, as we had in Korea and Egypt, was not justified. The main reason was the island's distance and isolation. If Castro were defeated, our pilots would be captured and become prisoners of war. There would be a scandal. He decided to send MIG trainers to Cuba. Let the Cubans first learn how to fly. In the meantime, Castro possessed only a few obsolete U.S. fighters. Most of them were left over from the Second World War.

The situation around Cuba grew increasingly tense. The first explosions and the first victims occurred on the streets of Havana. U.S. forces were moving closer and closer to the island. On April 4 the Cubans received a menacing warning. On that day Cuban Coast Guard ships two miles offshore stopped an intruder, the American ship *Western Union*, and decided to bring it into the nearest port. But they did not succeed. U.S. airplanes and ships literally surrounded the Cuban shore patrol's small cutters. There was no doubt that a fatal shot might ring out at any moment. Cuban authorities were forced to order the release of the intruder.

Father thought that an invasion was only a few weeks, or even a few days, away. Cuba didn't have a chance. Its defenders were reported to be preparing for a heroic death.

GAGARIN'S TRIUMPH

Well, Cuba was one thing, but that spring the impending flight of a man into space was the main event, awaited with bated breath. For those in the know, of course. Others could only speculate. The individual's name was not mentioned at the time. No one cared what it was. Simply that a man, the first man, was to fly into space.

I have heard stories of how Korolyov showed Father some pictures of candidates for the flight, and he chose Gagarin. That is one of those fairy tales that usually spring up around especially remarkable events.

However, they did talk about the date for the launch when they met right after the successful landing of the previous spaceship, which brought the dog Zvezdochka back from orbit. Korolyov was nervous. He was in a hurry. All signs indicated that the Americans would soon launch their experimental spaceship with a man on board. They had officially set the launch for the first half of May. Although the planned U.S. flight was in no way comparable to the Vostok program, Korolyov was intent on being the first. Americans would not fail to publicize their achievement in every possible way. They were moving cautiously. They had decided to start with a flight along a ballistic trajectory, so they would barely scratch the unexplored space beyond the atmosphere. Who knew what awaited men there? Korolyov worked according to different principles. He preferred to take the bull by the horns at once, and from the first step he acted in terms of a complete program. In case of failure, he planned to continue the attack until he gained his objective. From the very beginning Sergei Pavlovich planned a flight in orbit. But with only one circuit of the earth.

He explained that the shape of the apparatus selected—a round capsule—avoided many problems. Most important was that it eliminated the need for the pilot to control the launch and reentry into the atmosphere. After braking at a lower altitude, the pilot would eject by catapult. Then man and empty capsule would land separately.

Korolyov preferred that the crew take no part in controlling the spacecraft. He had good reasons for thinking along these lines. No one knew what could happen under conditions of weightlessness. In those days there was serious concern that the abrupt change in sensations might cause a "guinea pig" to go out of his mind. Of course, the pilot could take over under special circumstances. Various clever codes were put into the simple control board installed in the small cockpit of the *Vostok*, as Korolyov dubbed his spaceship. The pilot could assume control of the flight only by using them and by turning switches in a certain sequence.

The Americans chose a different strategy. Their pilot controlled the spaceship from the very first launch.

Korolyov gave a detailed report to Father about the previous flights. Just as earlier, not everything was immediately successful.

One experiment had been especially unsuccessful: the spaceship, ready to return to earth, instead changed direction and flew into a higher orbit. The dog on board the spaceship died. Korolyov claimed that changes had been made since then to prevent such a mistake. Besides, a man is not a dog. He could always look out the window and make sure the spaceship was going in the right direction. If, of course, he's able to evaluate his position in space. Korolyov had no doubt that the systems were perfected, the spaceship could be relied on, and everything would go extremely well.

Father smiled and asked again: "Is there a one-hundred percent guarantee?" Sergei Pavlovich repeated emphatically: "Everything possible has been done." He paused, and then added: "Of course, something unexpected is always possible in such a business, but we should launch a man. It's time."

It seemed that everything had been taken into consideration. Korolyov proposed launching a man during the last few days of April, timing the flight to coincide with May 1. Father was categorically opposed. He wanted it either earlier or later. The recent tragedy with Yangel's rocket had left an open wound. They had also been certain of success.

Korolyov didn't want to delay and suggested that the launch of a man into space take place in the middle of April. A few days later he called Father and said they were aiming for April 12. Father agreed. The chief designer had the last word in such matters. The date was kept very secret, just like everything else connected with rockets and satellites. However, everyone sensed that it would happen soon, any day now. It was a time of agonizing suspense.

A launch into space was all very well, but life continued on its accustomed rounds. At the beginning of April, on either the seventh or ninth, Father left on vacation. That spring he had decided to go to Pitsunda, for the fresh air and the pine forests. He planned to catch up on work he'd had no time for in Moscow. The next party congress was planned for that autumn, and he had to think about the report. In general, there was a great deal to do during the vacation.

Father didn't spend much time thinking about the launch. Nothing depended on him, and Korolyov would report from the launch site.

I remained in Moscow.

April 12, 1961, was a warm sunny day in Moscow. The ground was virtually free of snow, and in some places little buttons of yellow coltsfoot had appeared.

I won't describe the events of that memorable day. They are now familiar to everyone, down to the smallest details. Perhaps only one thing: as Father's aide later described it, Korolyov called Pitsunda immediately after the launch took place and reported that everything was going well. That day Father was working with speechwriters on the report to the forthcoming congress. You couldn't really call it work, that hour and a half spent in nervous expectation while Gagarin circled the earth. Father kept looking at the telephone. When it finally rang, Father rushed to it and, hearing Korolyov's voice, shouted: "Just tell me, is he alive?"

After hearing the reply, he leaned back against his wicker chair with relief and began asking Sergei Pavlovich how the pilot was feeling; the term "cosmonaut" had not yet been coined.

I called Father that evening after returning from work.

I already knew every detail about how Gagarin had landed on the Saratov steppes and been taken to the cosmodrome. The experimental flight had ended successfully, and Korolyov was celebrating victory. I was sincerely happy for him. But no more than that. I didn't appreciate the significance of what had happened.

Naturally, this time our conversation was all about Gagarin, Korolyov, and the launch. Unlike me, Father was exultant. He supplied some details associated with the landing and told me that he had talked with Malinovsky that morning. The marshal had proposed awarding the brave pilot the title Hero of the Soviet Union and the rank of captain.

Father approved the idea in principle, but joked that the minister of defense was too stingy. He should be more generous. Adopting a more serious tone, he proposed skipping a rank and immediately promoting the senior lieutenant to major. Malinovsky didn't object—let him be a major.

Father suggested that the pilot be told as soon as he landed.

"Let him be happy," he said, employing a familiar phrase, which I knew connoted his own feeling of special satisfaction as well.

"That exhausted the minister's imagination," continued Father. "Major, Hero—we have so many of them, and on this occasion I'd like to think of something special."

Father recalled how the *Chelyuskin* and Chkalov crews had been feted when he was young,[11] and now he wanted to arrange something similar: crowds of people on the streets, showers of confetti, a huge gathering.

The fact that Father compared Gagarin with the *Chelyuskin* team shows that—just as four years before with the launch of the first satellite—neither Father nor the rest of us around him imagined how the world would react to the event. Reality exceeded all expectations. But at the time, on the day it happened, we had no idea that we were present on the first day of a new era.

Father said that he was flying to Moscow the next day. He wanted to greet the hero himself. He thought that the entire government should welcome the cosmonaut at Vnukovo Airport, as if he were the most honored foreign guest. A motorcycle escort should accompany Gagarin along the streets of the city.

According to Father's initial plan, only the hero of the day and his wife would sit in the lead car. But other members of the Soviet leadership thought differently. His associates vied with each other in urging that Father sit next to the cosmonaut. Father refused, then pretended to be unsure, and eventually allowed himself to be persuaded.

And then came the culmination: a mass celebration on Red Square. Nothing like it had ever happened that I could remember. As far back as Stalin's day the KGB was panic-stricken at the thought of a crowd. Holiday demonstrations were different. During them, columns of people walked along lanes assigned to them, with tight rows of "professionals" standing between the columns and staring intently into people's faces. Not the slightest suspicious movement could be hidden from them. Now this was going to be an unorganized crowd! But Father wouldn't hear of any objections.

From the meeting on Red Square the celebration would move to the George's Hall in the Kremlin for a grandiose reception in honor of those people, anonymous at the time, who had brought the dreams of visionaries to reality.

I was somewhat skeptical about Father's enthusiasm and his idea of organizing a national celebration. It seemed to me that people would not respond to it in their hearts. It would be just another official event, but with a theatrical touch. I didn't voice any of my doubts. I was mostly worried about Father's health. He had become extremely tired over the previous few months, had managed to get away for about two weeks of rest, and now he was planning to return after only three or four days. I tried to dissuade him, but he didn't want to listen. Father was simply dying to go to Moscow.

The day of the welcome for Gagarin can only be compared to the na-

---

11. *Chelyuskin* and Chkalov. The *Chelyuskin* (named for a famous eighteenth-century explorer) was the Soviet merchant ship used for polar exploration that tried to cut a route through the Arctic ice of the Bering Straits, between Chukotka and Alaska, in the 1930s. Its crew was saved in a dramatic rescue after it became stuck in the ice of the Chukotka Sea.

tional rejoicing on May 9, 1945, the day of victory over the Fascists. Hand-made signs with warm informal greetings overwhelmed the bold print of official slogans and banners. Sunlit streets were jammed with exultant Muscovites, and not only streets—balconies, roofs, windows, trees, any place from which you could see the hero, were crowded with people.

The appearance in the Moscow sky of the plane carrying Gagarin caused such an explosion of enthusiasm, it was as if the satellite was carrying him. The IL-18, accompanied by four fighters, described a circle over the city. It prepared to land, made the short passage along the runway, and the festive moment arrived. After the plane came to a stop across from a low grandstand put up overnight, Major Yury Gagarin appeared and with a military stride approached the crowd waiting for him. He was met by the Party Presidium and members of the government, headed by Father, the cosmonaut's wife and parents, ministers, marshals, ambassadors, and Muscovites waving flags of all sizes.

Gagarin had memorized the text of the report written for him, had time to practice during the plane's ceremonial approach to the airport and now marched with precision onto the red carpet leading from the plane's board-ing ramp to immortality. The carpet was a long one. The rather short major walked and walked—it seemed as if he would never reach the end of it. A minor mishap occurred halfway: one of the garters holding up his high offi-cer's socks came undone. The sock fell down, the garter slipped out of his pants and rose triumphantly up in the air with every step, then hit his leg painfully. The cosmonaut continued his ceremonial march without paying any attention.

At the end of his walk Gagarin mounted the two steps leading to the grandstand, delivered his report and fell into Father's embrace. Today you can't find Father's face on any film recording that moment. After his ouster he disappeared from all documentaries. For a quarter of a century Gagarin has been addressing his words to a vacuum.

Korolyov was right to hurry. He beat the Americans by only three weeks. But that was enough for him to go down in history. The May 5 flight by U.S. astronaut Alan Shepard, which took him to an altitude of 115 miles and covered a straight distance of 300 miles, didn't surprise anyone.

Father somewhat maliciously congratulated John Kennedy on the success of American technology. Perhaps it was then that the young president really decided to get his revenge.

THE BAY OF PIGS

Early on the morning of April 17, Father's sixty-sixth birthday, troops began landing in the Bay of Pigs in Cuba. That was his gift from the new U.S. president.

Reports stated that only Cuban émigrés took part in the operation. The U.S. fleet cruising offshore received orders not to interfere. Father didn't believe it. He thought it was a diplomatic smoke screen and that U.S. troops were already fighting on the island.

His mood darkened. He nourished no illusions about Castro's ability to repel an American invasion force. Father was certain of one thing, the final victory of socialism over capitalism—which in his mind certainly did not translate into a victory for a small socialist country fighting a large capitalist one in the here and now. Such a victory would come years later and would belong to the peoples struggling against the colonizers and for justice and freedom. Father regretted not having delivered enough weapons, especially planes, to the Cubans. They were virtually defenseless from the air.

Father decided to appeal to Kennedy directly. He dictated a letter, the first in their dramatic correspondence relating to the events around Cuba.

I will cite the letter in full.

Mr. President,

I write to you at an alarming moment which can endanger peace throughout the world. Armed aggression has started against Cuba. It is no secret to anyone that the armed bands that have invaded Cuba were trained, supplied, and armed in the United States of America. The planes that are bombing Cuban cities belong to the United States; the bombs they drop were given to them by the government of the United States.

All this evokes justifiable indignation in us in the Soviet Union, in the Soviet government and people. Quite recently, in exchanging opinions through our representatives, we spoke of the mutual desire of both parties to make joint efforts toward improving relations between our countries and averting the danger of war. Your statement, made several days ago, that the United States would not participate in military actions against Cuba created the impression that the government of the United States realizes what consequences, for the whole world as well as for the United States, aggression against Cuba would entail. How can you explain then what the United States is doing in reality, now that the Cuban invasion has become a fact?

It is not yet too late to prevent what might become irreparable. The government of the United States has an opportunity to prevent the flame of war, ignited by the interventionists in Cuba, from growing into a fire that will be impossible to extinguish. I turn to you, Mr. President, with an urgent appeal to stop the aggression against the Republic of Cuba. Military technology and the political situation in the world are such that any so-called minor war can cause a chain reaction throughout the world. As for the Soviet Union, there should be no misunderstanding of our position. We will provide the Cuban people and their government with all necessary assistance in repelling armed attacks on Cuba. We are sincerely concerned with relaxing international tensions. However, if others act to increase tension, we will respond in full measure. In general, it is hardly possible to conduct business so as to improve the situation and extinguish fires in one region while setting a new fire in another.

I hope that the government of the United States will consider our ideas, which are dictated solely by concern for preventing steps which would bring the world to a military catastrophe.

April 18, 1961   N. KHRUSHCHEV
                              Chairman of the Council of Ministers of the USSR

I felt as bad for Cuba as if our own country had been attacked. I kept the radio on constantly and caught every news broadcast relating to military actions. Despite Father's pessimism, I secretly hoped for a miracle, that the Cubans would win. Father understood my emotions and shared crumbs of information with me. He received news mainly from TASS reports based on bulletins from foreign news bureaus. Our ambassador to Cuba, Kudryavtsev, supplemented what we knew by his coded messages. He wrote about Castro's determination to fight to the end, and in case of defeat to retreat to the hills and resume partisan warfare. It was in those days that Castro publicly announced his preference for a socialist regime. He decided either to die or to win as a communist. On the one hand, Father disapproved of Castro's impracticality: "This isn't the time to do it. He burned all the bridges behind him. Americans will not let him off. There's no chance for negotiations." On the other, he was impressed by Castro's dedication.

Hours passed. Days passed. Castro held on. More than that—he gradually seized the initiative. The first encouraging news arrived: the landing force had bogged down as soon as it hit the shore and the Cubans had managed to bring up tanks. MIG trainers attacked the positions of the aggressors, sinking two barges with ammunition and communications equipment. The landing force's position became critical. Now there was hope, even if slight, of victory. Father cheered up noticeably.

There were no reports whatsoever of any U.S. regular troops taking part in the battles. U.S. Navy ships swept the seas offshore and planes from the carrier *Essex* cruised back and forth in the landing area, but did nothing more.

Father was constantly expecting reports of a landing by U.S. Marines and a massive bombardment of the island. He thought that once the president had decided to act he wouldn't stop halfway. But the Americans preserved their neutrality. One evening during our walk Father said with relief: "I don't understand Kennedy. Perhaps he lacks determination?" He didn't bother to continue.

Meanwhile reports were growing increasingly optimistic. The brigade of Cuban émigrés that had landed was tied down in the swamps and had virtually no more hope of victory. Their expectation of an uprising on the island proved to be unjustified. The entire Cuban people rose up to fight the "liberators." Castro abandoned his headquarters in Havana and threw himself into the thick of battle. Father disapproved of his action, muttering that it was childish. But childishness born of a revolutionary impulse appealed to him.

Finally, on the third day, April 20, came the joyful news. At 3:15 A.M. Havana radio reported that the mercenaries were routed, the people were victorious! The battle had lasted seventy-two hours. Equipment was captured, including Sherman tanks.

Father simply beamed. He sent heartfelt congratulations to his friend Fidel. Cuba had stood its ground or, as Father felt, gained a respite. He had no doubt that the Americans would not give up, especially now that Castro had gone over to the camp of their adversaries. Officials in Washington would take stock of their mistakes, choose their time, and then attack Cuba, this time with their regular army.

The defense of Cuba became a question of prestige, not only for Father but for the entire socialist camp. Either we would stand by our comrades in the Western hemisphere and show the peoples of Latin America that they could rely on the Soviet Union, or everything would remain as before and the United States would run the whole show.

Father was now obsessed by the thought: How could we help Cuba? What could we do? Arms deliveries increased immediately after the victory in the Bay of Pigs. And they were not obsolete weapons, as in the recent past, but the most up-to-date ones. However, that didn't solve the problem.

Father did place certain hopes in the possibility of reaching an agreement with Kennedy. However, that possibility became very remote after the invasion of the island. Some unusual solution had to be found. But what? This question now pursued Father relentlessly.

CRISIS

KHRUSHCHEV MEETS KENNEDY

When he proposed postponing the summit for several months, Father didn't conceal his intention of talking only with the new U.S. president. Conditions were not propitious for a meaningful conference of the four powers. Its success or failure would depend on agreement between the United States and USSR: neither the proud de Gaulle nor the cautious Macmillan wanted to repeat their experience as spectators of the squabbling between the leaders of the two superpowers. Both Father and John Kennedy, the newly elected U.S. president, thought that it would make sense for them to have a preliminary meeting, get acquainted, try to feel out the grounds for agreement, and in case of a positive result, prepare for a four-power meeting.

Father was very troubled by the lack of movement in negotiations on disarmament and the prohibition of nuclear testing. If the warheads weren't tested, the Soviet ICBMs—Yangel's R-16, Korolyov's R-9, and Chelomei's UR-200—could not achieve their maximum potential.

The world could swing toward disarmament or toward a qualitative change in armed forces, missile confrontation, and a balance of mutual destruction. The first course would require new thinking from both sides and the emergence of mutual trust. Father's assurances that war did not enter into our plans and that the Soviet Union would demonstrate the superiority of our socialist system by the power of example were not taken on faith. A change in thinking would take years, the reappraisal of "obvious" dogmas, a change in the system of values. Neither Father nor the U.S. president was ready for that approach. Both were only testing each other and groping for the path that might lead to an agreement, provided something irreparable did not happen first.

The absence of an agreement made the resumption of testing more likely.

The other sore subject remained Germany.

There were other possible subjects for discussion, but progress in any direction depended on resolving those two. On all other issues, the leaders would run up against either disarmament or the German question. Although the usefulness of a dialogue was still being weighed in both countries, President Kennedy took the initiative. Soon after his inauguration he proposed to Father that they meet on neutral ground. They had to decide where to hold the meeting. Geneva and Paris were rejected; four-power representatives had either met there or tried to do so. The Americans proposed Vienna. Father would have preferred Helsinki, but he didn't insist.

Father left for Vienna by train on May 27, 1961, making many stops along the way. He expected to spend some time during the trip deciding on his line of conduct and getting a little rest. He stopped in Kiev for two days. Father took the opportunity to visit Kanev (a small town near Kiev) and pay homage at the grave of Taras Grigoryevich Shevchenko.[1] He spent a day in Bratislava and arrived in Vienna on the eve of the date set for the talks, June 2.

The meetings went on intensively, one day in the U.S. Embassy and the next day in the Soviet Embassy.

The emotional approach of both parties left its stamp on the negotiations. John Kennedy was very fearful of being considered weak and tried to show off his power; he was not averse to flexing his muscles.

Father was never left behind in such a situation. He lost no time going on the offensive. At certain times, therefore, the discussions were reminiscent of speeches at a meeting, where each party tries vehemently to persuade the other that his way of life is superior and to demonstrate his inflexibility and determination. A style clearly unsuitable for such an occasion.

Father argued that the Soviet Union would soon leave the United States far behind and the capitalists would beg to be admitted to socialism. He thought that with one more push our economy, as well as the economies of the other socialist countries, would take off. In less than two months, on July 30, a draft program issued by the CPSU was to be published that would claim that "the present generation of people will live under communism" and that by 1980 we would overtake and surpass the United States of America in all economic indexes.

Father was not alone in this belief. Academicians, ministers, and Central Committee secretaries working on the program were making every effort to lay the groundwork to carry out these promises. I remember summer weekends at the dacha when they enthusiastically read aloud newly written sections of the document, which was lavishly decorated with entrancing figures. To question their computations appeared not just improper, but blasphemous.

Nevertheless, a worm of doubt ate at me. It all seemed too easy. I tried to drive away my doubts, but a feeling of discomfort persisted. Ever since my

---

1. Taras Shevchenko is Ukraine's greatest nineteenth-century poet and one of its national icons.

student days, I had tried and failed to understand what exactly communism was. I had read the classic works of Marxism, but discovered nothing that was clearly comprehensible. I had to be satisfied with the familiar slogan "To each according to his needs, from each according to his ability," and have faith that needs would not exceed abilities. A long time before, during my school years, I had tried to get Father to shed light on the nature of communism, but did not get any intelligible answer then either. I understood that he was not very clear about it himself. He made no claims to theoretical knowledge. His goal, or better his dream, was "to feed and clothe the people." After that I didn't try to discuss the subject with him. Not that I wanted to avoid putting Father in an awkward position. I was simply ashamed of my own ignorance.

That year, 1961, faith supplanted doubt. However, I secretly mistrusted the specific numbers. I wondered why we thought we could overtake the United States in 1980, but were calculating that American production figures in 1980 would not rise above current levels. I decided to pose that question during one of the breaks, when the experts working at the dacha were relaxing and sitting on summer wicker chairs under the pines in front of the house. My naïveté amused the authors of the document, and one (I think it was Boris Nikolayevich Ponomaryev) explained that crises would inevitably hold back the development of capitalism, while we would make steady progress. I had to take his words on faith.

Father also allowed himself to take them on faith. He very much hoped to see communism himself, but if that was not to be, he wished to give other people the opportunity to enjoy that unprecedented happiness. That was why, though so pragmatic in other matters, he readily succumbed to the magic of words and numbers.

In Vienna he failed to persuade President Kennedy that he was right, but he took away from the meeting the impression that Kennedy was a serious negotiating partner. Naturally, the president was pursuing his own goals, but he had a realistic grasp of the situation and, most important of all, made his own decisions independently. In Father's opinion, the ability and desire of a country's top leader to go into the complex details of foreign policy deserved the highest praise and recognition. Father never regarded Kennedy as a weak president. The idea, widespread in the United States, that he did so would prevent us from understanding the relations that developed between the two leaders. In Vienna Father saw before him a mature politician with whom he could do business—but who must not be allowed to step on our toes. Father did not intend to retreat one iota from his principles. Their conversations must be between equals.

Father's aide, Oleg Troyanovsky, told me that when Father was asked for his impression of the new U.S. president after the first day of negotiations, he replied: "This young man thinks that, backed by the might of the United States, he can lead us by the hand and make us dance to his tune. Nothing will come of it. He will have to acknowledge that we are no less a power than the United States and he has to talk with us on equal terms."

"Young man . . ." He also referred to President John Kennedy that way at a conference in Moscow, where he repeated his tirade that equality had finally been achieved between the USSR and United States: they were equally able to destroy each other.

A diplomat named Arkady Shevchenko was present at the conference. He later became a U.N. deputy secretary-general and gained fame when he defected to the Americans, to whom he conveyed the sensational news that "Khrushchev considers Kennedy to be a weakling."

Well, we shouldn't be too hard on Shevchenko. Defectors go to great lengths to interest their new masters. In that, Shevchenko was successful. To this day his version of Father's attitude toward John Kennedy is prevalent around the world, easily accounting for all the subsequent crises. Nevertheless, Shevchenko was wrong. Or rather, he correctly repeated what he heard, but he didn't hear very much. I allow myself to repeat: Father thought John Kennedy a worthy opponent, but did not for a minute concede that Kennedy could consider himself superior.

I wasn't taken to Vienna, so I can't describe my own impressions, but I base my account on Father's numerous descriptions of their encounter, which he remembered vividly.

Here is what another immediate observer, Pierre Salinger, one of the president's closest colleagues, writes: "Despite their failure to find solutions to most of the problems dividing East and West, both leaders left Vienna with increased respect and liking for each other. Khrushchev once later remarked to me: 'I liked your young president. He does a good job of presenting the subject he is speaking about.' John Fitzgerald Kennedy found the Russian leader to be 'harsh, but not reckless. His words are firm, but his actions are cautious.' Their mutual respect was later expressed through the celebrated exchange of personal messages, in which I served as one of the couriers."[2]

During those two days they managed to agree only about Laos.

Their talks about peaceful coexistence and disarmament achieved nothing new. In contrast to his previous meetings with President Eisenhower, Father brought no specific proposals to Vienna and was not planning to make any concessions. In 1959 at Camp David he was disposed to agree to partial aerial inspection of mutually agreed border regions as a first step. In 1960 Father took proposals for joint U.S.-Soviet space exploration to the Paris summit.

---

2. Pierre Salinger, *With Kennedy* (New York: Doubleday, 1966), p. 162.

Much had changed by 1961. Father's previous wish to believe in the honesty and peaceful nature of the White House had vanished without a trace.

"First the U-2, and then Cuba! What kind of trust can there be?" That was Father's attitude.

Nevertheless, when President Kennedy proposed joining efforts for flights to the moon (on May 25 he had sent Congress a message on the subject), Father at first agreed, though only in the most general terms. But the next day, during their meeting in the Soviet Embassy, he regretfully rejected the tempting idea. In the rocket field, defense was so closely interwoven with space that it was impossible to separate them. There could be no thought of sharing military secrets. Conditions were not ready for that.

When Father told me that he had rejected the idea of a joint landing on the moon, I supported him. How could we even dream of such a thing? Chelomei disagreed. He argued that we would gain more from cooperation than they would. Nevertheless, the matter was dropped.

Kennedy brought to Vienna a proposal to rule out war as a way of solving conflicts arising in the world. Father welcomed the idea put forward by his opponent, especially since the U.S. president cited estimates of the nuclear potential of our two countries by way of argument. They indicated that the United States possessed enough nuclear weapons to destroy our country more than once, while the USSR had only enough to partly destroy the United States. Where the Americans picked up their data remains on the conscience of the CIA, since at the time our rockets capable of delivering nuclear warheads to North America could still be counted on the fingers of one hand. They were right in one respect: even that number of potential thermonuclear explosions would cause any country to consider such losses unacceptable.

Father reacted with delight to the president's reasoning. For the first time the United States acknowledged parity in the nuclear might of the two states. As far as the multiple capability of the United States, he summed it up with black humor: "Unlike the Americans, we are not bloodthirsty. They intend to bomb corpses, while once is enough for us." He often repeated this later on. Now we know that the ratio of U.S. stocks of nuclear warheads to those of the USSR was 9.7:1.

The adoption of Kennedy's proposal could have advanced disarmament negotiations, which were thoroughly bogged down, but Father saw something he could not agree to: a pledge that our country would not help oppressed people in their struggle for independence. The early 1960s was a stormy period—bloodshed in Algiers, battles in the Congo, the first stages of a war against colonizers in Angola, clashes in Laos, and finally, the recent landing in Cuba. The list could go on. Father spotted (and he was not wrong) a veiled attempt to preserve the existing balance of forces. Proletarian solidarity did not allow for indifference. Our place was among the rebels. The world of socialism was confronting the world of capitalism, freedom was confronting slavery.

I deliberately use the terminology of those years. Father categorically rejected what he considered a provocative proposal and read John Kennedy a whole lecture on wars of liberation and their positive role in the development of human civilization.

The attempt to find a mutually acceptable decision failed.

Negotiations about Germany proceeded even more dramatically.

Father considered himself obligated to find a solution to the German question and a definition of the legal status of the GDR. In Vienna he tried one last time to convince the Americans to agree to separate peace treaties with the FRG and the GDR, with Berlin to be designated an independent free city. This question turned out to be the one on which Kennedy was least ready to come to an agreement with Father. Public opinion in the United States demanded firmness, including even the possible use of force.

Hoping that his opponent would waver, Father decided to exert the utmost pressure. However, he didn't even dream of using force, either then or in subsequent months. In his words, it wouldn't take any special effort or great intellect to occupy West Berlin. But then what would happen ?

It was easy to predict the consequences—war. That did not enter into Father's plans under any circumstances.

This is how he remembered the final day of negotiations:

> We parted in a state of heightened tension. I warned the president that if we did not meet any understanding on the part of the United States on the question of concluding a peace treaty, we would decide this question unilaterally and sign a treaty with the German Democratic Republic and then change the legal norms of access by the Western powers to West Berlin. I exaggerated the situation in order to put the Americans in an untenable position and force them to admit that our proposals made good sense. Otherwise a conflict would occur. But the president was not ready to reach an agreement under pressure. My appeals that he recognize the realistic nature of our arguments hung in the air. We remained on our old positions.

Pierre Salinger recalls the drama of that last conversation with Father. In answer to the president's statement that they would defend their communications with Berlin with the help of the armed forces, he retorted: "That is your problem."

The president replied: "You, not I, are forcing changes in the region."

Khrushchev shrugged. His decision was final.

"This winter, it seems, will be a cold one," were John Kennedy's last words.

Father understood that he had to take advantage of the moment, and he stepped up the pressure. After John Kennedy's departure (he had to leave for previously scheduled talks with Harold Macmillan in London), Father met with the Austrian state secretary, Bruno Kreisky. They knew each other well from when the State Treaty and the neutrality agreement, which ended the state of war between the two countries, was concluded in 1954. At that time they had developed close and confidential relations.

Kreisky played a notable role in social democracy in the West and supported close ties with Willy Brandt. Father counted on influencing the West Germans through him.

He dictated the following for his memoirs: "I repeated to Kreisky what I had said to Kennedy. I hoped that if I presented our position just as sharply, this would become known not only to the U.S. president, but to Brandt as well. And something depended on Brandt in the German problem. He was then mayor of West Berlin. I thought it possible that they might take the steadfastness of our intentions into account and decide not to raise the temperature around Berlin to the boiling point, but finally agree on sensible conditions in order to find a solution and come to an agreement."

And further: "We also took other steps after the meeting. Not so much in practice, as by advertising that we intended to carry out our proposals and sign a peace treaty. We acted rather energetically and exerted pressure through the press and during meetings. In a word, we utilized all the means available to us to give our opponents the impression that if they did not behave sensibly and agree with us, then we would carry out what we had said to the U.S. president."

In this, Father was mistaken. His opponent was prepared for forceful opposition. Any step he took to accommodate Father over Berlin would have been seen, both in Bonn and in Washington, as a manifestation of weakness, a capitulation in face of the Soviet Union. The president could not permit himself to be portrayed that way.

In Father's words, he and the president parted in a mood of gloom. Father said that it was obvious from John Kennedy's expression that he was extremely disappointed by the lack of specific agreements, by the fact that negotiations were deadlocked.

Father had a more philosophical attitude, but naturally he was also unhappy at the outcome. He said, in that connection:

I would have liked us to part in a different mood, but there was nothing I could do to help, since state policy is inflexible. Our class position made it impossible to reach agreement. . . . That drove us back toward an intensification and continuation of the 'cold' war. And for that we paid a price, since the arms race resumed. In a word, it was a policy already familiar to us, which put a burden on the budget and reduced our economic potential . . . and the living standards of our peoples.

It's not especially important who looked gloomier: Father and the president both understood that something unfortunate was happening, but both sides envisioned a final victory over the adversary, or the negotiating partner. I don't know which sounds right.

The Vienna negotiations did not yield any results. Father did not find a common language with the new president either. And that meant that the nuclear race continued.

The Ministry of Defense, as well as designers of rockets, planes, and other types of weapons, continued to deluge Father with requests to resume testing. Father hated to lose the moral and political advantage accumulated over the two and a half years of the moratorium, but now he was inclined to think that there was simply no other recourse.

Father was also worried by the fact that the Soviet Union would still be performing too many tests in the center of the country, in Semipalatinsk. No matter how carefully these tests were carried out, winds would spread clouds poisoned by radiation throughout the area. The Ministry of Medium Machine-Building was instructed to develop a variety of underground tests. The Americans were also moving in that direction. They proposed restricting tests to underground ones. Our nuclear specialists didn't like the idea and told Father that it was extremely difficult to verify the effectiveness of underground explosions. At that time structures were built at the test site, machinery was installed, and people watched what happened to it. With underground tests you had to rely on computations.

Minister Yefim Pavlovich Slavsky was particularly skeptical about the possibilities of testing large warheads underground. In those years every designer tried to surprise fellow designers, and especially the leadership, with the steadily increasing explosive force of his creation. Warheads went from three megatons to five, then to ten, then to fifteen, and now they were talking about twenty, fifty, and even one hundred megatons. There was no clear articulation of any possible military use of such monsters, but the numbers themselves were impressive. Even Father was influenced by them. He never tired of praising the achievements of designers. Of course, underground tests of such fantastically huge warheads were out of the question.

The Americans were not chasing after records. They stopped at a yield of about twenty megatons and began to reduce sharply the weight of both the warhead and its explosive force. A rational people, they thought that you could ruin more by studding the ground with relatively weak explosions (of several hundred kilotons) than by a single gigantic blow similar to a volcanic eruption, an explosion that would rapidly lose its destructive force as distance from the epicenter increased. In addition, their warheads were very well suited to underground testing.

The Ministry of Medium Machine-Building also objected to the increased cost of underground tests. A special shaft had to be dug for every explosion. And during those years dozens of warheads were being made.

Father asked that as many tests as possible be moved from Semipalatinsk to the Novaya Zemlya test site. Of course, it was incomparably more difficult to work in the Far North, but it was farther from populated areas. He ordered Slavsky to make another painstaking study of the technical aspects of carrying out underground tests and advised him to consult with people in the coal industry, as he had when underground missile launch positions were proposed. Father thought their experience might prove useful. They completed the experimental shaft, and it was possible to carry out the first underground explosion in that very year, 1961.

Although Father had reconciled himself to the need to resume tests, he wanted to verify the correctness of his decision one more time before making it final. Therefore, on July 10 he convened a large meeting of specialists, scientists, designers, testers, and military officers in the Oval Hall of the Kremlin.

At the time nothing was more secret than work relating to nuclear subjects. Father avoided discussing details, even with me. I therefore know very little about this conference.

Most of its participants supported the idea of resuming tests and thought that we had already lost too much time and had allowed the Americans to gain the advantage.

Father told me that Sakharov was the only one to speak out in opposition.

Father very much regretted his differences with Sakharov. It was not the first time that Andrei Dmitriyevich had opposed testing. His letters to Father on the harmful effect of nuclear explosions and their destructive effect on everything living had played an important role in the decision to announce a moratorium. Sakharov had objected to holding the series of tests in 1958. And now, anticipating the discussion at the conference, he sent Father a note in which he stated that the resumption of tests after the three-year moratorium would disrupt negotiations on ending tests and on disarmament and would lead to a new spiral in the arms race.

Father acknowledged regretfully that he lost his temper and spoke sharply to Sakharov.

"As if I didn't know all that already," Father told me as he unburdened himself the next evening. "But the Americans don't even want to hear about disarmament. Sakharov talks about humanism, but I have to think about the country's security. If a war began, how many people would die if we couldn't retaliate properly?"

Father thought that his situation was more difficult and more complicated than Sakharov's, since he was the one forced to make the final decision. And he made it, by coming out in favor of the resumption of tests.

Preparations began. An official announcement was planned for the end of August.

Now we know that the U.S. president faced a similar dilemma and that he too was tormented by doubts. The military were pressuring him as well, and he finally also gave the order to prepare for tests.

THE DESIGNERS FOLLOW FATHER TO THE CRIMEA

In July Father freed up some time and departed for a vacation in the Crimea. He was accompanied, as usual, by the whole family, including children and grandchildren. Chelomei made up his mind to visit Lower Oreanda, the sanatorium that adjoined Father's dacha. He knew that Father would invite the "neighbors" to spend some time with him, and Chelomei wanted to tell Father about his new projects. On the other hand, perhaps he was simply worried that his rivals had similar plans. Korolyov and Tupolev were already there.

Chelomei and the Global Rocket

That summer Chelomei was preoccupied by a new weapon, a global rocket (the GR-1) capable of overcoming an antimissile defense. He had first mentioned it during a meeting with Father in April of 1960, also in the Crimea.

Now the fantasy was being transformed into a solid engineering proposal. Chelomei wanted to describe it to Father and, with his approval, begin designing it. With the help of the UR-200, he proposed launching into orbit a nuclear warhead that, upon receiving a radio braking command from earth, would fall on an adversary's head along a surprise trajectory known only to the attacker. The military supported this project.

A great deal remained undefined in the very concept of this global missile. If the missile was launched for less than a complete orbit, then it was clearly that same ballistic missile warhead that was attacking the enemy along an unanticipated trajectory. But Chelomei also proposed building long-lasting bomb-satellites to orbit the earth for years at a time. However, what if no war took place? Should they be sent into a higher orbit and left as souvenirs for our descendants? And what if the Americans decided to knock them down or, even worse, developed spaceships capable of capturing them? Not such a preposterous idea. Then, to defend them, would military space stations filled with shells have to be launched into orbit? There were many unanswered questions.

When they met, Father spent a long time asking Vladimir Nikolayevich questions. They talked things over at length while sitting under a linen umbrella on the beach. Who could imagine that the subject under discussion in such a setting was the possibility of waging nuclear war in space?

Father gave his approval for work to begin on the project. It went on with a degree of secrecy unusual even by the standards of that time. But how could it be otherwise? We were making a weapon unknown to the world, one that was capable of changing the balance of power on the planet. The work went along as planned, and the time came to build experimental prototypes and begin testing.

Then, in the middle of August 1962, Father did something which I found inexplicable at the time. He talked about our project with American journalists. Even earlier he had mentioned the global missile in one of his speeches.

I considered such indiscretion to be intolerable and almost treasonable.

Choosing an opportune moment, I poured out my objections. At first he smiled slyly and avoided saying anything, but I persisted. He finally gave in.

"Don't you understand that no one would allow us to launch such a thing into orbit? Not only would it be dangerous, it would be crazy," growled Father in a didactic tone of voice.

In bewilderment I forced out: "Then why . . . ?"

Father smiled: "Let them rack their brains in Washington. Just the thought of nuclear weapons hanging over their heads should cool them off. So you're not working for nothing."

I didn't answer, but felt hurt and disappointed.

Development of a global missile ended with a set of blueprints. We did not proceed to its manufacture.

Washington's reaction was to increase spending on antimissile defense.

However, the idea proved to be tenacious. Korolyov followed Chelomei in becoming fascinated by the global missile. He had more "luck," and in 1964–65 he made several full-scale mockups of the GR-1 (Korolyov and Chelomei used the same designation). But its development did not proceed any further. It was those mockups which were usually carried in the parades through Red Square. As the archives testify, the Americans swallowed Father's bait and spent huge amounts of money attempting to create a defense against missiles that didn't exist.[3]

The next attempt to build a global missile was made by Yangel. He finally brought the project to its logical conclusion and created a flying model. But Brezhnev, who by then had replaced Father in the Kremlin, didn't dare to launch nuclear warheads into earth orbit.

---

3. Associated Press, "Soviets Fooled World with Dummy-Missile Parades," November 18, 1998.

KOROLYOV AND THE SPACE PROGRAM

Korolyov was another of Father's companions at "beach meetings." That year the subject of their conversations was once again a new heavy rocket capable of competing with the Americans in a race to the moon. After rejecting President Kennedy's proposal for a joint effort, we had to decide whether to go it alone. While Father didn't intend to yield our unquestioned superiority in space research, he was also thinking of the cost.

Unlike Father, Korolyov had no doubt of the need to compete in a race to be first to land on the moon. However, preliminary studies showed that more than seventy tons would have to be lifted into orbit. That seemed an infinitely large amount in those days, the equivalent of an entire railroad car. Father wondered which rocket would be capable of lifting such a large and cumbersome object. Korolyov replied that he planned to keep within a launch weight of 2200 to 2500 tons.

"About ten R-7s," said Father tentatively.

In the end he allowed himself to be persuaded. He had staked so much on our rocket achievements that it didn't seem sensible to refrain from further progress. Moreover, Father was just as much a dreamer as Korolyov. In that they were alike. Father was extremely eager to be a contemporary of the first man to step onto another planet. Especially a Soviet man. There were so many attractive prospects ahead: space, the moon, communism. Soviet power had raised people to such heights that it took your breath away!

The next version of the N-1 had already been formally included in a new government decree issued on May 13, 1961, shortly before their meeting. However, the decree didn't sound very encouraging to Korolyov: "On the reexamination of plans for space vehicles with a view toward implementing tasks of importance to defense." Although by nature an enthusiast, Father was nevertheless disturbed by the general fascination with space when the intercontinental missile so vital to national defense did not yet exist. He therefore decided to use that decree to restrain the hotheads.

Korolyov understood that the decree referred to him, but he needed Father's support. Now one government decree had appeared, but tomorrow there could be a new one.

He was satisfied with their meeting on the beach. Father had taken his side, although with reservations.

They agreed that Korolyov would continue his work and report to the Defense Council when estimates were ready. A final decision would be made then, possibly by winter of the following year.

As Korolyov was leaving, he superstitiously rapped on the wooden top of the small beach table while reminding Father that a space flight, manned by German Titov, would take place at the beginning of August.

To my surprise, Father asked (though he did not order) that the launch be carried out no later than the tenth. He usually tried not to interfere in such matters. On this occasion he changed his rule.

Korolyov readily agreed.

"Let's plan it for the seventh," he said with a smile.

"All right. Agreed," responded Father.

Father promised Korolyov that Titov would be welcomed back the same way as Gagarin. Just let him return unharmed.

It was only afterward that I guessed why he preferred the first ten days of August to the second ten. In his mind, Father wanted Titov's flight to coincide with the establishment of a border in Berlin, which was then a very highly guarded secret.

Tupolev and the Nuclear Airplane

I should also mention his beach talks with Tupolev. No matter how friendly and pleasant the meetings with Chelomei and Korolyov seemed, they were still reports to the chairman of the Council of Ministers. When he was with Tupolev, on the other hand, the atmosphere was more relaxed. These were two men who had lived extraordinary lives, who knew both their own worth and each other's worth, and could simply sit and talk.

The illustrious Tupolev design bureau was having a difficult time of it in those years. Father no longer considered it necessary to spend billions building long-range heavy bombers. He thought that in the confrontation with the United States, missiles were sufficient. Development of the bureau's last two planes—the TU-22 supersonic medium-range bomber and the long-range heavy interceptor TU-28–80, armed with air-to-air missiles—was coming to an end. No new military orders were foreseen.

Of course, there were still passenger planes. The TU-104, which had thundered around the world, hatched a whole family of TUs. But until then passenger aviation had been viewed as something like a stream deviating slightly from the main channel, which was military aviation. That's the way it was and, thought Andrei Nikolayevich, that was the way it would remain in his lifetime.

Entry into rocket technology seemed closed to him. Ustinov vigilantly guarded a firmly closed door. So Tupolev had to find another use for his bureau. On this occasion he proposed building a plane with nuclear engines that, without landing, would be able to fly around the earth more than once.

In those years the enthusiasm for nuclear energy was universal. More and more nuclear-powered submarines were being planned and built. The nuclear-powered icebreaker *Lenin* was staggering the imagination of veteran captains of the Polar seas.

Now a plane!

Nikolai Dmitriyevich Kuznetsov, Andrei Nikolayevich's long-time collaborator on the TU-95 and TU-114, undertook the development of a jet engine for a nuclear-powered plane. They had worked together to produce preliminary calculations and now had the opportunity to "report" to the "boss."

The Air Force did not support the new concept. They thought the plane would be dangerous to the crew and ground service personnel on the one hand, and did not promise any particular advantages in the air on the other. But it wasn't the first time that Tupolev and Kuznetsov had to circumvent the generals to push through their innovations. Father listened to Tupolev without interrupting. That was a sign that he wasn't enthusiastic about the idea. Tupolev understood that, but had no intention of retreating.

Father recalled his much earlier conversation with Andrei Nikolayevich about the impossibility of building a bomber capable of operating effectively against the United States. He repeated the questions he had asked seven years before: "What is the new plane's projected speed and flight ceiling? Could it overcome the air defense system deployed on the North American continent?"

Tupolev's reply amounted to the same thing. You couldn't expect miracles. Unlimited range came at a cost: nuclear power units were heavy in any case, and they would need additional shielding. The plane would therefore fly at about the speed of sound and at about the usual altitude, ten to twelve kilometers.

Father shook his head. "But you've said yourself, with those parameters there's no point in poking our noses into the United States. They could easily shoot it down."

"It's my job to think up technical solutions, but you're the one who must decide to buy them," Tupolev joked, both slightly offended and simply discouraged.

It was already clear to them both that the proposal would not be approved. However, Father didn't want to upset his guest. He asked whether it was possible to build a long-distance passenger plane with nuclear-powered engines. Andrei Nikolayevich simply waved his hand: absolutely not. Because it would require so much weight to shield the passengers effectively against radiation, the plane wouldn't even be able to take off. In addition, you'd have to contend with the problem of contamination at airports on takeoff and landing.

But the nuclear project was not abandoned immediately. Work continued for some time. They made a special flying laboratory, a plane with a mixed power unit, equipped with a nuclear turbine. However, the effort eventually came to nothing, and the most pessimistic predictions were realized. To operate such a plane was impossible, even with the casual attitude toward radiation prevalent at the time.

At their next meeting Father, who had completely lost interest in a nuclear-powered bomber, advised Andrei Nikolayevich to concentrate on passenger aircraft. He was particularly interested in the possible creation of a supersonic passenger plane. After that the design bureau's main focus became the TU-144, and it spent many years of intense work and many billions of rubles on its development.

I don't want to give the impression that Father examined such important matters, vital to the country's defense capability, only while reclining on the seashore or strolling along paths in the woods near Moscow.

It's simply that I was not present during his meetings with designers, military officers, and scientists in his Kremlin office. I heard only echoes of those conversations, comments by participants, and Father's reaction to good or, as he sometimes thought, worthless proposals. I know nothing at all about some events.

I am trying to describe in detail the events I happened to witness, which naturally, generally took place at our home.

THE BERLIN WALL

Father's thoughts constantly reverted to Germany. He no longer gave any serious thought to the unilateral conclusion of a peace treaty. It didn't pay to go overboard in the matter. Of course, thought Father, you couldn't avoid placing a strain on relations with the United States, but he didn't intend to exceed the framework permitted by the Potsdam Agreement.

After long vacillation, Father came to the conclusion that the only solution to the German question was to "plug up all the holes."[4] The decision was formulated there in the Crimea, during his vacation. He thought that once the door to the West was closed, people would stop rushing around and begin working, the economy would take off and it wouldn't be long before West Germans began knocking on the GDR's door. Then no one would be able to prevent the signing of a peace treaty with two German states.

In the meantime the first step was clear: stop the outpouring of people and take control of the situation. How could that be done? The most difficult place to divide was Berlin, since the sectors were sometimes separated only by a mutually agreed-upon line running down the center of the street. One sidewalk was in one sector, the other in a different one. Cross the street and

---

4. Contemporary Cold War historiography, based on documents, has concluded that the initiative for demarcation came from the Germans, not from Father. In later years Walter Ulbricht tried to promote the idea in every possible way. My account deals with the concluding phase, when Father was concerned with the details of carrying out the operation.—S.K.

you have already crossed the border. At the time sector boundaries were determined no one thought of borders, border guards, passes, or visas. Those lines existed only on paper and now Father was looking for a way to make them real.

Father asked our ambassador in the GDR, Mikhail Pervukhin, to send him a detailed map of Berlin with the demarcation lines marked on it.

Father recalled:

> The boundaries on the map were not drawn precisely. You couldn't tell whether it was possible to establish a definite border with border checkpoints. I decided that this was because the people who had marked the map were not fully qualified. That would certainly be understandable, since they weren't specialists.
>
> I called the ambassador again and asked: "Comrade Pervukhin, it's hard to make sense of the map you sent me. It doesn't help us to judge whether it's possible to establish borders. Invite over the commander of our forces (at the time the commander was Ivan Ignatiyevich Yakubovsky) and pass on my request that his staff make a map of Berlin with the borders marked and with comments on whether it's possible to establish control over them. After that report to Comrade Ulbricht. Let him take a look and say whether he would agree to discuss these questions."
>
> They sent a new map. The ambassador called me to say that Ulbricht was in full agreement. He thought that this was the right solution, that it would improve the situation and that it was the only possibility of controlling it.
>
> I looked at where they had indicated it was possible to set up control gates and concluded that it was possible to establish a border in Berlin. However, with great difficulty.

Father made up his mind. It seemed to him that the imposition of border controls should not provoke a particularly vehement reaction from our former allies. After all, their right of free movement among the zones was preserved. That was a crucial distinction from previous proposals and threats associated with the conclusion of a peace treaty and transfer of control functions to the government of the GDR.

Passes and other border formalities were to be imposed only on Germans, and there wasn't a single word about them in the Potsdam Agreement.

He understood that there was a certain risk. The most dangerous time would be the physical imposition of control at the border, the marking of lines dividing the sectors, and the construction of barriers at crossing points. A sudden shock might provoke thoughtless actions. Still, he felt that the risk was justified. There was no talk of putting up an impenetrable concrete wall. That was a purely German invention.

After receiving Ulbricht's approval and backing, Father decided it was time to act. He summoned Gromyko and his deputy Vladimir Semyonov, who was in charge of German affairs, to the Crimea. It was necessary to evaluate all possible diplomatic steps carefully. As a result, a plan of action was formulated that led to what was later widely called the Second Berlin Crisis.

Everything had to be prepared in the strictest secrecy. The minimum amount of time was allotted for building the installations. Work had to be completed before people on the other side could decide what to do. It's easier to interfere with work in progress than to knock down something already built.

"We didn't want our troops to stand at the border," Father dictated in his memoirs.

> That was the job of the Germans themselves. . . . The West Germans also guarded their own borders.
>
> A chain of Soviet troops was to stand behind the Germans at the border. Let the West see that, although the Germans stood in a thin line and it wouldn't take much to break it, Soviet troops would then take action.
>
> At the checkpoints . . . where representatives of the Western Powers would pass, one of our officers would stand and let them through without delay, just as before.

Father returned with this plan to Moscow. He presented his ideas to a special session of the Presidium of the Central Committee in the second half of July. On that occasion there was a minimum of outsiders present in the hall. The information must not leak through tightly closed doors.

No real discussion took place. Relying on Father's authority, speakers supported the proposed plan. "The comrades agreed that it was the only chance to create a stable situation in the GDR," Father noted.

He didn't want to act alone. All Warsaw Pact members were at risk, and he decided to discuss what he intended to do with the allies. They gathered behind closed doors in Moscow, in order to ensure secrecy. Not a line appeared anywhere in the press. No information filtered out to the West either. Only the first secretaries of party central committees and heads of government took part in the conference. The rest of their entourages stayed home.

At the time I had no idea what was being planned, so I return to Father's notes: "We explained these matters and expressed our opinion. All the socialist countries' representatives agreed enthusiastically and expressed confidence that we would carry out these measures successfully and that the Western countries would, to put it bluntly, swallow this 'bitter pill.' "

Publicly Father continued to bombard the West with various proposals. On July 1 the GDR advanced the so-called German Peace Plan. A joint commission of representatives of the parliaments and governments of both

Germanys should work out proposals for the conclusion of a peace treaty. But the idea of making West Berlin a free city stuck out like a sore thumb. The government of the FRG rejected the very idea of joint discussions. The GDR was missing from their maps.

On July 8, at a reception in the Kremlin for graduates of military academies, Father proposed convening a high-level conference to discuss problems of a peace treaty with Germany. After that there was a lull—no initiatives whatever, complete silence. In the GDR the Germans were quickly preparing fence posts. They had received tons of barbed wire from Soviet army warehouses, which they had dragged to the border, and were welding barriers. It was impossible to conceal such activities for long, but the workers themselves didn't know the purpose of what they were doing. The most improbable rumors spread.

Meanwhile, the tone of diplomatic documents changed and became sharper and more uncompromising.

On July 25 a statement by President Kennedy rang out like a peal of thunder. He warned that any steps taken to implement Father's threat to conclude a peace treaty with the GDR would encounter the determined opposition of the United States.

In his speech on television, Kennedy announced his readiness to fight for West Berlin.

The president backed up his words by taking decisive steps. He announced that 250,000 reservists were being called up for duty and that strategic aviation was being put on a fifteen-minute alert status.

On August 3 a Soviet government memorandum concerning a peace treaty with Germany was published in Moscow and sent to the government of the FRG.

Similar notes were sent simultaneously to the capitals of the victorious powers.

The memorandum's dominant theme was the assertion that at present neither a united Germany nor an overall German government existed. The division of the country had a societal basis and had to be recognized. It was an objective reality.

On August 7 German Titov flew into space. Father returned that day to Moscow, as he had promised Korolyov. That evening he intended to address the nation on television and deliver an emphatic answer to the president of the United States.

Rejecting the accusation that any threats had issued from his side, Father repeated the familiar points about a free city and communications. He said there was no question of a blockade of West Berlin. Nevertheless, he announced an increase in defense spending and an end to reductions in the armed forces, as well as the possibility of a future additional call-up of reservists and the transfer of several divisions from the country's interior to its western borders.

I watched his speech on television at home. Chills ran up and down my spine. I had the impression that real trouble was brewing and that the situation was heading toward war. I wanted very much to find out the particulars of what was being done, what Father's militancy signified.

At home he sounded far less bellicose than before the cameras. With respect to his statement about an increase in defense spending, Father told me that it was simply a reaction to Kennedy's statement and that it wasn't really necessary. No measures requiring additional expenditures were planned.

"We won't call up people and interrupt their work," he continued, "but we'll have to put a temporary halt to reductions in the army. After all, the Americans are really worked up."

Father was worried whether the U.S. president had strong nerves. Would he lose his grip?

Preparations for closing the border were virtually completed as this back-and-forth was going on. In Berlin they were waiting for the order from Moscow. General Yakubovsky reported to Father by telephone and requested agreement to begin the operation on the night of August 12–13.

Father joked that the thirteenth was an unlucky number, but immediately added: "Let it be unlucky for our adversaries."

The most difficult moment had arrived. How would the Americans behave? Father counted on their being reasonable, since all the work would take place on the territory of the GDR.

Clustered on their side of streets, the Americans watched as workers poured asphalt, set posts into the ground and strung barbed wire while a thin chain of German soldiers formed up along lines between the city's sectors. There were no attempts to interfere.

Father sighed with relief when he heard that. The danger had passed. Since they had not rushed in immediately, they would be even less likely to look for a fight after thinking things over.

But in the meantime peace was hanging by a thread. The report Washington received from Germany about the unusual construction project along the border inside Berlin was quickly followed by a request from the commander of U.S. forces for permission to send bulldozers and tear down the frail barriers. That was technically feasible, but the political consequences were impossible to predict.

Kennedy cooled off the hotheads. In Pierre Salinger's words, he thought that "the Ulbricht regime probably has the legal right to close its borders, and no one can imagine that we should start a war because of that."

Father was elated. He thought that the GDR had gained even more by establishing control over its borders than it could expect from signing a peace treaty.

Each day brought new reports. The Americans first decided to test the attitude toward representatives of the occupying powers. Beginning with the morning of August 13 several jeeps with officers and soldiers headed for East Berlin. They were allowed through without hindrance, but from the time they crossed the border they were tailed by two Volga cars filled with members of the East German state security service, which didn't leave them alone for a moment. The jeeps drove around the city. They had nothing to do there and returned just as freely as they had come.

However, a kind of war, one of threats and gestures, began that was no laughing matter. After sending a protest note claiming that the Potsdam Agreement had been violated, President Kennedy decided to make his determination more emphatic. Vice President Lyndon Johnson flew hastily to West Berlin and declared that "the life, the future and the sacred honor" of the United States were laid on the altar of defense of the city's inhabitants. Reinforcements—about 1,500 fully equipped infantrymen—crossed the border of the GDR from West Germany and advanced toward Berlin. Father was quickly informed when our command received notification of the impending passage of U.S. troops. Yakubovsky waited for orders. Malinovsky proposed that the Americans not be permitted to pass.

Father issued an unequivocal order to let them pass, create all conditions necessary for free transit, and behave with special courtesy.

Still, he followed reports on the convoy's movement with trepidation. Anything could happen. One chance shot and . . . His nervousness affected me as well. That evening we walked without speaking. As we approached the gate the duty officer jumped out of the guard post and hurried toward Father. My heart sank. What news did he bring? The officer reported that Malinovsky had called and asked to speak with him. Father went into the house and I waited for him on the street. My imagination ran wild. The several minutes Father was away seemed like hours. Finally, the front door opened and Father appeared on the threshold. He was smiling. Our alarm turned out to be needless.

"Everything's quiet. The Americans are moving along according to the procedures agreed upon," he said, replying to my unspoken question.

It all proceeded without incident, but Father breathed easily only after the column of trucks and armored vehicles had passed through one of the thirty designated crossing points onto the territory of West Berlin. There the new arrivals were greeted by Lyndon Johnson.

According to calculations made at the time, the government of the GDR saved more than three and a half billion marks annually as a result of closing the border. Father was informed that the food situation had eased dramatically, the GDR's budget was freed from the crowd of West Berlin buyers and the usual lines had disappeared.

It seemed that the right medicine had been found and the patient was starting to improve, but only the future could give the final answer.

Father decided to show the world that he was calm. In the middle of August he left for Pitsunda on vacation.

Life in the south took its usual course—bathing in the sea and reading official papers, taking short walks and reading still more papers and, of course, receiving foreign guests. Father thought that was especially important, since visits by foreign guests were indicative of the fact that the operation had concluded and that he was inviting Kennedy to renew their dialogue.

On August 25 Father received the American journalist Drew Pearson. He thought that Pearson's request for an interview provided an excellent opportunity to publicize the reasons for his recent actions and explain his viewpoint to the West. He was pleased with the interview, which was published on August 28 and distributed throughout the world.

The situation in Berlin had its complications. East Germans who had been working in West Berlin were given similar jobs in the Eastern sector. It seemed as if everything had been thought of: qualifications, wages, even time spent commuting. However, they completely overlooked the difference in labor productivity. German workers who had been well trained at Western enterprises simply couldn't imagine that it was possible to work in a different way. From the very beginning they began to exceed the norms by two and three times. Admonitions by colleagues, warnings to stop these provocations and begin working like everyone else or the administration would raise norms and lower wage rates—nothing had the slightest effect.

The East Berliners resorted to extreme measures. They simply beat up the newcomers. Ulbricht told Father about these incidents. Father only smiled sadly. Such reports were not pleasant. Soon everything returned to normal, and the newcomers adapted to "socialist work rules."

Meanwhile, preparations for nuclear tests were almost complete. On August 31 the Soviet government published a statement announcing that testing would resume. Father made the decision with a heavy heart.

The tension over Berlin and the corresponding need to strengthen our defense capacity was one factor cited in the statement.

The first test took place the following day, when a thermonuclear warhead intended for the R-16 was exploded.

Judging by the almost immediate response, the Americans were also moving quickly. Their first test took less than two weeks to prepare: on September 12 an underground explosion was set off in Nevada. The arms race went into still another spiral.

German Titov, newly returned from space, visited Berlin on September 1. Father thought that his visit would help defuse the situation.

In dealing with the German question, both sides during this period displayed a demonstrative inflexibility combined with a very high degree of caution and deliberation before they took any action whatsoever. Father continued threatening publicly to conclude a separate peace treaty with the GDR. At a meeting in Volzhsk on September 10, he stated that he would sign a treaty that year. But three days earlier, when he received an American journalist, the *New York Times* Paris correspondent Cyrus Sulzberger, he asked Sulzberger to convey to the president in confidence that the matter could only be resolved in a peaceful manner.

Father had a great deal of respect for Sulzberger. He considered him to be not simply a journalist, but a talented politician with an analytical cast of mind. He always read Sulzberger's articles (translated and supplied to him by TASS) with a great deal of attention. He also knew that Sulzberger was close to Kennedy, so Father decided to make use of this rather unusual method of communication.

The president demonstratively nominated General Lucius Clay, former commander of the U.S. Occupation Forces, to be his special representative in West Berlin. In so doing, he emphasized U.S. readiness to resort to the strongest measures, even to the use of weapons. Father immediately proposed sending Marshal Ivan Stepanovich Konev to Germany, appointing him nominal commander of Soviet forces in the region. Konev, together with Zhukov, had taken Berlin in 1945 and led the assault on Prague. So his nomination could have only one interpretation. Father was ready for anything.

But the instructions given the newly appointed commander could not have been more to the contrary. Father advised him to try to renew his friendship with his American colleague (at one time Konev and Clay had been on good terms) and not to avoid contacts and meetings.

A gradual warming was noticeable on both sides. When two U.S. F-84 fighters intruded into GDR airspace at the beginning of September, they were not shot down, although it would have been possible. Moscow's order not to commit any acts that might aggravate the situation was obeyed. Things also calmed down across the ocean. In a speech at the U.N. on September 22, President Kennedy, noting America's continued resolve on the question of Germany, said that

> it is absurd to suppose that we would unleash a war only in order to prevent the signing of a so-called peace treaty between the Soviet Union and East Germany. . . .
>
> The dangerous crisis in Berlin arose because of the threat to the vital interests of the Western Powers and the freedom of West Berlin. We cannot ignore that threat . . . , but we believe that a peaceful solution is possible.

Father appreciated this step. As an answering gesture of goodwill, *Pravda* reprinted an article about President Kennedy written for the *New York Post* by James Wechsler. The article had two main premises: the president had no illusions with respect to nuclear war and he was therefore searching for ways to achieve an honorable peace—although, like any human being, he was not immune to mistakes.

LINES OF COMMUNICATION

I allow myself a brief digression to describe how this unusual method of communication originated: how the leaders of two great powers began to write to each other via seemingly random individuals.

While meeting one-on-one in Vienna, they both complained that official correspondence through foreign policy departments—our Ministry of Foreign Affairs and the Secretary of State's staff in the United States—was very slow-moving and ponderous. The president proposed establishing a private and unofficial channel of communications that would bypass all formalities. On his side, Kennedy chose White House Press Secretary Pierre Salinger as a courier. Father proposed Mikhail Averkiyevich Kharlamov, who headed the Press Department of the Soviet Foreign Ministry. However, one man was always in Washington, while the other lived in Moscow. A trusted person was therefore chosen as the go-between—Georgy Bolshakov. He was permanently in the United States and combined three functions: journalist, superb interpreter, and Soviet military intelligence (GRU) agent. His candidacy suited both Father and Kennedy. Neither doubted that, possessed of such "versatility," Colonel Bolshakov could cope with his complex and extremely responsible new duties.

In September it came time to make use of the channel. The president was going to give his first speech to the U.N., the speech to which I referred above. Father was very concerned about what he would say. Would the United States turn toward war or toward a search for a way out of the stalemate? Father thought that his position should be communicated to Kennedy before the U.N. speech was delivered. There had been no reaction to the information conveyed through Sulzberger. The evening before the speech Kharlamov met with Salinger in the Manhattan hotel where the president and his entourage were spending the night. Because the U.S. reaction was uncertain, Kharlamov read Father's message without handing the text to Salinger, in order to leave no record of it.

In his message Father noted that the buildup of U.S. forces in Germany and the answering reinforcement of Soviet units presented a real threat to peace. He proposed that U.S. proposals on Berlin be reexamined at their next meeting. Meanwhile, he wrote, both sides should refrain from aggravating the situation and especially avoid handcuffing the parties with ultimatums. It's only a short step from an ultimatum to a real clash, since you never know how far your opponent is prepared to retreat.

Father proposed holding a meeting soon, since there was a constant threat of armed conflict in Berlin itself. Kharlamov stressed in particular that Father was very concerned that the U.N. speech not be as militant and categorical as the August 25 speech on television. Further escalation of the confrontation could lead to unpredictable and tragic consequences.

The president listened carefully to his press secretary. He had not received any messages from Sulzberger, who apparently viewed Father's method of communication between the two leaders to be too exotic. Kennedy therefore viewed this message, the first since the beginning of the crisis, to be of extreme importance. It would set the tone for their future relations. It was important to pick up all the nuances, to weigh everything, to display the necessary firmness but not go too far.

The president made Salinger repeat the main points several times. Then he stood for a long time at the window, deep in thought. Finally, he made a decision. "The message can have only one interpretation," said Kennedy. "Since Khrushchev is ready to listen to our viewpoint on Germany, he's not preparing to conclude a peace treaty with Ulbricht, not this year anyway. And that's not bad news."

Despite the late hour, 2 a.m., the president dictated an answer to Salinger for him to read the next morning to Kharlamov. Kennedy didn't leave a record either.

Kennedy gave careful consideration to Father's proposal for a meeting on Berlin, but he linked the subject to events taking place in Laos and Vietnam. He concluded by saying that the United States would adopt a waiting position and would follow the development of events closely.

The spirit of the message might even be called heartfelt. The president noted that Father's intention of reassessing his position on Germany was reassuring. He expressed the assumption that this would result in a general relaxation of tension.

Thus began an informal contact into which, apart from Bolshakov and Kharlamov on the one side and Salinger on the other, some entirely unexpected people were drawn, most of whom combined the professions of journalist and intelligence agent.

STALIN'S GHOST

October began. The Twenty-second Party Congress convened on the seventeenth. The polemics around the name of Stalin, his mistakes and crimes, which had died down, unexpectedly erupted with renewed force. Initially

Father had not intended to raise the subject again. His colleagues in the Presidium had persuaded him that enough had been said at the Twentieth Congress; the guilty were named, mistakes corrected and there was no point in stirring up the past. However, Father couldn't resist. Deviating from the approved text of the report written earlier, he made new revelations. He talked not only about Stalin himself, but also about his circle: Molotov, Malenkov, Kaganovich, Voroshilov, and Bulganin, who had remained members of the Central Committee Presidium after the Twentieth Party Congress.

No sooner had the harsh words condemning Stalinism issued from the mouth of the speaker than others on the schedule hurried to rewrite their remarks. Their prepared texts had not contained a word about Stalin or his assistants. Most of them were unhappy about being forced to join the chorus, but they didn't dare violate the unspoken tradition of perfect unanimity. In fact, they all tried to outdo each other in order to satisfy Father. All kinds of new crimes were dragged into the open; blood and filth were laid bare. It was now impossible to conceal them or hide them. What was said at the rostrum became part of history. The explosive situation demanded action. The Congress adopted a resolution to remove the embalmed body of Stalin from the Mausoleum. However, they didn't take it very far. During the night of November 1 it was buried in the Kremlin wall, among Stalin's most honored victims and confederates.

Marshal Konev was one of those present at the Congress. You might suppose that the Berlin Wall would have kept him in Germany, but in mid-October no one anticipated complications. Konev telephoned Father and, receiving permission to leave Berlin temporarily, arrived in Moscow. Father said that it was time, in any event, to think about his returning to his duties at the Defense Ministry. He wasn't going to sit in Germany and guard the Wall forever. At the Congress Konev listened with disapproval to the abuse directed at his former supreme commander. He belonged to the silent majority, who did not support the exposure of the crimes of past years which was now beginning.

A CONFRONTATION IN BERLIN

Meanwhile, the situation in Berlin was becoming alarming. General Clay showed some initiative.

The Americans planned an operation on October 28 to destroy the barriers at one of the checkpoints in Berlin. The forces deployed to carry it out were considerable: several jeeps with infantrymen, with an admixture of journalists eager to record the facts. The bulldozers accompanying them were supposed to remove the barriers, gates and lines of barbed wire that had grown up along both sides of the street. Ten tanks covered the operation.

General Clay didn't expect any shooting. East German frontier guards wouldn't risk opening fire on soldiers of the victorious army.

The Soviet command learned beforehand about both the timing of the operation and the forces engaged in it. The opportunity to prepare and think about how they should respond averted what would very likely have been a disaster.

General Yakubovsky reported everything to the minister of defense in Moscow. Malinovsky called Father at home that evening.

On this occasion the information sounded extremely alarming. No one could be sure that the U.S. commander would not decide to send larger forces into the breach. There was no mention of such an intention, but long experience had taught both Father and the marshal not to put all their trust in messages from the intelligence agency.

What was going on? Had the time come when we would be put to the test? It was essential that Father make precisely the right decision. To begin with, he doubted that the president had authorized such actions. And why had they decided to move now, more than two months after the border was established? Kennedy had just delivered an extremely reassuring speech at the United Nations. On the eve of the speech Father had sent the president a proposal to end the confrontation, evaluate the situation realistically, and return to the negotiating table. The message was sent through their private channel.

Father counted on the continuation of contacts, but suddenly this report about bulldozers and tanks . . . It seemed to Father that other forces, bypassing the president, were interfering.

Now the slightest mistake on Father's part could cost both sides dearly. Father supposed that Clay, acting on his own and without the backing of the White House, would not initiate an armed clash.

There was no time to write the president. Furthermore, Father thought such an appeal would be a humiliating display of weakness. An order was sent to the headquarters of the Group of Soviet Forces in Germany outlining the procedure and sequence of actions by our troops in case of a provocation. Now there was nothing to do but wait. There was a glimmer of hope that the report was false, that it was leaked to the agent in order to see what our reaction would be. That often happened.

But no. The message proved to be accurate. Everything began in accordance with the plan worked out by General Clay's headquarters. An unusual procession started out early in the morning to Checkpoint Charlie, at the Brandenburg Gate in the center of Berlin. Three jeeps with military personnel and civilians headed the column, with powerful bulldozers rumbling along after them. Ten tanks with closed hatches and exposed weapons brought up the rear.

If our forces hadn't known beforehand that they were coming, their appearance might have caused a panic, and it's conceivable that the whole plan was based on that. If so, it failed. The Soviet side initiated the plan prepared by General Yakubovsky's headquarters in accordance with orders received from Moscow. It called for concealed deployment of a battalion of infantrymen and a tank regiment in the side streets bordering on the checkpoint. They managed to get into position without being observed by the Americans.

The jeeps raced through the checkpoint unhindered. Just as the last jeep passed through the barrier, adjacent streets filled with the roar of tank engines. The terrible noise was amplified many times over by loudspeakers placed on the roofs of buildings. It created the impression that at least an entire army, not just a tank regiment, was converging.

After allowing the U.S. jeeps to pass through, the Soviet tanks began crawling slowly out of the side streets and turned to confront the bulldozers. Passengers sitting in the jeeps could see moving hulks of tanks, followed by a swarming mass of infantrymen, in every side street. A car with German police followed the jeeps closely. Onlookers observed a U.S. officer sitting in the front seat of a jeep shouting something into a microphone, obviously informing his commanders of the unexpected development.

The bulldozers halted short of the border on their own territory. The U.S. tanks were behind them. Soviet tanks immediately halted on their half of the street, as called for by the plan. The barrels of their weapons seemed to be trained on the bulldozer cabs.

The jeeps began driving around behind the Soviet tanks. Then, reversing direction, the jeeps returned through the lines of Soviet tanks without hindrance and without presenting any documents. Both Soviet and U.S. tanks remained where they were, but shut down their engines. A deafening silence ensued.

With this, both scenarios had been enacted. Improvisation took over.

We don't know if Clay contacted Washington. Yakubovsky made frequent reports on the situation to Konev in Moscow, and Konev quickly relayed the information to Father. His reports did not vary.

The first report: "They are remaining in place," caused joy.

The second, an hour later: "They are remaining in place," caused satisfaction.

Two hours later: "They are remaining in place." Satisfaction was replaced by perplexity.

The short October day came to an end in Berlin and it grew noticeably colder. The end of October is not the best time to spend the night in an unheated iron box. The Americans were the first to give in. The tank crews opened their tightly battened down hatches and spilled out onto the pavement. Stretching their legs, slapping their thighs and chasing after each other, they fought off the bone-penetrating chill.

Soviet tank crews quickly followed their example. Two small groups of young men—virtually boys—formed on the street, separated by the barely visible checkpoint barrier and not at all hostile to each other. This lasted for almost two days and nights.

Kennedy sought feverishly for a way out of the trap he had fallen into courtesy of Lucius Clay. The tanks had to be withdrawn, but in a way that would avoid losing face. The president decided to turn to Father for help, employing the recently tested channel that circumvented the State Department. In an oral message transmitted via the link by the president's brother Robert to Bolshakov, Kennedy asked Father to take the first step. Since the archives have been opened, this supersecret information has finally become available to historians.[5]

Father reacted favorably. In future there would be more than one problem that he and the U.S. president would have to solve together.

The situation was becoming idiotic. It was as if the two generals in Berlin were playing a game to see who would blink first. They could continue for a very long time, displaying their obstinacy.

Father proposed a solution. We had to make the first step, to blink, and the tension would be relieved. The Soviet tanks and accompanying infantry were ordered to pull back into the side streets and, after turning off their engines, remain concealed there.

Soon after it grew quiet the U.S. tank bringing up the rear of the procession turned around and began moving slowly away, followed by the entire column ending with the bulldozers.

The Second Berlin Crisis ended with this confrontation at the Brandenburg Gate.

This is what Father writes in his memoirs:

> Through certain channels we ascertained the West's opinion: let's consider this argument ended and leave the situation unchanged. That opinion then began to appear in the press.
>
> This was how we gained de facto recognition of the establishment of borders and the transfer of functions for guarding them to the German Democratic Republic. It ceased being a cause of aggravation in our relations.

TESTING RESUMES

In accordance with the plan to test nuclear weapons on Novaya Zemlya, preparations were under way that October to set off a nuclear blast of fantas-

---

5. Raymond Garthoff, "Berlin 1961, records corrected," *Foreign Policy*, no. 84 (Fall 1991).

tic power—fifty megatons. Three such monsters, of thirty, fifty, and one hundred megatons, had been prepared. It was decided to set off the middle one. An echo of the explosion should reach northern Europe as a threatening, but relatively harmless, roar. The world had never known such warheads. Ours was the first and only one. Our medium-machine builders were extraordinarily proud of their achievements and were very eager to demonstrate our might to Father.

Slavsky reported that preparations on Novaya Zemlya were going ahead full steam. Every calculation indicated that the blast would not cause any damage on our coast or affect our northern neighbors, although it would be perceptible. Father agreed: let them feel it and tell their NATO allies.

The blast was set for October 30.

Finally, the test took place. Returning from an evening session of the Congress (it was not by chance that the two events coincided), Father said proudly that results even exceeded those expected. Instead of the anticipated fifty megatons, it reached fifty-seven megatons. Father was elated. The problem was, there was no booster rocket able to lift such a heavy warhead.

A RESOLUTION, OF SORTS, IN BERLIN

In West Berlin panic arose soon after the barriers were erected on the border. It seemed to many people that the city's days of independent existence were numbered. Local businessmen began to curtail their activities and sell their enterprises.

Father was pleased to hear the news. He thought it would only hasten the inevitable appeal by the West Berlin City Council for assistance from the government of the GDR. His hopes were not realized. The situation gradually stabilized and capital investments slowly began returning to the city.

The Americans recalled Clay. Konev departed for Moscow.

According to Father's calculations, once the sovereignty of the national government was established over its territory, the economy of the GDR would pick up and there would be a dramatic improvement in living standards. He observed with some bitterness that this goal was not achieved. He mentioned indignantly that Ulbricht wanted to raise the price of the fishing boats being built for the Soviet Union. Father compared what we were paying the GDR and the FRG for the same commodities. It turned out that identical prices were set in the FRG and GDR, but that in the FRG they were producing at a profit, while in the GDR they were operating at a loss. Father complained bitterly that you couldn't make much progress under such conditions and with such management.

MISSILES, THE MILITARY, AND THE SPACE PROGRAM

With the uproar over Berlin going on, hardly any notice was paid to the modest newspaper reports about the launch of Soviet missiles over the Pacific Ocean on September 13 and 17. These were the final tests of the R-16 intercontinental ballistic missile. Construction of aboveground launch positions, which had begun six months earlier, continued without interruption. However, they were to serve for only a short time, until silos were ready.

Tests of Korolyov's R-9 continued, with no end in sight.

At the beginning of February 1962 Father left for Pitsunda on vacation. It was somewhat warmer there than in the Crimea, but more important was the fact that a seawater pool—an unheard-of luxury in those days—had been built for the government dachas. Father counted, not only on restoring his health, but on carrying out a review of missile development at the same time. A great many government decrees had been adopted during the previous few years. Some of them were out of date and some had not been implemented. Some duplicated each other, leading to the irrational loss of huge sums of money.

Father planned on holding an expanded session of the Defense Council, where he could, without hurrying, listen to military officers, ministers, and designers and investigate, consult, and adopt a missile program for the near future. In Moscow Father was simply unable to find the time. His days were taken up with daily business, receptions, and meetings, all without exception of "extraordinary" importance. He had therefore decided to gather everyone together during his vacation.

Father decided to hold the session in a sports hall. He thought that it would be easy to hang diagrams on bars along the walls and everyone could sit around simple garden tables.

Designers were to be accompanied by two representatives from each "firm." Chelomei decided to take me with him. Every evening we talked to Father over the telephone, and at the first opportunity I told him that I was coming. He didn't object. In fact, he was delighted. It was obvious that he was bored there, all by himself. Father joked that he would write a request to Chelomei to allow me to remain for a few days afterward.

We flew in on the eve of the appointed day.

The next morning began in a businesslike way. Lieutenant General Semyon Ivanov, the secretary of the Defense Council, was the first to appear in the heavily guarded sports hall. He looked around critically. He fingered the rickety tables and wicker chairs, shaking his head in disapproval. Then he concentrated on the problem of recording the speeches on tape. He had brought along a miniature tape recorder, which could record for many hours on a special wire—the latest achievement of General Staff intelligence. A colonel who had come with him helped out, speaking from different places in the hall. The task turned out to be beyond the tape recorder's ability. In one place it was too loud, in another a barely audible mumble was lost in static. Finally the general gave up and ordered the colonel to sit near him the whole time and take down speeches in a special secret notebook, sewn together with brown thread.

Meanwhile participants in the session were starting to arrive. Black Chaika limousines and Volgas pulled up to the doors, one after another. They had been collected from the entire coast to transport the high-ranking guests.

There was stocky Malinovsky, who arrived in the same car as Grechko, commander of the forces of the Warsaw Pact, tall as a beanpole; Biryuzov, the severe and composed commander of the Air Defense Forces, was next to the smiling head of the General Staff, Zakharov; and two more commanders in chief, lean and lively Moskalenko and Gorshkov, who resembled a round ball packed into his black Navy uniform. They were both scheduled to give reports, Gorshkov that day and Moskalenko the next.

After them were marshals, followed at some distance by a throng of generals. Our eyes were dazzled by the diamond stars on their collars, and the hall glimmered with the large and small stars of various styles embroidered in various configurations on their epaulets and their multicolored rows of service ribbons.

Ministers and designers entered, buttoned into official-looking dark suits, accompanied by people laden down with voluminous tubes of diagrams.

Everyone awaited Father. He appeared at about ten o'clock, a few minutes before the appointed time. He was followed through the door by Kozlov, Kosygin, Mikoyan, Ustinov, and some others—too many to remember. In contrast to the "Muscovites," Father was dressed in gray suit pants and a green sports jacket, as if to emphasize that he was on vacation.

We sat down. The doors were closed tightly. Admiral Gorshkov walked to a large map showing naval actions in the event of nuclear war.

During the previous few years submarines had become the Navy's main strike force. They were grouped along both coasts of the United States. Their mission was to launch ballistic missiles against enemy cities.

Submarines armed with cruise missiles lay in wait for U.S. aircraft carriers at the outlets of harbors. They lurked not only near the coastline, but in the open ocean as well, and were capable of striking an enemy from a distance of hundreds of kilometers.

The Navy's principal mission was to keep the Americans away from our shores. If they still managed to break through, shore defenses were capable of sinking any ship at great distances. There were also planes and patrol boats equipped with missiles and, finally, cruise missiles scattered along the coastline.

Father was pleased. They had not wasted time. The Navy had undergone a qualitative change. It had become lighter, more mobile, and most important, more powerful and less expensive. Father repeatedly stressed that last aspect.

Once again he described his argument with Kuznetsov and embarked on a lengthy account of all the circumstances of his fight against cruisers and aircraft carriers. Gorshkov nodded obsequiously in agreement.

Father finally stopped talking. Makeyev took the floor. He talked about destroying ground targets by submarine-launched ballistic missiles.

It may surprise some readers that our submarine fleet, equipped with ballistic missiles, was not given as important a role at that time as U.S. doctrine gave U.S. Polaris-armed submarines.

Clothes are cut to fit the cloth. In those years we had no missiles comparable to the Polaris. The range of our missiles was not quite half that of Polaris. Our submarines carried only two or three missiles, whereas U.S. boats carried sixteen. Originating with the R-II, naval missiles continued to be powered by acid. And I would not even attempt to describe what acid is like in the hermetically sealed space of a submarine on duty in the ocean depths.

The next speaker, Chelomei, talked about cruise missiles. In those years his design bureau was in the vanguard. It would be some time before similar weapons would appear in the fleets of the United States and other countries.

A whole phalanx of cruise missiles, launched from submarines, would line up. Some, launched on the open ocean, would travel very low, barely grazing the waves, approach harbors and naval bases inconspicuously and stealthily, and attack an enemy's seemingly invulnerable bases.

Others were designed for use against aircraft carrier groups on the high seas. Information on their location would be transmitted to submariners by a new satellite equipped with a super-powerful radar being developed by Chelomei's team. However, its accuracy in locating targets still left something to be desired. But that could be rectified. Having only an approximate idea of the enemy's location and composition, missiles would array themselves, automatically find the most important target in the carrier group, and launch a barrage at it.

Those launched from the surface had greater range and were launched from submarines that had surfaced at a safe distance. Others, with a somewhat shorter range, erupted from the water after being launched from a submarine at a safe depth.

The subject then turned to cruise missiles designed for use by surface ships, cruisers and destroyers. Like a magic wand, their large caliber extended the effective strike range by dozens of times. I don't refer to their accuracy—the target would be destroyed at the first volley, at worst at the second.

The question of shore defenses was not ignored. Installed on trucks, cruise missiles here on the Black Sea were capable of sinking hostile ships near Turkey itself. Chelomei waved his hand vaguely toward the nearest window, in the direction he apparently thought hostile shores were to be found.

"But those are of secondary importance," Vladimir Nikolayevich commented. "Submarines remain our principal weapon. When our plans have been carried out, the Soviet Navy will be able to confront the U.S. Navy on the high seas and without expensive aircraft carriers."

Father was interested and commented once again that tons of money would have been wasted if Kuznetsov's advice had been followed. But now they had succeeded in solving what had seemed an insoluble task, building a navy capable of competing with the U.S. Navy and saving many billions in the process. The hall buzzed approvingly. Gorshkov beamed.

Taking advantage of this pause, Chelomei asked Father for permission to describe the design bureau's proposals concerning space systems and rocket boosters. This subject was originally planned for the following day, but Vladimir Nikolayevich was feeling quite ill. The plane's ventilation had affected him and he thought that he might have to spend the next day in bed.

Father turned to those present: "Shall we meet him halfway?"

There was a murmur of agreement. After a brief pause to change the diagrams, Vladimir Nikolayevich began on what was supposed to be the next day's subject. It might have been better if his audience had heard the talk by the commander in chief of the Strategic Missile Forces, which was supposed to precede it. On the other hand, Chelomei had the advantage of speaking first and his proposals sounded fresher and more vivid.

Chelomei talked about his work on space systems, the UR-200 ballistic missile and launches. I have already mentioned most of these projects and will not repeat myself. Things were progressing very well, and the first launches of the UR-200 were scheduled for a year to eighteen months later.

Then Vladimir Nikolayevich outlined his new concept, a ballistic missile warhead with a homing system capable of precision targeting. He thought that if it was possible to assure a direct hit, the UR-200 could be modified to destroy enemy surface ships and we would not need a whole pack of expensive submarines, which were constantly in danger of being sunk. He had even thought up a name for it: the guided ballistic warhead, or UB for short. As the UB flew in space it would be controlled by guidance jet pulses. As it descended toward a target and the air became more dense—of aerodynamic force—it would tilt from side to side while approaching the target with great accuracy. The UB was, as it were, the logical conclusion of the whole concept of land-based cruise missiles designed to destroy the enemy at increasingly greater distances. Now a target would not only be unable to hide at the opposite side of the Black Sea, it would not be safe even on the far reaches of the Pacific Ocean. This was the first time I can remember hearing about the possibility of building a warhead with individual targeting.

The military reacted warily to this proposal. Admiral Gorshkov was the first to ask a question. He wanted to know which branch of the services—the Navy or Strategic Missile Forces—should be in charge of such antiship systems, whose launch positions would be located far inland. Father answered on Chelomei's behalf, saying that, in his opinion, the Navy should be in charge.

"But today the Strategic Missile Forces are the customer for the UR-200 and it's hard for us to influence its development," Gorshkov persisted.

They agreed to return to the question of dividing up spheres of influence later on, when the new weapon's technical capabilities were more clearly evident. In the meantime, the Defense Council approved the proposal and ordered preliminary development to begin. The appropriate government decree was issued a month later, in March.

Admiral Gorshkov had a good reason to ask his question. When he did not receive a satisfactory answer from the Defense Council, he didn't consider the new project to be fully his own. The project was without a sponsor.

Generally speaking, the Strategic Missile Forces didn't want to have anything to do with Chelomei, and certainly not when he was offering such an exotic product. They had enough of their own, "serious" tasks in the strategic area. Let the Navy deal with aircraft carriers.

Chelomei ran around from commanders in chief to state committee chairmen, to ministers, and finally to Kozlov. They listened to him respectfully. Kozlov promised to look into the matter and help, but the missile remained without a home. It survived only because of Father's support. In 1964 its last supporter was gone, while there were more and more technical problems. The project was eliminated at the first opportunity.

After completing his description of the UB, Chelomei began to outline proposals for developing a heavy booster rocket.

Vladimir Nikolayevich wanted to use it to launch space stations. He proposed initially to lift into orbit a heavy automatic station capable of observing both earth and space objects. As the project developed, these stations would begin to be manned and given more complex programs to carry out. The space station would be called Almaz (Diamond).

His projects could be realized only if payloads far greater than the R-7 carried could be delivered into space. The diagram Chelomei displayed to the Defense Council showed a space booster capable of lifting twelve tons into orbit. It was called the UR-500. The booster's launch weight was impressive, almost seven hundred tons.

Other diagrams displayed military aspects of the UR-500. Proposals called for using it as a ballistic missile, with the thirty-megaton warhead which had been tested in the recent past.

This was the first time that Ustinov heard about Chelomei's proposals, which Vladimir Nikolayevich had kept secret, even from Dementyev.[6] Dmitry Fyodorovich sat looking darker than a storm cloud. What's more, he spoke out against them. Not that he was totally against, but he thought that it would be a mistake to divide up our funds. We should create a powerful fist and beat with it at a single point. Naturally, Korolyov was understood to be the "fist." Knowing Father's stinginess, Ustinov counted on his support. And he probably would have received it, if Korolyov's recent desperate struggle against the R-16 had not been imprinted in Father's memory. Father didn't agree with Ustinov. In his opinion, a lively competition worked to our benefit.

"Where would we be if we had listened to Korolyov and not relied on Yangel to develop intercontinental missiles? Korolyov kept trying to drag us over to his side. He is a designer, he has his own goals, but we have to think on a broader scale and support a variety of projects. Furthermore, the goals set for Korolyov and what is being proposed today are different"—this is approximately what Father said.

Malinovsky supported him. The audience expressed its opinion by a murmur of approval. Ustinov gave in, but without giving up.

After a brief discussion, the Council adopted the decision to make the UR-500. Comrades Ustinov and Dementyev were told to prepare the necessary documents. This work was given official status in April. Relations between Chelomei and Ustinov became even more strained.

The following morning they gathered in the same hall. Marshal Moskalenko was the first to speak. His report emphasized that the armed forces were beginning to receive R-16 intercontinental missiles. He talked about the increased tempo of installing strategic missiles in launch positions. They were still based in the aboveground variant.

His talk was lengthy and detailed. Naturally, I don't remember all of it. I would like to mention only two points.

Moskalenko said that the existing R-16 had a long way to go before it met the demands posed by modern warfare. The main problem was the amount of time required to prepare it for launch. The prescribed sequence of preparatory operations took several hours.

After that, how could you talk about a retaliatory strike to a missile attack!

---

6. Pyotr Vasilievich Dementyev was the chairman of the State Committee on Aviation Technology. He was in charge of R & D, including design bureaus, among them Chelomei's, where Sergei Khrushchev worked.

He cited data for the U.S. Minuteman ICBM. Unlike the R-16, it could be prepared for launch in only a few minutes.

"Before we managed to move the R-16 and lift it into place, nothing would be left of us," exclaimed Moskalenko passionately.

Another serious shortcoming of the R-16 was the volatility of the corrosive components in its oxidizer tanks. If there was a launch delay, the missile could remain armed for only a few days. Then the fuel and the oxidizer had to be drained and the missile sent back to the factory for refitting.

"According to intelligence information, the solid fuel Minuteman can remain armed for years," continued Moskalenko. "As a result of these technical problems, the R-16 has become a first-strike weapon and not the retaliatory weapon that we need. It can be used if you know ahead of time when and where you want to launch it."

Yangel had not been able to fulfill the promises made to Father. The missile was incomparably less expensive than the R-7, but the problem of dealing with acid remained unsolved.

Moskalenko mentioned that all these complaints had been discussed with the chief designer, who had made certain proposals to satisfy them. Yangel would talk about that in his report.

The commander in chief went on to describe the situation that had developed around the alternative to the R-16—Korolyov's R-9. Korolyov had made heroic efforts to remain competitive. By lowering the oxygen temperature and using a profound vacuum in the thermal insulation system of his underground storage tanks (from which the rocket had to be fueled in case of an alert), evaporation losses had been reduced five hundred times. Reduced, but not eliminated. If a launch was delayed for some reason, the fueled rocket had to be constantly fed oxygen, just as before. In the enclosed shafts, the oxygen-saturated atmosphere itself became a major source of problems. Very serious ones. A fire broke out in an R-9 experimental silo the following year, on October 24, 1963, by sinister coincidence on the anniversary of the accident with Yangel's R-16 in 1960. It was caused by the careless use of electricity in the oxygen-saturated atmosphere. A soldier unscrewed a light bulb, which caused a spark. Nothing terrible under ordinary circumstances, but in those conditions there was a bolt of electricity and everything burst into flame, even things which don't normally burn. The fire was localized with difficulty, by battening down armored hatches. Six men died—those who were in the compartment ravaged by fire.

The problems didn't end there. Defects were discovered practically every time the rocket was launched. Tests of the R-9 were dragging on. Moskalenko didn't draw any conclusions. Putting down the pointer, he returned to his seat.

After a short break the designers spoke. Korolyov took the floor first. He began with missiles. His style was a study in contrast to Chelomei's artistic grandiloquence and Yangel's scrupulous thoroughness. Korolyov spoke concisely, in chopped-off sentences. His tone did not admit that his opinions might be open to question. Korolyov was confident that the future belonged to oxygen. He considered the R-9's failures to be a temporary setback. The missile would come into its own.

Having dealt with a subject he had to cover, Korolyov moved on to what really interested him. He walked over to the diagrams that illustrated his dream—the N-1 space booster—in various projections. Korolyov briefly discussed efforts to fulfill the 1961 government decree: The rocket weighed two and a half thousand tons and it lifted 75 tons into orbit. Korolyov thought that was sufficient to land a man on the moon and return. However, the final numbers would have to be determined when the preliminary design was completed.

I recalled Korolyov's meetings with Father in the Crimea, where he had "tried out" a first version of his ideas.

Two variants of engines for the rocket were being considered, one approximating the capabilities of the present day and one for the future. The country had no experience in building powerful rocket engines with hundreds of tons of thrust. Therefore, the initial proposal was to put twenty-four 150-ton engines on the first stage. The rocket's broad bottom would literally bristle with nozzles.

It was planned in the future to replace them with engines generating six hundred tons of thrust, like the ones the Americans envisaged for the Saturn. In the first stage, everything had to operate on oxygen and kerosene. "Exotic" engines operating on oxygen and hydrogen were planned for the upper stages.

On the subject of cooperation, Korolyov noted that he wished to have Nikolai Dmitriyevich Kuznetsov—not Glushko, as previously—develop engines for the N-1. They had already signed an agreement. Father gave a start. Kuznetsov's design bureau had no experience in developing such devices. He asked Korolyov to explain. Korolyov replied that Glushko was refusing to make the engines he needed. Moreover, he was already overburdened with Yangel's orders. Now he would be working for Chelomei as well.

Glushko, who had been sitting at the back, was summoned to the table. He gave a different reason for his refusal: the development of powerful engines with nitrogen tetroxide, an oxidizer which did not require a low temperature, was more promising. Spontaneous combustion occurred when it combined with fuel, engine structure was simplified and reliability increased. Nothing could be done about the fact that the components were more toxic. We simply had to accept it.

"If such a colossus exploded, nothing would be left in either variant," Glushko joked glumly.

Korolyov began to object vehemently. An argument ensued. The two highly decorated designers flew at each other like two bantam roosters.

Father had been silent all this time. Now he finally cut off the argument and ordered Ustinov to make a thorough investigation of the matter and prepare proposals. He had no objection to Kuznetsov participating, but thought that the truth couldn't be reached in the course of such a meeting.

A military use for the N-1 was also found. It was the only way to deliver a hundred-megaton nuclear warhead to a target. Korolyov touched only briefly on the subject. There was no serious discussion. The destructive force of this creation of the human brain was simply too unbelievable. Even the military couldn't find an appropriate target for it.

Korolyov had only the vaguest notion of how many billions his idea would cost. Ustinov was again instructed to calculate the necessary costs. The Defense Council approved the start of development of the N-1, limited for now to preliminary design work.

At this stage there were still technical decisions to be made, the spacecraft matched to a booster, associates (from microelectronic technicians to the builders of launch installations) to be given assignments in order to coordinate cooperation in the production process and ensure that many hundreds of collectives, tens of thousands of people, would work together harmoniously. All this was set out in appendices to a government decree in the form of mandatory commitments to carry out assignments.

In the case of the N-1, a whole series of decrees was issued in 1962 and 1963, and then in the first half of 1964. The project turned out to be very complex, requiring additional associates and postponement of the beginning of tests due to "unforeseen" delays. Not until August of 1964 did Father sign a fat document that seemingly specified down to the last nail everything that should be done for the successful landing of a man on the moon. Chelomei also managed to squeeze into this decree, but he wasn't allowed past the "door." He was supposed to send a cosmonaut around the moon with the help of the UR-500. But all this lay in the future.

Korolyov was triumphant. The project for sending a man to the moon was approved! The next triumph wasn't far off! That day in Pitsunda no one dreamed that an American would be first.

Only Chelomei was skeptical. He did not attend the second day's session. When I went to see him that evening to describe the meeting, he was reclining on a couch and reading a technical journal in German. He didn't look well and had a warm scarf wrapped around his throat. I told Chelomei about Korolyov's report. Vladimir Nikolayevich thought for a moment and then said: "I don't think the N-1 will fly."

I was surprised. Korolyov's report was so persuasive. Surely he couldn't be mistaken in the main point. Chelomei didn't go into details, but only said that to synchronize the operation of twenty-four engines was an impossible task, and in addition there would be vibration and interference from gases flowing from the nozzles at supersonic speed.

"The devil himself couldn't bring it off," Chelomei concluded.

I didn't say anything. We were hardly in the same weight division. But I could not agree with him. Korolyov was not a novice either. He knew what he was doing.

I have run a little ahead of myself. Yangel spoke at the meeting after Korolyov.

During a short break they changed the diagrams, which now showed a whole array of missiles: a row of one-stage and two-stage, ending with a huge three-stage missile, the R-56. The launch weight of 1200 tons was prominently listed below the diagram. Mikhail Kuzmich did not want to lag behind his rivals.

The somewhat stooped Yangel began his report with a detailed description of various shortcomings that had come to light as the military began working with the missiles. He spoke of the need to make changes and improvements in the serial production of missiles to make it easier for the military to operate the complex machinery. The speaker sounded like a diligent division commander, not a chief designer whose missiles had already been accepted by the military. Because of this concern, Mikhail Kuzmich was regarded with genuine affection and respect in the military.

Moving on from medium-range missiles, Yangel talked in detail about the R-16. According to him, the R-16 was entirely ready to be put into service. Ten to fifteen double launches would be carried out in the current year. Construction was being completed and everything was now in the hands of the assemblers. The factory would begin series production of the missile itself without delay. The necessary preliminary steps had been taken.

Father couldn't restrain himself and interrupted.

"But what about reducing the time needed for launch?"

Yangel asked him to wait a moment, saying that it was just that subject which he would now discuss.

Emphasizing that he was referring only to his designs, the R-12, R-14, and R-16, he said:

All the missiles now being delivered to the Army were made in accordance with the military doctrine and, most important, the technical possibilities of the 1950s. What was good in 1957 and even in 1959 is unacceptable now. The R-16 is the last missile of that generation.

What was the prevailing concept for using missiles in those years? Missiles were supposed to be kept in special hangars. They were transported to launch sites only after the decision was taken to launch.

Then the Americans, with their Minutemen, announced that they were always ready to launch. Preparations require only a few minutes. Missiles stand day after day on their launch positions during their entire period of service. No hangars, no personnel dragging them to launch positions after an alarm. The technology of a military launch has changed completely, both conceptually and technically.

Furthermore, the installation of missiles in silos, in order to protect them from possible missile or air attack, has become a rigid requirement.

Father grew animated and expressed his support of this view. He didn't miss the opportunity to remind people that he had been the initiator in this matter, outstripping the eminent designers.

After waiting for him to finish, Yangel continued: "Partial changes did not bring about the result we needed: it was impossible to keep first-generation rockets on the launch pad for long once they were fueled. Preparations for launch took a substantial amount of time, not least because operations are done manually."

Here Yangel paused and, stooping even further, turned, seemingly, to Father alone.

"We were not able to fulfill the obligations we assumed, Nikita Sergeyevich. The R-16 must be maintained dry. Otherwise it will not work." Yangel tried to justify himself: "Under today's technology the missile can stand fueled for only several weeks, and then it has to be replaced. We are trying to solve the problem of a strike response by speeding up the fueling process. There is no other solution. We promise to do it in a minimum amount of time."

Father stared gloomily in front of him.

He asked how much they could reduce the time needed to prepare for launch, as compared with the R-7. Brightening, Yangel began to rattle off numbers. The time saved would be considerable. Instead of a day, it would be a matter of hours, even tens of minutes.

Father nodded with satisfaction. Progress had been made after all. He asked Yangel to give more thought to what could be done to reduce the amount of time, to try to match the Americans. Yangel promised to do everything possible. He sighed with relief. Unpleasant explanations had been avoided.

For the future, Yangel proposed to ascertain the necessary minimum number of changes to make on existing missiles so that they could be installed in silos. Beyond that, no more time should be spent on them. They could serve in that condition until new and more modern missiles were built.

Marshal Andrei Antonovich Grechko, Ignatov, Brezhnev, Andrei Pavlovich
Kirilenko, Dmitry Stepanovich Polyansky, Father, Gennady Ivanovich Voronov, and
Kosygin. The Lenin Mausoleum from a seldom-seen perspective. May Day, 1960.

Father presents King Mohammed Zakhir of Afghanistan with a replica of the "Lunnik" sphere deposited on the moon in September. Kabul, February 1960.

Father and Marshal Malinovsky in Livadiya. Crimea, 1960.

Father, Todor Zhivkov, Kosygin, Nikolai Shvernik, Pyotr Prospelov (who did the
research for the 1960 "secret" speech), and Morris Torrez. Pitsunda, 1960.

Father, the ship's captain, Gromyko, and János Kádár on the *Baltika*
en route to New York. October 1960.

Father on the steamer *Baltika* playing shuffleboard with members of
his entourage during the voyage to New York to attend a meeting of the
United Nations General Assembly. 1960.

Father at the United Nations with the famous shoe in front of him. New York, 1960.

Andrian Nikolayev (future cosmonaut), Father, Valentina Ivanovna Gagarina,
Yury Gagarin, Mother, Mikoyan, Sergei Pavlovich Korolyov, and
Nina Ivanovna Korolyova at the reception in the Kremlin for Yury Gagarin.
Moscow, April 14, 1961.

Yury Gagarin, Marshal Malinovsky, Commander in Chief of the Air Forces
Marshal Konstantin Andreyevich Vershinin, Father, and Marshal Grechko at the
reception in the Kremlin in Gagarin's honor. Moscow, April 14, 1961.

Valya Gagarina, Yury Gagarin, Father, and Mother
looking over the article in *Izvestiya* about the welcome given to the first cosmonaut,
Yuri A. Gagarin, in the Kremlin. Moscow, 1961.

A historic handshake. Khrushchev and Kennedy meet in Vienna. June 1961.

Sergo Mikoyan, Valentina Tereshkova, Sergei Khrushchev, and Yury Gagarin
at the Kremlin. Moscow, 1962.

Van Cliburn. Moscow, 1962.

Andrei Tupolev and Artem Mikoyan, aircraft designers, and Father in
Lower Oreanda in Yalta. Crimea, 1962.

Father, with Rada's sons, Aleksei (to Father's right) and Nikita. On the far left, from front to back, Adzhubei and Aleksandr Ivanovich Alekseyev, the ambassador to Cuba. On the far right, from front to back, Raul Castro, Mother, and Sharaf Rashidov. The three women standing together in the back are my sisters (from left to right) Yelena, Rada, and Yuliya. Moscow, 1962.

Mobile S-5 cruise missile launcher. 1960.

A submarine of design type 644 surfacing.
This class of vessel was armed with P-5 cruise missiles. 1962.

The S-5 cruise missile, developed at Vladimir Nikolayevich Chelomei's design bureau, on parade in Red Square. Moscow, 1962.

A P-35 cruise missile launch from a cruiser. 1962.

Voroshilov and Father at the railway station. Moscow, 1962.

Kozlov, Brezhnev, and Father in the Great Hall of the Kremlin. Behind them are
Viktor Vasilyevich Grishin and Kirilenko. Moscow, 1963.

Recipients of the order Hero of Socialist Labor, in the Kremlin. Seated, from left to right: Sachkov, Kobzarev, Chelomei, Admiral Gorshkov, Pyotr Vasilyevich Dementyev, and Lifshitz. Standing, from left to right: Kazakov, Shumilov, Malikov, Sergei Khrushchev, Modestov, and Efremov. Moscow, 1963.

Mother and Father with Roswell Garst at the Lenin Hills residence. Moscow, 1963.

Brezhnev and Father. Father is speaking on the telephone to
the female astronaut Valentina Tereshkova. Moscow, 1963.

Father speaking with Tereshkova. From left to right: Leonid Vasilyevich Smirnov,
deputy chairman of the Council of Ministers; Ivan Dmitriyevich Serbin,
head of the Central Committee's defense industry department;
Dmitry Fyodorovich Ustinov; Mikoyan; Father; and Brezhnev. Moscow, 1963.

Castro and Father sitting on a concrete slab on the bank of Lake Ritsa. Castro is in
fatigues. Father is wearing an embroidered Ukrainian shirt. Abkhazia, 1963.

Father and Fidel Castro are guests of the Abkhazians. Castro is wearing a traditional *burka*. On the road leading down from Lake Ritsa, 1963.

Castro and Father at a table decked for a feast in the Abkhazian village on the road down from Lake Ritsa. Castro is holding his drinking horn. Abkhazia, 1963.

From left to right: Marshal N. I. Krylov, commander of the Strategic Missile Forces, Father, Marshal Malinovsky, and Fidel Castro. Ambassador Alekseyev is standing behind and to the left of Marshal Krylov. The man standing behind Castro is the interpreter, Officer (in the KGB) Leonov.

Alekseyev, the Soviet ambassador to Cuba; Father; and Castro. Moscow, 1963.

Autographed seventieth birthday greetings (April 17, 1964) to Father from
the cosmonauts. From left to right: Pavel Popovich, German Titov, Andrian
Nikolayev, Yury Gagarin, Valentina Tereshkova, Father, and Valery Bikovsky,
pictured standing at the Lenin Mausoleum. Red Square, Moscow.

Father's seventieth birthday celebration. To Father's left: Mother, Lena, Mikoyan, and Brezhnev. At the residence in Lenin Hills. Moscow, April 17, 1964.

Father's seventieth birthday celebration.
Father is seated at the head of the table with Mother and Lena to his left.
To their left are Mikoyan and Brezhnev. To Father's right are Podgorny and Suslov.
At the residence in Lenin Hills. Moscow, April 17, 1964.

Father and his aide Vladimir Semyonovich Lebedev, Andrei Gromyko, and Pavel Alekseyevich Satyukov (editor in chief of *Pravda*). The stenographer has her back to the camera. On board the *Bashkiria* to visit the Scandinavian countries, June 1964.

Father and Marshal Malinovsky at Baikonur.
Father had less than a month left in power. 1964.

The pensioner. Father sitting on a bench in the meadow, listening to the radio.
At the dacha "Further Petrovo," 1969.

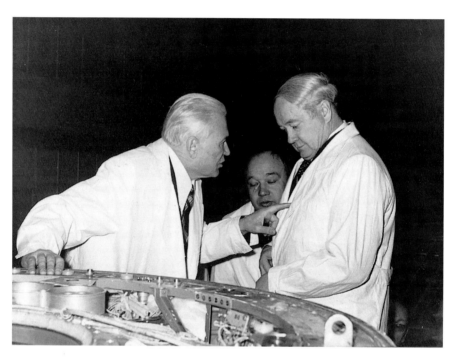

Chelomei (left) making a point to Smirnov, deputy chairman in the Council of ministers in charge of coordinating the defense industry. They are standing next to a mockup of the "IS" (satellite destroyer). The individual behind them is not identified. Design Bureau (OKB) "Mashinostroyeniye" (formerly OKB-52), 1970.

A model of Chelomei's lunar booster, the UR-700. 1965.

A launch of the Proton. Baikonur, 1967.

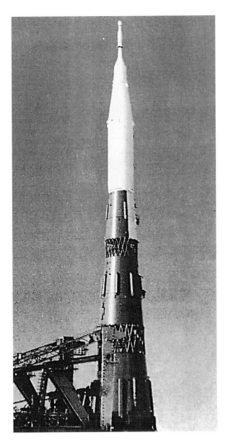

The Soviet lunar rocket: N-1. Photo courtesy of Peter Gorin, private collection.

Two UR-100s. 1970s.

The UR-500 Proton on the launching pad at Baikonur. 1970s.

Once again Father nodded approvingly, noting that it would be necessary to continue installing missiles in the aboveground variant until the situation with silos became clearer. There was a murmur of approval from his listeners.

Yangel walked over to the next diagram. He thought it was possible for the present time to keep the R-12 and R-14 to hit targets in Europe, and to concentrate all other resources on intercontinental missiles that would meet modern requirements.

He proposed, within the next year and a half, to develop and begin testing a new missile, the R-36, which would incorporate all the latest achievements in the field. The proposal provided for automatic pre-launch preparation, including fueling, the construction of dispersed underground launch sites controlled from a single command center, and naturally, a higher degree of precision in hitting the target. The R-36 was comparable to the U.S. missile Titan-2. They lifted approximately the same thermonuclear warhead, equivalent to ten megatons.

To Father's question of how long the new missile could be kept armed, Yangel could not say anything reassuring. They had not yet managed to deal with the corrosive effect of its components.

Father was not pacified: "If the Americans can find a solution, then why are we marking time?" Yangel explained that both the Minutemen and Polaris engines used slow burning "powders." The production of such powders was beyond the capability of our chemical industry. We would have to look for our own, unique design solutions.

That was how the Soviet Union and the United States followed different paths in the technological development of missiles. From then on each prayed to its own God.

With the R-36, Yangel concluded his discussion of the ballistic missile program and began to talk about research in space.

Chelomei wasn't the only one whose sleep was disturbed by Korolyov's successes and his worldwide recognition, even if only as an anonymous "chief designer." Yangel thought that he had the right to compete with his colleague in space. Of course, he didn't yet possess the unique opportunities offered by the R-7, but there were many applications where such record weights were an inadmissible luxury. He could send small payloads into space by adding stages to the R-12 and R-14. The new satellites were of various types. Some were research and civilian satellites, some were military.

Military projects were held in the tightest secrecy. It was as if they did not even exist. But you can't hide an orbiting satellite. A simple solution was found: they were all lumped together. Every satellite launched by Yangel's rockets (and not only Yangel's) was named Cosmos.

What was supposed to be Cosmos-1 had no relation to Yangel or to research into the space surrounding the earth. It was prepared for launch in Tyura-Tam. In circles where people had access to secrets, it bore quite another name, Zenit,[7] and was designed for photographic intelligence, just like its U.S. cousin, the Discoverer. But it came rather later than they did. The main reason for the delay was that during those months Sergei Pavlovich's attention was focused on something else entirely, and he was the only one who could return a payload to earth from orbit.

It should not be said that nothing whatsoever was done. At numerous meetings the military and Korolyov's team discussed requirements for photos from space, came to an agreement and approved a technical plan, and established a firm schedule for its development and tests. It was decided to use the Vostok to bring back exposed film from the Zenit. Of course, the return capsule made for a cosmonaut was rather large and expensive to carry out this new mission, but Korolyov had no time to design another. In Korolyov's mind, no intelligence information could compete with launching the first human being into space. And neither design bureau nor factory could pursue two such projects simultaneously. So the Zenit was never given priority. On paper and in government decisions and decrees this work was described as extremely important, but every chief designer knows what he can postpone without getting his head taken off.

Father was also in no rush, because of his generally skeptical attitude toward intelligence. And because, never doubting America's technical capabilities, he didn't try to discover the location or cost of strategic bombers, or how the deployment of new ballistic missiles to launch positions was proceeding. He could not influence any of that and was not tormented by curiosity.

Something important was always happening that caused work on the Zenit to be postponed. At first everybody was busy with Gagarin, then came Titov's flight, so again there was no time for the Zenit. The first Zenit was launched near the end of 1961, on December 11, but the R-7 did not function properly, and the satellite failed to reach orbit. Since it failed, there was no announcement about it. Those were the rules in those years. So the Zenit did not have the good fortune to become Cosmos-1.

On the eve of the February conference Yangel, much to Chelomei's envy, did launch Cosmos-1, his first satellite, from the Kapustin Yar test site. Its contents were entirely peaceful. However, because of previous military launches, it was decided not to publish any information about the satellite's purpose except what was impossible to hide, the parameters of the orbit. The announcement continued reassuringly: "All onboard systems are functioning

---

7. *Zenit* = zenith.

normally." No breakdowns, no failures, even if the pile of metal circling the earth failed to respond to a single signal. There must be no failures, and "there were none."

The next satellite was also Yangel's and was christened Cosmos-2. It was launched on April 6 from Kapustin Yar. It was followed by Cosmos-3, launched on the twenty-fourth.

But all of us who were involved waited impatiently for April 26 and the launch of Cosmos-4. The second attempt to put the Zenit into orbit was to take place that day. This time it was successful: the space spy flew off and over the course of four days photographed areas designated by the General Staff. After it landed the next day, the film was brought to Father. Through large, gray, grainy blotches you could make out small whitish crosses of planes at airfields, rectangles of factory buildings, warehouses, and a great deal else.

But the satellite didn't provide any important information, and not only because it was the first, experimental one. Some objects were completely obscured by clouds or hidden in the dark of night, while others could not be photographed because of the angle of inclination of the satellite's orbit.

The military sighed: If only we could launch on a polar orbit, like the Americans! But that would require the construction of a new test site, spending additional billions. Father did not respond to their request. He begrudged money "to look through keyholes." They managed to obtain funding only in 1964, after he was ousted.

Cosmos-4 was followed by other satellites: Yangel's had a 19-degree angle of orbital inclination, while the Zenits were steeper, at under 56 degrees. So anyone who was interested could easily distinguish between them.

Korolyov was never enthusiastic about intelligence from space. At the first opportunity he disowned it, transferring it to his new Kuibyshev branch established at the plant which made the R-7.

However, let us return to Pitsunda. Mikhail Kuzmich decided to go for broke. Following Chelomei and Korolyov, he proposed cooperating with Glushko to build a space booster, the R-56, to be similar to the initial version of the N-1 in its parameters and delivering about thirty tons into orbit. The project had been worked out thoroughly, as was always the case with his organization; everything was calculated with an intelligent reserve capacity. The proposal called for the appropriate payload for space, a heavy orbital station. He also planned a warhead of fifty megatons.

If Yangel had succeeded in being the first to submit a bid, I think that his proposal might have won support. But now . . .

Father tried to sweeten the pill and, turning to Yangel, said that his design bureau was a leader in guaranteeing our defensive capabilities, and that was more important than any launches into space. Therefore, thought Father, we should not distract his team from its main mission.

After a short discussion the guests were dismissed and the Defense Council began to discuss its own, purely military, matters.

THE DEFENSE OF CUBA: THE BEGINNINGS OF A PLAN

It seemed to Father that, with the erection of barriers and the establishment of border controls, the problem of the GDR had been to some extent resolved. Now his attention was directed toward Cuba. The situation unfolding there was increasingly threatening.

American newspapers were peppered with threats against Fidel Castro and his government. Information came through secret channels about President Kennedy's adoption of a wide-ranging plan, "Mongoose," to destabilize the situation in Cuba. It included sabotage of the country's economy, explosions in ports and oil storage areas, and the burning of sugarcane fields. Its authors didn't hesitate at more decisive measures: murder of the country's leaders, first of all Fidel himself.

Every day the Cubans expected a new invasion, this time not just by émigrés but by the U.S. Army. Cuban president Oswald Dorticos had warned Father about this during their meeting in September of the previous year.

Father thought that U.S. preparations were extremely serious and that Cuban apprehensions were well founded. He became increasingly nervous. He saw Castro's possible defeat as his own defeat.

But how could he help? Some major surprise move was required. The responsibility weighed heavily on him. But, "in for a penny, in for a pound." If the Soviet Union was to be recognized as a great power, it must inevitably assume responsibility for the security of its allies. Otherwise, no one would believe it to be a world leader. If not leader of the world, a role for which the Soviet Union did not qualify at all—it was unable to catch up to the United States even in per capita consumption of meat and milk—then at least leader of the socialist segment of the globe. Father understood all this perfectly. The burden of leadership that he himself proclaimed sometimes seemed unbearable.

His thoughts kept going back to Berlin, to how the U.S. president had risen to its defense without a moment's doubt or hesitation, with complete determination and had unhesitatingly staked his country's security. "Now it's my turn," flashed through Father's mind. He must think up something equally effective. Something that would discourage the Americans from encroaching on Cuba. But what?

Cuba was so far away. Thousands of miles away, it was virtually unreachable, even by plane. Only the TU-114 passenger craft and its older brother, the TU-95 strategic bomber, could fly that distance nonstop. And all the routes by sea ran past countries whose governments could not be expected to support the effort.

There were many factors to take into consideration. But Father had no intention of giving up. He wasn't going to abandon the young revolution, which had just celebrated its third anniversary, to the hostility of the United States. Such treachery was contrary to the very essence of proletarian internationalism.

On May 14 Father left on a long-planned visit to fraternal Bulgaria. Cuba was constantly on his mind while he was there.

> Something had to be done to make Cuba safe. But what?
>
> By Declarations, which we could make in the form of Notes or TASS statements? None of those was very effective. . . . Such actions might even do some harm. . . . If you issue empty threats, you teach the opponent that you're just a chatterbox. . . .
>
> Something more effective had to be done. This problem preoccupied me greatly.

In his search for a solution, Father thought about the subject day and night, even while he slept. In other, less important matters he willingly shared his thoughts and doubts with others. In this case he kept everything inside. Outwardly Father was, as always, the personification of activity: he gave speeches, took an interest in the successes of his Bulgarian friends, talked a great deal with Todor Zhivkov. But he would suddenly fall silent and they could only guess how far away his thoughts had drifted. No one dared break the silence, and they waited respectfully for their guest to "return," whereupon the conversation would resume where it had left off.

According to the schedule, on May 17 he was to have a brief rest on the shores of the Black Sea at Varna. Protocol obligations were relaxed, and Father wandered among the paths of the residence provided for our delegation, walking now and again toward the sea and then turning back into the vast park.

Usually he loved company on his walks and would invite the whole delegation to come along to talk and ask questions. Those accompanying him were accustomed to that. This time he spent the time alone. Members of the delegation, not wanting to bother the premier, wandered off in different directions.

The "idea" was born there, on the paths of the Varna park. Not yet a plan—only an idea of how to save Cuba.

"I was traveling around Bulgaria, but I was haunted by the thought: What will happen to Cuba? Will we lose Cuba?" It was precisely the subject of

Cuba with which Father began to dictate his memoirs four years later, after the events described.

> It was not a simple matter. It was very hard to think of a way in which we could oppose America.
>
> I, as chairman of the Council of Ministers and secretary of the Central Committee, was obliged to find a solution that would not draw us into war. Any fool can start a war, and then even the most intelligent of men don't know how to stop it.
>
> There was another option: simply yield to intimidation from the United States and begin a verbal duel. That would hardly be worth doing under conditions of the class struggle. The United States would then announce a policy of splitting off, i.e., of removing, one country after another from the socialist camp. The goal would be to isolate them and subject them to American influence, but since capitalist ideology is no longer particularly attractive to most peoples of the world, they would rely more on force, on military force.
>
> America has surrounded the Soviet Union with its bases; it has installed missiles around us. We knew that U.S. missile forces were based in Turkey and Italy, not to speak of West Germany, and assumed that they might also be in other countries.
>
> I thought: What if we also install missiles with nuclear warheads in Cuba, of course after reaching agreement with the Cuban government. I thought that this would keep the United States from taking military action. If things turned out that way, it wouldn't be so bad: as the West put it—a balance of terror.
>
> If we install the missiles secretly, then when the Americans find out, the missiles will already be in place, ready to fire. Before making the decision to eliminate them by military means, the United States would have to think twice. America could knock out some of those installations, but not all. What if a quarter, or one-tenth survived . . .
>
> I paced back and forth in thought and the idea gradually took on shape in my mind. I didn't tell anyone what I was thinking. This was my personal opinion, my inner torment.

Yes, Father realized that the United States would do everything possible to prevent the open deployment of missiles in Cuba. The winner would be the one who was better at concealing and deceiving. After the incident with the U-2 and the president's lie, Father had no qualms of conscience. President Eisenhower had given him an object lesson. One bad turn deserves another. Furthermore, the deception was in a good cause, defense of the weak against the strong, of the victim against the aggressor.

Father's miscalculation was somewhere else. He often repeated that the

Americans had surrounded us with their military bases, they threaten us on all our borders, and we have the right to respond in kind. But we were accustomed to this encirclement, just as the Italians are used to living on the slopes of Vesuvius and Etna and the inhabitants of islands in the Atlantic and Pacific Oceans are used to the frequent onslaught of hurricanes and typhoons.

To Americans, the appearance of missiles close at hand was bound to be a shock, to puncture their illusions of absolute security, which were based on the "imperial" traditions of their right to make decisions affecting adjacent regions. Though the latter was true of both superpowers in those years.

We should refer here to the provisions of the Monroe Doctrine, which do not admit anyone else's armed presence in the Western hemisphere. Taking all these factors into consideration, it's not hard to predict the reaction to the appearance of our missiles. It was bound to exceed many times over the reaction Father anticipated. It was not just the government and the president—an enraged public became the main actor. In that kind of situation, both arguments and reason are impotent.

I can only express my own point of view. If Father had correctly diagnosed the reaction of the American public—not of the president, but of the people—he would probably have chosen a different and less dangerous policy. However, that is only conjecture.

En route back to Moscow on May 20 Father shared his thoughts with Gromyko, who was a member of the delegation. Andrei Andreyevich listened as usual without saying anything, pursed his lips, indicative of deep thought, and only then expressed his support. He thought that the U.S. government would not risk war. There was not sufficient cause, just as in the case of the recent establishment of a border in Berlin. Unfortunately, the foreign minister also failed to attribute proper importance to the Monroe Doctrine or to the specific attitude of Americans to their region of the world. But Gromyko should have known that. He had spent years in the United States and should have developed a feel for all nuances of the national character.

Perhaps he had his doubts, but couldn't bring himself to express them. That was not in his nature. The Stalinist school of diplomacy instilled obedience. So the first supporter of the plan to install missiles in Cuba appeared. Father refrained from sharing his thoughts with anyone else in advance of discussing such a delicate matter in the Presidium of the Central Committee.

The Presidium met that very day, as was customary after Father's return from a trip. This happened by itself, since all its members thought it was their duty to meet him at the airport, and from there they headed as a group to the Kremlin. On such occasions Father usually began with his impressions of the meetings in distant or nearby countries and asked what had happened at home while he was away.

This time, after greeting everyone Father announced that he had some important ideas he wanted to present to his colleagues. He thought that the airport was not the place to mention the subject.

This is how he later described their meeting:

> The comrades heard me out. As soon as I finished presenting my ideas, I said: "Let's not decide now. I've only expressed my ideas and you're not ready to make a decision. You must think over everything and I'll think about it some more. We should meet a week from now and discuss it further. We have to weigh everything very carefully. I think it's my duty to warn you that this action will have many uncertain and unpredictable consequences. Of course, we want to do all we can to make Cuba secure, to prevent Cuba from being crushed, but we could be drawn into war. You must keep that in mind.
>
> . . . "We have to act in a way that will preserve our country, not allow war to break out and not allow Cuba to be crushed by U.S. forces. . . . We have to make Cuba a torch, a magnet attracting all the destitute peoples of Latin America, who are waging a struggle against exploitation by American monopolies. The blazing flame of socialism in Cuba will speed up the process of their struggle for independence."
>
> The meeting broke up.

Aside from Father's account and a very few official documents, there are no other real sources providing information about the details of events unfolding in those days. I was especially interested in finding out if there were any arguments or objections. During the past few years a great deal of speculation and conjecture has arisen about the decision to install missiles in Cuba. However, everyone who had any connection with the decision, who was present at various meetings, who was close to the leadership, including Gromyko and Alekseyev, the Soviet ambassador to Cuba, claimed that there was no opposition to Father's proposal.

Rumors of some mythical debates or clashes spread later, after Father's removal from office in 1964. Some people quickly began to reexamine their position and change their views.

The Presidium next met on May 24. This time the military made their first contributions. They had made initial estimates of how much it would cost to install our missiles in Cuba.

I return again to Father's account:

> A week went by. I brought up the question again. I asked:
> "Well, comrades, have you thought it over?"
> "Yes, we have."
> "Well, what do you think?"
> Comrade [Otto Vilmovich] Kuusinen was the first to speak. He said:
> "Comrade Khrushchev, I have thought it over. If you introduce such a

proposal and think we need to make such a decision, I trust you and I vote with you. Let's do it."

So . . . On the one hand I was flattered, but on the other—it was a very heavy burden. His answer placed the entire responsibility on me. I had a great deal of respect for Comrade Kuusinen and was conscious of his honesty and sincerity; so I took his words in a friendly way.

During that period the Presidium generally relied on Father. His word was final. It wasn't even a matter of personality. Everything was determined by the structure of centralized power, which was just beginning to change. Everything depended on the top person. Even Presidium members tried not to push themselves forward unless their vital interests were gravely affected. Those interests were not necessarily personal, but perhaps affected areas where a particular Presidium member felt himself to be in charge. In such cases a skirmish could occur—perhaps not very sharp, but a clash nonetheless.

But Cuba didn't affect anyone's interests.

Mikoyan stood out against the background of general placidity and unanimity. He had his own point of view on every subject. With Father he always behaved as an equal. He had spent considerably more years at the top of the pyramid of power.

This time Mikoyan shared his doubts.

Comrade Mikoyan expressed his reservations. On such an occasion there had to be reservations. His opinion was that we would be taking a dangerous step. I had said that myself. I even phrased it more crudely. This step bordered on adventurism. The risk lay in the fact that in wanting to save Cuba, we could be drawn into a very terrible and unprecedented nuclear missile war. That had to be avoided by every possible means, and to consciously provoke such a war would really be adventurism.

I am against war. But to live only under the pressure of thinking that every action we took to defend ourselves or our friends could provoke a nuclear war—that would be to paralyze oneself with fear. In that case, war would become probable. An enemy would immediately sense your fear. Or sense that you will yield your position without war and give him the opportunity to achieve his aims; your fear and compliance would so embolden an enemy that he would lose any sense of caution and fail to perceive the limit beyond which war is inevitable.

This problem existed and still exists. . . .

We adopted the decision that it was advisable to install missiles with nuclear warheads on the territory of Cuba and thereby confront the United States with the fact that if it decided to invade, Cuba would be able to deal a crushing retaliatory blow. . . . That would restrain those with the power to do so from invading Cuba.

We all reached this conclusion after a second discussion of my proposal. I myself proposed that we not be in a hurry to make the decision and that we allow it to crystallize in everyone's thinking, so that everyone makes the decision consciously, understanding its consequences, understanding that it could lead us into a war with the United States. The decision was adopted unanimously.

Procedures called for the relevant department to be made responsible for implementing the decision. In this case the job was assigned to the secretary of the Defense Council, General Semyon Pavlovich Ivanov.

He was given the responsibility for preparing to install missiles in Cuba. The operation was given the code name Anadyr, in order to mislead the adversary.[8]

A final typed copy of the document was circulated. One after another, members of the Presidium wrote "For" and signed their names. There was an opportunity to express a contrary opinion and vote "Against," but it was purely theoretical. I can't recall a single such instance. Everything went smoothly: "For," "For," "For." Mikoyan was the only Presidium member to return the document with just his signature. Ivanov tried to suggest that a more specific response was necessary, but Mikoyan only waved him off, ending the discussion.

Candidate members of the Presidium and the secretaries of the Central Committee were not supposed to express their opinions. Their signatures simply attested to the fact that they had read the text. That was how they acted on this occasion.

After finishing the "operation," Ivanov telephoned Father and reported that everything was in order. Then, hemming and hawing, he added: "Only Anastas Ivanovich didn't put 'For.' He probably forgot."

That put Father on guard and he asked: "Was he the only one? Or was there someone else whose memory failed?"

"Not at all, everything is in order," reported the general. He added: "However, the candidate members of the Presidium and the secretaries didn't vote for the resolution, but that isn't required."

"Call on Mikoyan again. I will telephone him," said Father. "And at the same time have the candidate members and secretaries vote. It's an important matter and they have no business sitting on the fence."

The second round didn't take much time and there were no doubters left.

I heard about the missiles soon after that memorable session. Father and

---

8. "Anadyr" is the name of a river, town, and gulf in Russia's extreme far northeast.

I went to the dacha and, without going into the house, headed for the bank of the Moscow River to enjoy the spring weather. Father was not one of those people who keep things bottled up. He needed to share his ideas with those close to him, to hear words of approval or, if worst came to worst, objections. On this occasion he decided to share his thoughts with me.

At first we walked in silence. Father was enjoying the clear, warm scent of the May evening. Then he abruptly began talking about Cuba, about the danger of an invasion, and suddenly disconcerted me by saying: "We have just adopted a resolution to secretly install our nuclear-armed ballistic missiles on the island." At first I was stunned. Until then we had not risked shipping nuclear weapons outside our territory. A small number of tactical nuclear warheads for the Lunas and Fives were an exception. Our units stationed in Germany were equipped with them.

But here he was referring to strategic warheads. I caught my breath. Then doubts began to emerge: What if the Americans captured them? How could we let such powerful and—most important—secret weapons out of our hands? Castro was there today, but what about tomorrow?

I threw all these questions at Father. Possibly they were why he brought up the subject, to some extent. In the Kremlin everyone always agreed with him. That worried Father somewhat. He was conscious of the fact that they might overlook obstacles that were not immediately apparent.

Father began eagerly to share his plan with me. As soon as the missiles were on the island, it would be just as dangerous for the Americans to attack Cuba as to attack the Soviet Union itself. He didn't intend to transfer nuclear weapons to the Cubans. Father thought that only regular units of the Soviet Army, under command from Moscow, should have control of the missiles.

I gradually became enthusiastic. The Americans would finally find themselves in the same position they had put our country in for the past few years. Furthermore, if we ever had to deliver a retaliatory strike, it would be an important advantage. The number of R-16s to be added to the military arsenal that year was extremely modest. Father didn't share my enthusiasm in that respect. He thought that a temporary advantage in the global confrontation did not justify the expenditure of money and material resources necessary for the deployment of missiles in Cuba. His reasoning was simple: How many missiles could you put on the island? At most several dozen. You can't stick them all over the island, like spines on a hedgehog. Missiles had to be serviced and, most important, protected against possible surprises. And all this under the nose of the United States, three seas away from the Soviet Union. Of course, Father did think that deployment of the missiles had a certain strategic importance, but the principal aim of the operation was to defend the Cuban revolution. He was strongly of the opinion that the entire operation was expedient only because it might prevent a new landing on the island. When I asked how many launch sites would be equipped, Father answered that the military were exploring their possibilities.

After that we had many conversations about installing missiles in Cuba. I waited until we were alone—secrecy had to be observed—to ask the latest news. I was the only member in the family to be let into the secret. Some information reached me from other sources. Because of my work, I associated with many high-ranking military officers. I had only to hint that I was in the know for tongues to loosen and a lively discussion to ensue. Most of the people I talked to supported the plan. I didn't hear any objections. Perhaps those who disagreed with Father didn't want to talk to me, but in all likelihood there were no such people.

After taking into account what was available at the time, it was proposed that no fewer than half a hundred missiles be installed on the island. The number kept changing. Some missiles on their way to the Army were diverted, but most of the missiles were removed from launch positions. It was decided to carry out the operation without delay, without waiting for factories to fill orders; there was no time to lose. As a result, the strike force aimed at Europe was weakened, which didn't please everyone. Some thought that we were concerned with Cuba's security at the expense of our own.

The decision was finally made to install 24 launch sites with 36 R-12s and 16 sites of 24 R-14s—altogether, five regiments, 60 missiles. All missiles were equipped with one-megaton warheads. They decided not to risk sending new, recently tested upgraded two-megaton warheads. In any case, production of them had just begun.

Appetites gradually increased. More and more voices were heard in favor of increasing the number of R-14s. But at the time there were simply none to be had. Father said that plans called for eventually replacing the R-12s with R-14s. In view of the fact that there were constant U.S. intelligence flights over Cuba, he was especially concerned with the problem of how to conceal the missiles from the inevitable aerial observation and photographing.

The Cubans were not yet aware of Father's plans. The time had come to share his idea with Fidel Castro, to make a decision and begin carrying out the operation. Or to postpone it, if the Cubans weren't pleased with the idea of having nuclear missiles installed on their island. Father didn't expect that reaction. He was convinced that his proposal, which was intended to ensure their security, would be greeted with approval in Havana. Our country was taking a risk on their behalf.

A delegation, half political and half military, was appointed.

Sharaf Rashidov, first secretary of the Communist Party Central Committee of Uzbekistan, was made head of the delegation. He was entrusted with the political negotiations. For some reason it was thought that representatives of our border republics would be better at finding a common language with the leaders of peoples fighting for liberation.

Marshal Sergei Semyonovich Biryuzov, who had replaced Moskalenko as commander of the Strategic Missile Forces in April, represented the delegation's military side and had his own instructions. Father had known him since Stalingrad, where he had been chief of staff in Malinovsky's Army. Biryuzov had a reputation for being reliable and reserved, a man of few words. The episode with Powers had also added to his authority. Of course, the marshal did not shoot down the U-2, but Father thought the fact that our defense system was so well organized that the adversary had not escaped was an achievement by our high command. In those years Biryuzov was among the military leaders who enjoyed Father's highest respect and trust.

According to the procedures followed in such cases, the military were disguised; they wore civilian clothes and were issued passports with false identities. Marshal Biryuzov was renamed engineer Petrov. He took along two generals, Air Force Lieutenant General S. V. Ushakov and Major General N. B. Ageyev from the General Staff, to assist him. Their main mission was to carry out a survey of the island and, most important, find a way to conceal the missiles, to hide them from curious eyes not only from the air, but on the ground.

Another delegation member was Aleksandr Ivanovich Alekseyev, that same smart journalist from the KGB who, by virtue of his professional duties as a KGB intelligence officer, as well as his personal qualities, had been the first Soviet citizen to visit Cuba after the victory of the revolution. He had long enjoyed the reputation in Father's eyes (and not only in his) of being the most competent person involved in relations with Cuba.

He arrived in Havana on October 1, 1959, in the capacity of TASS correspondent and immediately began working intensely. By October 12 he was already meeting with Che Guevara, and on the fifteenth with Fidel Castro. In February of 1960 he organized a Soviet industrial trade exhibit. Apart from brief TASS reports, Alekseyev sent detailed official dispatches to Moscow about everything he saw. To a considerable extent they shaped Father's image of the Cuban revolutionary leaders, with whom Alekseyev developed personal, friendly relations. Certain difficulties arose after the establishment of diplomatic relations. Their source was the newly appointed ambassador extraordinary and plenipotentiary, Sergei Mikhailovich Kudryavtsev. He conducted himself in an official manner and observed his distance, as prescribed by protocol. He did not find a common language with the Cuban leaders.

The Castro brothers and Che Guevara continued to turn to Alekseyev when they had problems. Alekseyev had meanwhile been reclassified from journalist to one of the counselors at the Soviet Embassy in Havana. His coded messages went straight to Father's desk, along with the ambassador's dispatches. They traveled through KGB channels and were placed in folders of a different color. Father increasingly preferred Alekseyev's, taking note of his grasp and his analytical mind. Most important of all, he maintained close ties with the republic's leaders.

A duumvirate emerged in the Embassy. Official papers, properly transmitted through the ambassador, Fidel often left unread. He knew that important messages would come from Alekseyev. It worked the same way in the other direction.

Kudryavtsev sealed his own fate. At the beginning of April, Father commented that our ambassador to Cuba was requesting armed guards to protect him. The "Mongoose" operation was gradually gaining strength and the situation in Havana was unstable.[9] Sometimes there were explosions or a burst of machine-gun fire. Father was indignant: "What will the Cubans say? They are fighting against enemies, while the ambassador of a socialist country is hiding, having barricaded himself in the embassy building!"

Then he summed up everything: the ambassador's passivity, his inability to maintain direct contacts with Fidel Castro, his bureaucratic approach to diplomacy. Without wasting time, the Presidium of the Central Committee decided to rearrange personnel in accordance with the situation: to appoint Alekseyev ambassador and transfer Kudryavtsev to a safer place by recalling him to Moscow.

In May Alekseyev arrived back in Moscow in response to a telegram from Gromyko. Father wanted to consult with him about the situation in Cuba and have one more talk with him before his forthcoming appointment. Alekseyev arrived in the very thick of events. As a specialist on Cuba and a person who enjoyed Father's total confidence, he plunged headlong into discussions about problems related to the planned installation of missiles.

In his first meeting with Father, Alekseyev expressed doubt that Fidel Castro would agree to the proposal. Castro was preparing to defend the revolution together with his entire people, relying on his own strength and the support of public opinion in the countries of Latin America. It would hardly suit him to replace the lofty patronage of one great power with that of another.

Father began hotly arguing his position, then suddenly stopped, as if he realized that this wasn't Fidel in front of him. He continued in a conciliatory tone of voice, saying in that case we would provide other forms of assistance to Cuba. However, it was doubtful that they would stop an aggressor.

At the very end of May a TU-114, flying along the northern edge of our

---

9. Mongoose—code name for the CIA operation to overthrow Castro. Derived from "MO," the CIA two-letter code for Thailand.

hemisphere along a route that did not take it over any other country, delivered Father's emissaries to Cuba. They took no documents whatsoever with them. Who knows what might happen in the air.

They were forbidden to communicate with Moscow by radio about the subjects under discussion, even in code.

Alekseyev has said that he felt ill at ease, accompanying such a high-level delegation. The changing of the guard at the Soviet Embassy had not yet taken place. It was only two weeks later, on June 12, that Kudryavtsev was to be officially recalled and Alekseyev appointed. But this awkwardness proved to be temporary. On the day they arrived, Alekseyev met with Raul Castro. Formalities didn't have to be followed. They were friends and a telephone call sufficed. Castro undoubtedly understood that such high-ranking guests were not visiting by chance. His curiosity was only piqued by the veil of secrecy surrounding the visit and Father's coded telegram asking him to receive his representatives about a special matter.

Without explaining anything of substance, Alekseyev asked Raul to arrange a meeting of the delegation with his brother as soon as possible.

That same evening Fidel and Raul Castro received Father's emissaries. Rashidov spoke first. He communicated the essence of Father's proposal. Then Marshal Biryuzov explained the military aspects. Fidel appeared deep in thought. Then, looking at Rashidov through his glasses—which made him appear unfamiliar, since he normally did not wear them in the excitement of meetings—he said firmly that he thought it was an especially interesting idea, because it would serve the interests of world socialism and oppressed peoples in their confrontation with insolent American imperialism, which was trying to dictate its will throughout the world.

Alekseyev's misgivings proved to be unfounded.

The next day they summed up the results. On this occasion the meeting had an official character. The Cubans were represented by the country's main political leaders and commanders of its armed forces: Fidel and Raul Castro, Ernesto Che Guevara, Oswaldo Dorticos, and Ramiro Valdes.

In essence, there was nothing to discuss. The Soviet proposal was accepted without reservation. Only details had to be decided. They would be negotiated in Moscow. The Cubans appointed Raul Castro as their plenipotentiary representative in those negotiations.

Rashidov was in a hurry to get back to Moscow, since Father was waiting impatiently for information on the results of the negotiations. However, there was still one more, no less important, matter. Biryuzov had to visit the areas where the missiles might be based and make some estimate of how difficult it would be to conceal the operation from CIA professionals.

Rashidov didn't give the marshal enough time for a real reconnaissance of the area. He managed only to drive around in the vicinity. The places seemed open and exposed, though there were small groups of unfamiliar trees in some locations. The marshal was especially struck by the sight of coconut palm trees, which he had never seen before except in pictures. He thought that their bare trunks, stretching toward the sky, looked like ballistic missiles sitting on their launch pads.

BLOODSHED IN NOVOCHERKASSK

At the beginning of June Father had no time to think about Cuba. A bloody turmoil broke out unexpectedly, stupidly, in Novocherkassk. But then, such events are always unexpected, always spring from someone's thoughtlessness.

On June 1, 1962, Father gave a public address on television. He said that it was necessary to increase retail prices for meat by 30 percent and for butter and other livestock products by 25 percent. For years the cost of producing these commodities had exceeded purchase prices. The state was increasingly subsidizing farmers. Economists, specialists in Gosplan and the Council of Ministers, had been trying for a long time to persuade Father to raise prices and bring them into line with actual costs. Then, as they put it, agricultural production would become profitable. Farmers would have a profit, a stimulus, they would make giant strides forward and finally realize Father's dream of surpassing the United States in per capita production of meat and milk. The experts' conclusions sounded convincing, and Father reluctantly agreed, issuing an order to prepare for an increase in wholesale prices and a subsequent rise in retail prices.

Today we know that in a centralized economy everything is organized differently than in a market economy and that a price increase has virtually no stimulating effect on producers. But we have paid dearly for that knowledge. We gained in wisdom only after the Kosygin and Gorbachev reforms. But at the time it was thought that you had only to give managers more freedom, establish "sensible" prices, and all would go well.

Father decided to announce this change himself. Father's aide for international affairs, the cautious and diplomatic Oleg Troyanovsky, tried to dissuade him, advising him to protect his reputation and order Mikoyan or Kosygin to speak. But Father objected sharply: "I am the first person in the state and it's not appropriate for me to hide behind somebody's back, especially when the subject relates to unpalatable decisions. I am responsible for everything and must be the one to tell people." Oleg said nothing, but didn't change his opinion.

Naturally, Father's speech was not received sympathetically. People grumbled quietly. On the evening of June 1, when I tried to tell Father what was being said in Moscow, he only brushed it aside sadly: "I know everything. It couldn't be otherwise."

That day he didn't tell me that there was more than grumbling in No-vocherkassk, in the south of Russia, in Aleksandrov and Murom in central Russia, and in Temir Tau, in Kazakhstan. In those cities workers had held spontaneous protest meetings.

In most places the situation ended peacefully. Local leaders found a common language with the protesters and somehow pacified them. The crisis was resolved.

The situation developed differently in Novocherkassk. By a tragic coincidence, work norms at the Electric Locomotive Plant had been increased in February, which led to a decline in workers' wages, in some cases up to 30 percent. Now, a price increase on top of that. On the morning of June 1 workers in the foundry shop went on strike and demanded to see the director. The plant director, Boris Kurochkin, could not have conducted himself more boorishly. In answer to the workers' complaint that now they wouldn't have money to buy meat, he retorted insolently: "If you don't have money for meat, buy cabbage pies."

Provoked by his words, the crowd flocked to the plant administration building and were joined on the way by workers from other shops. The number of strikers quickly rose to three thousand people. Placards appeared: "Meat, butter, raise our wages!" The strikers also hoisted a large portrait of Lenin. The crowd gathered in the plant square, blocked railway lines, stopped a train.

Instead of trying to cope with the situation themselves, the frightened city and province leaders appealed to the Army for help.

On June 2 Father came home looking grim. When I asked what happened, he replied: "In Novocherkassk the workers kicked up a row and the local idiots started shooting." In Father's vocabulary, the word "row" meant that the workers refused to work. He often recalled how he had refused to work at the Bossa Factory in the Donbas before the Revolution. But a row didn't have serious consequences if people were handled skillfully. Father put the blame for what happened in Novocherkassk, not on the workers, but on the local party leaders, who had, as he said, lost any connection to the people.

At this point, with the situation in flames, the center had to intervene. Father said that Andrei Kirilenko and Aleksandr Shelepin had flown to the city, but had not managed to carry out their instructions. They'd gotten cold feet. They were even afraid to go out and meet people, preferring to take cover in the provincial committee building in Rostov.

Father then sent a whole landing party: Frol Kozlov, Anastas Mikoyan, and chief party propagandist Leonid Ilyichev. Father put particular hope in Mikoyan, in his ability to reach agreement even, as Father joked, with the devil himself. They were not successful either. The conflict was settled by force and people died. The most active demonstrators were arrested, accused by Colonel General Pavel Ivashutin, first deputy chairman of the KGB, who went to the city, of "attempting an armed insurrection and hooliganism resulting in substantial destruction in the city." In evidence he sent an album of photographs, of buildings with smashed windows, rooms with broken furniture, crowds of people on the streets.

Father brought the photographs home and thrust them at me: "If you wish, take a look at what's going on there." He didn't want to answer any questions and just brushed me off, saying "Don't pester me."

I gradually learned about what happened during those days from disconnected and inadvertent remarks let slip by participants in the tragedy. Eventually, a certain picture emerged as if from a mosaic, though naturally it was far from complete. The chairman of the KGB, Vladimir Semichastny, said that those who instigated the disorders were tried, and the most recalcitrant were shot. His words gave off the sepulchral stench and chill of the 1930s.

Then Mikoyan's son Sergo told me why his father had failed in his mission. According to him, Frol Kozlov, then second secretary of the Central Committee of the CPSU—next after Father in the hierarchy of power—completely excluded Mikoyan from what was going on. The harsh Kozlov was thirsting to use force and totally rejected Mikoyan's proposal to address the crowd. It's quite likely that Kozlov, a coward by nature, was afraid to appear on the square himself and didn't allow Mikoyan, fearing that he would gain the laurels of a peacemaker. When it was over, Kozlov not only demanded that demonstrators be severely punished, but ordered the deportation to Siberia of those who had been arrested for no reason. Mikoyan objected and threatened to complain to Khrushchev. In reply, Kozlov forbade Mikoyan to call Moscow and at the same time ordered that railroad cars be brought to Novocherkassk for people to be deported. It was only after Mikoyan raised a furor that he was permitted to telephone Father. Father was angry at Kozlov's arbitrariness and the deportations did not take place. Kozlov and Mikoyan couldn't stand each other from that time on.

That is essentially everything that I managed to find out. A more or less detailed picture of what happened during those days in Novocherkassk did not emerge until 1990 when, by order of the First Congress of Soviet People's Deputies, a thorough investigation was carried out by the Military Prosecutor's Office. Of course, the results of that inquiry were not fully objective either. The military tried to whitewash themselves and place all the blame for the bloodletting on the KGB, but the facts they assembled are persuasive.

Materials in the case show the following. The provincial committee leaders, headed by Provincial Committee Secretary Alexander Vasilyevich Basov, arrived in Novocherkassk in the afternoon of June 1, when the meeting had already grown in size. Basov came out onto the balcony of the plant administration building. The crowd quieted down. People waited for him to begin speaking about what was upsetting them, about wages, about problems at the plant, about his vision for the immediate future. But Basov, at a loss for the appropriate words, started to read the official announcement of the price increase. The crowd reacted with a hostile murmur, and someone threw a bottle at Basov. The members of the provincial committee withdrew into the building and ordered the militia to clear the square. But the militia could not carry out the order, even with the help of troops from the Ministry of Internal Affairs (MVD). They turned to the Army. Defense Minister Rodion Malinovsky, citing Khrushchev's instructions, ordered the district commander, General Issa Pliyev, to call up troops on an emergency basis and concentrate them in the area of Novocherkassk.

When General Pliyev arrived at 5 P.M., Andrei Kirilenko ordered him to help out Basov, who was trapped in the plant administration building. In issuing orders to his subordinates, Pliyev emphasized: "No force or weapons should be employed in carrying out the operation." What's more, soldiers were not issued ammunition for their submachine guns. Soon the airborne reconnaissance company of the Eighteenth Division brought the province leaders out the back door of the building and took them to Kirilenko. It should be said that the troops entered the building openly, even though the crowd was agitated. People grabbed officers by the sleeve, asking: "Who are you for?" They overturned two trucks. But the strikers did not follow the soldiers into the building.

By this time the tanks summoned by Kirilenko were approaching the square. They received a far more hostile reception from the demonstrators, who tried to stick metal bars into the caterpillar tracks of the lead tank, broke its headlights and periscope, and immobilized it by covering it with a tarpaulin. Noticing the tanks, Pliyev's deputy, General Mikhail Shaposhnikov, immediately ordered them to leave the square.[10] He didn't know that they were there on orders from Kirilenko.

At about this time Malinovsky again called the staff of the Military District from Moscow and ordered: "Tell Pliyev: Bring in the division. Do not remove the tanks. Impose order. Report." Toward evening Frol Kozlov flew in from Moscow and took over command, not only of civilians and the mili-

---

10. There were many press reports about a general who refused to bring tanks into the city despite an order issued from above. The investigation found no evidence that this was the case. It is true that when Rostov Provincial Committee Secretary Basov called Colonel Shargorodsky, commander of the 18th Tank Division, at 12:30 on June 1, before Kirilenko's arrival in Novocherkassk and before Malinovsky's order, and commanded him to establish order at the factory, Shargorodsky refused. He was not subordinate to the Provincial Committee. The district military staff reacted the same way to Basov's call. They decided not to do anything without Pliyev. General Pliyev approved the action, or rather, the inaction, of his officers. The troops intervened only after orders from Minister of Defense Marshal Malinovsky. No instances of orders being refused were found.

tia, but also of the Army. He intended to act decisively. The newcomers gathered where the tank division was deployed. At their very first conference Kozlov stated: "Weapons should be used. A thousand people should be placed in railroad cars and removed from the city." (Sergo was right.)

Aleksandr Shelepin testifies that as they left Moscow, Father ordered him and Andrei Kirilenko to resolve the situation by peaceful methods alone. What he said to Kozlov is unknown.

When it grew dark the strikers went home. On the morning of June 2 workers again gathered on the square in front of the factory administration building. They debated what to do next. Finally, they formed into a column and began crossing the bridge spanning the Tuzlov River and moving toward the city party committee building. The column was an impressive sight. As documents from the investigation attest, it resembled the demonstration of workers who marched, caps in hand, to petition the tsar on January 21, 1905. But this time red flags and portraits of Lenin, Marx, and Engels, rather than banners and icons, waved over the crowd. We can summon up the memory of what happened when soldiers opened fire on the demonstrators being led to the Winter Palace in Petersburg by the priest Gapon. If the tsar and his generals had not panicked, if they had not ordered troops to fire, perhaps all of Russian history would have been different. The demonstrators were, after all, going to ask the tsar to defend them. If he had come out onto the balcony, had spoken with representatives and accepted their petition, people would probably have dispersed. But that's not what happened and history can't be rewritten. Everything would have depended on the wisdom of political leaders. Shots, blood—they roused the people to fury. So began the First Russian Revolution.

On the bridge, the unarmed demonstrators were confronted by the tanks sent by Kozlov and by ranks of cadets, also unarmed, from the Rostov Military School. The people didn't risk a confrontation and forded the river. No one stopped them. By 10:30 the column had reached its goal and emerged onto Lenin Square, where the city party committee and the city executive committee were located. The local "leaders" ran away in a panic, and no one came out to speak to the strikers. Entry into the building was blocked by ranks of Volunteer Militia and soldiers. Angry people easily smashed the cordon, forced the doors, and ran up to different floors. The first speakers from among the demonstrators appeared on the balcony. They talked about what had prompted them to strike. The temper of the crowd gradually heated up. Someone suggested going to the militia to free those who had been detained the previous evening. About three hundred people collected outside the premises of the militia and the KGB (the two offices were located in adjacent rooms). A few people tried to climb over the brick wall into the inner courtyard. Shots rang out in response from soldiers of the 505th Regiment (MVD). They fired over people's heads—along the wall, but not at people. The demonstrators stopped trying to get into the courtyard and jumped from the wall back into the street. However, the shots didn't frighten the attackers. They broke down the doors onto the street and got inside, but didn't find the prisoners, who had been taken out of the city during the night. Finding a handful of soldiers in the corner of the duty room, they began to beat them and they took away Private Repkin's submachine gun. Aside from that gun, the demonstrators had no other weapons, either then or later.

Another private, Sharaf Azizov, seeing what was happening, shouted: "They're beating our men!" He began firing into the air and was joined by his comrades. The crowd rushed to the nearest door. It led to that same courtyard where the soldiers, frightened by the previous attack, had gathered. They opened fire. The regimental commander, Pyotr Malyutin, who had hurried there when he heard the shots, brought the firing to a halt with some difficulty. Five people were killed as a result. Another two died later of their wounds. The total number of wounded was not ascertained.

Meanwhile, Kirilenko and Shelepin, who had come into Novocherkassk from where the tank division was posted, ordered garrison commander General Ivan Oleshko "to clear the 'pogromists' from the city committee building. If necessary, fire warning shots into the air." That was the terminology used. By twelve o'clock tanks and armored personnel carriers of the Eighteenth Division, students from the Artillery School, and other units had reached Lenin Square. They formed a semicircle around the demonstrators. The city committee building was cleared without difficulty. There were only thirty or forty people inside, and they offered no resistance.

General Oleshko went out onto the balcony. Through a loudspeaker he demanded that the crowd disperse or the troops would use their weapons. "They're trying to scare us, they won't shoot," said someone in the crowd.

"Soldiers, move away from the crowd, move to the wall," ordered Oleshko, and a little later: "Fire a volley in the air!"

There was a rattle of machine-gun fire, but the crowd didn't move.[11] "Don't be frightened, they're firing blanks," shouted someone.

But then the soldiers fired a second volley. In the absence of orders, according to military investigators. With a groan, people in the crowd reeled back and began to scatter. Running over each other, people rushed around the square and into adjacent streets. After using up their ammunition, the soldiers stopped firing.

Heaps of people lay on the square. Fortunately, not many were killed. The shooting was random.

---

11. A version widely disseminated in the press alleging that the soldiers, firing into the air, killed many little boys who had climbed into a tree was not substantiated.

It remained unclear who had fired into the crowd. Some witnesses claim that the soldiers fired, that they had "gradually lowered their automatics." The servicemen themselves swear that they fired only into the air. Other witnesses testify that some civilians fired from roofs, including firing from machine guns. They cite the fact that some people on streets far from Lenin Square were wounded as confirmation. It would have been impossible to hit them if the firing was from ground level, but from roofs nothing would have been easier. In general, those guilty were not identified. It is also unclear who gave the order to open fire on people, or even whether there was such an order.

Investigators did not find any documents from that time relating to the bloodshed on Lenin Square. Former KGB chairman Vladimir Semichasny insolently told investigators: "No one wants to take responsibility in such cases." And he's certainly someone who knows what to say and what not to say. He was the man who coordinated all actions by the special services from Moscow, and three of his deputies were acting on the spot. Semichastny sent Father reports on the struggle against "hooligans and pogromists." Well, nothing else could be expected from Semichastny, particularly not the truth. The same was true of his predecessor as chairman of the KGB, Aleksandr Shelepin. That pair long ago decided what to say and how to say it to curious journalists, inquisitive historians, and conscientious investigators.

It has been determined that Father had given no order to fire. This is what the document states: "Materials of the investigation allow one to conclude that the decision made on the spot by members of the Presidium of the Central Committee of the CPSU to use firearms was not agreed upon beforehand with Khrushchev. As already noted, initially Khrushchev was against the use of extreme measures. Then, as the situation deteriorated, he began to demand that order be restored by any methods, up to the use of weapons—however, with the proviso: if government offices are seized."[12] But that is poor consolation. Blood was spilled, and the person standing at the head of the country is responsible, regardless of what position he occupied. Father himself never denied responsibility.

"According to data collected by the investigation, twenty-five people in all died on June 1–2, 1962, in Novocherkassk. More than fifty were wounded by gunfire. More than twenty civilians were injured and hurt. Nine of the eighty-six servicemen injured in the clash were hospitalized."

Twenty-five killed. That was all. Against a background of the hundreds, if not thousands who died on October 3–4, 1993, in President Boris Yeltsin's

12. Yuri Bagreyev, senior assistant to the Chief Military Prosecutor, and Vladislav Pavlyutkin, journalist, "Novocherkassk, 1962. Tragedy on the Square. Materials from the Investigation of the Chief Military Prosecutors' Office, 1992," *Krasnaya zvezda*, October 7, 1995, p. 7.

storming of his own parliament; 40,000 peaceful inhabitants killed by the Russian army in pacifying Chechnya in 1994–96, tens of thousands killed in the Armenian-Azerbaijani conflict of 1990–96, a hundred thousand who have died to date in the ongoing civil war in Tajikistan! But in Novocherkassk only twenty-five! After all, don't "they" say that sometimes it is necessary to use force to keep order?

"They" may say it, but in this case Father did not. The Novocherkassk bloodshed tormented him to the end of his days. He had lived through two wars and seen many deaths, but had never grown used to them. That was probably the reason he did not write about Novocherkassk in his memoirs. He did not think he had the right to justify himself, and he could not adopt the position of an indifferent observer.

THE DEFENSE OF CUBA: THE PLAN TAKES FORM

As talks were going on in Havana, people in Moscow were preparing to act. Malinovsky proposed putting General Pliyev in charge of the operation. The choice has always remained a mystery to me. A cavalry officer of the old school, in the saddle from the time of the First World War and the civil war, he had risen by the end of the Second World War to the rank of cavalry corps commander. What did he have to do with missiles? And not only with missiles, but with modern war in general? In answer to my bewilderment, Father replied that he was Malinovsky's candidate, that Father knew him, but not very well. He had run into him during the war. A general like other generals, no worse than others, and a minister knows his own people.

As the plan was worked out in more detail, the enormity of its scale became more and more apparent. It might not seem that difficult to install four or, say, five dozen missiles. But with every passing day, so much "flesh" accumulated on the missile "skeleton" that the center of gravity of the operation began to move in the direction of a unified command.

The reasoning in the General Staff was simple and uncomplicated. Since the missiles would be in our hands, we would naturally have to ensure their safety. Father told me that initially the idea was to have only an infantry contingent, but it appeared that this would not solve the problem. If an invasion took place, there would be a clash with well-armed units of the U.S. military, who could be resisted only by a force of equal size and with equal equipment. A guard battalion would not do. You needed artillery, you needed tanks. Step by step, the sixty missiles expanded to include more than fifty thousand troops—about four full-strength divisions. To be exact, records compiled by the General Staff show that it was proposed to send 50,874 men.

Any invasion would undoubtedly begin from the air. There was virtually no air defense system on the island. So it had to be created. In the first instance, there was talk of antiaircraft missiles. They were to be the most modern missiles, the kind that had shot down Powers—a total of 114 launch complexes, with all the necessary equipment. In other words, two divisions. It was a complex weapon. Furthermore, it was highly secret. Father decided that it too must remain in our hands. Rapid-firing antiaircraft guns capable of destroying a target at low altitudes were delivered to the Cuban army, which had some experience in their use.

The most advanced supersonic MIG-21 fighters completed the air defense system. At the time you could count the number of such fighters in our units on the fingers of one hand, but Cuba was given the highest priority.

A shore defense had to be organized if the island were to be made impregnable. For this purpose, Father proposed sending Sopkas, the shore defense version of his favorite Kometas, to the areas most vulnerable to landing forces. Although the Sopka was by then rather obsolete, the Navy had nothing better to propose. Gaps between missile batteries would have to be covered from the sea by high-speed Komar (Mosquito) patrol boats armed with P-15 homing missiles.

It was proposed that IL-28 bombers patrol the coastline. Depending on their mission, they could carry bombs, including atomic bombs, or torpedoes could be hung from their bellies.

All these decisions about organizing the defense of Cuba were made gradually, as more and more new tasks appeared. The pie was composed of many pieces.

By the time the first estimates by the General Staff were complete, Father's emissaries had returned from Havana. He talked for a long time with Rashidov and Biryuzov and questioned them about Castro's reaction. Everything was normal as far as that was concerned. Father heaped questions on Biryuzov about the possibility of concealing military infrastructure, since the scale of the operation was constantly expanding. And the main problem was, how to hide the missiles?

Biryuzov hesitated. He had not really carried out that part of his assignment. He finally was forced to speak and said that, in the opinion of specialists—in which he concurred—the missiles could successfully be disguised as coconut palms. He had seen them himself in Cuba: the same straight barrel trunk. Only the warhead would have to be crowned with a cap of leaves.

To this day I can't understand how Father believed such primitive reasoning. The whole time he talked about the missile-palms, I couldn't take it seriously. I expressed my doubts to Father, but he didn't want to listen. He retorted that professionals were at work there and they understood the matter better than we did. I couldn't find any objections. For some reason I remembered the occasional landings by our plane at the plant airfield in Voronezh. After our monotonous life at the test site, the plant smokestacks stretching into the sky against a background of runways had more than once subconsciously reminded me of rockets ready to be launched. I reassured myself. Here smokestacks, there palms—maybe it would work. But I still couldn't rid myself of the feeling that this was a slipshod solution to the problem.

Father forgot about the auxiliary infrastructure specific to missiles: launchers, trailers, fueling trucks. But they, after all, are what make it possible to identify a launch position, even in the absence of missiles. If they are present, a missile is concealed nearby.

Transport was a problem. Huge amounts of cargo had to be moved in a short period of time and we had practically no ships, much less specially equipped ones.

Father summoned the minister of the merchant marine, who reported that to carry out the assignment would require cancellation of the entire annual shipping plan, which had already been approved. Naturally, there was no extra capacity anywhere. We would have to spend hard currency to ship goods on foreign vessels.

Father gave his approval. The Ministry of Finance was instructed not to spare the money.

There was feverish activity in Black Sea and Baltic ports. Sailings were canceled, cargoes readdressed. "Ordinary" cargoes to Cuba and other destinations were transferred to foreign vessels. There was simply no alternative.

Our ships, Soviet freighters, passenger liners, tankers—everything that was available—were refitted to transport arms, personnel, and fuel. Many problems had to be faced for the first time. Rockets, thermonuclear warheads, highly volatile and toxic rocket fuel and oxidizer, had never been shipped across the ocean. Not only must everything be delivered safe and undamaged, but secrecy had to be maintained.

The rockets were dealt with rather briskly. They could easily be stored in the latest model freighters of the *Poltava* type. Broad hatchways made it possible to load the rockets in the holds, where they were lashed down in case the ship rolled. It was decided to put agricultural machinery, seeding machines, cultivators, and combines on deck. The Americans, who flew over our ships in the open ocean, should not have the slightest idea of what the ships were really carrying.

Emotions ran high over the nuclear warheads. Their very presence on ships, which could be stopped, seized, or interned, violated our country's requirements for secrecy and security. Even within the country, warheads were moved in special railroad cars camouflaged as passenger trains and accompanied by numerous guards. No one wanted even to imagine what might happen on the high seas near foreign shores. This was reported to Father. He proposed sending them on submarines. That seemed an attractive idea, but it was difficult to carry out. Not only did it seem impossible to create the necessary conditions for storing them, but the crew would simply have no place to hide from the radiation.

After lengthy discussion, it was decided to send the warheads on surface ships, but not until the very end, when the rockets were already in Cuba. The thinking was that if nuclear warheads were delivered then, they would be more secure—otherwise, if an invasion occurred before the missiles were ready for launch, our atomic secrets might fall into U.S. hands.

Malinovsky reported to Father that, according to his staff's estimates, it would take about four months to install the rockets. If shipments began in July and August, installation couldn't be finished before October or November. This schedule suited Father. He was in no hurry to announce the deployment of rockets in Cuba. Let the U.S. elections be over. He thought that hotheads might gain the upper hand in the polemical heat of interparty struggle for seats in the Senate and House of Representatives. When everything quieted down, in November, he planned through private channels to test the mood of the president, to prepare him, and then to sound the bell. So the schedule for completing the operation was born: the end of October, beginning of November.

INTERMEZZO

What else remains in my memory from the events of that summer? Actually, not very much. I do remember that in the middle of June the American pianist Van Cliburn visited Moscow. Father was charmed by his performance. He had become very popular in Moscow in general, ever since his victory in the Tchaikovsky competition. Father never missed an opportunity to hear good music. On this occasion they met after the concert in the Main Hall of the Conservatory. After thanking the pianist for the pleasure given by his performance, Father invited Cliburn to visit the dacha the following Sunday.

The day turned out to be sunny and warm. Father showed his guest the garden and the cornfield. Cliburn smiled shyly. Having disposed of agriculture, they went for a boat ride on the Moscow River. Father took the oars, allowing his guest the privilege of steering. Then we had lunch in the garden, under the trees. The atmosphere was steeped in goodwill. In summer our family was always served *okroshka* (a brown beverage made from dark bread and water, very much like a nonalcoholic beer), a cold soup made from *kvass* with chopped meat, or vegetables. Our guest asked about this unfamiliar novelty, tried it, and started to ask how it was prepared. Father threw himself into explanations, but immediately ran into a stumbling block. The American simply couldn't understand what *kvass* was. Father became absorbed in the details. All in vain. What Cliburn thought is a mystery, but he politely pushed away the plate with this exotic substance and the whole rest of the meal he tried to avoid looking at the jar of *kvass* sitting in the middle of the table.

After lunch our guest was in a better mood.

He and Father said good-bye warmly, as friends. Father joked: Wouldn't our guest like to take along a glass of *kvass* for the road?

Cliburn put out his hands, as if pushing something away.

"*Kvass*, never," he said. They both burst out laughing.

THE DEFENSE OF CUBA AND OLEG PENKOVSKY

Father planned a trip to Bucharest at the end of June. Following it, Raul Castro was expected to fly into Moscow. On July 2 he was met at Vnukovo Airport by Mikoyan and Malinovsky. The next day the Cuban defense minister, barely recovered from a flight across eight time zones, was taken to see Father.

Negotiations, which began July 3 in Father's office, continued in a relaxed atmosphere at the dacha. Rashidov and Alekseyev came there with Raul.

They talked about preparing an official agreement. Naturally, a completely secret one. Aside from Rashidov and Alekseyev, Soviet defense minister Malinovsky, Marshal Biryuzov, and two or three generals participated in the negotiations. Alekseyev served as interpreter. An attempt was made to keep participants to a minimum for security reasons. Raul Castro's final meeting with Father took place on July 8. Father attributed particular importance to the secrecy of the proposed operation. Every conceivable step was taken to ensure this. It got to the point that many documents were handwritten. All in single copies. All decisions regarding access to the planned operation were made by Malinovsky himself.

Meanwhile, one of the most important spies of the Khrushchev period, Oleg Vladimirovich Penkovsky, was firmly entrenched in the Chief Intelligence Administration of the General Staff, the very heart of the Ministry of Defense. He worked for both British and U.S. intelligence. I have always suspected that Penkovsky played an important role in the Cuban or Caribbean Crisis. He knew a great deal.

The opportunities available to him were considerable. A highly placed Soviet intelligence official, in the State Committee on the Coordination of Scientific-Research Work, Penkovsky specialized in obtaining foreign technical information related to the development and production of precision instruments for missile guidance: hydroscopes and accelerometers.

After being assigned the job of collecting information in the field of hydroscopy, Penkovsky asked British intelligence to organize a tour by Soviet specialists to British factories in that field. Such an opportunity would increase his authority in the General Staff as well as the KGB. Until then our people had not been allowed within shooting range of such establishments. The matter was not decided immediately. Consultations began. The factories were contacted. The British engineers with whom MI-6 spoke only laughed at their concerns about security—there was an enormous distance between seeing something done and being able to do it oneself.

Companies independent of the British government agreed to permit a visit by our instrument specialists. The Soviet delegation was taken around shopfloors, shown laboratories, and given brochures. They were delighted when they returned home, but after looking over things more closely, it turned out that they had learned nothing new.

The trip had great repercussions.

Penkovsky became the hero of the day. Legends grew up about our penetration of the inner sanctum of the British military industry. Penkovsky, who had doors open to him even before, now became a very familiar figure among rocket scientists. He often visited design bureaus and went to the Tyura-Tam test site more than once. He explained his curiosity by saying: "If you want to gain information, you must have a good grasp of the subject—otherwise they're bound to trick you and palm off junk."

He won respect for this serious approach to his work. People confided things to this man from the "organization" that they would not always tell their own associates.

Penkovsky enjoyed equal access in the Army. Apart from everything else, he was close to Chief Marshal of Artillery Varentsov, commander in chief of Missile Forces and Artillery, who at one time had recommended him to his old friend, General Serov, head of the GRU.

Today it's hard to say what Penkovsky knew specifically, or what he transmitted to the Americans and when he did it. But there's no doubt of one thing: he kept the CIA informed concerning Soviet missile potential on a regular basis. Father was absolutely incorrect to think that his comments concerning incredible Soviet power were still being taken at face value at the White House. The Americans had precise knowledge that the Soviet Union had just begun to deploy R-16s, and that there were not hundreds of them, but only a few.

Information received from Penkovsky and from other sources enabled them to calculate the ratio of nuclear missile strength in 1962 as 18:1 in favor of the United States. U.S. arsenals contained about five thousand nuclear and thermonuclear warheads, as against our three hundred.

The quintessential information obtained from Penkovsky was that the Soviet missile program was not progressing nearly as successfully as the West supposed and that the Soviet Union did not possess intercontinental missiles. It had as yet only medium-range missiles at its disposal. Armed with this information, Kennedy could resist Soviet pressure when the Americans discovered launch sites for medium-range missiles in Cuba.

Let's look at the matter from a different aspect. Did Penkovsky have the opportunity, technically speaking, to transmit information? Here the answer is an unequivocal yes.

Those five months between May 20, when Father returned from Bulgaria, until October 22, the day of his arrest, Penkovsky was under constant surveillance by KGB agents. All his meetings, all his fleeting contacts, were carefully recorded.

The fact is that over a long period of time counterintelligence knew that highly secret information was flowing to the West from the General Staff.

In particular, the record of a highly secret conference at staff headquarters of the Group of Soviet Forces in Germany "returned" from the United States. The lists of participants were checked. Just as in a detective story, a substantial number of people fell under suspicion, but as the process of "screening" went on they became fewer and fewer, and finally the choice was down to only a few. One of them was Penkovsky. Each of the officers was put under surveillance. At first they found suspicious contacts made by Penkovsky, then suspicions became certainty. But all of this took time.

Here is a list of the meetings Penkovsky had with his foreign colleagues, excerpted from the information that figured in the trial process. We'll begin with the end of May.

We can eliminate his meeting with Anne Chisholm, the agent who was his liaison, at a British embassy reception on May 31. On that day Penkovsky could not yet have known anything.

On July 2 and in subsequent days he was in constant touch with Greville Wynne, an intelligence officer and "businessman" from Britain. That was a simple matter; the Englishman came on trade matters and negotiations with him fell within Penkovsky's official duties.

In those days, and even after Wynne's arrest, no one guessed that he was not a businessman or a low-level liaison type, but an experienced British intelligence agent—Penkovsky's handler from the British side.

It was only years later that the Soviets learned that Penkovsky and Wynne, his British intelligence supervisor, had agreed beforehand that, if apprehended, they would try to persuade investigators that Wynne was only a liaison. When they met, Penkovsky was supposed to give a sign, such as running his hand over his hair in a certain way, indicating that his interrogators had believed him. They did believe him. The accused exchanged the agreed-upon gestures. Court documents indicated that Wynne was an insignificant figure.

When those meetings began, information about all the secret activity around the subject of Cuba could have reached Penkovsky's ears, although it remained accessible to very few until Raul Castro's arrival. But after all, Penkovsky's "patron," so to speak, the man who recommended him for a position in the GRU, Varentsov, was a marshal, the highest rank in our military.

By the end of August Penkovsky simply must have been aware of the operation in progress. Troops were being transferred, dozens of ships were leaving for an unknown destination. Who would think of concealing information available to hundreds of people from one of the highest-ranking officers, moreover one trusted by the top leadership of the GRU?

And it was precisely at the end of August, as shown by testimony from the surveillance service, that Penkovsky—after obtaining the necessary permission—was a guest at the home of the U.S. agricultural attaché Khorbeli, where a meeting with CIA representative Rodney Carlson had been arranged. There they had the opportunity to talk. Besides, Penkovsky gave Carlson seven exposed microfilms and data about some Soviet missile. The accused admitted this in court. What did he not admit? Probably a great deal.

After Penkovsky's August meetings with CIA and MI-6 representatives, the KGB had no doubt that he was the foreign agent. Counterintelligence stayed literally on his tail.

Penkovsky sensed that disaster was looming. He asked for urgent evacuation. A rather good scenario had been prepared for this eventuality. Wynne had begun his trip with several trucks containing a mobile exhibit of his company's products. He was to travel from Hungary to the Soviet Union, to stop in Moscow, and continue on to Helsinki. A hiding place had been fitted out under one of the trucks, where Penkovsky could hold out in relative comfort from Moscow to the Finnish border. However, the operation fell through.

THE DEFENSE OF CUBA: THE PLAN IS IMPLEMENTED

Father knew nothing of this during those July days. Our missile secrets seemed safely hidden. In the middle of July the draft agreement for the deployment of missiles in Cuba, endorsed by the two defense ministers, Marshal Malinovsky for the Soviet Union and Raul Castro for the Republic of Cuba, was presented to the top leaders. Father approved the text. It could hardly have been otherwise, since Malinovsky called Father to consult over every single point that seemed to him of the slightest importance. The treaty provided that all types of missiles—ballistic, combat, antiaircraft, and shore defense—would remain under Soviet command.

The time had come to obtain Fidel Castro's consent. On July 17 Raul Castro flew home with the draft document in hand.

During those days I was away from Moscow. Demonstration exercises by the Northern Fleet were scheduled for July. Father and the country's entire top leadership were planning to attend. Our design bureau was the focus of attention. Almost all of the Navy's cruise missiles had originated within the walls of Chelomei's design bureau. Feverish preparations were going on along the entire coast, from Murmansk to Arkhangelsk. I was sent to Severomorsk, where our cruise missiles were being readied for live firing.

We lived on a floating submarine base, a huge gray ship, part dormitory, part repair shop, part warehouse. We quickly found a common language with the Navy men and became friends. One evening during tea in the wardroom the commander told his officers that after the exercises the base would leave on a long cruise lasting many months. At the time he wasn't authorized to divulge its destination and purpose, and possibly he didn't know himself. The following days were filled with discussions, guesses, suppositions. Fantasies were played out. Only the thorough and reliable boatswain maintained a mysterious silence. He thought I could be trusted and told me that he had been issued a lightweight, tropical uniform. His conclusion was unequivocal: the base was heading for Cuba.

I didn't fail to mention this episode when Father arrived and I began to tell him about my days in Severomorsk. He smiled: "It's impossible to keep a secret. At headquarters any mention of Cuba is forbidden, but the boatswain already knows everything!"

By that time it had been decided that our submarines would play a more important role in bolstering the island's defense. That would also solve the problems we had in maintaining submarines on patrol along the U.S. coast. If they could be based in Cuba, their battle positions would be only a stone's throw away.

No special consideration was given to how the Americans might react to this step. It was thought that if everything went well with the missiles, no one would pay any particular attention to a submarine base. After all, the U.S. Navy based ships in Scotland, Italy, Greece, and other European ports.

A colossal operation began in July to transfer what were in essence several Soviet divisions. Staffing of the units went on for an entire month, with some of the men in civilian clothes and some in the uniform of the Cuban revolutionary armed forces. No Soviet military must appear in Cuba. Soldiers and officers were disguised as technical specialists, tourists, and who knows what else. Troops and equipment were moved inconspicuously to ports to be loaded onto ships.

The main flow was to Black Sea ports, Feodosiya, Nikolayev, and Poti. General Ivan Statsenko's strategic missile division, a combined force, was loaded on a ship in the Sevastopol Naval Base, which was closed to outsiders. His division was composed of the most highly trained regiments, those which had acquired experience in practice launches. A year before, in June 1961, one of the regiments had "bombarded" the Novaya Zemlya test site with nuclear warheads fired from a combat launch position in the region of Vorkuta. Two missiles were released, one with a nuclear warhead, the other with a thermonuclear warhead. The force of the explosions met expectations. Now the regiments were to prove themselves in Cuba.

To preserve secrecy, it was decided not to take on board the Turkish pilots who usually accompanied ships through the Bosporus and Dardanelles. Presents and bribes were prepared for them. These were handed over right in the pilots' launch. The appropriate entry was made in ship registries, and the sides parted well pleased with each other.

The Baltic merchant fleet played no less a role than the Black Sea merchant fleet. Ports there were located even more conveniently; it was easier to disperse the shipments. Some were loaded in Kaliningrad or, more exactly, in Baltiysk, others in Liepaja, and others in Kronshtadt.

However, those ships had to sail in full view of all Europe, through the Danish Straits, the North Sea, and then the Channel. There was no way for them to hide from the curious eyes that would be watching the entire way. But that was not particularly important; with modern technology, you couldn't hide on the high seas either.

A smaller stream of freight—just a brook compared to the first two streams—flowed from the North, from the port of Murmansk and the North Sea Military Base. The most sensitive freight left from there: nuclear warheads for rockets, atomic bombs for bombers.

Rocket and artillery units subordinate to Marshal Varentsov were loaded on in the west. They included jet launchers for the short-range Lunas, without their nuclear warheads. Special warheads were, as I just mentioned, transported separately.

The mass sailings from Soviet ports began in July. All imaginable precautions were taken: loading was done at night at especially isolated piers. Access was blocked to outsiders.

No one was told where the ships were headed. The most improbable rumors were deliberately spread; captains were given false destinations and charts of totally different regions of the ocean. In some cases personnel were handed warm clothing upon embarkation, also in the interest of disinformation. Soldiers were quartered in holds that had been hastily equipped with cots and hammocks. Portholes were sealed from the outside for greater se-crecy and the men were allowed to go on deck only in the open sea and in the dark. Agricultural machinery was placed on the decks of all ships carrying military personnel. The entire Ministry of Agriculture seemed to be moving to Cuba.

To keep information from leaking beforehand, those taking part in the loading operations were then sent off on lengthy official trips to test sites and distant garrisons. There they were forced to while away the time until autumn, until November. Local commanders didn't know what to make of it—what kind of disaster was this? Why such a number of commissions, in-spectors, and simply uninvited consultants and assistants? No amount of questioning helped. Having been strictly briefed, their guests maintained an enigmatic silence.

Soldiers and officers crowded into the holds of departing ships were also left in ignorance until the last minute. The High Command wanted them to learn the truth only when they were on the high seas. Captains were handed packets with wax seals. Some were to be opened when ships entered the North Sea, others when they passed Gibraltar.

However, you can't hide an eel in a sack. Despite these measures, all of Odessa knew that ships were being secretly fitted out for Cuba. It was dis-cussed at the local flea market and provided gossip for women peddlers around the port. Even the reserved Balts couldn't keep the secret. But they tried not to spread the information around too much, saying, "Let them go to Cuba if they have to."

The first ships in various ports were loaded and went to sea at virtually the same time. A crush developed in the Danish straits. The same picture was seen in the Bosporus and Dardanelles. Never had such a number of Soviet freighters sailed from the Black and Baltic Seas. At first the phenome-non only caused perplexity, which turned to surprise and finally suspicion. West German intelligence became concerned—not one of the ships was en-tering a European port.

Surveillance began. By observing the ships' courses, it was discovered that all of those passing into the North Sea turned toward the Atlantic, some through the Channel and some by roundabout routes skirting the British Isles. Ships leaving the Black Sea were behaving similarly. They were all being drawn toward distant shores, like eels to the Sargasso Sea.

The situation aroused deep suspicion. Fears were confirmed by intelli-gence information: ships were being loaded in Soviet ports under conditions of the tightest secrecy, and then heading in an unknown direction. The Ger-mans thought it necessary to warn their American allies about the unusual migration of the Soviet merchant fleet toward the Western hemisphere. The information was sent to the CIA in the middle of September. The Americans themselves were not sitting on their hands. Their surveillance planes over-flew the ships in the open ocean, but discovered nothing suspicious. Photo-graphs showed only civilian cargo.

The Americans then asked their allies to try to find some pretext to in-spect the ships. But nothing was discovered then either. The captains said nothing that would have justified further action, and a superficial inspection confirmed that there was agricultural machinery on board, just as ship docu-ments stated. Meticulous CIA analysts made some calculations. It turned out that in July of that year thirty ships flying the Soviet flag had arrived in Cuba, as compared with fifteen the previous year. Even more arrived later on. In August there were fifty-five, as against twelve in the same month of 1961, in September sixty-six, and about forty were counted during only the first half of October. According to our data, in July ten ships carrying military cargoes docked in Cuban ports, the first being the *Mariya Ulyanova* on July 26. In all, eighty-five ships took part in the operation, completing two hundred forty-three runs in the course of two and a half months. So the CIA was not off by much.

The Cubans were feeling their strength. At a gathering to celebrate the anni-versary of the storming of the Moncado barracks, Fidel delivered an emo-tional speech that went on for hours. In it he threatened the United States that any attack on Cuba would mean the start of a new world war, and he referred to the support and assistance provided by socialist countries and especially the Soviet Union. He was shooting off his mouth. Any hint in those days was fraught with danger.

Alekseyev, appointed the Soviet ambassador to Cuba on June 12, didn't get there until August 13. First there had been the negotiations with Raul Castro. Then it seemed that no one could manage without him. The Central Committee, the Ministry of Defense, and the KGB all needed information and advice about Cuba.

After arriving in Havana, Alekseyev gave Fidel still another version, which he had brought with him, of the text of the agreement on installing missiles. It differed somewhat from the one that Raul initialed in Moscow. The changes did not affect Cuba's interests, they only reinforced its ability to resist an attack because additional modern types of weapons would be delivered. Fidel kept the document. Soon new changes appeared. As a result, yet another round of negotiations was required.

The Americans were not sitting idly. On August 10, CIA director John McCone warned President Kennedy of the possibility that Soviet medium-range missiles might appear in Cuba. From then on Cuba was under a micro-scope. Every change, every step was registered. In August they noted the appearance of twelve Soviet Komar missile boats in the port of Mariel. The information was precise. The appearance of antiaircraft missiles on the island was noted at the same time.

But they failed to discover the most important objects: ballistic missiles. There were simply none of them on the island as yet.

CIA director John McCone was troubled by dark premonitions. Why were the most advanced means of air and shore defense suddenly being delivered to Cuba? Logic indicated that the main force, very possibly ballistic missiles, must follow. That was, after all, precisely the same sequence by which the Americans themselves equipped Thor and Jupiter emplacements in Turkey, Italy, and Britain.

On August 22 McCone shared his suspicions with the president. But when Kennedy asked him directly whether there were any such missiles in Cuba, he had to answer in the negative. So far no one had seen any. At a press conference that day Kennedy said that he had no knowledge of any landings by Warsaw Pact troops in Cuba. However, reports about secret events occurring on the island aroused his suspicion and the following day he issued Order No. 181 to his National Security Council, asking it to consider possible reactions to the growing activity of the "Soviet bloc in Cuba." He asked for study of the potential military, political, and psychological effect of the deployment in Cuba of missiles capable of reaching U.S. territory and of military options that might enable the United States to destroy those missiles.

Kennedy was thinking along global lines when he evaluated Father's possible initiative as an effort to reduce the gap in nuclear missile potential. That Khrushchev could have had other, no less powerful, motives for such a step didn't enter his head. Kennedy made a mistake in evaluating our position. He simply could not imagine that such risky actions might be taken only to defend a small people who were an ocean and three seas distant from the Soviet Union.

Meanwhile, the situation in Cuba was heating up. The "Mongoose" operation was intensifying. By all indications, an invasion was not far off.

During the night of August 24 two small unidentified boats sneaked into Havana harbor under cover of darkness and opened fire with their twenty-millimeter guns on houses and hotels along the shore. Such a pinprick couldn't cause much damage, but the incident put Cubans on their guard—no one would fire at a neighbor for no reason.

Senator Capehart called on Kennedy to order an invasion of Cuba.

The president calmed things down at a press conference. He declared: "I think it would be a mistake to invade Cuba. Actions of that kind, which could result from a very impulsive proposal, might lead to very serious consequences for many people."

The president's words were published in the Soviet Union, but they did not inspire much trust in Father. Intelligence services reported that the noose around Cuba was tightening. The Americans would continue to be agitated, and we could expect decisive actions. But where and when? Father became nervous and was worried about being too late. He thought that, without cutting through the Cuban knot, it would be impossible either to move off dead center in disarmament negotiations or to count on the possibility of relaxing tensions in the world in general.

Father did not mean to aggravate relations with the United States, which were already far from ideal. Now, in the heat of the operation, he avoided any actions that might provoke unforeseen complications in any part of the world. A fire could be set off by the slightest spark. Therefore, when a U.S. U-2 spy plane flew over Sakhalin on August 31, no attempt was made to shoot it down. It's hard to say now whether that was even technically possible, since it spent only nine minutes in our airspace.

The Soviet government limited itself to a protest note and accepted the routine explanation: the pilot was blown off course by strong winds.

NUCLEAR TESTING

Cuba occupied considerably less space in correspondence between the two governments and in newspapers than did nuclear tests, violation of the moratorium, oversight and inspection, complete and universal disarmament.

Renewal of tests by the Soviet Union and then by the United States moved the block of ice from its place and, gradually picking up momentum, it was rolling downhill. If not stopped in time, it threatened to knock down and flatten any barrier standing in its path. It became increasingly obvious that shaky unilateral promises and moratoriums would not lead to resolving the problem. A treaty was needed, and as soon as possible.

Father very much wanted to stop the tests at one stroke, to freeze the development of this technology and not allow any possibility of evasive maneuvers. He continued to be skeptical about the U.S. proposal to allow underground testing only. That would permit the race to continue, but by more expensive methods.

Meanwhile, we had only begun to prepare for the next series of tests. Several dozen explosions were planned, including super-powerful multi-megaton ones. However, Father began to question the advisability of the latter. It was too difficult to foresee their consequences. Reverberations from the previous year's fifty-seven-megaton test on Novaya Zemlya were felt around the planet, provoking a storm of protests, especially in Scandinavia.

The Americans firmly retained a qualitative advantage, and it was in their interest to stop our tests as soon as possible.

We, on the contrary, were racing to score points before the dialogue resumed. It was thought impossible to catch up with our rivals—Father had no illusions on that score—but he was trying to gain everything that our technology could provide.

At the time we didn't take the possibility of inspection seriously. It continued to be perceived as a kind of legal espionage enabling the United States to confirm its manifold superiority. In Father's opinion, such inspection would not move us away from war, but push us toward it. For the time being, if the Americans contemplated a nuclear strike they could only guess at the response. Their calculations were based on their own capabilities and of necessity exaggerated the potential of their adversary.

Once convinced of our weakness, they might not resist the temptation to deal with the Soviet Union before it gained in power. In Father's opinion, inspection would become effective only under conditions of disarmament, when the capabilities of the parties were equal.

On February 25, 1962, President Kennedy again called on the Soviet Union to stop testing.

In his reply of March 7, Father agreed only to a meeting of the U.S., Soviet, and British foreign ministers. It was to convene in less than a week, so there was no time to think of any serious preparation or development of new positions. The ministers met in Geneva with slightly refurbished documents used numerous times before. Gromyko brought with him a draft treaty for complete and universal disarmament under effective international inspection. No one, including the author himself, believed in the possibility of its adoption.

In response the Americans presented an ultimatum: either we accepted the inspection conditions, or in the last ten days of April they would begin atmospheric tests over islands in the Pacific Ocean. The uncompromising tone of this statement was a signal that tests would begin.

They resumed on April 26. Everything pointed to careful preparations having been made. Explosion followed explosion at intervals of two to three days. By June 10, a month and a half later, there had been seventeen.

By June 17 the number rose to twenty.

High-altitude explosions were the key feature of this series. In previous years atomic bombs had been exploded above ground and underground, on the ocean surface and underwater. Now it was the turn of space.

The possibility of explosions outside the atmosphere had been discussed for a long time. Now the Americans justified their actions as a necessary search for ways to fight the global missiles Father had threatened. However, no one had as yet launched global missiles, and one could only guess what they would be like. According to specialists, the purpose of an explosion in space was to disrupt radio communications and blind radars. It would also deprive both an adversary and oneself of the ability to relay commands to military devices orbiting the earth, and not to them only.

FATHER VISITS THE NORTHERN FLEET

Father arrived in Murmansk on July 19. In advance of the naval exercises, he wanted to visit fishermen, look the city over, and learn about how people lived in the north. His reception proceeded with pomp. By that time a certain ritual had developed, one that largely transformed a working trip into a ceremonial procession. Father frowned, but couldn't summon up the will to act forcefully to put a stop to all the adulation.

While the ceremonial speeches were being delivered in Murmansk, preparations were being completed in Severomorsk. Navy vessels took their assigned positions.

The Navy intended to show off everything that it had achieved in the seven years since it was announced that the submarine fleet would become its principal strike force.

Father was greeted by Admiral Kasatonov, the new commander of the Northern Fleet, who by chance was also the officer who had demonstrated the sailors' achievements in 1959 in Sevastopol.

The schedule for the demonstration had acquired its own traditions over the previous years; first a display of the mockups of weapons on land, then a demonstration of their capabilities in action.

A staggering array of weapons was on display in the Fleet warehouses, now transformed into exhibit halls.

One structure held a display of ballistic missiles, from the first, with its modest firing range of 150 kilometers, to the latest, launched underwater to a distance of many hundreds of kilometers. Here Viktor Petrovich Makeyev was in charge.

Chelomei ruled over the next exhibit hall, which held cruise missiles. His missiles were installed on submarines and cruisers and in shore batteries, and were intended for firing on coastal installations and at ships. He had recently adapted them for motor launches as well.

Next door were Mikoyan's Kometas and Bereznyak's P-15s. Both were soon to become familiar with the seas around Cuba.

Further on were torpedoes, depth charges, and numerous other weapons. All, or almost all, were designed so that they might be fitted with nuclear warheads. Virtually every speaker, whose reports had been approved by the Supreme Command and repeatedly rehearsed, talked about the different degree of destructive power of "his" type of weapon armed with the "old" warhead, as compared to the "new" nuclear warhead proposed for tests. They were all in favor of carrying out one more series of explosions and were only waiting for Father's signature. He added it without discussion. That evening the document went to Moscow and on July 22 all newspapers published the Soviet government decision.

The Americans carried out their tests in response to Soviet tests, and we in response to theirs.

There, in the North, Father saw nuclear-powered submarines with his own eyes for the first time. Early models were equipped with torpedoes and had just begun to explore the hitherto almost inaccessible seas bordering the United States. The Navy had also acquired its first missile-equipped submarines. However, none could compare with the U.S. "Patrick Henry" type submarine, which we viewed with envy. They carried sixteen missiles, while Makeyev had managed to squeeze in only three. But it was only the beginning. Long-range submarines were already under construction, and Makeyev promised to improve their firing range.

An especially pleasant ceremony brought the first day to an end. Government awards were presented to the nuclear submarine crews who had made the first long-distance voyage under the northern ocean's polar ice without surfacing in the history of our Navy. Father presented the stars of Hero of the Soviet Union to Rear Admiral Aleksandr Ivanovich Petelin, commander of the submarine flotilla, and to the hero of the day, Captain Second Grade (U.S. Navy equivalent is Commander—Trans.) Lev Mikhailovich Zhiltsov, the submarine commander who had brought his boat to U.S. shores undetected by foreign eyes.

On the morning of July 21, Father, Kozlov, Brezhnev, Kirilenko, and Ustinov, accompanied by Minister of Defense Marshal Malinovsky and Admiral Gorshkov, the Navy's commander in chief, came on board the cruiser *Admiral Ushakov*, flagship of the Northern Fleet, to the sounds of an orchestra. After the welcoming ceremony was over, the other participants in the demonstration, both civilian and military, followed in single file. The broad deck of the cruiser filled with a diverse crowd and began to look something like a cruise ship. However, the weather was severely northern. Although it was July, the air was crisply invigorating and autumnal. When the sun was hidden behind a cloud, it became positively cold. The military had on overcoats and foresighted civilians wore topcoats. Less prudent passengers, who had pinned their hopes on the calendar, were issued pea jackets from the ship's stores.

Eight years had gone by since Father's Pacific voyage on the cruiser *Mikhail Kalinin*. Since then, there had been a striking change in the Navy. Gone were the attacks by torpedo boats, sneaking up to the very side of the flagship under a smoke screen. Gone also was the rapid fire from destroyers driving them off.

A different war was on display. An enemy located at a vast distance over the horizon had to be defeated. After the cruiser sailed into the open sea, one of the first Soviet nuclear submarines came alongside and then submerged. The submarine, with three ballistic missiles on board, moved to its firing position farther off, to the left of the cruiser's course. It was to demonstrate the latest achievement—the underwater launch of a ballistic missile. Those present clustered at one side of the deck, some indifferent and others feeling the tension and identifying with the crew.

Finally a missile, looking like a miniature from that distance, leaped from the water far to the right of where people were looking. At first it tilted a little to one side. Everyone froze. Then the engine let out a roar, the missile leveled off and a few dozen seconds later only a small bright star was visible high up in the sky.

Viktor Petrovich Makeyev received congratulations. Underwater launches, which only recently had seemed a fantasy, were now a reality. The submarine had truly become an underwater weapon.

I won't try to describe the numerous torpedoes, with both conventional and nuclear warheads, and the helicopters and planes designed to attack submarines. The day was filled with events. There was one attack exercise after another.

As the feverish activity continued, the cruiser gradually skirted the Kola Peninsula and approached the mouth of the White Sea. On the way it stopped briefly at various naval bases and other places along the coast. The day's schedule called for the guests to make such visits.

Then it was time for cruise missiles. The destroyer *Grozny* (whose rank was later upgraded from destroyer to cruiser) began to circle the flagship cruiser at high speed. Instead of the traditional cannon, it had cumbersome four-tube cruise missile launchers towering over its prow and stern.

The *Grozny* was one of a series of new strike ships on which traditional high-caliber artillery had been replaced by Chelomei's cruise missiles, the P-35, which could sink enemy ships at the previously unimaginable distance of 250 kilometers (160 miles).

The *Grozny* reduced speed and allowed the heavyweight flagship to catch up. The tubes rotated smoothly across the ship's side and the bulging covers of the gigantic launch containers opened noiselessly. No crew members were visible. There was first a low penetrating whistle as the missile's engine began to warm up, which developed into a steady roar. The sound grew until it was almost unbearable. With an even louder roar, the powder boosters ejected a graceful missile from its tube. The missile's small wings unfolded instantaneously, too quickly to be seen. Everything was over in a few seconds, and the missile disappeared over the horizon.

The announcer's voice had a ring of triumph as he said: "The target is destroyed."

Father congratulated Vladimir Nikolayevich. The latter decided to take advantage of this favorable opportunity to raise an issue that was troubling him. The problem was that initially a large number of such ships were going to be built. But viewpoints had changed. Cruisers and destroyers were no longer "fashionable." Instead of the dozens of ships planned earlier, the decision had been made to stop with the four already under construction.

Addressing himself to Father alone, Chelomei began describing the advantages of the missile. He spoke of how, with its appearance, the surface fleet was undergoing a qualitative change. Firing range had increased and there were very few misses. New destroyers were a formidable threat, and it was not sensible to limit their number.

Father liked the missile. Still, he was in no hurry to agree with the general designer's conclusions.

He asked: "Isn't it possible to put this missile on submarines?"

I understood from his tone of voice that he would not be deciding in favor of destroyers.

Chelomei replied that missiles for submarines had specific design features. They were already in existence and would be shown in action about an hour later.

Father nodded with satisfaction. He asked: "How can your *Grozny* defend itself against air attack? It's not unsinkable, is it?"

Now his attitude was obvious to everyone. Chelomei replied that the destroyer had antiaircraft missiles and antiaircraft guns, but of course they didn't guarantee complete invulnerability.

"We're not going to waste money," Father said in conclusion. "For us such surface ships are an unacceptable luxury. Let's stick to submarines, as we decided."

Mounting his favorite hobbyhorse, Father began a long and detailed recital of the advantages that a submarine fleet had over a surface fleet for the Soviet Union, a land power. These arguments had died down long before. Everyone knew them by heart, but no one was bold enough to interrupt Father. Finally, coming to the end, he snapped: "We'll limit ourselves to four destroyers, one for each of the four fleets."

Meanwhile, it was almost time for the next launch. Chelomei invited Father to the cruiser's side. In a few minutes the submarine was going to execute the underwater launch of a cruise missile, the "Amethyst." Not even the Americans had been able to do that. Everything went smoothly. Almost without disturbing the water's surface, a short-winged missile broke from the depths and sped off with a deep roar.

Toward evening on July 22 the cruiser tied up at a berth in the port of Arkhangelsk. The following day, Father met with the provincial committee and then continued to familiarize himself with new weapons. There was talk of future plans. Drawings and mockups of cruise and ballistic missiles, in various designs and for various purposes, covered tables and display panels made for this special occasion and located in the staff quarters of one of the naval units.

A separate section was devoted to the military use of space: intelligence, navigation, communications. At the time these seemed like exotic novelties.

There the group examined a mockup of one of Chelomei's satellites, which carried a powerful radar for observing ships on the ocean surface. Because of its function, the satellite required an unusually large amount of power. Solar batteries were not powerful enough. It was decided to install a portable nuclear reactor. Until then such devices had not left the earth.

The question of security was of particular concern. When its period of service expired, the satellite was supposed to burn up in the atmosphere. Specialists claimed that nothing tragic would happen, but Chelomei didn't want to take the risk. He decided that the spent reactor should be separated from the rest of the satellite and lifted to a higher orbit by means of a solid-fuel rocket. It would then rotate the earth in an orbital dumping ground until our descendants figured out what to do with their unpleasant inheritance.

This decision suited everyone. However, their satisfaction proved to be premature. The equipment was prone to failure and one time it played a trick. During tests of a modification of the satellite the command did not go through and the reactor failed to separate. A backup emergency channel didn't function either, and the satellite soon made no response whatsoever to hysterical calls from earth. There was a certain amount of panic in Moscow and an endless series of conferences, some searching for culprits, others insisting that the developers produce a document guaranteeing security. As if a document could shield anybody.

The need to inform the world about what had happened made people especially nervous. Specialists could not predict where the uninvited guest might fall, and what the consequences might be.

The reactor's chief designer, Mikhail Makarovich Bondaryuk, refrained from comment. Finally, under pressure from the Central Committee, Bondaryuk wrote that a nuclear explosion was ruled out, but that he would not presume to predict other consequences. In a postscript at the very end of the document, he admitted laconically that if the shielding was not destroyed, an extremely low-grade thermal explosion, no more than five kilotons, was possible. However, the likelihood of such an explosion was virtually nil.

People in the Central Committee tore their hair and demanded that the postscript be withdrawn, but the chief designer held his ground, saying: you asked for my opinion. I described all the theoretical possibilities. You decide yourselves whether to make it public or not. They decided not to publish it.

Days of anxious waiting ensued. With each rotation the satellite dropped lower. At any moment it would be caught by the atmosphere and come tumbling to earth. There was a glimmer of hope that it would land in the ocean and the pieces disappear under the water. But no such luck. The satellite disintegrated over Canada, and its fragments scattered like rain over the North American tundra. Fortunately there was no explosion. No one was hurt.

But all this lay ahead. Meanwhile, arguments were raging about what type of reactor should be installed. It should combine reliability and minimal weight.

Academician Aleksandrov favored a thermal reactor, saying it was more reliable. Corresponding Member Aleksandr Ilyich Leypunsky considered Aleksandrov's arguments laughable. In his opinion, a fast-neutron reactor must be placed on the satellite. They couldn't reach an agreement either at their ministry or with the military.

The very experienced Aleksandrov chose Father as arbiter. At the conclusion of the display officer's report, when Father was already about to walk on, Aleksandrov intervened and began to describe the advantages of the thermal variant. Father listened in some surprise, but did not interrupt him. He regarded Aleksandrov with tremendous respect as one of the fathers of nuclear-powered vessels, both submarines and surface ships.

Aleksandrov's remarks were confusing and sometimes slipped into technical details intelligible only to the specialist.

"Comrade Aleksandrov, you want me to decide what kind of reactor to install? But what are you paid for?" said Father with a good-natured smile. "Don't tell me unnecessary things. You decide yourself, you be responsible, and don't try to make me your accomplice."

Father leaned forward and clapped the tall academician a little below the shoulder, which was as high as he could reach, and drew him toward the mockup of the next satellite.

People's feet always tire more quickly in museums and at exhibits. Father was very tired after visiting the exhibits. He tried to look cheerful and hide it, but finally gave in. Captain First Grade (U.S. Navy equivalent, Captain) Konstantin Konstantinovich Frants, one of the theorists of naval strategy in the space age, was giving a report on building a global intelligence system. Father listened attentively. The display seemed to be the last one in that hall. When Frants concluded his remarks, Father didn't move on but, looking around, inquired (or requested, it wasn't quite clear): "You wouldn't have a chair?"

Someone brought a chair from the next room and put it down in front of Father. He was about to sit down when he looked around at the "suite" crowding around behind him and the specialists standing in front of the displays, and suddenly felt uncomfortable. Father described a circle with his hand: "For everyone, everyone."

And added, quite as if he were at home: "Let's sit down for a bit and rest. My feet won't hold me up any longer."

Chairs were brought and the confusion usual on such occasions quickly subsided. A silence ensued. No one felt entitled to break the silence in Father's presence.

"You have produced a great number of unusual things," he began, glancing at one person after another. "It's simply a marvel. Only God forbid that we ever have to use them."

Father fell silent and seemed deep in thought. Then he aroused himself and began to talk about his meeting with Kennedy in Vienna the previous year.

Father had several such stories about events that had produced an especially strong impression on him and were forever engraved in his memory.

One of them concerned the circumstances preceding the encirclement of our forces near Kharkov, in the spring of 1942. At the time Father was a member of the Front Military Council. The hopelessness and feeling of personal impotence, the impossibility of influencing the headlong movement of events, all stayed in his memory down to the slightest detail. Time and again he returned to the telephone calls to Stalin, who didn't want to listen to him or to Marshal Timoshenko. They pleaded with him to stop the advance of the troops, an advance that had become disastrous, and to withdraw them to their original positions before the impending German blow. Probably this move would not have succeeded, but at least they could have tried. The Germans began their encirclement of the Soviet armies on the following morning. A feeling of guilt for those wasted lives remained in Father's heart forever.

Father repeatedly returned to the subject of Stalin's death. In those days no one knew what path the country would take, how the destinies of those in the narrow circle around the tyrant would unfold. No one doubted one thing: a fight could not be avoided.

The story of Beria's arrest was still another frequent theme.

Now a new chapter was added: the meeting with President Kennedy in Vienna.

Father's description in Arkhangelsk has faded from my memory in the mass of similar ones heard in other places. But I was recently reminded of its content by a leading designer from our bureau, Mark Gurevich, who was in charge of the mockup of one of our intelligence satellites.

A man of the utmost subtlety and intelligence, he remembered not only the words, but even the intonation of the speaker. Father began his account with an evaluation of the approach of various world leaders to the problems of war and peace. Every one of them—Eisenhower and de Gaulle, Eden and Guy Mollet, Nasser and Mao Zedong—had his own views and peculiarities, but in Father's opinion they all emerged from the Cold War and now could no longer rid themselves of ossified stereotypes. "To believe in the reality of life without war you have to look at the world on another plane, in a new way," Father pontificated. "That is very difficult."

Father fell silent for a moment. The room was quiet. He continued: "So it was all the more pleasant for me to talk with the new American president. Kennedy looks at the world in a different way; you feel that he really wants to find a way out of this impasse."

Father added at once that there was a great deal which John Kennedy didn't understand, some things because of inadequate political experience and some things because of the narrowness of his class thinking. The first could easily be corrected; experience would come with time, but the second we would have to take into account, since there was nothing we could do about it. As an example he gave the president's position when he spoke in Vienna against wars of liberation by enslaved peoples.

"Nothing can be done about it, he's a representative of his class," Father repeated, with a smile. "But that's not important; the main thing is that he wants peace. It's possible to work with him. He holds American policy firmly in his hands."

The room fell silent once more.

What was Father thinking? Where had he gone? Who knows? As if regaining consciousness, he suddenly said quietly: "Kennedy is a man born to be president. He has everything: culture, the ability to carry on negotiations, a firm understanding of his goals, and a sober evaluation of his opponent's intentions."

He paused a little longer and concluded unexpectedly: "Only he's too good for the Americans. They'll get rid of him."

Father didn't wait for a reaction. It seemed as if he didn't even notice his listeners. A few moments went by and Father rose with deliberation—the rest period was over. Everyone else started to get up too, chairs scraping the floor.

"Let's go on. What else do you have for us?" Father turned to Gorshkov, speaking in an entirely different tone. The entire group moved on.

The following day Father returned to Moscow.

FAREWELL TO A RESPECTED ADVERSARY

A day later, on July 25, Father received the U.S. ambassador, Llewellyn Thompson, for a farewell call. Father was rather sorry that Thompson was leaving Moscow. He was used to him, respected his intellect, his perspicacity, self-possession, and above all his effort to get at the essence of what was going on in our country and to find solutions mutually acceptable to our countries. Also important were purely human feelings. Father had sincerely come to like not only the ambassador, but his affable and friendly wife Jane.

On the other hand, Father didn't hide his satisfaction at Thompson's new appointment. He was to deal with questions relating to Russia in the Kennedy administration. A person who knew our life, not by hearsay, but by having experienced the Moscow "kitchen," a person who knew almost everything and everybody, would be constantly by the president's side.

Father had already warned Mama that he was inviting the ambassador with his family to have a farewell dinner at the dacha. Not even the representatives of friendly countries had been granted such a sign of exceptional hospitality.

The day of the farewell visit coincided with the start of the mass departure of our ships with military cargoes to Cuba.

The atmosphere at the dacha was relaxed, almost familylike. The ambassador's two daughters presented their drawings to "grandfather," just like children in every country.

No serious conversation went on at the table. Father reminisced about his visit to the United States, talked about the American people's hospitality and openness, and told of his meeting with President Kennedy in Vienna. However, he didn't fail to complain that his interlocutor did not understand the inevitability of change in the world and instead was trying to "preserve" the old order, but no one has ever succeeded in doing that.

They talked a little about the ambassador's new appointment. After lunch Father and Thompson went for a walk, while Mama remained with Jane on the verandah, where they carried on their own conversation.

The farewell was friendly, I would even say warm. Father joked that the president had made a good choice. The ambassador politely thanked him for his hospitality.

Jane Thompson was among those who sent condolences upon Father's death in 1971.

A ROYAL VISIT

At the beginning of August Father prepared to go to the Crimea on vacation. The king of Afghanistan, Mohammed Zakhir, promised to meet him there. The king usually went to Italy or the Cote d'Azur on holiday, but Father had so praised the charms of the Black Sea and the Crimean beaches that it had simply become awkward to ignore the invitation.

Father considered the king's arrival to be his personal victory. Strengthening ties of friendship with the kingdom had been a strategic goal for a long time. The complex and mountainous region along the border needed tranquillity. To reinforce the border and maintain troops there would cost the Soviet Union billions of rubles. Father undertook his first attempt to establish mutual understanding with Mohammed Zakhir as early as the end of 1954, when he and Bulganin stopped in Kabul on the way home from India. The king received them with fitting honors, but did not agree to a rapprochement, as he was rather afraid of communists. Father described how the king rejected all, even the most neutral, proposals to provide assistance, specifically for building a bread factory and hospital. Other countries accepted gifts with gratitude, but in Afghanistan an expression of thanks was followed by a polite refusal.

It took years of diplomatic persistence before the king believed in our friendly disposition and the sincerity of our intentions, and finally stopped being afraid of some trick or even an invasion from the north.

By 1962 I would call our relations with Afghanistan friendly. The king trusted us to such an extent that he agreed to the construction of a road from Kabul to the border separating our countries. He didn't even object to a cautious probe about the possibility of building a branch line from the main road to the Iranian border. If the main branch served purely trade purposes and to supply the city with commodities from the Soviet Union, then the possibility of an outlet to the Iranian border would ensure flexibility in case of military conflict. Father viewed construction of the road as a supreme manifestation of intergovernmental trust, since it could easily be transformed from a trade route to a strategic line of communication.

That summer Father devoted a great deal of effort to convince our neighbors of our peaceful intentions. He spent all his free time with the king. They traveled into the mountains, admired the deer in the Crimean nature preserve, and toured the entire southern coast. They met almost daily. They swam together and often dined in the family circle. The king came to the dacha with his heir, leaving the women of his family at home.

It seemed that everything was going well. We could stop worrying about our southern border.

TESTING AND ANDREI SAKHAROV

It had finally been possible to reach an agreement in Geneva. Father retreated—he realized that he would not succeed in persuading the United States to agree to a complete cessation of tests. In his opinion, it was not a matter of inspection. The world was simply not ready for such a decision. It was not possible to stop so abruptly.

On August 30 President Kennedy announced during a press conference at the White House that he was prepared to stop all nuclear weapons tests, except for underground tests, on January 1, 1963. Of course, on the basis of reciprocity with the Soviet Union.

On September 3 our representative in Geneva, Vasily Vasilyevich Kuznetsov, received instructions to agree to a ban on three types of tests.

At the same time Yefim Pavlovich Slavsky was ordered to make preparations to work under the new conditions. To dig into the ground.

In the days remaining before the start of the new year both sides tried to outdo each other, since there would be no more such opportunities. The roar of explosions at Novaya Zemlya, Semipalatinsk, and the Pacific islands was almost constant.

The only person upset by the decision to hold a new series of tests was Andrei Dmitriyevich Sakharov. Again he left no stone unturned; he warned, he demanded, but everyone took his protests as capricious, as the whims of a theoretician—none of whom, it was said, is wholly of this world.

After the previous year's July clash with Father in the Oval Hall of the Kremlin, Sakharov understood that the tests would not stop. But this time he had a specific reason to be concerned. Another explosion on Novaya Zemlya seemed pointless to him. In his opinion, he stood alone—the other specialists had expressed themselves "in favor."

Desperate, Sakharov decided to call Father. That turned out to be difficult. At the time Father was making a trip through the Central Asian republics, without staying long in any one place. From September 26 to September 30 his route lay through Turkmenia: Ashkhabad, Mary, Nebit-Dag.

Sakharov managed to catch Father in Ashkhabad. When his aide reported who was calling and asked what to reply, Father guessed what the subject was. He remembered the previous year's argument, which had left an unpleasant trace in his mind. Like most normal people, Father didn't like unpleasant conversations and tried to avoid them whenever possible. In this case, any explanation seemed pointless. The government, after weighing all the factors, had made a decision. Even the other scientists had been in favor of the test. Only Sakharov was again opposed.

He felt a momentary desire not to take the phone; his aide could find some plausible excuse. But Father rejected the cowardly thought. After last year's spat, his refusal to talk would acquire special significance. Sakharov could not be treated that way. He had to be listened to, and if he were wrong, then there must be an attempt to explain, to persuade, to argue, finally.

Of course, I cannot reproduce the conversation. Father was in Ashkhabad and I was in Moscow. I only remember what he said about it. He did not accept Sakharov's conclusions, which seemed to him to be naive.

Sakharov for his part didn't understand Father. How could momentary advantages, military or political, be more important than the fate of all mankind?

Father tried to persuade Sakharov that he was exaggerating the danger of the explosion, that all his colleagues, no less professional than he, guaranteed success and reasonable safety. The argument reached a dead end, and Father decided to resort to guile. He proposed that Sakharov lay out his conclusions to Kozlov—let him look into it. He would assign that to Kozlov. The conversation ended, leaving both men dissatisfied.

Father immediately asked to be connected with Slavsky. The latter once again assured him that the test was necessary and that everything had been checked and rechecked. Sakharov was just panicking.

Slavsky proposed moving up the date of the explosion. With everything accomplished, there would be nothing to argue about. Father agreed.

When Sakharov knocked at the designated doors in Moscow, a subject for argument really no longer existed; it had vaporized along with the metal tower.

Father didn't brush aside his disagreements with Sakharov. He did not agree with him, but he didn't consign him to the camp of his opponents either. Father believed that he himself was right in a political sense, and he forgave the scientist's "naive delusion." Neither one changed his mind. During those far-off years when he was in power, Father often talked about his conflicts with Sakharov. And in retirement, when both men fell into the ranks of dissidents, Father did not change his evaluation of the events of previous years.

I don't think that Sakharov and Father could have ever reached an agreement. They belonged to different times and judged the same events in different ways. In one way they were alike. Each in his own fashion tried sincerely to find the path that would deliver mankind from destruction, that would lead to justice and a better life.

According to established custom, extensive lists for awards were drawn up after the tests against which Sakharov had protested so vehemently. The bureaucrats did not include Sakharov's name. Everyone knew about his sharp clashes with Father.

Father was outraged.

"You have to talk with people like Sakharov, persuade them, not fight them," he repeated the words that I had heard before.

Sakharov was awarded his third star as a Hero of Socialist Labor.

Soon after Father's telephone conversation with Sakharov and the test of the powerful warhead, Slavsky again brought up the subject of exploding a hundred-megaton warhead. This time Father refused unequivocally: there was no place on earth where that could be done without harm. The superpowerful warhead would be retained solely as a means of political pressure.

THE DEFENSE OF CUBA: THE BUILDUP

When Ambassador Thompson arrived in the United States, nothing pointed to a new outbreak of tension. A long-awaited decree transferring some units of servicemen into the reserves was published in the Soviet Union.

The muted dispute over Berlin had not ended, only temporarily subsided. It flared up in connection with the anniversary of the establishment of the border line, which by now had acquired an increasingly solid material embodiment in the form of a wall of reinforced concrete blocks.

The Soviet government continued its old habit of pressuring the West, brandishing the threat of a separate peace treaty with the GDR. From time to time slogans were accompanied by demonstrative acts. In August the USSR announced the abolition of the commandant's office in Berlin. On August 28 the Soviet government informed the U.N. secretary-general that it intended to sign a peace treaty with the GDR in the immediate future. However, the date for concluding the agreement was prudently not indicated.

When I asked if Berlin wouldn't interfere with what was planned in Cuba, Father only smiled enigmatically and didn't reply. But to be honest, by then I was very tired of hearing about the fuss over a free city and all the problems associated with it, and I didn't take them too seriously.

As became clear later, the Berlin splash was intended by Father as a diversion. Washington had begun focusing its attention too intently on Cuba. His craftiness worked. Through already tested private channels, the Americans sent a request not to aggravate the situation in Europe until the election was over. Father agreed with alacrity—all right, let it be after the election.

In a word, the world continued on its usual course.

The stream of ships heading for Cuba expanded with every passing day. The freighters under foreign flags we had chartered usually docked in Havana and other major ports. They carried foodstuffs, equipment, fuel, and other ordinary cargoes. Ships under the Soviet flag tried to disappear into the night as they approached the Cuban coast. They didn't tie up at crowded docks, but at remote and secluded moorings in specially selected Cuban ports: Casilda, Mariel, Cabanas, Cienfuegos, Santiago de Cuba, and others.

These places were not easy to reach overland. All approaches were guarded by people who were armed, wore civilian clothes, and did not speak Spanish. Unloading went on at night, and was also carried out by foreigners in mufti.

All kinds of things were brought by those ships. Out of the holds, through special gates in the sides, crawled tanks with barrels protruding like elephant trunks, strangely shaped trucks, armored personnel carriers. Those same civilians drove them skillfully off the ships.

The many-wheeled "forty-wheelers," with strange-looking semicircular gun turrets on their backs, attracted particular attention from specialists, who immediately recognized them as launchers for the Lunas, tactical battlefield missiles. The missiles themselves, in their crates painted a dirty green color, were unloaded nearby. Special preparations were made for the arrival of nuclear warheads.

The Lunas were intended for defense of ballistic missile launch positions. Their mission was to defeat a possible landing force by using conventional explosives. Special, i.e., nuclear, warheads were to be mounted only in an extremity, or if the Americans were the first to use nuclear weapons. It is ever so. Orders always look feasible on paper. But in the heat of battle a commander knows only one order: "Hold out to the end," and more often than not he has to make his decisions about how to do that.

However, no one was thinking about that at the time. The Lunas rumbled toward their destinations, designated by marks on a map. Cranes unloaded a multitude of crates in various sizes and shapes, which were quickly moved to temporary storage sites nearby. From there lines of ZILs, GAZ, and MAZ trucks spread out over the entire island, like columns of ants.

Small planes, similar to the MIGs already familiar on the island but without cockpits, were removed from boxes at prearranged points along the coast. Some were mounted on catapults, transported to the coast, and then camouflaged, so that shore defense missile batteries were now prepared to repel an invasion from the sea. Others were taken to the island's interior. If the Lunas were able to fire at a target a couple of dozen kilometers away, these combat cruise missiles—which was what this modification of the pilotless MIG was called—could hit a target almost 180 kilometers (112.5 miles) away, all the way to the Florida coast. As with the Lunas, they could be equipped with two types of warheads, ordinary and special.

Strange-looking Komar patrol boats entered Cuban ports during the night. Instead of the torpedo gear usually mounted on the stern, they had some kind of humpbacked small sheds resembling chicken coops. The launches anchored far from curious eyes. Only those especially entrusted with the secret knew that these small structures contained miniature cruise missiles capable of sinking a warship armed with the most powerful cannons from a distance of several tens of kilometers. Meanwhile, the launchers themselves were invulnerable to the adversary's artillery. If its luck held and it was not attacked from the air, such a patrol boat could even confront an aircraft carrier. The Cubans were especially pleased with these small boats, which made them a match, as it were, for their mighty neighbor.

Special measures were taken to protect against air attack. If the Americans decided to attack, they would first of all launch a bomb strike against the missiles. Antiaircraft batteries were set up around the entire perimeter of Cuba, and were especially close together on the side facing the United States.

Pale young men, their bodies not yet tanned by the tropical sun, dressed in lightweight sport shirts and blue pants, energetically dug emplacements, sometimes with the help of "Belarus" excavators, but mostly with shovels, as we usually do. The launchers were driven into the emplacements and camouflaged with nets, according to regulations.

The antiaircraft complexes, just like the ballistic missiles that were on their way, would be manned solely by Soviet servicemen and were subordinate only to Soviet command.

The antiaircraft missiles were placed in a line along the coast, like a fence. Only on the western end of the island, across from Guantanamo, did they have to be installed in depth. The U.S. base was considered the most likely source of attack.

Antiaircraft guns were transferred to the Cuban army. They would have to defend the island against low-flying aircraft, primarily obsolete ones, like the B-26. It would be impossible to violate the Republic's airspace without encountering the barrels of antiaircraft batteries jutting into the air. Soviet instructors were exhausted after moving from one position to another, preparing the weapons for action and teaching the Cubans how to operate them.

Planes supplemented and reinforced land defenses. Five air bases, or more precisely, simple airports, were located at approximately equal intervals along the entire length of the island. Three were close to the island's center, to protect Havana against possible air attack and, most important, to protect launch positions of ballistic missiles, which were invulnerable in the air but completely defenseless on the ground.

Supersonic MIG-21 fighters were assembled there after being delivered in crates. Their mission was to intercept the adversary's planes as they attacked.

IL-28s were stationed at the two outer airfields, on the island's western and eastern extremities. They were not meant to fly beyond the zone covered by their antiaircraft defense, since it was feared that they would become easy prey to the adversary's fighters. By flying along the coastline, they could carry out patrols effectively and if necessary attack any landing party that might be discovered.

These resources were intended to ensure that the ballistic missiles were invulnerable. There were many missiles: eighty combat cruise missiles, almost one hundred and fifty 75s, and thirty-four Sopkas. In addition, there were nine Lunas. All these missiles could be armed with nuclear warheads. This arsenal of weapons was supplemented by forty MIG-21s and forty-two IL-28s. Twelve Komar patrol boats, each with two P-15 homing missiles on board, could offer serious resistance to any landing party.

Ballistic missiles. They were the center of all plans; the whole grandiose operation was carried out because of them. Most shipments went to places where they would be installed: San Cristobal and Guanajay at Cuba's western end, and Sagua la Grande and Remedios closer to the island's center. A great deal of preparation was necessary before the missiles arrived: quarters found for the troops, of whom there were many, launch installations equipped—everything that is meant by the all-inclusive phrase, "organization of defense." These were the places where tanks and artillery were concentrated and defense lines for infantry units were drawn. In the event of a clash, the missiles must not fall into the adversary's hands.

All preparations were made in close cooperation with the Cubans. Fidel Castro took an interest in the most minute details of the operation. Any flaws, inevitable in such a large-scale operation, were corrected immediately.

All the threads involved in operational control over the project were joined together in Soviet military headquarters in Cuba, in the hands of General Pliyev. He looked rejuvenated, as he recalled former years and military operations. Just as then, you had to hurry everywhere, check everything, keep an eye on the entire operation. Almost every evening, and sometimes several times a day, he called Fidel to give him the latest news. Father was simply delighted with Pliyev.

The Americans didn't exhibit any particular activity and took no countermeasures to our movements. Father attributed that—though only partially—to superb camouflaging. He didn't rule out the possibility that the Americans had decided that actions being carried out to strengthen Cuba's defense capabilities were not very important.

Father was increasingly confident that the operation would be completed successfully. Several times he praised Pliyev and commented that he deserved the rank of Marshal of the Soviet Union for his work. Father would have enjoyed carrying out his intention immediately, but decided to await the final step.

I asked him again how they intended to conceal signs of the missiles' presence from American eyes. This time Father simply waved me off.

In Washington McCone was trying to detect any signs that would confirm or allay his fears that there were ballistic missiles in Cuba. For that purpose a U-2 took a long flight over Cuba, including over San Cristobal, where Soviet sappers were already preparing to build the first R-12 launch positions. However, when the photographs were developed they didn't clarify the situation. There were no signs of ballistic missiles. On the other hand, the photographs revealed 75s in various parts of the island. Their launch positions were springing up like mushrooms after the rain. Analysts made still another discovery. Construction of launch positions for antiship cruise missiles was beginning on the Cuban coast facing Florida. Something was certainly going on in Cuba, but what?

It's hard to say what reports were reaching the CIA from its agents, who were undoubtedly present on the island. But ordinary letters sent by Cubans to their relatives who had emigrated to the United States contained quite enough information. Persistent rumors were spreading across Cuba about the arrival from the USSR of "strange Soviet weapons."

However, at that point the U.S. administration didn't attribute any special importance to this disturbing information. Apparently Kennedy couldn't imagine that the Soviet Union would dare to intrude its missiles into the Western hemisphere. And possibly he didn't even consider them such a threat to his country's security.

However that may be, on September 5 the president, replying to questions from journalists, said that the United States did not possess any information on the presence in Cuba of surface-to-surface missiles or of any other offensive weapons.

This statement was preceded by a meeting between the president's brother, Robert Kennedy, and the Soviet ambassador, Anatoly Dobrynin. I have already mentioned that Father and Kennedy had made use of trusted individuals, Mikhail Kharlamov and Pierre Salinger, to exchange especially urgent and delicate messages during the Berlin crisis.

The two leaders decided that Robert Kennedy and Dobrynin would meet unofficially, to set up a new channel of communication. That would bypass the State Department bureaucracy, which, in Father's words, the president didn't particularly trust. And if necessary, Dobrynin could contact Father directly, skipping intermediate stages.

Robert Kennedy voiced his concern with the growing Soviet military activity in Cuba.

The ambassador replied readily that he knew nothing about it. In fact, he had not been told of the plan, which was entering its final phase. Dobrynin relayed to Robert Kennedy Father's assurances that no offensive weapons, in particular surface-to-surface missiles, were based in Cuba.

As a result of the squabble with Eisenhower over the U-2, Father understood that deceit was a customary tool in the arsenal of U.S. politics. He now decided to make use of the lesson he had been taught.

Kennedy was satisfied with the clarification from Moscow. Father didn't display any special uneasiness either; everything was proceeding according to plan. At the end of August he left for the Crimea, and from there to Pitsunda to make the most of his remaining vacation, which had been interrupted when he went to greet the latest returning cosmonauts, Andrian Nikolayev and Pavel Popovich. His departure from Moscow coincided with Kennedy's press briefing in Washington. It seemed as if both leaders had agreed to maintain a calm atmosphere.

Furthermore, a new U-2 flight on September 5 had not made any sensational finds. It surveyed areas around Sagua la Grande, where agents had reported that some kind of construction was in progress, but nothing suspicious was discovered. The photographs did show the first MIG-21s, but that was not unexpected. The Cubans had long been flying MIG-15s and MIG-17s. Then MIG-19s had appeared. Now it was the MIG-21s' turn.

Meanwhile Che Guevara was negotiating with Malinovsky. He had flown to Moscow on August 26 carrying the text, approved by Fidel Castro, of a secret treaty on the deployment of missiles in Cuba. On August 30 he met with Father in the Crimea. The Cubans brought a proposal from Castro that an announcement about the missile deployment be made immediately. They thought this would enhance the prestige of the agreement and improve Cuba's standing in the eyes of the world community as well. Who would dare to interfere with the conclusion of a treaty between two sovereign states?

Father only smiled in response. He thought Castro's idea was naive, to say the least. He began to explain to Che that a right was a right, but power was power. And at present power lay with the United States. Only when the missiles were in position, and no sooner, would Cuba be able to talk with its neighbor on equal terms.

But if the Americans learned of what we planned, they would find a thousand ways to prevent it from being carried out. What good would it do then to refer to international law and sovereignty?

The treaty signing was put off until the end of the year, to November. Meanwhile they decided to be guided by the plan initialed by Malinovsky and Che Guevara. The absence of formal signatures had no effect whatsoever on practical implementation of the operation. Father and Fidel Castro trusted each other's word.

Plans called for holding the signing ceremony of the agreement in Cuba. Father wanted very much to visit the island—not so much to pique the Americans, although that desire existed, as to see with his own eyes what was going on in the first country in the Western hemisphere to choose socialism. A great deal depended on its successes, or failures, since the other peoples of Latin America would begin to compare themselves with Cuba. They would look toward Cuba as they chose a road to the future. In Father's opinion, not everything was going the way it should. Castro, absorbed in the revolutionary struggle, was not paying enough attention to developing the national economy. That really bothered Father. He planned to take a look around himself, and then speak frankly with Fidel.

But that was for the future. First, the missiles had to be installed. He would have to wait for November. Che Guevara bade a friendly farewell to Father and left for Havana.

THE DEFENSE OF CUBA: THE AMERICANS GROW SUSPICIOUS

Despite the reassuring official statement, disquiet grew in the United States. Aggressiveness toward Cuba increased at the same time.

On September 6 Dobrynin was visited by Theodore Sorensen, special assistant to the president. He dearly wanted to find out what was going on in Cuba. What was all the activity about? The ambassador didn't know any more than Sorensen and assured him that routine operations aimed at strengthening the Cuban defense capabilities were proceeding, in accordance with a long-term agreement reached some time before. He stressed that Soviet military assistance was of a purely defensive nature and that Cuba could in no way threaten its powerful neighbor. To reinforce his words, Dobrynin cited Father's message, which contained assurances that the Soviet Union would refrain from any actions "likely to complicate the international situation before elections to the Congress of the United States."

Despite Father's reassuring statement, Kennedy decided to make a warning gesture, and on September 7 he asked Congress to approve the call-up of 15,000 reservists. The action served, as in the case of Berlin, to demonstrate the gravity of the administration's intentions.

The Soviet Union reacted quickly. The text of a TASS statement written by the Foreign Ministry, with the headline "Put an End to the Policy of Provocation," was sent to Father in Pitsunda. Such a document could not be published without his approval. The paper spent several days en route and the statement was broadcast on the radio only on the evening of the eleventh. It appeared in newspapers on the morning of September 12. The statement both asserted that Soviet ships were bringing peaceful cargoes to Cuba and stressed that the United States had surrounded the USSR with its military bases and that our country was fully within its rights to carry out measures strengthening its defensive capability. In conclusion, it pointed out that an abnormal situation continued to exist around West Berlin.

Tension over Cuba continued to increase. Father began to get the impression that the United States was preparing public opinion for a possible landing on the island.

Decades later, at a meeting in Moscow devoted to the lessons of the Caribbean Crisis, former defense secretary Robert McNamara said that the Kennedy administration had no intention of invading Cuba, but that he thought measures carried out at the time gave the other side every reason to suppose that such a plan existed and was close to being implemented.

"In your place, I would have drawn exactly the same conclusion," added McNamara.

Participants in the discussion tried to find out whether, after the failure of the expedition at the Bay of Pigs, there was such a plan to land U.S. troops in Cuba. The former secretary of defense avoided a direct answer. He said that a good headquarters staff must have plans for every eventuality in life, and joked that he even had a draft contingency plan in case of war with France.

The decisive moment was arriving. The missiles were expected to arrive in Cuba any day. Of course, I didn't know the exact date. Nerves were stretched to the limit—God forbid the plan failed!

When the missiles did arrive, sometime in the middle of September, the number of guards during unloading was tripled. It seemed that not even a fly could escape notice. But you can't hide an eel in a sack. Long wooden crates and extremely long trailers are bound to attract attention. The conclusion would seem to be obvious.

But even then the CIA failed to discover the missiles. As is usually the case in such matters, everything was hanging by a thread—but it did not break.

CIA agents in Cuba reported: "We have seen Soviet missiles. Very close up. We could almost touch them."

An example: in the middle of the night of September 12, one of the spies noticed a long Soviet transporter with a load carefully wrapped in a tarpaulin leaving an area near the port of Havana (actually the port of Casilda) and heading for San Cristobal. He decided that the missiles had probably been delivered by the *Omsk*, which had docked at the island on September 8. Comparing the description of the R-12 in reference materials sent from the center, the agent had no doubt—this was it! The CIA knew everything about the R-12. Penkovsky had done his job well. The information reached Langley on September 21. The agent was absolutely right. The *Omsk* delivered the first six missiles to Cuba.

Another agent reported that the *Poltava* had arrived at the port of Mariel. He saw ballistic missiles, to all appearances again R-12s, being unloaded. Between September 15 and 17, at least eight long, narrow trailers went in that same direction, toward San Cristobal. He was also right—another eight missiles arrived on the *Poltava*.

Quite a few such reports, more or less credible, came in, if we are to believe declassified official U.S. documents.

However, who puts much faith in messages from intelligence agents? Their reports are, as a rule, the last thing taken into consideration. It is only years later, when all questions have been answered, that historians begin to construct suppositions about why a particular report—whether arriving in good time or at the last minute—attracted no attention in the Kremlin, at the White House, or on Downing Street.

When reminiscing about the war, and not only the war, Father said that such reports are disregarded except when they confirm what people already think or when they clarify some particular detail. And even then, they are treated with caution. There are always doubts: was the information leaked deliberately, was the agent turned, was he mistaken? That happened near Kharkov in 1942, when German pilots landed among our troops with maps revealing plans for an offensive, as well as in many other cases.

This time too the CIA decided that fear has big eyes—that what the agents thought were ballistic missiles were actually the far smaller 75s.

However, that didn't resolve the matter. The information had to be checked. For that U-2 photographs would be useful. But just at this point there was a new complication: a high-altitude U.S. spy plane was shot down over China by one of those Soviet 75s. Flights over Cuba had become dangerous. The next day participants at a meeting in McGeorge Bundy's office in the White House decided to act more cautiously. The U-2 would not fly back and forth in the sky over Cuba, as it should, but cut across the island from west to east, so that its stay in Cuban airspace was reduced to a minimum. In addition, they decided not to have it fly over the western tip of the island in order to avoid the greatest concentration of antiaircraft defenses. That area would be examined from beyond the limits of Cuban territorial waters. However, not much can be seen from that distance.

Meanwhile, the operation to install the missiles was proceeding according to plan. Construction of the launch platforms was nearing completion. The missiles themselves were temporarily concealed by camouflage netting. Everything seemed to have been taken into account. But is it possible to think of everything? The most important phase began, when days, hours, minutes, and of course, chance are decisive.

Which would happen first? Would the missiles be in place, or would the entire operation be discovered by the adversary?

Moscow sent still another reminder: "Pay special attention to the camouflage." Pliyev passed on the order: "Check the camouflage."

I waited impatiently for Father to return from Pitsunda.

Father returned from the Black Sea coast in the middle of September. He went straight from the airport to the Kremlin—not that his presence was urgently needed, but he had followed that routine lately in order to save time.

Only his luggage arrived home. We met that evening, and the moment we were alone, I besieged him with questions. Unlike me, Father was calm. He thought that everything was going according to plan, and there was nothing to worry about. Of course, the Americans were becoming suspicious and were searching, but they wouldn't find anything. Tension would peak in November, when the presence of the missiles would be made public. But even then, "they will make a fuss, make more of a fuss, and then agree," as he put it.

His words had a confident ring, but I was still left with a feeling of apprehension. I had learned from naval officers that submarines were deployed along the routes taken by our ships, and especially on the approaches to Cuba, in order to secure the operation. The ships would not be defenseless. This action struck me as meaningless. What could submarines actually do?

Father didn't stay in Moscow for long. After disposing of current business, he flew to Central Asia to see for himself how the cotton harvest was progressing.

The Americans continued to wonder what we were really shipping to Cuba. Pressure continued to grow from all directions. On September 20 the Senate adopted a resolution calling for the defense of the Western hemisphere from aggression originating in Cuba, including, if necessary, the overthrow of the Castro regime. The voting was virtually unanimous: eighty-six in favor, and only one against.

The following day Gromyko, speaking at the U.N., warned that any attack on Cuba would automatically mean war with the Soviet Union.

Nevertheless, the House of Representatives voted to support the Senate resolution by a vote of 384 to 7. The mood in the United States grew increasingly agitated. Whereas the previous year Americans had been talking about distant Berlin, now they were beginning to imagine that Russian tanks might suddenly appear on the streets of their cities.

It was no secret that a large number of the ships sailing to Cuba were foreign vessels chartered by the Soviet Union, and that some of them belonged to American allies. At first no one paid much attention to that fact. However, when the flow of shipping increased many times over, it became obvious to the CIA that the Soviet Merchant Marine had been given a task that it simply could not handle. The Americans began to view the participation of ships from other countries in supplying Cuba as a hostile act. They understood correctly that Soviet ships were carrying weapons, while the foreigners were carrying everything else.

A feverish search continued for an answer to the main and most important question: are they shipping missiles across the ocean? And if not, what are they shipping? How does the Soviet Union count on defending Cuba in view of the absolute U.S. control over the lines of air and sea communications?

A joint assessment of intelligence information titled "Military Deployments in Cuba," transmitted to the president on September 19, noted that Soviet political doctrine never envisaged the deployment of nuclear forces on foreign soil. Considering that, as well as the risk associated with carrying out such an action, intelligence officials thought that it was unlikely that missiles were being installed in Cuba.

Then what was on all those ships?

U.S. Navy planes were ordered to double their surveillance and to fly at the lowest possible altitude over all ships heading for Cuba. However, nothing was learned this way either. The move was not unexpected. The possibility had been discussed in Moscow as early as that summer. At the time Father expressly warned against placing anything on deck that even camouflaged might give away the operation. Who knew what instruments U.S. planes might be carrying?

However, exceptions had to be made. There was just no way to fit missile-firing patrol boats and IL-28s in the cargo holds. After lengthy discussions in the General Staff, it was decided to put them on deck in huge wooden crates lined with metal plates. But such ruses didn't help. Photo interpreters at the CIA, looking at photographs taken on September 28, quickly deduced that the crates cluttering the deck of the steamship *Kasimov* contained IL-28s.

The U-2 flight scheduled for September 10 and then hastily canceled took place a week later. It was repeated on the twenty-sixth. Again nothing special was discovered. On the first flight thick clouds interfered with camera work, and pictures from the second showed nothing more than the already familiar antiaircraft missiles and their launchers.

Nevertheless, the Americans decided to impose sanctions. They demanded that their allies prevent their ships from carrying cargoes to Cuba.

THE DEFENSE OF CUBA: THE "CARGO"

It was in this impossibly overheated situation that the nuclear warheads were sent on their long voyage.

Father thought that a ship might be seized if the Americans found out what it was carrying. Not necessarily by American hands, but by some unidentified ship, unknown "pirates"—then we could protest, search, write as much as we pleased. The rockets would turn into useless toys and the carefully prepared operation would come to naught in its final stage.

All possible variants were rehearsed repeatedly in the staff headquarters of the Navy, the Strategic Missile Forces, and the General Staff before final approval was granted. The commanders in chief—Marshal Biryuzov of the Strategic Missile Forces and Fleet Admiral Gorshkov of the Navy—together with Minister Slavsky and nuclear scientists ran through all possible variants meticulously. They reported to Minister of Defense Marshal Malinovsky, but did not take responsibility for the final decision.

Just as a month before, the idea of shipping the warheads on submarines had been put forward. It seemed very tempting. It would guarantee the safety and secrecy of the cargo. However, scientists voiced their doubts once again. There were so many negative factors.

Besides, how many warheads would fit into a submarine? Two? Three? But more than two hundred had to be delivered. It would take an entire submarine flotilla.

Protection of the crew from radiation was no less serious an obstacle. They would have to work and live next to this unpleasant cargo for many days. Men would have to be moved from the compartments holding the warheads and special shielding installed. All that would involve a great deal of additional work.

The idea of underwater transport was finally abandoned, with great reluctance.

There remained the surface variant, with all its uncertainties and risks.

They reported to Father.

Father again conferred with Slavsky and then ordered: "Don't try to be clever and don't argue; send the warheads in specially equipped ships." Several ships would be chosen, but only some would have the "cargo." They must not differ in any way from those already familiar to the Americans. The number and identities of the ships were kept secret. I didn't know at the time which actually contained the "cargo" and which were used to divert attention. That information has now been declassified. The nuclear warheads were shipped on the *Indigirka*, the *Lena*, and the *Aleksandrovsk*.

It took a long time before they could bring themselves to send off the nuclear warheads without any kind of guard. Gorshkov proposed sending two or three submarines with each transport ship. In case of attack submarines could defend the "cargo," and if the situation became hopeless, they could assume command and sink the warheads together with the ship. At first Father agreed, but after giving the matter some thought he rejected the plan as too risky. He thought that once the ships were near the U.S. coast, the Americans could not be stopped by one, two, or three submarines. The submarines themselves would be sunk and that would be the end of it. Moreover, they would help the Americans pick out "the" ship from among a mass of others.

Father spoke against any kind of escort. He again emphasized that our main weapon was camouflage. The ships should look ordinary; they should be indistinguishable from the rest of the fleet.

That was how the matter was decided.

The ships carrying warheads were scheduled to arrive in Cuba at the end of September or beginning of October, when work on the missile installations would be almost finished. Special storehouses for the warheads were being built. The nuclear warheads required "hothouse" conditions at launch sites. They would be installed on rockets immediately before launch. When the alert was over, they would be removed at once and lowered again into their den to "hibernate."

The first ship to depart on its perilous journey was the *Indigirka*, carrying the bulk of the arsenal of ninety-nine nuclear weapons: forty-five warheads for the R-12, thirty-six warheads for combat cruise missiles, six nuclear bombs, and twelve warheads for the Lunas.

The records of the General Staff include a document showing that at exactly 10 A.M. on September 17, 1962, its chief, Marshal of the Soviet Union Matvei Zakharov, informed Khrushchev: "The cargo has left as ordered."

It only remained to wait for the coded signal that they had arrived. Radio communications during the voyage were forbidden. An incautious word—or, even worse, coded messages—could ruin the entire operation. The only communications permitted were between dispatchers, which were necessary to ensure that the voyage proceeded safely.

Father flew to Ashkhabad on September 26.

On October 1 newspapers published a statement from the Cuban Revolutionary Government titled "The Cuban People Will Not Be Crushed!" Again, as in April 1961, Cubans prepared to fight to the end, and then to retreat into the hills to carry on partisan warfare.

By coincidence, that same day McNamara convened a meeting of the Joint Chiefs of Staff. There was only one item on the agenda: possible alternative actions with respect to Cuba. Their discussion revolved around the steady stream of Soviet ships that for three months had been transporting something to the island. The question was whether to stop them. The problem would then disappear of itself—The Soviets on Cuba itself couldn't hold out for long without resupply. Admiral Dennison, commander of the U.S. Atlantic Fleet, was ordered to carry out preparations for a naval blockade of the island, if it proved to be necessary.

Meanwhile, construction of the first missile launch positions continued at San Cristobal and elsewhere. Concrete was poured for the launch platforms, structural parts for the missile storehouses were assembled, and a bunker was dug for the warheads. All of this was done in the strictest secrecy. The area was surrounded by Soviet troops, and camouflage nets concealed both construction site and rockets from aerial observation.

But you can't think of everything. Ruts worn into roads that had been thoroughly surveyed from the air would suddenly disappear—and reappear one hundred yards further on. Then too, troops didn't always manage to keep track of the large number of machines, such as bulldozers, cement mixers, trailers, and missile erectors. They were moved from place to place, and sometimes a tractor or a conspicuous trailer dolly was left out in the open. Luckily, storm clouds were hanging over Cuba. Summer weather was over.

The *Indigirka* arrived in Cuba on October 4 with the first shipment of nuclear warheads. The *Lena* was halfway en route. The last ship with a nuclear cargo, the *Aleksandrovsk*, left Severomorsk on October 5.

That same day Father sent President Kennedy his sincere congratulations on the successful completion of a space flight by astronaut Wally Schirra on the Sigma-7, which splashed down in the Pacific Ocean on October 3.

He himself was continuing his trip in Central Asia. On October 5 he visited Almalyk, the center of Uzbek ferrous metallurgy.

Gromyko, who was taking part in the regular session of the U.N. General Assembly in New York, met with Dean Rusk, the U.S. secretary of state, on October 6. They talked about everything, including Cuba, but their attention was focused on the problems of Berlin and a ban on nuclear testing. As if to confirm the hard line taken by the secretary of state, American troops in West Berlin began to practice—or more precisely, to demonstrate—what is nowadays called military operations in urban terrain, in full view of numerous witnesses. At the same time, in Washington the Senate approved a resolution declaring that the United States would resist by any means necessary, including force, any violation of its rights "both within Berlin and with lines of communications to it."

For the time being Cuba remained one of a number of international problems dividing the two great powers. For the time being.

High-altitude reconnaissance flights carried out over Cuba on October 5 and 7 did not discover anything new. There were more antiaircraft missiles, but the Americans were already used to them. Furthermore, they behaved peacefully and didn't interfere with the picture taking.

On October 9 President Kennedy approved the next U-2 reconnaissance flights over Cuba. However, thick cloud cover over the island made photographing useless. The flight was put off from one day to the next.

Emotions ran higher and higher. On October 10 Senator Keating gave another speech claiming that military bases equipped with medium-range ballistic missiles were being built in Cuba. He accused the U.S. government of inaction.

Father returned to Moscow on the tenth.

General Pliyev reported that the first R-12s would be operational toward the end of the month. Work was going according to schedule and in compliance with all the measures to preserve secrecy.

Pliyev met the deadline of October 20–31 set by Moscow for completing work. The only exception was the R-14s, which had not yet arrived in Cuba. The delay didn't particularly concern Father. Everything would be finished in November, if not in October.

According to the approved plan, twenty-four launch complexes, each capable of receiving three missiles, were to be built in Cuba. It was assumed that the missiles could be moved quickly to reserve positions in case one of the sites was discovered, or in some other eventuality. That provided some flexibility. The possibility of building fake launch sites was also considered, but so far there had been no time for that.

If everything went well, the General Staff planned to bring all the sites to capacity eventually, but not by denuding Europe or removing missiles from launch sites inside the Soviet Union. Missiles coming off the production line would gradually be added to empty launch sites, according to plan.

But that was for the future. No decisions were made at this time and Malinovsky did not report his preliminary ideas to Father. Once he referred to something in passing, but Father only grunted disapprovingly: "Don't put the cart before the horse."

During a stroll in Lenin Hills one day, Father said almost casually that he had given it some more thought and decided to communicate the unpleasant news to the U.S. president around the twentieth of November, after our October Revolution holidays and when their election fever would have died down.

He had already begun to mull over the arguments he would use in an especially secret and personal message. It was very important to persuade Kennedy that our objectives were exclusively defensive and that we were trying to protect a still weak republic from attack. Most important was to keep him from taking an impulsive first step prompted by emotion and not by reason, and to enlist him in a dialogue. Father expected the conversation to be difficult, but he didn't believe that there was any possibility of armed conflict over Cuba. Over and over again, he drew a parallel with himself: we live with U.S. missiles, and they will live with ours. In the final analysis, a country's fate is not determined by missiles at military bases, but by the will of politicians in their capitals. But the conversation would be difficult.

I awaited the outcome with a sinking heart.

THE DEFENSE OF CUBA: THE AMERICANS LEARN THE TRUTH

Meanwhile, events were following their own timetable.

Meteorologists predicted good weather over Cuba for the morning of October 14. Major Richard Kaiser took off in his U-2. He was to photograph suspicious sites located to the west of Havana. The flight took place on a Sunday, which suited the pilot—there was less chance of being hit by an antiaircraft missile. Flights had become very dangerous, even at such high altitudes.

By a strange coincidence, at the very moment the U-2 set a course for Cuba the president's national security adviser, McGeorge Bundy, speaking on the ABC television program *Issues and Answers*, said in response to Senator

Keating that the government had no reliable evidence that there were any Soviet offensive weapons in Cuba.

On the morning of October 15 the developed U-2 film arrived at the National Center for Photo Intelligence for examination. Most of the stills from the long film were not of any interest: fields, beaches, sugar cane, the familiar Soviet antiaircraft positions, not operating despite the flight of a foreign spy plane.

In the region of San Cristobal the photo analysts immediately noticed a difference from pictures taken by the same plane on August 29. Their attention was attracted by a large area covered by camouflaged awning.

Of course, it's possible to argue over whether a ballistic missile resembles a palm tree. You can poke fun at the idea. But in real life Biryuzov's assumption was not put to the test. The U-2 photographs revealed, not missiles with short skirts of palm leaves, but instrument setters, fueling trucks, and trailers, left without any concealment from the air. If they had been stored on the ramps designed to hide military hardware, as required by regulations, perhaps the crisis would not have begun for several weeks. But even the most strict orders and instructions cannot overcome our characteristic lack of discipline and reliance on luck.

The secret was revealed. The missiles themselves were undoubtedly under the awning, waiting to be installed on the launch platforms. Possibly the launch mechanisms were hidden there as well. That was not so important.

A month earlier than Father had planned—and not from him—the Americans discovered that Soviet missiles were in Cuba. The most serious crisis of the decade began.

Moscow suspected nothing. In Washington, on the other hand, there was frenzied activity.

At 8:30 in the evening of that ill-fated October 15, CIA deputy director Ray Cline called McGeorge Bundy at home and hinted that he had found what he had been looking for. The telephone was not secure, so they were not supposed to discuss classified subjects on it. Bundy decided not to disturb the president until the next morning. McNamara waited for the information in his office at the Pentagon. At midnight he was shown the interpreted photographs: some kind of dots, barely visible stripes, tiny hooks—it all looked quite harmless. However, specialists claimed that it was indeed a missile base under construction. He had no reason not to believe them.

The next morning, at 8:45, Bundy reported the bad news to the president. Kennedy was astounded. Despite the persistent rumors, he had believed the many assurances, relayed by the Soviet ambassador in Washington, by the minister of foreign affairs, and by many other less informed but no less trusted persons, that there were no Soviet offensive weapons in Cuba.

There now began a kind of verbal game of hide-and-seek. Father considered the ballistic missiles with nuclear warheads being installed in Cuba purely defensive in nature. However, he didn't consider it shameful to mislead an "adversary" by a direct assertion that "surface-to-surface" missiles were not being deployed on the island.

The deception wounded Kennedy deeply. One of the numerous versions that sprang up around the events of those two weeks claims that the president would not have asserted so categorically in September that he would not tolerate the presence of Soviet ballistic missile in Cuba, if not for Father's assurances that there weren't any. He would have conducted himself more cautiously and not have issued such far-reaching threats to use force. At the 1989 meeting in Moscow I referred to earlier, people who were close to Kennedy in those years said that the categorical nature of those statements had tied the president's hands. Well, it's more apparent to them. Personally, I don't believe in that interpretation of the possible course of events.

After listening to Bundy's report, Kennedy summoned his closest advisers to the White House for a meeting at 11:45 A.M. As soon as Bundy left, he called his brother Robert and asked him to come immediately.

"We're in real trouble," said the president.

Robert hurried to the White House. He found his brother in his office. The news stunned both of them. Robert went back over his recent meetings with Dobrynin. How could he have believed the assertions that there were, and would be, no offensive weapons in Cuba? And convinced the president of that?

At 11:45 those invited met in the president's office. CIA experts spread out the huge and very clear photographs on a table and began to describe them. After their explanations, details—trailers, a launch pad under construction, rutted roads leading to it—stood out, as if revealing themselves for a second time.

The question arose: What should be done? Not react? After all, one sovereign state was building a military base on the territory of another sovereign state. That approach was rejected from the start.

Those present had no doubt that what the Soviet Union and Cuba were doing must be stopped by whatever means necessary. The United States must demonstrate its will and determination. But how?

They agreed to meet in the second half of the day in a larger group, to include the military and diplomats. Almost all the president's assistants were present. Special hope was placed in the newly appointed expert on Russian affairs, Llewellyn Thompson. He was the only one experienced in associating with the Soviet leadership and could predict what course of conduct they would choose in Moscow.

Opinions diverged. Representatives from the Joint Chiefs of Staff recommended an immediate air attack, to be followed by an invasion.

Robert McNamara thought that the consequences of such a decisive step were impossible to predict, but would undoubtedly be frightful. He proposed the imposition of a naval blockade of Cuba as a first step. In his opinion, it would never be too late to take the last step.

He was supported by Robert Kennedy.

The president was especially worried about possible retaliatory steps by the Soviet Union. Would Moscow look on quietly while napalm and bombs fell on their soldiers' heads? How would they react to humiliating searches of their ships? The Americans expected retaliatory measures in the center of Europe. Berlin remained a vulnerable spot. It would be easy to seize—or, in response to the more moderate variant of a blockade, to set up their own blockade.

No decision was made that day.

Meanwhile, in Moscow Father received the new U.S. ambassador, Foy Kohler. As reported in the newspapers, the meeting was held in an atmosphere of frankness and mutual understanding. Kohler seemed to Father to be more dry and formal than Thompson, and on first acquaintance no special rapport was established. That evening Father said that we might have more occasions to regret the changes in the U.S. Embassy. I can't say that he was pessimistic, because he added immediately: he'll get used to us, he just needs some time. The question of Cuba did not come up during their meeting. Neither Father nor the ambassador expected the sensational disclosure that was only days away.

By 1962 Father's correspondence with Kennedy through unofficial channels was well established. They exchanged messages once or twice a month. In the middle of October it came time to send another letter. Among other matters, Father turned again to the question of installing our weapons in Cuba and emphasized that they were of a strictly defensive nature. On October 17 Georgy Bolshakov called the Department of Justice and asked Robert Kennedy for a meeting. It was held that very day. Unlike their previous meetings, it was brief. The president's brother was not interested in news from Moscow and, coldly thanking Bolshakov, promised to take the letter to the addressee immediately.

THE DEFENSE OF CUBA: CALM BEFORE THE STORM

Pliyev reported that work to install the missiles was proceeding according to plan. He made no mention of the U-2's flight over the island, thinking that it was not worth Father's attention. The strict order to use camouflage was being followed, and they were accustomed to U-2 flights. No one gave any thought to the changes that had taken place on the island since the previous reconnaissance flight. It didn't enter anyone's head to fly over the construction site himself.

In Moscow all was calm.

In Washington there was a rash of meetings. New photographs showed with increasing clarity the contours of launch sites for either sixteen or thirty-two missiles, depending on whether the launch platforms were dual. At the rate work was progressing, they would be operational within a few days.

The president's conference on Thursday, October 18, began with a report from the CIA. Its experts stated that the detected missiles comprised no less than half of the strategic potential of the Soviet Union. According to their estimates—in my opinion based primarily on information from Penkovsky—there were about fifty operational intercontinental ballistic missiles in the Soviet Union. That figure was confirmed by McNamara in Moscow in 1989.

In reality, by October of 1962 there were about twenty R-16 launch positions, plus six positions for the R-7. That was all. In retrospect, we couldn't even dream of basing our policies on some mythical superiority in this type of weapon. They knew that in Washington, but Moscow didn't suspect that Washington knew. The Americans also knew that it took a considerable amount of time to prepare the missiles for launch. Penkovsky had managed to find that out as well.

The number of megatons on each missile and the number of missiles in silos sometimes seems a rather abstract and academic subject, even to government leaders burdened by the weight of responsibility. Until then no one had given serious thought to actually using this terrible weapon. It was enough to brandish it. On Thursday everything changed—targets, retaliatory strikes, radii of destruction, millions of dead. They all became absolutely real to President Kennedy. Such was the price that might have to be paid to destroy the missiles in Cuba.

Father considered such a price reckless. Kennedy judged it to be unacceptably high, but he put a still higher value on the honor of the United States. The missiles must be removed from Cuba at any cost. It was preferable that the cost be an acceptable one. But what would that be? Experts thought that 80 million American lives would be lost in a nuclear exchange with the Soviet Union.

The military demanded an attack. In that, the members of the Joint Chiefs of Staff were unanimous. Only armed intervention and an immediate bomb strike could finish off not just Soviet missiles, but Castro as well. General Curtis LeMay, the Air Force chief of staff, was especially zealous. He was impatient to show off what his bombers and low-flying attack aircraft could do.

Their decisiveness didn't suit the president. Kennedy asked LeMay how he thought the Russians would react. Without thinking, the general snapped back: "Not at all! They wouldn't dare."

The president was doubtful: "After all their statements, they can't sit with their arms folded and watch how we seize their missiles and kill quite a few Russians in the process. If they don't act in Cuba, they certainly will in Berlin."

McNamara told Kennedy that military forces could attack at dawn on the twenty-third, the following Tuesday. Military units and planes were on the move toward Florida.

According to General LeMay's plan of action, the first stage alone called for more than five hundred sorties to bomb and fire missiles, not just at launch positions, but at airfields, ports, artillery bases, and other targets that might be important points of resistance to a landing party.

After presenting a factual description of the preparations for military action, McNamara spoke against it. He was in favor of a blockade, which would give both the president and his opponents greater freedom of choice. Robert Kennedy supported the secretary of defense. So no decision was made that day.

By a twist of fate, the meeting with Gromyko was set for that same day.

Following his meeting with the president, the Soviet minister of foreign affairs was to attend a dinner hosted by the U.S. secretary of state.

Gromyko knew all the details about the missile deployment in Cuba, but he didn't suspect that the Americans knew them as well. An intriguing situation developed. Andrei Andreyevich began by expressing surprise at the fuss raised in the American press over Soviet assistance to the Republic of Cuba. He spoke in measured tones, without hurrying, giving weight to each word, as befitted his rank as the foreign minister of a great power.

Gromyko asserted that our principal aim was to help Cuba develop its agriculture. For that reason we were delivering farm machinery and were building a fishing port. Those claims corresponded to the facts. As far as military assistance was concerned, said Gromyko, it was of a purely defensive nature. And there too he did not deviate from the truth. It all depends on how you interpret the word "defense."

Gromyko conveyed Father's assurances to the president: neither the Soviet Union nor Cuba was thinking of attacking the United States. No preparations for such an attack were being made in Cuba and no offensive weapons were being delivered there.

I permit myself a small digression. Both leaders got tangled up in terminology. Nuclear missiles with megaton warheads cannot be considered either offensive or defensive—or they may be considered both. That is completely beside the point, since they are annihilating. After their use both terms, "offense" and "defense," lose any meaning whatsoever.

Gromyko did not mention missiles.

President Kennedy, still agitated after the argument between LeMay and McNamara over how to deal with the Soviet missiles, choked with indignation. But—he restrained himself. He decided not to ask about the missiles directly. The longer the Soviet Union remained in ignorance, the more time the United States would have to evaluate the situation and make decisions.

It was as if the word "missile" had been banished from the lexicon of both men. They spoke only of defensive and offensive weapons.

Andrei Andreyevich was often asked later: "Why didn't you tell the president about the missiles?" He would dodge the question and refer to the fact that Kennedy had not asked him. But the answer was simple: he had not been instructed to. The time to show our hand was still ahead. Both men were playing in the dark.

The president noted that deliveries of weapons to America's closest neighbor could not but cause alarm, and he read excerpts from his September 4 statement, where he warned that installation of offensive weapons in Cuba would have the gravest consequences.

It is interesting to read excerpts from Gromyko's recently declassified, top secret coded telegram. In it he writes: "Kennedy and Rusk both emphasized that the United States was not preparing to attack Cuba, but that the massive shipment of weapons which began in July was causing concern. Kennedy read an excerpt from his press conference in which he stated that he believed the USSR and that there were no offensive weapons in Cuba. In speaking about Cuba, Kennedy formulated his thoughts slowly and with great care, obviously weighing every word. During our conversation Rusk sat silently and was as red as a lobster."

Naturally, the subject of Cuba came up again at the dinner with Rusk. The secretary of state's nerves were apparently weaker than the president's. Father recalled:

> Comrade Gromyko later told me: The conversation was polite, but Rusk kept insisting: the military are giving us data proving that you are installing missiles. You should take into account the fact that we can't accept that. The president cannot ignore the reaction developing inside our country. A dangerous situation is being created, and it would be better if you get out of Cuba.
>
> That was not a warning so much as a request not to aggravate the situation.
>
> Dinner followed. During dinner Dean Rusk drank a lot and continued to dance around the subject. He allowed himself to use expressions such as: we would do anything, we would stop at nothing, we have no other recourse, and therefore we ask you to judge the situation accordingly and take steps to avoid

a fatal clash. It could occur if the missiles really turn out to be in Cuba, which we're convinced they are.

Today it's hard to say whether the secretary of state had let the cat out of the bag or wanted to warn his colleague. The evening's conversation was private and no one on the Soviet side recorded it. There remain only Gromyko's reports in Moscow, written hot on the heels of the visit.

Father didn't attach any special importance to Dean Rusk's words or suspect that the secret was out. In those days everyone was expressing the most fantastic conjectures about Soviet weapons in Cuba.

"Well, it was just the usual verbal skirmishing," Father commented four years later about that much earlier conversation.

> Both knew what they were talking about, but both were defending their own viewpoints and wanted moral and legal justification for their actions.
>
> We had greater legal and moral grounds than Dean Rusk. Of that, there can be no doubt whatsoever. At the time U.S. missiles with nuclear warheads had long been based in Turkey and Italy.
>
> Rusk understood that, but he saw a difference in one respect, though he only hinted at it and didn't say it straight out:
>
> "You've already gotten used to living surrounded by our missiles, but we have faced this for the first time. That's why we've gotten such a shock. We cannot recover from that shock."
>
> Gromyko reported all this to the government, but we continued to complete shipping and installing the missiles. We went on with our work.

The group of advisers continued to meet in the absence of the president and secretary of state. According to Robert Kennedy, opinions fluctuated from an immediate military attack to doing nothing and waiting, and then swung back to favoring an attack. By evening viewpoints had polarized, with the majority against military action and in favor of a blockade.

They left to report to the president. It was already late, about 9:15 P.M., an unlikely time for meetings. A cavalcade of government limousines might arouse the curiosity of journalists prowling around the White House. To maintain secrecy, they all crowded into the attorney general's car—the attorney general and driver in front, Robert McNamara and Maxwell Taylor next to them. The other six members of the group squeezed into the back seat.

During the meeting with the president, the apparent consensus fell apart again. Opinions began to change, irrefutable arguments suddenly no longer seemed convincing.

There was a good reason for that. An incorrect recommendation could put the world on a course toward destruction. Not for nothing did Robert

Kennedy note sadly: "I now know how Tojo felt when he was planning Pearl Harbor."

Allied reaction still had to be considered. The previous evening, in response to a U.S. warning of a possible attack on freighters steaming toward Cuba by ships belonging to Cuban émigrés, the British Admiralty had stated that Her Majesty's Navy would defend its cargo ships.

The president hesitated. He simply could not decide.

His advisers set off for home to continue working on proposals. He himself planned to leave the next morning for Cleveland, where he was scheduled to give some preelection speeches. If Kennedy failed to appear there it would cause speculation and might draw unwanted attention to events going on around the White House. From Cleveland the president planned to fly to the West Coast. He seemed to want to avoid the necessity of making an immediate decision, trying to give them time to talk things over and let off steam in his absence.

That entire day, Friday, October 19, was spent arguing. From time to time members of the group seemed to reach agreement, only to erupt into arguments based on diametrically opposite opinions. Robert Kennedy, trying to bring them together, repeatedly called his brother on the telephone.

They finally set a deadline. The president would speak to the nation on Sunday and announce his decision. Kennedy understood that it was time for him to return.

While the arguments were going on, the commander of the Atlantic Fleet was carrying out the order he received from the Department of Defense to prepare for a naval blockade of Cuba. Naval vessels were on the move and were massing near the island. Father began to worry that we were too late. Perhaps this was a run up to the long-awaited invasion. He didn't connect the naval activity with the missiles. How could the Fleet be related to them? The reaction in that case would be very different—public and sharp. But it all seemed to fit a more potent repetition of the Bay of Pigs landing, this time under U.S. leadership and with the participation of the U.S. Marines. There was nothing Father could do in response. He could only wait for events to develop and voice his attitude—I use his words—"by means of protests in the press."

The fate of its cargo ships in the Caribbean region continued to concern Britain. It warned the United States that if it could not assure the safety of navigation, the ships of Her Majesty's Navy based in those waters would be reinforced to the extent necessary to protect their ships against attack by "pirates."

On Saturday, October 20, the group of advisers, short of sleep and rest, gathered again at the State Department. And again they failed to arrive at a unanimous decision.

Robert Kennedy, McNamara, and the president's assistants were solidly in favor of a blockade. In their opinion, it would allow them to calculate the possible course of events a few steps ahead.

John Kennedy promised to return at once. Pierre Salinger announced that, because of a "slight cold," Kennedy was interrupting his trip and returning to Washington.

While the president was on his way, preparations for both actions began. McNamara called the Defense Department and ordered that four squadrons of tactical aircraft be put on alert for an attack. At the same time Robert Kennedy, McNamara, and Dean Rusk tried to compose the text of a government statement on establishing a blockade to prevent the delivery of offensive weapons in Cuba.

John Kennedy returned to the White House at 1:40 P.M. on October 20. While he was freshening up, Robert filled him in on the latest developments. A meeting began at 2:30. The entire National Security Council and many other insiders were present. The circle of those in the know had expanded considerably. There seemed less and less sense in maintaining secrecy. Their decision would be known to the entire world on the following day.

Both points of view were discussed thoroughly. McNamara spoke in favor of the blockade, the military in favor of an attack. Emotions flared up with renewed force. A member of the Joint Chiefs of Staff began to insist on using an atomic bomb to destroy the missile installations.

Adlai Stevenson, who had not taken part in the previous debates, proposed a diplomatic solution to the problem: the United States would remove its Jupiters from Italy and Turkey; it would also close the base at Guantanamo; the Soviet Union would remove its missiles from Cuba. The military reacted to this proposal with a burst of indignation. They considered that his idea violated the spirit of the nation. Kennedy also thought that such a proposal was premature, although he himself had often remarked that it would be advisable to dismantle those bothersome missile bases in Europe.

The meeting continued for two and a half hours. Having listened to the mutually exclusive proposals, the president brought the meeting to a close at 5:10, saying that he had to think and would let them know his decision that evening. He remained alone with his brother.

On October 20 the first regiment of the missile division was ready for action.

That day life in the Kremlin was proceeding according to schedule. On October 20 Father received Aleksandr Trifonovich Tvardovsky, poet and editor in chief of the journal *Novy Mir*, who had been seeking a meeting for a long time. Both censors and Central Committee ideologues had been exerting more and more pressure on him, endeavoring to close down what was then the only outlet for free thought. Father loved Tvardovsky the poet. His verses, especially about Tyorkin, with his peasant musicality, awakened memories of childhood and carried Father far away, to the Kursk region and his native Kalinovka.

His relations with Tvardovsky the editor had their ups and downs. Sometimes Father backed him completely; sometimes, under pressure from Suslov and Ilyichev, he unleashed the thunder and lightning of ideological accusations at the journal.

On this occasion the tone of the meeting was friendly. "I was greeted more kindly than ever before," said the poet later.

They talked about various things: about Stalin, about Beria's arrest. Father praised the civic importance of Yevtushenko's poem, "Stalin's Heirs," and complained that not all members of the Presidium of the Central Committee approved of Aleksandr Solzhenitsyn's *Ivan Denisovich*.

Tvardovsky tried to persuade Father to abolish censorship. After all, he said, "Some supervisor's opinion about a work of art often depends on chance circumstances, poor digestion even. Let them replace me if I'm not qualified to be an editor, if I'm not trusted." Tvardovsky assured Father: "You know, Nikita Sergeyevich, all that is best in our intelligentsia is solidly behind you in the struggle against the cult of personality." Father found the poet's arguments convincing. As if musing out loud, he said: "We have to think it over. Maybe you're right. Actually, a year ago we abolished censorship of foreign correspondents' reports from Moscow. And you know what? They started to lie and slander us less often."

This conversation was held before the notorious and regrettable meetings with the intelligentsia. The entire ideology department of the Central Committee rose up in defense of censorship and persuaded Father that it was precisely censorship that was defending Soviet power to the last bastion. Father wavered and retreated; then a year later the struggle to suppress the penetration of bourgeois culture into our sterile socialist sanctuary was in full swing. You certainly couldn't avoid censorship in that effort.

But I mention the poet's meeting with Father for another reason. At the end of the conversation Tvardovsky suddenly surprised him by asking: "Would it be possible to delay my trip to America? I want to finish a poem and work on my own personal plot, so to speak."

Kennedy had invited him to the United States, and plans called for the poet and president to meet. Only Father could free Tvardovsky from his lofty mission.

Father didn't object: "Of course, of course . . . Relations with America are bad at the moment. But go in the spring. They'll give you a fine welcome then."[13] Father was thinking of the coming storms in November, not suspect-

---

13. V. Lakshin, "*Novy Mir* in the Khrushchev Years," *Znamya*, no. 6 (1990).

ing that they had already begun. It is also interesting that he didn't foresee a serious and prolonged disagreement over the missiles—he was sure that by spring everything would have quieted down.

THE DEFENSE OF CUBA: THE CONFRONTATION BEGINS

On the other side of the globe there was far less optimism and certainty. The Kennedy brothers still couldn't make up their minds: invasion or blockade, blockade or invasion. Finally John Kennedy decided to order a blockade, but he still didn't feel absolutely certain. He decided to resume discussion on Sunday morning. A small group gathered at 11:30. Robert McNamara and Maxwell Taylor were there, along with Robert Kennedy and the president. General Walter C. Sweeney, who commanded tactical aviation, delivered his report. As was to be expected, he did not absolutely guarantee that all missile positions could be destroyed. A launcher suddenly coming to life could spit out a megaton warhead toward New York or Washington.[14] The president felt reassured that his decision was correct.

His speech to the nation was rescheduled for seven o'clock Monday evening. Some time was needed to prepare the text, as well as to bring at least the most influential of the allies, British prime minister Macmillan and French president de Gaulle, into the picture and to inform the leaders of Congress.

The news was already becoming almost impossible to contain. It was leaking out. John Kennedy asked Orville Dreyfuss of the *New York Times*, who enjoyed his personal confidence, to help distract the public's attention from the signs of impending crisis. The information must not slip out before the president's speech. It might create chaos. The first signs of a leak appeared Monday morning. The *Washington Post* published an article about the unusual degree of activity at the White House. In the author's opinion, it had to do with Cuba, although he did not rule out Berlin.

That article did not go unnoticed. Soviet newspapers referred to it. After receiving Gromyko's report on his talk with the president and an account of his dramatic conversation with Dean Rusk, Father became even more concerned.

He was especially apprehensive about the movement of warships in the Caribbean Sea. Enormous forces were being concentrated there. There were constant meetings at the White House. Clearly, something was going on. But what?

---

14. Michael R. Beschloss, *The Crisis Years: Kennedy and Khrushchev, 1960–1963* (New York: HarperCollins, 1991), p. 461.

At such a distance, Father could not intervene and events were developing according to their own inner logic. He could only observe, put things right where possible, and wait for the moment of decision when he would be forced to say: "Forward!" or "Stop!"

To all my questions he replied tersely: "We have to wait."

What especially worried Father was how the ships carrying nuclear warheads would pass through the U.S. warships concentrated in such numbers around all the approaches to Cuba. He feared a provocation. There was good reason for the American warning of possible piratical acts by Cuban émigrés. Here too he could only wait, hope for luck and put his trust in the inviolability of the national flag of a great power.

On Monday the White House Press Office managed to restrain the press only with great difficulty. In some cases it required the president's personal intervention. The morning papers reported only that the country was facing a crisis, but without identifying it. That evening's speech should dot all the "i's."

In the morning the president signed Order No. 196, which established the Executive Committee of the National Security Council under his chairmanship to govern the country in the crisis. The members of this committee had been meeting as a group since Tuesday, only now their meetings had acquired official status.

Precisely at noon on Monday, White House Press Secretary Pierre Salinger announced that President Kennedy would make an important statement at seven o'clock that evening, which would be carried by all the country's radio and television stations.

At that moment it was already 8 P.M. in Moscow. Father was immediately informed of this disturbing event at home. As it happened, we were taking an after-dinner walk when he was called to the phone. Without removing his coat, he went into the living room, while I waited for him in the hall. It was a brief conversation, and I could make out nothing from his disjointed questions and answers. But I could tell from his tone that something unpleasant had happened.

Father hung up the phone and we went out again into the courtyard. I waited to see if he would tell me the news, or if it was something I shouldn't know. He seemed to be mulling over the information he had just received. Finally, as if returning from far away, he said absent-mindedly: "In Washington they've announced that the president will deliver an important speech tonight. They've probably discovered our missiles. We can't assume anything else. In Berlin everything's quiet, and if they were getting ready to invade Cuba they wouldn't be saying anything."

I gave a start. "What will happen?"

Father laughed. "If I only knew. Most of the missiles aren't operational as yet. They are defenseless and everything could be destroyed from the air at one blow."

I froze with horror.

Father, speaking more to himself than to me, said that an air attack was unlikely. They would not have announced that ahead of time either.

He said, somewhat more cheerfully, that Kennedy apparently wanted to deal with the matter through diplomatic channels.

"Tomorrow morning you'll know," he said, as if to summarize.

He fell silent and, sensing that I was about to question him some more, said: "Don't bother me. I have to think."

We walked for a long time, each deep in his own thoughts. Father was evidently trying to put himself in the president's place and calculate his probable actions. Finally, he broke off our circuit around the courtyard and headed into the house. Without pausing in the hall or removing his coat, he went to the room with the telephones, picked up the Kremlin line and dialed a number.

"Call the members of the Presidium of the Central Committee and ask them to meet me in the Kremlin in one hour," Father said tersely.

After listening to the response, he replied: "What is it about? I will tell them when we meet. And also"—he hesitated—"invite Malinovsky and Kuznetsov from the Foreign Ministry, Gromyko's deputy."

The conversation ended. Father picked up the next telephone and said briefly: "Order a car."

Then he turned around and, noticing me, explained: "We have to consult. Don't wait for me; I'll be late."

We went back out in the courtyard. Father didn't utter a single word until the car arrived.

When I left for work the next morning, I noticed that Father's coat was missing. Apparently he still hadn't returned home. Or left early. Either way, it meant that events were breaking fast.

Night had fallen in Moscow, and in Washington last-minute preparations were under way. Phrases of the president's address were being polished and consultations with NATO countries and members of Congress were concluding. The latter were furious. They thirsted for blood. A blockade struck them as an extremely weak action and there was one word on their lips— "invasion."

Even such a cautious and wise (in Father's opinion) politician as William Fulbright favored military action. The president was being pressured from all sides, but he stood firm.

Military preparations went ahead simultaneously with activity on the diplomatic front. Troops were transferred to the southeast from states in the
country's interior. An armored division moved from Texas to Georgia. Five
other divisions were mobilized and prepared to move to Florida.

Intercontinental missiles were armed; bombers were put on airborne
alert, with full bomb loads. When one landed to refuel, another would take
off, creating a continuous nuclear carousel.

Warships moved to their starting positions to establish the blockade. The
zone for seizure of ships bound for Cuba was set at a distance of 800 miles
from the island.

The new U.S. ambassador in Moscow received instructions to hand Father a
letter from President Kennedy and the text of the forthcoming speech, sent
by code from Washington, one hour before the speech was to begin. This
marked the start of a daily exchange of letters during the crisis period.

Foy Kohler tried to carry out his instructions, but, as Robert Kennedy
wrote, "he was not able to meet with a single high-placed official." That was
not surprising, since they had overlooked the fact that at six o'clock in the
evening in Washington it is 2 A.M. in Moscow. The duty officer at the Ministry of Foreign Affairs politely advised the ambassador to wait until morning.
The ambassador entrusted Embassy Counselor Richard Davis with the job
of persisting. The contents of the message were not conducive to tranquillity.
By morning it might already be too late. Davis finally managed to hand over
the letter.

Such mix-ups occurred more than once during those days. I was told that
our submarines in the seas near Cuba were ordered to surface in the middle
of the night, between midnight and 2 A.M., to communicate with Moscow, in
order to preserve secrecy. It was thought that at that hour lookouts were
sleepy and might miss a submarine transmitting messages from the surface.
However, they overlooked the fact that the order referred to Moscow time,
when it was broad daylight in Cuba. This was corrected only on the following day, when a submarine reported that it had to transmit in full view of the
entire U.S. fleet.

Ambassador Anatoly Dobrynin was asked to meet with Secretary of State
Dean Rusk at the same hour that Foy Kohler was supposed to visit the Soviet
Foreign Ministry. He was handed the text of the president's forthcoming
speech and an explanation of the U.S. government's position.

Deployment of the missiles had been kept highly secret. Many years of
experience had shown that leaks of information occurred most often through
the Embassy, whether intentionally or not. For that reason Gromyko, after
consulting Father, had not informed the ambassador of the operation. The
news hit Dobrynin like a bolt from the blue. According to reporters on duty

at the State Department entrance, he emerged gray-faced from the secretary of state's office.

At 7 P.M. on Monday, October 22, all Americans were glued to televisions and radios.

You can view the president's appraisal of the situation in various ways. You may believe, or you may doubt, that Cuba could threaten life in the Western hemisphere, even with help from the mighty Soviet Union. Everything depends on one's point of view. In my comments I don't want to embark on a polemic after the fact. Kennedy's words belong to history.

I find the attitude of his listeners to be more interesting. You might compare it to the American reaction after the Japanese attack on Pearl Harbor: shock, followed by demands for immediate retaliation. The stance of the Joint Chiefs of Staff received powerful support. Americans, it seemed, were all prepared to perish, just as long as they could evict those uninvited guests from their neighbor's territory. No one mentioned that they were talking about another, sovereign state. Americans joined in a single anti-Cuban and anti-Soviet outburst.

The president announced "a strict quarantine on all offensive military equipment under shipment to Cuba. All ships of any kind bound for Cuba from whatever nation or port will, where they are found to contain cargoes of offensive weapons, be turned back. This quarantine will be extended, if needed, to other types of cargo and carriers. We are not at this time, however," continued John Kennedy, "denying the necessities of life as the Soviets attempted to do in their Berlin blockade of 1948. . . . I have directed the Armed Forces to prepare for any eventualities. . . . We are asking tonight that an emergency meeting of the Security Council be convoked without delay to take action against this latest Soviet threat to world peace."

Immediately after the president's speech the armed forces of the United States were moved from DEFCON (defense condition) 5 to 3, which ensured that they were prepared to engage in military operations immediately. This top secret order from the commander in chief, ordinarily highly classified, was on this occasion transmitted unencrypted to overseas posts by radio. The president addressed it more to Father, to the Kremlin, than to the commanders of military bases and Air Force units.

That night three additional Marine battalions were airlifted to the base at Guantanamo. Families of military servicemen were evacuated on the return flights. All this was shown on television, demonstrating the president's determination to the American people.

However, not everything was reported on television. The meticulous McNamara was calculating what would be needed to invade Cuba. A quarter of a million soldiers would be required, plus an additional 90,000 Marines and commandos for the first assault wave. Losses of personnel were estimated at about ten percent, i.e., from 25 to 35 thousand men.

Two thousand aircraft sorties would be needed to crush Cuban resistance and ensure a safe landing.

The committee of the Joint Chiefs considered it necessary to have the landing party reinforced by Honest John tactical nuclear missiles. The president agreed, but stipulated that they had to obtain special permission from him before installing nuclear warheads.

At eleven o'clock that evening the Pentagon received word that the first fifteen Jupiters at the base in Turkey were armed and ready to fire.

THE BOOK IS CLOSED ON PENKOVSKY

By a strange coincidence, that was the day Oleg Penkovsky was arrested. Two months had gone by since his last report to Washington. Hemmed in by a dense circle of counterintelligence agents, he was physically unable to transmit new information. Those days he had no time to think of Cuba or missiles, Khrushchev or Kennedy. It became clear that Wynne would not arrive in time and that counterintelligence was breathing literally down his neck. Penkovsky began to panic. He dialed the telephone number given him earlier. It only remained to send his last farewells to his new friends. Or should we say masters? Or employers? A prearranged signal had been agreed upon at the very start of their collaboration. Every agent has such instructions, and every agent hopes that he will never have to use it. Now the time had come.

But Penkovsky did not send the prearranged phrase signifying his own exposure. He sent a totally different one, also agreed upon earlier. This one meant that the Soviet Union was about to carry out a nuclear strike on the United States. Was it a mistake? Or a desperate attempt to do away with himself and world civilization at one blow?

Fortunately, the fuse sputtered out. The CIA agents who received Penkovsky's signal assumed it was just one of those mistakes or distortions that invariably crop up in channels of communication. They didn't even report the panicky warning to the president.

THE SOVIET RESPONSE

Father crossed the threshold of his Kremlin office at about eleven that evening. It might have been the first time since Stalin's death that he had to come to the office at such a late hour. Not everyone had arrived in the conference hall, and its solid double doors opened and closed repeatedly as those invited to the session entered. A combination of surprise and alarm was reflected on all their faces. Everyone knew the reason for the unusually late and urgent meeting. But what precisely had happened? An ominous uncertainty hanging in the air oppressed and weighed them down as they sat waiting.

When everyone had arrived, Father repeated the news about the U.S. president's forthcoming speech. The others had already been informed of it. He went on to say that the speech was apparently going to deal with our missiles in Cuba.

Father looked around at those present, and his glance stopped at Malinovsky.

"We missed our chance," he said with regret.

The stout marshal started to rise from his chair, preparing to justify himself, but Father just waved his hand: "What is there to say? Sit down."

There appeared to be no point in discussion. Conversation lagged. All they could do was wait for news, and the time passed with unbearable slowness.

Oleg Aleksandrovich Troyanovsky, Father's assistant for international affairs, sat in a corner of the hall behind a small, rectangular polished table. At about 2:30 A.M., half an hour before the time set for the speech, he was summoned to the telephone. Dobrynin was calling from Washington.

Oleg Aleksandrovich was still speaking with Washington when a call came from the Foreign Ministry, from Gromyko's office, informing him that the U.S. chargé d'affaires in Moscow, Richard Davis, had just brought an urgent letter for Father. Troyanovsky asked them to read the text. The duty officer spoke slowly, trying not to miss a single word. The letter added nothing to Dobrynin's report—it was also about Kennedy's impending speech on American television. Troyanovsky was gone for a long time; it seemed an eternity. He finally returned, holding a sheaf of hastily scribbled pages.

"What have you got? Read it out," Father said, forcing a smile.

Troyanovsky, hesitating and sometimes stopping to check his notes, read President Kennedy's statement. Strangely enough, it evoked a feeling of relief among those present—it did not mean war. After those hours of agonizing suspense, when they were prey to the most somber suppositions, a blockade seemed like a kind of deliverance. Of course, only for the first few minutes. According to Troyanovsky, Father received the report calmly. The term "quarantine" sounded odd. Neither Kuznetsov nor Malinovsky could explain what it meant in real terms. But one thing was clear: they were threatening us.

By this time the Foreign Ministry had delivered the original of the U.S. letter. Father asked Troyanovsky to read it aloud. Perhaps some important details had been lost over the telephone. When his aide had finished, Father, glancing around the table, proposed that our answering statement be published quickly. It should demonstrate a determination to answer force with force and warn that we possessed a nuclear strike force no less powerful than the U.S. one.

Here again we have to remember Penkovsky. According to the information he had transmitted to the United States, our strike force was much weaker. However, a different calculus applies here. The two dozen missiles we had available were enough to destroy dozens of U.S. cities. Would a U.S. president consider that an acceptable price to pay for the removal of missiles from Cuba?

Father himself dictated the text of the answering letter and statement. His assistants went away to put it into so-called "fair form." Everyone agreed to resume the discussion at ten the next morning. Though it was time to leave, Father kept putting off his departure. Something still bothered him.

"Let's stay here until the morning," he said finally. "Foreign correspondents and intelligence agents are probably prowling around near the Kremlin. It doesn't pay to show that we're nervous. Let them think we're peacefully asleep in our beds."

No one objected. Father went to his office, where a bed had already been prepared for him on a couch. Deputy chairmen of the Council of Ministers were in a privileged position, since their offices were located in the building. Those with offices in the Central Committee building on Staraya Square had to while away the night on chairs in the conference hall.

In the morning everyone looked rumpled and unrested. The assistants read the edited texts of the answer to Kennedy and the Resolution of the Council of Ministers. The Resolution was left almost unchanged, but Father virtually rewrote the letter to Kennedy, making one correction after another. Other participants in the meeting occasionally made suggestions. Vasily Vasilyevich Kuznetsov decided to make his contribution. In essence, he proposed that we ourselves exert pressure on Berlin in response to U.S. pressure on Cuba. Kuznetsov thought that Father would approve, but he didn't. In fact he reacted with surprising sharpness.

"Keep that kind of advice to yourself," he snapped roughly. "We don't know how to get out of one predicament and you drag us into another."

Obviously, Father did not want to raise the level of tension.

They finally finished the letter. It was already almost lunchtime. It was decided to respond to the president via the Embassy. The government statement and orders to the troops of the Warsaw Pact, however, were read over the radio. They were read by Yury Levitan at 4 P.M.

In the Council of Ministers of the Union of Soviet Socialist Republics. In connection with the provocative actions by the government of the United States and the aggressive intentions of the U.S. armed forces, on October 23, 1962, the Soviet government in the Kremlin heard a report from Soviet minister of defense, Marshal of the Soviet Union, Comrade R. Ya. Malinovsky, on steps taken to raise the military readiness of the armed forces and has issued the minister of defense the necessary instructions, including:

1. Transfer to the reserves of eligible personnel in the Strategic Missile Forces, antiaircraft defense forces, and the submarine fleet will be postponed.
2. Cancellation of vacations for all personnel.
3. Combat readiness and vigilance in all branches of the armed forces will be increased.

This was followed by a similar statement concerning forces of the Warsaw Pact: "In the Staff of the Unified Armed Forces of the Countries of the Warsaw Pact. On October 23, 1962, Marshal of the Soviet Union and Commander in Chief of the Joint Armed Forces of the Nations of the Warsaw Pact A. A. Grechko summoned representatives of the participating armies and issued an order to carry out a series of measures raising the level of combat readiness of troops forming part of the Joint Armed Forces."

The order to arm the strategic missiles provoked an unexpected call to Father from Korolyov. The following day, October 24, Korolyov had planned to launch his first unmanned probe toward Mars. Launch preparations were almost complete and the rocket was on the launch pad when an order came from the General Staff to replace the space vehicle immediately with a missile.

Korolyov rushed to the phone and called Malinovsky. The latter sympathized, but answered that there was nothing he could do, he was just following government orders. Then Sergei Pavlovich asked to be connected with Father. Naturally, Father knew about the Mars launch. He reassured Korolyov: "Don't get upset, continue working. The Mars launch is more important than arming yet another ballistic missile. I will arrange it."

A SHOW OF COMPOSURE

First to react to the crisis over Cuba was the British philosopher Bertrand Russell. That very night he sent both leaders an appeal not to commit any acts that might push the world toward nuclear catastrophe. Fidel Castro was the next to act. Late that night Cuba requested an immediate meeting of the Security Council.

I was at work when I heard over the radio about the developing crisis. From the report it was impossible to tell what had happened. I waited for evening with impatience and apprehension.

I expected Father to explain everything when he came home. But he appeared only briefly, announcing from the door that he was going to the theater. I thought to myself: The theater?! But out loud I only said the usual: "Are we going with you?"

Father loved the theater, opera more than ballet. He favored the dramatic theater also, especially the classics, Ostrovsky and Tolstoy. He was not so fond of contemporary plays, though for some reason he was enthralled by Alexander E. Korneichuk's stilted works. He also enjoyed going to concerts. Usually the whole family attended, but official visits by foreign guests were an exception. Then the appearance of his children or household members in the government box was, naturally, out of the question. That turned out to be the case now. A Romanian delegation led by Gheorghe Gheorghiu-Dej was visiting Moscow. A visit to the Bolshoi Theater was planned, in accordance with the usual procedure for official visits. They decided on *Boris Godunov* in an American production, an unusual event in Moscow. Neither Father nor, certainly, officials in the Ministry of Foreign Affairs, suspected that on Tuesday they would hardly have time to go to the theater.

However, Father decided not to change his plans. He thought that a theater appearance might even be useful. The whole world would see that the U.S. president's threats had not disturbed the Kremlin's equilibrium. Moreover, the Romanians' sensitivity to insult had long been the talk of the town.

And the fact that it was an American performance, he thought, also came in handy. It showed that we didn't want to quarrel with anyone. That signal would be noted. To reinforce the impression, Father proposed that several other members of the Presidium of the Central Committee also have a "change of scene."

We had about forty minutes before he had to leave, and we began to stroll around the house. Father looked tired. Nevertheless, we had hardly walked outside when I began to deluge him with questions. In fact, he couldn't tell me very much: the Americans had discovered our missiles, but at this point it was hard to tell what they knew or whether their information was accurate.

On that first day Father still had some hope that reports received by the White House were vague and based on rumor. By evening he was sure that they would not have begun to act so decisively without irrefutable proof. We would have to adjust to the new situation.

I was surprised: it turned out that we had no carefully thought-out plan of action in case our missiles were discovered prematurely. Now we would have to improvise.

Despite everything, Father thought that construction should continue. Work to make the missiles operational should go forward even more rapidly. Then the Americans would be put in the position envisaged by our initial plan. They would be forced to think things over. Of course, the fact that now there was such a furor made it more difficult to make judicious decisions, but

Father hoped that the president would still reconcile himself to his unpleasant neighbors.

The appropriate order was sent to Cuba. There was not much work left. It was literally only a matter of days before the first launch sites would be ready for the R-12s. The R-14s were to follow.

At the same time Pliyev was ordered to investigate and send in a report on how the Americans could have observed what was going on. There was no immediate response. It took them some time to think things over and decide how best to explain this latest misstep. Too late, they checked on the camouflage, then concealed the machines that had been left day and night under the open sky in violation of all instructions.

Our walk came to an end. I still didn't have any reassuringly clear idea of what was going on.

The theater visit was mentioned in the U.S. ambassador's regular report to the State Department. Father was accompanied in the box by Kozlov, Kosygin, Mikoyan, and Brezhnev. The choice of "theatergoers" was not accidental. Father made the point that no one was left in the Kremlin. They were all at the Bolshoi. After the performance the artists, both Soviet and American, were invited to the former tsarist box, now reserved for official visits by heads of foreign governments. Father thanked them for the performance. Champagne was served, and they all drank to peace around the world, to pure voices, and a clear sky overhead.

THE BLOCKADE

While Father was preparing to go to the theater, a hectic day was dawning in Washington. At 10 A.M. on October 23, the first official meeting of the newly created Presidential Executive Committee convened. It was chaired by John Kennedy.

The Americans were now inspecting the launch positions daily. In his report on changes in Cuba over the last few days, McCone noted that the island was calm and that only Soviet personnel were allowed onto the missile bases. His report about the sudden and hurried camouflaging of missile installations was met with surprise. Why only now?

The Americans couldn't think of a satisfactory explanation. Father also got no sensible answer from Pliyev. I didn't hear any more enthusiastic remarks from him about the general, or references to awarding Pliyev the rank of marshal.

When McCone showed photographs of Cuban military sites taken the day before, John Kennedy was surprised to see that planes were lined up in straight rows on military airfields, as if to simplify the work of aerial attackers.

He joked that this was a manifestation of the military's penchant for order and pattern and commented that you could probably find something similar at airfields in Florida. General Taylor immediately sent a plane to inspect U.S. bases from the air. The president proved to be correct: there too, planes were parked wingtip to wingtip in exact geometrical patterns.

That same evening, after consultation with representatives from the Organization of American States, the decision was made to impose a naval blockade at 10 A.M. on October 24.

Uncertainty about the blockade was Father's greatest worry. Kennedy's statement referred only to the imposition of a quarantine. When would they decide on practical steps? This was immensely important to Father, since the last thirty ships were approaching Cuba.

Father thought that we, as a great power, could not yield to dictation by the United States and that it did not have the right to inspect our ships on the high seas. All captains were ordered to continue on their course, not to obey commands from U.S. ships, and not to come to a halt. A confrontation was beginning. The least mistake could lead to something irreparable.

The Americans kept careful track of all communications, both open and encrypted, between our ships and the continent. On the evening of the twenty-third they noticed an unusual number of coded messages. Robert Kennedy writes that the CIA could not decode them—they didn't know then and don't know now—what orders the captains received from the center. The Executive Committee simply recorded that the ships did not change course. For the present they were not stopped. U.S. destroyers only swung around their silent weapons as they observed the freighters, tankers, and less often, passenger ships, flying the Soviet flag. The extreme tension affected everyone on those ships, from captain to sailor. It was only after the quarantine line was left astern that they sighed with relief. The danger was past.

Some of the ships with military cargoes, including the "nuclear" *Aleksandrovsk*, slipped through the quarantine zone at the last moment. To get out of harm's way, the *Aleksandrovsk* hurried to the nearest port, Isabel, instead of Mariel, as listed in the ship's documents. It transmitted a coded signal, an inoffensive message to shore, containing the prearranged phrases so anxiously awaited in Moscow. However it was worded, the meaning was: "We made it."

Father was informed at once. He calmed down somewhat. He even nourished some hope that the Americans were only making empty threats and would not dare to stop ships on the high seas. Father was increasingly preoccupied by the possibility that the Americans might decide to inspect Soviet ships. That was where he saw the greatest danger of a clash. Father began to seethe when he pictured foreign sailors rummaging through our ships, scurrying about the decks, opening doors to cabins, prying into ship documents.

He regarded such actions as piracy, and that very day he dictated an indignant letter to President Kennedy, his first letter since the crisis began. In it he noted: "I would like to give you a friendly warning that the measures announced in your statement represent a grave threat to peace and security in the world. The United States is openly and crudely violating international norms of freedom of shipping on the high seas, and committing aggression toward both Cuba and the Soviet Union."

And further on, without being specific about what was being placed in Cuba, he reasserted: "We confirm that the weapons now in Cuba . . . , intended solely for defensive purposes, serve as a defense of the Cuban Republic against possible attack by an aggressor."

The terminological war continued.

That same day the Soviet Union requested a meeting of the Security Council "in connection with the violation of the U.N. Charter and the threat to peace resulting from actions by the United States." On the desk of U.N. Acting Secretary-General U Thant now lay requests from all three parties to convene the Security Council to discuss the same question, with very similar mutual accusations.

The evening of October 23, I asked Father the most important question: "Will there be war?" He answered: "It's one thing to threaten with nuclear weapons, quite another to use them." In his words, the announcement of a higher level of military readiness in the Soviet Army was only a political response to U.S. actions.

Nevertheless, our intercontinental missiles, however few they were, stood fueled and armed, ready for immediate launching. At airfields pilots were on duty in their planes, prepared for immediate takeoff if the command were given, and Army units were issued ammunition.

Both Father and Kennedy were aware, not only of their personal responsibility, but of how important it was to keep control over events in their own hands, to keep anyone else from acting rashly and starting the war they both hoped to avoid.

At six o'clock that evening, October 23, the Executive Committee again gathered in the White House to discuss the practical aspects of imposing a blockade.

In Moscow it was late at night. Father had fallen asleep long before.

The president cautioned against precipitate actions that might result in the destruction of ships and deaths of their crews. He assumed that the captains of the Soviet ships, following Moscow's orders, might ignore U.S.

warnings, and then the question was: Who would win? If the ships do not obey U.S. orders, then either they will be allowed to pass or . . . we open fire. In the latter case, Kennedy insisted: "Fire only at propellers and only by my personal order. No individual initiative."

John Kennedy tried to clarify his position to Father. In answer to the message he had received that morning, he wrote that the United States did not intend to open fire on Soviet ships, but anything could happen if the ships ignored the rules of the blockade that had been established.

U Thant proposed his good offices to resolve the conflict. Both parties verbally accepted his proposal to mediate, but with certain reservations. John Kennedy agreed to engage in contacts in an attempt to clarify the possibilities for holding negotiations. Father agreed to U Thant's idea to bring a halt to the progression of events and promised to end military shipments to Cuba in return for lifting the blockade. There were as yet no possibility of reaching agreement, but any dialogue was better than a clash.

The meeting of the Executive Committee ended late. It still had not made a final decision on how and on what grounds to stop Soviet ships or to let them pass.

The situation became even more complex: Soviet submarines were assuming battle positions in the Caribbean Sea. My friend the boatswain from the submarine base in Severomorsk had been correct. However, the floating base itself was still at home.

As early as September 25 the Kremlin had decided not to send surface warships to Cuba. Their appearance would only put the Americans on guard. Only submarines would be sent. Four diesel torpedo submarines left for Cuba on October 1. Their commanders were Captains Second Grade Arkhipov, Dubivko, Ketov, and Shumnov. Each boat had six torpedo tubes and eighteen torpedoes in reserve, including a single nuclear one.

They arrived at their destination with some difficulty, having overcome three antisubmarine lines: at the North Cape, in the area of Iceland, and the last and most difficult stretching between the Azores and Newfoundland. Three of the submarines arrived at their destination. One had to turn back halfway because of a breakdown.

Now they were ready for anything. Ryurik Ketov, commander of one of the submarines, recalled many years later that, as he saw them off, Northern Fleet chief of staff Admiral Rossokha said: "Use the special weapon [nuclear torpedoes] in the following cases: first, if they bomb and hit you; second, if they force you to surface and shoot at you on the surface; third, on orders from Moscow."

When the others had left, the president asked his brother to meet with Dobrynin.

Robert hurried to the phone. The meeting was held at the Embassy at 9:30 in the evening. It was not an easy conversation. So much had happened since their last talk that it seemed as if the world had turned upside down. At their last meeting the ambassador had persuaded the president's brother not to even imagine that our missiles were present in Cuba.

Now Kennedy was seething with indignation as he enumerated the reassuring TASS statements, Father's letters, Gromyko's assurances.

"The president trusted you and you deceived him," was the dominant theme in his approach to Dobrynin.

All this reminded me of the history with the U-2, but it was as if the sides had switched places, with one essential difference: in May 1961 Father limited himself to loud pronouncements, whereas now the U.S. president was preparing for decisive actions.

Dobrynin had not managed to get new instructions from Moscow and continued to deny the obvious. In his words, there were no missiles in Cuba.

Finally, emotions were exhausted, and Kennedy asked the question he had come to ask: "Will Soviet ships continue to go through to Cuba despite the announcement of a blockade?"

Dobrynin confirmed: "Their instructions have not been changed."

"But this can end in war," said Robert Kennedy somberly.

Dobrynin simply shrugged in reply.

In parting they agreed to hold such meetings regularly, but only late at night to avoid attracting the attention of curious journalists.

After saying good-bye, Robert Kennedy hurried to the White House.

The ambassador began preparing a coded message to Moscow.

That was not a simple matter. In those days not only was there no direct communication between the two governments, but information from the Soviet Embassy reached the Kremlin by a roundabout route.

Many years later Dobrynin humorously described how it was done. The writing of dispatches, the formulation of proposals that might affect the fate of both countries, and then encryption—those were not the most difficult aspects. The main problem came afterward. Since the Embassy lacked a communication line with Moscow, it had signed an agreement with Western Union to transmit its messages. That, by the way, simplified the work of the CIA, which did not have to bother with radio interception—copies of the messages reached Langley before the originals reached Moscow.

The dispatch of a telegram began with a call to the company's local office summoning its representative. After feverish, often nocturnal work, there was a tedious wait for the messenger. He would finally appear. It was usually a carefree, smiling black man traveling around on a bicycle. A message from the president to the chairman of the Council of Ministers or a report on a conversation in the Justice Department would be put into his bulky satchel next to telegrams about weddings, births, and funerals. After signing for the envelope in a record book, the messenger continued on his route.

At this point, Dobrynin added, as if by chance: "When the papers were especially important and urgent, one of the Embassy's brighter employees would go off after the messenger. It was his job to make sure that our letter didn't get held up in some bar along the way, along with the messenger. This never happened, but we were always on watch for it."

In the White House the president was impatiently waiting for news. That day the blockade, or more precisely its implementation, was John Kennedy's main concern. It all seemed perfectly clear to the Joint Chiefs of Staff and the commander of the Atlantic Fleet, unanimously supported by the press: stop and search every ship crossing the patrol line, shoot pointblank at any obstinate ones. Fortunately, it was not up to them but to the president to make the final decisions, to slip between Scylla of war and the Charybdis of appearing weak.

As the evening of October 23 drew to a close, it was already the morning of the twenty-fourth in Moscow. Father also faced that most important and complex question. The threatening word "blockade" was hanging over him as well as over the president. The previous evening, after discussions in the Presidium of the Central Committee, he had issued the order to go ahead, no matter what. The flag of a great power must not dip before arbitrary Yankee actions on the high seas. They were relying on force, but we were not weak. The decision was made, but did not confer any peace of mind. Father confronted the very same dilemma: how, without compromising the dignity of a great power, to refrain from taking a fatal step, making a fatal miscalculation, stepping over the line between peace and war.

That line was rather transparent, almost invisible.

Robert Kennedy's visit to Ambassador Dobrynin did not bring any feeling of relief. When he returned to the White House, he found his brother with the British ambassador, David Ormsby-Gore. They were talking quietly in front of the fireplace. The subject was, of course, Cuba, the blockade, Khrushchev. Ormsby-Gore was an old friend of the president, one of the few whom he trusted without reservation. The president had called him in order to hear an opinion "from the outside." He believed that his advisers had been too close to the situation for too many days in a row and it had dulled their perceptions.

Unconstrained by the ambassador's presence, Robert gave a detailed account of his conversation with Dobrynin. The situation was clarified, but not eased. To avoid a mistake, they had to know what the thinking was in Moscow. Otherwise the game would proceed in the dark and a false step could be made at any moment.

John Kennedy proposed arranging an immediate meeting with Father. A face-to-face talk should clear up any misunderstandings.

The same thought had occurred to Father. In his reply to Bertrand Russell, he wrote that a way out of the current crisis might be found in an immediate high-level meeting. Father was being somewhat devious. To organize a meeting would take time, a few days at the very least. During that period the missiles would be deployed and the conversation could proceed as between equals. Father needed those few days. At present, Cuba remained essentially unarmed and hostage to the United States.

Possibly the same thought occurred to Kennedy. Or perhaps he had other reasons, but after some thought he himself rejected the idea of a meeting.

The decision to impose a blockade went into effect at 10 A.M. on October 24. At that moment clocks in Moscow were chiming 6 P.M. Very little time was left to evaluate the situation and make decisions. They were running out of time. The Soviet vessels were in the immediate vicinity of the screen of U.S. warships. Any haste would increase the probability of some impulsive and mistaken decision.

The sensible Ormsby-Gore advised Kennedy to give Moscow more time to think things over by moving the blockade line closer to Cuba.

The president accepted his advice. He called McNamara immediately and ordered that by morning the line of interception be set up at a point three hundred miles, rather than the present five hundred miles, from the island. That hectic Tuesday then drew to a close.

In fact, the new decision made little real difference. There was a constant stream of Soviet ships, and some of them had just passed the eight-hundred-mile mark and were already approaching the five-hundred-mile point. They hadn't thought of that in the White House. The balance of time offered to Moscow had not increased.

Today there are fewer and fewer participants in that grandiose epic. Each one's evidence is worth its weight in gold. I was able to contact Ivan Fyodorovich Sepelev, who commanded the freighter *Volgoles* in 1962. He made two voyages bringing arms to Cuba. The first took place in early September. The *Volgoles* ("Volga lumber"), as befitted a ship with that name, was in the British port of Hull unloading timber from Arkhangelsk when Sepelev received a coded message from Moscow ordering him to complete unloading quickly and make full speed for Kaliningrad. The captain was surprised by an unusual postscript: "Families of the crew should not visit the port of call."

Massive concrete slabs were loaded into the hold of the *Volgoles* in Kaliningrad. Sepelev was puzzled: Why were these "bars" so important? It was only later that he learned that the slabs were to form support platforms for the launch sites of ballistic missiles.

From Kaliningrad the ship sailed to neighboring Baltiysk, a naval base. "Traders" were not usually allowed there. An exception was made on this occasion. The *Volgoles* was to take on extremely secret MIG-21s. A fighter regiment made its own way directly from Moscow, where it had taken part in the air show at Tushino. In those days it was the only unit of the Soviet Air Force that knew how to fly the new planes. The bulky crates filled all the holds and some had to be placed on deck.

Three dozen Air Force pilots, dressed in civilian clothes, were housed in the crew's quarters, crowding the crew. Neither the pilots nor the seamen, including the captain, had any idea where they were going. Sepelev was to open a secret packet only upon leaving the Baltic, while crossing the Skaggerat. There he found that they were to head for the Cuban port of Isabel. The voyage proceeded calmly. Unloading as well. On September 11 the *Volgoles* was on its way back. It was already expected in Baltiysk.

The second trip to Cuba turned out to be more nerve-wracking. The holds were filled with enormous crates. Military lorries, with carefully covered cargoes, were rolled onto the deck. This time the captain was not told what was concealed inside. Only as it approached the island, when U.S. destroyers surrounded the *Volgoles*, did a laconic and somber man accompanying the cargo warn through clenched teeth that they must be prepared for anything. The cargo was—unusual. Sepelev still didn't understand what he was carrying: nuclear warheads or, perhaps, rockets? On the other hand, there was no doubt what was meant by: "Be prepared for anything." Orders received from Moscow were that if the ship was in danger of capture by foreign pirates, as U.S. warships were referred to, the *Volgoles* must be scuttled, along with its cargo.

Fortunately, it didn't reach that point. On Sunday, October 22, the ship's officers sighed with relief as they entered the roadstead of the port of Havana. But there they seemed to have been forgotten. No one rushed to unload the ship. The seamen languished in uncertainty. The radio was their only contact with the outside world, and what broadcasts they heard did not inspire any optimism: first Kennedy's announcement of the blockade, then Castro's call: "The Motherland or death." Moscow was silent.

Almost two weeks passed in this manner. It was not until November 3 that the crates and lorries were hastily transferred to shore and Sepelev was ordered to sail to the port of Mariel and begin loading rockets. Now they had to be shipped back.

Today we know that there were no nuclear warheads on the *Volgoles*. Apparently it was one of the "cover" ships, and all this secrecy was designed for foreign eyes and ears if they were suddenly found in the vicinity.

Now it is reliably known that forty-two out of sixty ballistic missiles and all the nuclear warheads were delivered to Cuba before the imposition of the blockade: about a hundred one-megaton warheads for ballistic missiles, eighty 120-kiloton warheads for tactical cruise missiles, eight 120-kiloton nuclear bombs, twelve 20-kiloton warheads for the Lunas and another four naval mines.[15] The last twenty-four nuclear warheads for R-14s and forty-four nuclear warheads for combat cruise missiles were delivered by the last of a trio of nuclear-powered freighters, the *Aleksandrovsk*.[16]

The enormous containers were unloaded in conformance with all precautionary measures. The security agencies admitted only the most reliable and verified workers. Perhaps it was just these special measures that gave rise to new talk: "something" was being delivered to the island. Fortunately or unfortunately, these rumors did not reach Washington and the CIA was left in ignorance. I say "unfortunately," since if the White House had been certain that nuclear warheads were on the island, the members of the Executive Committee would probably have behaved with still greater circumspection.

If one is to believe the declassified figures, the bulk of the nuclear cargo was transported on the *Indigirka* and *Aleksandrovsk*, while the *Lena* carried none of it, or almost none. It's possible that the *Lena* played the role of a decoy, to draw the attention of Americans. It's also conceivable that the "special" cargo was distributed among the ships in a rather different way.

It was decided not to unload the *Aleksandrovsk*, and it lay idle all those days in port. When the crisis was over, the ship with its cargo returned home to Severomorsk without attracting anyone's attention.

Against all this strain on the nerves, the failure at launch of the Mars probe went unremarked. However, not by everyone. In his book about Korolyov, the American historian James Harford writes that the U.S. early-warning system almost interpreted the explosion that blew the Soviet rocket and

---

15. From a book recently published in the United States and based on several Soviet secret documents made available to researchers: Aleksandr Fursenko and Timothy Naftali, *One Hell of a Gamble: Khrushchev, Castro and Kennedy, 1958–1964* (New York and London: W. W. Norton, 1997). For some reason the authors reduced the explosive power of all nuclear warheads (except for the R-12 and R-14) by a factor of ten. They probably diligently copied the documents that fell into their hands. I remember that a ruse was employed at that time to mislead undesirable readers—instead of 50 they wrote 5, instead of 120, 12. It was thought that the proper numbers would be familiar to those who needed to know, and the others. . . . Apparently the ruse worked, at any rate with the book's authors.

The "old" nuclear warheads for combat cruise missiles had an explosive force of 56 kilotons, which increased to 120 kilotons after the tests in 1961. The "old" bombs had an explosive force of 80 kilotons, the new 120 kilotons. Shells for the Lunas were not modernized, since their explosive force suited the military perfectly.—S.K.

16. D. A. Volkogonov, *Seven Leaders* (Moscow: Novosti Publishing House, 1995), 1:424–28; A. Dokuchayev, "100 Days of a Nuclear Crisis," *Krasnaya zvezda*, November 6, 1992. Specialists viewed this second work with distrust, but archival data now compel one to believe that the figures given in it are close to reality.

spaceship into small pieces as the beginning of a missile attack. Fear has big eyes! However, the confusion lasted only a few moments; the fragments fell, but certainly not on the territory of the United States

Harford embellished the picture somewhat. There was no explosion. Three stages of the rocket operated normally and lifted the spaceship into orbit, but the fourth, start-up interplanetary stage did not ignite, so the ship became a satellite of the earth. In the Soviet Union it didn't occur to Father or to the military that in the extremely tense situation of those days the Americans might have their own interpretation of the launch of a space rocket.

Such a failure of the imagination was not restricted to the Soviet Union, but affected the Americans as well. The routine launch of a ballistic missile from its Florida test site was also briefly thought at the time to be a missile attack on the east coast of the United States. The mistake was discovered only after radars showed that the missile's trajectory was taking it over the empty expanses of the Atlantic Ocean.

On the morning of October 24, Moscow learned from American radio reports that the quarantine would come into force later that day, at 6 P.M. Moscow time. Next came the message from Dobrynin. He emphasized that the president's brother was extremely concerned by the possible consequences of contact between our ships and the quarantine barrier. They might be unpredictable.

During the night Father had already begun to doubt the advisability of the evening's decision to continue straight ahead. It was made in the heat of the moment, dictated by the heart, not the head. The morning's news made him hesitate still further. The risk of a conflict with U.S. warships appeared to be absolutely unjustified. Now he based his argument in favor of changing the decision by saying that everything necessary had been delivered to Cuba, except for the R-14s.

At the morning session of the Presidium of the Central Committee, Father proposed issuing a new order to the ships carrying weapons: to stop. The ministers of defense and of the merchant fleet should decide which ships should stay at sea waiting for the blockade to be lifted, and which would be better off returning home or heading for the nearest ports.

Since the president's statement referred only to offensive weapons, ships with civilian cargoes were ordered to continue and to answer inquiries from Americans, but not to allow them on board under any guise whatsoever. They were our sovereign territory, sanctified by the Soviet flag.

The military were especially concerned about tankers. We could make do with the armored troop carriers and tanks that had already been delivered, but without fuel our planes could not take off and our military vehicles could not move. Missiles also required fuel.

Father wavered. On the one hand, the tankers' cargo was to supply the troops, but on the other—that was not obvious. The Americans could interpret it either way, depending on their inclinations. Father felt he didn't have a choice; without fuel the entire operation was doomed. It was finally decided that the tankers should stay on course, but under the same conditions: not to resist the Americans, to satisfy their curiosity, but not to let them on board.

The day was drawing to a close by the time their discussion ended and a coded message was ready. Father grew nervous—the first clash could occur at 6 P.M. Submarines were moving to implement the previous day's order, to break through by any means. In the event the Americans employed weapons, they were instructed to act according to the situation.

Finally, at just after 5 P.M., he was informed that the coded message had been sent. The approximate hour in reserve was quite sufficient. Father sighed with relief. The decision had not been easy. Someone was sure to accuse him of giving way to the imperialists, of insufficient firmness, but that would pass. It would be more terrible if shooting began. Then the situation would be out of his hands and events would be out of control. Father waited impatiently for reports from the Atlantic. How would the Americans behave?

Naval personnel were ordered to report immediately all suspicious maneuvers by the opposing side. It only remained to wait until six o'clock.

Like Robert Kennedy, Father didn't want to provide food for idle conjecture. He proposed moving the meeting to his residence.

"Journalists are camped out on Red Square counting how many windows are lit up in the Kremlin. Let's not give them any satisfaction," he joked humorlessly.

They settled into the large dining room at No. 40 Lenin Hills. The doors, usually wide open, were shut carefully. Conversation was barely audible. Finally, there was a loud ring from the government phone in the living room adjacent to the dining room. Father hurried to answer it.

This whole time I was sitting in my room reading, or trying to read. All I could think about was what was going on in the dining room across from my door. Every once in a while I caught myself listening to indistinct voices from there. However, it wasn't possible to make out what they were saying.

On the other hand, I could clearly hear what Father said over the phone. From his words I understood that no clash had occurred.

Soon the guests began to leave. After their departure Father and I went out for a stroll. He looked tired, walked along without saying anything, and I didn't try to pester him with questions.

Father grew nervous, as did the Americans. In the morning President Kennedy asked first of all about the behavior of Soviet ships. On the ocean nothing had changed, as if there had been no address to the people, no decisions by the Organization of American States, and no proclamation about establishment of the blockade. The ships, as if nothing had happened, were continuing on their course and coming closer with every hour to the line separating today's world from yesterday's.

There was nothing to do but accept Father's words in the previous day's letter from Moscow—that they did not recognize as lawful any piratical actions that violated the universally recognized rules of the freedom of navigation on the high seas. The time had come to decide: either board the ships and seize their cargoes or let them pass, admit that his own statement, a decision by the president of the United States, was untenable.

The retreat from the five-hundred-mile line had not helped. It was estimated that the two sides would make contact no later than noon. Then word came that the first Soviet ship would cross the blockade line between 10:30 and 11:00.

THE CONFRONTATION AT SEA

Across a quarter of a century, Robert McNamara recalled how the president ordered him to get in touch with the fleet commander once again. John Kennedy had begun to doubt that the admiral had understood his last message: "Fire only with the president's approval." A mistake could be very costly.

McNamara immediately called Atlantic Fleet headquarters. Admiral George Anderson had been there around the clock for the last few days. He seemed somewhat surprised by the secretary of defense's question about what he would do in case Soviet ships did not submit. He replied firmly and distinctly that he intended to act according to standard instructions: first a warning shot would be fired across the bow, and if that had no effect, they would fire on the ship.

McNamara gasped! The president's suspicions were justified. The admiral had just explained how he was planning to unleash the third world war!

"Open fire only after receiving an O.K. from the White House," ordered McNamara, controlling himself.

"What, have you decided to rescind Navy rules?" Anderson questioned, with a certain degree of mockery.

"That's the president's order," McNamara snapped.

This reference to the commander in chief had its effect, and the admiral reacted testily with a curt: "Yes, sir."

What if it hadn't occurred to Kennedy to double-check how headquarters was interpreting his decision?

Meanwhile, Soviet ships were continuing their calm motion forward, toward the point clearly demarcated by the line of U.S. warships which, if crossed, would force the White House and Kremlin into a decision. Which one? As yet neither Kennedy nor Father knew.

Two ships were in the lead in this potentially fatal race, the *Gagarin* and the *Komiles*. I don't know what cargo was on the *Komiles*, but we know that the *Yuriy Gagarin* was carrying fuel trucks and cranes for one of the missile division's regiments, as well as the regiment's staff, headed by its commanding officer. A ship named in honor of the first man to fly in space was now about to be the first to cross, or attempt to cross, a quite different boundary.

"The moment had come for which we prepared, although we hoped that it would never arrive. The perception of danger and anxiety hung over us all like storm clouds. The President particularly felt it"—this is how Robert Kennedy described the atmosphere that morning in the White House.

The situation soon became even more complex. The cruiser appointed to make the initial interception reported that the distance between the two leading Soviet ships had narrowed and they were moving side by side, while between them the screws of a submarine had been detected.

McNamara reported to the president that the aircraft carrier *Essex* had sailed immediately to assist the cruiser and that its antisubmarine helicopters had taken off. According to their current orders, they would demand by sonar that the submarine come to the surface; if it did not obey they would begin dropping depth charges with small explosives, which were not capable of damaging its hull but would create an unholy racket.

This method had always produced results under other conditions. The submarine being pursued would surface. Its captain would climb on deck and was able to express his opinion on what had happened. But then both sides had known that it was a game. And now? What instructions did the submarine commander have? It was hardly likely that he had orders to obey commands from a U.S. aircraft carrier.

Only the words of a witness allow one to describe, even if approximately, what was going on then in the White House. Again Robert Kennedy:

> There was a steady hum of voices, but I couldn't make anything out until the President's voice rang out: "Isn't there some way we can avoid having our first exchange with a submarine?"
>
> "No," answered McNamara. "There's too much danger to our ships. There is no alternative. . . ."
>
> We had come to the time of final decision.

And further:

I think these few minutes were the time of gravest concern for the President. Was the world on the brink of a holocaust? Was it our error? A mistake? Was there something further that should have been done? Or not done? His hand went up to his face and covered his mouth. He opened and closed his fist. His face seemed drawn, his eyes pained, almost gray. For a few fleeting seconds, it was almost as though no one else was there and he was no longer the President.

One can imagine the feelings of the captains of the two small freighters and the commander of the threatened submarine, over which loomed the 180-ship armada of the U.S. Atlantic Fleet.

They were only a few miles from the blockade line when the radio operators on the *Gagarin* and *Komiles* reported to their captains that an urgent coded message had come from Moscow. They ran to get the cryptographer. He was new and had been on only one voyage. The *Gagarin* and *Komiles* had never associated their fate with state secrets and never would again. Time passed—it seemed an eternity while the cryptographer fiddled with his codes. The U.S. ships were approaching rapidly. They felt a great urge to slow down, but orders from Moscow had been to ignore this great concentration of forces. Finally the cryptographer, his shoes clattering on the steel ladder, flew onto the bridge. His face was pale and a piece of paper with the decoded order was visible in his hand.

"Here," he gasped. The coded message consisted of only a few lines. The captain caught the gist without reading to the end and immediately called the engine room. A bell rang acknowledging his order to stop.

The ships came to a halt, as did the submarine. It had no communication with shore. According to orders it had received the day before, the submarine was to follow the freighters and assist them, depending on circumstances and if weapons were needed. The submarine's commander was at a loss to understand why the ships he was guarding had come to a standstill. The U.S. aircraft carrier, cruiser, and accompanying destroyers were audible at a distance and, judging by the sound of their screws, were clearly not preparing to attack.

Eduard Aleksandrovich Zagalny, captain of the *Komiles*, whose name I learned by chance, now reread his instructions carefully. He was ordered to move to a safe distance, drift, and await further orders, without entering into contact with the U.S. formation and without crossing the line of quarantine.

Brief commands were issued, and both the *Gagarin* and *Komiles*, as if joined together, described a smooth semicircle and headed in the opposite direction. The submarine followed them.

A message flew to headquarters from the *Essex*: "The Russians are withdrawing!"

The decision made in Moscow had reached its destination at the very last moment. How much time remained before a clash? An hour? Thirty minutes? Or less? Fortunately, today we can only guess. Why fortunately? Because we are alive, and so we are able to guess.

When did this happen? There is an exact note of the time. It was made in the White House by Robert Kennedy:

> 10:25 A.M. A messenger brought a note from CIA Director McCone: "Mr. President, we have a preliminary report that seems to indicate that some of the Soviet ships have stopped dead in the water."
>
> 10:32. "The report is accurate, Mr. President. Six ships which had almost reached the blockade line suddenly stopped or have turned back. A representative from the Office of Naval Intelligence is on his way over with a full report."
>
> "So, no ships will be stopped or intercepted," said the President.

Prudence won out in the first round, and both sides received a breathing space.

The commander of the Atlantic Fleet was sent an urgent message to do nothing, to give the Soviet ships the opportunity to turn back.

Anxiety in the White House lessened somewhat, but soon news came that only sixteen ships had turned around. The rest, mostly tankers, were holding their course.

The Executive Committee was faced with another decision. The tanker *Bucharest*, flying the Soviet flag, was the first to reach the quarantine line. Pugnacious members of the Executive Committee, aroused by what they saw as a victory, wanted to make a show of determination and detain the ship, even though no types of fuel were covered by the previous day's declaration. Success was beginning to go to the heads of some people. Their more sober colleagues thought there was no need to raise the level of tension.

The president adopted an intermediate position. After the ritual process of identification, that tanker, as well as those following it, was allowed through the screen, but a U.S. destroyer shadowed them closely right up to the harbor.

In his memoirs Father noted respectfully that despite the sharp and aggressive press campaign against our country, U.S. leaders displayed a sober evaluation of the situation and did not challenge the inviolability of the Soviet flag.

Of all the ships heading for Cuba, one attracted particular attention from the Americans—the cargo ship *Poltava*, which they thought had left from the port of Odessa, but had really left from Sevastopol.

The CIA had been informed by its agents that missile warheads were on board the *Poltava*. Now, when many secrets have been revealed, we can say with certainty that the *Poltava*, like four other freighters (the *Almetyevsk*, *Nikolayev*, *Dubna*, and *Divnogorsk*) which failed to attract close attention from the Americans, carried R-14s and their associated equipment.

U.S. intelligence recorded every stage of the ship's journey. It even knew that the *Poltava*'s documents gave Algiers as the first point of destination.

The Americans followed the *Poltava* doggedly. They determined that instead of Algiers it had headed for the Straits of Gibraltar, and then sailed into the Atlantic Ocean. Their suspicion grew and became almost a certainty when the ship was observed meeting three Soviet submarines that belonged, the CIA believed, to the Northern Fleet.

Its further course lay toward Cuban shores. The *Poltava*, *Almetyevsk*, *Nikolayev*, *Dubna*, and *Divnogorsk* were among the ships that received orders on October 24 to return home.

SURVIVING WEDNESDAY

Construction was going ahead smoothly in Cuba. Reports from Pliyev breathed optimism. Father remained firmly convinced that the best policy was to play for time in order to complete the installation of the missiles. The message received October 24 from U Thant was therefore very welcome. It proposed that weapons shipments to Cuba be halted for several weeks and that the blockade be removed during that same period, while an attempt was made to reach a mutually acceptable solution. Father seized on this idea and again proposed a summit meeting.

Now Kennedy rejected any possibility of a dialogue. Meanwhile, the missiles remained in Cuba.

He sent the same reply to Bertrand Russell. The elderly philosopher thought that the U.S. measures were too harsh and their uncompromising policy was dangerous. He called on the parties to look for a way toward reconciliation. Kennedy wrote in his message: "I think your attention might well be directed to the burglar, rather than to those who caught the burglar."

Here the president went too far. It was only a case of an unwelcome (to him) guest visiting a neighbor.

Father took advantage of every opportunity to convey his understanding of events to his opponent. On that anxious Wednesday he received American businessman William Knox. Father wasn't interested in his business proposals, but wanted to use the meeting with Knox to explain his position to President Kennedy.

Father emphasized that both the ballistic and antiaircraft missiles were under Moscow's strict control. Not a single Cuban was present on the missile bases. Father told Knox that times had changed; America's exclusive situation was over and it had to get used to having Soviet missiles in Cuba, just as we had learned to live with the U.S. Jupiters next door to us in Turkey.

With respect to the blockade, he adopted a tough position: there would be no compromises that might humiliate a great power. If Soviet freighters were subject to attack—which is how he described their stoppage and inspection—we would take retaliatory measures and, if there was no alternative, we would sink the aggressor.

Father's words were heard in Washington. Not a single Soviet ship had been stopped. The State Department asked the U.S. ambassador in Ankara, Raymond Hare, what the Turkish government's reaction might be to the removal of the Jupiters. A similar message went to NATO headquarters.

SURVIVING THURSDAY

Thanks to the restraint shown by both leaders, that critical Wednesday ended without incident. Despite militant statements, mutually acceptable conditions for honoring the blockade were tacitly established for the next couple of days: the Soviets did not try to send prohibited cargoes; the Americans let our remaining ships through without interference. This equilibrium was very fragile.

Now reconnaissance planes flew over Cuba every day—not only U-2s, but eight low-flying planes visited twice a day, morning and evening. They recorded the minutest details. The exposed film amounted to tens of thousands of yards. For example, on October 24 it was twenty-five miles long. Of course, it was impossible to process all of it, but the most important objects were studied, primarily photographs of known areas.

On Wednesday intelligence data showed significant progress in construction. Pliyev was keeping his promise to Father. The objects being built were revealed one after another. What yesterday had been only vague contours, today were clearly visible as almost completed installations: launch positions, missile nuclear storage sites, bunkers. Specialists concluded that the missiles would soon be fully operational. It was a matter of days, and no longer than a week.

They were mistaken. One regiment of R-12 ballistic missiles had been operational and nuclear capable for five days already. It was joined on October 25 by a second regiment and one battalion of a third.

Alarm grew in the White House. The president ordered strategic aviation to be raised to DEFCON 2, the second level of readiness, for the first time in the postwar era. DEFCON 1 would signify the start of military operations. Kennedy's decision didn't indicate that he intended to take another step toward a nuclear attack. It was a warning gesture that should be evaluated by Moscow. As in the previous case, every effort was made to ensure that the order was known in the Soviet Union almost before it arrived at Air Force units themselves. Their calculations were correct. But more about that later.

After that stormy Wednesday, it seemed that détente arrived on Thursday, October 25. The sense of relief on both sides of the ocean was obvious. Of course, that was only on the surface. The situation was still deadlocked. But even that was good, since Thursday saw no American actions. It became increasingly clear that the situation could not be resolved head-on and that circuitous ways had to be sought. Compromises would be unavoidable. As soon as emotions over the establishment of the blockade and the shadowing of the *Bucharest* died down, John Kennedy decided to answer Father's latest letter. That was his first act on Thursday. The letter was sent that night, at 1:45 A.M.

In his message the president enumerated all the recent events and re-ferred to his September statement and the fact that deployment of offensive weapons in Cuba was unacceptable to the United States. He expressed genu-ine resentment at the fact that he had been deceived. He had believed Father's assurances and "had begun to restrain those who had insisted at the time on taking immediate steps." Now those people turned out to have been correct. The message conveyed between the lines was that this had under-mined his prestige. Kennedy called for efforts to search for a mutually ac-ceptable way out of the impasse. The tone of the message was not belligerent, but it made clear that no agreement could be reached unless the missiles were removed.

Father received the letter before noon. He was touched by the sincere tone of the message. The brevity and toughness of its wording left no doubt of the president's resolve and decisiveness. Now a great deal, in fact every-thing, depended on Father: he would have to make the one correct decision. The old policy no longer applied. The risk was too great. That Thursday was when a change took place in his thinking, a turn toward the search for a solution to the defense of Cuba not by brute force, but as a result of compro-mise. For the moment Father tried to explore the basis for that. Simply re-moving the missiles under the uproar of a worldwide scandal would inevitably be viewed as a defeat, a retreat. That, Father could not permit. But only a madman would persevere.

At a session of the Presidium which convened after lunch, Father talked for the first time about the possibility of removing the missiles. Of course, under the condition that the U.S. president promise to guarantee the inviola-bility of Cuba, not only from the United States, but from its Latin American allies as well, not to speak of the Cuban émigrés. No one in the Kremlin believed for a moment that they would dare to lift a finger or open their mouths without orders from Washington.

But that didn't seem enough to Father. Our enemies would try to discredit us by saying that of course, the USSR took away its missiles as soon as the United States said "Stop it!" Guarantees would be of no consequence.

Father proposed that still another condition be included in a letter to the president: a quid pro quo, the Cuban missiles staked against the Jupiters based in Turkey and Italy. It was decided not to push too hard by mentioning the Thors, which were deployed in Britain.

Presidium members agreed with Father's new approach just as unanimously as they had to sending our missiles to Cuba five months before.

Gromyko left for the Foreign Ministry to carry out instructions. It was decided that the Presidium would examine the answer the next morning. Given the eight-hour time difference, it would arrive in Washington that same morning, making it possible to gain an entire working day. Work went on in both capitals as if on a sliding schedule. The KGB report that it had intercepted an order putting U.S. forces on a heightened level of readiness, transmitted by strategic aviation headquarters, compelled haste. Father reacted simply to the news that it was not encrypted: "They're trying to intimidate us." Intimidate or not, it would be extremely thoughtless to ignore this unequivocal warning.

Now Father had to calculate what it meant. A bluff? Or an honest warning? Are they going to attack?

He himself didn't hesitate to bluff, and therefore he sensed with particular clarity that under superhuman tension and when such forces were put in motion, even a simple threat can sometimes suddenly, against its author's will, turn into an inevitable reality. After all, an order doesn't vanish into thin air! It affects thousands of people and hundreds of planes. One more coded word and this entire armada would throw itself on the Soviet Union. It could not be held back.

The importance of the decision he would have to make was overwhelming, but Father did not give way to panic. He decided to wait. While Gromyko was occupied with the letter the situation would become clearer. Only, in which direction? But morning is wiser than evening.

It was with such melancholy thoughts that Father returned from the Kremlin.

At home I was waiting for him. As usual, we went out for a breath of fresh air. Naturally, he didn't reveal all of his doubts, but that evening I heard for the first time that we would probably have to remove the missiles. Of course, under the condition of appropriate U.S. promises and international guarantees that Cuba would be safe from attack by forces of the United States or its allies, or by Cuban émigrés located in neighboring countries. Father said not a word about Turkey and Italy.

I was shocked and could hardly restrain my anger. To my mind, retreat was associated with national humiliation. In answer to my questions, Father explained patiently that pressure was being exerted on the president from all directions: the military, the press, Congress. All were demanding military action. Kennedy might not be able to resist such pressure. And then what would happen? They would attack Soviet troops in Cuba and we would attack them in Berlin? It would be stupid and nothing would be gained. Once you begin shooting you can't stop.

I couldn't understand how Father had decided to trust the word of a U.S. president. I sensed that he simply had no alternative. Until then Father had held the opinion that the imperialists, especially Americans, could not be trusted; they will deceive you. And he would at once refer to his experience with Eisenhower, the episode with the U-2. Now he had softened. He was ready to be satisfied with paper assurances. He thought that the president would not bring himself to violate them.

He did not convince me. Father was trying to persuade himself, painfully reconsidering the principles he had followed in recent years. Something new had to emerge. He had already almost agreed. But he wanted to be asked—let the proposals originate with the Americans, not with him. They should be the ones to suggest the idea.

Father felt trapped. If Soviet missiles in Cuba were attacked, he had no retaliatory actions in reserve. Such an attack must be averted at all costs. Not for a moment did he contemplate a nuclear strike on the United States. The atomic bomb was fine for newspapers. Father considered any action in Berlin to be unduly dangerous. Against his wishes, it could lead to a great war. He ruled out war as a way of resolving quarrels. There was no other answer to be found. And since it was impossible to respond in kind to the use of force, such a possibility must be averted no matter what the cost.

When we returned from our walk, Father drank tea with lemon, glanced idly through the newspaper, which vilified the American naval pirates, and climbed heavily up the stairs to his bedroom on the second floor. I also retired to my room. Although my heart was heavy, I was not afraid that a conflict was inevitable. I had no doubt that Father would find a way out of the situation.

SURVIVING FRIDAY

On the morning of Friday, October 26, unpleasant news awaited Father in his Kremlin office. The information had arrived late the previous evening, but had taken most of the night to make its way through the KGB offices on Lubyanka Square. No one dared to wake Father, and the report from the "source" was placed in the usual gray-blue folder, along with other reports from the same department.

After reading the first few lines, Father understood: here was confirmation that yesterday's announcement of a military alert of strategic aviation was not a bluff. Or, more precisely, was probably not a bluff.

This is what had happened. The day before, Wednesday, a member of our Embassy, a professional intelligence agent, had followed his usual habit of dropping in at the National Press Club to chat and try to ferret out the latest news. The club was crowded with journalists, all talking about Soviet missiles in Cuba. They were speculating about what the White House would do. Attack or not? And if so, when?

Our agent was "lucky." He came across the trail immediately. *New York Herald Tribune* correspondent Rogers was saying a noisy good-bye to his friends. He was leaving that day for Florida to report on the landing of U.S. Marines in Cuba. Military actions would begin the following day. Our agent, who knew Rogers well, picked a suitable moment and drew him aside to a separate table. Rogers repeated: "Yes, things are moving right along; we begin tomorrow." He spoke confidently. Furthermore, information gained from him previously had always proved reliable. And now he mentioned details, said something about landing craft and planes with bombs hanging from their fuselages. They were all just waiting for tomorrow's order to go forward.

After circulating a little longer around the press club, our agent hurried to his office. The disturbing information must be sent without delay to the center, to Moscow.

Today it's hard to tell whether this was simply not very accurate information, or carefully crafted disinformation intended to reinforce the previous day's order to strategic aviation. The latter is more likely. The White House and Langley were doing everything they could to undermine the Kremlin's position.

On this occasion Father hesitated, even though he tended not to believe reports from intelligence agents. How could he ignore such a report? Father decided to take the intelligence report from Washington seriously.

Leafing through the remaining pages, he found nothing of any importance. Important, that is, measured against the yardstick of that "black" Friday, when he had either to turn away from the abyss or they would all fall into it together, the just and the guilty, the leaders and the led.

As agreed earlier, around 10 A.M. members of the Presidium of the Central Committee began entering his office, along with the two constant participants in the vigils of that week, Malinovsky and Gromyko. They all arranged themselves along a long conference table, covered by a fine green "Kremlin" cloth. The draft answer from the chairman of the Council of Ministers of the USSR to the president of the United States, printed on special paper, lay in a folder by the foreign minister. Andrei Andreyevich walked toward the desk where Father sat a little apart. He wanted to show him the document, but Father stopped him with a gesture. "Now we'll all listen together," he said.

A few minutes later Gromyko began to read the message. Usually Father didn't leave a speaker in peace. He would interrupt with corrections and additions, which were immediately written down by the Presidium stenographer, a middle-aged, dark-haired woman, who looked a little like a gypsy. This time he didn't interrupt, only looking up at Gromyko when he began to speak about the U.S. missile bases in Turkey and Italy. Gromyko finished, cleared his throat, waited uncertainly for a few seconds and then sat down.

The rest were silent. Father's unusual reaction, or rather lack of reaction, unsettled them.

Father rummaged through the paper folders scattered on the desk, finally found the gray-blue one he was looking for, and took out a couple of thin sheets of paper fastened together with a paper clip.

"We have been warned that war could start today," began Father. His voice sounded unusually hollow. "Of course, it's possible the information was planted, but the risk is too great. America is gripped by a real frenzy and the military are thirsting for action. I therefore propose that we not involve U.S. missiles in Europe in the argument at this time. They're not bothering anyone. We have to concentrate on the main point: if the United States, their president, pledges not to attack Cuba, we will withdraw our missiles, despite the unpleasantness. Otherwise the situation becomes too dangerous."

None of the meeting's participants objected. Gromyko droned: "That's right."

Father proposed that a new answer be composed immediately, right then and there. There was no time to wait. As it was, more than twenty-four hours had passed since arrival of the message from Washington.

"Nadezhda Petrovna," said Father, turning to the stenographer.

"I'm ready, Nikita Sergeyevich," replied the woman.

Father stood up and started to dictate. He talked about responsibility for the fate of the world, for people's lives, which rested on the shoulders of the U.S. president and on his, the chairman of the Council of Ministers. He went on to discuss which weapons could be considered offensive and which defensive and called for prudence and calm. At the end he proposed an agreement whereby the Soviet Union would withdraw its missiles, while the United States would guarantee the security of Cuba.

Unlike president Kennedy's letter, Father's was long, like many of his speeches, not always consistent or focused. However, there was no doubt about its main point: its author was searching for a way out of the crisis and sincerely striving for peace.

They decided that Nadezhda Petrovna should immediately write out the text from her shorthand and Father's assistants, together with the diplomats, should put it in good form. After lunch, at about two or three o'clock, it was to be ready for final review and signing. Nadezhda Petrovna left the room and was replaced by a colleague. In Washington people still slept.

There was really no other item on the agenda, aside from the letter. Father proposed hearing from the military, from Malinovsky, about the damage Americans might cause the Soviet Union and what we could do to oppose them. Of course, that had been discussed more than once, but now war was transformed from a specter into a real threat. Malinovsky looked bleakly around at those present and answered that materials, maps, and diagrams could be ready by the following morning. As for the rest, the armed forces had been put on the alert and no enemy would take them by surprise. Father agreed that tomorrow would do. In any case, nothing could be radically changed in the hours remaining. The important thing now was not to think about how to wage war, but about how to prevent it.

On that note the morning meeting of the Presidium came to an end. Father detained Gromyko, who was heading for the door. He had thought of giving some advance notice of his letter. A great deal of time would pass while the letter was being typed, edited, rephrased, transmitted, and approved. But no one knew how much longer peace would endure. So Father decided to resort to an already tested method—use a trusted individual to transmit, not the message itself, but a hint that it was coming.

Gromyko endorsed Father's idea. Father at once picked up the phone and dialed the telephone number of the KGB chairman. Semichasny himself answered. That telephone to the secretaries was always manned. Father briefly explained what he wanted. Shelepin replied that such a person could of course be found, and that he would immediately issue the necessary instructions. An order to sound out the Americans went to Washington.

A man named Aleksandr Fomin[17] was told (through nondiplomatic channels) to meet with someone who had connections with top-level officials and to sound out this person's opinions on several matters. Fomin's choice fell on journalist John Scali, who was close to people at higher levels of the State Department.

Father's initiative did not mean that work stopped in Cuba. Everything was taking its normal course there. Father thought that if the Americans sus-

---

17. Aleksandr Fomin was actually Aleksandr Semyonovich Feklisov, now a retired KGB colonel. At that time he was KGB Station Chief in Washington, D.C. Earlier, in the 1940s, he was the controller for the Soviet espionage ring in the 1940s that was responsible for acquiring U.S. atomic secrets.

pected that we would cut them some slack, that we would show a lack of determination, then they would be unmanageable. Pliyev's reports were brief: installation of the launch sites was proceeding according to plan. U.S. aerial photographs confirmed his words. Construction of the missile sites was progressing at an extremely rapid pace.

From the first day Father kept Castro informed of every step that he took and reported Washington's reactions. It would appear that Castro had good reason to be nervous, but according to Alekseyev, he maintained an enviable composure. He took a tough position and thought that, if the Soviets displayed firmness, the Americans would not dare to carry out their threats. The ambassador agreed with him. He believed that Castro had made a thorough study of American psychology.

Father had a different point of view. He thought Castro was so resolute because he overestimated the "weight" of the missiles. In the eyes of its leader, Cuba finally seemed, if not equal in strength to its hated northern neighbor, at least able to put up a fight.

During those days the island looked like a besieged fortress. Its coast was dug up into trenches and communications passages and bristled with the barrels of weapons. They awaited a landing, tomorrow if not today. Castro toured the installations and encouraged the fighters. The summons to "Motherland or Death" became the leitmotif of his speeches.

If talk of a possible exchange of Cuban missiles for Turkish ones was heard for the first time in the White House on Wednesday, October 24, by Thursday such proposals poured forth as if from a horn of plenty. The analogy was obvious. The famous political commentator Walter Lippmann devoted a long article to the subject. Austrian foreign minister Bruno Kreisky promoted the idea as well.

The proposal came up again at the evening meeting of the Executive Committee in the White House. However, they decided to put off discussing it until a response came from Europe.

It didn't take long to appear. Thomas Finletter, U.S. ambassador to NATO, was the first to react. He described Turkey's position with the utmost clarity: the Jupiters are seen "as a symbol of the alliance's determination to use nuclear weapons in the event of a Russian attack by conventional, as well as nuclear, weapons, and therefore the Turks have a profound interest in the presence of missiles on their territory."

Finletter's statement concerning the Turkish argument for basing Jupiter missiles in Turkey sounds to me like a duplicate of Father's argument for basing missiles in Cuba.

Friday, October 26, brought new disturbances, and not to Father alone. The short breathing space, if one may use such a word, was over. That morning the Executive Committee was particularly concerned with the problem of the blockade. It had been in effect for three days. Ships of the Atlantic Fleet had formed a line in the sea, but they had not stopped anyone yet. The few ships clearly heading toward Cuba were crossing the blockade line without hindrance.

The president continued to oppose inspection of ships flying the Soviet flag. "If we are not absolutely certain that missiles or other weapons which might be considered offensive are on board, then it's better not to tease the goose," he decided.

A chance to show some determination seemed to appear toward evening on Thursday. The *Volker Freundschaft*, a passenger ship flying the East German flag, was nearing the quarantine line. But here too Kennedy decided against action. If things did not go well, it would be impossible to justify firing on an unarmed passenger vessel.

Finally, a compromise was found. Atlantic Fleet headquarters was ordered to stop the first ship that was neither a passenger vessel nor flying the Soviet flag. Early on the morning of October 26 a ship appeared that fit that category, the Swedish freighter *Kollangatt*, chartered by the Soviet Union. But they decided to let it through. The White House didn't want to antagonize the government of traditionally neutral Sweden. They decided to pick a simpler and more modest target.

The lot fell to a Liberty ship, the freighter *Marucla*, Panamanian-owned, registered in Lebanon, and bound for Cuba under Soviet charter to deliver a cargo from Riga to Havana. Everyone was certain that it was not carrying weapons and that there would be no conflict. Two destroyers, the *John Pierce* and the *Joseph P. Kennedy, Jr.*, followed the *Marucla* throughout the night. Apparently the latter destroyer was chosen to please the president.

As soon as the ship crossed the quarantine line, at 6:50 A.M. on Friday, it was ordered to stop its engines. The destroyers lowered motor launches with a boarding party. There were no incidents, no weapons were discovered, and the *Marucla* proceeded on its way.

The White House considered that this interception would "graphically demonstrate to Khrushchev that we are moving to strengthen the blockade." At the same time, as if to show restraint, Soviet ships were left untouched.

The letter to the U.S. president was already on its way to Washington when news reached Moscow that the *Marucla* had been stopped.

The CIA's report on Friday, the twenty-sixth, indicated that one more step had been taken toward finishing work on the Soviet missile bases. Despite everything, construction workers were continuing to pour concrete, workers were assembling parts, and electricians were laying cables. Hour after hour, day after day.

The president ordered an increase in the number of flights from two a day to twelve. Changes in the situation were now being monitored virtually every hour. Night photography was about to begin. However, all this made it possible to record the situation, but not influence it. The military increased its pressure on the president, and the press accused him of indecisiveness. Kennedy gradually weakened. Voices calling for a military solution to the problems grew ever louder in the Executive Committee.

Friday morning President Kennedy ordered the State Department to begin outlining immediate steps to set up new government agencies in Cuba after its occupation by the U.S. Army. The Joint Chiefs of Staff began practical preparations for invasion. Troops moved toward points of embarkation, and civilian ships were ordered to leave the danger zone. Honest John missiles were prepared for firing. All that was necessary was to mount the nuclear warheads.

In Cuba the Soviet Lunas and tactical cruise missiles were readied to face a landing party. The final operation, to install the nuclear warheads, was not carried out. That required Moscow's agreement, as long as communications were maintained. If they were broken, the entire responsibility would rest on Pliyev's shoulders.

Preparations for a landing did not go unnoticed. Intelligence reports reaching Moscow during Friday pointed to one thing—an invasion was imminent.

There was an increasingly noticeable smell of gunpowder in the air. The Foreign Ministry and KGB asked for permission to warn its overseas representatives, mainly those in the United States, of the emergency. That meant that they should prepare for the possibility that war would break out, which meant, among other things, that they were to prepare their secret documents for immediate destruction and await a special order concerning the transmission of coded messages. Father approved the alarm signal. He thought that it couldn't do any harm and might even help avert a war, since U.S. counterintelligence would certainly detect the signal and understand what it meant.

The Presidium of the Central Committee met again after lunch. They waited for the text of the letter to Kennedy. As always, work went on to the last minute before the typing and checking was complete.

Finally everything was ready. The letter sounded confused; even Father sensed that, and he added several changes in his own hand; however, he didn't think there was enough time to retype it, much less make a thorough revision.

Picking up a pen, Father lifted his head: "Is everyone agreed?" Members of the collective leadership nodded their heads in unison. Father scrawled his signature and, holding out the paper to an aide, half-ordered, half-requested Gromyko: "Please, get it off without delay."

"Of course, Nikita Sergeyevich," rumbled Gromyko. He didn't need to say that—what delays could there be?

But in fact, everything turned out differently. Father's concern proved to be justified. According to U.S. diplomatic records, the letter from the chairman of the Council of Ministers was received by the U.S. Embassy in Moscow at 4:43 P.M. It was delivered by courier directly from the Kremlin. It took a little more than two hours before all the procedures, including translation, were followed and at 7 P.M. the message arrived at the Moscow International Telegraph, along with all other government and diplomatic documents and coded messages. In Washington it was 11 A.M. the same day and a stormy session of the Executive Committee was under way.

I don't know what happened at the telegraph office. But the letter did not go out. It is to weep. They even reported the delay to Father. But what could he do? Only advise them not to harass the workers at the telegraph office—then they would become completely flustered in the presence of so many high officials. The long message went through in sections.

The decision to attack was not made on Friday. At the morning session of the Executive Committee, McNamara presented the conclusion of experts that they must be prepared for grave losses. McCone warned that an invasion would be far more dangerous than most people had previously realized. General Taylor saw no alternative. He was supported by the Joint Chiefs. The president was doubtful: "We are going to have to face the fact that, if we do invade, the missiles will be pointed at us before we fight our way through to launch installations. Furthermore, we have to be ready for the fact that those missiles will be fired as soon as military actions begin."

It was a paradox: to ensure the security of his people the president would condemn them to destruction.

Another tragedy occurred at 2 p.m. that October 26, although in the fever pitch of emotions of those days it was viewed as a routine misfortune: a U-2 crashed as it was heading toward Cuba over the Gulf of Mexico on an intelligence mission. Its pilot, Joe Nayd, was killed. No one suspected either the Cubans or Russians of malicious intent; it was simply a routine accident. It wasn't the first accident to result in deaths in the Caribbean Crisis. Three days earlier, on Tuesday, in the hurried transfers typical of preparations for any large-scale military operation, a KC-135 transport plant crashed on landing at the U.S. base at Guantanamo. Seven men were killed.

Friday, October 26. Evening had come in Moscow. Father felt a nagging apprehension. He seemed to have done everything in human power to prevent an explosion, but his anxiety remained. I waited in vain that evening to ask him more questions. His secretary called and said that he would be staying overnight in the Kremlin.

The thought flashed through my mind: Could it really be so serious? Until that phone call my fear had been suppressed by an inner conviction that Father would find a solution. Now it emerged. But I didn't share my distress with any of the family. What could they do? What good would it do to upset my Mother and sisters?

Mama telephoned Father. He said that there might be urgent reports during the night, so he had decided to stay there and avoid having to get up and go in. The answer satisfied Mama, but not me.

In his memoirs, Father writes that he did not believe that there might be a war over Cuba, that there was only one night when he was truly worried and stayed in his office at the Council of Ministers. He doesn't say which night, but it was that Friday night.

While Father was in his office that evening, prepared for the most unpleasant news, John Scali was lunching with his old acquaintance Aleksandr Fomin.

During lunch Fomin asked Scali if he could find out what high-level State Department officials would think of resolving the crisis under the following conditions: the USSR removes the so-called offensive weapons from Cuba and takes them home; the United States is able to verify those actions; the United States and its allies make a solemn promise never under any guise to invade Cuba; the Soviet Union promises not to deliver any offensive weapons to Cuba in the future.

In Fomin's opinion, the best way to put forward these proposals was through Adlai Stevenson, the U.S. ambassador to the United Nations. Zorin, the Soviet ambassador, would support his proposal.

Scali wrote nothing down. Professionals don't do that. Neither did he express his own opinion. They agreed to meet that evening, at 7:30. By then Scali would know what the State Department thought of Mr. Fomin's initiative.

Another lunch was proceeding nearby. Well-known Soviet diplomat and Deputy Foreign Minister Georgy Konstantinovich Korniyenko, in those days a Soviet Embassy official in Washington, described it twenty-seven years later. Either the Embassy doubted the information given by Rogers about a landing in Cuba on October 26, or they simply had instructions to verify such a grave warning. In any case, Korniyenko was told he should try to invite Rogers to lunch. He called Rogers that morning. The journalist was in his office and accepted the invitation willingly. That meant he was still in Washington, and either the invasion was going to take place without a representative of the *New York Herald Tribune* or it was postponed—therefore, today and tomorrow it was still possible to try to do something.

Rogers made no secret of his assignment. It was postponed for an indefinite, but very short time, possibly several days. He didn't use the word "invasion," but emphasized that the president wanted to be convinced that there was no alternative. The White House was not looking for a pretext to invade, but the inner conviction that invasion was the only course of action. The world should be in no doubt that there was simply no peaceful solution to the crisis.

Korniyenko sighed with relief—war was not yet in sight. He quickly brought the conversation to an end so that he could send the information to Moscow. In parting Rogers stressed that, in his opinion, there was an opportunity to resolve the matter peacefully, but negotiations could not drag on.

Night had fallen in Moscow by the time Korniyenko returned to the Embassy.

Father's message to the U.S. president was still making its way through the unreliable contacts of teletypes of the Moscow Telegraph, while Father himself was tossing and turning on the couch in his Kremlin office, listening half-asleep for the ring of telephones that might break the quiet with news of trouble. The telephone didn't ring, and the secretary, keeping vigil in the reception area as usual, didn't interrupt the premier's sleep.

Father began the morning as usual, without agitation or hurry. He took a shower and shaved. After breakfast he began looking at papers. The workday hadn't yet begun, and the telephones were silent. Father became absorbed in reports that had come in during the night about Turkish missiles. It seemed that yesterday everyone, both in the United States and Europe, had been talking about them. There were Lippmann's article and Kreisky's proposals, and intelligence reports about discussions of this question at the highest level in Washington and consultations with the Turks and NATO. Father later told me that someone close to high-level U.S. officials openly hinted that such a proposal coming from Moscow would get a favorable reception.

After carefully reading the mail, Father even became a little upset. Obviously his nerves had given way the previous day, and he had hurried to send the president a letter after deleting from it any mention of Turkish and Italian missiles. He took the news from Washington as a good sign, a proposal for an equivalent exchange.

After the passage of decades it's impossible to confirm whether such an alternative exchange was considered, whether there actually was a trial balloon from the U.S. side. Today all U.S. participants are unanimous in saying that such proposals were not discussed. I have my doubts. There was a great deal of talk about those famous Jupiters going on at the time, both within the Executive Committee and outside it. Tape recordings of the Executive Committee discussions have recently been declassified. You can find evidence in favor of the proposed exchange in them. For example, in one of the meetings, then Vice President Lyndon Johnson spoke in support of Father's proposal to withdraw the missiles from Cuba, viewing it as a good deal and saying that they had "feared" that he (Khrushchev) would never propose that (the exchange of Cuban missiles for Turkish missiles), but would want to trade over Berlin. Deputy Secretary of State George Ball seconded him: "We thought that if we managed to gain that [withdrawal of the missiles] in exchange for Turkey, then we would have made an easy and very profitable deal."[18]

However, you can also find directly contradictory remarks in the stenographic records, if you look for them. Finally, there is no direct evidence that the Americans were preparing to advance such proposals, and apparently none will appear.

However, I have gotten ahead of myself. Evening was just beginning in Washington. Fomin was preparing for another meeting with Scali. He was impatiently waiting for a call "from the other side."

After six in the evening the White House began receiving the so-called first letter from Father. It arrived in sections, as the telegraph machine produced each portion in turn. This letter, which has always aroused great interest among historians and is justly called a key document, has now been published. I have already said that it was long and freighted with emotion and digressions. I have decided not to reproduce it here in full. But I can't resist quoting the excerpts given in Robert Kennedy's *Thirteen Days*. They show not only Father's train of thought, but also what received special attention in Washington.

"We must not succumb," wrote Father,

> to petty passions or to transient things. We must remember that if indeed war should break out, it would not be in our power to stop it, for such is the logic of war. I have participated in two wars and know that war ends when it has rolled through cities and villages, everywhere sowing death and destruction.
>
> The United States has nothing to fear from the missiles. They will never be used to attack it, and they are on Cuba solely for the purpose of defense. You can be calm in this regard, that we are of sound mind and understand perfectly well that if we attack you, you will respond the same way. But you

---

18. October 27, 1962: Transcript of the Meetings of the Extraordinary Commission for International Security, Winter 1987/1988, vol. 12, no. 3, p. 76.

too will receive the same that you hurl against us. And I think that you also understand this. . . . This indicates that we are normal people, that we correctly understand and correctly evaluate the situation. Consequently, how can we permit the incorrect actions which you ascribe to us? Only lunatics or suicides, who themselves want to perish and to destroy the whole world before they die, could do this.

. . . We want something quite different . . . not to destroy your country . . . , but despite our ideological differences to compete peacefully, not by military means. . . . There is no purpose in seizing Soviet ships bound for Cuba, because they are not carrying weapons. The weapons are already in Cuba. . . .

If assurances were given that the President of the United States would not participate in an attack on Cuba and the blockade lifted, the question of the removal or destruction of the missile sites in Cuba would then be an entirely different question. Armaments bring only disasters. When one accumulates them, this damages the economy, and if one put them to use, then they destroy people on both sides. Consequently, only a madman can believe that armaments are the principal means in the life of society. No, they are an enforced loss of human energy and what is more are for the destruction of man himself. If people do not show wisdom, then in the final analysis, they will come to a clash, like blind moles, and then reciprocal extermination will begin.

This is my proposal: no more, as you call them, offensive weapons in Cuba and we will remove and destroy those which are already there. In response you would promise to lift the blockade and not to invade Cuba. Not to carry out piratical acts against Soviet ships.

If you have not lost your self-control and sensibly conceive what this might lead to, Mr. President, we and you now ought not to pull on the ends of the rope in which you have tied the knot of war, because the more the two of us pull, the tighter that knot will be tied. And a time will come when the knot will have to be cut. What that would mean I need not explain to you, because you yourself know perfectly well what terrible forces our two countries possess. Therefore, if our intention is not to pull on the knot and thereby condemn the world to the catastrophe of nuclear war, let us not only relax the forces straining on the ends of the rope, but take measures to untie the knot. We are ready for that.

There is the long excerpt. It reflects not just logic, but also Father's emotional mood on that day when he felt that war was crawling out of the masses of paper threats and becoming a reality.

In the White House they read and reread the letter, trying to discern a hidden meaning, to guess at Father's real intentions. The discussion dragged on until morning. The president felt a renewed hope that he might succeed in avoiding military intervention. However, the Joint Chiefs thought differently and grew more and more emphatic with every passing hour.

At a little after six o'clock, just as they began reading Father's letter, Dean Rusk was told that Scali was insisting on being seen in order to transmit some urgent information from Moscow. So much activity by the Kremlin was clear evidence that they were seriously alarmed. In leaving the Executive Committee meeting, Rusk managed to exchange only a few words with the president and receive clear instructions from him. What Scali conveyed to Fomin would be in essence a preliminary answer to the letter they had received.

Scali was amazed by the secretary of state's muted reaction to his sensational report. Nevertheless, Rusk did not assume the responsibility of a final decision. Seating the journalist in his limousine, he took Scali to an entrance in the rear wing of the White House. As luck would have it, when they were approaching the door to the Oval Office, they crossed the path of Pierre Salinger. He almost attacked Scali—all they needed that day were journalists at the Executive Committee meeting. But Rusk whispered something in his ear, opened the door, and invited Scali to enter.

Scali was not surprised to discover that the president was waiting to see him. He repeated his story to Kennedy. The president ordered Scali to tell the Soviet representative that "at the highest level of the government of the United States" they viewed his proposals as a basis for negotiations and that representatives of the United States and USSR at the United Nations "could begin discussion of these problems both with U Thant and with each other."[19] As they parted, Kennedy warned him not to use his name, to speak only of the "government." He was very anxious to prevent the Kremlin from sensing how tense the situation in the White House had become.

Fomin and Scali met, as agreed, that evening at 7:35. Scali relayed the message word for word. After listening attentively, Fomin promised to inform the Kremlin immediately.

In the late evening of October 26, there was another meeting, probably the most important. The Soviet participant, then ambassador Anatoly Dobrynin, did not break his vow to keep silent about it until January of 1989. According to him, Dean Rusk was not the only one to leave the Executive Committee meeting discreetly that evening. The president was afraid of making a mistake, and Robert Kennedy decided to talk to the ambassador in the attorney general's office.

The subject of the conversation was, of course, obvious. In those days everything revolved around the missiles. The ambassador knew the contents

---

19. Beschloss, *Crisis Years*, p. 521.

of Father's last letter and, as a disciplined diplomat, kept within its framework. But uncompromising statements are one thing, and a trial balloon is something else entirely. Perhaps something else could be gained by the trade? Dobrynin had, of course, read numerous press reports about the Turkish missiles. Washington's negotiations with its allies had not been kept all that secret. In the course of the conversation about possible conditions for the withdrawal of our missiles, he only hinted at possibilities concerning "a state adjacent to the Soviet Union."

Robert Kennedy's reaction was unexpected. He didn't answer, and simply asked to make a call from the next room, without witnesses. The ambassador was accustomed to such calls. The conversation was brief. Returning, Robert Kennedy relayed the words of the person to whom he had been speaking: "The president said that we are prepared to examine the question of Turkey. Favorably."

The ambassador had not dreamed of such a reply.

On Cuba matters were taking their course. During the night of October 26–27, General Pliyev ordered that nuclear warheads be moved from their storage area 500 kilometers away and placed closer to where missile regiments were billeted.

SURVIVING SATURDAY

Meanwhile in the Kremlin, on the morning of October 27, Father read the latest reports over and over again.

He couldn't shake the thought: "If the Americans are so insistent on a trade, why not take advantage of it?" Though experience teaches that what is done is done. But what if it could be changed, after all?

Father called the Ministry of Foreign Affairs. Although it was early morning, Gromyko picked up the phone. He usually arrived early. Father asked whether the letter had been received and when. Andrei Andreyevich hesitated: "The letter got to the U.S. Embassy without any delay, but then . . ." He was looking for the right word, afraid of Father's anger. "Technical problems with the telegraph appeared, unforeseen difficulties arose and it took many hours to transmit the letter."

Gromyko fell silent. But the premier was not angry. It seemed as if this unpleasant news suited him. Father didn't respond in any way. He started talking about Turkish missiles. As always, the opinion of the foreign minister coincided with that of the chairman of the Council of Ministers.

When asked whether the Americans would agree to remove their missiles, Gromyko didn't give a direct answer. If not for yesterday's letter, then very likely, but now it's doubtful—but on the other hand . . .

The conversation ended.

Father decided to try to change horses in midstream, so to speak, to return to the old version of the letter, the one that they were preparing on Thursday. Of course, it would have to be rewritten, since two days had gone by. That was a long time when every minute was precious. Father decided to cut his demands in half and omit mention of the Italian, as well as the British, missiles. Now it was all logical: the base in Turkey in exchange for the base in Cuba. It seemed as if the White House might agree to this offer. There must be a good reason that they had made so many hints.

Calling Gromyko again, he asked them to prepare a new letter, or rather, revise the old one. Andrei Andreyevich expressed some surprise: How should they deliver it? While the new message is traveling along telegraph wires, the White House will already be replying to the previous day's message.

Father had what seemed a good idea at the time: the new letter should be published immediately, without waiting for it to reach President Kennedy. Father became increasingly excited with the plan. It seemed to him that if you stretch out your hand publicly, there, across the ocean, they would take it willingly, while a statement made known to the whole world would facilitate a dialogue with both Turkey and NATO.

Gromyko didn't warn Father. He even completely supported his idea. He promised to prepare a draft of the new message by two or three o'clock that afternoon, at about the same time they planned to hear the report by the military. Father thought that one would not interfere with the other.

It was decided to begin the meeting of the Presidium of the Central Committee immediately after lunch.

Meanwhile, messages from Fomin and Dobrynin arrived. They reinforced Father's feeling that he was right to send a second letter. What was there to argue about, if the president gave his approval? A line in Dobrynin's telegram about the conversation between Korniyenko and Rogers was reassuring. Yesterday's information proved to be false. However, the Pentagon was not obliged to inform journalists of its plans, so the fact that Rogers was not in Florida did not necessarily mean anything.

Before lunch Father worked with his aides and read his mail. Telegrams arriving from all over the world were all on the same subject—Cuba.

Pliyev reported that work on the missile bases would be completed in a few hours. This information didn't give Father the satisfaction that he would have had only two weeks before. Now it was not particularly important. He called Malinovsky and asked him to repeat the order: missile units in Cuba must obey the premier's orders, and no one else's. Father was nervous, and tried to be as cautious as possible. That was especially true with respect to nuclear warheads. He ordered that their storage and transport be kept under special control. In a coded message sent the same day by Malinovsky to Pliyev, the minister of defense forbade the "use of nuclear weapons on all types of missiles and planes."

Reports from intelligence agents in the United States were causing concern: the concentration of troops and landing ships was continuing. Soldiers were being issued ammunition. There were persistent rumors that an invasion would begin in the next few days or hours.

Too much still remained unclear.

In contrast to coded messages from the United States, Alekseyev's reports from Cuba sounded optimistic: Castro was full of energy and confident of victory.

An oppressive period of waiting began. Father paced the floor of his Kremlin office. At times he would stop by the window, though it's unlikely that he saw what was going on outside.

Father called Gromyko for the third time that morning. He asked him to get in touch with our ambassador in Turkey and ask the ambassador to find out what the Turkish government thought about the possible removal of U.S. Jupiters in exchange for security guarantees provided by the Soviet Union.

Gromyko promised to contact Ankara immediately.

Before the meeting Father requested that couriers be available, so that as soon as the letter was in final form it could be delivered immediately to the radio and to *Izvestiya*, our only national evening newspaper.

Almost all the participants in the upcoming meeting gathered for lunch at the Kremlin cafeteria. This time they ate in silence, without any of their usual joking remarks, and even without discussing urgent matters. Cuba pushed everything else into the background, but they couldn't talk about the crisis. There was nothing new, and to bring up old news was painful.

That day's meeting was moved from the office to the conference room, so that there would be space for everyone. Gromyko was late because of the letter. Father entered last. The massive oak doors opened and closed quietly behind his stout figure. The meeting began with the report by the military.

The couriers, A. A. Kharlamov and M. G. Sturua, from *Izvestiya*, were kept waiting in the reception room. Time passed very slowly. What was happening there, behind the tightly closed doors? What fate awaited us? From time to time worried aides popped into the reception room, either with papers or to telephone urgent instructions somewhere.

During those few seconds when the doors were open, they could hear a few alarming words. Malinovsky reported possible targets for U.S. planes and missiles on our territory, possible numbers of casualties, and of course, how we would retaliate. Our response didn't seem very convincing: circles representing targets and radii of destruction resulting from nuclear attacks were scattered far apart on a map of the United States hanging on the wall.

In Europe the circles were much closer and in some places even merged. But Europe was not the focus of attention.

Father listened to Malinovsky with half an ear. The solution must be sought in diplomacy, not in military plans, so that when Gromyko appeared Father suggested interrupting Malinovsky's report and listening to the foreign minister.

Forty minutes later the couriers were given copies of Khrushchev's so-called second letter to Kennedy, freshly typed, with hand written corrections.

That evening Moscow radio interrupted its scheduled program and began broadcasting the message. *Izvestiya* quickly changed its front page. They had been told in advance to leave room for a government announcement, although no one had known how much space would be needed. Therefore, they had to cut out some of what was already planned.

Father sent a conciliatory response to U Thant's appeal the same time he sent the message to the U.S. president. He agreed with the U.N. secretary-general's proposal to halt all deliveries of weapons to Cuba and not to raise the level of tension. His letter states that the Soviet government condemns the U.S. refusal to listen to the voice of reason and to lift the blockade. Nevertheless, Soviet ships were ordered to leave the area where U.S. naval vessels were located, in order to avoid provocations.

Kennedy had acted more quickly. His message to the U.N. had been delivered the day before. He agreed with the secretary-general and assured him that "our government will accept your suggestion and treat it with respect. Our ships in the Caribbean Sea will do everything possible to avoid a direct confrontation with Soviet ships in the near future, to reduce to the minimum the risk of any unwanted incident."

On Friday the Executive Committee had still not arrived at a decision. They agreed to continue their discussion of Father's letter on Saturday morning, October 27.

However, that morning everything seemed to go wrong. An avalanche of information about unexpected events fell on the White House. Under other circumstances, every one of those events would have been enough to provoke a small crisis.

Early in the morning FBI director J. Edgar Hoover called Robert Kennedy and said he had been informed that Soviet diplomats in New York spent the whole night apparently destroying secret documents. Such actions could only be interpreted as preparations for war.

At one of the meetings devoted to problems of the Cuban Missile Crisis, Georgy Korniyenko said: "The rumors that the documents were burned at the Embassy were false. Nothing like that happened. But naturally, we were preparing ourselves for all kinds of surprises."

Robert Kennedy writes that on the way to the White House he was wondering how to reconcile those actions with Father's letter, in which he proposed a way to settle the conflict—or could the message be simply camouflage?

Each side suspected and distrusted the other, but at the same time each side was counting on the other for a last-minute miracle.

The morning meeting of the Executive Committee began at the White House at ten o'clock, as usual. McNamara spoke first. His report gave no grounds for optimism: the Russians were working day and night to complete the bases. He could follow their work hour by hour. It was interrupted only when the low-flying spy planes roared over the construction sites.

This lack of respect infuriated Fidel Castro. "Cuba is, after all, a sovereign country and will not allow the Yankees to humiliate it," was his emotional response to appeals from Moscow, relayed by Alekseyev, that he keep calm and show restraint.

As long as the planes made two flights a day, Castro put up with it. But starting with the previous day, something unimaginable began to happen. Yankee planes acted as if they were at home, as if Batista was still around. Castro's injured pride demanded revenge. He said repeatedly that reasonable arguments would not work with his northern neighbor. They only respected force.

Late in the evening of October 26, Castro ordered Cuban antiaircraft guns to open fire and shoot down the intruders. This order was brought to Colonel Voronkov, the commander of antiaircraft missiles. Voronkov was subordinate to Pliyev. Neither had permission to act without orders from Moscow.

A few hours earlier Pliyev had sent a coded message to Malinovsky. In it he asked permission to use his antiaircraft guns "in case of a strike by American strategic aircraft units"—in other words, in case the planes were preparing the way for an invasion.

After receiving the message, Malinovsky hurried to see Father. In response, sometime on the morning of October 27, Moscow informed Havana that Pliyev had permission to open fire in case of a massive air attack. The key term in Moscow's response is "massive."

The antiaircraft missiles were not yet considered fully operational: installation was being completed at launch sites. Electronic devices were being checked, radars adjusted. One more step remained, half a step—and the Americans would not go unpunished.

Colonel Voronkov received Moscow's order, relayed by Pliyev, and Castro's order at almost the same time. He didn't like Moscow's orders, but he was enthusiastic about Castro's. He told his subordinates to redouble their efforts to make the antiaircraft missiles operational. The warheads were mounted on the rockets and they were deployed at launch sites. Now it was up to the technicians and, of course, to headquarters.

McNamara continued his report. He said that, in addition to the missiles, Soviet specialists were hurriedly assembling IL-28 bombers and preparing them for operation.

Each party had its own interpretation of the other's actions and intentions. Sometimes the conclusions were mutually exclusive. Erroneous evaluation of the other side's intentions led repeatedly to new levels of escalation and new mistakes.

At 11 A.M. McNamara's report was interrupted by an urgent message. The radio broadcast another letter from Moscow. These two letters, which historians call the first and the second Khrushchev messages, have given rise to a great number of interpretations and suppositions. I have tried to describe the history of their origin and now I would like, in spite of its substantial length, to give the complete text of the second message.

> Dear Mr. President,
>
> It was with great satisfaction that I studied your reply to Mr. U Thant on the adoption of measures in order to preclude contact between our ships and thus avoid irreparable and fatal consequences. This reasonable step on your part reinforces my belief that you are concerned with the preservation of peace, and I note this with satisfaction.
>
> I have already said that the only concern of our people, our government, and me personally, as chairman of the Council of Ministers, is that our country develop and take its rightful place among all peoples of the world in economic competition, in the development of culture and the arts and in improving the living standards of our peoples. That is the most noble and necessary field for competition and it will be good for the losers, as well as the winners, since it means peace and an increase in the means by which people live and enjoy life.
>
> In your statement you said that your main goal lies not only in reaching agreement and adopting measures to preclude contact between our ships and, consequently, a deepening of the crisis, since such contact could ignite the fire of a military conflict, after which any negotiations would be superfluous because other forces and other laws would begin to operate—the laws of war. I agree with you that this is only a first step. The most important thing is to normalize and stabilize the position of the world between states and between peoples.

I understand your concern for the security of the United States, Mr. President, because that is the primary obligation of a president. However, these same questions also disturb us; as chairman of the Council of Ministers of the USSR, I have the same obligations. You have been concerned that we assisted Cuba by supplying arms intended to strengthen its defense potential because Cuba, no matter what weapons it has, cannot compete with you, the difference in size is too great, the more so given modern means of destruction.

Our purpose was and is to help Cuba, and no one can dispute the humanity of our motives, aimed at helping Cuba to live peacefully and develop as its people desire. You wish to ensure the security of your country, and this is understandable. But Cuba wants the same thing. All countries want to be secure. But how are we, the Soviet Union, our government, to assess your actions, which have been to surround the Soviet Union with military bases, surround our allies with military bases, set up military bases literally around our country, and station your missile weapons there? This is no secret. High-ranking American figures make demonstrative statements about it. Your missiles are stationed in England and in Italy and are aimed at us. Your missiles are stationed in Turkey.

You are worried about Cuba. You say that it worries you because it lies ninety miles across the sea from the coast of the United States. But Turkey lies right next to us. Our sentries pace back and forth and watch each other. Do you believe that you have the right to demand security for your country and the removal of those weapons which you call offensive, while not recognizing that we have that right? You have placed devastating missile weapons, which you call offensive, literally right next to us. How then can you reconcile acknowledgment of our equal military capabilities with such unequal relations between our two great states? They are impossible to reconcile.

It is good, Mr. President, that you have agreed to have our representatives meet and start negotiations, apparently with the mediation of U.N. Acting Secretary-General U Thant. He consequently assumes to some extent the role of mediator, and we believe that he can cope with that responsible mission if, of course, every party involved in this conflict demonstrates goodwill.

I think that it is possible quickly to eliminate the conflict and normalize the situation; then people would heave a sigh of relief, considering that the government leaders who bear the responsibility are of sound mind, are aware of their responsibilities, and have the ability to resolve complex questions and not permit the situation to result in a military catastrophe.

I therefore make this proposal: We agree to remove from Cuba those weapons you regard as offensive. We agree to do this and to state this commitment at the U.N. Your representatives will make a statement to the effect that the United States, for its part, bearing in mind the anxiety and concern of the Soviet state, will remove its analogous weapons from Turkey. Let us reach agreement on the period of time you and I need to put this into effect.

After that, authorized representatives of the U.N. Security Council can check on the spot whether these commitments are being honored. Of course, the Cuban and Turkish governments will have to agree to admit those representatives into their countries so that they may verify that this commitment undertaken by each side is being implemented. Evidently it would be best if those representatives enjoyed the trust of the Security Council, the United States, and the Soviet Union, as well as Turkey and Cuba. I think that it will evidently not be difficult to select people who enjoy the trust and respect of all the interested parties.

In assuming this obligation so as to give satisfaction and hope to the peoples of Cuba and Turkey and strengthen their confidence in their security, we will make a statement within the Security Council framework to the effect that the Soviet Union gives a solemn pledge to respect the inviolability of the borders and sovereignty of Turkey, not to interfere in its internal affairs, not to invade Turkey, not to allow our territory to be used as a springboard for such an invasion, and will also restrain those who might think of committing aggression against Turkey, either from Soviet territory or from the territory of Turkey's neighboring states.

The United States government will make the same statement within the Security Council framework with respect to Cuba. It will declare that the United States will respect the inviolability of Cuba's borders and its sovereignty, will promise not to interfere in its internal affairs, will not invade Cuba or allow its territory to be used as a springboard for invading Cuba, and will also restrain those who might think of committing aggression against Cuba, either from the territory of the United States or from the territory of Cuba's other neighboring states.

Of course, for this we will have to agree and set a time limit. Let us agree to give it some time, but without any unnecessary delay—say, within two or three weeks, not more than a month.

The weapons in Cuba to which you refer and which, as you say, alarm you, are in the hands of Soviet officers. Therefore, any accidental use of them which might be to the detriment of the United States is excluded. These weapons are stationed in Cuba at the request of the Cuban government and solely for defensive purposes. Therefore, if there is no invasion of Cuba or attack on the Soviet Union or our other allies, then, of course, these weapons do not and will not threaten anyone. They are not for purposes of attack.

If you accept my proposal, Mr. President, then we would send our representatives to the U.N. in New York and give them detailed instructions in order to reach an agreement more quickly. If you also appoint your people and give them similar instructions, then this matter can be resolved quickly.

Why would I want to achieve this? Because the entire world is now apprehensive and awaits reasonable actions from us. An announcement of our agreement to eradicate this conflict would bring the greatest joy to all the world's peoples. I attach great importance to this agreement, since it could serve as a good beginning and, in particular, facilitate reaching agreement on a nuclear test ban.

The problem of tests could be solved at the same time, though without linking one with the other, since they are different problems. But it is important to reach agreement on both problems in order to give people a wonderful present, to let them rejoice in the news that a nuclear test ban agreement has also been reached, thereby preventing further contamination of the atmosphere. Our and your positions on this issue are very close.

All this could perhaps also serve as a strong impetus in the search for mutually acceptable agreements on other controversial issues on which we are exchanging opinions. These issues have not yet been resolved, but they are awaiting urgent solution, which would clear the international atmosphere. We are ready for that.

These are my proposals, Mr. President.

Respectfully yours,
N. Khrushchev

While such a letter might have been greeted with enthusiasm the day before, on that day it provoked disappointment and surprise.

The Executive Committee didn't know what to make of this second message, on the same subject as the first but with more pressing demands. They had not been able, even before, to agree on an answer, and now Turkish missiles were added to the picture. Moreover, no one except the president knew about Robert Kennedy's meeting with the Soviet ambassador the previous day. The brothers understood that it was evidently Robert's telephone call to the White House that played the decisive role in Father's change of position. But they had not expected him to publicize it around the world. Confidential correspondence was one thing—you could allow yourself to be open and call things by their right names—but to address the entire world was quite different. Now public opinion and the press had entered the game and it would be impossible to disregard the response from NATO headquarters and the telegram from Turkey.

Moreover, after this public demand by the Soviet Union, many would view any agreement by the president as a manifestation of weakness, as a capitulation, and that could not fail to influence the outcome of the elections.

John Kennedy didn't want to tell the Executive Committee about the previous day's contact with the Soviet ambassador. He preferred to wait, listen to the others, and only then make a decision. That day he was beginning anew, as if from a blank page.

Father had made a mistake. But people in the Kremlin were accustomed to a tame national press, which only published viewpoints formulated there or at the Central Committee offices on Staraya Square, and which supported only what it was told to support. They simply could not conceive of another world, where the president was not free to make decisions without taking the changeable views of voters into account. Our country was just starting out on the road to democracy.

Father had been in too much of a hurry, and now the game entered a new phase. Confidential negotiations between the two governments became the property of all; secret messages were transformed into feature articles in the newspapers.

The issue was no longer the real military significance of the Turkish missiles or their weight in the total balance of strategic forces. The rules of a political game were beginning to operate.

Kennedy did not attach much importance to the Jupiters based in Turkey. The first nine Minutemen, which would become operational on October 30, and the Polarises, could reach virtually all targets in the Soviet Union. However, Kennedy didn't want to remove the Jupiters from Europe under pressure. He thought that would compromise the dignity of a great power.

Father's recent letters, just as previous documents, continued to avoid the short word "missile," instead using the tortuous phrase, "weapon which you consider to be offensive." That was neither capricious nor a mistake. Father wanted to emphasize that the missiles in Cuba were intended solely for defense. However, such phrase-making gradually pushed him into a corner. In this case, the effort to avoid calling things by their names and the habit of using ambiguous expressions freed American hands. We ourselves stopped understanding what was under discussion aside from missiles. Our adversaries could describe any weapon delivered to Cuba as an offensive weapon.

If Kennedy understood the reasons that prompted Father to send the new letter, the other Executive Committee members were puzzled: what had happened in the Kremlin during those hours? Someone pointed to a stylistic difference between the first and second messages. Some jumped to the conclusion that Father hadn't even written the second letter; the phrasing, the sentence structure, the very spirit of it seemed far too formal. That was, at any rate, the conclusion drawn in the White House. There was endless speculation. People who thought straightforwardly favored the version that there was a split in the Soviet leadership and that a hard-line policy had won out, resulting in the dispatch of a second letter disavowing the first.

The Executive Committee was confused. Its members didn't know what to do or how to answer. One thing was clear: delay was out of the question. A decision had to be made quickly. The White House didn't want to hear of the two or three weeks mentioned in the letter. The president simply didn't have that much time to solve the Cuban issue.

A new sore point had emerged—Turkey. Judging by the tone of the letter, an invasion of Cuba would automatically trigger an attack on Turkey by the Soviet Union and its allies. That would lead inevitably to war in Europe.

In reality, Father did not intend to start military operations against Turkey under any circumstances. The only war that Father was ready to wage was a war of nerves.

McNamara was called to the phone in the heat of the discussion. The Strategic Air Command reported that a U-2, which had taken off from Alaska, had gone off course and since 10:15 that morning had been in Soviet airspace over the Chukotsk Peninsula. Realizing that he was lost, the pilot had asked for assistance, since his navigational system was barely operating. An F-102 had flown to the rescue. There were now two intruders over Soviet territory.

U.S. radar operators detected Soviet fighters on their way to intercept. It would all be over in a matter of seconds: either the F-102 would manage to lead the slow-moving reconnaissance plane out of Soviet airspace or the U-2 would have to land at a Soviet airfield. Anyone can get lost, and that shouldn't cause any particular trouble—if not for the scandalous reputation of the U-2.

According to his instructions, the pilot was strictly forbidden to land at foreign airfields and let his highly secret plane fall into foreign hands. That meant a dogfight! As luck would have it, that day the F-102s on duty were armed with air-to-air cruise missiles with nuclear warheads. What decision would the pilot make in the heat of battle?

Fortunately, disaster was averted. The Soviet interceptors dawdled. At the last moment the F-102 and the U-2 crossed the frontier. The U.S. pilots saw the interceptors turn sharply and head back toward Chukotka. The time in Washington was 11 A.M.

Washington and Moscow only found out later that everything ended without incident. At the time, witnesses say, "McNamara grew pale, and turning toward the president, exclaimed excitedly: 'This means war with the Soviet Union.'" The president remained calm. He only muttered a phrase which later became a Kennedy refrain: "There is always some son of a bitch who doesn't get the word."

Fortunately, the danger passed. But not for long. About an hour later came new, and this time truly tragic, information: a U-2 had been shot down over Cuba and its pilot, Major Robert Anderson, had been killed. The report shocked participants in the meeting. Many of them wondered: "Has it begun?!"

No one in the White House doubted that the action was premeditated.

The letter just transmitted by radio had stated clearly that all missiles were in the hands of Soviet officers subordinate only to Moscow. And the attack coincided with President Kennedy's receipt of the Kremlin's message.

The more hotheaded and hawkish Executive Committee members demanded that antiaircraft batteries in Cuba be bombed. Now, after the death of an American pilot, they were supported by a majority. Even temperate supporters of a blockade spoke in favor of an attack. Kennedy himself wavered for a time. However, statesmanlike wisdom won out over emotion. "It isn't the first step that concerns me," said the president in restraining the more zealous members, "but both sides escalating to the fourth step and fifth step—and we don't go to the sixth because there is no one around to do so. We must remind ourselves we are embarking on a very hazardous course."

The outburst of aggressiveness alarmed the president. There was some danger that the situation would slip out of control. Kennedy did not issue an immediate order to destroy Soviet antiaircraft installations. He proposed that the question be discussed later, when they had more information.

Kennedy's uneasiness found expression in a strict order sent to the U.S. missile sites in Turkey: "Remove explosive devices from the rockets." They were to be replaced only by a personal order from the president of the United States. Kennedy had no intention of letting the reins slip from his hands.

Major Anderson's U-2 flight that day was exactly like the ones on previous days. Photographing Soviet missile installations had become a routine mission. Nothing especially new was expected and no particular apprehension was felt—another flight, another few miles of film.

However, on the ground everything was completely different from the day before. Fidel Castro had forcefully and unequivocally ordered his antiaircraft gunners: "Shoot down intruders without warning." The Soviet antiaircraft commander had agreed with this decisive approach. Work at the bases was finished and antiaircraft battery commanders reported that they were operational. Like Castro, the Soviet generals viewed the unpunished U.S. flights over Cuba as a personal challenge. Furthermore, the destruction of the first air pirate over the island would be noticed in Moscow. Of course, it would not match the incident with Powers, but it would not be routine.

It was almost noon when Colonel Voronkov reported the U.S. reconnaissance plane. The early warning and guidance radar station was just beginning to operate and adjustments were still being made, while Cubans were being trained at the same time. The antiaircraft installations would eventually be transferred to their control, after all the commotion over ballistic missiles had died down.

When the blip from Major Anderson's U-2 appeared on the radar screen, operators were initially suspicious, thinking it must be a mistake or interference. How could it be?! The radar is turned on for almost the first time and immediately there's a target! The uncertainty didn't last long. The light dot persisted and numbers began flashing across the screen: azimuth, altitude, distance, speed. Their doubts vanished—it had to be a high-altitude reconnaissance plane.

They called headquarters, which replied: "Keep tracking the target and prepare missiles for firing. Don't shoot without orders."

As the U-2 flew over the designated areas, Colonel Voronkov began trying to find his commander. Pliyev was not at staff headquarters, so Voronkov reported the intruder to Pliyev's deputy, General Stepan Grechko. Grechko rushed off to look for Pliyev, who seemed to have vanished into thin air. Luckily, another one of the commander's deputies, General Leonid Garbuz, was at headquarters. Garbuz didn't know where Pliyev was either. He had talked about visiting the troops, but which troops?

Voronkov called again: the intruder had flown over the ballistic missile positions under construction and was heading toward an area where Soviet combat forces were deployed.

Grechko told him to continue tracking the plane.

"What should we do?" He turned to Garbuz.

Garbuz only shrugged. Both generals knew there was not enough time to contact Moscow. In a few minutes the intruder would be gone.

"Shall we fire?" Grechko rephrased his question.

Garbuz hesitated. On the one hand, they shouldn't let the American leave with valuable information; then too, there was Castro's order. On the other hand, they were supposed to obey only orders from Moscow. Garbuz knew that Pliyev had asked Malinovsky several times in the past few days for permission to shoot down U.S. spy planes. However, he had received clearance to act only in case of a massive attack. One U-2 could hardly be considered a massive attack.

At that moment Voronkov called again: "The target is leaving. We have only two minutes."

"We *will* fire!" Grechko no longer asked, but asserted. His eyes sparkled with determination. Garbuz nodded. "As well be hanged for a sheep as a lamb."

Two (as prescribed) 75s tore from their launchers and, dropping their boosters, raced into the clear blue sky. A few dozen seconds later a small white ball expanded overhead.

The operator said the prescribed phrase: "The target has been hit." The plane's blip disappeared from his screen.

Their victory was immediately reported to Voronkov, who relayed the good news to Grechko at headquarters.

To say that the mood in Soviet staff headquarters in Cuba was festive would be misleading; it was more like dismayed. Moscow had to be informed. And how would they react "at the top" to this "individual initiative"?

Pliyev at last appeared, but only growled at Grechko: "You were in charge, so you report." The general composed his report with excruciating difficulty.

Cuban antiaircraft gunners were the first to inform Castro of what had happened. They had watched the drama unfold from start to finish. Castro's joy was indescribable. Asking to be connected by telephone with Pliyev, Fidel congratulated the Soviet commander for the bold and effective actions of his subordinates. Pliyev mumbled some words of thanks. The old and experienced Pliyev was nervous. It had all happened without permission from the center. In such cases you never knew whether you were going to be praised or cursed. In his heart, he hoped for praise.

As soon as he received the coded message, Malinovsky immediately called Father and asked to be received. He must be the one to report what had happened. Malinovsky understood that praise was unlikely.

Father was inwardly pleased that another U-2, which had inflicted such humiliation on our country, had been downed by a Soviet missile. But that was only a momentary reaction, to be replaced by profound disquiet. How would the White House interpret this action? They must be just receiving the letter, which stated that such a thing was impossible without his personal permission.

It was at that very moment—not before or after—that Father felt the situation slipping out of his control. Today one general had decided it was a good idea to launch an antiaircraft missile. Tomorrow a different one might decide to launch a ballistic missile—also without asking Moscow's permission.

As Father said later, that was the moment when he felt instinctively that the missiles had to be removed, that disaster loomed. Real disaster.

Father grimly asked Malinovsky: "Did the general consult with anyone? Did he ask permission to launch?" Malinovsky replied that there wasn't enough time, and the general had decided to follow Fidel Castro's orders to Cuban antiaircraft forces.

Father exploded: "Whose army is he in, the Soviet or the Cuban? If it's the Soviet Army, why does he allow himself to obey a foreign commander?"

His fury was momentary. The problem didn't lie with General Grechko or General Pliyev. The very possibility of lethally dangerous clashes must be eliminated. That was not easy to accomplish at a distance of seven thousand miles. A single order, no matter how strict, might not be enough. What decisions would Pliyev make if there was a U.S. landing or an air strike on the missile bases?

In case of an invasion, communications with Moscow would be problematical. The fate of mankind would be in the hands of generals. God forbid that they would act with determination. But what else could you expect from them? Fighting was their business. It was what they had been taught.

These, or similar, thoughts raced through Father's mind. Malinovsky waited, shifting from one foot to the other. "Is there something else?" said Father, looking up.

Malinovsky continued: "Another violation of airspace has been detected, this one over Soviet territory. A U-2 crossed the Soviet frontier. For some reason it happened over Chukotka. What could he be looking for there? He flew over our territory for almost forty-five minutes. Interceptors were sent up, but they didn't catch him. The network of airfields there is very thin."

Father actually seemed pleased at this news. On a different occasion, the defense minister would have been subjected to more than one reprimand.

"The plane violating our airspace was probably lost," said Father. "There was nothing for him to do over Chukotka."

However, he admitted that it could have been a provocative act by U.S. generals.

"Is it possible," he continued to speculate, "that they wanted to see if there are troop concentrations there? After all, Chukotka is the closest place to America. But in Washington they're not such fools as to think that the Bering Strait is the best place to cross."

Father was inclined to think that it was a mistake. It was lucky that they had not shot it down.

Father told Malinovsky to order the country's air defense forces not to intercept reconnaissance planes violating our airspace without explicit permission from the commander in chief. "This applies in particular to our forces in Cuba," he stressed. "They're not likely to poke their noses in here. You tell our general that he should follow Moscow's orders only, even if Castro comes to him in person. He should be polite, but nothing more."

"Only Moscow's orders," Father repeated as they parted. "No independent initiatives. Everything is hanging by a thread as it is."

Malinovsky didn't intend to scold the generals. He would have acted the same way in their place. When the moment of decision arrives, a commander must display initiative. That's why he's a commander.

The coded message sent to Cuba was brief: "We think you were in too much of a hurry to shoot down the U.S. U-2 reconnaissance plane at a time when an agreement on a peaceful way to deter an invasion of Cuba is already taking shape." That was all, except for the signature: "Director."

Secrecy forbade use of the defense minister's name in correspondence, even in secret messages. That had been the custom ever since the Second World War.

Receiving this reply, Pliyev bit his lip, called Voronkov and ordered curtly: "No independent initiatives. Let the Americans fly as much as they like. Track them, but don't open fire."

Then he called Grechko and Garbuz and silently showed them the telegram. Any comment would have been superfluous.

When the door closed behind Malinovsky, Father looked at the clock, which showed almost ten in the evening. Saturday was drawing to an end. He planned to go home that night. Father was somewhat ashamed that he had panicked the day before and spent the night in the Kremlin. He had given way to nerves and had upset his colleagues.

At this time, he thought, there was no reason to expect surprises. Washington had already received his new message. Now it was their turn to think, to calculate their options and prepare a reply. It was the middle of the working day there. He must have a clear mind the next day, so he needed a good night's sleep. And how well can you sleep on a couch?

Father called Kozlov and asked him to warn members of the Presidium that tomorrow he proposed to meet in Novo-Ogaryovo, not in the Kremlin. The meeting was set for 10 A.M. After all, it was a Sunday.

However, Father was in no rush to leave the Kremlin. He asked for a stenographer. The U-2 incident worried him more and more. It must not be repeated. Who knows how the Americans would behave? Moreover, it would be awkward if Castro met with a refusal from Pliyev. He should be given an explanation. Father decided to prepare a draft letter to Havana. It would save time, and they could discuss it tomorrow morning.

"We would like to recommend that you now, at this critical moment of crisis, not give way to emotion, that you display self-control," dictated Father. "I must say that we understand your feelings of indignation at the aggressive actions of the United States and their violations of the elementary norms of international law."

Father felt himself getting angry. But he paused, as if regrouping. "But now it is not law which is operating, so much as the recklessness of militarists in the Pentagon," he went on in a completely different tone. "At present, when an agreement is emerging, the Pentagon is looking for an incident to disrupt that agreement. That is why it organizes provocative flights of planes. Yesterday you shot down one of them. . . ." Father hesitated for a moment. "Yesterday you shot down one of them," he repeated and continued, "whereas previously you did not shoot them down when they flew over your territory. Such an action can be used by the aggressors for their own purposes.

"Therefore we would like to give you some friendly advice: Show patience, self-control and once more, self-control."

After dictating a few more sentences, Father dismissed the stenographer. Today he had been unusually brief.

Leaving his office, he warned his secretary: "If something comes up, call the apartment at any hour."

Father came home at about eleven. He refused dinner, but asked for tea with lemon. While drinking it, he said that he would be busy the next day, from the morning on. "We're meeting outside the city," he observed, "so you should go to the dacha, and if nothing happens I'll come there, too."

The dacha?! Well, we never argued with Father. After breakfast the next morning he left for the meeting and we all went to the dacha. I felt a clawing anxiety. It didn't seem the proper time to leave the city, but there was nothing I could do about it.

We now return to Washington, to the meeting of the Executive Committee interrupted by news of the incident over Cuba. Kennedy proposed that the State Department prepare a draft reply to Father's message by that evening. Then General Taylor spoke on behalf of the Joint Chiefs of Staff. His main point was that the past few days' events proved that the military were right; that if force had been employed immediately the problem itself would no longer exist. The Joint Chiefs were unanimously of the opinion that it was not too late to correct this mistake and to bomb launch positions before they became operational. The troops were ready for action and only awaited orders. He proposed that an air attack be carried out on Monday, followed immediately by an invasion. Tactical nuclear weapons would be employed if necessary.

The president resisted, but restraining the military was becoming ever more difficult. Newspapers and television were filled with calls for decisive action. The masses thirsted to teach the "Reds" a lesson. Pressure was growing and members of the Executive Committee were wavering. Preparations for military action continued. The Fifth Marine Brigade was transferred to the area where troops were being concentrated for a landing on Cuba's west coast.

The next meeting of the Executive Committee was set for four o'clock.

Meanwhile, the president couldn't find the answer to a crucial question: Why was the U-2 shot down? If it signified an escalation, other actions should have followed. But everything had been quiet since that single firing incident.

What if it was a misunderstanding? Then some peaceful solution had to be found. It all came down to: What are they thinking in Moscow?

However, there was no one to ask why a U-2, after violating the airspace of a sovereign state, had been destroyed. They could only speculate.

However, the Executive Committee did not cancel flights of U.S. planes over Cuba. Six F-8U reconnaissance planes took off on an intelligence mission at three in the afternoon, in accordance with their flight plan. The pilots already knew of the tragic incident. That kind of news spreads quickly in the aviation circles of every country. The pilots had no doubt that they would be met, as the U-2 had been, with antiaircraft fire. Therefore they hugged the ground and tried to make use of any higher areas for concealment. Surprise and speed were all that could save them—to roar over the heads of defenders and then disappear. Their flight path was the usual one, over San Cristobal and Sagua la Grande, and their assignment was the same: to photograph the missile sites under construction.

Two pilots were lucky. Their planes began to act up on the approach to the island and had to turn back. The remaining four were met by Cuban antiaircraft fire. The Cubans didn't succeed in shooting any down, but when the planes returned to base technicians found several holes in their wings made by 37-millimeter shells.

Kennedy was informed. It seemed to confirm that the U-2 downing was deliberate. The conflict was heating up. Supporters of an immediate attack on antiaircraft positions now had yet another argument in their favor. The decision would rest with the Executive Committee. It was to convene in half an hour.

Dean Rusk simply couldn't understand why Father's second letter referred to the Turkish missiles, and he decided to try to get at the truth. He asked Scali to meet Fomin and attempt to clarify the situation. Neither Rusk, Scali, nor Fomin knew about the previous evening's conversation at the Soviet Embassy. The meeting had taken place at 4:15 P.M. Scali pressured Fomin, shouted, accused him of playing a double game. Eventually he warned: "The invasion of Cuba is now only hours away." Fomin tried to justify himself, referred to poor communications, and asserted that the misunderstanding was about to be cleared up: the ambassador was expecting a message from Moscow at any moment. However, he didn't say what message from Moscow, and he had nothing new to say. The latest message had just been transmitted by radio and through diplomatic channels, and now Washington was about to receive the text signed by Father and already broadcast throughout the world.

With this they parted. Scali immediately typed a brief report and passed it to Dean Rusk. They were unable to meet because the Executive Committee was already in session.

Fomin didn't waste any time either. In his coded message to Moscow, he warned that the situation was becoming explosive. An invasion force could land very soon, possibly the next day. In addition, he passed on Scali's question about the Jupiters in Turkey.

In Moscow it was past midnight. Sunday was beginning.

I must allow myself a small digression. There is much that is unclear in the history of the meetings between Fomin and Scali, and there are various interpretations of what occurred. The participants themselves think that they were the ones who saved the world from destruction. In the Occidental, a Washington restaurant, there is a memorial plaque above one of the tables with the portentous inscription: "During a tense period of the Cuban crisis, in October 1961, there was a conversation at this table between a mysterious Russian Mr. X and a correspondent of ABC Television, John Scali. On the basis of this meeting, the threat of nuclear war was averted." Not a bad advertisement for the restaurant and for the participants in this "negotiation."

However, Georgy Korniyenko doesn't think that Fomin accomplished anything. He and the ambassador didn't even bother to report what Fomin said to Moscow. Naturally, I didn't hear Fomin's name from Father. The intelligence reports in their gray-blue folders didn't provide names, even to the chairman of the Council of Ministers. They just said "a source reports," and that's all. And of course, Father wouldn't have remembered the obscure Fomin, who was not his only source.

No one doubts that the inscription on the plaque in the Occidental is an exaggeration. Fomin did not play an important role in the drama of those thirteen days. Robert Kennedy, Dobrynin, and to some degree, Bolshakov were the leading players.

"Fomin" carried out his assignment. He was a backup person. In Feklisov's memoirs much looks different. For example, the proposal about guarantees to Cuba and lifting the blockade in exchange for removing our missiles supposedly originated in the White House. There are other discrepancies. When I heard him (still under the name Fomin) speak at a Moscow meeting in 1989 devoted to the Cuban Missile Crisis, I had the distinct impression that his memory had really deteriorated. Therefore, I will describe the events in the way I see them, reconstructed on the basis of my own impressions and Father's accounts.

I cannot agree with Korniyenko. The KGB station chief did not need the ambassador's approval to send messages. Feklisov himself writes that Dobrynin "studied the draft telegram for three hours" and refused to sign it. What then? "After witnessing the ambassador's hesitation, I signed the telegram and gave it to the code clerk to be sent to my superiors." Naturally. At no time was the KGB dependent on the Foreign Ministry. So Fomin's telegrams reached their destination.

When the Executive Committee meeting resumed at 4 P.M. in the White House, the president opened the session by saying that "tomorrow, Sunday, there will be no attack." He wanted to make another attempt to explore possibilities for a peaceful outcome. The State Department submitted a draft reply to Moscow. It outlined objections to Father's demands for the withdrawal of U.S. missiles from Turkey. In Washington their reasons sounded completely persuasive, but it was unlikely that they would produce the same effect in Moscow. Cuban missiles were right next to the United States, and Turkish missiles were right next to the USSR.

Opinions diverged. The president himself was inclined to accept Father's second letter. After all, Kennedy had approved the exchange of R-12s for Jupiters. However, only his brother, the attorney general, supported him. There was a chorus of objections from the other members of the Executive Committee, who knew nothing about the agreement with Dobrynin reached the day before. NATO's approval would be needed for such a decision, and Turkey would have to be persuaded. The reaction in Europe had been negative so far. John Kennedy was trapped: On the one hand, he had given his agreement to Moscow, but on the other he didn't want to quarrel with NATO. His opponents' arguments sounded more than convincing.

When it seemed as if they couldn't find a way out, Robert Kennedy came up with a crazy idea. He thought that in his reply the president should not argue with his opponent, but should work toward achieving a positive decision—even if some important details were left out. Why argue about missiles in Turkey? The first letter hadn't even mentioned them. Therefore, it was better to respond to the first letter and see what happened. Ted Sorensen and some of the others agreed with him.

But the president thought that such an approach was unrealistic. How could the Soviet premier agree to ignore his own message, one that Moscow radio had just broadcast around the world? At this point Thompson, the former ambassador to Moscow, intervened. He thought that fears of Khrushchev's inflexibility were groundless. Thompson had studied Father rather well. In his opinion, such a sharp change in position from the first letter to the second indicated the superficial nature of the renewed demand for an exchange of missiles. It was a momentary consideration and a pragmatic politician—as the former ambassador described Father—would not cling to it. Provided, of course, that he thought the situation sufficiently grave.

Thompson thought that Father had made his decision when he signed the first letter. But then something had induced him to toughen his position. The ambassador didn't know what that was, but his calculations were correct. Only the Kennedy brothers knew what prompted Father to write a second letter.

The president trusted Thompson and proposed that his brother and Sorensen compose a new version of the reply. They had enough material to choose from.

In the meantime the Executive Committee discussed plans for the following day. The main question was what to do about reconnaissance flights. No one was in favor of ending them, but they felt it was impossible to expose the pilots to such danger. They talked again about ordering a single air strike to destroy the antiaircraft sites. That would make the skies safe, not only for reconnaissance flights but for a future invasion as well.

Opinions diverged. The decision was left to the president. An attack on the antiaircraft batteries was postponed. At the same time, they canceled the U-2's morning flight. It was clear that altitude no longer protected the U-2s and they had become ideal targets for missiles.

Maneuverable, low-flying reconnaissance aircraft had more chance of slipping past antiaircraft positions and surviving. Missiles were ineffective at low altitudes.

The members of the Executive Committee knew that the antiaircraft missiles were under Soviet control, and the antiaircraft artillery was under Cuban, but it didn't distinguish between the Soviets and the Cubans. Washington was convinced that Castro was blindly following orders from Moscow.

The immediate destruction of antiaircraft positions would follow another attack on the planes, since it would remove any doubt about the intentions of the Soviet command.

That was a potentially fatal mistake. Father had given the Soviet contingent strict orders not to fire on U-2 flights, but these orders did not apply to low-flying planes, which were relatively safe from missiles but vulnerable to antiaircraft. Cuban antiaircraft gunners had every intention of obeying Castro's command to "destroy any foreign plane which appears over the island."

The first flight on Sunday, October 28, was scheduled for ten that morning.

Meanwhile, a second version of the reply to Father was born. It sounded much more substantive than the first: no questions, no arguments. The president agreed on all points, though with a few reservations. The president himself corrected the final version. It was a short letter. Half an hour later a freshly typed copy was brought in. John Kennedy signed it, then handed it to Dean Rusk to send. At 8:05 P.M. Washington time, 4:05 A.M. in Moscow, the message was received by the U.S. Embassy in Moscow. Ambassador Kohler didn't even try to call the Foreign Ministry. There was good reason for that. Following Father's example, Kennedy had given the letter to the press immediately, so that it could hardly pass unnoticed in Moscow.

The Foreign Ministry did not officially receive the text until 10:30 Sunday morning.

The president wrote:

Dear Mr. Chairman,

I have read your letter of October 26th with great care and welcome your desire to seek a prompt solution to the crisis. However, the first thing that needs to be done is for work to cease on missile bases in Cuba and for all missile systems capable of offensive use to be rendered inoperable, under effective United Nations arrangements.

Assuming this is done promptly, I have given my representatives in New York instructions that will permit them to work out this weekend—in cooperation with the Acting Secretary-General and your representative—an arrangement for a permanent solution to the Cuban problem along the lines suggested in your letter of October 26th. As I read your letter, the key elements of your proposals—which seem generally acceptable as I understand them—are as follows:

(1) You would agree to remove these weapons systems from Cuba under appropriate United Nations observation and supervision; and undertake, with suitable safeguards, to halt the further introduction of such weapons systems into Cuba.

(2) We, on our part, would agree—upon the establishment of adequate arrangements through the United Nations to ensure the carrying out and continuation of these commitments—(a) to remove promptly the quarantine measures now in effect and (b) to give assurances against an invasion of Cuba. I am confident that other nations of the Western Hemisphere would be prepared to do likewise.

If you give your representative similar instructions, there is no reason why we should not be able to complete these arrangements and announce them to the world within a couple of days. The effect of such a settlement on easing world tensions would enable us to work toward a more general arrangement regarding "other armaments," as proposed in your second letter which you made public. I would like to say again that the United States is very much interested in reducing tension and halting the arms race; and if your letter signifies that you are prepared to discuss a détente affecting NATO and the Warsaw Pact, we are quite prepared to consider with our allies any useful proposals.

But the first ingredient, let me emphasize, is the cessation of work on missile sites in Cuba and measures to render such weapons inoperable, under effective international guarantees. The continuation of this threat, or a prolonging of this discussion concerning Cuba by linking these problems to the broader questions of European and world security, would surely lead to an intensified situation on the Cuban crisis and a grave risk to the peace of the world. For this reason I hope we can quickly agree along the lines outlined in this letter and in your letter of October 26th.

John F. Kennedy

After the letter was sent, John Kennedy announced a break until nine that evening. He remained alone with his brother. After this new turn of events, interest in another meeting between Scali and Fomin evaporated. Turkish missiles were no longer on the agenda. Furthermore, they were unsure if Saturday's contact in Washington would be given the proper importance in Moscow. Did the Kremlin realize fully just how explosive the situation had become?

The president was nervous. Without a positive response from Moscow, advocates of an invasion could win out. Furthermore, it was essential that the Kremlin recognize the White House's emphatic position on the destruction of the U-2. Silence on this matter could be construed as weakness. A mistake in evaluating the intentions of an adversary could come at a high price. Another chance for survival might simply not present itself.

The president asked his brother to have an urgent meeting with the Soviet ambassador and give a frank description of the situation in the White House. It was time to work together to solve the impasse.

It's difficult to say what else the president was thinking at that time. What, if any, political steps was he holding in reserve?

The majority of eyewitnesses and historians agree that Saturday's opportunity was truly the last one. If Moscow refused to remove the missiles on Monday, Tuesday at the latest, an invasion would follow. And then Father would have either to swallow that pill or . . . I don't know what that "or" might have been.

Judging by the evidence of President Kennedy's closest aides, he cannot be accused of recklessness. Even on Saturday, he thought that an invasion of Cuba was not the only solution. He talked about the need on Monday, and even on Tuesday, to try to undertake diplomatic initiatives.

Ted Sorensen, Robert McNamara, and McGeorge Bundy referred to that at the Moscow meeting in 1989. Today we can only speculate about what those initiatives might have been.

During those days the American press teemed with reports of Soviet missiles in Cuba and photographs of launch sites under construction. Americans were in the grip of fear. It seemed as if the end of the world had come.

Soviet newspapers contained no mention of the word "missiles." The Kremlin thought there was no reason to alarm people. Some guessed what was really behind the headlines of political articles in *Pravda* and *Izvestiya*: "Peoples of the world reject the aggressive policies of the United States," "The Soviet Position—Bulwark of Peace," "Cuba on Guard!" Of course, vague rumors spread around town but, with the exception of a few people behind the high walls of the Kremlin, no one had any concept of the real danger.

Most of the Soviet people found out what had happened only much later, when the Cuban Crisis was history and when people talked about the danger of mutual destruction as a threat that had been successfully averted.

We return to Washington. At 7:15 that evening, Robert Kennedy called Anatoly Dobrynin and invited him to his office in the Department of Justice. The ambassador needed no explanation. He said that he would arrive in half an hour.

The meeting took place at 7:45.

There are two versions of the meeting: Father's, based on Dobrynin's report, and Robert Kennedy's. Both were written when their meeting was fresh in their minds. Their descriptions do not disagree in substance, but are strikingly different in emotional tone.

I would like to cite both, beginning with Father's. His account is not always very precise in describing specific details, but he presents a vivid description of his feelings.

> The culmination came when Dobrynin, our ambassador to the United States, reported that the president's brother, Robert Kennedy, had come to see him on an unofficial visit. He described his appearance: Robert Kennedy looked exhausted, and you could see from his eyes that he had not slept for days. He himself described that later. Robert Kennedy told Dobrynin that he had not been home for six days and nights and had not seen his wife and children—he sat with the president in the White House while they struggled with the problem of our missiles.
>
> He said:
>
> "We are under very severe stress. The danger of war is great. I want to ask you to inform your government and Khrushchev, so that they take this into consideration. The president is preparing a message through unofficial channels and he very much wishes Khrushchev to accept his proposals."
>
> He said frankly that the situation is very threatening; therefore the president is writing the message himself. Robert Kennedy said that the president himself didn't know how to resolve the situation. The military is putting great

pressure on him, insisting on military actions against Cuba and the president is in a very difficult position.

He said:

"You should take the peculiarities of our state system into consideration. It's very hard for the president. Even if he doesn't want or desire a war, something irreversible could occur against his will. That is why the president is asking for help to solve this problem."

I don't have the documents now and I am describing everything from memory, but the essence stands out graphically in my memory. I lived through this and remember everything very well. Because I was the person responsible for this action, from beginning to end. I was its initiator and I formulated the entire correspondence between me and the president.

Later on Father refers to the Turkish missiles: Kennedy asked that Khrushchev be informed that, because of considerations of prestige and obligations to NATO allies, he could not unilaterally announce their removal, but that he would do so in the very near future.

Robert Kennedy describes the meeting in somewhat more detail, with many factual references and with an eye to his future voters.

We met in my office at 19:45. I told him first that we knew that work was continuing on the missile bases in Cuba and that in the last few days it had been expedited. I said that in the last few hours we had learned that our reconnaissance planes flying over Cuba had been fired upon and that one of our U-2s had been shot down and the pilot killed. That was for us a most serious turn of events.

President Kennedy did not want a military conflict. He had done everything possible to avoid a military engagement with Cuba and with the Soviet Union, but now they had forced our hand. Because of the deception of the Soviet Union, our photographic reconnaissance planes would have to continue to fly over Cuba, and if the Cubans or Soviets shot at these planes, then we would have to shoot back. This would inevitably lead to further incidents and to escalation of the conflict, the implications of which were very grave indeed.

He said the Cubans resented the fact that we were violating Cuban airspace. I replied that if we had not violated Cuban airspace, we would still be believing what Khrushchev had said—that there would be no missiles placed in Cuba. In any case, I said, this matter was far more serious than the airspace of Cuba—it involved the peoples of both our countries and, in fact, people all over the globe.

The Soviet Union had secretly established missile bases in Cuba while at the same time proclaiming privately and publicly that this would never be done. We had to have a commitment by tomorrow that those bases would be removed. I was not giving them an ultimatum but a statement of fact. He should understand that if they did not remove those bases, we would remove them. President Kennedy had great respect for the Ambassador's country and the courage of its people. Perhaps his country might feel it necessary to take retaliatory action; but before that was over, there would be not only dead Americans but dead Russians as well.

He asked me what offer the United States was making, and I told him of the letter that President Kennedy had just transmitted to Khrushchev. He raised the question of our removing the missiles from Turkey. I said that there could be no quid pro quo or any arrangement made under this kind of threat or pressure, and that in the last analysis this was a decision that would have to be made by NATO. However, I said, President Kennedy had been anxious to remove those missiles from Turkey and Italy for a long period of time. He had ordered their removal some time ago, and it was our judgment that, within a short time after this crisis was over, those missiles would be gone.

I said that President Kennedy wished to have peaceful relations between our two countries. He wished to resolve the problems that confronted us in Europe and Southeast Asia. He wished to move forward on the control of nuclear weapons. However, we could make progress on these matters only when the crisis was behind us. Time was running out. We had only a few more hours—we needed an answer immediately from the Soviet Union. I said we must have it the next day.

I returned to the White House. The president was not optimistic, nor was I. He ordered twenty-four troop-carrier squadrons of the Air Force Reserve to active duty. They would be necessary for an invasion. He had not abandoned hope, but what hope there was now rested with Khrushchev's revising his course within the next few hours. It was a hope, not an expectation. The expectation was a military confrontation by Tuesday and possibly tomorrow.

Probably there is a certain degree of embellishment after the fact in both of these recollections. Once the threat is past, one wants to appear a little more impressive to the historians. But the facts agree. When these events were taking place, the four—John Kennedy, Father, and their representatives—were not thinking about external effects.

One more vitally important detail should be singled out in the conversation between Robert Kennedy and Anatoly Dobrynin. For some reason, neither party records it, but in his account of the events of those days Father often returned to it.

The Americans warned that they would consider any attack on reconnaissance planes as the initiation of military actions by the Soviet Union. I have already mentioned that their first flight was scheduled for ten o'clock Sunday morning.

Pliyev and Major General Statsenko, commander of the ballistic missile division, reported to Malinovsky that as of the evening of October 27 the last missile battalion of the third regiment was ready for action and that testing of the nuclear missile warheads was fully completed.

THE TURN TOWARD RESOLUTION

At the dacha in Novo-Ogaryovo, participants in the Sunday meeting arrived early. They waited for Father. He arrived exactly at ten.

It wasn't the first time that Father arranged for such a meeting on a day off. However, he didn't abuse this prerogative. The meetings were ordinarily devoted to a discussion of some major reform or another equally important event, when they needed time to talk over everything without haste and without being interrupted by reports and phone calls. Before getting down to business, they usually joked and sometimes went for a walk.

This time everything was different. Father greeted everyone coolly and without his usual smile. Turning abruptly to his aide, who was standing nearby, he asked: "What's new?"

"A letter has come from Kennedy. It was broadcast during the night on American radio," he answered. "There's some information from the ambassador in Washington, and something else besides." The aide paused—of course, he knew everyone there, but he still hesitated to mention intelligence reports.

"Let's go, we'll look at them there," said Father, pointing at the door of the two-story house, Malenkov's former dacha, where they were going to work that day. He went in first and the others followed.

The meeting was held in a large dining room meant for receiving high-ranking guests. That day the white tablecloth on the long table was covered with folders in various colors: red, pink, green, and gray-blue. Each of the meeting's participants picked up a stack of mail delivered early that morning by a courier.

When everyone was seated, Father proposed that they begin with the president's letter.

They decided to have it read aloud, even though a meticulously typed TASS copy lay in front of everyone. Father's aide for international affairs, Oleg Aleksandrovich Troyanovsky, began to read. A funereal silence enveloped the room except for his flat and monotonous voice.

Less than five minutes had gone by when a door opened noiselessly and the duty officer slipped through and whispered something in Gromyko's ear. Andrei Andreyevich coughed politely. Troyanovsky paused in the middle of a sentence and all heads turned toward the foreign minister.

Gromyko coughed again and said quietly: "They've called from the Foreign Ministry. The U.S. ambassador is asking to be received."

He looked inquiringly at Father.

"You don't need to waste time," said Father in answer to the silent question. "He's probably bringing the message which we are reading. Let your deputy meet him and call us if it's something important."

Gromyko went quickly to phone and Troyanovsky, returning to the beginning of the sentence, continued his reading. It took about half an hour. Finally, the aide read: "Signed: John Kennedy." And added, with a note of surprise: "This time without 'Sincerely' or 'Sincerely yours,' which he included previously."

There was a pause. Father was deep in concentration, thinking over the text he had just heard. He seemed to be trying to imagine, to resurrect, the U.S. president's train of thought, to put himself in his place. No one dared disturb him, and the others buried themselves in the papers lying before them.

Finally, Father stirred, glanced around at those present and asked for their opinions. However, no one was in any hurry to be first. There was a heavy silence, broken finally by Troyanovsky: "We also received a report from Ambassador Dobrynin about his talk with Robert Kennedy. Very curious."

"Read it," ordered Father.

Troyanovsky picked up some thin, transparent pages resembling cigarette papers, which had a warning in red ink at the top of each page against making copies, and continued his recitation.

Father stared intently at Troyanovsky, listening to every intonation and several times asking him to repeat passages that had particularly attracted his attention.

I have already described the conversation that took place at the Department of Justice.

Later on, when Father would recount the story of how Robert Kennedy appeared to Dobrynin, he always added with a smile: "And we didn't look any better."

The president was calling for help: that was how Father interpreted Robert Kennedy's talk with our ambassador. The tone of the conversation was evidence of the fact that to delay could be fatal. The temperature in the Washington boiler had apparently reached a dangerous point and was about to explode.

"What else?" Father turned to Troyanovsky.

Oleg Aleksandrovich opened a gray-blue folder. The first page contained a report from Washington: the "source" (Fomin-Feklisov) reported that his interlocutors were extremely disturbed by the sudden emergence of the question of Turkish missiles. Furthermore, the correspondent referred to the fact that the issue was raised directly by Dean Rusk.

Father looked up in surprise. "The right hand doesn't know what the left hand is doing," he said with irritation.

"Anything more?" He looked at Troyanovsky again.

Intelligence reports from various parts of the globe pointed to an increase in tension, with the most disturbing information coming from the American continent: Marine detachments, the Air Force, and Army troops were ready for action and were only waiting for the order to begin an attack.

In fact, there was no need to look at secret reports. Every American newspaper was trumpeting the news of an imminent invasion—if not today, then tomorrow.

"That's everything," said the aide, closing the folder.

"So, what do you think?" Father repeated his question.

Did no one answer this time either? Well, Father didn't really need any advice. A clear picture was emerging. They had to accept Kennedy's proposal now, before a war started. They had to be satisfied with his guarantees not to attack Cuba and begin removing the missiles. Otherwise he might not be able to resist the militarists, and if the dam broke there would be innumerable victims. Judging by Rusk's questions reported by our intelligence agent, the secretary of state knew nothing about Robert Kennedy's meeting with Dobrynin the day before. Apparently the president could not take the risk. He simply could not inform his circle of the promise he had given. And that was a bad sign. Everything indicated that he was reaching the limit of his strength. A trade was no longer feasible. There was no use harping on the Turkish missiles. They were not what counted. The idea of a trade would have to be given up. It was a shame. But life was more important than prestige.

Of course, Father would have wished to receive a more ceremonial assurance from the U.S. president concerning the inviolability of the borders of Cuba—in the form of a written agreement or a decision within the framework of the U.N., for example. The two or three weeks mentioned in his last letter were intended for the implementation of just such a procedure. But evidently the situation in Washington was too volatile.

That was Father's general train of thought. He spoke for about an hour, returning constantly to the premise that Kennedy's word should be trusted and that he would be in the White House for a long time, at least six more years. A great deal could be done during that time, mountains could be moved. Cuba would become impregnable, wealthy, happy.

And the Turkish missiles? Forget about them. Kennedy would remove them sooner or later. In his last talk with our ambassador, Robert had confirmed that and only asked not to be pressured.

Father broke off and looked around at those present. The members of the Presidium of the Central Committee supported their first secretary with their usual unanimity. He resumed his monologue.

While Father was persuading the others—and primarily himself—Troyanovsky slipped from the room. The duty officer had opened the door a crack and beckoned to him. Suslov, Gromyko's aide, was calling from the Foreign Ministry with some new information. Propping the phone in place with his shoulder, Oleg Aleksandrovich made some hurried notes about the information, which he was to report at once, without waiting for a courier to deliver the documents.

When Troyanovsky returned to the room, everyone turned toward him, as if on command. What else could happen? It must be something important for anyone to dare summon the chairman's aide during such a meeting. Finishing his sentence, Father broke off and invited Troyanovsky to speak.

The aide first reported: "The U.S. ambassador handed over President Kennedy's message—the same one, nothing new." This information was greeted with some relief. That day no one expected good news.

However, the next report was from Washington and was cause for concern: rumors were circulating around the city that the president would deliver a new and important speech at 5 p.m. About what? That was not known, but it was easy to guess. On black Monday, October 22, he had announced the blockade. Now, on Sunday the twenty-eighth, the next step would be an invasion. Yesterday's warnings by Robert Kennedy were being realized. They had broken the president. He was unable to hold out.

"At five o'clock whose time?" asked Father. Troyanovsky only shrugged. General Semyon Pavlovich Ivanov, secretary of the Defense Council and a regular participant in the previous days' meetings, came to his assistance. He had been called to the phone at about the same time as Troyanovsky, and now he was waiting his turn to report information received by military intelligence. Their dispatches confirmed the report of Kennedy's upcoming speech at five o'clock.

"Moscow time," asserted the general.

No one knows whether their messages really included this detail, or if Ivanov assumed the responsibility, having decided that it was better to be early than late. The general's words removed the last doubts—only a few hours were left before the catastrophe.

Ivanov returned to his seat in the corner of the room.

Fear has big eyes! American TV was reporting that the president's speech from the previous week, the speech of October 22, would be repeated that Sunday. We can only speculate why the report from the intelligence station in Washington suddenly transformed that into a new address to the nation by the head of state.

After the "clarification" introduced by Ivanov, Father spoke again. He thought that our agreement to withdraw the missiles should be broadcast immediately over the radio, like the previous one, so that it was not late in arriving. After giving a speech to the nation, Kennedy would not reverse himself.

Father was ready to begin dictating letters immediately. Stenographers, who were sitting at a small table along the wall, made their preparations.

However, Troyanovsky had some additional news to report.

"Nikita Sergeyevich, a very disturbing message has come in from Castro." As always, Oleg Aleksandrovich spoke in quiet and measured tones, not allowing himself to hurry after onrushing events. "The text itself is still at the Foreign Ministry, but I wrote down its main points."

"Yes," said Father impatiently.

"Castro thinks—and in his opinion, the source of his information is reliable—that war will begin in the next few hours," said Troyanovsky, looking at his notes. "They don't know exactly when, possibly in twenty-four hours, but in no more than seventy-two. In the opinion of the Cuban leadership, the people are ready to repel an imperialist and aggressive attack. They would sooner die than surrender."

Oleg Aleksandrovich sighed and continued: "In Castro's opinion, in face of an imminent conflict with the United States, the imperialists must not be allowed to deliver a strike"—he looked down again at his pad and repeated—"allowed to be the first to deliver a nuclear strike."

"What?!"

"That is what I was told," Troyanovsky responded without visible disquiet.

"What? Is he proposing that we start a nuclear war? That we launch missiles from Cuba?" said Father, somewhat more calmly.

"Apparently," confirmed his aide. "The text will be delivered soon, and then it will be easier to tell what Castro really has in mind."

"That is insane." Father still hadn't calmed down. "We deployed missiles there to prevent an attack on the island, to save Cuba and defend socialism. And now not only is he preparing to die himself, he wants to drag us with him."

Malinovsky, who hadn't said a word the entire time, now tried to put in his two cents: "The missiles in Cuba aren't operational yet. Only a few of them could be launched. Besides, nuclear warheads are not mounted on them and are kept separately, under close guard. It would take several hours to prepare the missiles for launch."

"I know that myself," Father dismissed his comment. "The point is not whether or not his proposal could be carried out, but how can he even think of such a thing?"

Whatever doubts Father might have had earlier about the timeliness and correctness of his decision to withdraw the missiles, they now vanished completely. "Remove them, and as soon as possible. Before something terrible happens."

The meeting's participants stared at each other incredulously. To start a third world war in such a way, so simply! It was becoming obvious that events were slipping out of control. Yesterday they had shot down a plane without permission—and today they were thinking of a nuclear attack.

To general approval, Father ordered that an immediate order be sent to Pliyev through military channels: "Allow no one near the missiles. Obey no orders to launch and under no circumstances install the warheads." Father began to feel a little easier. Pliyev was a reliable and disciplined officer. He wouldn't permit arbitrary actions. But if there were an invasion and communications were cut off, who knew what some of the younger commanders might do?

Malinovsky went to a neighboring office to issue the necessary orders.

The sharpness of our perceptions are smoothed over with the passage of time. Events that took place many years before begin to be viewed differently, especially since we know the sequel. But even a quarter of a century later, Oleg Aleksandrovich couldn't talk about it calmly. The apocalyptic sound of Castro's message, he said, made a shocking impression on him.

What had happened in Cuba? The situation was becoming more tense with every passing day. Castro wasn't bluffing when he talked about being ready to die, together with most of his countrymen. He thought constantly about when it might begin.

He thought not only about tiny Cuba, which had its score to settle with the Yankees, but about the fate of the Soviet Union, which had come to Cuba's assistance when the imperialists threatened to invade it, and about the entire socialist camp. They might all collapse because of Cuba! That thought gave Castro no peace.

If the Americans launched an attack, which he now did not doubt, their blows would fall not only on the Cubans prepared to defend themselves, but on Soviet regiments, batteries, and squadrons. After his visits to Soviet Army units, Castro was convinced that they were just as determined as the Cubans to resist to the end.

But a blow here would inevitably bring a response there, across the ocean. Whether it was in Berlin or Turkey was unimportant. A great war would break out and the use of nuclear weapons could not be avoided. Everything would be decided in hours, minutes, and seconds. The one who struck first would win. Castro didn't know anything about McNamara's statistics showing an eighteen to one ratio of nuclear warheads, and not in our favor. In general, never having seen a nuclear explosion, he had no clear picture of what one was like. He didn't realize the consequences, not only for the losers, but for the winners as well.

It seemed to Castro that if the Soviet Union struck the first blow, it would be the end of the imperialists, the end of his arrogant northern neighbors—who for decades had been humiliating his Latin American brothers—and of all other oppressors. An era of freedom and prosperity would begin.

For the sake of this bright future, Castro resolved unhesitatingly to sacrifice Cuba. Cuba would perish, but socialism would be victorious. Perhaps it was for this, for this minute, that he had agreed without hesitation to base foreign missiles and foreign military units on the island. "The motherland or death! We shall be victorious!"—that became the meaning of his existence. It was why Castro preserved an unshakable calm in the face of impending danger. Alekseyev guessed at Castro's sacrificial resolve, but didn't realize how far it had gone.

That was why Castro regarded ideas of exchanging U.S. missiles in Turkey for Soviet missiles in Cuba, ideas put forward in the previous few days and hours, with extreme disapproval and even suspicion. Again, just as at the beginning of the century, the Yankees were arranging a trade behind Cuba's back. They were trying to exchange a sacred idea for some missiles!

He had to inform Moscow as quickly as possible of his decision to sacrifice Cuba. Let them be aware, as they drew up their plans, that Cuba was ready to perish for the sake of victory.

During all the preceding days, Castro's thoughts revolved around this idea of a great sacrifice. But his message to Moscow wasn't turning out well. He simply couldn't find words that were modest, lucid, and profound, but not excessively heroic. And time was pressing. Mirra Cordona's circle of Cuban exiles was not the only source of disturbing reports of an imminent invasion. On October 26 Castro received reliable information from Brazilian president Goularta that an invasion would occur within forty-eight hours. That source could not be doubted. The United States would have to report the invasion to members of the Organization of American States, to which Cuba until very recently had belonged. The hour of decision had come!

So what precisely was going on in Havana? Documents from those days have been preserved. At the international conference in January of 1991 devoted to this event, Feliks N. Kovalyov, chief of the Foreign Ministry's Department of Archives, discussed the contents of some recently declassified messages sent by Ambassador Alekseyev. From time to time Alekseyev himself, who attended the conference, commented and enlarged upon his coded messages.

Castro, like Stalin, often confused day and night, rejecting the rhythm of sleep and activity decreed by nature and destroying the usual pattern for all his associates. This was true even during ordinary times, and in that turbulent October period he entirely stopped distinguishing between daylight and darkness.

"On October 27, at two o'clock in the morning [Cuban time, of course], Dorticos called me," reported the Soviet ambassador in one of his coded messages to Moscow. "He informed me that Fidel Castro was on his way to the Embassy to see me. He wanted to discuss the latest events."

The message doesn't say whether Alekseyev was asleep at the time, but he greeted his friend Fidel with his usual hospitality. Castro looked extremely worried. He said that the time for decisions had come and that he had to dictate a letter to Khrushchev. Only a few hours were left before an American invasion.

A nervous Castro began dictating to the secretary who accompanied him. Alekseyev knew Spanish, although not perfectly, and often interpreted at important talks. That day he could barely grasp Castro's meaning. Fidel got mixed up, became angry, stopped in the middle of a sentence, and started over again from the beginning.

Alekseyev seized an opportunity to leave Castro and sent a brief coded message to Moscow. In it, he reported that Fidel was at the Embassy preparing a personal letter to Khrushchev. The Foreign Ministry received this message at 2:40 P.M. on Saturday and began to wait for the text of Castro's letter. Evening came, night came, and still no further word from Havana.

Meanwhile, Fidel was struggling with the letter. He couldn't find the right words. The letter was clumsy and flat. It lacked heart and emotion.

Alekseyev had understood for some time what Fidel was trying unsuccessfully to express. But it seemed so terrible that it didn't fit into normal human perceptions. Finally the ambassador steeled himself. "You want to say that we should be the first to deliver a nuclear strike?" he asked his friend, and held his breath, hoping profoundly for a storm of protest or at worst a simple shake of the head. Castro froze, then, as if weighing every word, he said with unusual slowness: "No . . . I don't want to say that directly. No. But the situation is developing in such a way that it's either we or they. If we want to avoid receiving the first strike, if an attack is inevitable, then wipe them off the face of the earth."

Alekseyev said nothing. He was crushed. He didn't want even to think about such a possibility. The world seemed to be coming to an end.

Without waiting for an answer, Castro resumed his attempts to express his feelings on paper. It was only toward seven in the morning that he thought he had been successful or decided in despair not to test fate any longer. The letter was, in my opinion, something like a last testament, a farewell.

So much has been said about this letter that I feel I should include its full text.

Dear Comrade Khrushchev!

After analyzing the current situation and the information which we have in our possession, we have concluded that aggression will almost certainly take place within the next twenty-four to seventy-two hours.

This aggression will take two possible forms:

(1) More likely is an attack from the air on particular targets, with the only objective being their destruction.

(2) Less likely, though possible, is a direct invasion of the country. I think that a large force would be required for this variant, and that could restrain the aggressor. Moreover, world public opinion would be outraged by such aggression.

You may be assured that we will resist firmly and decisively, whatever form the aggression may take.

The morale of the Cuban people is extremely high, and they will face the aggressor heroically.

Now I would like to express in a few words my personal opinion on the events which are taking place.

If the second type of aggression occurs and the imperialists invade Cuba with the intention of occupying it, then the danger posed by such an aggressive policy would be so great for all of mankind that in that event the Soviet Union should under no circumstances allow conditions to be created which would permit the imperialists to deliver a first nuclear strike on the USSR.

I say this because I think that the aggression of the imperialists is becoming extremely dangerous.

If they carry out an attack on Cuba it would be a barbarian, illegal, and immoral act. In those circumstances and in view of the lawful right of self-defense, it would seem the appropriate time to think about putting a permanent end to such a danger. No matter how difficult and terrible this decision is, in my opinion there is no other solution. That is my opinion, provoked by the development of that aggressive policy by which the imperialists—regardless of public opinion, principles, and rights—blockade our seas, violate our airspace, and prepare to invade while, on the other hand, disrupting any possibility of negotiations, despite the fact that they are well aware of the gravity of the consequences.

You are and will remain an indefatigable defender of peace and I understand how bitter these hours must be, when the fruits of your superhuman efforts in the struggle for peace are subject to a grave threat.

However, we will remain hopeful to the last minute that peace will be preserved, and we will do everything within our power to preserve it, but at the same time we evaluate the situation realistically and are ready to face any test with resolution.

Once again, I express infinite gratitude and appreciation on behalf of our entire people to the Soviet people, which has been so fraternally generous to us. We also express our admiration and deep gratitude to you personally and wish you success in your tremendous and responsible work.

With fraternal greetings. Fidel Castro

Today it is for historians to decide whether Father correctly interpreted the meaning of the letter, or if there was something he did not fully understand. Furthermore, we should keep in mind that it was Troyanovsky's words about a nuclear strike, uttered even before the text of the message arrived, which lodged permanently in Father's brain. They were the words ringing in Father's ears that day; on October 30, when he composed a detailed reply to Castro; half a year later in May when they met in Moscow; and five years later when he started working on his memoirs. He remembered the most important words, "preemptive strike."

One more thing: history is as capricious as the people creating it. We have already seen how, in the episode about the Turkish missiles, the main actors began insistently and on the very next day to manipulate their answers to different questions.

Coded messages from Havana reached Moscow even more slowly than those from Washington. That was understandable: first the text was encrypted by hand, the old-fashioned method used in the last century. Then there were problems with the telegraph. And finally the same kind of decoding process had to take place in Moscow. It was easier when the writer liked to be brief. But what if, like Father or Fidel, he suffered from volubility? So it was not surprising that the text, arriving in the hands of the Embassy's code clerk at seven in the morning Havana time, did not leave the code room of the Foreign Ministry until 1:10 A.M. on Sunday morning.

"Remove them, and as quickly as possible," repeated Father, referring to the warheads on the missiles in Cuba, addressing everyone present, but seemingly no one in particular.

Then he suddenly thought of something and turned to the foreign minister.

"Comrade Gromyko, we don't have the right to take risks. Once the president announces there will be an invasion, he won't be able to reverse himself. We have to let Kennedy know that we want to help him." Father hesitated at the word "help," but after a moment's silence repeated firmly: "Yes, help. We now have a common cause, to save the world from those pushing us toward war. Send a message to Dobrynin in Washington. Let him meet with Robert Kennedy and advise him to wait for our answer to yesterday's letter from the president. Emphasize that the answer is a positive one."

"I'll do it, Nikita Sergeyevich," said Gromyko in a muffled voice as he rose from behind the table.

Dobrynin received the coded message at 3 P.M. Moscow time, 8 A.M. in Washington.[20] After reading Gromyko's instructions, the ambassador at once called Robert Kennedy. They met literally a few minutes later.

Meanwhile the conference in Novo-Ogaryovo was continuing. Father broke a painful silence by turning to the stenographer with his usual phrase: "Let's begin, Nadezhda Petrovna."

Father began to dictate. The stack of pages grew higher and higher. Father was getting carried away and the letter was growing in length. Apparently he sensed this and decided to cut it short, beginning to search for some sentences to bring it to a conclusion: "We must be extremely careful now and refrain from any steps which would not benefit the defense of states involved in the conflict, but which could only cause irritation and even serve as a provocation for a fateful step. Therefore, we must display sanity, reason, and refrain from such steps."

The passage seemed to be successful; two more paragraphs and Father said, as he looked around at his colleagues sitting silently at the table: "That seems to be everything." Father didn't even mention the Turkish missiles, as Kennedy had not in his letter. As if they didn't even exist. For now . . .

His aide prepared to read through the text. He held only the first few pages. The rest was being hastily typed in the next room. Father asked about the radio station and was told that they were already waiting. The announcer had been called and was waiting for the text.

"Well, and the couriers? Yesterday's? Are they still waiting?" Father smiled. His usual joking manner was coming back.

"Sturua from *Izvestiya* is here," reported Troyanovsky. "But Kharlamov hasn't come. They couldn't find him. He's off today. We'll send it with the messenger service."

At this point, the story goes, some initiative was displayed by Leonid Ilyichev, the Central Committee secretary for ideology, who was present during the discussion but had not said a word the entire day. I began this book with an account of his trip. He volunteered to deliver the package to the radio station. Father nodded. He didn't really care who carried the letter, as long as it was delivered in time.

Final editing of the letter was quickly accomplished. The aide read it aloud. Father interrupted him now and then, changed words, inserted whole phrases. Other members of the Presidium occasionally interjected something. A stenographer made all the corrections. The letter was retyped one

---

20. On Sunday, October 28, the United States went off daylight savings time and the time difference between Washington and Moscow was reduced from eight hours to seven.

more time, the last, now quite insignificant changes were made, and the final version was ready.

Father nodded. "It can be sent," and stopped suddenly. He had remembered Castro. But he hesitated only a minute. "Send it at once," Father repeated.

Half a year later Father explained it this way to a still irate Castro: he interpreted the Cuban message that an invasion was expected within a few hours essentially as agreement, since there was no time for formalities.

That was certainly true. The situation required an immediate decision. And it was not exactly true. Castro's proposal to deliver a preemptive strike on the United States had shocked Father. Only at that moment did he really grasp the difference in how they looked at the world and the values they placed on people's fates and lives. If Castro had resisted, which seemed quite possible, negotiations with Washington would have been cut off and the moment irretrievably lost.

Father decided to present Havana with a fait accompli. If the world was not destroyed, relations with Castro would eventually improve.

In my opinion, time has shown that he was right.

Today Cubans still feel insulted that they were not asked to participate in the negotiations, and they consider Father's instantaneous reaction to be a mistake. In their opinion, he should have insisted on negotiations. Or on perishing.

A Central Committee Chaika limousine and an *Izvestiya* Volga carried the couriers with the good news. News of the triumph of reason and of life.

Father finally cheered up. He proposed that they all have a snack together while waiting for the radio broadcast.

Opening the door slightly, he called down the hall: "Is there any lunch?"

The head guard suddenly appeared out of nowhere. "Yes, Nikita Sergeyevich. But the table isn't set." He glanced at the table, where the meeting's participants were still sitting. They began moving around and talking to each other. The entire atmosphere changed, the way it does when the sun suddenly comes out after a thunderstorm.

Father suggested taking a walk while the waiters set the table. The whole crowd went out into the park.

That morning we, the members of his family, knew nothing about any of this. We went to our dacha, which was only a ten-minute drive from where the Presidium was meeting, but on that day those minutes stretched into an eternity.

What were they doing? And why was it taking so long?

We weren't supposed to call. Anyway, what could the duty officer say?

I walked aimlessly around the house. Mama sat in front of the television, but what could she see on the screen?

I finally couldn't hold out and called Father's office at the Central Committee. His secretary's answer was unenlightening: "They're still at the meeting, which is not being held here. We don't know when it will end."

That was all. Again, an agonizing wait.

It was almost time for lunch. Should we wait or not? On weekends Father always had lunch at home. Mama was beginning to worry, and I decided to call the dacha where the meeting was being held. Now I had a reason to call and maybe I could find out something. The news was not reassuring. Litovchenko, the head of the guards, said that the end of the meeting was not in sight and they would probably interrupt it to have lunch. I couldn't help asking: "What's new?" although I knew the answer in advance. I heard on the other end: "Nothing." The conversation was over.

We had lunch without Father.

Before lunch, I had turned on the radio. Nothing important or disturbing was being said, but I left it on and tried to stay close enough to hear it. We had no other source of information. This went on until afternoon. At about four o'clock Moscow Radio's call sign came on. Since the war it had always preceded important government announcements. The seconds dragged on endlessly. Finally we heard the customary words, "This is Radio Moscow," and Levitan began reading Father's letter to the president of the United States, John Fitzgerald Kennedy.

> Dear Mr. President:
>
>   I have received your message of 27 October. I express my satisfaction and thank you for the sense of proportion you have displayed and for realization of the responsibility which now devolved on you for the preservation of peace throughout the world.

The noted announcer's voice, which had sounded slightly shaky as he said the first few words, regained its usual resonance.

I listened intently. Judging by the first sentences, it did not mean war.

>   I regard with great understanding your concern and the concern of the people of the United States of America in connection with the fact that the weapons you describe as offensive are formidable weapons indeed. Both you and we understand what kind of weapons these are.

Levitan's steely intonation stressed the word "what," which suddenly grew in size and became truly threatening.

In order to eliminate as rapidly as possible the conflict which endangers the cause of peace, to give an assurance to all people who thirst for peace, and to reassure the American people, who I am certain, also want peace, as do the peoples of the Soviet Union, the Soviet government, in addition to earlier instructions on the discontinuation of further work on weapons construction sites, has issued a new order to dismantle the arms you describe as offensive, and to crate and return them to the Soviet Union.

"Well, that's it," ran through my mind. "We retreated!"

I understood that the situation could have ended in war, but at the time I thought of war in abstract terms, like a map with arrows depicting strikes and circles showing the radii of destruction. The removal of the missiles seemed like a concrete and humiliating retreat, a surrender of positions.

I stopped listening carefully. The crucial part had already been read. The announcer was talking about the peaceful nature of our intentions, U.S. connivance at Cuban émigré attacks on Havana, and the constant threat of aggression.

Then something that seemed important again attracted my attention:

... We have supplied the means of defense which you describe as offensive means. We have supplied them to prevent an attack on Cuba, to prevent rash actions.

I regard with respect and trust the statement you made in your message of October 27, 1962, that there will be no attack, no invasion of Cuba, and not only on the part of the United States, but also on the part of other nations of the Western hemisphere, as you said in your same message. In that case, the motives that induced us to render assistance of such a kind to Cuba disappear.

The last words emphasized that Father had achieved the goal he had set himself. If the Americans lived up to their word, there would never be an invasion of Cuba. My mind interpreted this part of the announcement as a victory, but I still felt a profound sense of injury.

In those years I wasn't the only one who thought in straightforward concepts of victory or defeat, us or them. It is only today that we can place a true value on the courage and wisdom of John Kennedy and Father, who rose above the conventional wisdom of their time.

Robert Kennedy recalled how that Sunday a member of the Joint Chiefs angrily proposed, without considering the consequences, that the United States carry out an invasion despite the Soviet Union's agreement to remove the missiles. He had everything prepared, and he was eager to teach both the Russians and the Cubans a lesson.

The message went on to discuss the need to reduce tensions in our time, with its surfeit of weapons and conflicts; referred to violations of our airspace by U-2s over Sakhalin and Chukotka, and then to U.N. participation in the final settlement of the conflict.

Finally, the last sentence:

> The Soviet government has sent First Deputy Foreign Minister V. V. Kuznetsov to New York to assist Mr. U Thant in his noble efforts to resolve the present dangerous situation.
>
> Respectfully yours,
> N. Khrushchev

When the announcer finished reading, he seemed to give a sigh of relief and, in a different tone of voice, said: "We have broadcast a message from the chairman of the Council of Ministers of the USSR, Nikita Sergeyevich Khrushchev, to the president of the United States, John Kennedy."

Ceremonial music began to play.

My earlier distress about the need to remove the missiles changed to relief. Only then did I really begin to comprehend what a great work had been accomplished and that a catastrophe had been averted at virtually the last moment.

The following week I heard from Father about the events that transpired at the guest dacha on that calm autumn morning and afternoon. Not all at once. He described first one episode, then others.

The lunch (in Russia lunch is usually eaten between two and three in the afternoon, not at noon, as in the United States) was brief and businesslike. Father asked that the plates be removed, and the meeting continued. The couriers hadn't yet reached their destination, and Father instructed the head of the guards: "When they begin the announcement, come in and turn on the radio."

After lunch they turned to a subject postponed because of work on the urgent message to Washington: antiaircraft fire on U.S. reconnaissance planes over Cuba. Father thought that this was precisely what might cause new and unpredictable problems. If another plane were shot down, who knows what would happen in the United States, with its unregulated press exerting such influence on the government.

He gave his colleagues a brief account of the draft letter to Fidel Castro he had been working on the previous evening. A report on the decision made that day must now be added and the letter sent off to Havana without delay. As it was, in Cuba they would hear everything unexpectedly over the radio, and not from our ambassador or the chairman of the Council of Ministers.

There was neither time nor energy left for a detailed letter, which was left for later, when the situation became somewhat more relaxed.

Father asked that the notes to Castro he had made the previous evening be read aloud. They sounded convincing, at least to those present. A few sentences were added at the beginning about Kennedy's message, in which the president pledged not to invade Cuba with his armed forces and to restrain his allies from such actions. The letter urged Castro to show restraint and concluded by assuring him of the continued support of our country and our people.

They decided to limit it to that. The message was sent to be retyped, and then it was time to listen to the broadcast. After a warning knock on the door, Litovchenko entered and turned on a radio standing in the corner.

After a few moments, the spacious room seemed to fill with a loud and crisp voice: "Attention. This is Radio Moscow. We have the following important announcement." It was 4 p.m. Moscow time.

Yury Levitan, clearly articulating the words and sentences, read the message from the chairman of the Council of Ministers of the USSR to the president of the United States.

Father listened intently to Levitan's voice as he read the message over the radio—as though he had not dictated it only a few hours before. In some places he nodded his head, as if in agreement. He was testing himself. He wanted to make sure that he had not made a mistake. No—in such a situation, there was simply no other way out.

Total silence reigned in the room. It seemed as if everyone had even stopped breathing.

Finally the announcement was over. Father got up from his chair, the others also: "Why don't we go to the theater?" Father suggested unexpectedly. "We'll show the whole world that there's nothing more to fear."

Such sudden proposals had long ceased to astonish anyone. As usual, no one objected to the idea. A newspaper was brought in and Troyanovsky read through the listings of that evening's performances and mentioned that it was the final day of a tour by a Bulgarian troupe.

"That's good," said Father, for some reason taken by the idea. "Let's go see the Bulgarians."

So that's what they decided to do. It was almost six o'clock and Father barely had time to drop by our dacha and change his shirt.

Litovchenko called to say that Father was coming to take us to the city, to the residence, and then they—the entire Presidium of the Central Committee—would be going to the theater.

The next day newspapers carried an announcement that Father and other comrades had attended a play at the Kremlin Theater titled *At the Foot of Vitosh*, the Ivan Vazov National Theater's final performance in the Soviet Union.

It was then nine in the morning in Cuba.

Alekseyev did not expect an answer that day or night to Castro's message warning that an invasion was imminent. Toward morning he fell asleep. It seemed only a few minutes later when he was awakened by a telephone call. President Oswaldo Dorticos was asking, or more precisely demanding, that he explain why Moscow Radio was broadcasting that the Soviet Union had agreed to remove its missiles from Cuba. The mere fact that Dorticos, and not Fidel, was on the phone was indicative in itself. The ambassador had no answer for the president. In his words, he "felt like the most miserable person on earth, especially when he pictured Fidel's reaction."

The reaction was indeed volcanic. A furious Fidel left to visit his troops: no matter what Moscow thought or decided, Cuba's armed forces were able to repel aggression without any outside assistance. For four days he refused to meet with the Soviet ambassador. Alekseyev simply couldn't find Fidel Castro, who communicated with him exclusively through Oswaldo Dorticos. "As if I were a leper," Alekseyev thought.

The coded message from Moscow did not reach the Embassy until midday. It didn't clarify anything. In essence, it simply stated that the letter had been sent to Kennedy. Most of it consisted of appeals and requests that U.S. planes be left in peace. Alekseyev thought that Castro would reject Moscow's proposal and consider it to be insulting.

But he was mistaken. That very evening he received Fidel's answer to Father's message. The fact that neither Fidel nor anyone else in his entourage even called required no explanation, but the tone of the letter itself was calm.

Castro wrote:

Earlier the violation of our airspace occurred secretly, without legal grounds. However, yesterday the government of the United States tried to explain its legal right to violate our airspace at any hour of the day or night. We cannot accept that, because it would mean that we were giving up our sovereign prerogatives. However, we agree to avoid incidents at this particular time because they could inflict a great deal of harm on the negotiations. We will therefore issue orders to Cuban batteries not to open fire, but only during the time the negotiations are being held, and without changing our decision, published yesterday in the press, to defend our airspace.

At the same time, the danger that incidents may occur accidentally in the current tense situation should be taken into consideration.

From the start Castro rejected in principle any talk of the possibility of allowing inspections on Cuban territory. The Cuban people were the masters there, and they would allow neither Moscow nor Washington to give orders.

As for the most important thing, Fidel decided to follow Father's example. His letter began by referring to the sweeping statement Khrushchev had made that same day. As a counterweight to the Soviet message to the U.S. president, Castro advanced his own five points:

1. Termination of the economic blockade and of all the measures of economic pressure being carried out by the United States against Cuba in various parts of the world.
2. Termination of all types of subversive activity, including the infiltration of spies and armed saboteurs.
3. Termination of piratical flights over Cuba from U.S. military bases.
4. Termination of violation of the Republic's airspace and territorial waters by U.S. ships and planes.
5. Withdrawal of Americans from the military base at Guantanamo and the return of Cuban territory occupied by the United States.

Father would have been glad to add these, in his opinion, justified demands to the agenda for negotiations at the U.N., but after Sunday's message he was powerless to change anything.

Kennedy decided not to hold an Executive Committee meeting on Sunday morning, October 28. He wanted to wait for Moscow's reaction. It would determine his decisions.

His waiting was interrupted by his brother's phone call. He said that Ambassador Dobrynin was requesting an urgent meeting. Again a tedious wait.

The meeting between Robert Kennedy and Anatoly Dobrynin was brief. Moscow's reaction was unequivocal—the storm had passed. Robert thanked the ambassador and assured him that they did not intend to make any move before receiving the text of the letter. Now he must inform the president at once. After a brief conversation, the older brother remained in the White House to wait for Father's message, and Robert, for the first time during those crazy fourteen days, took his young daughters to a riding stable, to look at the horses. He had promised them long before, but until an hour earlier had not dreamed that it would be possible.

At nine o'clock the Americans began taping the message to the president being broadcast over Moscow Radio. As Robert McNamara described it at the meeting in Moscow in 1989, his first reaction, even before consulting the president, was to cancel the morning reconnaissance flight over Cuba. Naturally, he didn't know about Castro's order to shoot down the planes, but his precaution may have saved everyone from disaster.

Dean Rusk found Robert Kennedy at the stable. The attorney general listened to the news with extraordinary calm. The secretary of state didn't realize that it was not really news to his colleague. After sending the children home, Robert Kennedy hurried to his brother.

I can't say what they talked about. That is probably not so important; the most important thing is that the world survived, and the process of recovery began.

Relief would most appropriately describe the mood in the White House on Sunday. They felt the same way in the Kremlin or, more precisely, in Novo-Ogaryovo.

John Kennedy decided to ignore diplomatic procedure, and he sent off his answer to Father before receiving the official text of the message from Moscow. It also went out over the radio. It seemed as if the people in both capitals wanted to put an end to the crisis and escape from the mortal terror of the previous two weeks.

I would like to quote the complete text of his answer:

Dear Mr. Chairman!

I am replying at once to your broadcast message of October 28, even though the official text has not yet reached me, because of the great importance I attach to moving forward promptly to the settlement of the Cuban crisis. I think that you and I, with our heavy responsibilities for the maintenance of peace, were aware that developments were approaching a point where events could have become unmanageable. So I welcome this message and consider it an important contribution to peace.

The distinguished efforts of Acting Secretary-General U Thant have greatly facilitated both our tasks. I consider my letter to you of October 27 and your reply of today as firm undertakings on the part of both governments which should be promptly carried out. I hope that the necessary measures can at once be taken through the United Nations, as your message says, so that the United States in turn will be able to remove the quarantine measures now in effect. I have already made arrangements to report all these matters to the Organization of American States, whose members share a deep interest in a genuine peace in the Caribbean area.

You referred in your letter to a violation of your frontier by an American aircraft in the area of the Chukotsk Peninsula. I have learned that this plane, without arms or photographic equipment, was engaged in an air-sampling mission in connection with your nuclear tests. Its course was direct from Eielson Air Force Base in Alaska to the North Pole and return. In turning south, the pilot made a serious navigational error which carried him over Soviet territory. He immediately made an emergency call on open radio for navigational assistance and was guided back to his home base by the most direct route. I regret this incident and will see to it that every precaution is taken to prevent recurrence.

Mr. Chairman, both of our countries have great unfinished tasks and I know that your people as well as those of the United States can ask for nothing better than to pursue them free from the fear of war. Modern science and technology have given us the possibility of making labor fruitful beyond anything that could have been dreamed of a few decades ago.

I agree with you that we must devote urgent attention to the problem of disarmament, as it relates to the whole world and also to critical areas. Perhaps now, as we step back from danger, we can together make real progress in this vital field. I think we should give priority to questions relating to the proliferation of nuclear weapons, on earth and in outer space, and to the great effort for a nuclear test ban. But we should also work hard to see if wider measures of disarmament can be agreed and put into operation at an early date. The United States government will be prepared to discuss these questions urgently, and in a constructive spirit, at Geneva or elsewhere.

John F. Kennedy

This letter brought to a close the period of "openness" in Father's correspondence with the president of the United States. Relations gradually resumed their normal course, letters again traveled through diplomatic and not entirely diplomatic channels, encrypted or hidden in the suitcases of emissaries traveling with passports that allowed them to avoid curious eyes when crossing borders.

Sunday evening Fomin again met with Scali. A record of that meeting exists in official U.S. documents and there is no reason to doubt it.

"I have been instructed to thank you," said Fomin. "The information you supplied to Chairman Khrushchev had a great impact and impelled him to act quickly. That includes your outburst on Saturday."

He was referring to Scali's verbal assault on Fomin, when he warned that an invasion was only hours away. Possibly he sensed a weakness in the KGB station chief and added the information about a speech the president was supposedly preparing to deliver. I think that Fomin somewhat exceeded his authority in this matter. It's hard to imagine that Father would have used such candid expressions to someone who was far from being the most important source of information in Washington. However, the phrase is worded in such a way that you can interpret it as coming either from Fomin himself or from his immediate superior.

That night, after the theater, Father's thoughts returned to the Turkish missiles. Father wanted very much to get written guarantees, in case Kennedy tried to renege on the promise he gave at the height of the crisis. No, it wasn't so much that he did not believe the president. On the contrary, Father was very well disposed toward him and felt a much higher degree of confidence in him than would seem justified by the adversarial relationship between our two countries, standing, as they were, on opposite sides of the front line. Father was now himself striving to achieve that "special" relationship between two leaders that Kennedy had hoped to establish when he left for the meeting in Vienna two years before. Moreover, White House promises to remove the missiles would come in very handy for foreign consumption, to counter those people who would inevitably rant and rave that he had retreated under pressure from the imperialists.

Father decided to write Kennedy a personal, confidential letter. Ambassador Dobrynin handed this message to Robert Kennedy on Monday, the first day after the crisis passed its peak. Robert looked through the pages handed to him, shrugged, and withheld comment. This message was very different from previous ones. Father stressed mutual trust and, what was completely unusual, returned again and again to the idea that there was now a special relationship between him and the president of the United States.

Father drew the correct conclusion from reports by Dobrynin, Bolshakov, Fomin, and other sources unknown to us: in talks with them, the Kennedy brothers had gone considerably beyond what they had allowed themselves to discuss in Executive Committee meetings at the White House. Now Father was trying to reinforce the trust that had arisen, to build on his success.

The main part of the letter dealt with the question of removing missiles from Turkey. Dobrynin had the impression that Father was overdoing it and ignoring various factors, but he didn't say anything. The ambassador's apprehensions were soon justified. The next day he had another meeting with Robert Kennedy. Kennedy returned the letter. In Robert's words, the president had already begun to act and he would fulfill his promises, but it would be better not to talk about official agreements. That would only complicate the matter.

Father was not offended. He understood: President Kennedy didn't want to leave any traces to go down in history and he was afraid of being accused of catering to the communists. Nothing could be done about that. The return of the letter was only a tactical step: the important thing was that they, the president and Father, understood each other's aspirations and could trust each other. The first real indications of trust had appeared. But a difficult and thorny path still lay ahead.

The White House kept its word. On October 29 McNamara issued an order to close the Turkish bases by April 1, 1963.

CASTRO'S WOUNDED PRIDE

Cuba itself now became the main source of Father's concern. It was paradoxical: the entire venture had been undertaken to defend the Cubans from U.S.

aggression, but now that the crisis was being resolved and progress was being made, Castro was mortally offended. Why? Because he had not managed to engage in a fight with the Americans. He had made up his mind to die a hero, and to have it end that way. But Moscow was trying to find a way to smooth over relations with its obstinate ally.

Alekseyev tried to discuss the matter with Fidel personally to persuade him that Moscow was right. He resorted to every trick he could think of in those post-crisis days. Every day he called Oswaldo Dorticos numerous times and dropped in on him without warning, hoping to find Castro there. Without success.

Alekseyev's messages from Havana sounded more and more distressed. Not a trace seemed to be left of the Soviet ambassador's former friendship with Fidel. Father felt deeply hurt, not only by the apparent deterioration in the relations between our country and Cuba, but also by the rapprochement taking shape between Cuba and China. After the announcement that the missiles were being removed, Castro's "revolutionary spirit," his extremism, was actively encouraged by Beijing. Fidel didn't want to accept Father's arguments. He viewed the removal of the missiles simply as a retreat, cowardice, capitulation. He was not alone in this opinion: the Chinese were blasting Father for yielding to a "paper tiger" and the American press was loudly celebrating a victory over the "Reds." With that in the background, Father's arguments appeared unpersuasive to Fidel. We suffered an important moral loss. Our reputation in Cuba did not rise, but fell sharply. Castro considered Father a traitor.

The "Cuban problem" came to a head on Monday, October 29. A message from Alekseyev vividly depicted Fidel's stormy reaction and complained about his own isolation. Something had to be done urgently. Father proposed sending Mikoyan to Cuba. He had been there before and had established good relations with Castro. And most important: Father thought that "there was no better diplomat than Mikoyan for such an occasion."

The rest of the Presidium of the Central Committee agreed with Father, but the final decision was left to Anastas Ivanovich himself. In those days he had no time to think about Cuba. His wife, Ashkhen Lazarevna Tumanyan, with whom he had spent more than forty years and had raised five sons, was lying near death in the Kremlin hospital. The doctors said that her condition was hopeless and the end could come within a few days.

Anastas Ivanovich hesitated. During this sorrowful time it was not just understandable human emotion and affection that required his presence at home, but the purely Armenian cult of the family. On the other hand, for a revolutionary, which he remained throughout his life, nothing was more important than the Cause, service to the party, the people, the fatherland. And the Cause required him to fly to Cuba.

There was an oppressive silence in the Kremlin meeting hall of the Presidium. Mikoyan said nothing. The lengthy pause weighed on those gathered there, who stared down at the papers in front of them.

Father was the first to give in. He urged Mikoyan to go, saying that Ashkhen Lazarevna was beyond help and that, without him, the situation in Cuba was going to be very grave.

Having witnessed many deaths of relatives, close friends, and simply good people during his long life, Father regarded this last stage of earthly existence without sentimentality, as something natural and inevitable. Life is life, and death is one of its attributes; it is not a tragedy, one flows from the other. In those years I completely disagreed with him, and to me death seemed like a gigantic catastrophe, perhaps comparable to the end of the world. Father and I never discussed this subject. It was only during his last years that Father sometimes started talking about the inevitable end. With superstitious dread, I tried to persuade him not even to think of such a thing; it seemed to me that talk of death could bring on disaster. Father laughed. He didn't argue and let me change the subject. Even in his last days Father didn't change. In taking his leave of life, he remained calm; he thought of those who remained here on earth, didn't cling to his medicines, or try desperately to lengthen his days.

"Anastas," continued Father, "if the worst comes to pass, we'll take care of everything. You don't need to worry."

Mikoyan yielded. His departure was set for the following day, October 31. His flight went through New York, where he would stop over and meet with Adlai Stevenson and John McCloy, the U.S. representatives to the U.N. President Kennedy had authorized them to carry on negotiations with our country to work out procedures for dismantling and removing the missiles. They had been dealing with Kuznetsov until then, but his authority was clearly inadequate.

Mikoyan took along his younger son Sergo, a historian by profession. Sergo helped Mikoyan with documents and acted as his secretary. Sergo has told me some details about this difficult trip.

On the eve of Mikoyan's departure, Father sent Castro a long letter, the first since that memorable Sunday. In it he tried to convince his distant and unbending correspondent that he had made the only possible decision, one that benefited Cuba and the entire world.

The letter has been published, and I will cite a few passages from it. "We considered," wrote Father,

> that it was necessary to make use of all our opportunities to defend Cuba, to strengthen Cuba's independence and sovereignty, to thwart military aggression and prevent a thermonuclear world war in our time.

And we have accomplished this.

Of course, we made concessions and accepted a compromise, acting according to the principle of give-and-take. The United States also made a concession, committing itself before the whole world not to attack Cuba.

Even after the dismantling of the missile installations, you have powerful weapons to repel the enemy on land, in the air and on sea approaches to the island.

As if sensing that his arguments wouldn't convince Castro, the next day Father wrote him yet again—not a letter, but a message consisting of many pages, where he analyzed the approaches and positions of the parties, the sources of decisions, where he drew conclusions and made recommendations.

The goal . . . was that revolutionary Cuba should have on its territory the means to restrain the aggressor from invading . . . and we achieved that,

repeated Father.

Our missiles deployed in Cuba would, of course, have played a role in overall strategy. But only a subsidiary role, because the quantity of missiles we placed in Cuba was not of decisive importance, and moreover could not have such importance. One must not place one's main forces close by an adversary, especially not where the geographical conditions make it difficult to deploy the most modern types of weapons in secrecy and, consequently, to use such weapons in general.

Father was also bothered by the fact that virtually the entire adult population of Cuba was under arms:

The enemy has now set itself the aim—which it talks about openly—of starving Cuba, and to do it in such a way that assistance to Cuba exhausts the Soviet Union. That is their goal. Therefore it is important that people—perhaps not now, but soon, without delay—get to work in factories and plants and in the fields. After all, people must be fed.

And the Soviet people are now making every effort to improve their economic potential, to elevate it above that of all capitalist countries, to secure the world's highest living standards. That will be graphic evidence of the truth of the teachings of Marxism-Leninism. There is no other yardstick.[21]

And so it went, word after word, page after page. But the letters did not convince Castro. Moreover, the Americans rejected Father's appeals for calm and sent planes flying low over the island several times a day. They were not fired upon, and the aerial spies conducted themselves more and more bra-

---

21. *Bulletin of the USSR Foreign Ministry, 1990*, no. 24.

zenly. Castro could barely restrain himself, but had not yet ordered that they be shot down.

The U.S. military behaved more and more aggressively, I would even say insolently, and not only toward the Cubans.

On Sunday, literally one day after the conciliatory exchange of letters, the commander of the Atlantic Fleet decided to deal with the Soviet submarines, which hadn't given him a moment's peace. He was fortunate that the president was no longer keeping track of every move made by the admirals.

U.S. destroyers had been shadowing Soviet submarines since October 30. They tried to force the submarines to surface in their presence, as if to admit their defeat. Small depth charges were dropped methodically from the destroyers. Their explosions didn't damage the submarines, but crews were deafened by the unbearably loud explosions. This went on for hours at a time, even for a day or two. Diesel submarines, which predominated in the Navy at that time, could not win the contest, of course. They rose to the surface accompanied by whoops from sailors crowding their tormentor's deck. One witness of such an unpleasant scene told me how he was seized by an overwhelming urge to send a torpedo below the waterline of the ship with the ranting Yankees—a secret, nuclear torpedo. He conceived a lifelong hatred of Americans. But Admiral Rossokha's order about the possible use of weapons was rescinded as early as October 23, at the same time that ships carrying weapons were ordered to turn back. Now a new and no less strict directive from Moscow came into force: not to respond to provocation. And they did not respond. They just gritted their teeth.

Neither Father nor Kennedy was aware of what was happening. As Kennedy said, "there's always some son of a bitch." It couldn't be expressed any better.

Planes, submarines—that was not so very serious. But the Americans were eager to get on the island and demanded that they be allowed to go there. As victors! Negotiations threatened to break down before they began. The stumbling block was inspection, on-site verification that we were fulfilling our promises. Father had emphasized from the very beginning that access by representatives of foreign states to the territory of Cuba was possible only with the consent of its government.

The Americans absolutely refused to carry on a dialogue with Fidel Castro. They demonstratively ignored him. Castro, in turn, refused to hear of allowing foreign inspectors onto his territory. "We have not broken any law, have not committed any aggression against anyone. Therefore inspection is one more attempt to humiliate our country. We will not accept inspection"—that was how the Cuban leader explained his position in a speech on Havana television.

He would not agree either to transfer inspection duties to U.N. representatives. The agreement achieved with such difficulty threatened to crumble.

U Thant took on the difficult task of negotiating with Castro. He landed at the airport in Havana the same day Mikoyan arrived in New York. All problems were resolved easily with Soviet representatives, though there were some curious aspects. For some reason the Ministry of Defense decided to maintain secrecy and not introduce Pliyev to U Thant. Major General I. D. Stetsenko, acted in his place. He commanded a ballistic missile division in Cuba. Stetsenko assured the secretary-general that all forty-two rockets would be dismantled within the next few days and sent to ports to be loaded onto Soviet ships.

But the Cubans dug in their heels. U Thant realized that inspectors, no matter what they were called, would not be allowed on the island. Some indirect methods had to be found.

According to Father, when Castro was in Moscow half a year later he admitted that he had been too hot under the collar and he agreed that the presence of U.N. officials would not have injured the national dignity of Cuba. But that was six months later. At the time every attempt at persuasion was met with a resounding "No!"

An agreement was urgently needed. Even though we were no longer on the threshold of war, U.S. warships had not moved from their blockade and antisubmarine patrol positions. The eastern seaboard of the United States remained crowded with invasion forces. In the Soviet Union, as in the United States, armed ICBMs were still smoking on their launch pads, shrouded in clouds of oxygen.

New York's greeting to Mikoyan was not a friendly one, but resembled that accorded representatives of a hostile power. Negotiations were difficult from the start. The Americans conducted themselves with increasing obstinacy and their demands grew more and more inflexible.

Mikoyan considered it premature to decide anything, or even propose anything, until he consulted with Castro and coordinated their viewpoints and approaches. Anastas Ivanovich's purpose was to clarify his opponent's viewpoint and obtain information. But the Americans pressed insistently for virtually instant agreement to their daily increasing demands.

Naturally, Mikoyan's negotiations in New York revolved around how to verify that all Soviet missiles were sent home and the launch sites destroyed. Anastas Ivanovich had to find the answer to that question in Cuba.

On the day of his departure for the island Stevenson and McCloy came to his hotel to say good-bye. They met downstairs in the lobby.

Suddenly, when everything had seemingly been discussed, his hosts made new demands. McCloy read out a whole list. They included IL-28 bombers, missile patrol boats, "air-to-ground," "ship-to-shore," and "ground-to-ground" missiles, as well as mechanical and electronic equipment for their use, warheads, and fuel.

Probing had even begun somewhat earlier. During negotiations the day before, McCloy tested the waters by raising the subject of withdrawing anti-aircraft missiles from Cuba. Mikoyan expressed surprise: "How could those be considered offensive weapons?" They couldn't answer his question, and the subject of the 75s was dropped.

That day the Soviet side had to pay for their euphemisms and reluctance to call things by their proper names. In his letters Father had never referred to missiles as missiles, but only as weapons which the opposing side considers to be offensive. Now this game of terminological evasion turned against him. The Americans stated that they had always classified these weapons as offensive ones. And what you—that is, Father—had in mind, that was your business: the Soviet government had agreed to remove offensive weapons from Cuba.

Today it's difficult to say when and why the top levels of the U.S. government began to change their position. It seems to me that, sensing weakness, they decided to grasp at more.

But where did this list come from altogether? The IL-28 bombers had been mentioned back in the president's speech on "black" Monday, and in his book Robert Kennedy writes that they were discussed by the Executive Committee. But until Mikoyan's arrival not a word had been said about the rest. In January 1991, I asked Raymond Garthoff, who was involved in compiling the list, how they were selected.

His answer was remarkably simple: they included in the document all types of weapons which could technically be referred to as offensive. That was why the obsolete bombers, but not the latest MIG-21s, became an object for haggling.

It's my guess that they compiled the list the night before, which is why they had to hand it to Mikoyan in the hotel lobby. Anastas Ivanovich flatly refused to discuss the newly hatched idea, saying that he was authorized to discuss proposals found in the documents, which referred only to ballistic missiles.

After parting coolly with Stevenson and McCloy, Mikoyan left for the airport. But then came a new twist. The Americans were in a hurry to legalize their demands in some way. A State Department representative rushed breathlessly up to Anastas Ivanovich in the airport and tried to hand him an envelope with some message, which evidently consisted of the demands he had just rejected. Mikoyan was amazed: to hand over important documents this way, on the run, at the last minute! It violated every diplomatic norm. He pushed aside the envelope held out to him and, without a backward glance, headed for the departure lounge.

The document was handed to Kuznetsov that same day. The IL-28s and patrol boats were the subject of just as many discussions as the matter of inspection.

The report of Washington's new demands was received in Moscow on the following day. Father was informed. The American move made no particular impression on him. He felt deceived, but not especially injured. Like a person who has been asked to hand over a wallet the thief does not know is empty. He'd had to give away the money earlier.

Father's position could be expressed simply: the missiles had been Cuba's main defense against invasion. We had reached an agreement and were now removing them. President Kennedy's word became the chief guarantee against aggression.

The IL-28s and missile patrol boats played an auxiliary role. All they could do was hold up an invasion. That was why they were there. If there was not going to be an invasion, it wouldn't matter if they stayed there or not. He didn't consider outdated planes and patrol boats to be offensive weapons, much less able to threaten the United States. But what could he do?

Nevertheless, quite an argument developed. Threatening notes again surfaced in the correspondence between Moscow and Washington. The Americans even hinted at a possible attack on the airfields where IL-28s were based. Father fell between two fires. He very much wanted to avoid offending Castro even further, but on the other hand it wasn't worth teasing the Americans for the sake of outdated bombers, thereby undermining renewed contacts and trust.

President Kennedy increased the pressure. Father didn't think that he was really ready to carry out his threats, violate his word, and invade Cuba. No. Father remained calm, but again it was up to him to find a solution.

I asked Raymond Garthoff: "Why was there such an uproar over the IL-28s? From the military point of view, those planes didn't represent a real force."

He agreed. No one in the Pentagon thought the bombers presented any real threat. It was a matter of prestige.

Father tried to bargain and proposed exchanging the bombers for a withdrawal of U.S. troops from Guantanamo. In his opinion, the base was of no more importance than the IL-28s under modern conditions. It's difficult to say whether he had any real hope of success. When I asked him about it, he only sneered: "Of course, the Americans don't need the base, but it's a very convenient way to exert pressure on the Cubans." Perhaps deep in his heart Father counted on his new relationship with Kennedy, but he miscalculated.

A demonstrative show of support for Castro's five points was his main purpose in raising the issue of Guantanamo. Even if it was not successful.

The White House was not prepared to make any concessions. Guantanamo had indeed lost its importance, but not in the eyes of public opinion, which would consider its evacuation to be a serious concession by the president. Father had to give up his idea. The negotiations dragged on through November.

After nerve-wracking talks lasting many days, the question of the missile patrol boats was dropped.

On November 1 Fidel met with Alekseyev for the first time since the shock caused by the news that the missiles would be removed. Mikoyan was flying in the following day. In a speech on television that same day, Castro publicly expressed gratitude to our country for its support at a difficult hour:

> We should recall in particular that at all difficult moments, when we met with American aggression . . . we always leaned on the friendly arm of the Soviet Union. For this we are grateful to it and we must always express that gratitude at the top of our voices. The Soviet people whom we see here . . . have done a great deal for us. In addition, Soviet military specialists, who were ready to die along with us, have accomplished a great deal in instructing and training our armed forces.

Excerpts from Castro's speech were published in Soviet newspapers. Father viewed his speech as a good sign. The Cuban leader was beginning to realize who his true friends were, who had risked not only their welfare but their lives as well for the sake of people living on a faraway island.

Nevertheless, Mikoyan received a very frosty reception in Havana when he landed on November 2. The ritual called for by protocol was observed, but it was as if a cold and transparent wall had grown up between the hosts and their guest. Mikoyan was upset. For the sake of Cuba's inviolability we had entered into a conflict with the United States and brought the world to the brink of nuclear destruction. Now we were meeting hostility from both the Americans and Fidel.

During their first meeting, held at the Cuban government guest house where Anastas Ivanovich was staying, the feeling of discomfort became intense. It seemed as if Fidel Castro could barely hold back harsh words. Mikoyan was disheartened.

That evening, Anastas Ivanovich invited Pliyev and the other generals to the guest house. The dismantling of launch positions had begun. Evacuation lay ahead, and although the Defense Ministry in Moscow was in charge of everything, Mikoyan wanted to know the details. Otherwise, how could he conduct the negotiations?

The next day began just as gloomily. At nine o'clock everyone met in Fidel's apartment, where the negotiations were to be held that day. There were very few people: Mikoyan, Alekseyev, and an interpreter on the Soviet side, only Fidel on the Cuban. He thought that would make it easier to speak frankly. Mikoyan understood how the situation was developing and prepared himself to defend Moscow's point of view and not allow the "ship" to be washed onto the rocks.

The conversation began haltingly. After a while Castro became more talkative, but that didn't make things easier. "The Cuban people do not understand how deals can be struck and a country's fate decided behind its back, without even consulting them," said Fidel repeatedly.

Anastas Ivanovich went over the reasons given in Father's letter: there hadn't been enough time to consult him, and the most important thing was that their objective was achieved and Cuba was saved. But Castro didn't listen and didn't want to listen: they had not taken Cuba into consideration, and no one had the right to decide its fate! Castro worked himself into a rage. Mikoyan held his ground. He didn't allow himself to become rattled and kept monotonously repeating his arguments.

When Father insisted at the Presidium meeting that Anastas Ivanovich should be selected to go on the mission, he had emphasized just this quality: Mikoyan's unshakable equanimity when confronted by a storm of emotions. But what this must have cost Mikoyan, a man of great sensitivity and possessed of a southern temperament besides! But his strength of will, his self-possession, prevailed.

The conversation had gone on for more than an hour when Alekseyev was called to the phone. It was the Embassy. The code clerk had received a telegram for Mikoyan from Father with the news that Ashkhen Lazarevna had died.[22] The ambassador whispered to Mikoyan that an urgent message had come in. He didn't say what it was about, but Anastas Ivanovich guessed everything. He had been expecting this bitter news from day to day, even on the day he flew out of Moscow. He asked the ambassador to drive over to the Embassy and bring the telegram. The two buildings were not far from each other, and it took only five minutes to make the trip by car. Alekseyev didn't want to leave Mikoyan and Castro alone together at such a moment, but it was also impossible not to go. He couldn't bring himself to send anyone else.

Through Fidel Castro's secretary in the adjacent room, Alekseyev passed Castro a note informing him of what had happened and requesting him to take a break in the working meeting.

Half an hour later the ambassador handed the telegram to Mikoyan. In

---

22. There is an inaccuracy in Alekseyev's memoirs. He says that the negotiations had not yet begun. However, the protocol of the conversation between Mikoyan and Castro preserved in the Foreign Ministry's archives makes it possible to be precise about the timing.

it, Father expressed his condolences and left it to Anastas Ivanovich to decide whether to return to Moscow for the funeral. The negotiations broke off. Fidel's vehemence subsided. His guests apologized and left. At the guest house, Anastas Ivanovich asked to be left alone.

The uncertainty lasted about an hour. The door to Mikoyan's room remained tightly shut. Alekseyev, the interpreters, and the few people who accompanied Mikoyan conversed in low voices in the hall.

Mikoyan finally appeared. He looked gray and drawn. His small body seemed to have shrunk.

"I will stay," Anastas Ivanovich said hoarsely. "I would no longer be of any help there, but here . . ."

For a moment he remained silent.

"Sergo will fly to Moscow. Send him on the next plane," he asked the ambassador, and repeated: "I'm needed more here."

Pravda published an announcement of Ashkhen Lazarevna's death. Father asked an aide to supervise preparations for the ceremony, although there was no particular need for that. The administrative department of the Council of Ministers knew what had to be done.

Father himself did not go to either the wake or the cemetery. He couldn't bear to go to funerals.

Mikoyan didn't say a single word of reproach to his friend, but he never forgave him.

Negotiations in Cuba resumed the following day. The sad event and Mikoyan's self-sacrificing decision to remain relaxed the tension, and Fidel kept the reproaches he had prepared to himself.

Nevertheless, agreement was reached with enormous difficulty. U.S. representatives followed a hard line, which produced a sharp reaction on the part of the Cubans. Everything was complicated by the fact that direct negotiations were out of the question. All proposals, arguments, and finally, points of the agreement traveled a complicated route from New York, where Kuznetsov was in contact with McCloy and Stevenson, to Moscow, from there to Mikoyan in Havana for him to discuss with Fidel, and then back the same way.

In Moscow every step had to be reported to Father. Cuba took a tremendous amount of Father's time and required his unflagging attention, but its problems were gradually pushed aside by new, and no less important, issues.

THE CRISIS FINALLY ENDS

By November 10 the tension around Cuba had abated. The question of inspection remained the last stumbling block. It became increasingly a purely political problem, rather than a technical one. After all, changes at the former missile positions were meticulously detected by the U-2s. No one interfered with their flights over Cuba. They took miles of film. The photographs showed that the dismantling of launchers was going ahead at full speed. Some things were dismantled, others cut apart, while the concrete foundations were simply blown up. The Soviet side didn't intend to conceal anything. Father had issued strict orders: No tricks. We're leaving for good.

Finally, immediately after the October Revolution holidays (November 7–8), the U.S. Defense Department announced officially that "all ballistic missiles of medium and intermediate range which are known to have been deployed in Cuba have been dismantled."

Final evacuation of the missiles took only four days and eight ships. The operation began on November 5. The *Divnogorsk* was the first to take on cargo, followed by the *Bratsk*, the *Ivan Polzunov*, the *Labinsk*, the *Mikhail Anosov*, and the *Volgoles*. The *Igor Kurchatov* and the *Leninsky Komsomol*, which left the port of Casilda on November 9, brought up the rear.

The Americans still had to be convinced that all missiles had left the island. The U-2s were not able to do that.

The Cubans continued to resist inspection. They wouldn't allow anyone on their territory—not just Americans, but no one else, even under the auspices of the U.N., and even on the Soviet ships in their harbors. Castro explained his position firmly to Mikoyan: "You can agree with the United States and you can make concessions to them. It's easier for you, a great power. We are a small country and won't allow ourselves to be humiliated, particularly since we didn't violate any international norms."

An agreement was eventually reached with the United States that Americans could count the missiles as they were being transported onto the ships. Here too Fidel was unyielding. "Do whatever you want, but outside Cuban waters. No inspections inside our territorial waters."

They decided to arrange for the transports to rendezvous with U.S. Navy ships on the open ocean. But Father refused to allow foreign inspectors to board our vessels, which were sovereign territory of the Soviet Union. A new compromise was found.

The missiles were secured on deck, in full view. The Americans could come alongside and photograph them, but couldn't handle them. On November 11, Deputy Defense Secretary Roswell Gilpatrick announced that they had counted forty-two missiles in this manner, exactly the number that the CIA supposed had been in Cuba. But a shadow of doubt remained: without carrying out an inspection, the United States "could not be certain that forty-two was the exact number of missiles transported to Cuba." Again, the question of inspection.

The Americans had no cause for concern. There really were forty-two missiles. Six were for training purposes only and could not be launched.

The nuclear warheads returned as they had arrived, without fanfare or inspection. U.S. intelligence never found out whether they were on the island, or if they had just imagined it. No one tried to persuade the CIA to the contrary. Well wrapped and concealed in cargo holds, they returned to the Soviet arsenal which they had left two months before under conditions of the most profound secrecy.

Following the missiles, a stream of ships headed for home loaded with ground equipment. The soldiers who boarded the ships traveled light. Everything they had brought to Cuba was left on the island, including tanks, weapons, and armored personnel carriers, not to speak of machine guns, submachine guns, and even tens of thousands of Cuban army uniforms sewn in our country, which our military personnel had worn to preserve secrecy.

However, ammunition wasn't the only thing left in Cuba. One of the Soviet motorized brigades remained there for many years. In the event of a landing by enemy forces, it was ordered to "show the flag" and enter the fight from the very beginning. Of course, three thousand men, no matter how well trained and equipped, could not determine the outcome, but the very presence of a Soviet regular military unit would immediately transform a local, inter-American realignment, to which the world had long grown accustomed, into a conflict of global significance.

Though the White House didn't object, it categorically refused to make any public statements, even the most cautious—just as with the Turkish missiles. The brigade was simply ignored. U.S. intelligence was instructed to ignore what it shouldn't notice.

After the missiles were removed, the focus turned to the IL-28s. Kennedy pressured, insisted, threatened. Hotheads in the Executive Committee again proposed attacking the airfields. And the press simply ranted and raved.

Ships of the U.S. Atlantic Fleet were arrayed in a line and continued to enforce the blockade. U.S. planes still swept over the island at low altitudes several times a day. Their cocky impudence was especially irritating to Castro. Under the roar of their engines, he became more and more stubborn. He didn't even want to hear about withdrawal of the IL-28s. Relations in general grew increasingly strained. Even Anastas Ivanovich kept his temper with difficulty. However, outwardly he remained pleasant and unperturbed.

Nevertheless, it almost came to an open break. When the argument about the IL-28s was in full swing, Castro casually informed the others that there would be no meeting the next day. He was leaving for several days on urgent business to inspect agricultural regions. Fidel advised his guests to look at livestock farms. His words sounded openly derisive. Mikoyan tried to object, but without success. The following day Anastas Ivanovich, gritting his teeth, went to visit a dairy farm. A day later the prime minister's office politely informed him that Castro had not yet returned. He still wasn't back on the third day.

Mikoyan began to get nervous. He had no intention of flying into a rage or breaking off the negotiations. He was used to finishing any business he started. But how could he do so in this case? His opposite number had disappeared.

The fourth day also passed in enforced idleness. Then Anastas Ivanovich decided to take an extreme step. That evening he dined with his old friend Nuñez Ximenez, the director of agrarian reform. They talked about the harvest, about animal husbandry. In parting Anastas Ivanovich said that he would soon be leaving, perhaps in a couple of days. His mission was apparently coming to an end.

His host was surprised and dismayed. He had heard that the negotiations were far from complete.

Anastas Ivanovich complained that days had gone by and he had not managed to meet with Castro. There was only one possible explanation: he was not the person with whom the Cuban leadership considered it possible to hold negotiations. That was too bad, but there was nothing he could do about it. He was therefore thinking of returning to Moscow so they could send some more suitable person in his place.

Castro "unexpectedly" appeared the next day. It seemed that he had already completed his inspection of agriculture. Their conversation, which began with a discussion of bean crops and milk yields of cows, quickly reverted to its usual subject.

Castro disconcerted Mikoyan by saying that he had sent U Thant a letter on the question of inspection—or rather, about how they should not even dream of carrying out any inspections on Cuban territory. That would be useless. Mikoyan heard him out. It was the same old stuff, which he had gotten sick and tired of hearing long before. He only complained that he should have been shown the letter before it was sent, since it would be better if both countries began to coordinate their actions.

Castro retorted that he had proposed nothing new. However, he had warned the U.N. and the United States that his moratorium on firing air defense weapons at U.S. planes was canceled. From now on any violator of Cuban airspace would receive the punishment he deserved. Antiaircraft forces had been put on alert and fighters were patrolling at a low altitude in the air corridors favored by U.S. spy planes.

Mikoyan almost leaped from his chair. "That will cause a new escalation in tension." Castro responded curtly: "Cuba will not permit violations of its sovereignty. We've had enough. We're fed up."

The order went into effect at 11 A.M. on November 18. It was announced over Havana radio.

Kennedy displayed prudence. There were no more low-altitude flights over Cuba. Now they had to rely on the U-2s.

Mikoyan managed somehow to talk Fidel into agreeing to the return of the IL-28s to the Soviet Union. On November 19 Castro informed U Thant that he had no objection: if the USSR wanted to, it could remove the IL-28s. But he warned once again that he would not tolerate any inspections or any flights over Cuban territory.

The last obstacles were removed, and on November 20, 1962, President Kennedy announced the ending of the blockade:

> I have today been informed by Council of Ministers' Chairman Khrushchev that all of the bombers now in Cuba will be withdrawn within thirty days. He also agrees that these planes can be observed and counted as they leave. Inasmuch as this goes a long way toward reducing the danger which faced this continent four weeks ago, I have this afternoon instructed the Secretary of Defense to lift our naval quarantine.
>
> . . . According to the evidence we now have in our possession, the dismantling of offensive missile installations in Cuba has been completed. The missiles and their associated equipment have been loaded on Soviet ships. Inspection of these departing ships, which we have carried out at sea, has confirmed that all missiles reported by the Soviet Union as having been brought into Cuba, and which closely corresponded to our own information, have now been removed. In addition, the Soviet government has stated that all nuclear weapons have been withdrawn from Cuba and more will not be introduced.
>
> . . . The record of recent weeks shows real progress, and we are hopeful that further progress can be made.

A short government announcement appeared in Soviet newspapers on November 22: "To end the status of full combat readiness in units of the Soviet Army . . . in connection with the order by U.S. President John Kennedy to lift the quarantine (blockade) of the Republic of Cuba."

Marshal Grechko issued a similar order to the Warsaw Pact troops he commanded.

I still remember the state of purely physical relief which I felt at the time.

The Cuban Missile Crisis ended at the same time as the work of the Plenum of the Central Committee that had convened November 19. That day Father delivered a lengthy speech on urgent measures to improve the structure of economic management.

By a strange coincidence, on the same day that the status of military readiness ended, November 22, the Plenum adopted the decision (referred to earlier) on reorganizing the structure of the party apparatus, namely the division of party committees along production lines. Former party function-

aries criticize it to this day. Then too, party committees viewed it as infringing on their power. Muted grumbling spread throughout the party apparatus.

The Plenum's decisions not only contributed greatly to Father's ouster
from power, but I think that they also paved the way for what today we call
"stagnation." The influence of the apparat increased still further. The external crisis was replaced by an internal one—not as noticeable, but more dangerous.

In the days, weeks, and months to come there was endless talk from the left
and the right about Father's defeat, retreat, and capitulation in the face of
imperialism. Such comments were most prevalent in China and the United
States. However, the president himself thought differently. Robert Kennedy
testifies:

> He made no statement attempting to take credit for himself or for the admin-
> istration for what had occurred. He instructed all members of the Executive
> Committee and government that no interview should be given, no statement
> made, which would claim any kind of victory. . . . If it was a triumph, it was a
> triumph for the next generation and not for any particular government or
> people.

Father thought that, having received a promise that Cuba would not be
invaded, he had achieved his goal:

> The governments of capitalist countries place a dollar value on everything.
> So, if you look at it in terms of money, this was a very profitable operation.
> We incurred expenses only on the transportation of military equipment and
> several thousands of our soldiers. That was the cost of guaranteeing the inde-
> pendence of Cuba. We did not spill blood, either our own or that of foreign-
> ers. We prevented war. We prevented destruction and atmospheric pollution.
> Of that I am proud.

The Cuban Missile Crisis came to an end; the parties agreed where it was
possible to reach agreement. Those elements of the confrontation impossible
to resolve at the time were left to future generations.

I would not undertake to judge President Kennedy. But for Father those
thirteen days in October were very significant. It was the end of an era, the
era of American superiority in the world. Now force opposed force. Any
crisis could lead to mutual ruin.

If we look at the events of those years through the prism of the past
decades, we see that as a result of the Cuban Missile Crisis Father achieved
what he was striving for all those years: American de jure recognition that
the Soviet Union was its equal in destructive power.

History loves to present us with paradoxes. American recognition of parity can be credited mainly to the American press. Two weeks of intense fear, the expectation from one minute to another of a nuclear apocalypse, dramatic details describing the lethal power of the "Cuban" missiles—all left a permanent mark on the nation's historical memory.

The possibility and expediency of dealing a preemptive nuclear strike on the Soviet Union—advocated periodically by the more zealous U.S. generals, primarily General Curtis LeMay, who commanded the Strategic Air Command—was never again contemplated.

The Cuban climax of confrontation had to be replaced by a peaceful competition between the sides and preservation of the status quo. Without yet acknowledging it to himself, Father had inwardly made a step toward the proposal John Kennedy made in Vienna.

The situation in Berlin also quieted down somewhat after the Cuban Crisis. Both leaders behaved more cautiously and more wisely.

They had gotten to know each other during the conflict and were filled with mutual respect. This is how Father remembered President Kennedy:

> Of course, as far as you can vouch for someone with different political views, I trusted Kennedy both as a person and as a president. . . . Of all the presidents I knew, Kennedy was the one with the greatest intellect. He was a clever person and stood out sharply in comparison with his predecessors. I never met Roosevelt. Perhaps Roosevelt was his superior.
>
> I have the best memories of . . . the president. He showed himself to be levelheaded; he didn't let himself become frightened, but also didn't let himself be intoxicated by the might of the United States. He didn't go for broke. It doesn't take great intellect to start a war; he showed wisdom and real statesmanship; he did not fear condemnation by right-wing forces and he achieved peace.

And these are the words Robert Kennedy used to describe the U.S. president's impressions of Father: "President Kennedy believed from the start that the Soviet Premier was a rational, intelligent man. . . . He respected Khrushchev for properly determining what was in his own country's interests and what was in the interest of mankind."

Despite the difference in style, they used very similar words.

After spending almost a month in Cuba and doing everything within his power, Mikoyan prepared to go home. The negotiations ended in a compromise, which was why they sent a "master" compromiser. Although he had not persuaded Fidel Castro to agree to all points, he managed to put out the fire that had threatened to turn into a conflagration. Only the smoking coals remained. Some would die out by themselves, while others had still to be extinguished.

After giving a farewell speech over Havana television on November 25, Mikoyan left for New York. His arrival coincided with a statement from Secretary of Defense McNamara that all armed force units had returned to their bases.

On November 29 Anastas Ivanovich met with President Kennedy in Washington. This was the first meeting between a member of the Soviet government and the U.S. president since the crisis began. Unfortunately, I don't know any details about their conversation.

Mikoyan returned on December 1 to a snowy Moscow.

CASTRO VISITS THE SOVIET UNION

In my view, the history of the Cuban Missile Crisis would not be complete without an account of Fidel Castro's first visit to the Soviet Union and his meetings with Father. A real battle was waged for Castro. Castro wavered. Father anguished. He had given his heart to the bearded leader and now regarded him almost as a son.

I first heard about the possibility that Castro might come to the USSR in the winter of 1962. Rumors would spread, almost prove to be justified, then fade away. Finally, in the early spring of 1963, Father reported that they had definitely agreed on a visit. The situation around Cuba had calmed down and Castro could leave the island without apprehension. It was decided that he would fly on one of our TU-114s and arrive by May 1. Father wanted to show his guest our holiday, and besides the weather would be warmer.

During the last few days of April a TU-114 left Moscow for Havana under a curtain of secrecy to pick up Castro. Both "professionals" and Father thought that there was a real possibility of an "accidental" attack on the plane carrying Fidel over the ocean. It was well known that one of the aims of the "Mongoose" operation was his physical elimination, so it was decided to make Castro's visit public after any danger was past, with the plane already on the ground in Murmansk.

A gala reception, with a meeting on Red Square, was organized—the same as those given for the cosmonauts. People didn't have to be urged to go there. The noisy meeting, the May 1 parade, with the bands playing and people marching, came to an end. Castro seemed to be captivated by the sincerity of the friendly feelings expressed by the people. On May 2 Father brought him to visit us at the dacha. Father's grandchildren clung to Castro the minute he arrived. My son Nikita, who was not yet three, captured our guest and dragged him off to a clearing to hear the bumblebees buzzing.

Father didn't talk about any business matters. Serious negotiations were to begin on the following day. Father planned to take Castro out of Moscow and try to win him over in a small circle of colleagues. He didn't succeed right away. It took time and effort.

Fidel spent thirty-five days in the Soviet Union and at least half of that time with Father. He toured almost the whole country, visiting Volgograd and Tashkent, Bratsk and Kiev, Tbilisi and Sukhumi. Father and Fidel developed a teacher-student relationship.

Father tried to persuade Castro that the U.S. president would keep his word and that Cuba was guaranteed six years of peaceful development, which was how long Father thought Kennedy would be in the White House. Six years! Almost an eternity! During those years Cuba, with its beneficent climate, combined with the advantages of a socialist economy, would achieve unprecedented successes and would be transformed into a rich and flourishing state. All of Latin America would be trying to keep pace with it. The new presidents who succeeded Kennedy would not dare to commit aggression, since Cuba would become too strong for them. All that was necessary to achieve this was to get down to work.

Father would not have been true to himself if he had not begun immediately to talk about what should be done. From the very first day he tried to persuade Castro of the need to mechanize sugarcane harvesting. Father simply dreamed of manufacturing agricultural machinery for harvesting sugarcane. He had already ordered one of our research institutes to produce a design for a combine. When it became available, people would not have to bend their backs and cut stubble with a machete. Work would become enjoyable. Castro kept nodding agreeably.

Father's other hobbyhorse was fishing. He couldn't understand why Cuba did not have its own fishing fleet. The ocean was right there, but they had always imported fish from the United States. A fishing port was already being built in Cuba—the one the Americans stubbornly referred to as a naval base. Father thought that it could provide the basis for an entire branch of industry capable not only of feeding Cuba, but its neighbors as well. Father described to his guest herds of fat cows, grazing on eternally green meadows, providing Cubans with an abundance of milk and meat.

Castro listened attentively to what Father said. He agreed.

Only once did Fidel show his temper. One day he drove with Father and Marshal Malinovsky from Sukhumi to Lake Ritsa. Father wanted his guest to enjoy the beauty of the Caucasian mountains. He himself very much loved the region. During his first visit to the Caucasus, in the 1920s, he had hiked to the lake along a trail. In those days no one even dreamed of a highway. Those mountains, which he saw then for the first time, were a source of delight for the rest of his life. Now, traveling in a comfortable ZIL limousine, the trip took less than an hour. They walked along the lake shore, ate shish kebab, and had their pictures taken. It's difficult to say who enjoyed the trip the most, the guest who admired the scenery or the host who was exposing him to the beauty of nature.

Nature is nature and scenery is scenery, but the conversation veered, like those in the preceding days, toward war, invasion, Americans, and crisis.

It was at this point that Father insulted Fidel by saying that if regular U.S. troops had invaded the island the Cubans would not have been able to resist them, and that the agreement he reached with Kennedy had, as it were, saved the life of the Cuban revolution.

Castro exploded. "They would never break us."

Father insisted. He called on Malinovsky for support and asked him how long he thought an organized defense of the island could hold out.

Malinovsky took some time to respond, as if making estimates and calculations.

"Two days," he said confidently.

Castro was furious and began trying to prove that in the mountains they would be unconquerable. CIA director John McCone agreed with him on that, by the way. At one of the sessions of the Executive Committee he had commented pessimistically: "It would be damn difficult to chase them out of the mountains; the experience of the Korean war showed that clearly." At first Father objected. He tried to persuade Castro that a partisan war is an underground one, whereas he had been referring to control over the island. But then he decided to drop the argument and not offend his guest any further. No one changed his opinion.

There was an amusing episode on the way back. Local Abkhazian officials were waiting along the road for their honored guests. The limousine came to a halt. They were informed that a village nearby was inhabited by people who had survived to a great age. Tables had been set up, and they would be insulted if such high-ranking visitors didn't stop, at least briefly. Father was always suspicious of such "spontaneous" events, especially in the Caucasus. Even a younger and healthier person could pass out after being treated to the local hospitality. But now he wanted to please Castro and to surprise him with hospitality surpassing any fantasy, especially after their recent argument.

I won't describe the variety of Abkhazian food. Even professional writers have not always managed to do it justice. Fidel was ecstatic and tried one dish after another. Father abstained. Whenever he sat down at a table in those years he thought about his kidney stones, and only then decided what to eat.

New wine was brought to the table and each guest was presented with a huge horn filled with wine. Castro smiled, thinking it was a joke. How could anyone drink so much all at once? He was told that he could—and should. He appealed to Father for protection, but Father laughed and threw up his hands: "I have no authority here. This is the empire of the toastmaster."

There was no escape. Fidel emptied the horn, accompanied by a murmur of approval. He immediately received the horn as a gift for his "exploit."

Now it was Father's turn. He was hoping to use his age as an excuse, but that didn't work. As Father later described it, they brought up a man old enough to be his father, who took the horn from Father with great self-assurance and emptied it in one draught.

A minute later the refilled horn was handed back to Father. He was trapped.

The company buzzed happily and Father whispered to Castro: "Now let's quickly get to the car and go home."

Castro talked about their funny adventure the whole next day. The quarrel was completely forgotten, so Father considered his sacrifice worthwhile.

After they returned to Moscow Father suggested to Castro that they go to see an R-16 intercontinental missile and hear about its features. This was a sign of the highest degree of trust on his part—no foreigners, and only those Soviet citizens with top-level clearances, were allowed to visit launch positions.

Fidel was delighted. They went by car. It was not very far from Moscow. Malinovsky and Biryuzov were waiting for them.

The commander of the missile division showed them the launch position, the warehouses, and the command center. Not surprisingly, Castro was already familiar with them from Cuba. The chief designer for both missiles was the same, and the engineering features remained the same.

In conclusion, they conducted an exercise. They chose the most spectacular stage of preparing the missile for launch—mounting the missile on the launch platform. The operation went smoothly. The missile moved from the hangar on the missile installer, which rotated on the launch area, moved backward, and then began to raise the missile skyward. The operation was over in a few minutes. The missile was vertical and firmly supported by clamps of the multi-level service tower.

Castro thanked the commander, then turned to Father and, with a sly smile, asked whether it was a real missile or just a mockup.

Malinovsky, who was standing nearby, assured him that it was as real as it could be. The previous October it had stood fully ready to be launched, but he couldn't say what the target was. The General Staff did not divulge that secret information to anyone. All he could say was that the target was located on the territory of the United States.

Suddenly Castro asked if it would damage the missile to put his signature on it. "If it is used, God forbid, let the U.S. imperialists know that it's a greeting from Cuba."

Father nodded. Castro was given a piece of chalk and he sprawled his signature on the body of the missile.

Then they had their pictures taken, but with neither the missile nor its launcher visible. Their eyes are riveted on empty space. Fidel Castro appears with the Gold Star of Hero of the Soviet Union and Order of Lenin on his chest.

Father and Castro parted as friends.

Castro visited the Soviet Union more than once again. In January 1964 he was still received by Father, after that by his successors. But a meeting like the first one could never be repeated. In 1963 the country greeted a Hero, and not simply the leader of a friendly country.

DEPARTURE

IVAN DENISOVICH

Events sometimes take a peculiar turn. The Cuban Missile Crisis had just ended when a different subject caused a wave of excitement in Moscow. In November 1962, *One Day in the Life of Ivan Denisovich*, a novel by a totally unknown writer named Aleksandr Solzhenitsyn, was published in the eleventh issue of the journal *Novy Mir*.

It made a stunning and crucial impression on me: knowledge is one thing, emotion another. Father's speech at the Twentieth Party Congress exposed Stalin's crimes. The numbers and names of those who perished were given, but abstractly and coldly. You could not visualize their fate. What are numbers? You add a zero and the number is ten times larger. But what are we talking about? The number of pounds of crops harvested—or the number of people buried side by side in trenches?

Ivan Denisovich exposed all the horror of inhuman lives and inhuman fates. It foreshadowed a crisis. A struggle was beginning, a struggle not just against particular features, shortcomings, and distortions in the system, but against the system itself, which had given rise to all those horrors.

For me, at any rate.

The novel undoubtedly had not the slightest chance of being published. Even such a harmless thing as Emmanuil Kazakevich's *The Blue Notebook*—which described Lenin's well-known stay in hiding in Razliv near St. Petersburg, during which he wrote *The State and Revolution*—could not be published because Grigory Zinoviev's name was mentioned in it. The fact that there was someone with Ilyich in the cabin was not mentioned anywhere for many years.

Suslov was adamant. Only Father's intervention kept the novel from being left in the drawer. He used to laugh when he remembered how Suslov objected to its publication. Suslov wouldn't allow the writer to have Lenin call Zinoviev "comrade."

"But what else would he call him? They were in hiding together," said Father, cutting off pointless arguments. *The Blue Notebook* was published uncensored.

This time the situation was more complex. The writer was more threatening. Aleksandr Trifonovich Tvardovsky, the editor-in-chief of *Novy Mir*, gave the manuscript to Father's aide, Vladimir Semyonovich Lebedev, as early as that summer. Among his many responsibilities was to keep an eye on literature. Fortunately, he was a conscientious, perceptive, and discriminating person.

Ivan Denisovich became not the first, but one of the most complex, works he promoted. Lebedev promised Tvardovsky to find an opportunity to inform Father. He was sure that Father would react positively. He just had to present it properly. Aides generally try to avoid reporting "problems." Every failure hurts their reputation.

A suitable moment did not come until September, when Father went to Pitsunda to finish his vacation, interrupted by the flight of cosmonauts Nikolayev and Popovich.

One evening, in answer to the question "What else do you have?" Lebedev responded that Tvardovsky was asking for advice about a novel by a young writer who survived Stalin's camps. Lebedev explained that Aleksandr Trifonovich praised the literary qualities of the book, but the theme itself was complicated and required political evaluation.

"Well, go ahead, let's read it," Father said amicably.

Lebedev began to read out loud. Father enjoyed listening to such readings. They allowed him to relax and rest his eyes, which were tired from going over hundreds and thousands of typed pages. If it was boring, he let himself doze off. This time, Father listened with growing interest.

Vladimir Semyonovich has said that Father didn't have the slightest doubt, that he thought the truth about the camps must be told and the novel must be published. Perhaps he himself sensed for the first time what had really happened during those horrible years.

After the Twenty-second Party Congress and the removal of Stalin's body from the Mausoleum, Father had made up his mind to act decisively. But he didn't want to make the final decision alone. He wanted to express his attitude to the collective leadership.

Copies were made and immediately distributed to all members and candidate members of the Presidium. Red seals placed on the cover of each copy prohibited duplicating the book, taking it away, or lending it to anyone else. All copies were to be returned to the General Department of the Central Committee after being read.

Father's colleagues already knew that he had read and liked the manuscript. Therefore, if anyone had doubts, he kept them to himself, because he would have to argue with the first secretary, not with the unknown Solzhenitsyn or with Tvardovsky. A few days later the book received unanimous approval and was recognized as being useful.

The novel was published ahead of the usual schedule. In September it was "approved" and by November it was already being read by the journal's subscribers. The editor in chief was in a hurry.

KOROLYOV AND CHELOMEI COMPETE FOR RESOURCES

With the start of work on heavy launchers and space systems, the design bureaus of Korolyov and Chelomei became increasingly inadequate. They both needed new personnel, infusions of new blood.

In the military field Father finally and definitively put his reliance on missiles. Orders for new planes and cannons were cut back. Enterprises that had taken years to build up were left idle.

The design bureau of Vasily Gavrilovich Grabin sprawled over a large area in Kaliningrad, near Moscow. Cannons were made there. After the war Korolyov was given some work space at a small artillery plant nearby. The authorities didn't want a rocket facility to impinge on Grabin's serious organization. Now that small plant had grown into an industrial giant; in fact, it had swallowed up all surrounding space. There was no room for expansion. On one side workshops merged with apartment buildings, on the other they came right up to the railroad tracks.

Grabin's bureau was located on the other side of the railroad tracks. Legends had grown up around him, but only among those privy to secrets. The general public, especially young people, knew hardly anything about him. Grabin was responsible for important design work during the war: out of 140,000 field weapons used by our side during the war, 120,000 were made from Grabin's designs. Now he was "outdated." It was time for him to leave the stage.

Two claimants to Grabin's heritage appeared immediately, Korolyov and Chelomei. Chelomei applied first, but Korolyov was unconditionally supported by Ustinov.

The contest lasted for about half a year. Chelomei didn't want to give up. Ivan Dmitriyevich Serbin, head of the Central Committee's defense department, took his part. The issue threatened to reach the Presidium. Ustinov didn't want to take the risk. He had to neutralize Chelomei. He found a solution at the expense of aviation. Ustinov summoned Vladimir Nikolayevich and proposed that he "swallow" Lavochkin's firm. During the two years it had been left without a chief designer, it had withered and gradually lost focus. Chelomei happily agreed. He could only have dreamed of such a gift: an organization with a tremendous aviation culture and now a rocket culture as well. How could even the best cannon-makers be compared to it?

The bargain was struck.

A FEW LOOSE ENDS

After the confrontation over Cuba, the world gradually returned to normal. Problems that had seemed less important again took center stage. Just as before—but not exactly as before. Both sides seemed to have grown older and wiser.

On December 12, 1962, Father returned to the problem of Germany in his report to a regular session of the Supreme Soviet on the current international situation and Soviet foreign policy.

He repeated what he had said earlier: if the West continues to refuse, we will sign a separate peace treaty with the GDR. However, the tone of his speech had changed. Although not abandoning the idea of a peace treaty, Father said that there was no need to hurry and we could wait until conditions were ripe.

A month later, on January 16, 1963, Father explained his reasoning in a speech at the Sixth Congress of the Socialist Unity Party in Berlin. He said that there was no reason to push for the signing of a peace treaty, no reason to threaten opponents with a hundred-megaton bomb, which could have no target in Europe because it would kill one's own people as well as the enemy.

The outline of a compromise was taking shape: John Kennedy promised not to invade Cuba and Father effectively relaxed any pressure on Berlin. In his opinion, the establishment of control over the borders of the GDR—the Wall—stabilized the situation. Conclusion of a peace treaty could be postponed. Was Father planning to put pressure on the West's weak point in the future? I think the time for that had passed.

FATHER PROPOSES A RADICAL RESTRUCTURING OF THE MILITARY

At the beginning of February, Father convened a regular session of the Defense Council devoted entirely to the subject of missiles. He wanted to see what we had achieved since the last gathering in Pitsunda. Many questions had accumulated.

The focus was now to be on missiles, in contrast to the previous meeting, which was largely concerned with heavy launchers.

What was of particular concern to Father? The R-36 (SS-9) was far superior not only to its older brother, the R-16, but to everything else Soviet designers had built. However, it was becoming increasingly clear that it would not solve the problem of creating a nuclear shield. The missile was large and heavy, as expected. The silo and auxiliary premises also had to be expanded. Only a few such launch sites could be built—but the General Staff required the destruction of hundreds of enemy targets. The country's security could not be guaranteed otherwise.

During the previous two years there had been a marked advance in technology. Advances gained through nuclear testing had enabled designers to reduce the weight of warheads. The creation of new gyroscopes promised a substantial increase in accuracy, which in turn made it possible to forgo multi-megaton thermonuclear charges. All this created new opportunities for designers.

Father proposed that the Defense Council meeting be held in Myasishchev's former design bureau in Fili, which was now one of Chelomei's work areas. The meeting was later christened the Council of Fili.

Besides listening to reports, Father wanted to see the production area with his own eyes.

I will concentrate on the most important decision: to build a mass-produced intercontinental missile as technically advanced as the U.S. Minuteman.

Yangel and Chelomei delivered reports. Both of them had just completed preliminary designs. They presented their calculations, components, and mockups. Whichever was judged the better missile would be selected for development. It was a difficult choice. The designs were remarkably similar. That often happened in engineering—the same level of expertise, the same technology. Coincidentally, designers have similar ideas. Externally, models can look almost like twins. The insides differ.

Each design had its supporters, its boosters, among the military and officials of different ranks, up to the very top, the Council of Ministers and Central Committee.

Yangel spoke first. His missile looked elegant. It was extremely accurate and could remain fueled in launch position for a much longer time. Like all his earlier designs, it used components of fuel and oxidizer, based on nitrogen compounds. But now Yangel seemed to have solved the problem of controlling the corrosive acid. His data sounded convincing.

After answering numerous questions, Yangel sat down. Chelomei spoke next.

Chelomei's main goal for his new design, the UR-100 (SS-11), was that the missile operate autonomously for an extended period of time and that its launch be fully automatic. Until those problems were solved, large-scale deployment of ICBMs would continue to be unattainable, since it would require all the nation's technical and human resources. He cited an example involving material resources: during prelaunch preparations, the control officer had to make a great number of measurements. It was estimated that connecting all the launch sites planned by the General Staff with their command centers would take more than the annual cable production in the Soviet Union, even if all, including the thinnest, cable was employed for that purpose.

Father looked at Chelomei with amazement. Despite his habit of interrupting speakers, on this occasion he remained silent.

The question of performance was an even more complex subject, continued Vladimir Nikolayevich. It was not just a question of ensuring a virtually instantaneous launch. That was an obvious requirement. But there was also the fact that every additional year a missile was in service saved the state enormous sums of money. As long as a missile was standing, it didn't "ask to be fed," so to speak. But the minute it had to be taken down for maintenance, repair, and eventual replacement, there were huge expenses. Costs amounted to many billions of rubles.

Father listened carefully. He liked such an approach, which took the monetary aspect into consideration. He nodded from time to time, as if to encourage the speaker.

"What determines the period of service for missiles?" asked Chelomei, and answered his own question: "Primarily, the corrosive nature of its components."

He didn't discuss the problem in any depth, simply mentioning that across the ocean the use of solid-fuel rockets made possible a constant state of readiness and a prolonged period (up to ten years) of service. Our attempts to design intercontinental solid-fuel rockets within the next few years were doomed to fail. That fact must be faced and not ignored. In his opinion, we needed to focus our efforts on areas where we were strong, not where we were weak.

"During the past few years we have acquired considerable experience in working with nitrogen compounds," said Chelomei, shifting to his main subject. "Despite all their negative features, we have learned how to work with them, and if we use some engineering ingenuity, we can control them. Let the Americans work on solid fuels—we will rely on acid."

Special treatment of tank interiors, a system of especially acid-resistant pipelines, superb membranes—all that, combined in a multi-stage design, would make it possible for the rocket to be stored safely for ten years and to be used at a moment's notice.

"Our missile," Chelomei continued, "somewhat resembles a soldered ampoule. Until needed, its contents are totally isolated from the outside world; only at the very last moment, upon the command to launch, will the missile's membranes break, its components rush toward the engine, and the launch will occur. Because of these measures, and despite the fact that its contents are so dangerous, it is as safe to maintain in a state of readiness as a solid-fuel missile."

Chelomei fell silent.

Judging by the reaction of those present in the hall, he was winning. At any rate, Father clearly liked him. Dementyev smiled triumphantly. Ustinov stared gloomily in front of him. His report was followed by an endless series of questions. Chelomei answered confidently and precisely. He had clearly put his whole heart into developing the missile.

The first part of the meeting ended. Its participants split up into groups and, accompanied by specially assigned guides, went to look at the exhibits.

At the workshop entrance Father suddenly recalled that a few years earlier he had examined Myasishchev's M-3—perhaps in this very workshop—and had tried to get a positive answer to the question of whether it could reach America. At the time, the Western hemisphere, shielded by the ocean's expanses, was unreachable.

Father began talking about what strides technology had made in the past few years. He couldn't stop talking—missiles had become his latest favorite subject. Those present listened attentively, though many of them had heard it all before.

Finally Father stopped, was silent for a moment and then, turning to his host, said: "Let's go on."

There were many exhibits in the halls of the design bureau.

Father's attention was drawn to a section on naval space intelligence. The Navy had ordered a whole range of specialized satellites capable of gathering various types of information. After listening attentively to the guide's account, Father said some encouraging words to Gorshkov and turned his head, as if looking for someone in the crowd. But whoever it was, he didn't find him.

Pointing to the next room, where the Ground Forces had their materials displayed, he asked someone from the design bureau: "Find that tall marshal and bring him here."

A few minutes later, Marshal Grechko, the commander in chief of the forces of the Warsaw Pact, entered the room with a broad smile. But Father was not in the mood for pleasantries. He pointed to the mockup of a reconnaissance satellite, then to Grechko's stomach: "You don't have anything," he said to him threateningly. Then, smiling and pointing to Gorshkov, he continued: "He has everything. Why?"

Grechko was silent. He lost his smile and stood there with his head hanging like a guilty schoolboy. But you could tell from his expression that he didn't take the reprimand seriously.

"Because you don't work. You're lazy," said Father, after not getting any answer to his question. "Follow the Navy's example."

Grechko nodded agreeably, demonstrating by his entire manner that he was ready to follow anybody's example.

"Let's go and see what you've got," Father said to Grechko.

Mockups of nuclear and conventional battlefield weapons were mounted in the next room. Grechko brought Father over to the mockup of the advanced Luna tactical missile launcher. Next to it was a poster depicting a cannon with a long barrel. Those present could guess what they would talk about. Grechko had long advocated equipping army units at the corps and even division level with nuclear weapons.

Now he cited the latest U.S. data: in addition to Honest John missiles, their army units were well equipped with long-range cannons able to fire nuclear warheads. Infantry units had nuclear mortars and land mines. It was rumored that they had a mobile nuclear warhead that could be shoulder-launched.

In Grechko's words, the Soviet Army was in a catastrophic situation. Apart from the Lunas, we had virtually nothing to rely on. Grechko began getting angry and tried to persuade Father that without tactical nuclear weapons, the army could not confront the probable enemy. Without using tactical nuclear shells on the battlefield—very small ones (at this point he used his hands to indicate how small they could be) of one or two kilotons— without such warheads it would be impossible to win a modern battle.

This time his eyes were not smiling. The subject was a serious one. It didn't concern some space trifle. Grechko had little faith in such things and thought of them as toys. He confronted Father like a bull, looking down at him from his height of almost six and a half feet. Father retreated. He didn't want to talk to someone if he had to look up.

"Move back a couple of steps"—he was tired of backing up.

The atmosphere grew less tense.

"And don't try to persuade me. I don't have the money," continued Father. "You can't have everything."

Father obviously didn't want to get into an argument. Everything had already been discussed repeatedly. Father didn't like tactical nuclear weapons. He did not think of nuclear weapons as instruments of war, but as a factor in political battles, a method of exerting pressure, threats, and even blackmail. But to use them!?

Father's objectives were met by hundred-megaton warheads, for which Europe was too small. The megaton warheads of missiles of varying ranges, targeted at the capitals of potential enemies, were an effective deterrent to any hotheads.

All these "small things" struck Father as being very dangerous because of their down-to-earth quality, which lowered the threshold of fear. Moreover, such "treats" could be extraordinarily expensive. Slavsky reported that the charge for a nuclear cannon equivalent to one and a half kilotons cost no less than the megaton warhead for an intercontinental missile. If we intended to equip the army with nuclear weapons, it would require, not thousands, but tens of thousands of weapons.

Father held his ground: "No!"

However, two experimental long-range cannons were built. They were capable of hurling a nuclear charge about thirty kilometers. Twice a year they took part in parades on Red Square. During exercises they fired with a tremendous roar. But that was the end of it. Father instantly rejected any proposals that they be produced. Neither the marshals nor Ustinov could shake him. So those two monster cannons remained a single pair.

The Luna was less of a problem. It was put into serial production, usually with a conventional warhead. A few nuclear warheads were produced.

Father didn't even want to hear about mortars or land mines. References to the Americans had no effect on Father, who was used to warnings that if money weren't allocated we would lag behind the Americans. Father held to his point of view: if you spend all your money on those "toys," you will definitely lose. If the Americans want to waste their money on them, let them. In Father's opinion, in a nuclear war there would be no battlefield.

When Father was forced to retire, Grechko had no trouble obtaining Brezhnev's approval. Leonid Ilyich "understood" the situation. Since that time more than seven thousand nuclear cannon have been built; the number of nuclear warheads also rose into the thousands, then into the tens of thousands, and continued moving upward.

After lunch, everyone gathered again in the conference room. They still had to talk things over and come to some decisions.

They began with the missiles. Who should receive the go-ahead? During lunch Father discussed the subject with Kozlov and Brezhnev. He liked Chelomei's proposals, but he wanted to get some support for his decision. Besides, Father was mindful of the fact that I worked there, and my presence created certain difficulties for him. Someone could always say: "We know why he's tending in that direction." There was a lot of gossip in those days, and it became rampant in subsequent years. There were malicious officials who were happy to ascribe their own mistakes to Father's "understandable preference" for "one famous firm." It's not for me to justify Father. And to justify myself is improper and senseless.

Kozlov and Brezhnev supported Father.

At the session Father came out in favor of Chelomei. Yangel looked simply crushed. Ustinov was upset. Wishing to support Mikhail Kuzmich, Father said some kind words about his great achievements and the importance of his work on the "36" rocket. His words were not comforting, but just rubbed salt in the wound.

The history of the creation of genuine Soviet missile power began with this meeting of the Defense Council. A government decree issued on March 30, 1963, set out time limits and specific parameters for the first Soviet mass-produced intercontinental missile.

The meeting continued with a discussion about personnel changes.

Father was thinking of promoting Ustinov and putting him in charge of co-ordinating Soviet regional economic councils throughout the country. The plan was to create a new body—the Supreme National Economic Council—and to make Ustinov its chairman, with the rank of First Deputy Chairman of the Council of Ministers. Father proposed appointing Leonid Vasilyevich Smirnov, the director of Yangel's plant, to replace Ustinov. When Father visited the plant two years before, he noticed how well the plant was maintained, that its director was a good manager. Moreover, he was a rocket specialist.

For some years Father had tried to promote to top positions people from production, who had not become bureaucratized in ministerial chairs and were not accustomed to playing interoffice games of intrigue.

The meeting seemed to be coming to an end. The main issue of a new missile was settled and only some details were left. However, what sometimes seems to be only a detail can stimulate a discussion and turn into a problem.

Malinovsky began to talk. Until then he had maintained a gloomy silence. He had said hardly anything during the entire meeting.

In his opinion, the situation in the Army was unfortunate, particularly with respect to personnel. By the mid-1960s, children born during the war were going to be inducted into the Army. But what kind of birthrate was there during the war? The men were all at the front. Now there were not enough men to call up for military service. Units did not have enough personnel. The Defense Minister thought that various privileges, such as deferments or the refusal to serve, were especially damaging.

Grechko supported Malinovsky. He viewed student deferments as the main problem. He argued that a student who served in the Army would become a real man—the service would be good for him. Grechko was also against military departments at universities, which turned out officers for the reserves. He didn't like them because of their civilian behavior, their inability to command, and their ignorance of military service. Those departments should be closed down and the recruitment of students to military schools should be increased instead.

Grechko was in such a hurry to talk about what bothered him that he sometimes jumbled his words. He said that another mistake which we would regret was the reduction in service from three to two years in the Army, and from four to three in the Navy. That was an unforgivable decision. The technology was becoming more sophisticated and more time was needed for training. Soldiers barely began their period of service when they were demobilized. It wasn't real Army service, but a two-year training course. He proposed that the old system be restored and that service be extended to four or more years in branches of service where the technology was particularly complex.

Grechko finished talking. A tense silence ensued. The marshals sitting around the table stared at Father. It was obvious that this was not a new issue and that they were all of the same opinion. They just couldn't convince the commander in chief. Father was silent. Though smiling shortly before, he now looked gloomy. His small brown eyes swiveled from Grechko to Malinovsky. Grechko shivered and tried to make a joke, but Father didn't copy his frivolous tone of voice and he subsided.

Father collected his thoughts and stood up. At first he spoke slowly, with long pauses, as if thinking things over.

He began with a rhetorical question: Who serves for whom? The Army for the people or the people for the Army? He thought that there was a good reason why the period of service had been reduced—and only after lengthy discussions. The national economy needed working hands, which were in short supply everywhere. Meanwhile, young people in the Army only consumed, without producing anything.

"Have you ever thought about how many useful things will be produced by people who leave the Army a year sooner?" He stared at Grechko. Grechko fidgeted. He didn't know what to answer, but Father didn't expect an answer.

Father said that of course one can learn military skills better in three years than in two, and even better in five. Then he reminded his listeners that under Nicholas I soldiers served twenty-five years. Could that be the ideal to which the marshal aspired?

Grechko, with feigned terror, shook his head.

Father began talking about how it was necessary to think primarily about strengthening the country's economy. If it was healthy, no imperialists would frighten us. Of course, we couldn't do without the Army at present, but we should approach everything sensibly and strike a balance in which neither the economy nor the Army would suffer.

Father agreed that only well-trained specialists could work with complex technology, but then even five years might not be enough. In his opinion, new ways had to be found and we shouldn't knock on a closed door.

"We have to think, to try new things." He smiled for the first time. Grechko smiled in response. Malinovsky continued to look gloomily at the floor. The other military leaders fidgeted in their chairs and were clearly dissatisfied.

"As for the students," continued Father, "you simply do not understand. Otherwise you wouldn't ask such a stupid question. Just think—we spend billions training urgently needed specialists, and you want to take them and 'Hup, toop, threep . . . !'"

Father was so indignant that he even broke out in a sweat. He said that something had to be done if military training departments were unsatisfactory and turned out unqualified people. But to draft students would be harmful. We live for the interests of the people, for the interests of the state, which needs qualified engineers, agronomists, and other specialists, people who make people's lives better. The Army is obligated to guard their work. But Grechko was, as Father put it, trying to turn everything on its head. If everyone was drafted into the Army, there would be nobody to protect and no need of an Army.

"We need specialists, and we will train them at institutes. The Army's problems must not be solved at the people's expense," Father concluded, then added after a moment's thought: "There are things to think about. But to draft students would be an unforgivable waste. How can you not understand that?"

The subject of students was dropped, but only for the time being, since neither Malinovsky nor Grechko considered themselves defeated. They brought it up repeatedly to Father—each time unsuccessfully. It was only after Father's resignation that Grechko managed to convince the government.

Father continued, as if thinking out loud. He had recently become increasingly preoccupied by the question: What kind of Army should we have in the future? For the time being we could only dream of disarmament. What could we do to keep the Army, as it provided for our security, from being a heavy burden on the country? He thought that it was time for an innovative approach to the question of the country's defense. We still thought in the categories of the Second World War: tanks, airplanes, armored personnel carriers, the number of weapons per kilometer of front. It was all reminiscent of the prewar situation, when we relied on glorious but hopelessly anachronistic cavalrymen, with their sabers, and on machine guns transported on carts. We realized too late that those days were gone forever. To gain that knowledge had cost us a huge quantity of blood. Now missiles and nuclear warheads were making our previous military experience obsolete.

The time has come when he who is successful in preventing war wins, not he who counts on military victory. Then Father said some absolutely unusual things—things that seemed to me not only seditious, but improbable as well. He thought that the Army's structure was hopelessly outdated. Missiles had drastically changed the balance of forces and altered all concepts of war.

"Take tanks, for example," he said, elaborating on his thoughts.

During the last war they served as the nuclei for offense and the fulcrum in defense. They were invulnerable to small arms and could be destroyed only by cannons, which had a hard time hitting them. It wasn't clear which would destroy the other, the artillerymen hitting the tank or the tank crews hitting the artillery battery. It was a fight between equals. By the end of the war everything had changed. The Germans torched tanks with their shoulder-fired antitank weapons, while remaining almost invulnerable themselves. It was simply that our superiority was so great in those months that we didn't feel these changes. But to use those antitank weapons, soldiers had to come right up to their target. Today antitank rockets can destroy armored cars at the extreme limit of their own range, from several kilometers away. Tanks, self-propelled artillery, and armored personnel carriers are simply traps for their crews, so why are we mindlessly ordering more and more of them? We are spending billions.

Planes have also virtually lost their former importance. Antiaircraft missiles are drastically reducing their combat effectiveness. While ground-to-air fire used to be ineffective, today it only takes one or two missiles. Here too we need to revise established views.

Father focused especially on helicopters. At the time there were a lot of arguments over their potential combat effectiveness. Would they be introduced into the Army primarily as combat weapons or as a means of transport, including evacuation of the wounded?

Father was a skeptic. In his opinion, helicopters would lose in any competition with antiaircraft missiles. They were clumsy and likely to crash.

Father moved on from particulars to his main point: "The basis of our defense is strategic missiles. Intercontinental and medium-range missiles can strike anywhere on the territory of an enemy, regardless of how far away it is or how well it is defended. Even if someday people learn how to shoot down missiles, some of them will always penetrate, and even a few warheads are enough to scare off any aggressor."

Father looked toward Marshal Zakharov, the head of the General Staff, and added maliciously: "You plan hundreds of targets, but even a dozen missiles with thermonuclear warheads are enough to make the very thought of war senseless."

In his opinion, not a single politician would think of engaging in war if threatened with inevitable retaliation.

If missiles with nuclear warheads made war between the great powers senseless, then, as a thrifty manager, he didn't see any point in spending money on a gigantic army. "We, a socialist country, are not colonialists. We're not planning to invade anyone," he emphasized.

Father was getting carried away—not so much arguing any longer, as looking into the future.

"If missiles are able to protect us, then why should we maintain such an army?" he repeated. No one said anything. The marshals obviously didn't like the question.

"We can put the money that we spend on defense," continued Father, "to better uses."

He began talking about housing, fertilizers, and harvests. Then, as if remembering what was being discussed, he returned to the subject.

In his opinion, the entire structure of the armed forces had to be reexamined, with only a very small, but very highly qualified, army as the result. The word "professional" was not used then, as if they were unaware of it. I won't use it either, so that I don't leap unintentionally from the 1960s to the 1990s. The nucleus of this army—the strategic missile forces—would restrain potential aggressors. A small and very mobile group would be deployed around them, with the mission of protecting launchers and securing them against any sudden attacks.

The rest of the army, in Father's opinion, should be organized on the basis of regional militias. Its soldiers could live at home, do useful work, and spend some time on military training. They would be mobilized only if the country was really in danger.

Father fell silent.

A tense hush ensued. No one supported Father, but no one ventured to object.

"In that case, students would be no problem." Father smiled. "And we wouldn't have to lengthen the period of service. If a person lives at home and works, he can spend as many years in military training as necessary."

Then, as if reconsidering, he added: "Of course, as long as it doesn't interfere with his work."

Father said that he was just thinking out loud and that the subject deserved some consideration, but the main thing was that this plan could be carried out only after we had enough missiles.

The military brightened up.

"By the way, speaking of missiles," Father said, turning to Ustinov, "we have to think about the future. We don't need an unlimited number of them. A few hundred? But then what? Will the plants stop producing? That's not economical. Think about it, Comrade Ustinov—what useful thing could they do later on?"

Ustinov nodded and made some notes. Now he had to view the subject from a different angle.

"For example, Comrade Yangel has a huge plant," said Father, pursuing his thought. "Besides missiles, the plant produces tractors. But we don't need so many tractors, and tomorrow we might have too many missiles. Perhaps they could also learn to build ships? We really need good ships for our rivers."

Everyone was staggered by this idea. Yangel looked at Father with astonishment and a certain degree of alarm. He tried to say something, obviously in protest, but reconsidered and sat without moving.

Kozlov intervened, commenting that everything should be weighed with great care.

Father didn't object and nodded. "That's a matter for the future. Meanwhile, let's make good missiles."

Father's time in power was running out. The missiles were made. For a long twenty years no one remembered either the reorganization of the Army or the transition of work at missile plants to peaceful production. Today it's called conversion.

Father's speech concluded the meeting. He said good-bye to everyone and left for the Central Committee. He had some business to attend to there. Kozlov left with him.

Brezhnev gave Chelomei a lengthy and emotional handshake, congratulating him on his well-deserved success.

Ustinov nodded coldly at the others and left for his office in the Kremlin.

FROL KOZLOV

Kozlov was acquiring more and more power. After replacing Kirichenko as second secretary of the Central Committee in May 1960, he began gradually putting down roots and drawing provincial committees and departments of the Central Committee under him.

As I wrote earlier, the replacement of the second secretary had not had any political implications. And no one would put Kirichenko and Ignatov "to the left" of Kozlov. As history showed, all the new members of the Presidium of the Central Committee selected by Father held approximately similar views. It couldn't have been otherwise. They had all emerged from under Stalin's overcoat. They had all grown up in Stalin's stable. Every one had gone through Stalin's school of power and not one could claim that he had committed no "sins" that, after the Twentieth Party Congress, no one wanted to remember.

They "exposed" Stalin's crimes with greater or lesser enthusiasm and remembered the innocent victims, not because of any inner compulsion, but because of circumstances, of their need to follow in Father's steps.

Not much changed in the party apparat itself in those years. And it couldn't change. People moved from one chair to another, sometimes losing their positions and being replaced by men with the very same outlook. Father was unable to cope with all of them. It sometimes seemed to him that everything would fall into place after yet another reorganization—that honorable people would finally occupy party and government positions, and yet he used occasionally to complain to his old friend Aleksei Vladimirovich Snegov[1] that

---

1. A. V. Snegov, an active member of the Communist Party during the 1920s and 1930s. He

"as he walked down a hall he sometimes felt looks that could kill" directed at his back. However, there was nothing he could do about that.

The replacement on May 4, 1960, of key people in the Secretariat of the Central Committee did not spring from a "struggle under the carpet," as Sir Winston Churchill sarcastically called bureaucratic games, but was another of Father's attempts to find better qualified associates. That was difficult to accomplish. There were very few candidates to be found on the microscopic platform at the top of the pyramid of power. He had practically no one to choose from: five, ten, or twenty people at the most.

The crude Kirichenko had moved offstage. In those years, Kozlov seemed, not more intelligent, but more able and skillful at adapting to the political situation. Not only was he good at adapting to a situation, he planned to manage it. Whereas Kirichenko followed Father blindly in everything, Kozlov gradually developed his own policies and shifted a little to Father's right. But that wasn't the case in 1960 or even in 1962. During the Cuban Missile Crisis he didn't take a different position, and together with the others was solidly "in favor."

At the beginning of 1963, there was an almost imperceptible change. Frol Romanovich began to act a little more independently of Father. There would have been nothing unusual about that in relations within any normal circle of leaders. But in those years in Moscow everybody carefully observed nuances. Possibly others noticed the symptoms even earlier, because changes in relations among those in the leader's entourage first affect lower-ranking officials.

It is only now, from a distance of decades, that we can see how slowly we crawled out of Stalin's tyrannical boots. After eliminating despotism, we made the first timid steps toward democracy. In the years of "collective leadership," it was regarded as a significant achievement that everyone voted unanimously for the proposals of the "first among equals." Probably it really was.

Was opposition to Father growing in 1962 and 1963? I find it difficult to say. There was always dissatisfaction with Father. But dissatisfaction and the jokes it provokes are one thing, and when a nucleus begins to crystallize in an amorphous environment you have a very different situation. Personally, I doubt it.

Father liked Kozlov. He assumed responsibility for solving many specific problems, supervised the process, was organized and efficient, and didn't need petty oversight. The fact that he sometimes objected and argued with Father elicited Father's respect rather than irritation. After all, without argu-

---

worked with Father in the Ukraine for a number of years. In the 1930s he was arrested and only released from prison after Stalin's death. Snegov was active in rehabilitating the victims of Stalinist repressions.—S.K.

ments, without differences of opinion, work becomes not only more boring, but more difficult, especially for someone with Father's character. Endless nods of approval, eyes either cast down submissively or eating you up with admiration were annoying and put you on guard.

During previous years, Mikoyan was the only one in the Presidium who failed to agree with Father about everything. Now he was joined by Kozlov. Deep in his heart, Father liked the appearance of an "opposition." Moreover, the "opposition" often took divergent points of view. Mikoyan was known as an experienced and cautious politician. Kozlov was known as an adminis-trator, a practical person, though somewhat unrefined, but someone who knew how to get things done, had the ability to apply pressure and raise his voice if need be. In politics, Kozlov reflected the views of the right—today I would say the views of Stalinists, but at the time he didn't declare himself openly. He preferred the apparat clichés: "there is an opinion," "let's not rush forward," or a stronger one—"not to deviate from policy."

That year there were many arguments in Moscow over Yugoslavia. The tanks on the streets of Budapest, like a dash of cold water, chilled the brief thaw in our relations. Time gradually healed the wound. By 1963 relations were again becoming friendly. But Moscow's conventional leaders didn't like it. In their hearts they were Stalinists and considered any deviations from dogma to be unforgivable heresy.

May 1 was approaching. In 1963, as in previous years, Party Central Committee slogans were published a couple of weeks before the holiday. The first pages of all central newspapers were filled with appeals, in bold print, to workers, the military, the intelligentsia, countries, peoples, and con-tinents. Every word in them was carefully selected. The Central Committee's ideology department scrutinized every word in these slogans, or, more pre-cisely, they rewrote them, using newspapers from past years, changing verbs from past to future tense, and making slight changes to suit the current situa-tion. Father didn't bother with those empty, dogmatic games and he happily gave Suslov and Kozlov supervision over the publication of these appeals. Gradually, Kozlov assumed control over such routine matters—and real power, along with it.

However, that doesn't mean that Father didn't keep track of what was published. Although he didn't read the pages with the trite slogans, there were always some informers who reported the slightest deviation in the slo-gans to him.

This time the appeals were published on April 8. The international sec-tion followed the domestic one. There was an exhaustive list of greetings to each and every allied country: "Fraternal greetings to the peoples building socialism." Third world countries, however, were urged to extend friendship and their peoples exhorted to "fight for socialism." There was a principled difference. "If people are fighting for socialism," it means that they have someone to fight against: usually those in power in their own countries who are preventing them from having happy lives.

Yugoslavia fell in between. *Pravda*'s appeal read: "Fraternal greetings to the working people of the Federal People's Republic of Yugoslavia! Let friendship and cooperation between the Soviet and Yugoslav peoples develop and strengthen in the interests of the fight for peace and socialism!"

In April Father was vacationing in Pitsunda. I was with him. He had grown used to taking an additional two-week vacation in winter or spring. The years were taking their toll. His doctors insisted on the extra time off. Their recommendations were reinforced by a special decision of the Presidium of the Central Committee. It also specified a shorter workday, but Father never took advantage of that privilege. However, he did get used to the additional vacation. He could think better away from the hectic activities in Moscow. Lately his thoughts had increasingly turned to the Constitution. In this revised version of the Constitution, he wanted to strengthen principles that would exclude any possibility that a new Stalin would appear.

In those days it seemed sufficient to proclaim a mandatory turnover of leaders by establishing two five-year terms for everyone in higher positions, from minister and up, and to hold elections with not one candidate, but several. Father naively thought that if people could only vote, everything would go smoothly. That April Father began taking preliminary steps. I also enjoyed a one-week vacation: sun and sea. I sat next to him on the beach, but didn't listen carefully to his conversations.

It was then that I became an involuntary witness to Father's conflict with Kozlov. The newspapers were brought. They reached Pitsunda at the end of the day. Father looked quickly at the first page and was going to turn to the inside pages when his aide drew his attention to that unfortunate slogan. He had already looked over the papers as he sorted the mail.

Father read the lines pointed out to him and became furious. "Again we're going back to zero! Is Yugoslavia building socialism or not?" He demanded that a call to Kozlov be put through immediately. The special phone was right there, on a small table under the awning.

After being connected to the Central Committee and brusquely saying hello, Father began reproaching Kozlov for his oversight. But Kozlov rejected Father's complaint and gave a substantive reason for doing so. From his viewpoint, what was written objectively reflected the real situation in Yugoslavia. Father shouted at Kozlov and accused him of being arbitrary: the Central Committee had officially confirmed the socialist basis of the Yugoslav national economy. No one had the right to revise that decision on his own. Further, Father allowed himself to question Kozlov's competence in theory. He was following the most reactionary dogmatists, shielding them with his authority.

In conclusion, Father demanded that there be a change, the sooner the better, before this incorrect formulation was distributed around the world.

A change in the formulation of an already published Central Committee appeal was unprecedented in those days. The rumor of Father's conversation with Kozlov quickly spread within the Central Committee. Probably Kozlov himself shared his anger with like-minded associates. In the corridors they gossiped about how unfairly and harshly Father had spoken to Kozlov and later whispered sympathetically that it was after this reprimand that Kozlov developed heart problems.

It took three days to compose a new slogan. On April 11 a correction appeared in *Pravda*, which explained that the appeal should be read in its new version: "Fraternal greetings to the working people of the Socialist Federal Republic of Yugoslavia, building socialism! Long live the eternal and unbreakable friendship and cooperation between the Soviet and Yugoslav Peoples!"

I remember another of Father's conversations with Kozlov. On May 11, 1963, Colonel Oleg Penkovsky was given the death sentence.

Two important military officers were involved in the scandal. Both of them were connected to Father in one way or another: the commander in chief of Missile Forces and Artillery, Chief Marshal of Artillery Sergei Sergeyevich Varentsov, and the head of the Main Intelligence Department of the General Staff, Army General Ivan Aleksandrovich Serov, in the recent past chairman of the KGB.

Varentsov had recommended Penkovsky for service in the GRU. He also occasionally shared with him some work-related news, classified, naturally. In other circumstances, that would not have been compromising. Both had held high positions in the Army.

Serov was accused because he had favored Penkovsky, not just because he had failed to detect a potential traitor in him. The fact that Serov's wife and daughter were with Penkovsky in Britain not long before his arrest was the most incriminating factor. However, the women had traveled as tourists. Doors to the West were opening slightly at that time. The first cruise ships sailed around Europe and it became possible to visit some foreign countries. Applicants were vetted more strictly than if they were applying to work in intelligence. A general's family didn't have such a problem, but a visit to a capitalist country provoked a certain amount of timidity. Serov, remembering that his subordinate was going on a business trip to London, asked Penkovsky to look after his wife and daughter and to help them in case of need. The colonel gladly performed this service, took them on a sightseeing tour, and helped them shop in stores. Now everything appeared in a different light. Somebody tried to expose the general and the colonel as co-conspirators.

Father was not inclined to take serious measures against them. He thought that they had been punished enough by what had happened, and that it wasn't written on Penkovsky's forehead that he worked for the British and Americans. He suggested that punishment be limited to an administrative reprimand.

Kozlov thought otherwise. He was extremely determined. His real motivation remains a mystery. Perhaps he could not reconcile himself to the fact that Serov and Varentsov had overlooked a traitor? That seems doubtful. He had sometimes ignored even more obvious "sins" and didn't belong among the "saints" himself. Then why? Did he want to remove from the game with one stroke two military officers devoted to Father? Why? Of course, we can speculate. I don't have any facts.

At the end of February and beginning of March, Kozlov, on his own initiative, called Father at the dacha and asked for a meeting. Father willingly agreed. A quarter of an hour later Frol Romanovich arrived at our place. His dacha wasn't far away. Father greeted Kozlov warmly and suggested taking a walk. Before his guest arrived, we were taking a walk together, so I stayed with them.

Kozlov looked searchingly at me from time to time. He began trying to persuade Father that Penkovsky had compromised both Varentsov and Serov. He had not simply served in their departments, but had intruded into their family lives. He had been a guest in Varentsov's home and performed services for Serov's family. It was then that I heard about those ill-fated London shopping excursions. Kozlov tried to make it almost a government crime. Father maintained a grim silence. That wasn't like him. Then he tried rather uncertainly to object, but Kozlov persisted stubbornly.

I wasn't present at the end of the conversation because Father asked me to leave them alone. Kozlov left about an hour later. Father didn't invite him to have dinner with us. We continued our walk so unexpectedly interrupted by our visitor. Father was frowning. He didn't even look around him, but stared at the ground. We were silent for about ten minutes. At last Father spoke. He said that, according to Kozlov, everybody—he didn't say who—insisted on holding Serov and Varentsov strictly responsible.

"Perhaps they're right," said Father doubtfully. "It's a pity, especially about Varentsov." I asked what would happen. "He'll be demoted to major general and forced to resign," concluded Father regretfully. It all sounded as if Father was submitting to Kozlov against his will.

On March 12, the Presidium of the Supreme Soviet stripped Varentsov of his title of Hero of the Soviet Union and reduced his rank from marshal to major general "for loss of vigilance and unworthy conduct." Serov's rank was also reduced to that of major general.

Could this event have signified the beginning of an opposition to Father?

Now it's difficult to say. There is no evidence left and almost no witnesses, and the remaining ones are not interested in the truth.

Father continued to have complete confidence in Kozlov. What's more, he saw Kozlov as his successor and didn't conceal that fact. When Kozlov was struck down by a sudden stroke in the prime of life, Father was genuinely upset. After he was discharged from the hospital, Father went to see the patient at his dacha. I went along. Kozlov looked bad. Only a shadow remained of the confident and healthy man he had been. He lay helplessly on a hospital bed, muttered something unintelligible and waved his hands about. He presented a miserable picture. Father stayed only a short time. After saying a few words of encouragement and wishing him a speedy recovery, he left the room.

When he asked about Kozlov's recovery, the doctors replied unequivocally: "He will never return to work. Any upset would probably have a tragic outcome."

At the next meeting of the Presidium of the Central Committee, Father informed his colleagues of the doctors' verdict. Referring to the medical opinion, he proposed that, in spite of Kozlov's inability to pursue political activities in the future, his position in the Presidium should be preserved out of humanitarian considerations. Everybody supported him.

The position of second secretary remained vacant. After long consideration and hesitation, Father decided on Brezhnev in the late autumn of 1963. His choice was a provisional one, dependent on the appearance of a more suitable candidate. One did not appear. The final decision to appoint Brezhnev second secretary of the CPSU Central Committee would be adopted by a Plenum of the Central Committee in July 1964.

KOROLYOV AND GLUSHKO

The decision to develop the UR-100 finally dotted the "i," in Father's opinion. The country received a reliable shield. The light UR-100, which could be launched at a moment's notice, and the powerful R-36, with its heavy warheads, gave us a retaliatory strike power equal to that of the United States. The dream was coming true. From now on the country could feel safe.

However, the situation in the space program was not as satisfactory. Father was worried about the lunar project. The quarrel between Korolyov and Glushko that began in 1957 when Glushko decided to work with Yangel on an intercontinental missile had turned into a feud. Neither exhortations in the Central Committee nor appeals to Korolyov's and Glushko's consciences had any effect. Father decided to intervene.

In the first half of June, he told Mother that he had invited Sergei Pavlovich and Valentin Petrovich to come to the dacha over the weekend. Father hoped to find a way to their intellect, if not to their hearts. How could it be otherwise? All quarrels and hostility should fade before the great common goal of conquering the moon.

"They have everything," said Father indignantly. "The people and government satisfy their every whim, even when it hurts, just so that they can work. But they decide to settle old scores. What childishness!"

Father could not imagine how they could put personal relations above the common cause. Father placed most of the blame on Korolyov and viewed the quarrel as Sergei Pavlovich's caprice, evidence of his jealousy and ambition. He thought of Glushko as the victim.

But in that period it was technology, the evaluation of technical possibilities, and not solely old grudges that pitted Korolyov and Glushko against each other. Korolyov insisted on equipping his N-1 with oxygen-kerosene engines, with one combustion chamber and a thrust of six hundred tons each. Glushko thought that design was unrealistic and doubted it could ever be technically carried out, and certainly not in the next few years. New technologies would be needed to create such giants; new ground test platforms would have to be built, and all that without any guarantee of success. Why should we just follow the Americans? In Glushko's opinion, we should rely on developing engines operating on acid. Not only did they have many advantages, but we had acquired a tremendous amount of experience in building and producing them.

The guests arrived in the morning. Father immediately took them off to the meadow to look at the crops. He wanted to have the serious conversation after their walk.

Sergei Pavlovich was in a good mood. They were joking with Father as they walked down the path leading from the house to the meadow where the kitchen gardens were planted. But I thought that Glushko looked gloomy and depressed, and he said nothing.

Korolyov suddenly remembered his youth and began telling how he and Glushko were arrested and sent to Butyrka Prison.

"To the tower where Pugachov was kept long ago"—I remember those words of Sergei Pavlovich. Glushko was silent and only nodded, as if in confirmation.

It was no coincidence that Korolyov began talking about his imprisonment. He suddenly stopped talking and turned toward Father: "And you, Nikita Sergeyevich, do you believe that we were unjustly accused?"

Father looked into his eyes attentively and unsmilingly and answered seriously: "I have no doubt of that."

"Thank you," Sergei Pavlovich said with relief.

Stalin's "school" had left its mark, even on such strong people.

After completing the ritual promenade around the meadow, from the clearing in the woods to the bank of the Moscow River, we returned home. It was time to get down to business. We settled in the dining room. Korolyov sat next to Father so that he could show him some pictures more easily. Glushko sat across from them and I found a chair a little to the side, trying to keep out of the way.

At first Korolyov reported, or simply described, his immediate plans: the next launch into space, this time of two people, a man and a woman. Naturally, Father was aware of Sergei Pavlovich's plans. They were no secret to me either. Korolyov decided that these launches would bring the series of Vostoks to a close. It didn't seem possible to gain anything further from them. Gagarin had demonstrated the general possibility of orbital flight, the ability of man to survive in weightlessness, under conditions of cosmic radiation or other still unknown factors. Despite several severe attacks of motion sickness, Titov had confirmed that nothing would happen even if the flight lasted many hours.

Now a woman would fly in space.

When Father asked what space science would learn from that, Korolyov answered evasively, referred to the special characteristics of the female organism and began talking about future cities in space, where we would create families under new conditions. It was time to start preparing for that.

Father listened skeptically, but did not object.

Korolyov then briefly described a new spaceship he was already building, which had room for three cosmonauts. His future program revolved around it. He was again adopting a different approach from the Americans, who were using one-man space vehicles at the time. Our superiority had received powerful confirmation.

Father grunted approvingly.

Korolyov went on to talk about the lunar program. He was confident of success.

Not long before, Chelomei had paid—somewhat cap in hand—a friendly visit to Korolyov. He had taken people from various departments with him. I went to represent guidance systems.

The problem was that work on the UR-200 was lagging. It turned out to be difficult for us—with no experience in the design of ballistic missiles—to send up a "cigar" filled to the top with bubbling liquid and curving in all directions. Deadlines were not being met. The date for the first launch was repeatedly postponed. It became clear that the missile was not going to be ready to test in advance of the satellites. An awkward situation emerged: the launcher would be ready at about the same time as the maneuverable satellite, at the end of the year. It was unreasonable to risk the satellite. Chelomei made a difficult decision, considering his pride: to ask Sergei Pavlovich to let him launch the satellite on the R-7. That would be necessary for only the initial stage of tests.

We were received as honored guests at Korolyov's design bureau. The first sign of respect was when we were admitted without having to show passes or documents. However, the meeting was not held in the main work area, but in some intermediate zone, in the small building where Korolyov's office was located. He and Chelomei greeted each other like friends who had not met for many years and shook hands warmly for a long time, calling each other "Seryozha" and "Volodya."

Despite increasing competition in their work, their personal relations remained friendly. That was an achievement, considering their complicated personalities.

It didn't take long to settle the business. Korolyov called over one of his people and ordered him to seat Volodya's "rider" on his "horse."

They talked a little about the N-1. Korolyov didn't want to go into detail. A great deal in the project remained unclear and besides, he was sitting with a potential rival. Korolyov had no doubt that once Chelomei started working on heavy launchers, he would not stop with the UR-500. That would not have been in his nature.

After this meeting, our previously unrelated organizations developed, not exactly cooperation, but what might be termed "interrelations."

Closer acquaintance revealed just how different were the styles of the two designers, the two schools. Chelomei moved ahead cautiously, making a program more complex with each step, each stage. First a mockup, then the simplest flights, and only then, after some experience had been gained, would he undertake full-scale launches. That was the way designers always worked in aviation.

Korolyov operated differently. This is how Mark Gurevich, one of our leading designers, who was in charge of work on a reconnaissance satellite, described his first meeting with Korolyov:

> After reaching agreement in principle, Vladimir Nikolayevich sent me to Sergei Pavlovich to sign the decision—which had been thoroughly prepared and approved by all departments on both sides, ours and theirs—to launch our first offspring on the R-7. Korolyov didn't keep me waiting long in the reception area, but received me very quickly. He was friendly, but there was a shade of "patronage" in every word he said.
>
> Asking me to sit down at the table, Korolyov seated himself across from me. He began asking detailed questions about the satellite, including who ordered it and the purpose of the tests.
>
> He was surprised that only a couple of launches were planned on the R-7

and that the satellite was far from what it would be by the end of the program. We planned to test only the system of stabilization and orientation.

Leaning back in his chair, Korolyov asked curiously: "And where are you from? From aviation?"

Upon receiving a positive answer, he seemed satisfied and delivered a little lecture:

"That's obvious. Why have you and Volodya thought up all those stages? You should wait until the subcontractors give you supplies, assemble five satellites and launch them in accordance with the whole program. That's the only way to act in our business."

For some reason, Korolyov asked: "Do you think I would agree to repeat photographing the other side of the moon?" Gurevich remained silent. He was not a young man and had more than one project to his credit. He had gone through Lavochkin's school, headed work on the "Burya" from the very beginning, experienced the bitterness of failures, and had taught it to fly. When work on the "Burya" was shut down, Gurevich moved over to Chelomei and took charge of one of his most important and complex projects. What Korolyov was now saying contradicted the experience of his entire life. He couldn't agree with the chief designer, but didn't want to argue and was therefore trying painfully to think of a reply. But Sergei Pavlovich didn't expect an answer, and said didactically: "Rocket technology is not like aviation." As if suddenly remembering that he had other matters to attend to, he asked: "Where are your pieces of paper?"

Gurevich added: "He signed the agreement without comment."

Naturally, Gurevich reported the whole conversation to Chelomei after returning "home." Vladimir Nikolayevich was not surprised and commented only: "They're going to have a lot of trouble with the N-1."

I return to my narrative of Korolyov's conversation with Father, from which I digressed. As it happened, Sergei Pavlovich began talking about the main subject, the N-1.

Korolyov had prepared a so-called General's set of schematics for Father. These were not detailed blueprints, but drawings showing only the basic design. They were comprehensible to the nonspecialist and impressive to the layman.

These really were good enough to arouse great enthusiasm. The first drawing Sergei Pavlovich spread out on the table showed the new rocket stretching almost one hundred meters into the sky. Its first stage had an elegantly flared skirt, which made it look like the queen in an old chess set. It was being prepared for the enviable destiny of being the first rocket to deliver a man to the moon.

Korolyov began talking about it. Father listened attentively, his eyes focused on the picture. "The launch weight of the rocket is about three thousand tons—two thousand eight hundred to be exact, with three stages. The first operates on oxygen and kerosene, the next two on oxygen and hydrogen."

At these words Glushko grimaced involuntarily, but didn't say anything.

"But that's if the engine builders don't disappoint us," said Korolyov, glancing at Glushko. "Just in case, we are also preparing a spare, using the engines we already have. We'll begin flight tests in 1965, or no later than 1966."

The technical decision made in Pitsunda to install twenty-four engines was still in effect, but Korolyov hesitated momentarily and continued: "Maybe we'll use thirty of Kuznetsov's 150-ton engines. As the parameters of the interplanetary spaceship become more exact, its weight is increasing, so that we will have to lift somewhat more than 75 tons into orbit. Therefore, we will have to increase the thrust of the rocket and add engines." Without turning from his papers, Korolyov again darted a glance at Glushko. Father pretended not to notice.

"At the first opportunity"—Korolyov had talked about this before— "150-ton engines will be replaced by engines generating six hundred tons of thrust. That can't happen right away. They wouldn't be ready in time. We still need a lot of work on design and ground testing in order to have superpowerful thrust. Besides, such gigantic ground testbeds do not exist in the Soviet Union, and to build them is an additional problem."

According to Sergei Pavlovich, there was an advantage to having many engines in the first stage. If one failed, it wouldn't be a catastrophe. A special system would turn off the engine on the opposite side, to avoid any imbalance, and the remaining engines would complete the operation. There would still be excess thrust, even in the event of such a failure.

Father asked why they should develop six-hundred-ton engines if there was a simpler solution. Korolyov replied that he was not going to dwell on the numerous technical problems, but that work on powerful engines was necessary. Father didn't probe—if it had to be done, let them do it.

Sergei Pavlovich picked up the next page. It dealt with stages of the flight toward the moon. He proposed that the interplanetary spaceship launched into earth orbit have a two-man crew. The N-1 simply could not lift three people, as provided for in the American project.

Otherwise, the flight followed the same plan as the Apollo project. It's hard to imagine any other solution, since the laws of mechanics are the same for all.

A Soviet cosmonaut was to descend alone from moon orbit to its surface. His partner would be left in the orbital module to keep watch. If something happened to the cosmonaut on the moon, he could not count on any assistance. Korolyov's rationale was simple: If dust on the moon's surface was as deep as a five-story building was high, it wouldn't matter how many cosmonauts were there—they wouldn't be able to extricate themselves. If the surface was hard and the moon lander alighted without damage, a cosmonaut would not be frightened to be alone. His words sounded convincing, but I felt uncomfortable at the very thought of being alone on a strange world hundreds of thousands of kilometers from earth. What if he fell down? A cosmonaut might not be able to get up, in his bulky spacesuit. He might remain lying on his back, waving his arms and legs like a clumsy beetle turned over with a twig by a mischievous child.

The plan called for the lunar module to fly around the moon first, with the landing coming afterward—just as was the case with automated lunar stations.

All this put Father in a good mood. This briefing sounded so much more specific than previous ones. He could trace the progress of the stages, and the function of each stage was clear. There seemed to be a real opportunity to leave the Americans behind once again. Korolyov's ideas appealed to Father more and more, but he didn't forget his concerns here on earth. He wanted to know how much the whole project would cost. This time Korolyov had all the estimates on a separate piece of paper. According to his calculations, it would take several billion rubles (I don't remember how many, but that's not so important) to carry out the project. Korolyov was simply not able to calculate the real expenditures. Each state committee and regional economic council paid for work in its own way, some raising and others lowering actual expenses, depending on their own departmental advantage. The most that Sergei Pavlovich could do was to summarize his own requirements and those of his closest associates. But even that figure caused Father to shudder.

By the way, the amount spent by the Soviet Union on the moon program is not known to this day. Korolyov's successors think that 3.6 billion rubles had been spent by the time work stopped in January of 1973. It's just as unclear now as it was in 1963 what was and was not included in this 3.6 billion. I have a hunch that if one could make an accurate count of all expenditures, the amount would be four or five times as great.

Meanwhile, Korolyov was continuing his report. He put another sheet on the table from his seemingly endless stack of papers. It showed the rocket's layout. In cross-section, it resembled a toy pyramid. Pipelines were threaded through spherical tanks of diminishing size.

I was surprised that Sergei Pavlovich had rejected the traditional layout, in which the outer shell of the rocket also served as a tank for the fuel or oxidizer, thereby saving precious and much-needed kilograms. But in his design, the sphere-shaped tanks were covered by the cone-shaped outer shell. Korolyov began to explain that there was a good reason for this unusual solution—it was the result of a profound analysis of design. This spherical modular layout made it possible to extend the rocket by adding another stage underneath, or to decrease its height. Each succeeding stage of the rocket, from bottom to top, could be used independently without modification.

The huge diameter of the stages was a vulnerable feature in all powerful launchers. The size of rockets was of necessity largely dependent on the ability to transport them.

Sergei Pavlovich proposed that the rocket be assembled in one place. He planned to build an assembly workshop, or rather a plant, at the launch site. There, mega-liter sphere-shaped tanks of different diameters would be welded onto a structure and the launcher assembled. No matter how you looked at it, a real plant would have to be built, one that would require thousands of people—workers and highly qualified engineers—as well as hundreds of thousands of square feet. Everything would be located in the Aral desert, which would entail the construction of housing and provision of other services.

Father was noncommittal.

"Think about it and prepare some proposals. We will discuss them in the Presidium and decide then."

It was time to have lunch. The other end of the table where they were meeting was already being set.

The conversation for which Father had invited the scientists was still to come. The atmosphere was tense. His guests were wondering when he would start, but Father didn't want to cast a pall over the meeting. His role as a mentor, scolding negligent students, was at odds with the deep respect and affection he felt in his heart for both designers. The lunch provided an excuse for delaying the unavoidable discussion and Father grasped at the chance. He summoned his guests to the table with a smile, accompanying his gesture with the words: "Business can wait. Let's not ruin our appetites."

Korolyov and Glushko were obviously relieved at the delay.

The lunch proceeded without any toasts, in a businesslike atmosphere. They each drank one shot-glass of cognac, about fifteen grams apiece. Father said: "We still need to work." When we left the table, Father said: "We must have a private conversation," and drew Korolyov and Glushko into the next room, closing the door. I went to sit in the living room.

They were absent for about forty minutes. It was only later, after they left, that I heard about their discussion.

Father emerged from the room first. Heading across the living room toward the staircase to the second floor, he apologized, not very politely, that he had to leave because there were some documents requiring his immediate attention.

Korolyov and Glushko followed two or three steps behind Father. Both looked deflated. Korolyov was explaining something to Glushko. As they passed by me, I heard a sibilant whisper: "You're a snake in the grass."

Glushko didn't answer and turned away.

Father went upstairs. He usually didn't allow himself be so casual with his guests. No urgent documents had arrived. The head of the guards would have reported it, but he had not come to the house. Father simply wanted to cool off after such an unpleasant conversation, so he invented urgent business.

Glushko defused the situation. He remarked to no one in particular that he wanted to get some fresh air and was going to take a walk in the woods. Valentin Petrovich went out onto the verandah.

Korolyov remained where he was for a few moments and then moved toward me. He sat down next to me on the couch and said nothing for a long time. His silence made me uncomfortable. I fidgeted and again felt myself to be out of place. Suddenly he said: "Volodya is making a big mistake. Nothing good will come out of this space circus."

He was talking about Chelomei. I didn't understand what he meant by "space circus" and waited silently for an explanation. "Phased systems, interceptions in space . . . All these chases after who knows what? Spaceships assembled in orbit are only good for science fiction. In life we should be realistic. Is it possible even to imagine that up there"—he pointed upward with his finger—"two specks of dust can find each other? It might be possible in the distant future, but for now it's simply a fantasy."

I should explain something in this context. During those years of romantic aspirations toward distant worlds, both we and the Americans had seriously discussed the technical possibility of sending a manned spaceship to Mars. Design work showed that such a spaceship would be heavy and bulky, and most specialists agreed that it would have to be assembled from parts delivered directly into earth orbit by rockets. Chelomei was known to be the main proponent of assembling ships in space. Sergei Pavlovich, it turned out, supported the opposite point of view.

"Volodya is mistaken," Sergei Pavlovich continued. "A rendezvous in orbit is something for the next generation, no matter what our officials promise. . . . Therefore, Braun's Saturn, your UR-500, and all those rockets with their attached strap-on fuel tanks are a dead end. The money will run out and you'll reach the limit of strength. The Saturn is approaching it. Three thousand tons! Another thousand, or two, three at the most, and . . . kaput. The shell won't hold and the rocket will fold up like an accordion.

"We, on the other hand, will assemble everything on the ground and deliver it into space, without resorting to tricks. We won't have to engage in endless searches for lost modules or assemble them under absolutely impossible conditions. How are you going to test it? What if something fails?"

He paused.

"The only correct solution is to assemble rockets on the spot, like ocean-going ships. They are built on ways and launched into the water. That's what we will do: weld the tanks, assemble the rocket right at the launch site, and test and launch there. Otherwise it won't work. Today's N-1 is already hard to move from one place to another, and the next one will weigh seven thousand tons. Then twelve thousand, and after that, eighteen thousand tons."

Korolyov had finished what he had to say and lost interest in me. We could clearly hear the sound of unhurried steps from somewhere above. Apparently Father was coming down the staircase. He looked into the room.

"Here you are," said Father, as if he had been looking for us all over the house.

He smiled brightly. It was obvious that he didn't intend to continue any unpleasant discussions.

"Let's go and have some tea," said Father to Korolyov, and added: "Where is Glushko?" I explained that he had gone for a walk. "Find him and bring him to the verandah for tea. And you come too," ordered Father, as he drew Korolyov toward the door. I found Valentin Petrovich in the woods. He was sitting on a bench, enjoying the quiet. I called him and we returned to the house.

The tea drinking proceeded in a calm atmosphere. Nothing interfered with the peacefulness of that warm, quiet summer evening. Father gave up trying to reconcile the two.

THE TEST BAN TREATY

Negotiations on banning nuclear tests entered their final phase. It seemed that both sides had tested to their heart's content, were persuaded that testing was harmful, and had decided to stop it. After our two series of explosions in the atmosphere and the U.S. experiments with nuclear weapons in space had been completed, all ambitions were satisfied and the military were provided with "everything essential" for years to come. However, something interfered at the last minute every time, and the already negotiated agreement seemed about to fall through.

We began the new year, 1963, with optimism: the agreement was supposed to be signed any day.

In an interview with the newspaper the *Daily Express*, published January 1, Father expressed his readiness to stop testing.

But that last step didn't come easily.

There were more stumbling blocks than anyone anticipated. Two were especially large. Father tried again to go back to his old idea of a total ban on testing. He attempted to persuade Kennedy that the opposing sides had quite enough weapons and that it was time to stop. But he immediately tripped over the question of inspection. There was general agreement that explosions in the atmosphere could not be concealed, but detection of underground explosions was in dispute.

After conducting experiments, our scientists claimed that it was possible to identify an underground nuclear explosion without leaving one's own country. However, American scientists were afraid of missing something and demanded on-site inspection. That we were extremely reluctant to accept such an initiative in those years is quite well known.

Father was very averse to "crawling underground." I have already said that he thought underground tests were too expensive and hurt the Soviet economy. Therefore he decided to try again to reach a compromise. The Americans insisted on inspections. With great reluctance, Father forced himself to agree and, in a letter to Kennedy dated January 9, 1963, he proposed limiting inspections to two or three a year. However, the Pentagon, the Atomic Energy Agency, and the Department of Energy wanted dozens of on-site inspections—and at any sites on Soviet territory they chose. The president decided to accept their position. Nevertheless, he didn't give up hope of an agreement. Simultaneously with his reply to Father, Kennedy publicly announced a moratorium on conducting underground explosions during the negotiations. Father considered the U.S. position to be unacceptable and complained: "Give them an inch and they take a mile."

The moratorium didn't last even two weeks. The president announced that, in view of Moscow's inflexibility, he was forced to resume testing. Forced.

Father complained bitterly about the U.S. position in an April interview with the Italian newspaper *Il Giorno*. Eventually, he gave up. Underground tests were fated to continue for many years, as did the problem of control over them, including inspections.

Another complication arose with the appearance of new nuclear powers, Britain and France. Father was worried about being deceived if the Americans began setting off nuclear charges after repainting them in British or French colors. We would begin to lag behind, as in previous years, and the issue of resuming our own tests would resurface. An agreement was finally reached on this matter as well. Britain accepted the conditions of the agreement, and Father just ignored France. De Gaulle had not been getting along with Washington and London for a long time, and Father hoped that Americans would not be given access to French test sites.

After that things progressed more quickly. Intensive negotiations resumed in April. Details were worked out and sharp edges smoothed over. Finally, both sides were pulling in the same direction.

On April 23 Father received the U.S. and British ambassadors, Foy

Kohler and Sir Humphrey Trevelyan. They discussed the main provisions in the agreement. Averell Harriman flew to Moscow immediately afterward. Though the main subject of the negotiations was confirmation of the Vienna Agreements on Laos, the test ban was also on the agenda.

Father agreed to move forward and President Kennedy met him halfway. On June 12 *Pravda* published a report of the president's speech at American University in Washington.

Kennedy said: "We are separated by an abyss. . . . We have to coexist." And he went on to give the world hope, confirming the U.S. ban on further tests in the atmosphere and informing his audience that he, Khrushchev, and Macmillan had finally agreed that their representatives would meet in Moscow to reach an agreement on testing. So it was from the lips of the U.S. president that the Soviet people heard this extremely important news.

Father occasionally enjoyed using this method. On the one hand, everybody understood the significance of the fact that something was published; on the other hand, he himself had said nothing and committed himself to nothing.

The decisive moment was at hand. Averell Harriman and Lord Hailsham, the British government's representative, arrived in Moscow on July 13. They were to thrash out the final details with Gromyko. It was agreed that the signing ceremony of the treaty would be held in Moscow.

Father was extremely pleased. I would even say happy. I still entertained some doubts. Were we being deceived? Wouldn't the Americans leave us behind because of their extensive experience in underground testing? Father dismissed that with a joke. He repeated what he had said in Vienna: If we can already destroy the United States, why should we waste resources on destroying them many times over?

Finally, on August 4 in Moscow, Gromyko, Hume, and Rusk signed an agreement between the USSR, the United Kingdom, and the United States, banning nuclear tests in three places: the atmosphere, underwater, and in space.

Father was present during the signing ceremony, together with U.N. Acting Secretary-General U Thant. That was when they agreed to establish a direct communication link, the "hotline," between Moscow and Washington, to be used in case of unforeseen situations. Now there would be an opportunity to discern the true intentions of the parties without resorting to intermediaries, such as ambassadors, intelligence agents, and journalists.

The next day Father flew to Pitsunda for his vacation. I stayed in Moscow. Father invited Dean Rusk to have dinner with him there, on the shores of the Black Sea, and to have a rest at the same time. It was an informal—almost friendly—meeting. It was the first time since Father had said good-bye to Ambassador Llewellyn Thompson that he gave such a warm reception to an

American guest, as if he meant to forget the past and open a new page in our relations.

I am convinced that signing the agreement on test limitation was one of the lessons our top officials drew from the Cuban Missile Crisis. A situation in which you have to make decisions, not just talk about them, brings home a sense of responsibility as never before. After the crisis many things appeared in a different light and the dominant emotion was one of apprehension: What if we had waited too long!

Since he trusted the U.S. president, Father was ready for a long period of cooperation with John Kennedy. He thought that since they had reached an agreement without damaging the dignity of their countries and had survived such a serious test as the Cuban Missile Crisis, they could cooperate in solving other problems.

Father did not idealize the president. He didn't expect that Kennedy, a representative of a different ideology, would become a real friend. No, he was thinking of ways to survive on this planet, since fate had decreed that we would live as neighbors in what he called peaceful coexistence. He referred more and more often to his simple calculation that six years still lay ahead, based on his conviction that Kennedy would be reelected to a second term. In this dynamic world, that was a considerable period of time.

KEEPING VIETNAM AT ARM'S LENGTH

Meanwhile, a new problem had appeared. The Americans were being drawn more and more deeply into the war in Vietnam. The Cuban lesson did not extend to Southeast Asia; Hanoi and Saigon were a long way off, both from the United States and the USSR.

Father followed the development of events attentively, but was in no rush to interfere. He was afraid that the Chinese would try hard to force a confrontation there between us and the Americans. I don't know whether he was overestimating Chinese influence on Vietnam, but in this case it was better to overestimate than to underestimate.

Father was also in no hurry to provide military assistance. When they launched an offensive in the south, the Vietnamese didn't ask our advice and acted at their own risk. So Father certainly preferred to wait and see on that occasion.

COOPERATION IN OUTER SPACE

In the autumn of 1963, Father returned several times to his conversation with Kennedy in Vienna about the possibility of working jointly on a lunar project. At that time, concerned about military secrets, he rejected the president's proposal to cooperate and limited himself to an agreement on joint peaceful research in space. It was more a statement about exchanging information than a serious program of cooperation.

Father's views gradually changed. The possibility of revealing some Soviet secrets to American scientists didn't seem quite so terrible anymore. Previously, Father had been especially concerned that the Americans would find out that the Soviet Union had so few intercontinental missiles. Moreover, the level of Soviet missile readiness couldn't be compared to that of the opposite side. Such information, in Father's opinion, might push the hotheads toward preventive measures. Before they missed their chance.

The situation had begun to change in 1963. R-16s were being deployed, one after another. The missile development program was acquiring a more polished look. It wouldn't hurt if they found out that the Soviet Union possessed a good number of intercontinental nuclear launchers. Father wasn't fazed by the fact that these missiles were only in the initial project stage. They would soon appear on their launch pads. The first step in that direction was taken that autumn. Flight tests of Yangel's R-36 began in September and were successful.

The meeting with Korolyov and Glushko made Father think again about the lunar program. Sergei Pavlovich was asking too high a price for his N-1. It was sometime during the second half of September that I first heard Father talking, or rather thinking out loud, about the possibility of concluding an agreement with the United States to implement a joint lunar program. Apparently the impetus was provided by the U.S. president's speech at a session of the U.N. General Assembly on September 20, in which he again proposed that we fly to the moon together. Father still didn't share his thoughts with anyone, but I knew from experience that if he were thinking along those lines he would eventually speak out. When he was ready.

The last time Father returned to this subject was in November, about a week before Kennedy's tragic death. He said that when Soviet ambassador Anatoly Dobrynin met with the U.S. president, Kennedy referred to the lunar program (along with a whole series of other issues) and asked Dobrynin to assure Father that his proposal to associate the lunar projects of our two countries was a serious one and that he would like to discuss it in detail in the future.[2] "I must think about it," said Father pensively, adding: "It's very tempting. We would save lots of money, not to speak of everything else." He didn't explain what he meant by "everything else." I can't say that I was

---

2. In his memoirs (Anatoly Dobrynin, *In Confidence* [New York: Random House, 1995], p. 106), Dobrynin writes that during his last meeting with the president on August 26, 1963, Kennedy "asked me to let Khrushchev know that it would be mutually advantageous for both countries to cooperate more actively in outer space, thus sharing our huge investment; in due course there might be a Soviet-American flight to the moon."

pleased by this information. It seemed to me that it would be very dangerous to reveal our secrets to an adversary.

Now they were driven by the myth of Soviet superiority: powerful launchers, mysterious fuel, fantastically precise instruments, and who knows what else. But we knew that our superiority didn't amount to much. Maybe our rockets were just as good, but they were certainly no better than those launched from Cape Canaveral. In 1957, and to some degree in 1961, you could talk about the unique payload capacity of the R-7. But that was all in the past: the UR-500 and the N-1 were substantially inferior to the Saturn. I had to express my concerns to Father. He agreed with my reasoning, but drew the diametrically opposite conclusion. Father turned it around to suit his own point of view: If we couldn't stay ahead, there was all the more reason to join efforts.

He didn't dismiss my fears concerning military secrets, but considered them exaggerated. Father again cited Kennedy's acknowledgment that we were capable of destroying the United States. But he rephrased his response somewhat:

> It doesn't make the slightest difference whether we use more advanced missiles or less advanced missiles. If the Americans believe that something like that is possible in principle, then other factors will be secondary. Kennedy is a clever politician. War doesn't enter into his plans, nor into ours. We will agree and decide matters peacefully. In six years, when he has to give up his seat in the White House, we'll have more than enough "100s." So our country will be too much for the Americans to cope with, even if their policy changes radically.

Father fell silent and our conversation came to an end.

FATE INTERVENES

Father found out about John Kennedy's assassination on the evening of November 23. It's difficult to say now at exactly what time, but it was already quite dark out, which was not surprising for the end of November. We had finished dinner, Father had read the evening mail and was planning to go up to his bedroom on the second floor when the government phone rang in the living room.

Evening phone calls to our residence were rare. Father thought that he should work in the office and rest at home—that is, if pouring over stacks of papers brought from the Kremlin every evening can be called rest. Father was disturbed only in exceptional circumstances.

"Good evening, Comrade Gromyko," said Father in response to the first words of the invisible caller. "What's the matter? What's happened?"

Father listened intently for a long time, his expression changing to one of deep concern. He finally said in a depressed tone of voice: "Call the ambassador. Find out more. Perhaps it's some mistake. Then call me again right away."

Father hung up and walked to the middle of the room, as if undecided whether to sit down at the table or wait where he was. He shifted from one foot to the other. A bitter expression was fixed on his face.

Since Father's behavior seemed very unusual I couldn't resist asking him what happened, though without really expecting an answer. One was not supposed to ask in such cases.

To my surprise, Father answered readily. My question interrupted his unhappy train of thought. He said that American radio broadcasts were saying that someone had attempted to assassinate John Kennedy. The president was on a trip around the country. It was not clear whether he was wounded or killed. Reports were contradictory. Of course, if there had really been an assassination attempt, it was hardly likely that reporters would have full information.

"I asked Gromyko to find out more from the ambassador," Father repeated what I had already heard him say over the phone. "Of course, he's not likely to have exact information, either."

After a pause, Father said somewhat distractedly: "If the president is alive . . ."

He didn't finish. What did he want to say?

Hearing what Father had said, Mama and my sister Lena, who were reading in the dining room, abandoned what they were doing and joined us. There was a heavy silence. A small, polished round table and three chairs stood in the middle of the room. Father circled around them. I sat on a chair by the phone. Mama and Lena sat down on a small couch against the wall.

The phone was silent. Father lost patience. He looked up Gromyko's number in the directory and dialed. The secretary answered that Andrei Andreyevich was at home. Father identified himself and asked that Gromyko call him at the apartment. A minute later the phone rang.

Sounding slightly annoyed, Father asked: "Why haven't you called me back?"

"We put in a call to Washington, but we can't seem to get through." Andrei Andreyevich started trying to justify himself.

"Why Washington?" Father was surprised.

"To the ambassador, as you ordered" Gromyko answered.

"I meant the U.S. ambassador, Kohler," said Father, beginning to get irritated. "They would have informed him immediately if something bad happened. Call him and then call me back immediately."

Father hung up and gave half a smile.

"What a dunce. He called our Embassy in Washington instead of the Americans," he explained. "He'll call back."

Father resumed his circling. This time he didn't have long to wait. Andrei Andreyevich reported that President Kennedy had been shot in Dallas, Texas. The president was dead.

Still holding the phone, Father paused, as if thinking something over. Then he began to talk about expressing our condolences and asked about our participation in the funeral ceremony. Gromyko said that the ambassador could represent our country, but that he could fly to Washington as well. He said that on the one hand, Kennedy was the leader of an imperialist country and we should not particularly grieve over him. On the other hand, the appearance of a Soviet minister would be appreciated. Gromyko referred to the precedent of his attendance at the funeral of John Foster Dulles.

Father had already managed to think over the matter. He felt that the ministerial rank was not adequate in this case. A president should be buried by a president, but since Brezhnev was little known in America, he thought that it would be best to entrust this sad mission to Mikoyan. Gromyko agreed immediately.

In conclusion, they decided that Andrei Andreyevich would find out when Father could visit the U.S. Embassy to pay his condolences. Father said that, in addition to the official protocol telegram to Johnson, the new president, he also wished to send condolences to Kennedy's widow, Jacqueline.

He thought for a bit and then added: "And from Nina Petrovna separately. They met in Vienna."

This was unprecedented. Mama accompanied Father on trips and people had gradually grown used to the idea, but that was the extent of her role in state affairs. By this gesture, Father wanted to emphasize as far as possible the sincerity and personal nature of his sympathy.

The next day Father, accompanied by Gromyko, visited Ambassador Kohler and signed the book. A message went out to Johnson, which read: "I will preserve the memory of my personal meetings with President John F. Kennedy, a leader of wide-ranging views, who had a realistic grasp of the world situation and who tried through negotiations to find ways to resolve the international problems now dividing the world."

Father wrote to Jacqueline Kennedy: "He inspired great respect in all who knew him, and meetings with him will remain in my memory forever."

Mikoyan arrived in Washington on the twenty-fourth.

A day later, President Johnson made a statement confirming his country's hard-line position toward Vietnam.

A few days later, during our evening walk, Father suddenly recalled his ideas about the moon program. He said bitterly that that was all over now.

He had trusted Kennedy and counted on mutual understanding. He had been ready for risky (for those times) contacts, but with Kennedy, not with the U.S. administration. Now Kennedy was gone.

He thought for a few moments, then added that everything would be different with Johnson.

President Kennedy did not have the six years that Father counted on. Father did not have them either.

DISCONTENT AT HOME

Father began the new year of 1964, his last year of active political work, with a peace initiative. He called on the heads of countries and governments to resolve all territorial matters under dispute by peaceful means. Such appeals had appeared before, but this time he referred to specific places where war threatened to break out: Germany, Vietnam, Korea, and Taiwan. I see this appeal as reflecting still another of the lessons from the Cuban Missile Crisis: the time for threats had passed.

It seemed that we had thought of everything with respect to Cuba: a treaty between two sovereign states, no different from many similar ones concluded with other countries—but then look what it turned into.

A new period of world history was beginning. A period when war ceased to serve as an instrument of policy. Not everybody accepted this metamorphosis at the same time. It was given to some to recognize it earlier, some later. Father was among the first, and he purposefully sheathed his sword.

Meanwhile, sometime during the first months of 1964 the seeds of a new crisis were emerging. A crisis that Father, as it turned out, was not fated to survive. This time events were not unfolding somewhere far away, but here at home, in Moscow. "They" had decided to get rid of Father.

He had devoted the past decade to attempts to improve and energize the mechanism of a centralized economy, to search out and demonstrate in real life its advantages over anarchy, over a market economy. The numerous reorganizations following one after another, the changes, the elimination of some departments and appearance of others on their ruins, the fight to reduce the swollen bureaucratic apparatus, to deprive its members of their real and imaginary privileges—everything was directed at achieving that goal. At first it seemed that progress was being made, but soon everything slowed down again; reforms came to a halt time and time again, as they ran into insuperable barriers. Shouts, trips around the country, and attempts to get to the bottom of issues didn't improve the situation. On the contrary, decisions made on the run and his interference in everything just caused more confusion.

Father didn't understand what was wrong. He grew nervous, became angry, quarreled, looked for culprits and didn't find them. Deep inside, he began subconsciously to understand that the problem was not in the details. It was the system itself that didn't work; but he couldn't change his beliefs. Father turned to the Yugoslav practice, but didn't find the answer there. He sought remedies from Professor Yevsei Liberman. Liberman, a pragmatist, came very close to understanding the need to introduce a market economy, calling it material self-interest; but as someone who had grown up while an irreconcilable struggle was being waged against any manifestations of freedom in the economy, he could not bring himself to pronounce the seditious word.

It was time to turn the page.

The Twentieth Party Congress, which had exposed Stalin's crimes and denounced the repressions, condemned the centralized system of administration to death. The fear that had supported it all those years disappeared, but nothing had emerged to replace it. That was only gradually understood, but the more it was recognized, the more the top echelon lost the ability to dictate its will. The apparat, obedient only yesterday, stopped carrying out—simply ignored—any of Father's orders it didn't like. The fear of death had disappeared, and all the other levers of power were in the hands of the apparat itself.

There were endless transfers from one official position to another; temporary demotions were compensated for by new promotions. Of course, there were some tragic outcomes. In the drive for early fulfillment of the plan to overtake America in milk and meat production, Ryazan provincial committee secretary Aleksei Nikolayevich Larionov decided not to bother raising livestock in his region, but to buy meat from his neighbors. His triumphant report was publicized around the country, but the falsification came to light. He had hardly managed to pin the star of Hero of Socialist Labor on his jacket when, overwhelmed by the disgrace, he shot himself in the head. Others peacefully and discreetly retired. The Stalinist era was over. In order to avoid trouble, you had only to stay within certain boundaries.

Everyone was fed up with the "Old Man" and his incessant activity.

His closest associates, most of them ten years his junior, waited impatiently for the time when they could grasp the levers of power themselves and be free of his supervision, exhortations, and reprimands. He was becoming unbearable, and they felt the urge to speed up the process.

The apparat longed for calm and stability. They were sick and tired of all those transfers and shakeups. They wanted to enjoy life, to forget the fears of Stalin's era, to relax from the constant, nervous expectation of reorganizations. They needed their own reliable person at the top, and the sooner the better.

The Army complained about reductions in force, which resulted not only in men going home, but in officers losing their jobs. Now they suddenly had to change their profession and begin new lives in middle age.

Meanwhile, there were rumors about a total reorganization: not just a reduction but a radical change in the structure of the armed forces. The generals yearned for a leader who would "understand" their hopes and protect their interests, and the sooner the better.

The intelligentsia had also lost their faith in Father. He managed to quarrel with many of his recent supporters. He told artists how to paint, poets how to write verses, directors how to stage plays and make films. Even musicians did not escape. Today we can try to determine his degree of responsibility and the true sources of inspiration for that witch-hunt,[3] but at the time Father was the only one visible. It seemed that everyone would breathe more easily if only he were gone. People are always impatient to get rid of what bothers them.

Convinced of the economic advantages of large, mechanized agricultural production, Father embarked on an energetic policy of reducing "inefficient" household and private plots. He felt that they tied the peasants' hands and would be a burden when the future brought abundance. The peasants thought otherwise and cursed this reformer, recently so popular. They expected only relief from changes coming at the top.

In a country overflowing with Father's portraits, his name was associated with every policy. People were fed up with the incessant paeans of praise to him.

Father had exhausted his resources. His time had run out. The experiment of building a society based on a centralized economy was coming to an end. Scientists say that a negative result is also a result, but that doesn't make it any easier for the guinea pig undergoing the experiment.

Analysis of the reasons and sources for the mistakes and defeats is a subject for history. Now something different had to be tried. But in what direction? Why take a path that led the country forward, but into the unknown?

Those who made the decisions and held the reins tightly in their hands longed, as did the apparat, for peace, not a tempest—for sufficiency, not prosperity. For all the people, of course, but if that was impossible, at least for the elite. The time of transformations had passed. An era of ponderous stability was arriving. They made the choice. They took a step back. That was how the historical pattern manifested itself.

THE OPPOSITION EMERGES

At the top they struck a bargain rather quickly. It turned out that two groups of Father's opponents were moving toward each other. On the one hand,

---

3. "Witch-hunt" reference is to repressive measures taken against the intelligentsia and the church during the last five years of Khrushchev's tenure.

there was the group of Muscovite Ukrainians who had followed Father to the capital, his "supporters" from the periphery. Brezhnev became their natural leader; the lines of communication with provincial committees, republics, the Army, and the KGB were in his hands. Podgorny and Polyansky sided with him.[4] They had joined the Central Committee and the Council of Ministers rather recently, but they felt sure of themselves.

The other group was headed by Shelepin, the leader of the younger members—the Komsomols, as they were called. His people had infiltrated everywhere, into the apparat, the Army, the KGB. When new personnel were added to the apparat, they came from the Komsomol or, more precisely, from its Central Committee.

Having met, they joined forces. The young people had to yield the leadership to Brezhnev. Without him, chances for success were sharply reduced.

Father's seventieth birthday arrived. On April 17, 1964, saccharine paeans of praise were heard on all sides as neighbor tried to outdo neighbor. After listening to all the assurances of devotion and wishes for long and productive work at one of the regular sessions of the Presidium, Father said that he planned to step down from active work. There was a chorus of protest. Without him, life would simply come to a stop. Father insisted and referred, this time in a public speech, to his desire to yield his place to the young. His intentions were serious, but he didn't set any date for his retirement. He once mentioned to me that he wanted to put it off until the Twenty-third Congress and then make a final decision. This uncertainty suited neither Brezhnev nor Shelepin. It was hard to decide on the first step, but now they didn't see any sense in stopping halfway.

Invisible and dangerous preparations to effect a change in power were launched immediately after the splendid birthday celebrations. Trusted people traveled to near and distant regions and began, as if by chance, to talk with provincial committee first secretaries about the "Old Man," sounding them out cautiously and ready at any point to retreat and turn everything into a joke. There was virtually no need to do so, since sooner or later they found a common language. Then a plus sign was put against someone's name on the list of the Central Committee members Brezhnev kept in his safe. There were hardly any minuses, since Brezhnev avoided talking with those sure to be unresponsive. At the decisive moment they would be blocked, and if necessary, isolated.

Unlike Kozlov, Brezhnev didn't argue with Father. On the contrary, he

---

4. Nikolai Viktorovich Podgorny, Presidium member and secretary of the Central Committee of the CPSU, who became chairman of the Presidium of the Supreme Soviet (technically, Soviet head of state) from 1965 to 1977. Dimitri Stepanovich Polyansky had been a full Presidium member since 1960.

became infinitely attentive. His public eulogies exceeded all bounds. The other members of the Presidium of the Central Committee copied him, each trying to outdo the other. Father frowned acidly, but didn't put a stop to the glorification. How could he stop them when any objection resulted in a new outpouring of praise, this time of his modesty?

After those syrupy eulogies, Brezhnev would summon KGB chairman Semichastny to his office and hold long and confidential talks with him. He simply couldn't bring himself to decide on a date. Fear was paralyzing his will. He dreamed of everything happening by itself, by other people's hands. Brezhnev thought that Father's physical elimination would be the simplest solution—with the KGB's help, naturally. They discussed every method you could think of. Brezhnev seized on one method, then another.

At first he suggested poisoning Father. That kind of death seemed more natural to him. However, the KGB chairman was cautious. Semichastny was sickened by the idea of murder. Besides, he belonged to the other group, the "Komsomols," who thought of Brezhnev as a transitional figure, just a stage. Why should he be handed the trump card?

Semichastny refused, saying that the proposal was impossible. He told Brezhnev that the woman who served meals to Father was devoted to him and had worked for him since the war, since Stalingrad. It was impossible to bribe her, as Leonid Ilyich suggested. Besides, the logic of the crime would necessitate the elimination of the murderer, and then the murderer of the murderer, and so on ad infinitum.

"Then it would be my turn," said Semichastny, smiling, "and then yours." He nodded at Brezhnev.

Leonid Ilyich withdrew his proposal, only to replace it with a new one. Crime attracted him like a magnet. His next idea was to arrange a plane crash during Father's return from a state visit to Egypt. I was also on that plane. And again, Semichastny managed to talk him out of it. He absolutely refused to participate in the mass murder of a plane's passengers and crew.

Brezhnev seemed to have a vivid imagination. He substituted an automobile accident for the plane crash. He thought that Leningrad, where Father planned to have a brief meeting with Tito at the beginning of June, would be the most convenient place. But nothing came of that either, since Semichastny firmly resisted the idea.

His last plan was simply born out of desperation. Leonid Ilyich suggested arresting Father in the outskirts of Moscow, while he was returning by train from a visit to Scandinavia at the beginning of July. Semichastny rejected this plan as well. Brezhnev couldn't answer the question: "And then what? What follows his arrest?"

Father returned safely to Moscow. Who knows, perhaps Brezhnev remembered his frustration when he decided later to replace Semichastny with Andropov?

Were there any attempts to warn Father? As the years go by it's increasingly difficult to answer that question. There are fewer and fewer witnesses. Some of them are not interested in the truth. One thing is clear: there were very few. Father was isolated.

What have I managed to find out? A woman called my sister Rada during the summer of 1964. Rada doesn't remember her name. Saying that she had important information, she insisted on meeting my sister. Rada did not agree to meet her and finally the woman, in despair, said over the phone that she knew of an apartment where conspirators were meeting and discussing plans to remove Khrushchev.

Rada answered: "But why are you calling me? The KGB takes care of such things. Call them."

"How can I call them when KGB chairman Semichastny is taking part in those meetings himself! That was just why I wanted to talk to you. This is a real conspiracy."

The information didn't seem serious to Rada. She didn't want to spend time in an unpleasant meeting and answered that, unfortunately, she could do nothing. She was a private individual, and this was a matter for government agencies. She asked the woman not to call her anymore.

Valentin Vasilyevich Pivovarov, the former head of a Central Committee administrative department, approached Rada with a similar warning. Because of his call, Rada consulted an old friend of our family, Aleksandr Mikhailovich Markov, at the time director of the Health Ministry's fourth main department. He advised her to pay no attention to this information, attributing it to Pivovarov's exaggerated sense of vigilance. Rada listened to this authoritative opinion and dismissed the episode.

I heard about another interesting episode during a conversation with Melor Sturua, the veteran *Izvestiya* correspondent. Every generation has its own main theme. Our generation, the "Men of the Sixties," is drawn to the subject of the first "thaw." And as Sturua and I were talking, the subject turned to Father.

In 1964 Davy, Melor's brother, was working as a secretary of the Georgian Communist Party Central Committee. That summer he came to Moscow, apparently in advance of the July session of the Supreme Soviet. He went straight from the airport to his brother's apartment. Melor had not seen him so worried for a long time.

"Something unpleasant and incomprehensible is going on," said Davy as soon as he walked in. "Some kind of trouble is brewing around Nikita Sergeyevich."

He told Melor that before leaving Tbilisi he had met with V. P. Mzhevanadze, the first secretary of the Central Committee of the Georgian Communist Party, who hinted that it was time to get rid of Khrushchev. Of course, he didn't say so openly, but the trained ear unfailingly catches such nuances.

Now Davy was asking his brother for advice. Should he warn Nikita Sergeyevich? Or say nothing? It was not a simple situation—treachery and denunciation are equally repugnant to a Georgian. And besides, who knew what the consequences might be?

Melor suggested that Davy meet with Adzhubei at once. Sturua had access to his office at *Izvestiya* at any time. But his brother should make up his own mind. In that family they were well aware of what could happen if Mzhevanadze, and especially those above him, found out who had exposed the conspirators. Davy hesitated for only a few seconds before saying curtly: "Let's go." Half an hour later they walked into the office of the editor in chief of the country's second most important newspaper.

Davy briefly described the suspicious conversation with Mzhevanadze. Adzhubei commented acidly that in general Georgians disliked Khrushchev.

With respect to Mzhevanadze, such a comment sounded strange at the very least.[5] Davy Sturua objected, saying that he was not referring to Georgia. All the threads led back to Moscow. Something serious was going on.

But Aleksei Ivanovich didn't bother listening. He only made some incomprehensible remark to the effect that he and Shelepin had known about all that for a long time.

Disheartened, the Sturua brothers left the office. What was known? Who knew it? What did Shelepin have to do with it, when it concerned Khrushchev?

They decided not to discuss such a dangerous subject with anyone else. Aleksei Ivanovich didn't say a word to Father about the conversation.

"ET TU, BRUTE?"

We had an unpleasant incident at home not long before Aleksei Ivanovich's conversation with the Sturua brothers. That day Father left for the dacha after work, as he did all the previous days that summer. He stopped by the apartment on the way and asked if anyone wished to go with him. Only Rada and I wanted to join him.

At the dacha we took our usual walk on a path running along the fence that surrounded the dacha. Then it was time for dinner. There was a simple meal set on the table. Father didn't like fancy foods. A freshly opened bottle of mineral water bubbled on Father's left in the corner of the table, next to

---

5. Throughout his life Vasily Pavlovich Mzhevanadze was considered Georgian in name only. In 1953, after Stalin's death and Beria's arrest, Father needed someone reliable and trustworthy. Then he thought of General Mzhevanadze, who had served in the Ukraine. He knew Vasily Pavlovich well from wartime. So the general was turned into a Central Committee secretary. Now Mzhevanadze had changed into one of Father's active antagonists. Evidently, his old Ukrainian connections came into play.—S.K.

tea glasses. Neat slices of lemon lay on a saucer. Everything looked the same as usual.

Father sat down at the table, fidgeted a little, and then asked the waitress to bring him some cognac. He seldom drank, from a small ten-gram bell-shaped shot glass, but the pantry always held a supply of Georgian cognac and dry Ukrainian wine.

In response to Father's request, the waitress muttered: "There isn't any."

"Why not?" asked Father in surprise.

"Aleksei Ivanovich drank it all," said the waitress somberly.

"Wha-a-at?" Harsh notes sounded in Father's voice.

Rada, who was sitting opposite Father, stared at her plate. She had not taken a walk with us, but disappeared upstairs as soon as we arrived and came down only for dinner. She looked terribly upset.

"He's been here since Sunday," said the waitress, no longer feeling it necessary to keep anything back. Obviously, Adzhubei had tried her patience with his demands. "He lies around in bed drunk and demands one thing after another." The girl's eyes filled with tears.

Father choked with anger. He did not tolerate disgraceful behavior in his own house. For a minute he sat silently, looking down at his plate, then rose and left the dining room. We heard the stairs squeak as he went up the stairs toward the room where my sister and husband stayed. Rada froze for a moment, then rushed after him. I remained alone in the dining room. After about fifteen minutes Father came back. Rada followed him, her head hanging. Father sat down at the table and began to eat. I followed his example. Rada didn't touch her food.

"He's disgracing all of us," Father began, staring at Rada. "And not only us. We [Father meant the Party Central Committee] have assigned him important work. He is supposed to educate people. But what kind of person . . ." Father hesitated, searching for a suitable word, didn't find it, and finally finished with a sigh: "What kind of example is he setting?"

A painful silence hung over the table. My sister didn't look up. Evidently what they had seen upstairs didn't provide grounds for any excuses.

"We can't leave it like this," continued Father angrily. "Today's Thursday. He hasn't been to his office since Monday. And nobody reported it."

"I called them and said that Alyosha was sick," Rada said in a small voice.

"Some sickness," thundered Father, then broke off, continuing more calmly a moment later: "We will remove him from his editorial position. Such people should not work at the newspaper. And we'll draw the appropriate conclusions." Without another word or saying good-night, he picked up the folder with papers and went to his bedroom.

In the morning the conversation at breakfast was halting. Father didn't look at Rada, Rada didn't look at Father, and sat with her head bowed. I tried to be as inconspicuous as possible. Finally Rada couldn't stand the silence and started crying. Father looked at her with dismay. Sniffling, Rada said that Aleksei promised that nothing like this would happen again and that he wouldn't forget this lesson for the rest of his life.

Father was obviously at a loss. The sight of a woman's tears flustered him. "And where is he?" said Father, interrupting his daughter's lamentation. "He's gone home," said Rada.

As soon as Father had retired the previous evening, Rada telephoned the newspaper for a car and sent Adzhubei out of his sight.

There was another silence. Then Father broke it, saying that he did not forgive Aleksei, but didn't want to ruin his life. If anything like this happened again, he would have only himself to blame.

We had concealed from Father the fact that Aleksei had been drinking for a long time and often showed up drunk at work. Had he known that, the consequences wouldn't have been so minor. But Father didn't know.

At home we didn't mention what happened at the dacha. I don't know if Father told Mama or preferred not to upset her. But, naturally, Aleksei Iva-novich himself didn't forget Father's warning.

The rapid rise in Aleksei's career was closely associated with Father, de-pended on Father, and was managed by Father. It couldn't have been other-wise in our politicized society, since Aleksei was becoming an increasingly prominent journalist and political figure, and not sowing grain or soldering wires in some design bureau. Aleksei found it oppressive to be constantly in Father's shadow. From the first day he appeared in our family, he took advan-tage of every opportunity to try to demonstrate his own importance, I would even say superiority, to everyone present. He was especially persistent in emphasizing his "independence" from Father, naturally in Father's absence. When Stalin was alive, he bored the guards with comments that the prov-inces were one thing—hinting at Father's Ukrainian background—and the capital something else entirely. They don't like hicks very much here. The guards didn't know how to react. They didn't want to slander their "boss," especially with his son-in-law. Aleksei also liked to talk about how close he was to Beria and his family and to emphasize that Lavrenty Pavlovich had stood far above Father in the Kremlin hierarchy.

Father liked his son-in-law. At the beginning he didn't distinguish be-tween Aleksei and his other children. On our walks he told Father, as we all did, about his studies at the university; he read the newspapers out loud and weeded the kitchen garden. In Father's presence Aleksei was markedly atten-tive, perhaps a little bit obsequious. As time went on he, the oldest, began to rise above us. Aleksei's conversations began increasingly to be about politics. He was intelligent, and Father gradually began to listen to him.

Father first took a real interest in Aleksei's stories after his trip to Austria in the summer of 1952, when Stalin was still alive. That year Aleksei began working at *Komsomolskaya Pravda*, the newspaper for young people. In Stalin's time a trip abroad, especially to a capitalist country, was considered a major event. Few were sent abroad and few tried to go, since it meant remaining forever in the files of the Ministry of State Security. Therefore, when a beaming Aleksei said that he was going to Austria for an international rally in defense of peace, Father was worried, rather than pleased. A new wave of repression was gathering force in the country. Father couldn't be sure that this trip might not be used against him, if someone wished to do that. But he didn't share his concern with Aleksei and simply asked who was sending him and why. Then he fell silent and only said: "Make sure [Father always used the formal "you" when speaking to Aleksei] that everything's in order, and if anything happens—behave the way you should." He didn't say what could happen.

The trip passed without incident. Aleksei wasn't alone, but was included in a delegation led by Pyotr Masherov, head of the Belorussian Komsomol organization. Masherov liked the young and witty journalist, whom he mentioned in his report to the Central Committee. We at home, including Father, were transfixed by Alyosha's stories about Austria.

After Stalin's death the danger associated with foreign travel receded into the past. Aleksei traveled abroad more and more often, and his accounts increasingly attracted Father's attention.

Adzhubei's career advanced rapidly in Father's shadow. First he became editor in chief of *Komsomolskaya Pravda*; then, in 1959, of *Izvestiya*. He was elected a member of the Party Central Committee. He proved to be an outstanding journalist, and *Izvestiya* went from being a run-of-the-mill newspaper to the most widely read publication in the Soviet Union. Aleksei acted with courage. He often published things that others wouldn't risk publishing. Of course, family connections helped there. He had an opportunity to carry out a preliminary test of any "bold" decision. It was he—with Father's approval and against Mikhail Suslov's objections—who published Aleksandr Tvardovsky's "Tyorkin in the Other World," Yevgeny Yevtushenko's "Stalin's Heirs," and several other "unacceptable" works.[6]

---

6. The case of Yevtushenko requires some explanation. It happened at the dacha. After a walk, the three of us—Father, Adzhubei, and I—drank tea in the dining room. As we finished, Aleksei drew a folded sheet of paper out of his pocket and asked if Father would like to hear a new poem by Yevtushenko, who was much talked about in Moscow.

"Well sure, go ahead and read it," said Father indifferently.

Aleksei began reading like an actor, with expression. Father sat with an absent look, as if he weren't paying any attention to the words. The reading ended. Father was silent. Adzhubei coughed and said that he would like to publish the poem, but he wasn't sure that the ideology department of the Party Central Committee would support him. Father still didn't say anything. There was a lengthy pause.

Adzhubei joined Father's inner circle and became a member of the so-called "Press Group." Aside from Aleksei, it consisted of Father's aides Grigory Shuisky, Vladimir Lebedev, Andrei Shevchenko, Oleg Troyanovsky, *Pravda* editor in chief Pavel Satyukov, TASS general director Dmitri Goryunov, Central Committee secretary Leonid Ilyichov, and Foreign Ministry Press Secretary Mikhail Kharlamov. Unlike speech writers in the West, they did not compose drafts of speeches. On the contrary, they edited what Father had dictated and gave it a final polishing. The Press Group was always available and provided Father with the mobility he couldn't obtain from the sluggish apparatus of the ministries or party central committee departments.

As time passed, the Press Group acquired an appreciable degree of political independence and became an increasingly influential power structure, though with vaguely defined authority.

Depending on what Father asked them to do, they were joined by specialists from central committee departments, such as the international, agricultural, and industrial departments. Once having performed their assignments, they disappeared. The group's nucleus remained the same.

The Press Group became Father's personal staff, as it were. Naturally, in the process of their work its members had the opportunity to exert a certain influence on shaping Father's views.

Materials prepared by the Press Group were then sent to the agency concerned to be polished further.

If there were no objections—and departments very rarely objected—Father would deliver the final verdict. He listened carefully to the opinions of professionals, but always remained the originator of his policies. As far as international affairs were concerned, this "division of labor" failed to arouse any enthusiasm at the Foreign Ministry. Antagonism gradually grew between the Press Group and Foreign Ministry officials. This became especially noticeable after Father's trip to the United States in September of 1959.

Step by step, Aleksei achieved a special position, and not only in the Press Group. It wasn't that he began to dominate his colleagues, since in his daily activities Father relied primarily on his aides. I would say that Adzhubei behaved with an increasing amount of independence, not only with respect to the other members of the Press Group, but also to the Central Committee apparatus and even to members of the Presidium. In international affairs, Aleksei became something like Father's unofficial emissary. Making use of

---

"It's a good poem, it's needed and very timely," he said finally. "But it should be published in *Pravda*, not *Izvestiya*. People will understand it more correctly if it appears in the central Party newspaper."

He went to the next room and called the editor in chief of *Pravda*, Pavel Satyukov. "Stalin's Heirs" was published in *Pravda* the next day, October 21, 1961, but on the initiative of the editor of *Izvestiya*.—S.K.

his position as a journalist, he could easily arrange appointments with foreign leaders who wanted to establish contacts with the Soviet Union, but not to make official commitments. Aleksei's position as son-in-law made him an ideal partner. When he talked with people, they assumed that what they said would reach Father's ears.

The initiative for Aleksei's trips to unfamiliar countries often did not come from Father. Frequently Adzhubei, who was well informed about Father's strategic thinking, prepared the ground himself, sizing up future interlocutors and then, choosing a suitable moment, "launched a trial balloon" at Father. The results of his trips were then widely discussed. Aleksei not only described his meetings to Father at home, but reported on them to the Presidium and published extensive articles in his newspaper. He knew how to present the material and how to mold the image of the person he had interviewed.

Aleksei's descriptions were not like those by party and government functionaries. Sometimes more superficial, they were always more exciting and lively. He often drew conclusions that went beyond those of the Foreign Ministry. He was not bound by the ministry's routine and Andrei Andreyevich Gromyko's extreme cautiousness, which weighed heavily on Foreign Ministry officials.

At the beginning of the 1960s Father decided it was time to break ground in the "diplomatic virgin land" of Latin America. He trusted that the example of Cuba, which had chosen socialism, would prove attractive to its neighbors. Father was also trying to improve contacts with the White House. All this was reflected, as if in a mirror, in the geography of the *Izvestiya* editor in chief's travels. In 1961 Aleksei and Rada flew to Mexico, where they met with President Lopez Mateos. An urgent telegram from Moscow interrupted their stay in Mexico and they flew to Washington. The U.S. president wanted to see Aleksei. Subsequently such meetings, sometimes with John, sometimes with Robert Kennedy or their confidential aides, became a regular thing. From Washington Aleksei and Rada flew to Brazil, where they were received by President Goularta.

Father turned his gaze to the countries of Southeast Asia, and in 1963 Adzhubei flew to Thailand, a country with which we were totally unfamiliar. In March of the same year Aleksei, in the role of "unofficial diplomat," as he began to call himself, traveled to Italy. Father asked him to meet with Pope John XXIII and see if the Holy Father might agree to work together with the "Number One Communist" in the fight for peace.

Adzhubei was by nature extremely vain. The external attributes of success attracted him. He wanted everything: positions, awards, titles. It took incredible effort on his part to have the highest literary prize in the Soviet Union, the Lenin Prize, awarded to those who reported on Father's visit to the

United States. Aleksei persuaded Defense Minister Marshal Rodion Malinovsky to give him, a lieutenant in the reserves, the rank of colonel. And he took an extraordinary amount of pride in that. He also approached Mstislav Keldysh, president of the USSR Academy of Sciences, with the idea of being elected to the Academy. However, there he was unsuccessful.

Aleksei's supreme ambition was to become foreign minister. But to achieve that behind Father's back was impossible, and Aleksei didn't count heavily on his cooperation. Father had no thought of replacing Gromyko, and to try to drive a wedge between them would have been not only difficult but dangerous. Father made jokes at Gromyko's expense and sometimes criticized him very crudely and tactlessly for not being sufficiently energetic, but he placed an extraordinarily high value on Gromyko's professionalism.

In his conversations with Father, Adzhubei never breathed a word about transferring to the Foreign Ministry, much less becoming foreign minister. He knew what the reaction would be. But he loved to talk along those lines behind Father's back. As the years went by he gave increasingly free rein to this florid fantasy. Members of the Press Group only ridiculed his big talk and nobody in the family paid any attention to it, but less knowledgeable people took Aleksei's words seriously. As a result, rumors spread and there was talk in Kremlin offices that provoked a shiver among high-placed officials in the tall building on Smolenskaya Square. Many considered it already decided.

To some extent Gromyko's super-cautious style of behavior furthered the spread of rumors. It was not so much that he accepted the patronage Aleksei persistently foisted on him, as that he didn't firmly reject it. When they met, Gromyko even began to flatter him. Sometimes there were curious episodes. Adzhubei liked to tell how Andrei Andreyevich once stopped him in a Kremlin corridor and, drawing him into a quiet corner, asked his advice about the following: Mila, Gromyko's daughter, had become involved with Svetlana Stalin's former husband, Grigory Morozov; they were having an affair. Gromyko looked extremely worried. The anti-Stalin campaign was going strong in the country and now he, the foreign minister, was put in this ambiguous position. It seemed to Andrei Andreyevich that he should immediately inform Father about what was going on. Aleksei laughed and said that there was no reason to tell Khrushchev anything. What business was it of his? He advised Gromyko to stop worrying. At first Andrei Andreyevich resisted this advice, but was eventually persuaded and thanked Aleksei sincerely and earnestly for his support. Adzhubei made sure that this story received wide circulation in Moscow.

By 1964 Adzhubei's reputation was firmly established. His favor was sought not only by Gromyko, but by others far higher up in the hierarchy. Aleksei was flattered by such obsequiousness. He liked to talk about how he was feeding Father new ideas and even went so far as to say that Father was nothing without him, that in essence he was the one shaping the country's policies. Party Central Committee secretaries Aleksandr Shelepin and Leonid Ilyichov, KGB chairman Vladimir Semichastny, not to speak of TASS director General Dmitri Goryunov and the Deputy Chief of the Central Committee Administrative Department Grant Grigoryan, all considered it a great honor to be invited to Adzhubei's home.

Gromyko tried increasingly to play up to Adzhubei. Whenever there was talk of sending an unofficial delegation with broad prerogatives to some foreign country, Aleksei was the first candidate he proposed. During Father's trips to Egypt and the Scandinavian countries (in May and June of 1964), Adzhubei almost openly demonstrated a patronizing and condescending attitude toward Gromyko. I think that, since he had a tendency toward autosuggestion, he believed that his goal was not far off. And now this incident at the dacha . . .

I don't think that Aleksandr Shelepin divulged the conspirators' plans to Aleksei, but he made every effort to assure him from time to time that he was included in the narrow circle of the country's "young" future leaders. Neither Shelepin nor Adzhubei doubted that it would be the "Komsomols" who would take power, not the clumsy Ukrainians. Aleksei saw himself at the very top of the pyramid of power in the new structure. But when? And how did he picture the "changing of the guard" at the Kremlin? Here we are on shaky ground and can only guess and speculate. All subsequent events testify to the fact that Adzhubei was not one of the conspirators. He was dismissed from all his positions right after Father's removal and was forbidden to write under his own name. Nevertheless, we can't be sure that Aleksei did not share the information he got from the Sturua brothers with Shelepin or Semichastny, and that they set his mind at rest, saying that they were in full control of the situation. But perhaps he never said anything to anyone.

Adzhubei miscalculated. Neither Father nor Shelepin was planning to make him foreign minister. Father had other prospects in mind for the "young." In particular, when he heard from me about the conspiracy being hatched against him, Father recalled that after the Nineteenth Party Congress Stalin surprised everyone by expanding the Presidium's membership to twenty-five, thereby drastically changing the balance of power at the top. Now Father made up his mind to add a large group of the "young" to the top party body, among them Aleksandr Shelepin, Yury Andropov, Pavel Satyukov, Mikhail Kharlamov, and Aleksei. Father told me of his intention that October in Pitsunda, when his time was already running out. Had Father known about the conspiracy in July, on the eve of the preceding plenary session, when the Sturua brothers visited Adzhubei. . . . But fate decreed otherwise. Aleksei Ivanovich kept silent.

SEEING AROUND CORNERS

Did Father himself suspect anything? I never thought so at the time. But now I've begun to wonder. I'll describe one incident. That summer Father visited Chelomei's design bureau. The visit was timed to coincide with the presentation of an award to the bureau for its achievements in developing missiles for the Navy.

As usual, an exhibit was set up for the guests.

Chelomei was famous for his attraction to engineering novelties, which were sometimes useful for our work, sometimes just curious inventions testifying to the possibilities of the human mind. During this period he was captivated by fiber optics. Vladimir Nikolayevich was interested in it from a purely utilitarian standpoint as well. Work on space stations was beginning. Fiber optics made it possible to transport an image not directly, which would alter a configuration, but around sharp angles. One stand was entirely devoted to this new engineering concept. The centerpiece was an intricate coil of fiberoptic cable. One end was casting onto a screen a small and very clear picture of the Spasskaya Tower of the Kremlin, which it had received from a child's projector attached to its opposite end.

Father, who loved technical novelties, was mesmerized. He stared at the screen from various angles and moved the transmitter about, while the picture shifted obediently. He was finally satisfied. As he said good-bye to the engineer who had shown him all these marvels, Father suddenly grinned and remarked: "I'll order one of these things for myself. I need to see around corners to keep an eye on some people."

He continued on, leaving bystanders puzzled. Brezhnev, who was standing next to Father and listening to every word, turned pale.

At the time Father's words were treated as a joke. Now I can't help but look for a hidden meaning.

THE DISTRACTIONS

The situation was remarkably favorable for Brezhnev's secret activity. Father was almost constantly away and visited Moscow only briefly.

During the first half of the year he traveled to Hungary and Egypt. He finally made a repeatedly postponed trip to Scandinavia. His entourage unanimously asserted that he simply had no right to refuse invitations; every visit was made to appear extremely important. Some people were sincere, others were trying to send Father far from Moscow, no matter the destination: Cairo, Tselinograd, or Prague.

On June 12, 1964, our country and the GDR signed a treaty of mutual assistance and cooperation. There was nothing unusual in the fact of signing the agreement. Similar treaties had existed for a long time between the Soviet Union and countries friendly to us. They were, so to speak, a guarantee of their sovereignty and announced that an attack on our friends would be interpreted in Moscow as a declaration of war against the Soviet Union.

Nevertheless, the treaty with the GDR was unique. It summed up the many years of dissension over West Berlin. It has to be viewed as one of the lessons learned from the Cuban Missile Crisis, after which Father rejected the policy of "pressure," which had become deadly dangerous.

June 12 put an end to the Berlin Crisis. The text of the treaty clearly registered the status quo. For example, Article 6 said: "The high negotiating parties consider West Berlin to be an independent political entity."

They also lifted the main threat by transferring control over communications to the jurisdiction of the GDR. The treaty specified: "Until the conclusion of a peace treaty, the United States, Great Britain, and France continue to bear the responsibility for implementing on the territory of the FRG the conditions and obligations stipulated by the governments of the Four Powers in Potsdam and other international agreements." Article 9 eliminated any possibility for ambiguity, asserting: "This Treaty does not affect the Potsdam Agreement."

That was not the end of the Berlin epic, but its continuation belongs to a completely different story. No one in 1964 was in a position to look ahead to the year 1989.

After returning from a trip to Saigon in the middle of May, Robert McNamara observed that "it might be necessary to send additional personnel from the United States." Warships of the U.S. Pacific Fleet were patrolling off the coast of Vietnam and U.S. planes, mostly bombers, were massing on the nearest airfields. More and more weapons were piling up, and it would only take one last jolt to set everything in motion.

The inevitable occurred on August 2. The U.S. destroyer *Murdoch*, patrolling in the Gulf of Tonkin, was attacked by three Vietnamese patrol boats—or it wasn't attacked and they only imagined it, at night, in a storm, when nerves are stretched to the limit. We can't solve that riddle today. Experts express contradictory opinions, while reliable evidence is lacking.

But that isn't particularly important. The point is that the destroyer opened fire as it fought off real or imaginary enemies. It's precisely the type of event about which people say: if it didn't happen, it deserved to be invented. Everything and everyone was prepared for an attack on North Vietnam. They were only waiting for the order. On August 5 President Johnson sent a message to Congress and almost simultaneously issued the order to attack. Heavy bombers were the first to swing into action. The war began.

What had been almost miraculously avoided two years earlier in the Caribbean broke out in Southeast Asia. The White House calculated that victory was not far off, but John McCone's gloomy prediction about Cuba, that "it will be devilishly difficult to smoke them out," turned out to be true in Vietnam. Indeed, it is difficult to defeat those who are protecting their homes, whether in Cuba, Vietnam, Afghanistan, or anywhere else.

At the time Father was touring the virgin lands. A good harvest was desperately needed after the previous year's drought. Father wanted to take a personal look at what could be expected. Speaking in Tselinograd, he reacted to events in Vietnam with an angry rebuke.

I hurried to see him as soon as he returned to Moscow. I thought that the Soviet Union should come to Vietnam's assistance at once and with all possible force. Father dampened my ardor. He was far from convinced that we needed to get involved in the fight, fearing that we could be drawn unwillingly into a war with the United States. Father expressed that thought constantly and in various forms.

In his opinion, the Vietnamese leadership was being strongly influenced by China, and he didn't exclude the possibility of deliberate actions designed to draw us into conflict with the United States. Father said that we could not leave Ho Chi Minh without support. We would help Vietnam, we would send them weapons and other supplies. However, it was a long way off and no one knew how the Chinese would behave, since the route to Vietnam passed through their territory. He would not contemplate the extensive use of freighters. Because of its supremacy at sea, the United States could impose a naval blockade, as it tried to do in the Caribbean. Caution and yet again caution—that was Father's position.

FATHER AND THE MINISTRY OF DEFENSE

In the autumn of 1964, the Ministry of Defense planned two major events: demonstrations to the leadership of the latest achievements in modern weapons. This time it was the turn of the ground forces. At the first event plans called for a demonstration of combat weapons—tanks, artillery, and helicopters—at a tank test base in Kubinka near Moscow. Then the group would travel to Tyura-Tam to see intercontinental missiles and space vehicles in action. Father had never visited the cosmodrome before.

Just as before, they adjusted the program to Father's schedule, which was incredibly crowded. He even had to postpone his summer vacation to the autumn.

A Supreme Soviet session convened in the beginning of July soon after Father's return from Scandinavia. Father delivered a speech titled "Measures to Carry Out the CPSU Program on Raising the Living Standards of the People." It referred in particular to the establishment of pensions for collective farmers. That would remove them from the category of second-class citizens. The government, for the first time in all the years of Soviet power, recognized them as having equal rights.

The program also called for raising the salaries of teachers, doctors, and other professionals in the non-industrial sphere. Father had tried to put aside funds for that purpose by economizing on everything during the entire previous six months. It was hard to make ends meet. But the money was found, and he announced the results with justifiable pride.

Immediately after the session Father left for Warsaw for the celebration of the Day of Poland's Rebirth. Then, after a brief stay in Moscow, a long trip to the virgin lands. On August 27 he was in Prague, at the celebration of the twentieth anniversary of the Slovak uprising against the Germans.

The demonstrations of new weapons were squeezed into the middle of September: he was to be at the tank proving grounds in Kubinka near Moscow on the fourteenth, and then fly to Tyura-Tam for a stay of two days.

Father Alienates the Ground Forces

The weather was chilly on September 14, 1964. In the distance, the leaves of birch trees along the edge of the woods were turning gold. Hazy sunshine was occasionally obscured by clouds moving overhead.

Father finally appeared. The cars drew up at staff headquarters and a crowd gathered immediately. It surged and pulsated; only where Father stood, in the center, like the eye of a hurricane, was there any free space, a small circle protected by the guards. With Father were Brezhnev, Kirilenko, Ustinov, Malinovsky, and several others.

Brezhnev accompanied Father everywhere, not leaving him by so much as a step and devouring his every word and gesture. He was ready to anticipate any wish. His devotion appeared so genuine that it was positively touching.

Father was interested in a shoulder-fired antiaircraft missile, similar to the bazooka. But he wasn't impressed by the Shilka antiaircraft machine gun. I couldn't agree with him. The gun looked extremely elegant: four barrels projected from the turret of a powerful-looking caterpillar tank. With one push of a button, two radio antennas rotated with a slight buzzing sound. The gun was ready to fire in seconds. The perfection of its engineering design attracted the eye. Nothing superfluous. Everything in its proper place.

Father praised the designers, but added that the time for barrel artillery was past. It couldn't compete with missiles. Turning to Malinovsky, he advised, rather than ordered, him to think about how the Shilka might be used, if at all.

"We have to save money," concluded Father severely.

Malinovsky nodded. "Yes, sir."

The next exhibit to attract people's attention was the Grad system, successor to the Katyusha. It looked particularly effective in action, when missiles flew one after another out of steel tubes with a piercing whistle, looking like flaming arrows as they disappeared into the sky. The firing went on for a long time. There were many tubes packed tightly into a rectangular box mounted on the body of a truck.

A few seconds later an endless series of explosions began somewhere in the distance.

"God forbid we should ever come under such fire," Father remarked, shaking hands with the designers. They smiled cautiously, looking sideways at their weapon. The telltale yellowish ends of misfires were visible among the rows of empty black openings. Father pretended not to notice.

Continuing on, there were rows of cannons, mortars, and other "marvels" with grooved and smooth barrels, which could scatter land mines or fire an assortment of shells: armor-piercing, concrete-piercing, fragmentation, and "special-purpose," i.e., chemical. Behind them were exhibits of machine guns, submachine guns, grenade launchers, and various other devices to destroy people. Father listened to the explanations in silence, without interrupting or asking questions. He was already starting to get tired.

Then came helicopters. I have already mentioned that their possible use in combat caused acrimonious arguments at the time. According to the officers manning the exhibit, this new type of weapon had a future: it would become an indispensable means of infantry support for both attack and defense. Father didn't agree with the professionals and repeated his view that the clumsy machines were very vulnerable to missiles, especially now that missiles were moving from truck trailers to the shoulders of infantrymen. There was a ragged chorus of objections. Father didn't attempt to argue. He suggested that everything should be reevaluated, that they think it over and return to the subject of military helicopters separately. With some irritation, he scolded Grechko, who was particularly vociferous in defending helicopters: The marshal wanted this, that, and the other thing, but didn't think about who would have to pay for it all. He, i.e., Father, had no money to spare; he couldn't buy everything and would have to give up something, whether he wanted to or not. The objective, therefore, was not to choose what they liked, but what they couldn't possibly do without.

As they talked, looked at exhibits, observed the firing of weapons, and arguments blew up and quickly died down, the day wore on to afternoon. Malinovsky invited them for a quick snack. We had lunch right there, in the field, on tables set inside large tarpaulin tents. Father set a businesslike tone, suggesting that they not sit for very long and drink no alcohol—there was still a great deal of work ahead.

The second half of the day began with what looked like endless rows of tanks and self-propelled weapons. I was simply dazzled. I had never seen so many tanks. I was familiar with the T-34, the KV, and IS-3. But here was an incredible variety! Turrets that a special system kept immobile, no matter how rough the roads. Cannons, some with long grooved barrels, others with smooth barrels, but with shells sprouting small and elegant wings. I felt a twinge of jealousy: we weren't the only ones who designed wings that opened in flight. Night-vision devices and gunsights were already in wide use. Each tank invariably carried several antitank missiles.

Father looked at the machines attentively, I would even say, critically. It was immediately obvious from his questions that he was concerned that the tanks were vulnerable. Would they withstand enemy fire? Wouldn't they become clumsy targets?

The designers demonstrated two- and three-layer armor, passive defense and active defense. Father listened attentively, then repeated the question: But will the tank survive a hit by an antitank missile?

The designers began shifting from one foot to the other, hesitated, and then gave a lengthy explanation with all kinds of "ifs." Yes, if it's hit at a certain angle in the front. If active defense is operating. If . . . If . . . If . . . Father frowned.

Then the tanks fired, striking targets at extreme distances. They looked simply magnificent. But Father was especially enthusiastic about the antitank guided missiles. We got the impression that tanks had no defense against them.

The demonstration came to an end.

Participants gathered in the small headquarters building to exchange immediate impressions. Father began by talking about the tanks and expressing admiration for what had been achieved.

"These tanks can't be compared to those which were in the war, even to the best ones. If we'd only had them then," he remarked.

Those present murmured approvingly, but Father's tone changed abruptly. He repeated what he had said at the Defense Council in the spring of 1963: We follow the experience of the Second World War without analyzing it critically. Father paused and looked around at those present. There was a tense silence. He went on to say that we should take a different look at the Army in general—at its mission and at the goals that we had set for ourselves.

"Are we planning to conquer anyone?" Father gave a piercing look at Malinovsky, who was sitting next to him, and then answered his own question: "No! Then why do we need the weapons that we saw today?"

Father expressed his appreciation to the designers, saying that their work undoubtedly deserved praise, but that they were doing what was "ordered."

"And they are the ones who place the orders," said Father, pointing to the throng of marshals. "They decide what we need and what we don't need. I have the impression that they need everything."

Father went on to talk about the characteristic features of modern warfare. He had been thinking about the subject for a long time and as early as 1959 had written about it in a memorandum to the Presidium of the Central Committee. He had also discussed it at the Defense Council meeting in Fili the year before. What had then seemed like conjecture had grown into conviction: War between our two countries, the USSR and United States, was impossible. Nuclear weapons made it meaningless; there would be no winner. But Father thought that the use of nuclear weapons could not be avoided in case of war, even if both sides were initially against their use. Eventually the side being defeated would be irresistibly impelled to alter the unfavorable course of events in its favor, to take revenge, and it would resort to the hydrogen bomb.

Father continued. In his opinion, if we excluded the possibility of a conventional war between the USSR and United States, the Warsaw Pact and NATO, then why did we need this heap of weapons? They were all very good, very modern, but they cost enormous amounts of money. The country didn't have extra money. We should therefore think very seriously about what kind of Army we needed, and only then decide what weapons to give it.

"Otherwise, we'll all lose our pants because of you"—Father tried to defuse the tension with a joke, and poked Malinovsky playfully with his fist.

The joke fell flat. Malinovsky forced a sour smile. No one said anything. Many of them remembered Father's speech at the Defense Council. His reversion to this subject foreshadowed a new reorganization, a reduction in the Army. The generals didn't approve—a powerful state is renowned for its army.

They were not mistaken. Father began to talk about a compact, highly professional army, a territorial militia, about freeing up the working hands so vital to the national economy.

Father emphasized that he was not talking just about what weapons to buy, but about how many. After all, weapons rapidly become obsolete, primarily in a moral sense. Why do we need thousands of tanks and thousands of planes if war is not on our doorstep? That money is taken from the people and thrown away.

No, he didn't think that we should disarm. That was a tempting, but as yet unrealizable, dream. The Army must have the most modern weapons, but in reasonable quantities. No more than that. The same thrifty approach to the variety of weapons was necessary. Mass production of various designs of tanks and cannons with similar combat characteristics would result in spending many millions, which could be avoided by selecting the one best tank, the one best cannon.

"But you want to have the reputation of being generous—at the people's expense. You don't want to spoil your relationship with designers and you take everything they give you," Father told his listeners reproachfully.

There was a subdued murmur of disapproval. Father talked a little more about saving money, about the Army existing to defend the people, not the people existing to defend the Army. He finally stopped talking. No other speakers were proposed.

Father thanked those present for their work.

Everybody got up, moving their chairs noisily, but didn't head for the doors. Father was allowed to leave first, followed by the marshals. I hurried after them. When I approached Father, he and Malinovsky were talking about something in low voices. The marshal looked depressed as he listened to what Father was saying.

From the military's point of view, the demonstration had been not just a failure, it had been a setback. Having boasted of his achievements, Malinovsky wanted to obtain approval for the purchase of new weapons. It all went the opposite way. New discussions lay ahead, and their outcome was totally unpredictable. Or to be more precise, it wasn't hard to guess their result: the commander in chief had decided to destroy the Army. That was the only way the marshal could interpret a transition to some kind of hypothetical territorial militia.

At that moment neither Father nor Malinovsky knew that nothing depended on Father any longer, that his proposals were of no interest to anyone, and that no one was planning to implement his orders. There was exactly one month left until the "end."

We drove home in silence. Father sat in front. Brezhnev and Kirilenko took seats in the back, along with the devoted head of the guards and me.

THE FRIENDSHIP OF ROCKET SCIENTISTS

A few days later Father left for Tyura-Tam. I stayed in Moscow with a very painful leg.

I don't know very much about what went on at the cosmodrome. Father's account faded in the stormy events that followed his return. However, I would like to mention a few, sometimes minor episodes.

Brezhnev stuck to Father's side in Tyura-Tam as well. He probably thought that in doing so he was somehow protecting himself and deflecting suspicion. The story of Father's hat seems like a sad joke. Piercing winds blow constantly and during all seasons in the steppes near the Aral Sea, varying only in direction and in the misfortune they bring: freezing cold or enervating heat. In September, as a rare exception, they brought a pleasant coolness.

The exhibit was mounted partly in hangars and partly in the open. Sections were separated by temporary boards with posters. As they walked up to the intelligence satellites, a treacherous gust of wind blew Father's hat from his head and took it toward the steppe. Father only lunged forward and tried to grab it, but missed.

First to rush after the hat was Brezhnev, displaying a speed that nobody expected from the sixty-year-old Central Committee secretary. Outstripping numerous and far younger guards, he caught up with the hat. It described somersaults and resisted capture, but he grabbed it, examined it carefully, brushed off the accumulated dust with his sleeve, and returned it to Father with an expression of ecstatic devotion.

It was just that expression of devotion that left an impression in Father's memory and made that insignificant incident stand out among so many other everyday occurrences.

There is something symbolic in the fact that Father's last trip in his capacity as chairman of the Council of Ministers was to the cosmodrome. Before the curtain came down, he was able to admire his handiwork. He was introduced to the crew of the new spaceship—a three-man crew, as Korolyov had promised: Komarov, Feoktistov, and Yegorov. They were in the last preparations for launch. Father wished them a successful flight and a soft landing. He would still have time for the traditional telephone conversation with them, but others would greet them on their return.

They showed Father the legendary launch site from which Gagarin was sent into space, and another one, built for the UR-100. From now on the UR-100 would have to learn how to fly directly from a silo. He observed launches of the R-36 and the UR-200.

An important discussion was held concerning these rockets. Only one of them was to be selected for production. A difficult way still lay ahead before tests would end, but there was already no doubt that both would fly.

They preferred the R-36. I don't know why, since the rockets seemed almost identical. I think Father felt uncomfortable about Yangel. In Pitsunda his heavy rocket had been "cut down" and at Fili, Chelomei's UR-100 was preferred. When Father returned home I tried to discover the reasons for this decision, which went against us. He didn't want to discuss it and just said briefly: "We made a decision. Yangel's rocket was better."

In the days to come I had no time to think about the UR-200.

Their discussions concerned the fate of Korolyov's R-9A, as well as the R-36 and the UR-200. The R-9A had fallen hopelessly behind its competitor, the R-16, and its tests were not completed until February of that year. No one could decide what to do with it. Smirnov and Ustinov were in favor of adding the R-9A to the military arsenal. Malinovsky remained diplomatically neutral. It brought nothing new, only additional work: different compo-nents, in one case oxygen and kerosene, in the other nitrogen compounds; new design; new simulators. Not to mention the old, and still unsolved, prob-lem of long-term storage of liquid oxygen. But—he was very anxious not to offend Korolyov and did not want to quarrel with Ustinov.

They left the decision to Father. He decided against the R-9A. The ban didn't last long. After his retirement they reviewed the unfavorable decision, and in May 1965 the R-9A was approved. It counted for nothing, since its time had passed.

In 1964, before his trip to the test site, Chelomei decided to try to take part in the moon race. The design bureau prepared posters showing a general view and the parameters of a new rocket. Vladimir Nikolayevich planned to decide whether or not to show them in Tyura-Tam, depending on the situation.

I thought that it was simply folly to propose yet another moon program. Even one would be hard to sustain. Chelomei insisted that the N-1 was a sham, at least technically. Even if the rocket took off, how could we seriously hope to land on the moon with only seventy-five tons orbiting the earth? At that weight the flight would become questionable, to say nothing of the nec-essary reserves. Not a single designer had ever built a machine that came in exactly at the planned weight. And to land a person alone on the moon, in a bulky space suit . . .

Chelomei called his rocket the UR-700. Chelomei was skeptical of Glushko's claim that there were insoluble problems in building a high-thrust engine using oxygen and hydrogen. He attributed their disagreement more to ambition than to technical matters. However, Chelomei had no doubt that Glushko had no chance of overtaking the Americans, since he was starting design of a new oxygen-hydrogen engine without the necessary margin of time. The work was complex and would break new ground. It had to be tackled gradually, step by step. Attempting to make a big leap would only result in misfortune.

Vladimir Nikolayevich planned to use asymmetrical dimethyl hydrazine and nitrogen tetroxide as fuel and oxidizer (the same as in the UR-500). That put it at a disadvantage in launch weight compared to the Saturn and the N-1. However, in Vladimir Nikolayevich's opinion that disadvantage would be more than offset by using advanced technical designs in the engines. In this he was fully supported by Glushko. Furthermore, continuity was preserved in the inevitable future transition from 150-ton thrust engines of the UR-500 to 600-ton thrust engines for the UR-700.

Vladimir Nikolayevich also needed additional tons and kilograms to en-sure smooth transportation of this monster rocket to the test site. He decided to make the first stage of the UR-700 in sections, according to the packet design familiar to the rocket industry. The rocket could easily be dismantled to meet all current transportation standards.

The UR-700 was considerably wider and taller, but the new rocket preserved its remote likeness to the UR-500. It weighed up to four and one-half thousand tons, one and a half times as much as the N-1. That seemed a lot, but it was based on a solid foundation of experience. Surprises during flight tests were reduced to a minimum.

Two cosmonauts were planned for the flight, and the spaceship was to land on the moon as a unit, not separate in lunar orbit. Considering the state of our electronics, Vladimir Nikolayevich preferred not to take the chance of undocking. What would happen if something failed after undocking?

Chelomei decided to talk about his new proposal at the display stand for the UR-500. That was a psychologically sound decision. The rocket was impressive. And with the way work at the launch site was proceeding, he was confident of meeting the date set for the UR-500's first launch, the middle of the next year.

First, Vladimir Nikolayevich talked about the UR-500 and its potential. In testing such a monster, Chelomei didn't think it was sensible to hurl useless pieces of metal one after another into space. He and Moscow State University physicists had decided to mount a twelve-ton Proton satellite, which would record cosmic rays, on the first four UR-500 rockets selected for testing. The Proton looked like a pie, with layers of film and lead screens. It cost relatively little and was easy to build, so to lose one would not be a disaster. And if it were successful, scientists hoped it would help them to discover those elusive quarks—semi-mythical elementary particles. The first launches were successful, but no quarks were found.

This satellite gave its name to the powerful Proton rocket that has delivered manned stations, supply ships, and all kinds of civilian and military satellites into orbit.

Father listened to Chelomei without interrupting. After talking about the UR-500, Vladimir Nikolayevich moved on to plans for the immediate future. He removed the top part of the rocket mockup standing on the table and planted another stage on top. This three-stage rocket would double the payload sent into space. When Father asked: "Why not make the rocket three-stage right away?" he replied that you're more likely to solve a problem on schedule by complicating it gradually, one step at a time. Father was pleased by such a thrifty approach, and asked: "What would be the next step?"

Chelomei, with the gesture of a conjurer, unfolded the posters of the UR-700. Everyone was taken by surprise, even Dementyev, not to speak of Smirnov and Ustinov. Vladimir Nikolayevich counted on surprise. Father listened attentively to his report. He liked Chelomei's conclusions. But where would the money come from?

They agreed that Vladimir Nikolayevich would work on technical proposals and make all the proper calculations. Then they would return to the discussion. Smirnov was ordered to prepare a draft decree for the Council of Ministers. It was eventually signed by Father's successor, Aleksei Nikolayevich Kosygin.

Chelomei celebrated victory. He thought that during the year or year and a half he would need to prepare his documentation, the N-1's engineering fallacies would become clearly apparent. When I asked how he hoped to win the competition with Wernher von Braun, who had been working on the Saturn for three years, he replied casually: "We shall see." At the time Chelomei was worried about Korolyov, not von Braun. Chelomei became Korolyov's principal rival during the next year.

I don't know any details about what happened at Korolyov's exhibit. Chelomei's initiative with the UR-700 had no effect on the status of the N-1. Work was well advanced, and Father considered the chief designer's authority to be indisputable. Smirnov and Ustinov strongly backed Korolyov, who was also supported by Brezhnev.

Korolyov's report was approved. Smirnov was entrusted with ensuring that the work would be completed on schedule.

That is all I really know about Father's last meeting with the rocket designers. After his retirement, none of the designers—the stubborn Korolyov, the reliable Yangel, or the courteous Chelomei—called Father a single time or congratulated him on holidays. Father didn't resent that, only remarking that they're very busy, they have no time for a pensioner. Perhaps he really was offended, but didn't show it. In retirement he liked to talk about many different subjects, but there were some he never touched on. His hurt feelings and disillusionment with people belonged to that forbidden area.

GALYUKOV'S WARNING

In Moscow I greeted Father with staggering news.

While Father was visiting the test site, Vasily Ivanovich Galyukov—the former chief of Nikolai Grigoryevich Ignatov's security guard—called the apartment on the government phone and said that his boss was traveling around the country recruiting Father's opponents. Father's removal from office was imminent. Galyukov planned to tell Father, but since Father was not at home he had to be satisfied with me. It's still not clear what would have happened if Galyukov had talked with Father. Would Father have talked to someone he didn't know at all about such a tricky subject? At first I myself had serious doubts. But caution won out and I met with Galyukov.

During an evening walk in the woods near Moscow, far from the eyes and ears of others, Galyukov told me such things that simply turned my world upside down. For almost a year Brezhnev, Podgorny, Polyansky, Shelepin, and Semichastny had been secretly preparing to remove Father from power. Unlike the arrogant Malenkov, Molotov, and Kaganovich in 1957, who had taken the support of the Presidium members for granted, these conspirators had prepared the ground thoroughly. Under one pretext or another, they had talked to a majority of Central Committee members and won them over. Some agreed immediately: they'd been fed up with reorganizations and transfers for a long time. Others had to be coaxed and persuaded, while still others were pressured by references to a majority that had already formed.

Galyukov said that they planned to move in October, before the opening of the next Central Committee plenum. Besides removing him from power, they had to prevent him from introducing the draft of a new constitution, which contained, at his insistence, several provisions they considered seditious, and from carrying out his plan to expand and rejuvenate the Presidium. There was almost no time left. The last ten days of September were beginning.

The year 1964 was somehow sinister in general. Leaders whose names were familiar to the Soviet people since childhood departed this life, one after another. It seemed as if an entire historical epoch was coming to a close.

That summer Maurice Thorez, the general secretary of the French Communist Party, planned, as usual, to vacation in the Crimea. This time he decided not to fly, but to take a slow cruise in the Mediterranean and Black Seas. On July 11 he died on board the liner *Litva*.

The head of the Italian communists, Palmiro Togliatti, came to the Crimea on vacation. Invited to a children's celebration at the Artek camp, the honored guest stood up, raised his hand in greeting, and collapsed on the ground with a severe stroke. He died a few days later, on August 21.

Exactly one month later, on September 21, the chairman of the Council of Ministers of the German Democratic Republic, Otto Grotewohl, died.

Like some kind of curse.

The deaths of Thorez and Togliatti ended an agreement Father had made with them: that he would not refer to the public trials in his fight against Stalin's heritage. They had both been present at the trials. By their names and their consciences, they had corroborated the legality of the sentences that were imposed. They persuaded Father not to show them up as liars who had covered up for a murderer. In Thorez and Togliatti's opinion, repudiation of the public trials could result in the collapse of the communist movement in the West. Bukharin, Rykov, Pyatakov, Zinoviev, and many others had to remain murderers, conspirators, and poisoners "in the name of victory in a just cause."

He had to take the leaders of the two largest communist parties in Europe into consideration. But he didn't think it possible to leave everything the way it was, without any change. Father wanted to know the truth.

He had appointed a special commission that, for the previous two years, had been digging through the archives, comparing documents, and looking for and finding evidence. The work proceeded with extreme difficulty. It seemed as if Father was the only one who wanted to know the truth, while others tried, sometimes secretly, sometimes openly, to get in the way. Still, the investigation made progress. By the middle of 1964 several volumes of documents had been compiled. Father said there were five. The accumulated facts proved unequivocally that the accused were innocent and that the public trials had been rigged. It seemed that now it was possible to publish the materials and rehabilitate the innocent. But time had passed. That era was ending. It had already ended! We were simply not yet conscious of that fact.

When I told Father about Galyukov's disclosures, he both believed them and didn't believe them. Not that he doubted me or Galyukov, but he doubted that such a thing was possible.

"Brezhnev, Shelepin, Podgorny—such different people . . ." Father thought for a moment and concluded: "Unbelievable!"

I myself wanted very much to believe that the warning was baseless. I had known Brezhnev for twenty years, since childhood, and Podgorny and Shelepin only a little less. Now former friends were turning into enemies. But I thought it my duty to tell Father everything. He alone must evaluate the information and take whatever steps were necessary.

Father asked me to keep everything secret. His warning was superfluous. Whom could I tell such a thing? But he himself behaved in a strange, illogical, and inexplicable way. The day after our conversation he told Podgorny and Mikoyan everything—as if he were trying to rid himself of delusions.

Perhaps it was all right to tell Mikoyan, whose name was not mentioned by Galyukov. But why Podgorny? His name had cropped up more than once in accounts of Ignatov's activities. Ignatov had consulted with Podgorny and received orders directly from him.

According to Father, Mikoyan said nothing and Podgorny energetically rejected his suspicions, simply ridiculed them. What did Father think he could gain? Did he want to hear a confession? At times he had behaved naively, but not in such a situation.

Apparently Father cared very much that the information not be confirmed. He wanted a denial from Podgorny's lips. Of course, he didn't believe Podgorny, but on the other hand, Father had helped him along for so many years, first in the Ukraine, then to Moscow and in Moscow. The treachery of friends is always devastating.

Father decided not to change his plans. That year he had no summer vacation and planned to go to Pitsunda after finishing urgent business. The Crimea is rather chilly in October.

He asked Mikoyan to see Galyukov. Anastas Ivanovich should talk to him and then fly to Pitsunda, where they would talk everything over. Father himself didn't want to meet with the informant or listen to him.

Although a little offended by Father's casual reaction to my warning, I was reassured. People don't behave that way in moments of danger. I hadn't had my own vacation yet, so I asked Father if I could go with him. I was very reluctant to let him go alone. He agreed gladly: I should introduce Galyukov to Mikoyan and then follow him to Pitsunda.

The last days of September Father spent working, as if there had been no warning. Before leaving Moscow on September 30 he met with President Sukarno of Indonesia, who was on an official visit to our country.

The following day Father landed in Simferopol. He didn't go directly to Pitsunda, since on the way he wanted to look at some new poultry factories that had been purchased abroad. He was very concerned by the fact that their efficiency was declining rapidly under our conditions. The amount of feed consumed per kilo of weight gained was doubling or tripling. What was the problem? Even at such a critical time, the search for an answer to this question seemed extremely important to Father.

Pyotr Yefimovich Shelest and other Ukrainian leaders met Father in the Crimea. Shelest knew everything. Brezhnev had talked with him for the first time as early as March. They visited the Yuzhny Poultry State Farm and then the broiler factory of the Krasny State Farm. Father behaved as usual, asked about everything, took an interest in how the chickens were housed and fed. Shelest expected a dressing-down, but didn't get one.

Many years later, in his memoirs, Shelest noted that Father seemed somehow depressed and less confident than usual. At least that's what he writes in his memoirs.

Father didn't stay in the Crimea for long. He complained to Shelest that it was bleak and cold, and he left for Pitsunda. He began the vacation by receiving a delegation from the Japanese Diet, headed by Mr. Iyitira Fujiyama, on October 3. The next day Father met with members of the Pakistani parliament.

Mikoyan arrived soon after. What did he tell Father about his conversation with Galyukov? Neither one of them talked to me about it.

Together they met with the local boss, Georgy Ivanovich Vorobyov, secretary of the Krasnodar Territorial Party Committee. He came to visit them and presented Father with a couple of turkeys. In Galyukov's account, Vorobyov was one of the main actors.

Perhaps he had been sent to see what Father was doing. No one knows what Vorobyov reported to Podgorny at the Central Committee. He spent a whole day with Father and Mikoyan and had lunch with them. They talked about everything. Father wanted to know details about how things were going in the Territory, about the results of the harvest. As he always did. Only at the end of the meeting Father asked, as if casually, what kind of conversations Ignatov had with him, Vorobyov, that summer. And, without waiting for a reply, he added: "People say you plan to remove me."

When I arrived in Pitsunda, probably on October 11, I found an idyllic and tranquil setting.

To my cautious inquiry, "What's going on?" Father described his conversation with Vorobyov. Noting that he had "denied everything," Father said listlessly that Galyukov was probably mistaken, or else was overly suspicious.

I asked what I should do with the record of Mikoyan's talk with Galyukov. I thought that Father would want to read it at least. No such thing. He didn't express the slightest desire to look at it, and only said casually: "Give it to Anastas this evening."

Anastas Ivanovich was also calm and composed. However, he looked attentively through the pages that I had copied by hand in block letters, for the sake of secrecy. On the last page he noticed that I had not reproduced his comment that the Central Committee believed and did not doubt the honesty of Brezhnev, Podgorny, Shelepin, and other comrades. I had thought the phrase pompous and omitted it. It seems that those words were freighted with meaning.

Then Mikoyan asked me to sign the last page. The notes should not be anonymous. He hid my pages in a safe place, in the closet under a pile of underwear.

Father's behavior evidently seemed puzzling to "Moscow." He took no action. Just in case, the conspirators informed Malinovsky of their plans. Father might think of turning to him. After listening to the information, Malinovsky asked a few insignificant questions and agreed that it was time for "the old man" to take a rest.

During those days Brezhnev was in Berlin, where he was heading the Soviet delegation at the celebration of the fifteenth anniversary of the GDR. In his absence Podgorny was in charge of the Central Committee and Polyansky occupied the position of acting chairman of the Council of Ministers. The threads were all gathered in their hands.

More than anything, Brezhnev was afraid Father would find out.

And the worst happened: Father found out. That unpleasant news was passed to Brezhnev in Berlin. It occurred on October 7. Brezhnev panicked. Fear almost drove him out of his mind. Nikolai Grigoryevich Yegorychev, who knew what was going on, recalls that at one point Brezhnev suddenly refused to return to Moscow. Fear of Father paralyzed his will. They had a hard time persuading him. He compensated for his fright in the speech he gave at the anniversary celebration. I have never read such a panegyric addressed to Father.

FATHER'S FINAL DAYS IN POWER

The cosmonauts were launched on October 12—exactly on time, as Korolyov had promised. While everything worked perfectly at Baikonur, in Pitsunda the usual ritual was violated. As a rule, Father was immediately informed of such a joyful event. First by Ustinov, as the deputy chairman of the Council of Ministers responsible for military-industrial affairs. Then Korolyov would call, though more often Father called him first with congratulations.

Smirnov, who had replaced Ustinov the previous year, was in no hurry to call on October 12. Or I should say, he never called at all. He had to be found. When Father asked about the launch, Smirnov said that everything went normally and the cosmonauts were in orbit. He simply had not had time yet to call. Father got angry. Whether in his heart he felt a stab of premonition or he simply flared up, the conversation ended on an acrimonious note. Father asked irritably whether the orders given to Smirnov at Tyura-Tam were being implemented. He promised to find out when he came back to Moscow. But he never had that opportunity. After hanging up the phone he seemed to forget about the squabble. At least, he made no remark whatsoever about it, and I didn't ask him. Such questions had lost their meaning.

During his telephone conversation with the cosmonauts after lunch, Father radiated good humor. He summoned Mikoyan and together they wished the cosmonauts a successful flight and promised a hearty reception on earth and a triumphant greeting on Red Square. The cosmonauts, in turn, confirmed their official readiness to fulfill any assignment from the government.

The triumphant greeting took place, but was delayed until October 19, after Father had been pushed out.

For days the cosmonauts wondered why they were detained at the test site. People simply had no time to think of them. In Moscow, crew commander Colonel Komarov, in reporting to a new and different premier, repeated his promise to fulfill any government assignment with honor. That's when the saying appeared: "Ready to fulfill any assignment from any government." The first joke of the post-Khrushchev era.

But that was all to come later. That evening in Pitsunda, the television crew had hardly managed to assemble their equipment—they were filming the historic conversation with the spaceship—when there was a phone call from Moscow. Who called? Today there are two different opinions on the subject. In my notes, made soon after the event, as well as in my memory, it was Suslov.

All other witnesses claim that it was Brezhnev. We may suppose that the memory of witnesses obligingly made a substitution: Brezhnev's primacy in the following years required that he be the one who called. I wouldn't doubt that I was right, except that something Semichastny has said makes me hesitate. In an interview featured in the film *The Coup (A Version)*, Semichastny claims that Brezhnev got scared and had to be dragged to the phone. Such a detail sticks in the memory and is hard to invent. So perhaps it was Brezhnev who called. Actually, it's not of the slightest importance who held the phone in Moscow.

Moscow insistently requested that Father interrupt his vacation and come to the capital. Urgent matters had to be dealt with in the field of agriculture. Father resisted: Why such a hurry? He could look into everything after his vacation. The matter could wait. Moscow stubbornly insisted.

Someone had to yield. Father gave in and agreed to fly to Moscow the next morning. Replacing the phone, he walked out to the park and said to Mikoyan, who was present during the telephone conversation: "They don't have any problems with agriculture. Apparently Sergei was right in his warnings."

I didn't hear the rest of their conversation. Father wanted to talk with Mikoyan alone.

And so, did Father believe Galyukov's information from the very beginning, or only now?

I think the former is more likely.

Perhaps he didn't believe it totally. He had doubts. He wanted to be mistaken. After all, the people mentioned were not only associates, but old friends. All their first appointments were connected with Father; they had worked together before the Second World War, gone through the war together, returned to peaceful work. He had brought them to Moscow from the Ukraine, seen them as firm supporters, people who could be trusted.

And now this! But that's politics.

Polyansky recalls his telephone conversation with Father. Father called the acting chairman of the Council of Ministers on some urgent matter. As he was saying good-bye at the end of their conversation, he asked what would seem to be a neutral question: "Well, how are you getting on without me?"

"Everything's fine," answered Polyansky. "We're waiting for you."

"So you're really waiting for me?" repeated Father, with sad irony.

Polyansky caught the unusual intonation and immediately reported the suspicious conversation to Brezhnev and Podgorny.

Then why did Father not even make an attempt to verify Galyukov's information? Mikoyan's conversation with Galyukov could hardly be considered a serious step.

In 1957, in a similar situation, he had acted effectively to bring the Army and security services over to his side. Galyukov had reported that Semichastny sided with the enemy. Well, what about Malinovsky?

Father had every reason to count on him. In 1943, after General I. I. Larin, a member of the Military Council, committed suicide, Stalin was holding an ax over Malinovsky's head. Father managed with great difficulty to ward off the blow. Malinovsky knew that.

However, Father didn't even call him.

He withdrew from the battlefield, providing his enemies with freedom of action. If he simply did not want to resist, why was that?

Father was tired. Immensely tired, both physically and psychologically. He no longer had either the strength or the desire for a power struggle. He felt that with every passing day the burden was becoming heavier, while his strength was waning. The changes he made did not produce the results he expected. The government machine had stalled. The apparat kept piling new problems on Father. Not a single decision was made without him. Where and what to build. How much and what to produce. Where and how to plow and sow. There was no time to think, much less rest.

I've already mentioned that after his seventieth birthday Father talked seriously about retiring. "Let the young do the work now," he would repeat.

Now, in this situation, Father had to choose between a former security officer no one knew and his tried and true comrades.

Let's suppose he had believed Galyukov and decided to fight. The situation in 1964 was radically different from that in 1957. Then he was fighting against open Stalinists. The issue was what path to follow: Stalinist, or return to one common to all mankind. The country's fate depended on the outcome of the fight. Father accepted the battle and won.

But now? His associates, people whom he had chosen during those seven years, were sitting in the Presidium of the Central Committee. He had tried to keep the best, the most capable, most devoted to the cause. No, he didn't consider those people to be ideal, but he had not managed to find any better ones. He and they were working for the same cause; some worked worse and some better, but they worked together and for the same cause.

He had meant to leave those associates in charge when he retired. They must continue on the course begun by Lenin.

Now they were accused of being impatient, of deciding to speed up the natural course of events in order to receive today what was intended for them tomorrow.

Was he now to fight with them, with his own people?

But what if Father could have won?

A rhetorical question. It was impossible for him to win in 1964. The apparat, the Army, the KGB—the real parties in the game—did not support him. Neither did the people, who were given seats in the hall, isolated from the stage by a deep "orchestra pit." Father's time was past. But he didn't know that.

Besides, if he had won such a fight, what would he have won?

He would have won the task of removing his defeated enemies from the political arena. I'm not saying how. Stalin preferred murder. In the civilized world, defeat means retirement or joining the opposition. But not staying in power. So Father would have to remove his closest associates, men he had selected himself and to whom he had planned to transfer power.

Then he would have won the task of looking for new people, all from the same place, the top of the pyramid. He had tried to find people at lower levels, but that experiment had not produced positive results, either with Minister Volovchenko or with Smirnov.[7] So he would have to look again in the same place, although he felt he had already selected the best people from there.

To energize the country, and after that to retire and leave the country in the hands of those new people? How could he avoid the thought: "Will they be any better than the old ones, whom I also selected? Is the game worth the candle?" Evidently Father felt that it was better to leave the decision to fate, and so didn't interfere in the natural course of events.

With such reasoning, everything makes sense. The departure for Pitsunda was the only logically explicable step. And no action after Mikoyan's conversation with Galyukov. And the meeting with Vorobyov. And the conversation with Polyansky, whom he scolded from a distance.

He didn't want to act. If Galyukov was mistaken, so much the better, he wouldn't have to accuse his friends unjustly. If not, let things take their course. He was ready to go at any time.

I never discussed this subject with Father. The memory of those October

---

7. I've already mentioned the appointment of Yangel's plant director Smirnov to the position of deputy chairman of the Council of Ministers, bypassing all the stages of the hierarchy. The same thing happened with Volovchenko, director of a Belorussian collective farm, who was appointed minister of agriculture after his successful speech at a meeting. Father hoped that he could invigorate agriculture. Volovchenko was unable to do so.—S.K.

days remained too painful for him all his remaining seven years. But I myself thought a great deal about the events of those days and weeks, and drew my conclusions. I returned again and again to the conversations in Moscow and Pitsunda. I cannot find any other explanation. Perhaps someone thinks otherwise. That's his privilege. We can only suppose, guess, infer. The truth has gone with Father.

Before leaving for Moscow the morning of October 13, Father received French politician Gaston Pavlevsky. They discussed issues related to the development of nuclear and space research, prospects for inspection and cooperation in that field. Their meeting didn't last long and Father looked distracted. He guessed that the whole conversation was a waste of time and that neither he nor Pavlevsky would gain anything by it.

Pavlevsky was unaware of that.

The commander of the Transcaucasian Military District accompanied Father to the airport. Just in case. KGB chairman Semichastny met him at Vnukovo Airport in Moscow. He told Father: "Everybody's at the Kremlin waiting for you."

The Presidium of the Central Committee met for two days. Father had to listen to many bitter words, sharp and sometimes unjust accusations. He decided not to fight back. Late on the evening of the first stormy day—or rather, that night—he called Mikoyan and said that he had decided to resign from all his posts and submit to the demands of the majority. The phone was undoubtedly bugged, and Semichastny announced the happy news to Brezhnev only a few minutes later.

So the second day proceeded calmly. One after another, Presidium members and candidate members and Central Committee secretaries rose to vilify the past and swear allegiance to the future. Father sat glumly, with head bent. What was he thinking? Only yesterday they had been praising him to the skies.

During a brief interval between sessions, he entered his Kremlin office for the last time. He asked his secretary to call Troyanovsky, the only one of his aides who had come up through the staff of the Council of Ministers and whose office was located in the Kremlin. Father's other aides were employed by the Central Committee, where real power and control over ideology, agriculture, and industry was concentrated. Their offices were outside the Kremlin, on Staraya Square.

Father paced up and down by the long table used for meetings, stopped for a moment at a window overlooking the Kremlin square, and then resumed his pacing. The door opened noiselessly and Troyanovsky's head appeared. "May I, Nikita Sergeyevich?" he asked quietly.

Oleg Aleksandrovich understood that he had been summoned to say farewell, but he nourished the hope that the "boss" might come up with his usual surprise.

Saying "Come in," Father went to meet him. They met halfway, in the middle of the large office, which was where Father usually greeted distinguished foreign guests. He looked Troyanovsky over from head to foot, as if they hadn't seen each other for a long time, and sighed deeply. Troyanovsky was silent. He thought it inappropriate to initiate the conversation. And what could he say? What words could he find?

"Well, here we are," said Father finally in a subdued voice. "You already know everything?"

Troyanovsky nodded and was opening his mouth to say some words of sympathy when Father forestalled him.

"My political career is over. Too bad it's happened this way, but there's nothing to be done." His voice regained its familiar confident ring. "Now the most important thing is to get through it all with dignity."

Father fell silent, as if listening to his own words and weighing them.

"Perhaps the mood at the Plenum will change"—Troyanovsky didn't believe what he was saying, but he wanted so much to support Father at this difficult moment. "In '57 . . ."

Father didn't let him finish and raised his hand, as if in protest. Oleg Aleksandrovich stopped.

"No. It's all over," said Father quietly, as if deliberating, and added after a pause: "Kaganovich once told me that I should meet with provincial committee secretaries more often, at least twice a week. But I neglected his advice and told others to do it."

Troyanovsky realized that there was no use trying to console Father, that he had already made up his mind and was reconciled to his fate. The retirement of his boss could radically change Troyanovsky's own fate, especially if they held a "serious" conversation.

"And did you part on friendly terms?" Troyanovsky decided to ask "his" question.

Father thought over the question for a few moments.

"Well, you could say on friendly terms," he said sadly, but with a smile. Then he added in a totally different, businesslike tone of voice: "You should probably return to the Foreign Ministry."

The former Khrushchev seemed to come to life. He was deciding, ordering. But it lasted only a moment.

"What am I saying? Nothing depends on me now. Thank you for everything, Oleg Aleksandrovich. We probably won't see each other again. Too bad the others aren't here. Tell them . . ." Father stumbled. "I can't find the words," he said in some confusion. "So many years together . . ."

"I'll tell them everything." Troyanovsky came to his assistance.

"Thank you," said Father with relief. Once more, his aide had taken the weight onto his own shoulders. "Well, let's say good-bye."

They hugged, but didn't kiss each other. Father was averse to sentiment. As Father expected, he never saw his aides again, and it was more than a quarter of a century later when Oleg Aleksandrovich described this scene to me.

The Central Committee Plenum didn't last long. Mikhail Andreyevich Suslov delivered the report. During the previous few years he had become skilled at making such speeches. At the Plenum he was the chief accuser of the "Anti-Party Group" of Molotov, Malenkov, and Kaganovich. He had delivered the speech accusing Marshal Zhukov. And now it was Father's turn. Without any debate or discussion on Suslov's report, it adopted the following decision: "To agree to the request by Khrushchev, N. S., to relieve him of the responsibilities of first secretary of the Central Committee of the CPSU, member of the Presidium of the Central Committee of the CPSU, and chairman of the Council of Ministers of the USSR in connection with his advanced age and poor health.

"The Plenum of the CPSU Central Committee elected Comrade L. I. Brezhnev to be first secretary of the Central Committee of the CPSU."

In those days I naively supposed that there would be protests, that at least people would show some sympathy for Father. How blind we can be sometimes in our delusions, especially at the top. No one grieved for Father. The news of his retirement was met with relief, with the hope for change.

Those changes soon arrived, but they were not the ones people expected. Society moved backwards.

STAGNATION

And so, in 1964 those who backed reform and change were defeated. I don't associate that defeat with Father's retirement. He had to go, and everything depended on those who replaced him.

I am not going to analyze the period that followed. Its development was interesting and complex. The word "stagnation," which we adopted much too easily, explains nothing. Society did not stand still; it developed. The goal changed, and social evolution proceeded in a different direction, toward a dead end. But since that end was never reached, it's difficult to imagine what it could have been.

Father's hopes that his successors would continue to reform the country were not realized. His former colleagues, who only the day before had unanimously supported all his initiatives, now fell back. It became increasingly apparent that they preferred the old, pre-Khrushchev way of doing things. But they couldn't bring themselves to turn back openly. It was as if they were afraid of something, so they acted surreptitiously. The most they dared to do was accuse Father of voluntarism and subjectivism—as if a person making the simplest decisions, not to speak of those which determine a country's fate, could be anything but a voluntarist, as if a leader forced to act on matters and in areas too novel or complex to be covered by any political theory could be anything but a subjectivist.

But that is by way of an aside. Criticism of Father did not go beyond such vague accusations. More important is the fact that his successors quickly curtailed all his innovations and experiments, especially in the country's administrative structure—the ones most hated by bureaucrats. Everything was put back onto the old rails: they restored unified provincial party committees, revived ministries, stifled economic reform. They talked about rehabilitating Stalin, about restoring his "good name." The vainglorious Brezhnev was very eager to feel that he was sitting in the office of the "genius leader of all times and peoples." He did not want to be regarded simply as the new boss in an office whose previous occupant was the indefatigable "corn-pusher" Khrushchev. But that made it necessary to scrub Stalin clean. They planned to time this operation to coincide with the fiftieth anniversary of the Revolution, in the autumn of 1967.

Father was painfully distressed about what was happening in the country, but said nothing, even to those close to him, and during our Sunday walks he talked only about the past. If some hapless guest tried to draw him into a discussion about the present, Father would cut him off abruptly, saying: "I'm a pensioner now and my work is over. You should talk about what's going on today with those who are making the decisions, not those who do nothing but talk." After such a rebuff, the inquisitive guest would subside and the conversation would revert to the war, Stalingrad, Kursk, Stalin's death . . .

Father returned constantly to the subject of Stalin. He was, it would seem, infected by Stalin; he tried to rid himself of that poison, but could not. He tried to understand, to comprehend, what had happened to the country, to its leaders, to himself. How had the tyrant managed not only to subjugate the country, but to make its people deify him? He searched in vain for an answer.

Father was simply staggered by the news of Stalin's forthcoming rehabilitation. He could not have foreseen such a development, even in his worst nightmares. How could you justify what Stalin had done: the concentration camps, the executions, the persecutions? Father decided that he had no right to remain silent, that he must talk about those times, must issue some warning—even if the likelihood that his warning would reach people was infinitesimal. So he began to dictate his memoirs. Memoirs that became the focal point of the last years of his life. Memoirs that gradually, step by step, evolved from the unmasking of Stalin to reflections about the country's fate, the reforms, the future.

However, the rehabilitation of Stalin ran into serious obstacles. How could such an abrupt change of course be explained to the people, to the world? Even if they had not read it, everyone knew the contents of Father's "secret" speech to the Twentieth Party Congress, which had never been published in the USSR. It didn't seem possible to dismiss, to ignore, the monstrous crimes which had been revealed. They had to find some solution. And they succeeded.

KGB professionals—who were highly skilled in disinformation—proposed that the speech be attributed to Father's personal resentment of Stalin, to an egotistical "pygmy's" seizure of power in order to avenge himself against a "titan." They say that one of the authors of this idea was Filipp Bobkov, a future supervisor of the KGB's fifth, "dissident" directorate and a future first deputy chairman of the KGB itself. But how could this interpretation be conveyed? They had to find an angle, some fact from Father's life that could be falsified. And they found such a fact. They seized upon the tragic story of my brother Leonid's death during the war. I have described earlier what happened to him.

They acted in the way accepted among such professionals—not straightforwardly, but circuitously. The deputy director for personnel of the Ministry of Defense, Colonel General Kuzovlyov, was told to spread the following version of events (he held the cards, since Leonid had been in the military). Rumors were circulated around Moscow that the general had discovered documents (which, naturally, no one saw) indicating that Leonid was not killed, but had surrendered to the Germans, that he began to cooperate with them and betrayed his country. In consequence, whether at the end of the war or somewhat later, he fell into the hands of Soviet counterintelligence, confessed to his crimes, and was sentenced to death by a court. Father allegedly begged Stalin on his knees to forgive his son, but Stalin refused, saying: "My son was also captured. He behaved like a hero, but I refused to exchange Field-Marshal Paulus for him. Your son, on the other hand . . ."

The KGB "makers of history" carried out their assignment, attributing Father's exposure of Stalin's crimes to personal and petty revenge.

It would seem that this fabrication didn't deserve to be believed. But that is why professionals are professionals—they know better than anyone the laws for spreading rumors. The story began to make its way around the world, acquiring more and more details; then it was published in newspapers, was "corroborated" in the memoirs of General Sudoplatov, Stalin's chief KGB murderer, who during Father's time was sentenced to a lengthy prison term for his crimes, and finally it even began to be discussed in scholarly publications, at first cautiously and then more boldly. And all that without one single piece of evidence, without one single document.

And now we, Father's heirs, have to look for arguments to disprove this slander. Fortunately, they are easy to find. Nothing is known of Leonid's fate, but what kind of treachery could a senior lieutenant commit? What did he know? The answer is obvious: nothing important. The only way he could be useful to the Germans was by issuing appeals to Soviet soldiers to surrender. Leaflets with such appeals, in the name of Stalin's son Yakov, of a real or imaginary nephew of Molotov, of General Vlasov and many others, were dropped widely by German planes over Soviet positions. Not a single leaflet with the name of Leonid Khrushchev has been documented and war veterans do not remember any. The point is not even that he did not write them; the Germans simply had no idea of his existence. My brother died anonymously near Zhizdra.

Such is the sad and unpleasant story. I don't think that my explanations will bring the subject to a close. It's hard, almost impossible, to fight against slander, but it has to be done.

In those years still another "myth" about Father was disseminated for the same purpose. Those same "specialists" from the KGB spread the rumor that, during his years in power, Khrushchev tried to cover up any traces of his participation in the Stalinist repressions by ordering all relevant documents and evidence removed from the archives.

That accusation is more difficult to disprove. In the first place, Father himself never denied that he had to put his signature on orders written by the NKVD for the arrest of people he worked with. That was the way life was organized in those years—let anyone refuse to sign such a paper! He even visited prisons and met with those under arrest. But his behavior was altogether different from the actions of others of Stalin's companions, such as Kaganovich, Voroshilov, Molotov—not to speak of Beria—who, after receiving the order "Forward, march!" from the "boss," spilled a sea of blood, put all their strength into the effort. Others, Father among them, displayed no zeal and tried as far as possible to reduce the number of victims and ease their lot. He wrote about all that in his memoirs.

During the Twentieth Party Congress he said frankly that all members of the country's leadership were involved in Stalin's crimes, but to different degrees, and the people would have to determine the guilt of each. At the end of his life Father said repeatedly: "When I die they will place my actions on the scales. The evil in one cup, the good in another, and I hope the good will outweigh the evil." But even after his death the devil's servants try to cast their false metal onto the evil side of the scales. And they do it so artfully that even I—no, I did not believe it, but I must admit that the rumor started by the KGB made me doubt, made me consider the possibility that Father's past might have been "touched up." I had to admit, though with the most profound reluctance, that it was possible.

It did not seem to correspond to Father's inner self—but human beings are weak. And every one of us wants so much to improve his image after the fact, to forget ugly actions in the past. And with the opportunities he had . . . It seemed a waste not to use them. It seemed . . . To tell the truth, I was resigned to the possibility. But then His Majesty Chance intervened. At a conference held at Brown University in the United States in December 1994, on the occasion of the centenary of N. S. Khrushchev's birth, papers were delivered that referred to Father's "purge" of the archives. I decided to track down the primary sources. The charges related to two periods in Father's career: the Moscow period (up to 1938) and the Kiev period (after 1938). In other words, if any archives were "purged," they were the Moscow Party Archive and the Ukrainian Party Archive.

I began with the Ukraine. Yury Shapoval, a historian who specializes in Father's career, asserted unequivocally in his remarks that many documents relating to Father's activities were missing from the Ukrainian archive and had been "purged." I asked him to look up primary sources. Shapoval became interested in this question. He is a relatively young man, not infected by the hostility toward Father of the party apparatus, which never forgave him for exposing Stalin's crimes. And what turned out to be the reality? A great deal connected with Father's name was indeed missing from the Ukrainian archive. The fact is that Father kept his own archive. He took it with him to the Ukraine from Moscow in 1938. His aides put what they considered to be the more important documents into that archive, sometimes forgetting to transfer them to the official archive. Father—or rather, his staff—took all those folders, more than two hundred of them, back to Moscow in 1950. After Father's retirement they lay in the archive of the Politburo of the Central Committee of the CPSU. Archivists of an independent Ukraine are now arguing with officials of the Kremlin Presidential Archive about who owns these documents. In Kiev Yury Shapoval found no traces whatsoever that documents were destroyed. (If someone would like to verify this, I recommend reading the book *Khrushchev and the Ukraine*, published in Kiev in 1995 by the Institute of History of the Ukraine. On pages 181 through 185, Doctor of Historical Sciences R. Ya. Pirog gives a comprehensive description of all the details about Father's personal archive in his article "The Archive of CP (b) CC First Secretary Nikita Khrushchev: Problems of Restitution.")

Encouraged by the results of the Ukrainian investigation, I turned my attention to the Moscow period of Father's career. I asked for help from Vladimir Pavlovich Naumov, author of a paper presented at the conference at Brown University and also the secretary of Aleksandr Yakovlev's commission investigating everything related to the repressions of the Stalinist, pre-Stalinist, and post-Stalinist periods. By virtue of his unique position, Naumov has access to every single archive, including the Presidential archive. However, the situation is complicated by the fact that Naumov himself is a former official of the ideology department of the Central Committee of the CPSU. Unlike Yury Shapoval, Naumov, like all former apparatchiks, even those of a democratic bent, does not sympathize with Khrushchev. For a long time Vladimir Pavlovich made no response to my request, and only after repeated reminders sent a reply. I quote it in full, to avoid false information:

> I ask your pardon for the long delay in sending you this material. It was caused by the fact that I tried to clarify the circumstances of the purging of the f. (former) archive of the Moscow City Party Committee and Province Party Committee. The matter turned out to be extremely complicated. There are various versions. They are all connected in one degree or another with N.S. Khrushchev. But *not one person* could confirm his version with any documents.

In translation from bureaucratese, this means that in the Moscow archive nothing was burned on Father's orders. Such things don't happen without leaving any trace. There have to be written instructions to destroy documents—a formal order, or at least a letter, giving the bearer authority to act. Otherwise the entire responsibility would rest on the keepers of the archive, who would not proceed without written instructions.

As a result of this investigation, the only destruction of documents that could be confirmed was of those found in Beria's safe after his arrest in 1953. Members of the Presidium of the Central Committee decided unanimously to burn them without reading them. Who knew what compromising material Lavrenty Pavlovich might have gathered about them? But Father wrote about this in his memoirs.

So the second falsehood was also disproved, although I think that we will face more than one attempt to revive it. Dirt washes off only with the greatest difficulty.

And there I will stop.

I would like to end my account with several projects killed off in their prime by October 1964.

Whatever sins Father was accused of, the work he began on intercontinental ballistic missiles continued without interruption. No one reviewed the decrees adopted in previous years. However, the attitude changed slightly: Father's enthusiasm was replaced by the bureaucratic severity of his successors.

Work on the UR-200 was stopped. However, a few of the rockets were ready for launch and permission was given to fire them. The first "consolation" launch occurred at the end of October. The rocket successfully covered the distance and struck right on target. On such occasions Chelomei had always called Moscow on the special phone to give Father a triumphant report and to receive his congratulations.

Chelomei was nervous: How would his relations with the new leaders work out? Would they remember that Khrushchev had liked him? At the time people speculated openly about a possible change in Chelomei's fate—some with cautious sympathy, others with malicious and unconcealed pleasure.

Vladimir Nikolayevich didn't dare to call Brezhnev. He and Ustinov were friends, and Chelomei feared that "evil influence." He decided to call Kosygin. Chelomei's reasoning was simple: the state of the country's defense capability was a primary concern of the chairman of the Council of Ministers. Vladimir Nikolayevich cherished the hope that—only if the conversation went well, of course—he would ask the premier to support the UR-200.

His call went through quickly; the secretary only asked who was calling. In response to Chelomei's greeting, Kosygin asked coldly: "What's the matter?" Vladimir Nikolayevich began to report: "We have carried out a launch of the intercontinental UR-200 rocket. Deviations from the target were minimal." He mentioned some figures, which I don't remember, of course.

Kosygin listened without interrupting, but didn't react at all, either with questions or congratulations.

Finally Chelomei fell silent. There was a pause. Realizing that he was finished, Kosygin asked: "What do you want?"

Vladimir Nikolayevich was at a loss. "I wished to report," he began uncertainly.

Before he could say anything else, Kosygin struck the final blow: "Don't you have a minister?"

"Yes, Dementyev," answered Chelomei, now completely embarrassed.

"Next time call and report to him. Rocket launches are his responsibility, not mine. He'll inform me, if that should be necessary. Good-bye." Kosygin hung up.

Chelomei continued for a few moments to listen to the distant crackling in the phone.

In the summer of 1963, when development of the UR-100 was in its initial stage, Chelomei was seized by the idea of making it the basis of an impenetrable shield to protect our country from ballistic missiles.

Again, he was intruding on someone else's domain. Grigory Kisunko and Pyotr Grushin were working on antiballistic missiles. They were the ones whose missiles intercepted the warhead of Yangel's R-12 in March of 1961. Father was referring to them that summer, when he said proudly that Soviet scientists could hit a fly in space. But an experiment is one thing, and shielding the country's major cities so that not one foreign "fly" could penetrate is something else again. A single thermonuclear warhead breaking through to its target would make all attempts to create an ABM defense meaningless. Kisunko's electronic system turned out to be complex and very expensive. Moreover, it was capable of intercepting only one or at most several missiles. But the objective was to intercept hundreds, if not thousands, of attacking warheads.

At the beginning of 1963 Father met with Kisunko and asked him whether it was possible to simplify the system, while also ensuring that a massive attack would be repelled. Kisunko promised to think about it and began revising his system, but couldn't solve the problem. The interception of warheads in relative proximity to the object being defended did not in principle allow for the creation of a genuine ABM defense. Quite apart from the incoming warheads, the nuclear warheads of the antimissiles defending Moscow, for example, would not only destroy the enemy, they would threaten to kill 30 to 40 percent of the Muscovites from the nuclear shock wave and from radiation. In the designers' opinion, that would be the price for saving the lives of the remaining 60 to 70 percent of the capital's inhabitants. It wasn't a matter of improving the system, but of changing the concept.

Naturally, Chelomei knew all about these problems, and he suddenly had an inspired idea: the interception should occur far away in space. His proposal was essentially very similar to SDI, the Strategic Defense Initiative, which appeared much later in the United States. In those days it seemed completely fantastic: Satellites would have to detect enemy missiles as soon as they were launched; then long-range radars based on Soviet territory would begin operating. On their command, thousands of specially equipped UR-100s would zoom into the sky to intercept the foreign missiles deep in space, crossing their trajectory. The interception would last fractions of a second. The flash of a nuclear explosion would be followed by a jet of soft X-ray radiation, which would heat and literally peel the thermal shield off the warhead. Neutrons formed in the explosion would enter the very core of an enemy warhead, baking its insides into a useless mass.

Those warheads lucky enough to penetrate the first defense screen would be broken up at the edge of the atmosphere by the maneuverable missile-interceptors designed by Kisunko and Grushin.

In those years lasers were brand-new and Chelomei was very interested in harnessing their potential. Lasers would solve the problem of antimissile defense, Vladimir Nikolayevich insisted, while his colleagues smirked condescendingly.

Critics reproached Chelomei for indulging in harebrained schemes, saying that the UR-100 was not an interceptor and that it wasn't sufficiently maneuverable. Chelomei just smiled in response: Why talk about maneuverability if the target was to be intercepted in distant space, at an altitude of more than a thousand kilometers? The stumbling block was precise targeting, not maneuverability.

Father strongly supported Chelomei. He thought that finally there was hope of finding the key to creating an effective ABM defense.

The government issued a decree authorizing preliminary research on the concept. A Council of Chief Designers was formed to work on his idea. Vladimir Nikolayevich recruited a designer of long-range radars, Aleksandr Mints; a nuclear warhead designer, Yevgeny Zababakhin; antimissile designers Grigory Kisunko and Pyotr Grushin (who agreed only under great pressure, however), as well as many others. For some reason the absolute defensive weapon was called the Taran. Work began in full swing. They calculated, drew, drafted, and rejected one variant after another. Eventually a draft project emerged. It came time to decide on the next step. And at that point Chelomei suddenly thought of the economy. They drew up estimates of how much the country would have to pay for its security.

Even if you didn't include all the costs of creating huge radars and anti-missile guidance stations, two UR-100s would have to be launched to destroy one target in space, i.e., two which would each cost as much as each attacking intercontinental ballistic missile. Furthermore, if you considered the possibility that several warheads might be mounted on a foreign missile—and the probability that it would eject false targets—the cost of defense would increase many times faster than the cost of attack. Building the Taran would bankrupt the country. The idea had to be discarded.

In July of 1967 a decree on installing UR-100s in silos was signed by the top leadership. That marked the beginning of a countdown to establish parity. Its costs mounted. During Father's time, the General Staff estimated that hundreds of warheads were needed for the country's defense. Now no one wanted to talk about anything less than a thousand. And that was only at the beginning. Appetites grew. Now that numbers have been made public, we refer to tens of thousands of warheads. From these heights, the two dozen R-16s of the Cuban Missile Crisis—which seemed enough for a reasonable person to consider the possible damage unacceptable to a civilized country—appear simply laughable. The R-36 was placed in service at the same time as the UR-100. From then on they worked in tandem.

A new problem soon appeared: the Americans invented independently targeted multiple warheads. We couldn't allow ourselves to lag behind. A competition was announced. Yangel and Chelomei again became the main contestants. Both new missiles were successful. Grechko, who had become defense minister by that time, simply couldn't choose between them. Ustinov backed Yangel, while Grechko himself "rooted" for Chelomei. He went to Brezhnev for advice. Brezhnev made a Solomonic decision: to add both missiles to the country's arsenal.

However, that doubled the cost. Everything had to be made in two variants: not just the missiles, but the launch silos, servicing systems, and spare parts. When I told Father about it, he only growled and asked me to change the subject. He didn't even want to hear about such an outrage.

The UR-100 has now been retired. Some years ago I was at a military training course. Reserve officers are usually shown old equipment, as we all know. We studied the UR-100. I was extremely pleased when our lecturer, an officer, called it the best Soviet rocket. It meant that Father had not made a mistake, back at the conference in Fili.

The first UR-500 was launched on July 16, 1965. Everything went well. Chelomei had learned how to make rockets no worse, and perhaps better, than the "cannon-makers." The satellite named Proton, describing lazy somersaults, circled the earth and tried to capture some quarks. That year Vladimir Nikolayevich's thoughts were entirely focused on the UR-700. No one had canceled Father's order to develop still another moon project.

The year 1965 marked the beginning of the moon race in the Soviet Union itself. However, the two competitors, Korolyov and Chelomei, didn't enter the fight as equals. Chelomei was allowed to work on a variant of a heavy rocket and to present his ideas to be judged by specialists and the leadership. Korolyov moved far ahead. He had already been working on a moon rocket for four years—or at least for two and a half, if you ignore the first forty-ton version.

From the beginning, Sergei Pavlovich was very worried about Chelomei, his unexpected competitor. It wouldn't be easy to dispose of him. After all, they worked in different agencies, Korolyov in the State Committee on Defense Technology, and Chelomei in aviation, under the protection of his minister, Dementyev. However, this "inconsistency" didn't last long. In 1965 ministerial rights were restored. New ministries were added to the old ones, including a rocket ministry: the Ministry of General Machine-Building. Sergei Afanasyev, who was an experienced specialist in machine-building but didn't know anything about rockets, was appointed minister.

Smirnov's former deputy, Georgy Pashkov, remembers that "specialists" from Korolyov's design bureau sent a memorandum to Minister Afanasyev proposing that Chelomei's project be closed down—which would throttle his idea in its cradle—ostensibly with the aim of consolidating efforts and preventing the dispersion of forces and funds. Chelomei grew very nervous. He had nothing with which to oppose this but the conviction that his variant was the only one that would be successful. But how to prove he was right? Korolyov had behind him not only Ustinov, but the first satellite and Gagarin. And time was passing. The year 1965 was coming to a close.

In one year Vladimir Nikolayevich completed the design of the UR-700 and "patched" together cooperation. Cooperation was especially difficult to achieve. Many of the subcontractors put off reaching agreement, waiting to see what the leadership would do. After Father's removal not everybody thought that Chelomei was a desirable partner. Fortunately, Glushko was firmly on his side. He promised to make new engines and, without waiting for an official decision, began to work on designs.

Chelomei planned on maximum use of proven designs and finished assemblies and instruments for the UR-700. Anything new was allowed only when already tested designs simply didn't work. Otherwise, he thought, it would be impossible to produce a rocket capable of reaching the moon before the Americans.

The competition between Chelomei and Korolyov reached a climax. A tried and true bureaucratic method was employed to resolve the situation. On August 25, 1965, Leonid Smirnov, chairman of the Military-Industrial

Commission of the Council of Ministers, appointed a panel of experts. It included members of both design bureaus, as well as officials and representatives of the Academy of Sciences. The commission was headed by the new rocket minister, Sergei Afanasyev, and the president of the Academy of Sciences, Mstislav Vsevolodovich Keldysh, "the theoretician of space science," as he was meaningfully and anonymously described in newspapers at the time.

The commission paid its first visit to Chelomei.

Before their guests arrived people in the design bureau went several nights without sleep. They drew, corrected what was drawn, drew once more. Vladimir Nikolayevich had never been easygoing, but now he was totally unnerved.

Finally, the commission arrived. They were met at the door by the design bureau's leading specialists involved in the lunar project. The minister shook hands with everyone. Then the guests rode up in the elevator to the sixth floor, while everyone else ran up the staircase. The investigation began in the morning and lasted for more than a day.

Finally, the inspection by experts ended. No conclusions were announced. They still had to visit Korolyov's design bureau. In bidding farewell, the minister again shook hands with the engineers, who were drawn up as if on a parade ground. With each handshake, he said: "Work . . . Work . . . Work." This was considered a good sign.

It meant they didn't intend to shut down our project. The mood at the firm improved.

Korolyov didn't like posters—for him they were just pieces of paper and wouldn't impress the leadership. Sergei Pavlovich loved mockups. They were easier to understand. You could feel them, open the top, look inside at the cleverly wound wires and scattering of incomprehensible parts.

An impressive reception was prepared for the commission. They were shown work in progress. In contrast to Chelomei's design bureau, many of their designs were already in production.

The minister became somewhat flustered. Listening to Chelomei, he had been impressed by the soundness of his arguments. It seemed that the rocket should be built exactly as Vladimir Nikolayevich described.

But here they were defending the opposite point of view, and no less persuasively. Afanasyev didn't know which one to prefer. Leaving from Korolyov's, he again shook hands with everyone. This time he said, in some perplexity: "Think . . . Think . . . Think . . ."

Before the final decision was made, all materials were to be sent to the ministry, which would pass them on to the commission. In the history of the lunar program, it became known as "The Keldysh Commission."

The evening that Chelomei was signing his "Technical Proposals," I happened to enter his office on some business. Vladimir Nikolayevich was in a gloomy mood.

Chelomei set aside the folders he had signed on the edge of his oak desk, which resembled the wing of a plane. Silent for a moment, he touched the folders with his hand, as if saying farewell.

"I'm not going to fight with them," said Vladimir Nikolayevich emotionally. "I'm too tired."

His words were totally unexpected. Chelomei had only recently turned sixty. He looked very well, aside from the fact that his hair had grown a little thin and turned completely gray.

The technical proposals were sent to the ministry. The commission began its sessions. Chelomei almost never went to them, sending his deputies instead. Perhaps he didn't want to be present at his own funeral. No one had any doubt what the result would be. Meanwhile, there was one session after another. Experts discussed, argued, and agreed to continue their work at the following meeting. Technical experts and scientists tended to support Chelomei, while the "politicians" firmly backed Korolyov. It's very interesting to read about this standoff between "technicians" and "politicians" in the commission's materials, but they are unfortunately not accessible to everyone.

Finally, the commission concluded its work, approved the N-1 project, and gave its approval to the launch of a lunar vehicle to land one cosmonaut on the lunar surface. By then, as Chelomei predicted, the weight of the lunar module had increased. They barely managed to keep it at ninety-five tons. They had to increase the launch weight of the rocket. This in turn necessitated adding another six engines. In essence, the entire first stage had to be redesigned.

Chelomei again predicted that even ninety-five tons would not be sufficient. They would have to redo it again. According to testimony by Yury Aleksandrovich Moszhorin, doctor of Technical Sciences, director of the main institute in a branch of the TsNIIMash,[1] and an immediate participant in the entire lunar epic, "just a little more was needed. . . . And then a solution was found: fueling with super-cooled oxygen and kerosene made it possible to take more fuel on board."[2] The last possibilities had been exhausted. A new government decree was issued on October 25, 1965, based on the conclusions of the experts.

Korolyov had not simply won, he had knocked Chelomei completely out of the ring. They even took the flight around the moon away from Vladimir

---

1. TsNIIMash—Central Scientific Research Institute of Machine-Building.
2. Supercooling the fuel reduced its volume. Yu. Moszhorin, "This Is the Way It Was. The Difficult Fate of the N-1 Project," *Krasnaya Zvezda,* January 13, 1990.

Nikolayevich. Now he was assigned an auxiliary role: the UR-500 was to lift Korolyov's spaceship into circular earth orbit, and that was all. Chelomei received his defeat stoically.

Korolyov was not fated to enjoy the fruits of his victory. In January 1966 he died, right on the operating table, during surgery on his rectum. Surgeons were preparing to remove a polyp, but as witnesses report, they found cancer. The news of Sergei Pavlovich's death struck us like a blow to the head. How could you think about competition, when such a man had died so prematurely! At the time Chelomei looked simply devastated.

Now the government decree had to be carried out without Korolyov. Even with Korolyov's energy, the schedule it mandated was impossible: to begin flight tests in six months and land an expedition on the moon in the third quarter of 1968. They were rushing to catch up with the Americans, which would require at least four launches a year to perfect the rocket, but the Kuibyshev Plant was barely capable of producing three rockets in two years.

We fell more and more hopelessly behind. Even if the tough schedule set by the decree had been met, by the time the Apollo made its first flight we would have managed to launch only one N-1. In theory . . .

In addition, there were purely personal problems.

The new chief designer, Vasily Pavlovich Mishin, the firm's former chief of ballistics, had a reputation for being soft, unable to pound his fist on the table, in the Korolyov manner, in offices where that was necessary. He was not a leader. He didn't have Korolyov's authority, and he had no managerial talents. Moreover, times had changed. Memories of how Ustinov set aside one week to approve diagrams of work related to government decrees had become legendary. Now it took many months and sometimes years to receive approval of documents. I remember one incident when, after receiving the final signature on a draft work schedule for the creation of Chelomei's orbital station, the chief engineer, Vladimir Abramovich Polyachenko, leafing through crumpled papers, announced sadly that the period for which the first signature was valid had already expired.

Everyone hoped for a miracle. They assumed that something would break down in the U.S. program, there would be failures and delays. But we would go on making progress.

In the second half of 1967, the minister decided to revive work on the UR-700. He ordered Chelomei to prepare a draft decree ordering the completion, within the course of a year, of a draft project of the UR-700 rocket and the LK-700 lunar vehicle for two cosmonauts. Vladimir Nikolayevich undertook the work with little enthusiasm. No, he did not refuse. Chelomei simply didn't believe that he would manage to accomplish much. Too much time had been lost.

By then the N-1 project had made progress. The first launch was planned for the beginning of the following year, 1969. The need for a reserve variant seemed to have disappeared. How much hope was invested in that raw and untested launch! They decided to launch the rocket right away, without going through the ground test stage. Suppose it works!? In the rocket field, bad luck is more common than good, and to "suppose" something just might work is almost the same as being sure it won't.

They docked the lunar module and the return capsule. If the spaceship went into orbit, they could carry out tests of the next stage as well. Naturally, on autopilot.

The launch took place on February 21, 1969, half a year before the U.S. launch. Seventy seconds into the flight a fire broke out in the tail section; something had happened in the engines. As they wrote in reports: "The flight ended." The launch site survived. Assembly of a second rocket began.

On its second launch on July 3, 1969, five months after the first, it was all over in a moment. A few seconds passed after the command "disconnect heel contact" and the rocket had barely lifted off when the oxygen pump in one of the engines collapsed. The KORD system became confused,[3] then alarmed, then switched off all thirty engines at once. The rocket sank heavily and crashed onto the launch pad, setting off a conflagration. The almost three thousand tons of kerosene and oxygen mixed together destroyed the launch pad completely.

The moon race came to an end on July 20, 1969, when Neil Armstrong and Edwin Aldrin landed on the moon's surface. Michael Collins waited in orbit.

You would think that it was time to stop. We'd lost, after all. Why waste money? But those in charge refused to see reason. The N-1 continued in its death throes.

The Americans carried out flights to the moon with enviable regularity. We were still trying to break free of the earth.

It took two years to resurrect the launch complex. A third launch of the N-1 was scheduled for July 27, 1971. This time the entire flight lasted ten seconds. Because of a gas-dynamic factor that had not been taken into consideration, the rocket began to rotate around its longitudinal axis. The mechanism limiting the angle of rotation began to operate and . . .

Another year and a half passed. For the fourth time the rocket was transported to the launch pad. No one knew yet that this would be the last time.

The test was scheduled for November 23. The launch proceeded normally and the rocket, as the saying goes, left. That was already viewed as an

---

3. KORD: "Coordinated Shut-off of Rocket Engines." In the event one first-stage engine broke down, the opposite engine was supposed to shut down to avoid a disparity in thrust, which could turn the rocket over.

achievement—the "ground" wouldn't have to be rebuilt. The flight lasted one hundred and seven seconds. The first stage operated ten seconds more when the entire huge assemblage began to vibrate and was finally destroyed.

It's not hard to imagine the feelings of a cosmonaut preparing to launch on the N-1, knowing that the previous flights had ended in crashes. Furthermore, there was no certainty that a fifth flight would go normally. There was only hope, just as illusory a hope as in the first, second, third, and fourth launches.

At the time Ustinov had no choice but to close down the N-1. He and Korolyov had originated the project, and every unsuccessful launch damaged his prestige. As an experienced official, he understood that failures could continue for a long time, and that nothing awaited at the end but a repetition of discoveries already made by the U.S. astronauts.

An announcement, in accordance with Soviet practice, was made that our concept of mastering space did not include landing a man on the moon. We were simply not planning to go there.

Today some things at the Baikonur Cosmodrome remind one of the N-1: the roof over the garage, made from the rocket's sheathing; gazebos made from halves of the huge fuel tanks; the delicate awning with large round openings hanging over the dance pavilion in the square.

And also an inescapable feeling of melancholy among the thousands and thousands of engineers of all ranks who devoted their lives to a machine which, it turned out, was not destined to fly. A melancholy that wordlessly seeks an answer to the question: Who is to blame? Such was the sad fate of the N-1.

In the years that passed not a single reference was made to Father's ideas about radically reorganizing the Army. They were not even criticized. Production of planes was quickly increased, aviation was resurrected. At shipyards, construction of naval surface ships, cruisers, and destroyers resumed. They even sneaked in a few aircraft carriers. The Navy began to feel cramped in coastal waters and headed toward other shores, following the example of its partners across the ocean—at first the Mediterranean, and then further on. How many billions did it cost us to show the flag, to which no one ever paid any serious attention? No one can say now. Billions? Tens of billions? Hundreds of billions?

Tanks came to be numbered in the tens of thousands. Planes too. Rockets in the thousands. I don't even remember how many warheads. There were enough for all of us. An intelligent man involved in the planning of weapons once commented bitterly: "We're equipping the Army as if we were preparing to fight tomorrow." And really, what sensible person could justify the production of such an enormous quantity of weapons that no one was planning to use? It contradicted all logic. But that's the point—not all logic. The distorted logic of a government department that has spiraled out of control is capable of even worse.

August 1989–June 1999
Moscow—Cambridge, Massachusetts—Moscow
Providence, Rhode Island

INDEX